Archaeology in the Dodecanese

Archaeology in the Dodecanese

Edited by Søren Dietz
& Ioannis Papachristodoulou

The National Museum of Denmark
Department of Near Eastern and Classical Antiquities
Copenhagen 1988

Printed in Denmark
by Special-Trykkeriet Viborg a-s

Lay-out: Jens Lorentzen.

The English was revised by
Mrs. Jennifer Paris, Wales.

ISBN 87-480-0626-2

Cover: Chart of Southwestern Coast of Turkey and the Dodecanese Islands by Gerard van Keulen, Amsterdam 1717. (Royal Library, Copenhagen).

Table of Contents

Preface

S. Dietz and I. Papachristodoulou

The Dodecanese Islands are situated at the crossroads of different geographical areas and civilizations. This explains their historical importance in all periods of antiquity and the variety of their cultural products and monuments. During the Minoan and Mycenaean period the islands, especially Kos and Rhodes, must have been important stations on the way from the Aegean to the Orient and vice versa. In late Mycenaean times, Rhodes was a flourishing centre of Mycenaean civilization, while in the first millenium it was mainly Lindos that played an important role within the colonization movement of the Greek city-states. After the synoecism and the formation of the new capital of Rhodes, the unified island state became one of the most important political, naval, economic and cultural centres of the Hellenistic World, while Kos, with the famous Asclepieion, was a flourishing centre of agriculture, industry, commerce and medicine, continuing to be a prosperous city in Roman times.

Rhodes, Kos and the other Dodecanese Islands attracted the interest of scholars and travellers very early, but the first period of active research took place in the nineteenth century, with L. Ross, C. Newton, W. Paton, V. Guerin and others, while A. Biliotti and A. Salzmann conducted excavations of dilettantish character at Ialysos, Camiros and in other parts of Rhodes. At the end of the century the publication of the Inscriptiones Graecae by F. Hiller von Gaertringen and his collaborators was an important milestone in research into the history and archaeology of Rhodes and other islands. Shortly thereafter the first systematic excavations in the Dodecanese were carried out at Lindos by the Danish Expedition and at the Asclepieion on Kos by R. Herzog.

The Italian occupation of the islands in 1912 was important for the development of archaeology in the Dodecanese. The Scuola Archeologica Italiana of Athens and the Italian Archaeological Service conducted extensive excavations on most of the islands, but their main efforts were concentrated on the necropolis of Ialysos and Camiros, and on the urban centres of Kamiros and Kos. Since the Second World War and the union of the islands with Greece, the Greek Archaeological Service has taken the responsibility for the continuation of the rich archaeological harvest which began in the last century. Now the main centre of interest is the capital of Rhodes, the city-plan of which deserved a special study. In recent years, much work has been done in the extensive cemeteries of the city of Rhodes and the city of Kos, while work has been resumed in the areas of Minoan and later Ialysos.

In connection with an exhibition presented recently in Rhodes and Copenhagen with the collaboration of the Danish National Museum and the Greek Archaeological Service, the two editors of the present volume conceived the idea of organizing a Symposium in order to discuss archaeological research in the Dodecanese from its beginnings up to today and to present recent finds in the area. We are pleased that this plan could be realized with success and that we are able to present the results of the Symposium in a relatively short time. We hope that the present volume will stimulate more research in the archaeology of the Dodecanese and give rise to new publications on the topics concerned.

The Symposium, which took place in Copenhagen from April 7th to 9th, 1986, could not have been held without the extensive goodwill and direct financial support of several institutions and foundations. In this respect the editors are most grateful towards the Greek Director of Antiquities, Dr. Ioannis Tzedakis, and the General Director of Antiquities and Director of the National Museum in Denmark, Professor Olaf Olsen, the Greek and Danish Ministries of Culture, the Carlsberg Foundation, Consul General Gösta Enbom's Foundation and the Danish Research Council for the Humanities. The three last mentioned foundations have generously provided the funds for the publication of the present volume.

Many colleagues and students have been involved in the preparation of the volume and it is impossible to mention all to whom we are grateful. It must be stressed, however, that the publication of the conference proceedings would have been seriously delayed if mag. art. Steen Ole Jensen had not made very special efforts in the preparation of most of the manuscripts for printing.

Copenhagen/Rhodes October 1987

Søren Dietz *Ioannis Papachristodoulou*

Chapter 1 . Prehistory

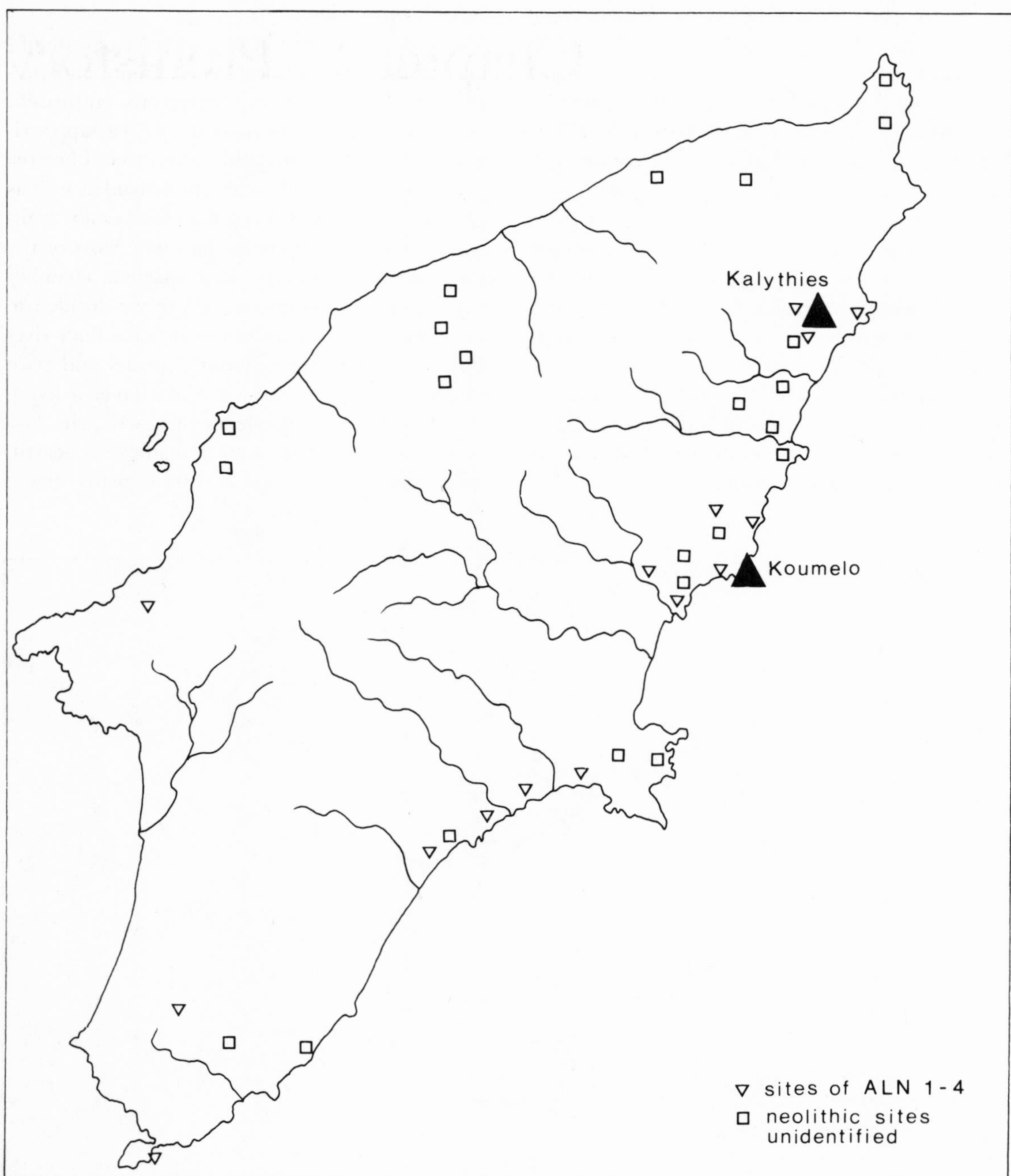

Fig. 1. Map of Rhodes.

Periodic and Seasonal Usage of Two Neolithic Caves in Rhodes

Adamantios Sampson

Until recently the island of Rhodes presented an image of unoccupied space during the Neolithic and Early Bronze Ages, despite the obvious habitational advantages. A systematic survey started in 1977 and, completing that of R. Hope Simpson[1], it indicated that there was continuous habitation on the island from the beginning of the Aegean Late Neolithic[2] until the Early Bronze Age (fig. 1). The most important neolithic remains were discovered in caves. In most of them, even the smallest ones, remains of use and/or occupation in these ages have been located.

Two of the caves were chosen for excavation, the Ayios Georgios cave at Kalythies (already known from rich surface finds) and the Koumelo cave near the village of Archangelos.

Ayios Georgios Cave

Situated almost on top of the limestone mountain of Psalidi, the location is remote and precipitous with a very dangerous approach. Geological surveys show that this was approximately the case in neolithic times too. The area below the cave is hilly with arable land as well as grazing areas. The sea is quite close, easily available to the inhabitants of the cave. Most of the remains were observed in a spacious chamber (fig. 2) near the entrance, where we decided to excavate. From the entrance the cave floor rises towards a chamber without deposits and with uneven surface. In the very first layer a living floor was found with plenty of hearth ash. At a depth of 15 cm there were remains of a hearth. The deposits consisted of ash remains mixed

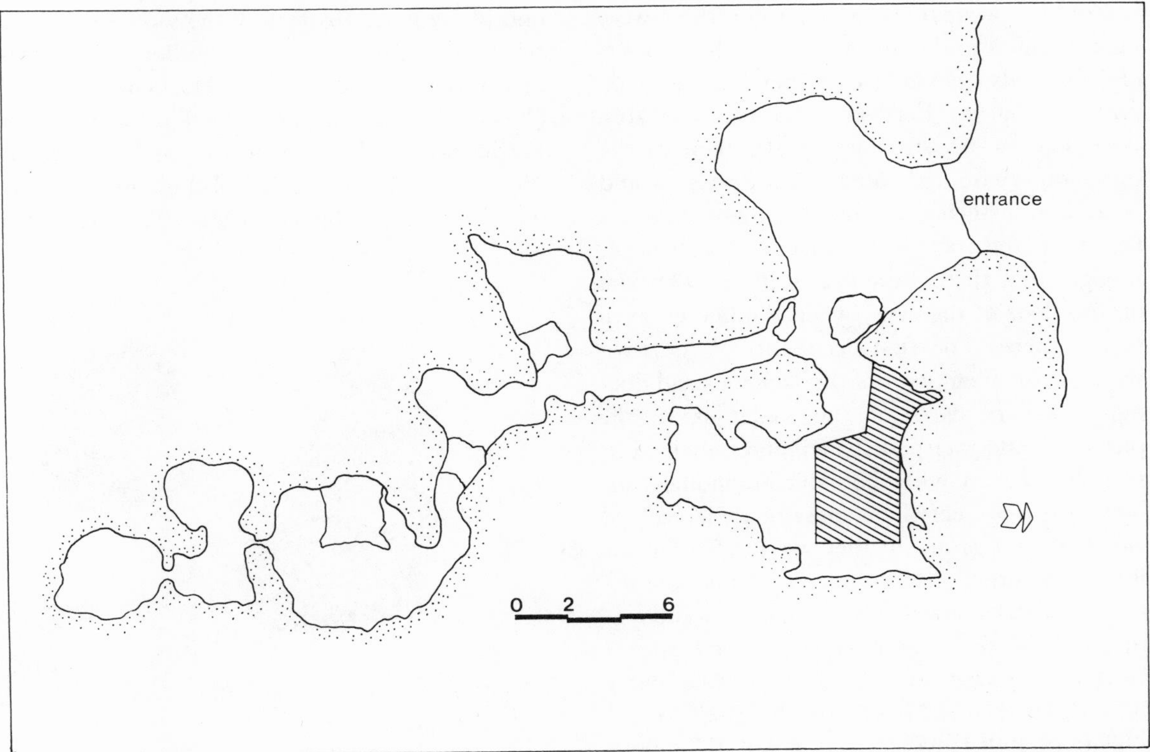

Fig. 2. Ground plan of the cave Ayios Georgios.

with small quantities of earth. The pottery was completely Neolithic except for traces of Hellenistic and late classic sherds found at the western side of the trench. At these stages it is possible that the cave was used as a sanctuary, if we can surmise from a niche hewn near the entrance.

The wealth of the pottery, the bone tools, the great number of querns and other stone implements as well as the animal bones and shells bear witness to intensive usage of the cave.

Stalactites and fallen rock impeded the excavation as we moved further down, and only at the western side of the trench were there thicker deposits. At the edge of the trench was a natural sink hole, which seems to have been used as a depository. This hole contained pottery, animal and human bones. Through dry sieving of the soil we were able to collect microfauna remains and seeds that give us important information about the subsistence habits of the inhabitants of the cave.

From the beginning we were puzzled by human remains found in the deepest layers. Particularly the presence of loose teeth, phalanges and metapodials, which seemed to belong to several different individuals, leads to the belief that the cave was used for primary burials, possibly before the occupation phase, since they were mainly found in the lower levels of the depository. It is also possible that these burials took place during an intermediate period. Probably the bodies were left lying on the floor of the cave; otherwise the occupation levels would have been disturbed by the opening of graves, a fact that was not substantiated. We believe, though, that there were practically no deposits on the floor of the cave, when the bodies were placed there. The first occupants of the cave were forced to empty it of the skeletons and during transport parts of the skeletons (teeth, phalanges and interpodials) fell and remained in situ. In contrast with the older individuals, infants are represented by most of their skeletal elements and probably they were left more or less undisturbed. Of course, a distinction between the mortuary treatment of infants and mature individuals is commonplace in prehistory[3]. In general, secondary burials have previously been discovered in Greek neolithic sites[4].

Pottery styles indicate that at Kalythies there are three phases of the Late Aegean Neolithic (1-3) that correspond to Late Chalcolithic 1-3 of Anatolia[5], except for the sporadic red-on-white sherds located at the deepest levels that have affinities with the Hacilar culture[6]. During the earlier phase (Kalythies 1) we distinguished a pottery with "mechanical slip"[7] and early white-on-dark, a decoration style very popular in the Aegean[8] (figs. 3, 4). The pottery of the second phase is approximately the same except for two new shapes and horned handles[9]. These two phases correspond to the Ayio Gala of Chios ("lower cave II", "upper cave I"), Saliagos and Emporio IX-X[10]. Characteristic of Late Aegean Neolithic 3 (Kalythies III) is the white designs on a red or black slipped surface. The shapes are

Fig. 3. White on dark painted sherds.

Fig. 4. Neolithic pottery from Kalythies.

shallow or deep bowls and pithoid[11]. These three phases cover a one-thousand-year period from the beginning of the 5th millenium to the beginning of the 4th millenium BC. The last phase of the Late Aegean Neolithic as well as the Bronze Age do not appear in the cave.

The variety and abundance of animal bones indicate that the occupants of the cave were mainly pastoralists. P. Halstead, who studied the bones, concluded that the animals were slaughtered outside the cave and subsequently transported piecemeal to it. Also the presence of molluscs and bird bones indicates a variety of food resources, since the sea is close by. The carbonized seeds as well as seed imprints on pottery show that cereals were also consumed. Hunting was also practised as evidenced by the deer remains that were found in the cave. We conclude that the cave was mainly occupied between the spring and the fall, if we are to judge by the age of the slaughtered animals and by the bones of migratory birds that pass over Rhodes during the fall.

Of course, we cannot completely exclude the use of the cave during the rest of the year. The inhabitants must have been members of the families belonging to a nearby settlement. In any case it is hard to explain how and why such an inaccesible cave was utilized. It is, however, very well protected and an excellent refuge in case of attack.

Fig. 5. Ground plan of the cave Koumelo.

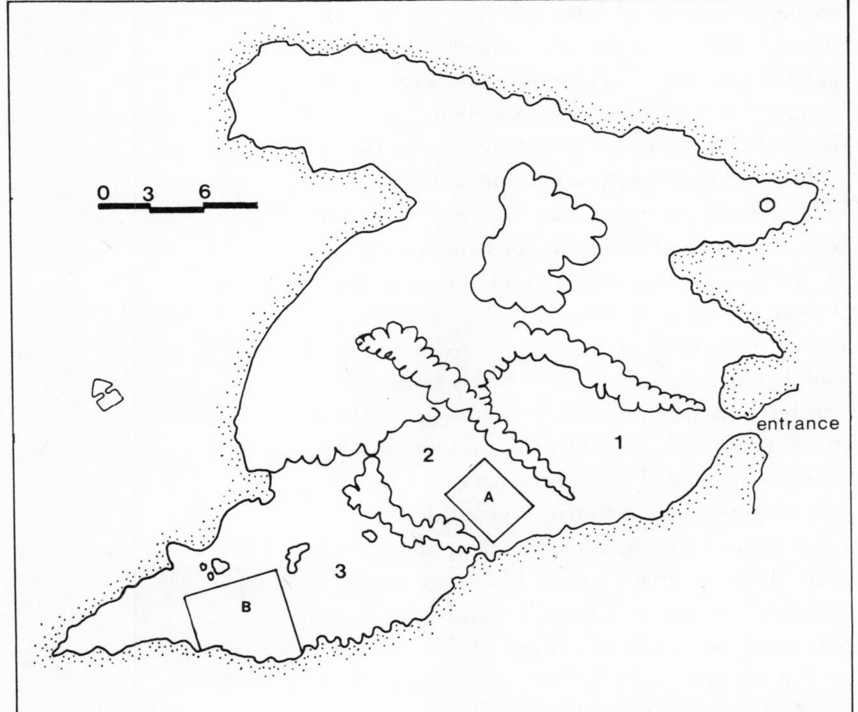

Koumelo Cave.

The situation of the second cave appear substantially different. It is located at an altitude of 140 m near the sea, one hour's distance from the village of Archangelos. Neolithic and Hellenistic sherds were observed as surface finds near the entrance. Rain water entering from the opening of the cave had filled in chambers 2 and 3 (fig. 5), making an even, level surface. No traces of ancient remains were found on the surface, indicating that a lengthy period without human activity had elapsed.

Our first trench in chamber 2 produced a very clear stratigraphy, quite different from that of Kalythies. The layers of later fill covered the living floors. At a depth of 15 cm, Hellenistic sherds were unearthed, while at a depth of 20-30 cm, a true living floor appeared. Under this layer there was an early Late Bronze Age level along with a layer of volcanic ash. Starting at a depth of 65 cm, an apsidal hearth was detected. The deposits on floor 2 represent a period of dry climatic conditions. After a layer completely void of evidence, we reached another living floor 3 at a depth of 85 cm, where abundant pithoi bear witness to food-storing activities (fig. 6). Special mention must be made of two human teeth, unconnected with other skeletal remains, on the lowest part of this layer. This was indication that here, too, secondary burials might have taken place. Possibly at a certain phase, while the cave was uninhabited, it was utilized as a burial ground; the skeletal remains having been subsequently transported to another site outside the cave proper. Following floor 3 there was an aceramic layer, while at a depth of 1.25 m we reached a new floor 4, one of limited activity. Under floor 4 fallen stalactites were located: these must be connected with a period of intense seismic activity. Subsequently, the excavation reached a depth of 1.80 m without encountering any sign of human habitation at this level.

Floors 3 and 4 represent an early and a late part of a neolithic phase corresponding to Late Aegean Neolithic 3 – Late Chalcolithic 3 (first half of the 4th millenium), in other words analogous with the last phase of Kalythies (III). Floor 2 (Archangelos II) corresponds to the last neolithic phase (Late Aegean Neolithic 4), not encountered at Kalythies, but quite common in Rhodes and other islands.

The layers of chamber 3 showed an equal sequence. This impressive cave chamber, darker and wetter than the previous one, with the most magnificent stalactitic background is connected with chamber 2 through a small opening. Down to a depth of 80 cm, there were thin layers of water-borne earth with a characteristic absence of pottery, indicating that no human activity following early Late Bronze Age can be successfully attested. At this point we were puzzled by the existence of a white, 70 cm thick layer starting at a depth of 80 cm. Laboratory examination of samples by the Freiburg Mineralogisches Institut proved that this was volcanic ash from Santorini. Comparable ash layers have also been detected in Crete[12], Kos (cave of Aspri Petra and elsewhere), Karpathos, Tilos[13] and recently at Chalki. These can be dated 1500-1450 BC, in other words about the time of the great Santorini eruption. It must be underlined that this tephra layer is considerably greater in the Dodecanese than in Crete, where at places it appears insignificant or not at all. It seems that the prevailing winds at the time of the eruption were NW or W, resulting in ash transport and subsequent deposition in the Dodecanese at a distance of approximately 250 km from the volcanic cone. It is calculated that a thick layer of tephra must have covered Rhodes and the other islands culminating probably in the destruction of both cultivation and animals. Doumas[14] believes that, despite its thickness, the tephra which fell on Rhodes had little, if any, influence on the settlement of Ialysos (Trianda).

The lower part of this layer in both trenches at Koumelo contained ceramics of early LBA including pottery of early Late Cycladic type fitting quite well with the estimated time of the eruption. It is quite possible that the ash layer in cave chamber 3 was formed by the transport and deposition of ash from the surrounding mountain side as a result of the torrential rains that must have followed the volcanic eruption. Careful geologic study revealed that this ash cannot be of aeolic deposition. This is also revealed by the fact that the lower segment of the layer is homogeneous and the upper mixed with heterogeneous materials. Chamber 3 contained larger quantities of ash because it is situated at a lower level than chamber 2. A detailed report on this matter is being prepared by a specialist.

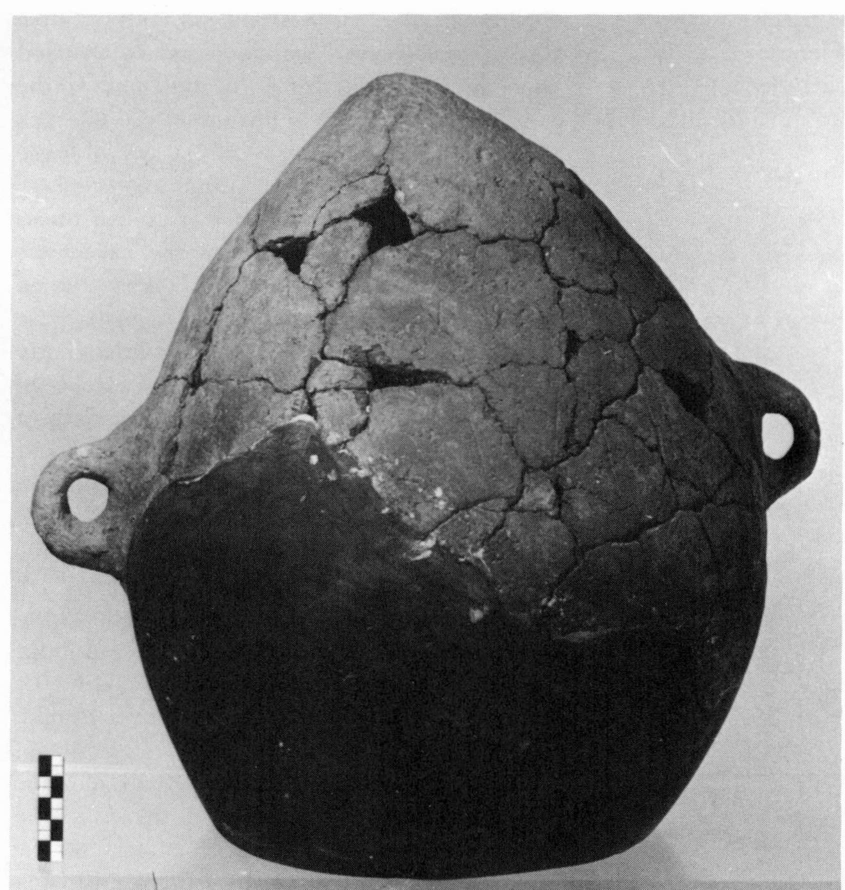

Fig. 6. Koumelo. Pithoid vase.

This ash had tightly sealed the neolithic layers in chamber 3. A living floor appeared at a depth of 1.55 m around a circular construction (figs. 7, 8) used as a hearth. Pottery and animal bones of the Archangelos II phase (LAN 4) were found. Down to a depth of 2.25 m, where the natural rock begins, we found other floors with several fire remains but practically no pottery. Above the natural rock we detected a layer of argil, which was created within the cave and presumably in a wet, warm climate. Neolithic sherds of Late Aegean Neolithic 4 were on the natural rock. The fact that phase LAN 4 was found at different depths in chambers 2 and 3 (0.65 and 1.55 m respectively) is a result of the difference in altitude and because there is a wall of stalagmitic material between the two.

Fig. 7. Koumelo. The trench in chamber 3.

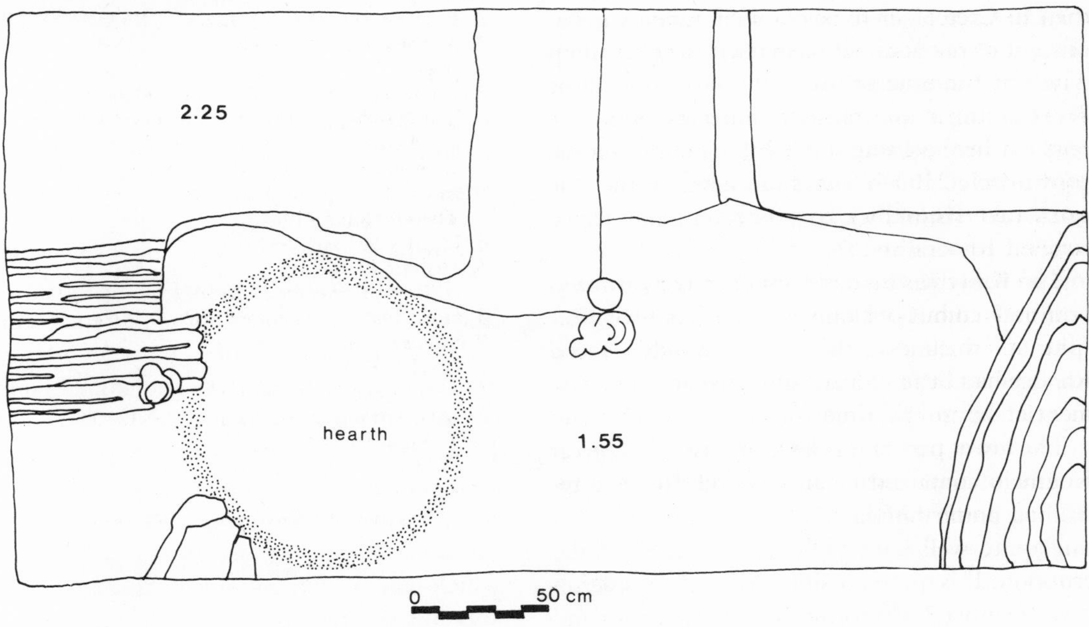

Fig. 8. Ground plan of a living floor in Koumelo.

Conclusions.

It appears that, in general, the cave chamber 2 was sporadically in use in phase LAN 3. In chamber 3 occupation started at the end of the Neolithic and there is more activity in chamber 3 than in chamber 2. This fact is hard to explain because chamber 3 is darker and wetter. Even lighting a fire would be difficult, unless conditions at that time were different. Characteristically, in Neolithic times, probably LAN 4, the opening between the two chambers was blocked up by means of small stones and ash mortar. There is no habitation attested for the Early and Middle Bronze Age, but briefly for the early Late Bronze Age and the Hellenistic times.

The restricted number of artifacts does not allow us to conclude that habitation of the site was continuous. The Koumelo cave, because of its location and orientation, is better suited for habitation than the Kalythies cave. Despite this fact signs show that it was utilized sporadically and circumstantially. Humans entered from time to time to bury the dead, to store food or to collect water from the dripping stalactites, and for other reasons. Near the cave there are two sites with neolithic remains, which presuppose the existence of small pastoral communities, because the area does not offer itself to cultivation. The same inhabitants seem to have used these caves at times and also the other caves of the region where we found Neolithic pottery on the surface level. But it seems more logical that the usual cave visitors were as they are today transhumant pastoralists.

The Kalythies cave was more actively utilized or inhabited but certainly not continuously. Our finds (a few hundred vases, a few hundred stone implements, a few dozen animals) are very few in relation to the time interval of a thousand years when the caves were in use. For great lengths of time during this period the cave remained uninhabited.

In my view, caves were not utilized for permanent habitation in Neolithic times as people could easily live in open-air settlements. For this reason the use of caves as burial grounds at these times is easily explained. It is believed that in Crete[15] caves were used exclusively as burial grounds. On the mainland[16] caves like Korykeio, Kitsos and Franchthi, Alepotrypa, Kastria at Kalavryta, Tharrounia and others, were occupied intensively during Neolithic times. But even then, in my opinion, they were utilized mostly by pastoralists, fishermen or food gatherers, seasonally or periodically, probably as a result of the new social conditions that prevailed at the time.

Adamantios Sampson
Chalkis Museum
El. Venizelou 13
Euboia
Greece

1. R. Hope Simpson – D. Lazenby, BSA 68, 1973.
2. A. Sampson, The Neolithic of the Dodecanese and the Aegean Neolithic, BSA 79, 1984, 239.
3. An example in Neolithic Dimini, Hourmouziades 1968.
4. T.W. Jacobsen – T. Cullen, A consideration of Mortuary Practices in Neolithic Greece, in Humphreys – King (eds.) Mortality and Immortality: the anthropology and archaeology of death, 1981; G. Hourmouziades in Theocharis (ed.) 1973.
5. Lloyd – Mellaart 1962.
6. Mellaart 1970.
7. A. Furness, ProcPS 22, 1956.
8. Hood 1981; A. Sampson, BSA 79, 1984.
9. Sampson 1986.
10. Hood 1981.
11. A. Sampson, AEphem 1983.
12. N.D. Watkins et al., Nature 1978, 122-126.
13. A. Sampson, AAA 12, 1980.
14. C. Doumas – L. Papazoglou, Nature 5780, 1980.
15. Zois 1973.
16. A. Sampson, Archaeologia 15, 1985.

Neolithic Skeletal Remains from the Kalythies Cave, Rhodes

Manolis Foundoulakis

Introduction

Before starting my lecture, I would like to mention some of the information that dental research can offer to palaeoanthropology and palaeopathology.

Sex and age of death of the individuals are usually indicated by the dentology, which contributes much to palaeoanthropological research.

It should be considered that the jaws and teeth are generally in better condition than the other skeletal bones, because of the density and hardness of their molecules (tissues). It is for this reason that the study of skeletal remains from archaeological excavations is often based on teeth and jaw fragments.

Thus, it is possible to combine extremely detailed information related to the causes of dental wear with poor alimentation, probable hypoplasias, caries, dental diseases and injuries, which considerably contributes to archaeological research in order to interpret culturally and demographically the "dental remains".

Last winter the Greek Ministry of Culture and the Ephors of Antiquities, Dr. Sampson and Dr. Papachristodoulou, gave me the opportunity to study the human skeletal material found in the Neolithic cave of Kalythies in Rhodes. It must be noted that Neolithic cave occupants were here found for the first time in the Dodecanese. Furthermore, the bones preserved after seven millenia are far fewer then expected from 20 burials.

Method

Firstly, very careful mechanical cleaning of the material was carried out to remove foreign matter, using soft brushes, thin dental instruments, and special bellows.

Then use was made of a magnifier lense 20X, a stereoscopic microscope 40X for the close examination, and the material was subjected to photography and radiography. After this systematic recording, calculation, classification and a detailed examination of the remains were performed. The modern view of anthropological investigation is that purification of the material and chemical preservation of the bones must be avoided. Otherwise, a future determination of skeletal A, B, O, typing, after a special elaboration of "spongy tissue" of the bones, would be quite unlikely.

Material

Unfortunately there is not one complete skeleton, no entire skull or long bones, but just small fragments. At this point we should mention that the composition of the soil, mostly "fire residues", and generally the good environmental conditions of this cave, preserved the material to a remarkable degree.

Description of Individuals

The skeletal remains from the deeper layers of the cave were examined as follows (Table 1). In this table the presentation of skeletal remains is very clear: (phot. 1,2) (Ζαφειράτος 1982).

- 55 different cranial fragments is a considerable number: a left brow ridge, and a right mastoid process.
- 13 children's cranial fragments.
- 2 vertebrae (one lumbar, one thoracic).
- a humerus fragment, from the diaphysis.
- 2 radius fragments.
- a fragment of the left Ulna proximal epiphysis.
- 1 patella.
- fragments of Femur and Tibia, diaphysis, and
- Metacarpal and metatarsal bones.

As we can see there is a complete lack of fundamental bones that would make it possible to record: stature, robusticity, alimentation and daily activity of the Neolithic inhabitants of Rhodes. (Angel 1959, Duday 1970).

HUMAN REMAINS FROM NEOLYTHIC KALYTHIES' CAVE - MEASUREMENTS

Table 1

MEASUREMENTS (In mm)	BROWRIDGE L	MASTOID PROCESS R	HUMERUS	RADIUS L	RADIUS R	ULNA L	PATELLA R	FEMUR R	TIBIA
MAXIMUM LENGTH	56	25	56	110	85	72	35	166	85
MAXIMUM BREADTH	20	16	16	14	12	17	40	29	25
MAXIMUM HEIGTH	15	13					19		
MAXIMUM DIAPHYSEAL DIAMETER			20	16	14	20		27	26
PROXIMAL EPIPHYSEAL DIAMETER				21		21			

Nevertheless close examination of the material allows certain observations to be made as follows:
Especially from the nature of the collection of teeth, it can be concluded that this Neolithic cave contained at least 20 individuals.

I assume this after Dr. Sampson's explanations about cave usage. To be more specific we have: 13 adults and 7 children. Table 2 gives us the relevant information. An effort to analyze this table, the burials in conjunction with the sex of individuals, could show:
- a child about three years of age.
- a five-year-old child, and another six years at death.
- a girl and a boy about eight years of age.
- a child (Inf. II) about ten and a boy 12 years old.

We also have 13 adults over the age of 17: four female, four male and five of indeterminable sex.

The sex of the adults and the age of the children were determined from comparative examination of the morphology and dimensions of 16 medial upper incisor pairs, and from the nature of teeth sperms and deciduous teeth.

The picture given by this collection also suggests a relationship between some of the individuals (Table 3). As indicated in Table 4 and in the Table 5 based on the dental wear (attrition) of 25 molars, the adults can be divided into three age groups at death. One group about 17 to 25 years old, a second 25 to 35 and a third 35 to 45.

AGE AND SEX DETERMINATION

SEX	AGE PERIOD: INFANT I 3 - 4	4 - 5	6 - 7	8 - 9	INFANT II 10 - 11	11 - 12	ADULTS 17 - 45	TOTAL
♀				●			(4) ●	5
♂				●		●	(4) ●	6
INDEFINITE	●	●	●		●		(5) ●	9

Table 2

It must be noted that I judge one male and one female as being from 35 to 40 years old (according to Brothwell's classification of group age, modified) (Brothwell 1981). Also 3 individuals were aged from 17 to 25, two were about 25-35 years, three about 35 years old and three about 35-45 years old at death.

We should have about 450-500 teeth in conjunction with the dentition of 13 adults and 7 children. However, the collection of teeth contains only one third of the normal number.

Dentition: Health and Pathology of Neolithic Rhodians.

The dentition of the occupants of the Kalythies cave gives the picture that the dental

KALYTHIES' CHILDREN DENTAL AGE DETERMINATION

AGE (YEARS)	TEETH - OBSERVATIONS		TOOTH SYMBOLIK NUMBER	INDIVIDUALS
3 - 4	1st L. Pe. Up. Mo.	Sperm's	16	1
	1st R. Pe. Lo. Mo.		26	
4 - 5	Decid. R. Me. Up. In.		51	1
6 - 7	Decid. L. Me. Up. In.		61	1
8 - 9	1st R. Pe. Lo. Mo.		46	1
	Perman. R. Lat. Lo. In.		42	
8 - 9	Decid. 2nd L. Lo. Mo.		75	1
	Decid. 2nd R. Lo. Mo.		85	
10 - 11	Perman. L. Lo. Ca.		33	1
	Perman. R. La. In.		42	
11 - 12	Perman. L. Up. Ca.		23	1
	Perman. R. Up. 2nd Pr.		14	
TOTAL	Teeth Sperm's :		2	7
	Deciduous Teeth :		4	
	Permanent Teeth :		6	

Table 3

health of these Neolithic people was comparatively poor (Table 6). I assume this because the following dental damage was observed on their teeth.

Caries: (Table 7). From this table it clearly appears that 34 of 150 permanent teeth showed caries, the most common dental disease. This means a high percentage of carious teeth (22.7%). This is almost a quarter of the number of teeth. The morphology of the carious teeth is detailed in Table 8. (phot. 3, 4, 5, 6) (Κρίνος 1935, Brothwell 1981, Ταραμίδης 1983).

Attrition: 134 of the 150 teeth appear worn. This high percentage (89.3%) is caused by the hard food of the Neolithic diet. The next three pictures show the teeth wear with pattern classification. (phot. 3, 4, 5, 7).

Pulp Exposure: This damage is caused by very advanced chronic attrition. In the 11 cases, 8 premolars appear exposed. (phot. 9).

Calculus Deposits: There are 30 teeth with a build up of calculus deposits, classified from slight to medium degree. It is obvious that these neolithic individuals suffered periodontal diseases. (phot. 10).

Reactive Elaborations: In six teeth we observe root thickening. This characteristic thickness of the root is an expression of traumatic occlusion. To be more specific this osteogenic reactive elaboration consists of secondary ostein and dentin. (phot. 11).

At the same time, we have an internal reactive elaboration which results in a diminution of the pulp cavity. The main reasons for this traumatic occlusion are considered to be the following:
- orthodontic abnormal occlusions,
- hard alimentation,
- bad habits, such as "teeth gnashing".

Disorders of Dendogeny: It is thought that the appearance of the disorders of odontogens on 22 teeth (14.6%), is due to alterations in the quantity of deposition of dental substances during odontogeny.

I consider the main reasons are:
- A short term disease, such as feverish infantile diseases.
- Deficiency in vitamin D.
- Traumatic shock to dentinoblasts and adamantinoblasts.

The reason for the discoloured enamel abnormality of tooth crowns was Ionic lack of calcium and phosphorus, and to alterations in the physiologic fluorine contents of the diet. Final conclusions can be drawn after a chemical analysis of the soil and water and determination of the Ph. This dental hypoplasia is clearly observable in these pictures. (phot. 12, 13, 14). We can also see the impression of layers of arrested growth, a kind of piles of enamel and ostein deposits (Redzius and Pickeril, stride). It should be noted that these 22 cases are derived from four individuals (2 children and 2 adults) 20%. (Duday, 1970, Δουβίτσας – Λαγουβάρδος1984).

Morphological Reduction: We observed that the four upper third molars appeared reduced. Two of them are reduced and the other two much reduced. This is an additional case of dental hy-

CLASSIFICATION OF KALYTHIES' DENTAL ATTRITION (MOLARS)

ADULTS AGE DETERMINATION

Table 4

DEGREE	ATTRITION (WEAR) PATERN					TOTAL	%	AGE PERIOD
	UPPER TEETH			LOWER TEETH				
	M_1	M_2	M_3	M^1	M_2			
B_2			4			6	24	17 - 25
Δ								
$Δ_1$						3	12	17 - 25
$Δ_2$								
E_1						2	8	25 - 35
ΣΤ								25 - 35
$ΣΤ_1$	2					9	36	
$ΣΤ_2$								35
$ΣΤ_3$					2			
Z		2				2	4	35 - 40
H_1								
H_2						4	16	35 - 45
H_3								
TEETH TOTALITY	5	7	4	5	4			

MORFOLOGICAL AND ALPHABETICAL CLASSIFICATION OF DENTAL ATTRITION

Table 5 (Key-Table)

DEGREE	ATTRITION (WEAR) PATERN	OBSERVATION
A		Absent
B	1, 2	Enamel only Polishing
Γ	1, 2	Dentine pointed with Enamel patern
Δ	1, 2, 3	Dentine only pointed to Excuesioned
E	1, 2, 3	Dentine Exposed
ΣΤ	1, 2, 3	Dentine Exposed
Z	1, 2	— Dentine very exposed — Partial loss of crown — (Bow - shaped) crown
H	1, 2, 3	— Considerable loss of crown — (Bow - shaped) crown — Pulp exposurs
Θ		Total loss of crown
I		Roots

DENTITION OF KALYTHIES' CAVE

Table 6

OBSERVATIONS		INCISORS	CANINE	PREMOLARS	MOLARS	TOTAL	%
ALVEOLI :	Available	2	1	1	3	7	—
TEETH :	Available	49	19	49	46	163	—
	Unerupted	—	1	2	—	3	1,8
	Erupted	2	4	4	3	13	8
	Permanent	47	15	45	43	150	92
	Wearless	2	4	2	4	12	8
	Cariousless	49	19	36	25	129	86
	Carious	—	—	13	21	34	22,7
	Attritious	47	15	47	25	134	89,3
Carious plus Attritious		—	—	12	18	30	20

DENTAL PATHOLOGY

Table 7

TEETH	UPPER I.	UPPER C.	UPPER P.	UPPER M.	LOWER I.	LOWER C.	LOWER P.	LOWER M.	TOTAL	%
CARIES										
— Occlusal			●	(4) ●			(4) ●	(4) ●	13	8,6
— Neck Interproximal			(4) ●	●			●	(7) ●	13	8,6
— Over - Neck Interproximal				(3) ●					3	2
— Under - Neck Interproximal			●					(2) ●	3	2
— Andvanset			●				●		2	1,3
PULP EXPOSURS			(3) ●	(2) ●			(5) ●	●	11	7,3
CALCULUS DEPOSIT	(6) ●	●	(4) ●	(5) ●	(8) ●	(2) ●		(4) ●	30	20
REACTIF ELABORATIONS	●		(3) ●				(3) ●		7	4,6
DISORDERS OF DENDOGENY	(2) ●	(8) ●	(5) ●	(2) ●		(2) ●	(2) ●	●	22	14,6
MORPHOLOGICAL REDUCE				(4) ●					4	2,6
MORHOLOGICAL LESIONS	(2) ●		(2) ●	●	●		(2) ●	(2) ●	10	6,6

Table 8

SHEMATIC REPRESENTATION AND CLASSIFICATION OF CARIOUS TEETH

CARIES	PREMOLARS	UPPER - MOLARS	LOWER - MOLARS
Occlusal			
Neck Interproximal			
Over - Neck Interproximal			
Under - Neck Interproximal			
Advanset (Hollowed - out) Dentine			

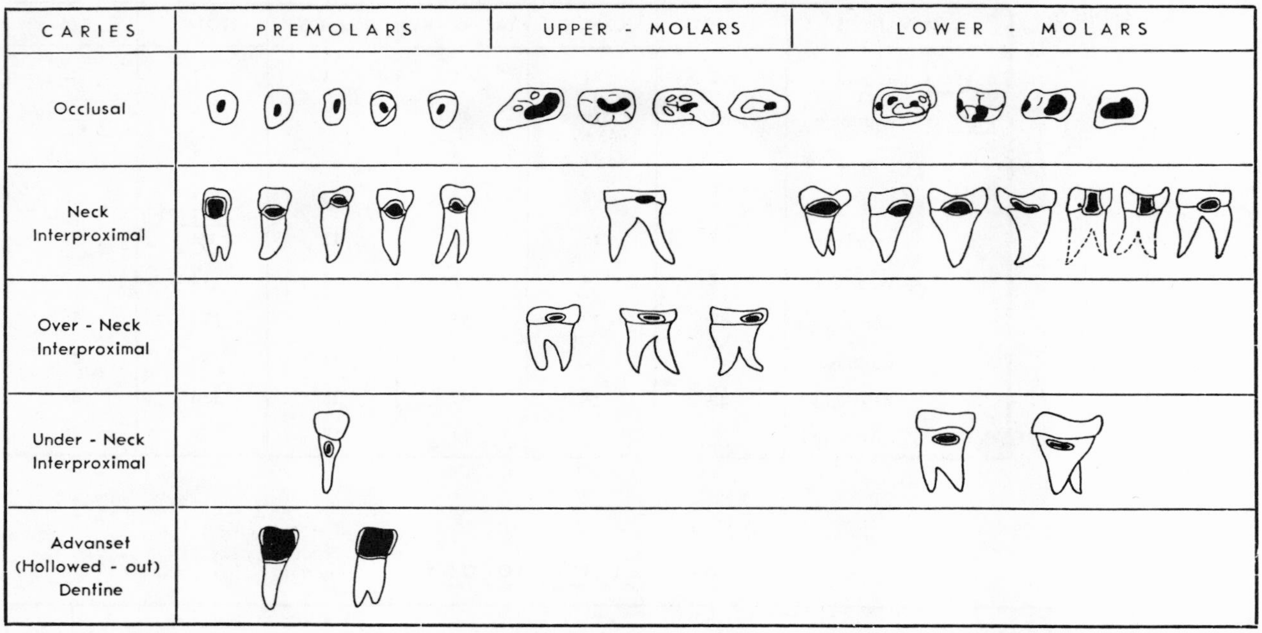

poplasia. (phot. 4: Upper row, 4th tooth from the left).

Morphological Lesions: We also observed some particularly characteristic attrition, as an expression of daily occupation activity. For instance, cutting of a thread and for alleviating the pain caused by periodontal disease.

Root Absorptions: These damages are caused by traumatic occlusions and abscesses.

Accidental Chipping of Crown: Caused by the effort to masticate hard foods (for example: wild nuts, hard roots, etc.). (phot. 8).

General Conclusions: The main conclusions drawn from this study are:

- That the Neolithic inhabitants of Rhodes had very poor dental health.
- Only hypothetical explanations can be given concerning lifestyle and the reasons for death or diseases.

At any rate, from the frequent occurrence of advanced dental attrition, pulp exposure, abscess, and the general oral diseases previously mentioned, (Table 7), we can conclude that the Neolithic inhabitants of Rhodes, compared (Shulte-Campbell 1979, Nyquist 1980, Fischer 1980, Lound 1983, Ταραμίδης 1983) with other prehistoric populations of the same general area, (Table 9) had worse dental, pathological problems (especially caries), and developmental problems, and they suffered from accute dental pains, caeosmia, etc.

Manolis Foundoulakis
Papanastasiou 12
Chalcis, 34100
Greece

Table 9

CARIOUS TEETH - AVERAGE PERCENTANGE OF PREHISTORIC POPULATIONS

REGIONS		TOTAL TEETH	CARIOUS	AVERAGE PERCENTANGE
NEOLITHIC	KALYTHIES	150	34	22,6
	KITSOS	84	3	3,6
	KHIROKITIA	853	12	1,4
	N. NICOMEDEIA	—	—	1,3
Early Bronge Age :	MANIKA	120	7	5,8
Midle Bronge Age :	LERNA	—	—	2,2
Early Iron Age :	PALAIPAPHOS	74	None	0

Photo 1. Human remains from neolithic Kalythies' cave.

Photo 2. Lower (left) and upper (right) childrens "jaws".

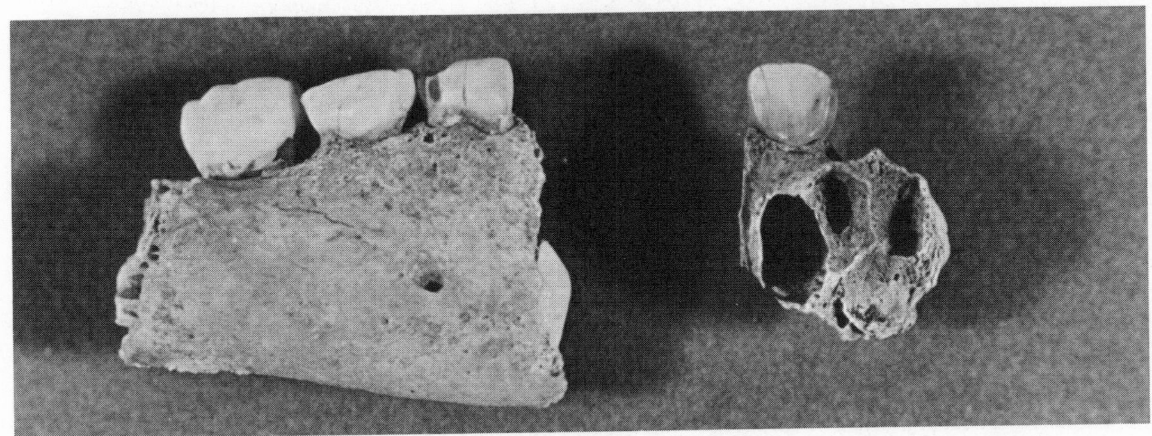

Photo 8. a. Dental wear (attrition) and b. accidental "chip-crown".

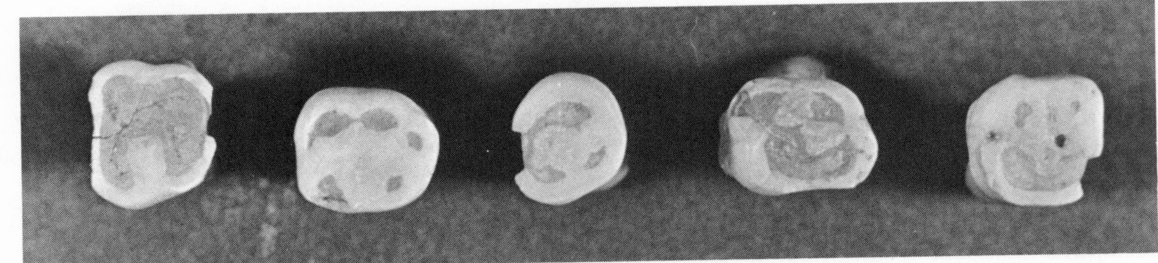

Photo 3. Attritious teeth with partial to considerable loss of crown.

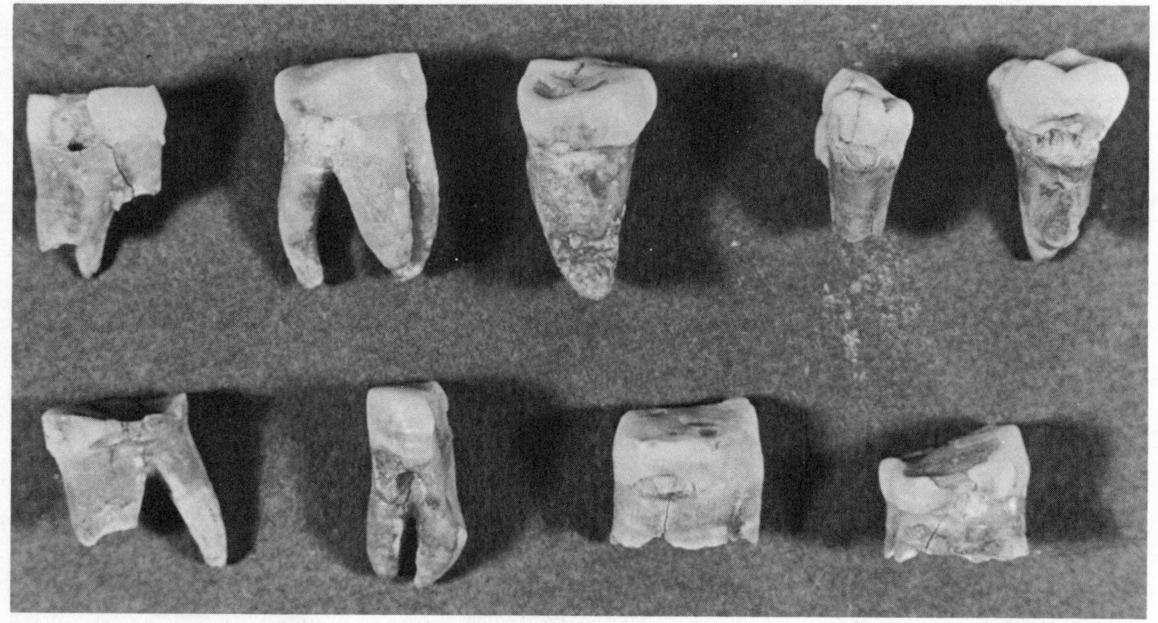

Photo 4. Carious molars (neck caries).

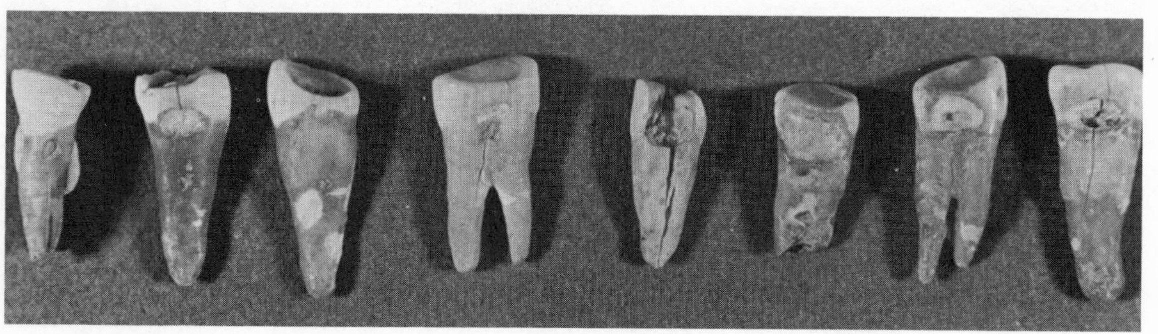

Photo 5. Carious premolars (neck caries).

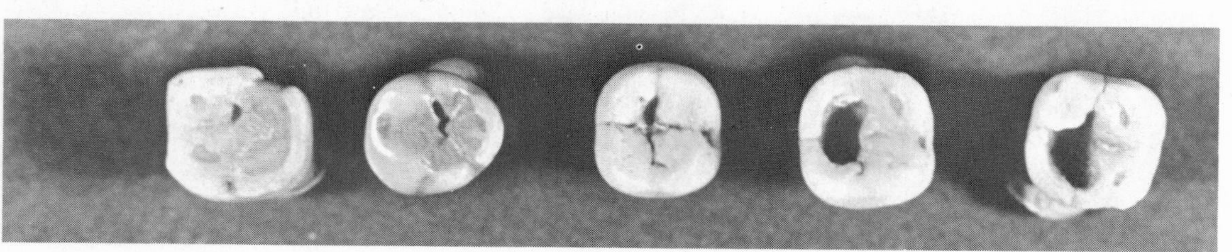

Photo 6. Carious molars (occlusal caries).

Photo 9. Molars and premolars with pulp exposures.

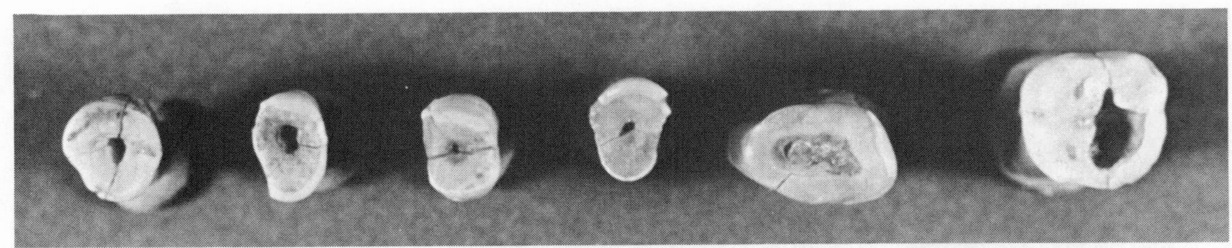

Photo 10. Teeth with calculus deposits.

Photo 11. Teeth (roots) with reactive elaborations.

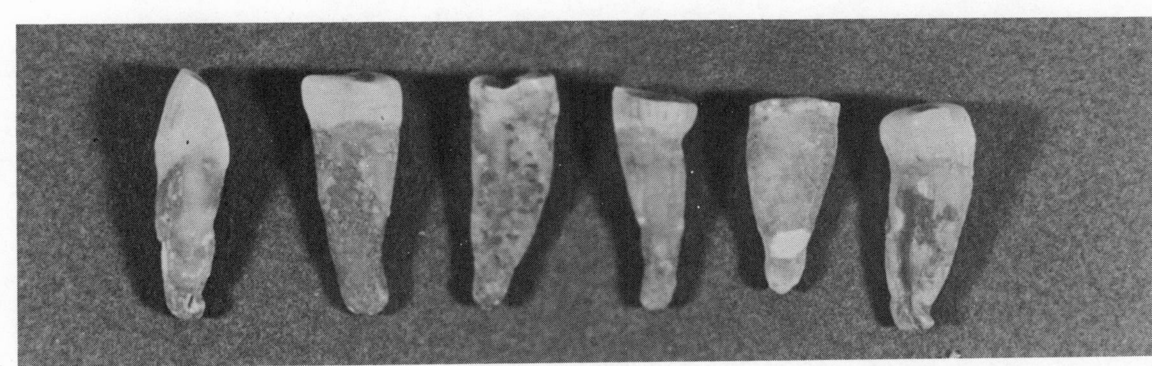

Photo 12. Teeth with disorders of dendogeny.

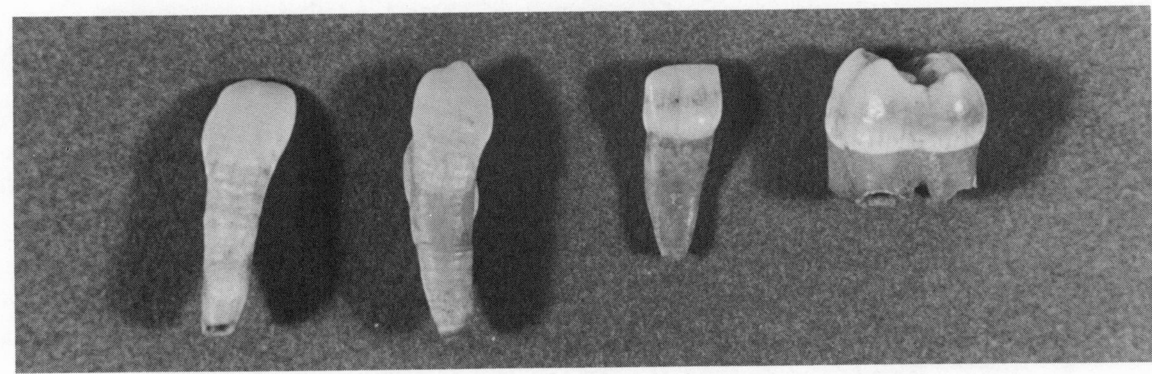

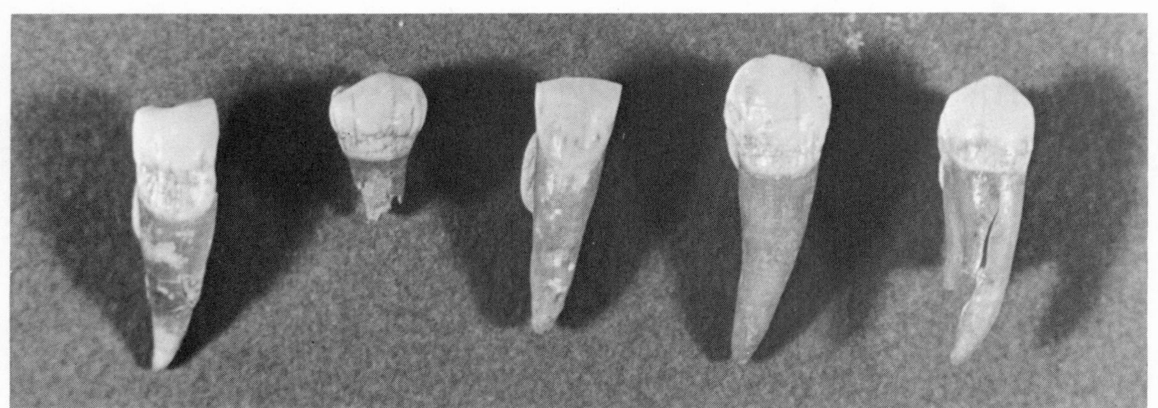

Photo 13. Teeth (permanent) with (wear) pattern classification.

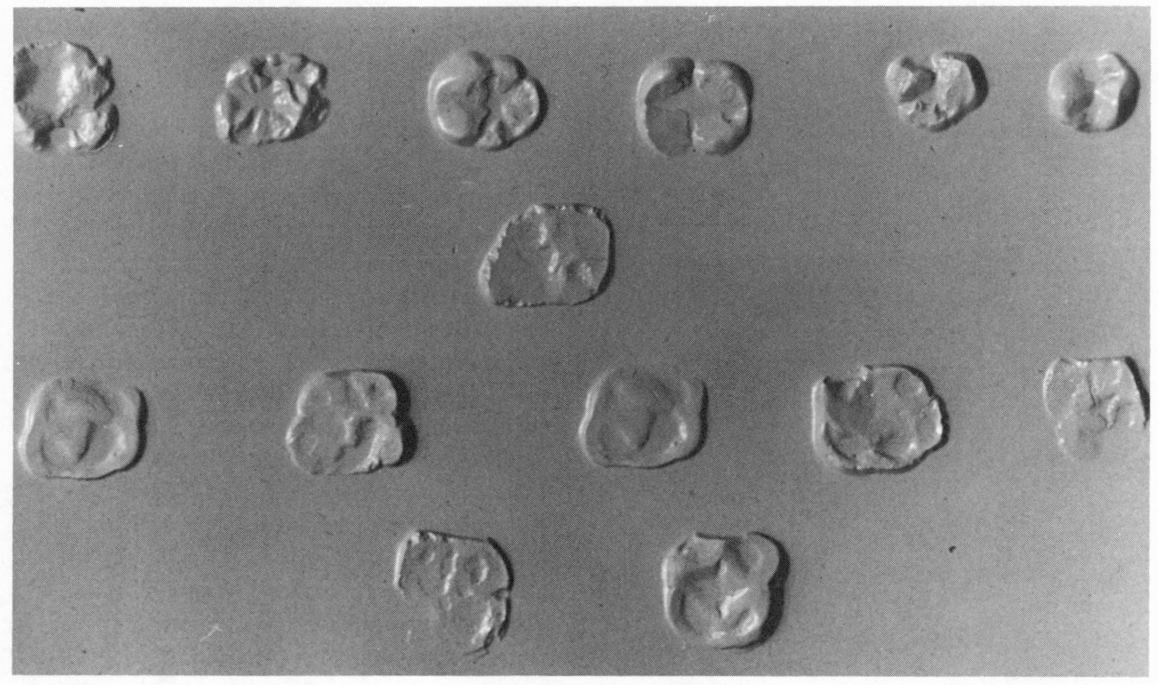

Photo 7. Tooth impressions with (wear) pattern classification.

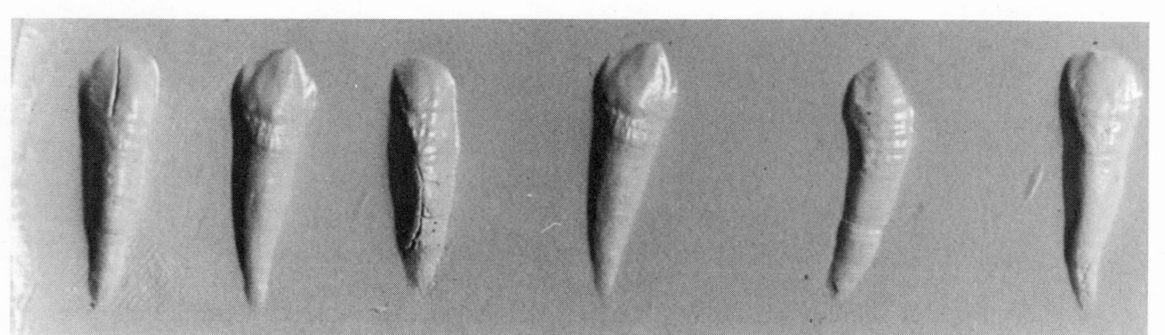

Photo 14. Teeth impressions with noticeable enamel hypoplasia layers of arrested growth.

New Evidence on the Topography and Site History of Prehistoric Ialysos

Toula Marketou

Today, fifty years after the Italian excavations at Trianda[1], and thirty-six years after Furumark's fundamental article[2], the general view of prehistoric Ialysos is widely changed. The Greek Archaeological Service began new excavations in 1978[3]. These excavations and recent field work in North-western Rhodes allow us to trace Minoan expansion during successive chronological phases and periods.

New topographical evidence in this part of the island provides a distribution map of the development of early settlement patterns and constitutes the basis for the analysis of the problem of Minoan expansion in Rhodes and its place in Aegean prehistory (fig. 1).

This paper is a preliminary report of our work[4], based on the up-to-date evidence, which comes from seven nearly unknown sites in addition to the well known Trianda settlement. The first Minoan evidence, mentioned by Coldstream and recently published by Benzi[5], comes from Mt. Philerimos. This evidence and that from the plain settlement of Trianda depict a development and growth which is complemented by the recently discovered site on Prophitis Elias, on the north-eastern side of Mt. Philerimos[6]. In the side of a ravine, widening from continuous erosion, near an abandoned church, we have found unstratified pottery of various shapes: jugs with high necks, high spouted jugs, black or red carinated cups, conical cups and others (fig. 2). The chronology is MM I – MM II, the character is local, some elements of the shape betray foreign influence[7].

A clay pipe projected from the edge of the ravine (fig. 3), while another pipe part had fallen down the slope along with several sherds. A small trench was dug. It revealed the clay pipe

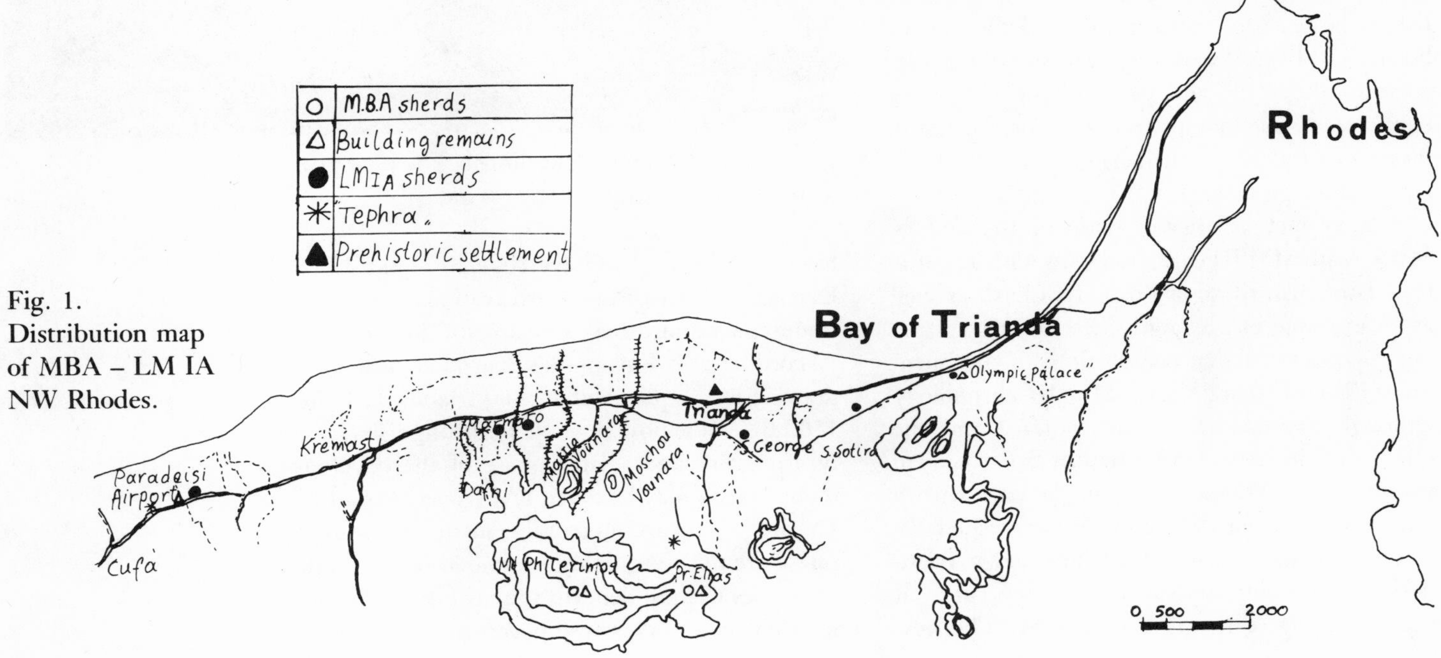

Fig. 1. Distribution map of MBA – LM IA NW Rhodes.

"in situ", running East-West along what seems to be a trace of a wall. In the trench the pottery was mostly LM IA early. It contained sherds of semiglobular cups and the neck of a spouted jug with knobs. It is likely that the pipe supplied water to the settlement situated somewhere to the east. The site of Prophitis Elias reinforces the argument that the earliest settlers of Ialysos first established themselves on Mt. Philerimos. The LM IA evidence near Mt. Philerimos, south of the settlement in the plain of Trianda, comes from test trenches dug in a building plot. Conical cups were found at a depth of 3 to 3.40 m from the surface. A layer of volcanic ash was revealed at just 0.9 m beneath which were LM IA sherds[8].

We come now to the main site of the Minoan expansion in North-western Rhodes, which is the settlement of Trianda. Trianda, together with Kythera, is one of the so-called Minoan colonies[9]. The colonial character of Trianda is still questionable but is outside the scope of this paper. The first occupation of the area coincides with the end of the MBA. The extent of this early town is not yet known (fig. 4). It was raised on the virgin soil of the area below what was to become the southmost area of the LM IA town. It seems that the main part of the settlement was focused on the area of plot 5 at the southern extent of the later town. Scattered remains of walls are revealed in the North sector of Plots 2 and 3. The only evidence of a catastrophe comes from a large burnt room in Plot 5. Fallen burnt beams and baked masses of clay from the upper parts of the walls and possibly the roof, give evidence of the first period. Part of the house was converted into a small cistern connected to a street drainage system[10].

The pottery is characteristic of the end of MBA, with MM III carinated cups with a profile type later than those of Prophitis Elias[11] as well as an example of a straightsided cup (fig. 5). A peg-top rhyton fallen on the floor of the burnt house (Room B) suggests a MM III chronology although the burnished dark surface and the quality of the clay differentiate it from Minoan prototypes[12]. Another example, a vase with a double neck, brings to mind Trojan parallels[13].

The second Minoan town (Furumark's Trianda I-IIA) was rebuilt over the previous ruins, at the beginning of the LM IA period. The new town is estimated to have covered about 12.25 hectares[14]. Four different excavations have been undertaken and three more are still in progress. According to Furumark's chronological diagram[15], it is equivalent to his Trianda I (1550-1500 BC). It is now possible to distinguish clearly an earlier and a later phase of the development, which may be dated LM IA early and LM IA late[16]. The architectural remains of the first phase are not thoroughly excavated because this phase lies exactly beneath the next one. Characteristics such as plastered pavements or floors of

Fig. 2. Sherds from Pr. Elias (Mt. Philerimos).

Fig. 3. Pr. Elias (Mt. Philerimos). The pipe projecting from the edge of the ravine.

Fig. 4.
Town plan of Trianda with plots 2, 3, 4, 5 and 6.

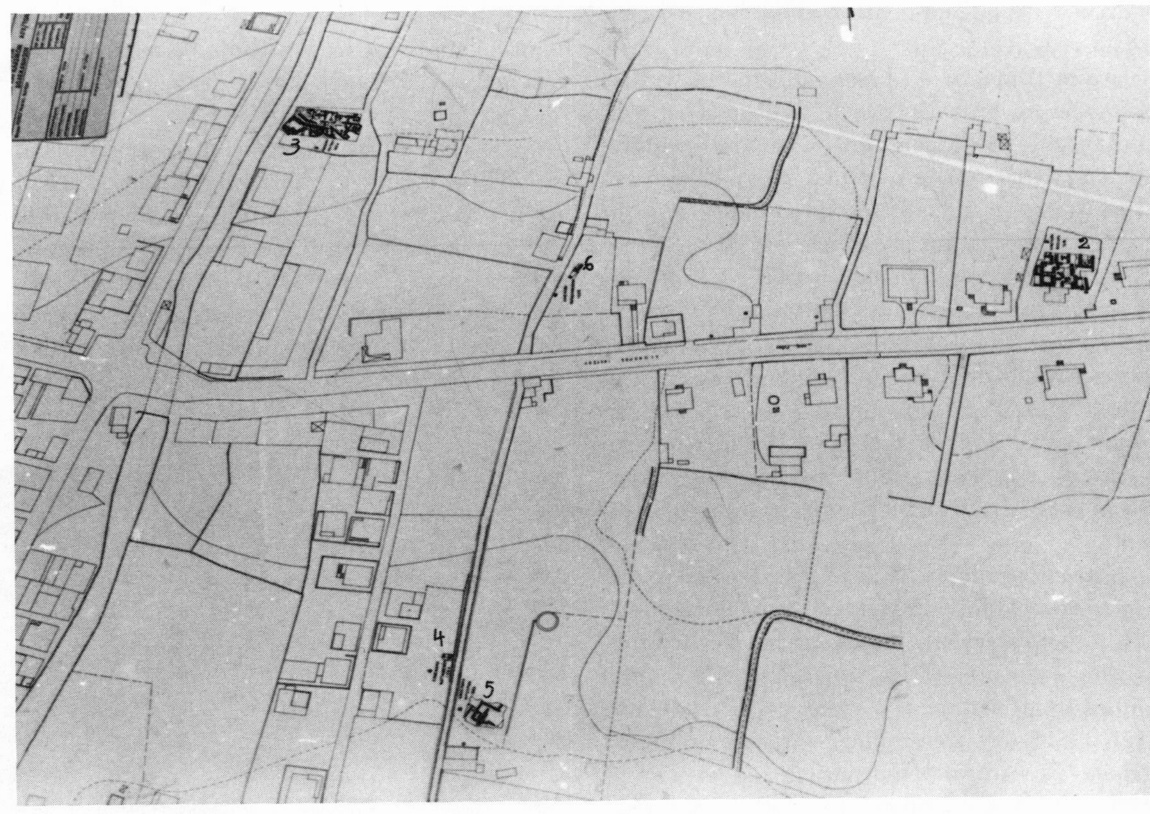

beaten earth and walls dressed with plaster are common to both phases. Walls of that early phase were usually repaired or sometimes reused. The orientation was also retained. Fundamental changes are visible in the North-western area of the town.

The Minoan evidence is strong during the second phase. It is obvious that the buildings of this phase are examples of a new town-planning on a larger scale. The renovation and rearrangement of the town were apparently necessary after the earthquakes[17] that had occurred at the end of the previous phase[18]. Excavation data allow us to detect the main area of the town.

Fig. 5.
Plot 3. MMIII cups.

Fig. 6. Plot 3. The polythyron.

This is between plots 3 and 6 in the North-western part of it.

Strong evidence of Minoan influence at Trianda is the *polythyron* in plot 3[19](fig. 6). This was built in the NW part of the town, shortly before the end of the LM IA period. It is of the type with four pier-and-door partitions and opens to the east onto a disturbed area and to the west onto an area open to the air, possibly a court, as is shown by the threshold found in the western side of the room. It was noticed that the polythyron was built on a sort of hilly area formed by rubbish from previous earthquakes. Another mound was S-SE of the *polythyron* in an open area, covered with tephra (volcanic ash). The thickness of the tephra layer ranges from 20 to 30 cm[20].

A polythyron is a kind of partition of space which admits fresh air and light from outside. In this case some tephra penetrated and covered the outside corner of the southern pier. This fact allows us to assume the direction of the wind blowing at that time. The Santorini tephra at Trianda is a distinct and measurable layer in a well defined stratigraphy. In another case, the layer of tephra rests on a court floor with scattered sherds and rubbish on it. A short distance SW of the polythyron (plot 6) we discovered the south-eastern corner of a building with an isodomic facade. The exterior face of the wall was built of carefully hewn blocks[21]. The inside was filled with rubble containing small poros stones. Pieces of coloured plaster were found inside this building.

G. Monaco, in his publication of Trianda, mentioned streets belonging to his "strato medio"[22]. A part of a "crossroad" was found in plot 5, where a narrow passageway with cobbled pavement was partially covered with volcanic tephra (fig. 8). This fact shows that it was never reused after the fall of tephra. The narrow passageway runs in the same direction as the earlier MBA/MM III street which was connected with the cistern.

The pieces of coloured plaster, some of them found in the interior of the building with the isodomic facade, bring to mind Knossian parallels; for example, a fragment depicting a white lily on a red background[23]. The blue ones with traces of yellow decoration show an advanced standard of technology. A fragment of a poros stone horn of consecration[24] was found among other stones, cut from a game board, in a well opened in the eastern corner of the polythyron.

Locally manufactured pottery of buff, pink-yellowish clay with grits and other admixtures of a quality inferior to the earlier local pottery of Prophitis Elias continues to be manufactured in old traditional shapes. LM IA imports occur as well as locally imitated LM IA patterns (see Doumas infra, fig. 3). There are also specimens of Light-on-Dark pottery in a clay differing from any local clay; it is a dark or lighter, highly

Fig. 7. Plot 6. SE corner of a building with an isodomic facade.

Fig. 8. Plot 5. General plan of the excavation.

Fig. 9. Plot 3. A part of the two parallel walls.

Fig. 10. A LMIB imported semiglobular cup and a sherd from close shaped vase decorated with locally imitated papyrus-motif.

micaceous, hard clay, similar to that of Seraglio in Kos[25]. The Seraglio Light-on-Dark appears in Kos in a large repertory of shapes and decorative motifs, locally manufactured. The examples from Rhodes are few and show us the possibilities of contacts between the two islands at that period.

Three bronze Minoan statuettes, found south of the building with the isodomic facade, reinforce the argument that the Minoan influence was stronger at the end of the LM IA period. The fact that they only rarely occur in the Aegean, outside Crete, indicates the importance of the building near which they were found[26].

After the fall of tephra the town of Trianda was partially reconstructed in some sections. The new town was:

- smaller in size
- the southernmost part of the previous town was abandoned. It was now located north; and
- new walls were erected over the tephra layer.

The incomplete LM IA houses show that the rebuilding and reorganisation of the LM IA town remained unfinished. Geological changes connected with the earthquake[27], which destroyed the LM IA town, probably forced the inhabitants of the new town in LM IB to replan with some changes (see C. Doumas infra, fig. 6). These changes appear in the North-western area near the river. LM IB is a new era for the settlement at Trianda. Two strong parallel walls were built on the tephra layer (fig. 9). Two interpretations of this wall system are possible:

- a retaining wall for the waters of the nearby river[28],
- a defensive system at the western end of the town.

There are LM IB imports such as pottery in the Marine Style and some (see C. Doumas infra, fig. 7) examples decorated with floral and reed patterns. These patterns are sometimes locally imitated[29] (fig. 10). Conical cups continue from LM IA. Interconnections with Cyprus are well documented by White Slip I ware[30] found together with LM IB pottery.

Here too the walls were plastered. An important piece depicting a golden double-axe with a sacral knot[31] was found above the tephra layer, but it may belong to the LM IA town. The upper strata of Trianda were disturbed by successive erosion and floods, as well as frequent reuse of the architectural material by later settlers. LM II pottery is mixed with the LH II/LH IIIA1/ LH IIIA2. During LM IIIA the pottery of Trianda became more Mycenaean in style, associated with new architectural remains. Another sort of retaining wall was built south of the double-wall system at plot 3 (see fig. 9) while this wall system was cut down and the material reused for a partially preserved paragonal building dated to the LH IIIA1 period. One characteristic house, found in the same plot, has two columns on either side of the threshold opening onto a court.

Besides LH IIIA1 pottery, there are sherds of LH IIIA2[32]. Some sherds, unassociated with architectural material, are as late as LH IIIB1[33].

The last evidence from Mycenaean Trianda is unstratified[34]. A fragment of a Base Ring I jug, however, should be contemporary with the White Slip already mentioned[35].

The LM IA expansion is now clear. During this period the Trianda town looks like a center for the Minoan expansion of which, according to recent field work, there is also evidence west and east of the main town. The sites are listed below from east to west (see fig. 1):

1. Traces of LM IA buildings were found and destroyed when foundations were laid for the "Olympic Palace" hotel at Ixia[36]. Conical and semiglobular cups as well as a piece of a ripple-patterned sherd were rescued from the site.
2. Some LM IA and Geometric pottery was found at Sotira, in the Treis area. No associated traces of walls were found.
3. Sherds of conical cups and a piece of a clay pigeon were found at the Ag. Georgios site west of the Trianda town. No associated architectural remains were found.
4. At Marmaro[37], NW of Makria Vounara and opposite the Hotel "Philerimos" some conical cups indicate another LM IA site.
5. In the summer of 1985 we were fortunate to find a thick, long tephra layer. This appeared during the opening of a sewer ditch along the highway of the International Paradeisi Airport at Vari (see C. Doumas infra fig. 1). The tephra layer was about 1000 m long and lay at a depth of 1.70 to 3.00 m; its greatest thickness was about 1 m. Seventeen vertical trenches were dug along it, so that we could examine the stratigraphy (see C. Doumas infra fig. 4-5). Underneath the thick, well preserved tephra layer was another of hard whitish clay earth, similar to the earth of Trianda, and this contained sherds of LM IA conical cups and one piece decorated with ripple pattern. The LM IA layer lay above the virgin soil, consisting of sand and pebbles. The only evidence for a building was part of a wall orientated south-north (see C. Doumas infra fig. 2). The exposed part of the wall was covered with tephra and some pebbles.

The following may be said in conclusion:

1. The earliest settlers of NW Rhodes were living on Mt. Philerimos in the MM I-II periods. This evidence is not purely Minoan. Local and other elements are visible in the pottery.
2. The Trianda settlement was first occupied at the end of MBA. The standard of living appears to have been high. Trojan influence shows us that it was still not thoroughly Minoanised and that there was a close relationship with North-West Anatolia. The question is still open and it will shed light on the origin of Dodecanesian civilisation before Minoan influence.
3. The fall of tephra occurred at the end of the LM IA period. The general plan of the large LM IA Trianda town belongs to two different phases. The second one seems renovated but partially unfinished before the tephra fall, as also indicated by rubbish and debris found covered with tephra.
4. The Minoan influence seems to have been more noticeable during LM IA late.
5. The LM IB-LM II town is smaller in size than the previous one. The southernmost section of it has been abandoned.
6. The later periods of Trianda town are complicated. There is evidence of LH IIIB and later occupation probably destroyed by erosion and successive floods.
7. The large LM IA town of Trianda seems to be the center of the expansion. Smaller settlements developed around the town. This pattern should be used for further study of the true character of Trianda and its interconnections with other Aegean sites and civilisations at that particular time.

Toula Marketou
Archaeological Institute of the Dodecanese
Rhodes
Greece

1. G. Monaco, ClRh 10, 1941, 41-183.
2. A. Furumark, OpArch 6, 1950, 150-271.
3. C. Doumas and L. Papazoglou, Nature 287, 1980, 322-324; A. Papagiannopoulou, AnatSt 35, 1985, 85.
4. No single building at Trianda settlement has been completely excavated and the final town plan is still impossible to detect. Excavations are still in progress, while the material from recent excavations, consisting of thousands of sherds, hundreds of vases and other finds, is still undergoing classification for final analysis and further study.
5. The earliest evidence from Mt. Philerimos is the socalled (by the Italian excavators) "Neolithic sherds" from Pilieria, the eastern area of the mountain. G. Jacopi, BdA 1926-27, 331-32; R. Hope Simpson and J.F. Lazenby, BSA 68, 1973, 137. For the MM evidence

from Mt. Philerimos a MM I chronology is suggested by J.N. Coldstream, BICS 16, 1969, 1 n. 6; for the type of high spouted jugs, see also in Coldstream – Huxley 1972, 258 (Ll) pl. 82,1; M. Benzi, Hägg – Marinatos 1984, 93-105.

6. The site was first discovered in the summer of 1983. The test trenches were dug in the autumn of 1985.
7. The clay of the high spouted jugs with a ring at the base of the neck is reddish-yellow according to Munsell, Soil Color Charts, Baltimore 1973, 5YR 6/6 with grits, some mica and small pebbles. The high-necked jugs with metallic flaring rim and the carinated and straight sided cups are made of a yellowish, clear, powdery clay, Munsell 1973, 10YR 8/4, 8/6. Of the same clay are the jugs with high neck, and one with curvilinear bands decorating the belly. The cylindrical, vertical bands are attached to the middle of the neck. For the ring around the base of the neck, see PMI 570 fig. 415B (N.E. Magazines). However these are of a later type, as also the jugs of Keos, J.L. Caskey, Hesperia 41, 1972, 381 (D78,83) pl. 85; in these cases they are not high spouted jugs. For carinated cups Levi 1976, pl. 205, 215; The rim is not so curved and the upper attachment of the handle is outside the rim. The type is of an earlier period than the examples of Mt. Philerimos and the later town examples A. Zois, AEphem 1965, 72, pl. 25 (8388).
8. Perhaps the volcanic ash layer (tephra) had been removed later from a higher area. The phenomenon of the continuous erosion of Mt. Philerimos brought down thick layers of whitish clay earth (aspropilos) which buried the plain settlement. The thickest layers were noticed at the southmost extent of the settlement, where we have met it as thick as 3.00-4.00 m, although the northern area was found at a depth of -1.50 m from the surface.
9. A. Furumark, OpArch 6, 1950, 180; C. Doumas in 150 Jahre deutsches archäologisches Institut 1829-1979, Mainz 1979, 95; K. Branigan, BSA 76, 1981,27. For further references see Hägg – Marinatos 1984.
10. H. Waterhouse in Krzyszkowska – Nixon 1983, 312; C. Doumas, AEphem 1974, 205.
11. M. Benzi in Hägg – Marinatos 1984, 96 n. 14, 15; the upper attachment of the handle inside instead of outside the rim is also observed at Keos J.L. Caskey, Hesperia 1972, 381 pl. 85, (D71) and at Kythera, Coldstream – Huxley 1972, 95.
12. The clay is usually red and the burnished surface is not connected with Minoan prototypes.
13. Podzuweit 1979, 180 pl. 10,2 NI, NII. Schliemann 1880, 553, 1175.
14. These are the largest dimensions according to the up-to-date excavations. J.W. Shaw in Doumas 1978, 431 note 3.
15. A. Furumark, OpArch 6, 1950, 179.
16. M.R. Popham, BSA 72, 1977, 195; M. Marthari in MacGillivray - Barber 1984, 132.
17. C. Doumas, Antiquity 48, 1974, 111.
18. G. Monaco, ClRh 10, 1941, 167; A. Furumark, OpArch 6, 1950, 179. Human victims were also found at Seraglio in Kos (forthcoming article).
19. Graham 1972, 86, 94, 165; J.W. Shaw in Doumas 1978, 434; J. Driessen, ActaALou 21, 1982, 27-92; Preziosi 1983, 34; N. Marinatos – R. Hägg, OpAth XVI:6, 1986, 57-73.
20. Tephra layers were found in thirteen areas of the excavated settlement. This is the thickest tephra layer to date.
21. G. Monaco, ClRh 10, 1941, 102 fig. 56; J.W. Shaw, ASAtene 49, 1971, 82 fig. 122, 205, 123.
22. G. Monaco, ClRh 10, 1941, 78, 95.
23. PM I, 517, pl. VI. A red lily on a whitish background is depicted on another frescoe from the Italian excavations at Trianda, G. Monaco, ClRh 10, 1941, 70 pl. VII; Atkinson et al. 1904, 75-6 fig. 64.
24. Dimensions: h.max. 0.39m/w.max. 0.31m. H. Sjövall, ARW 1925, 185; Effenterre 1980, 368, 440. The appearance of the horns of consecration may indicate a sacred nature Nilsson 1950, 184; Gesell 1972, 112. Gesell 1985, 35. Another game board reused as a threshold was also found at Trianda (plot 5).
25. L. Morricone, ASAtene 51, 1973, 296-326.
26. The first a female princely figurine with flounced skirt is similar to the Berlin statuette, Verlinden 1984, 190 ("Style des Princes"). The two others are a female and a male saluting figurines. A bronze saluting figurine was also found in Rhodes at Kalamona (Ammoudes), Papachristodoulou 1983, 109. A female saluting figurine was found together with the later objects from the still unpublished Ialysos deposit, Sapouna-Sakellarakis 1978, 26ff. The presence of Minoan bronze figurines outside Crete is not usual: J.L. Caskey, Hesperia 33, 1964, 328 pl. 56a-b; K. Davaras, BCH 93, 1969, 634.
27. Marinatos 1972, 44-5; C. Doumas, Antiquity 48, 1974, 110ff, Doumas (ed.) 1978-80.
28. This interpretation was also discussed with Prof. C. Doumas during the excavation.
29. For example, the papyrus motifs decorating an imported semiglobular cup, Niemeyer 1984, 54 fig. 16.13, are locally imitated for the decoration of a closed vase. For other imitations: A. Furumark, OpArch 6, 1950, 165.
30. Fabric, hard-baked, cement, buff-coloured clay white grits, hand-made, red decoration on whitish, lustrous background. A. Furumark, OpArch 6, 1950, 165, fig. 6,97 (stratum IIa) and G. Monaco, ClRh 10, 1941, 58-9; M.R. Popham, BSA 58, 1963, 91-2.
31. The motif is often depicted in pottery: Boyd Hawes 1908, pl. IX, 12, G1, the ivory relief from Palaikastro PM I, 432, 433 fig. 310d. For further references: Nilsson 1950, 210-11.
32. Before the publication of the excavation materials, we can give some parallels: A LH III A I goblet (FM 49:10) "curve stemmed spiral", Cummer – Schofield 1984, 484 pl. 56, a LH IIIA 2 kylix with "diagonal whorl shell", E. French, BSA 60, 1965, 169 fig. 2:2549.
33. "Myc.III Flower" FM 18, E. French, BSA 61, 1966, 225 pl. 48b 1.
34. It seems that the later Mycenaean settlement was destroyed by erosion owing to successive floods, see M. Benzi in this volume.
35. Finger prints are visible on the internal side of the handle P. Åström, Praktika tou Protou Diethnous Kyprologhikou Synedriou, T. A', 1972, 3. The vase is similar to P. Åström, SCE IV, 1c, 1972, fig. XLIX, 9, 10.
36. I am very grateful to Mr. Elias Kollias, Ephor of Byzantine Antiquities of the Dodecanese, who kindly allowed me to study the material. Papachristodoulou 1983, 85.
37. Papachristodoulou 1983, 85.

The Prehistoric Eruption of Thera and Its Effects. The Evidence from Rhodes

Christos Doumas

The late Professor Spyridon Marinatos' theory about Thera and its volcanic eruption has kept scholarly interest in this issue alive for several decades. According to his theory, published in 1939[1], the decline of the Minoan civilisation in Crete was caused by a tremendous eruption of the Thera volcano around the middle of the second millenium BC. Crete was supposed to have suffered then from earthquakes, tidal waves or tsunamis and tephra fall, all originating from the eruption. The same Greek scholar revived the issue in post-war archaeology[2]. With his excavations on the island of Thera, started in 1967[3], he produced abundant evidence not only of the standard of civilisation achieved by the Therans in the second millenium BC, but also of the magnitude of the eruption and its possible effects. International collaboration has been established for the study of the archaeological evidence and two international scientific congresses were organized (1964[4] and 1978[5]) to deal with these problems. Yet neither of these congresses confirmed the thesis that the collapse of the Minoan civilisation was due to the eruption. On the contrary, doubts have been expressed by an ever increasing number of scholars[6]. Since recent research tends to diminish or dismiss the effects of earthquakes[7] and tsunamis[8], we must examine those of the third agent, the tephra fall.

In recent years a number of investigations and research programmes have been carried out which shed more light on this problem. First of all the continuing excavations at Akrotiri[9] have confirmed the existence of three horizons of ejecta from the volcano around the middle of the second millennium BC: pumice, base surge deposits and chaotic tephra[10]. Moreover, it has been observed that the lowest horizon, pumice, consists of five distinct layers, obviously representing respective paroxysms of the same eruption[11]. The stratigraphy of the second horizon

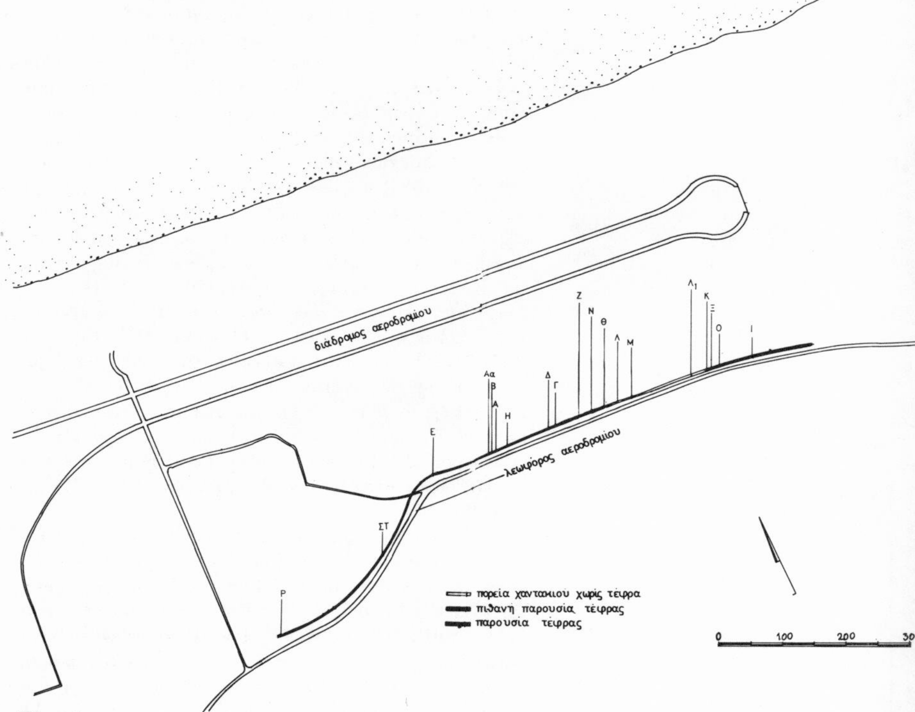

Fig. 1.

Fig. 2.

Fig. 3. Sherds found below the tephra layer in Trianda.

shows a similar pattern of consecutive paroxysms causing the violent horizontal dispersal of tephra round the crater of the volcano (base surge). Finally, chaotic tephra seems to have been ejected as a result of an enormous explosion, the magnitude of which is still to be gauged[12]. The evidence from Akrotiri might be of some help in this direction, for huge boulders, weighing several tons each, have been found in the chaotic tephra layer, suggesting that rocks were detached from the walls of the crater and flung far away[13]. Some of them fell on buildings in Akrotiri causing considerable damage[14]. From the trajectory of these boulders it should be possible to locate the site of the crater exactly, and, I suppose, the force which propelled them as far as the city of Akrotiri.

The chaotic tephra horizon in Thera has a thickness exceeding thirty metres in places. From the present morphology of the ground it is clear that the great mass of this fine material moved eastwards. Indeed the large plains extending along the eastern half of the island on either side, north and south, of the rocky ridge of Mesa Vouno (ancient Thera), were formed by this ash-flow. Such an eastward direction for the Theran ash had already been suggested by those scholars who conducted investigations along the Eastern Mediterranean[15]. More precisely, as Watkins and his collegues have stated, deep-sea sediment cores "indicate an easterly to southeasterly dispersal of tephra with the fall-out axis passing through Karpathos"[16].

Research was not restricted to the sea-bed only. Once the problem had been formulated, scholars concentrated their attention on the islands of that region. Indeed, research conducted on Kos by Professor Jörg Keller of the Albert-Ludwig Universität, Freiburg, located a layer of Theran tephra about 39 cm thick, north of Cape Aghios Phokas. Announcing his discovery at the Second International Thera Congress in 1978, Professor Keller stated: "Still wanted for our problem is the distinct tephra layer in well defined Late Minoan I stratigraphical position"[17]. This "wanted" stratigraphical position of tephra was discovered at Trianda on Rhodes at the same time, maybe the same day, as Keller was making this statement. The Ephorate of Antiquities was then conducting a rescue excavation on property of the late John Theocharis. The ruins revealed there were of Late Bronze Age date and undoubtedly belonged to the settlement of Ialysos. A preliminary report of the discovery was published in Nature, September 1980. Besides patches of tephra observed in several places on the plot of land investigated (about 90 m^2), a completely uncontaminated layer of this material was found about 1.80 m below the present soil surface. It covered an area of about 15m^2 and measured 10 cm in thickness. Analyses of the samples taken there were carried out by Professor Charles Vitaliano of Indiana University, Bloomington, USA and Professor Keller. Both were positive in that the tephra from Trianda was of Theran origin and was identical with that ejected in about 1500 BC. Subsequent research by Dr A. Sampson located more tephra deposits in cave sites on Rhodes as well as on the island of Telos[18]. Again the respective samples were identified by Professor Keller as Theran tephra[19].

Intensification of building activity in the Trianda region and the consequent archaeological rescue operations there brought to light more evidence of the tephra fall in Rhodes. Thanks to the hard work and alert eye of the Epimeletria Toula Marketou every operation there is under control and information is carefully recorded. So, now we are in a position to know not only that the prehistoric settlement of Ialysos was

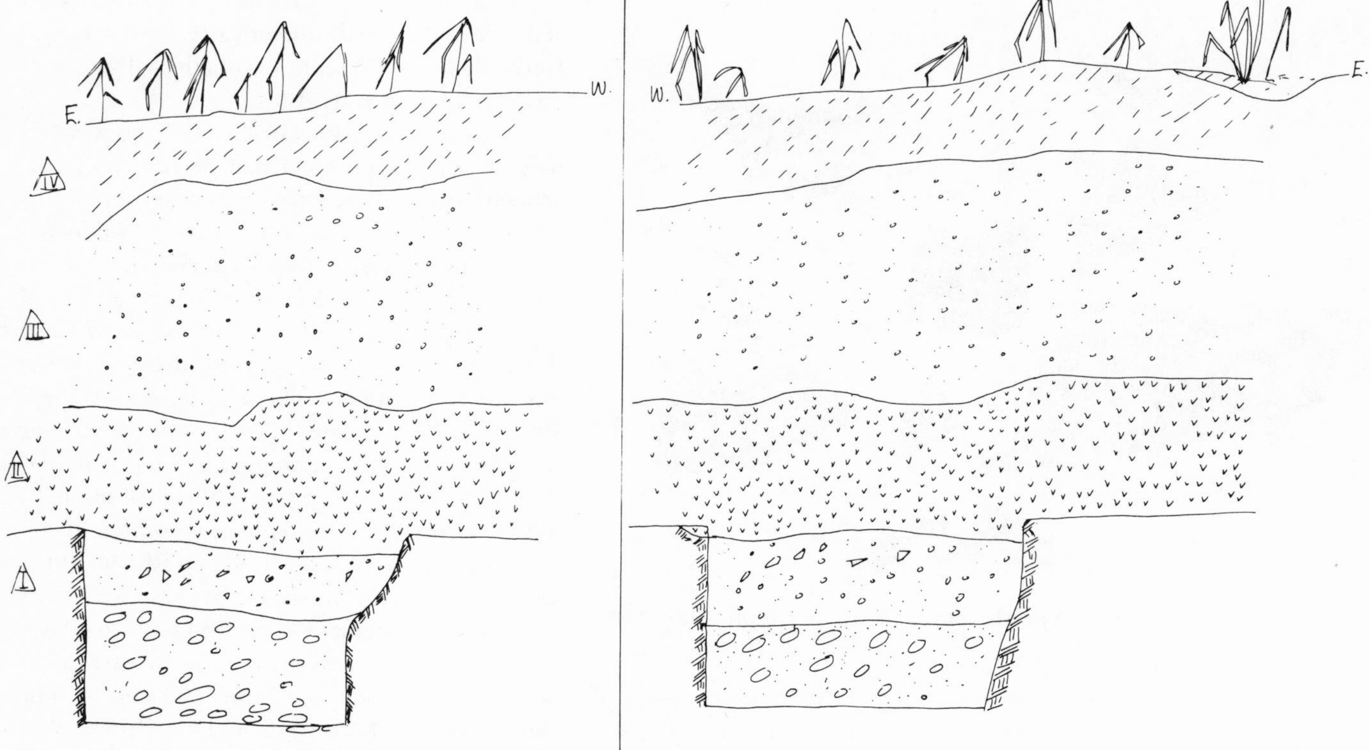

Fig. 4. Paradeisi Airport, Rhodos. Sections.

more extensive than so far believed, but also that tephra is present almost everywhere[20]. The most impressive discovery of tephra in Rhodes was made in the summer of 1985 along the northern border of the international airport. A ditch about one kilometer long was being excavated there for sewerage purposes (fig. 1). This operation did not escape Mrs Marketou's eye, and, among other things, she discovered, yet again, tephra deposits: all the way along the ditch at an average depth of about one metre from the present soil surface (fig. 2). The layer of tephra found in this ditch has an impressive thickness often exceeding half a metre (fig. 4-5). For inviting me to see all her discoveries in Rhodes, as well as for allowing me to present this evidence, I am much obliged to Mrs Marketou.

The importance of the discovery of Theran tephra in Rhodes is two-fold. First, it confirms the evidence from the sea-bed. There can be no doubt now about the south-eastward dispersal of Theran tephra. This means that at the time of eruption north-westerly winds were blowing. Such winds usually prevail in the Aegean at the very beginning of the summer[21]. Therefore, one could suggest such a time for eruption. And such a suggestion is in complete accordance with the evidence from Akrotiri: most of the storage jars found were entirely or nearly empty. Perhaps the eruption occurred before the harvest was completed[22].

The tephra deposits in Rhodes also demonstrated that the ash-fall did not seriously affect life on the island. Despite its thick deposition, the tephra does not seem to have caused abandonment of the settlement at Ialysos. On the contrary, the archaeological evidence suggests that life continued in the same place (fig. 6). This also suggests that the ash was not accompanied by poisonous gas, such as sulphur compounds, carbon oxides or fluorine.

In the light of this evidence from Rhodes it is no longer possible to maintain the view that the decline of Minoan Crete was due to ash fall-out from Thera. There is no place in Crete where a clear deposit of tephra has ever been found. Only molecules have been traced through various analyses[23]. Crete was at the margin of the zone affected by tephra, and it has been estimated that over the eastern part of the island a

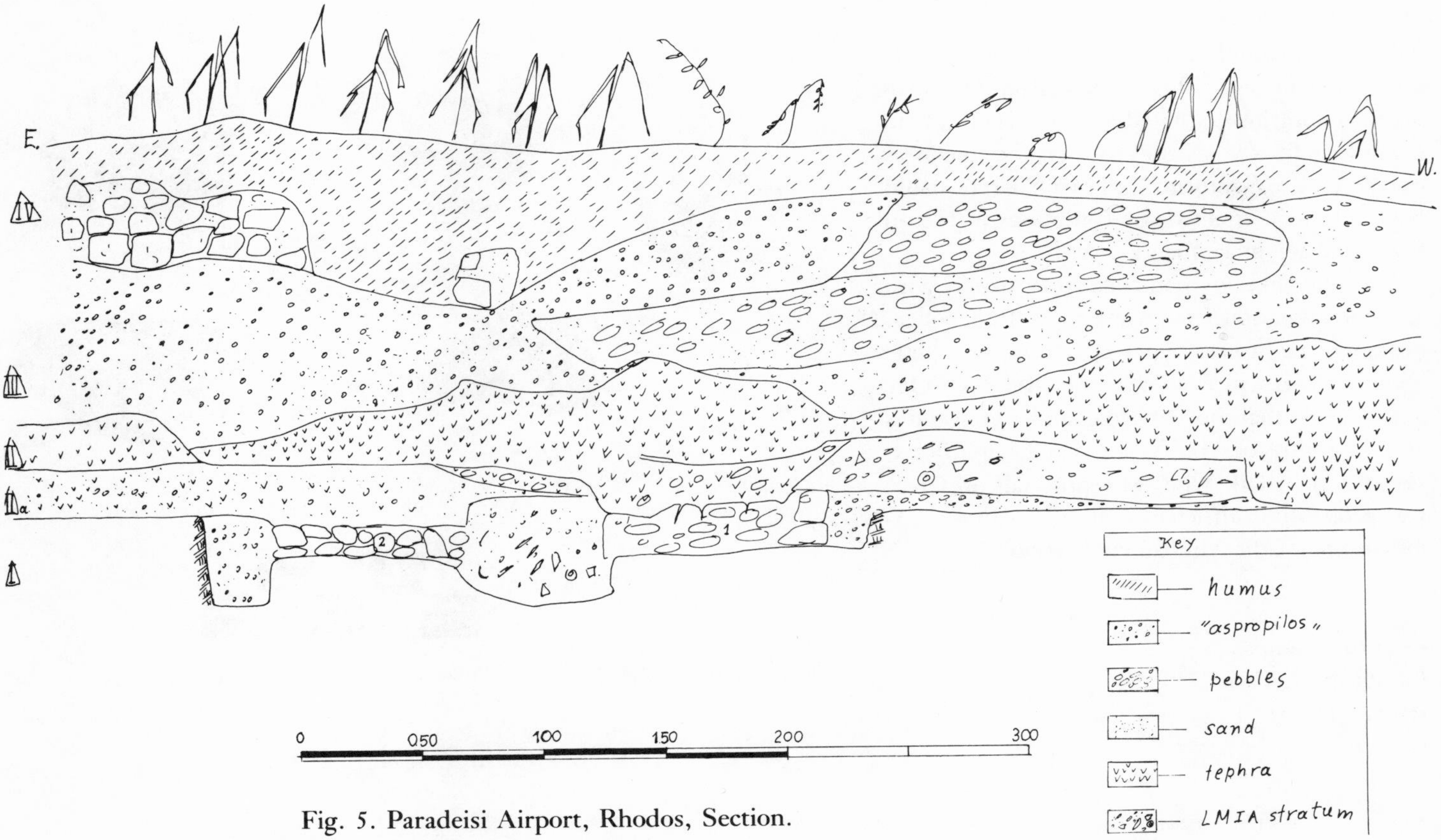
E.
W.
Key
humus
"aspropilos"
pebbles
sand
tephra
LMIA stratum
0
050
100
150
200
300

Fig. 5. Paradeisi Airport, Rhodos, Section.

"tephra"

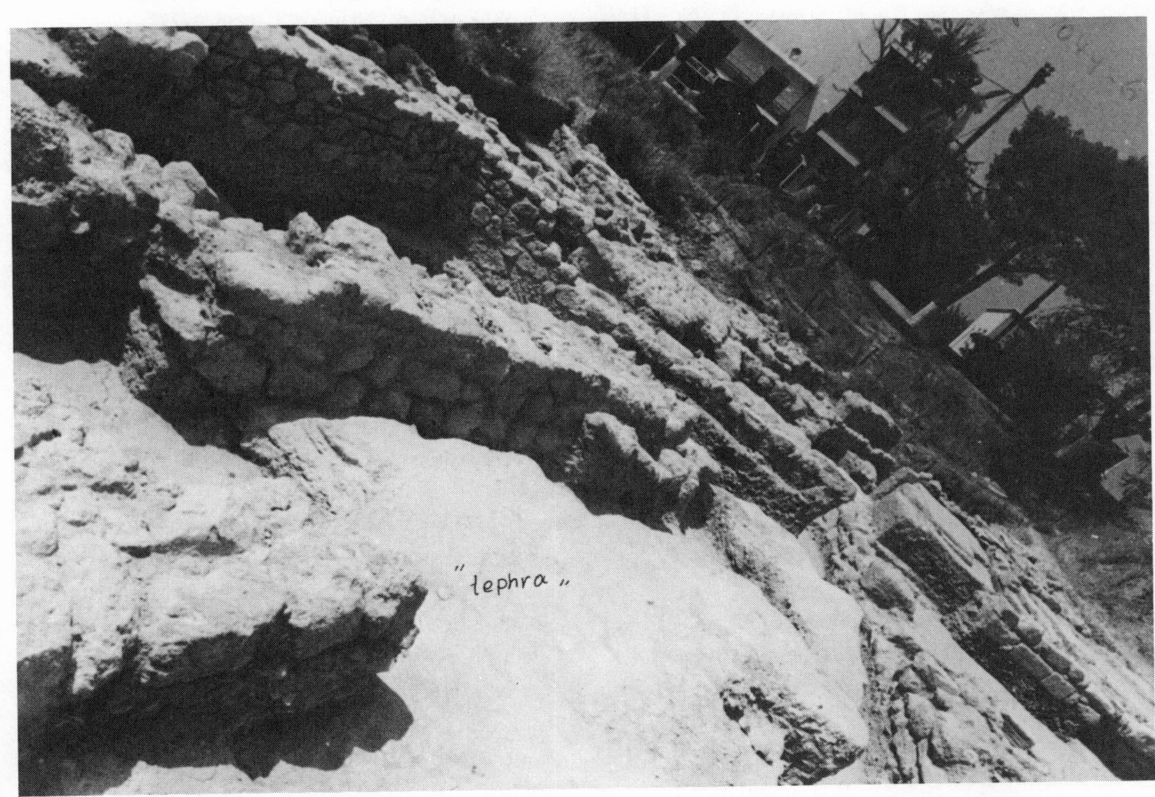

Fig. 6.

layer of ash would measure, when fresh, only 1-5 cm in thickness. This is the reason why Professor Thorarinsson stated at the Second Thera Congress: "it is very unlikely that the thickness per se of the Santorini tephra on Crete could have seriously affected the conditions of life on the island for more than a year"[24].

I would like to conclude this paper with another quotation from Watkins and his colleagues, who eight years ago were almost prophetic about our present evidence from Rhodes: "Our data suggest that the Minoan colonies on Rhodes and the south coast of Turkey may have suffered severe tephra-fall, whereas tephra-fall on Crete was probably insufficient in itself to cause a major decline of the Minoan civilisation"[25].

Christos Doumas
Lambrou Photiadi 27
Athens 116 36
Greece

Fig. 7. LMIB imports from Trianda.

1. S. Marinatos, Antiquity 13, 1939, 425-439.
2. S. Marinatos, in Europa: Festschrift für Ernst Grumach. Berlin 1967, 204-210.
3. Marinatos 1968-1976.
4. The International Scientific Congress on the Volcano of Thera, 15-23rd September 1969. Athens 1970.
5. Doumas (ed.) 1978 – 1980.
6. Doumas 1983, 140-147.
7. D. Vitaliano, in Ramage 1978, 148-149.
8. I. Yokoyama, in Doumas (ed.) 1978 – 1980, I, 277-283.
9. C. Doumas, Prakt 1975-1984.
10. C.J. Vitaliano et al., in Doumas (ed.) 1978 – 1980, I, 203ff.
11. C. Doumas, Prakt 1980, 294 Fig. 175b.
12. C.J. Vitaliano et al., in Doumas (ed.) 1978 – 1980, I, 204.
13. H. Pichler – W.L. Friedrich, in Doumas (ed.) 1978 – 1980, II, 24 fig. 6.
14. Op. cit. 19, fig. 2.
15. J. Keller, in Doumas (ed.) 1978 – 1980, II, 49-75.
16. Watkins et al., Nature 271, 1978, 122.
17. J. Keller, in Doumas (ed.) 1978 – 1980, II, 50.
18. Sampson 1986 (in press).
19. Personal communication.
20. T. Marketou, Supra, figs. 1 and 4.
21. Platon 1971, 277 attributes the eastward dispersal of the tephra to easterly winds and thus concludes that the eruption occurred during the winter when such winds often blow. However, this is incorrect because easterly winds would have blown the tephra in exactly the opposite direction, i.e. westwards, which is not the case.
22. Doumas 1983, 137, 139.
23. C.J. Vitaliano et al., in Doumas (ed.) 1978 – 1980, I, 218.
24. S. Thorarinsson, in Doumas (ed.) 1978 – 1980, I, 270-271.
25. Nature 271, 1978, 125.

Mycenaean Pottery Later than LH IIIA:1 from the Italian Excavations at Trianda on Rhodes

Mario Benzi

In recent years the Greek Archaeological Service has resumed excavations in the area of the BA settlement of Trianda. To the many important results of the new excavations must be added the discovery of a good amount of Mycenaean sherds later than LH IIIA:1 (T. Marketou, this volume). According to the main excavator T. Marketou, late Mycenaean sherds – either stray finds from the upper level or intrusive in lower strata – have been found at four of the new excavations.

Since the study of the new material is still in progress, it seems of some interest to reconsider in the meanwhile some related evidence from the Italian excavations, with particular reference to the disputed question of the settlement to be connected with the extensive LH IIB-IIIC Mycenaean cemeteries on the two neighbouring hills of Makra and Moschou Vounara.

Late Mycenaean sherds were found in four of the six Trial Trenches opened by the Italians in 1935 and in House 2 excavated by G. Monaco in 1936. All the sherds, now kept in the Rhodes Museum, carry markings which proved useful for attributing unpublished sherds to their find contexts.

Some sherds carrying no markings are also included, since they are stored with the remainder of the material.

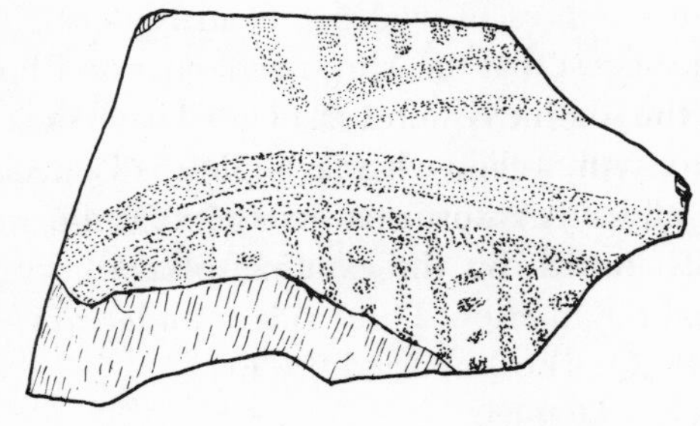

1

Trench I

This trench was excavated at Paraskeva, about 140 m SE of the main excavation area. The sherds were found in a thick layer (70 cm) east of the main North/South wall. No stratigraphic data are available. Monaco refers to the layer as a waste deposit, but this does not accord with the finds, which included several painted sherds and a substantial group of whole pots[1]. Of the 31 painted sherds published by Monaco no less than 17 are later than LH IIIA:1; to them must be added a fragmentary animal figurine. All sherds belong to open shapes: krater, mug, cup and kylix[2].

Kraters

1 Body sherd; l. 0.60; th. 0.008. Clay 7.5YR 7/6 reddish yellow with grits and a few mica; slip 10YR 8/3-8/4 very pale brown; semilustrous paint 10R 3/4 dusky red. FM 7 (Bird). FM 25 (Bivalve Shell). Imported. Fig.

2 Rim sherd, lip broken; l. 0.033. Clay 10YR 7/4-8/4 very pale brown; surface 2.5Y 8/4 yellow on the exterior, 8/2 white on the interior. Semilustrous black/brown paint. Floral motif (?). Local. Fig.

2 4

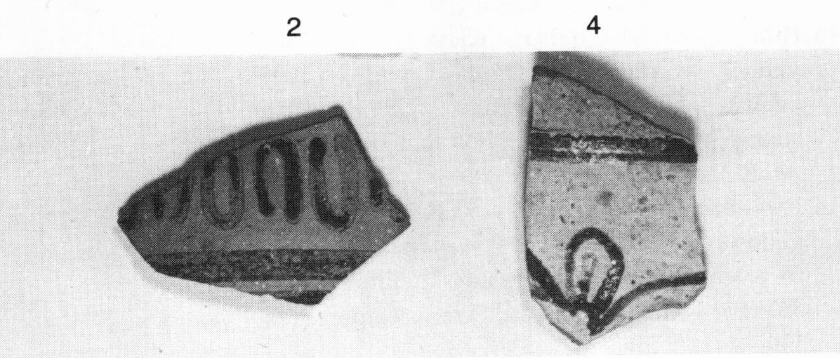

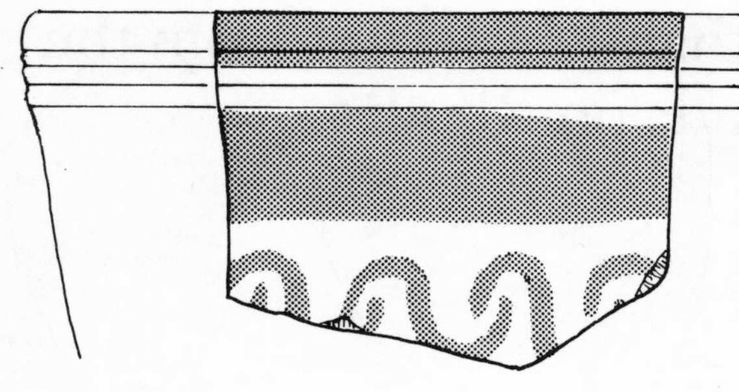

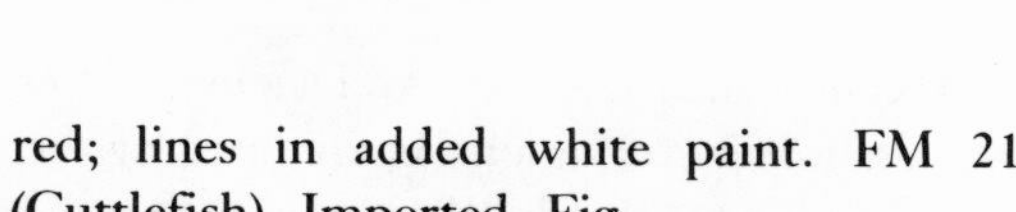

3

Mugs

3 Rim sherd; d. circa 0.145. Clay 7.5YR 6/6 reddish yellow; surface 5YR 6/6 reddish yellow; semilustrous paint 2.5YR 4/6 reddish brown on the exterior, black/dusky red on the interior. Three ridges under rim. FM 48 (Quirk). Imported (?). Fig.

Cups

4 Body sherd; l. 0.052. Clay 7.5YR 6/6 reddish yellow; surface 7.5YR 7/4 pink to 7/6 reddish yellow; matt paint 5YR 4/3 reddish brown to 3/3 dark reddish brown. FM 45 (U-Pattern). Fig.

5 Body sherd; l. 0.051. Clay 7.5YR 7/6 reddish yellow; surface 10YR 8/4 very pale brown; lustrous paint 2.5YR 3/4 dark reddish brown to 3/6 dark red. FM 58 (Parallel Chevrons). Imported. Fig.

Kylikes

6 Body sherd; l. 0.037. Clay 7.5YR 7/4 pink to 7/6 reddish yellow; surface 10YR 8/4 very pale brown; lustrous paint 5YR 5/8 yellowish red and black. FM 18C (Myc. Flower). Imported. Fig.

7 Rim sherd; l. 0.041. On the left, start of handle attachment. Clay 7.5YR 7/6 reddish yellow; surface 10YR 8/4 very pale brown. Semilustrous paint 5YR 5/8 yellowish red and black. FM 18C (Myc. Flower). Imported. Fig.

8 Rim sherd; l. 0.047. On the left start of handle attachment. Clay 2.5YR 6/8 light red; surface 5YR 7/6 reddish yellow; lustrous paint 10R 5/8 red. FM 19 (Mult. Stem). Local (?). Fig.

9 Lower body sherd; h. 0.040. Clay 10YR 8/4 very pale brown; surface 10YR 8/4 to 8/6 yellow; lustrous paint 2.5YR 4/6 to 4/8 red; lines in added white paint. FM 21 (Cuttlefish). Imported. Fig.

10 Body sherd; h. 0.076. Clay 10YR 8/4 very pale brown at center, 5YR 7/6 reddish yellow towards both surfaces; surface 10YR 8/4; lustrous paint 10R 4/6 to 4/8 red; bands in light red. FM 21 (Cuttlefish). Imported. Fig.

11 Rim sherd; l. 0.060. Clay 2.5YR 6/8 light red with a few mica; surface 5YR 8/4 to 7/4 pink; semilustrous paint 2.5YR 3/4 dark reddish brown. FM 23 (Whorl-Shell). Local. Fig.

12 Body sherd; h. 0.057. Clay 2.5YR 6/8 light red; surface 5YR 7/6 reddish yellow; matt paint 2.5YR 6/8 light red. FM 23 (Whorl-Shell). Probably local. Fig.

13 Rim sherd; estimated d. 0.165. Small hole (d. 0.003) through the wall probably due to an ancient repair. Clay 10YR 7/4 very pale brown at center, 5 YR 7/6 reddish yellow towards both surfaces; surface 10YR 8/4 very pale brown to 8/6 yellow; lustrous paint 2.5YR 5/8 to 4/8 red. FM 24 (Linked Whorl-Shell Pattern). Imported. Fig.

14 Rim sherd, lip chipped both in and out; l. 0.050. Clay 7.5YR 7/6 reddish yellow; surface 7.5YR 7/4 pink to 7/6; matt paint 5YR 5/6 to 5/8 yellowish red. FM 24 (Linked Whorl-Shell Pattern). Local (?). Fig.

15 Rim sherd; l. 0.043. Clay 10YR 7/6 yellow; surface 10YR 8/4 very pale brown; semilustrous paint 7.5YR 5/6 strong brown and black. FM 62 (Tricurved Arch). Local (?). Fig.

16 Rim sherd; l. 0.043. Clay 5YR 7/8 reddish yellow; surface 10YR 8/4 very pale brown to 8/6 yellow; lustrous paint 2.5YR 4/8 to 5/8 red. FM 62 (Tricurved Arch). Imported. Fig.

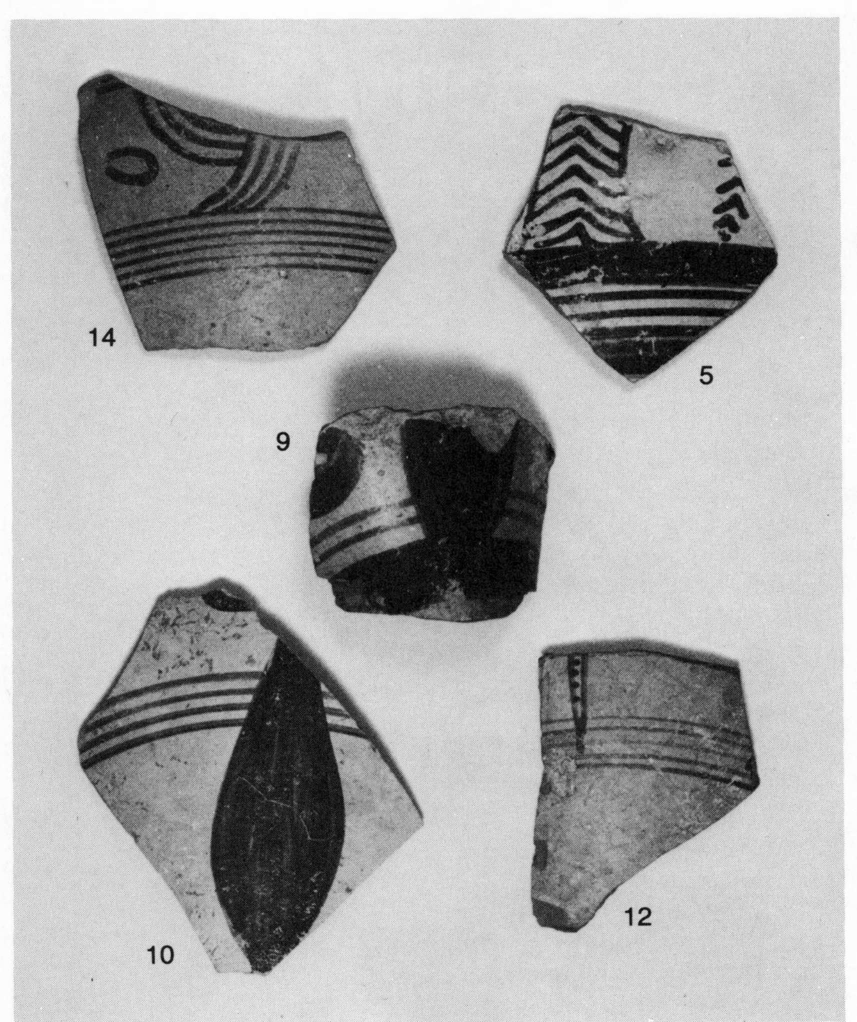

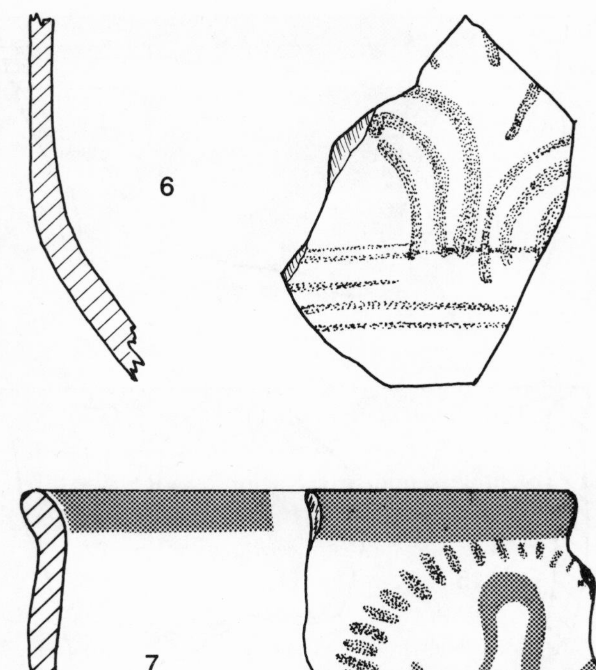

Miscellaneous

17 Rim sherd, broken lip; l. 0.025. Clay 7.5YR 7/6 reddish yellow; slipped surface 2.5 Y 8/4 pale yellow; lustrous paint 2.5 YR 3/4 dark reddish brown. FM 62 (Tricurved Arch). Fig.

Figurine

18 Animal figurine; head, legs and hindquarters missing; l. 0.043. Clay 7.5YR 7/4 pink; surface 10YR 8/3 to 8/4 pale yellow; lustrous paint 2.5YR 4/8 to 5/8 red. Wavy lines. Imported. Fig.

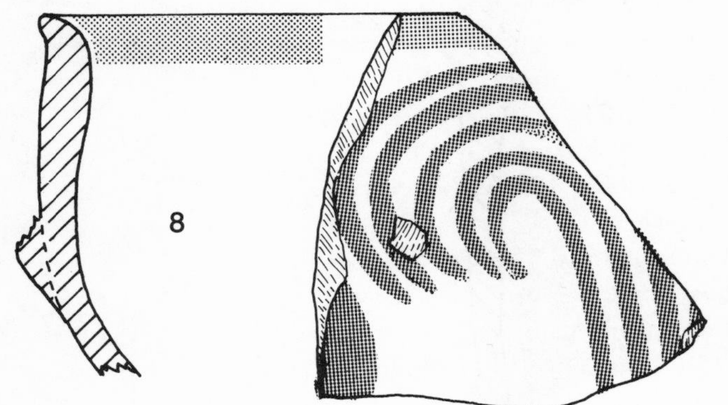

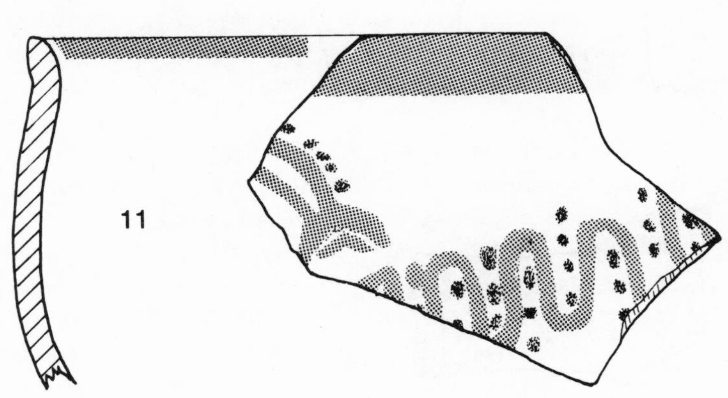

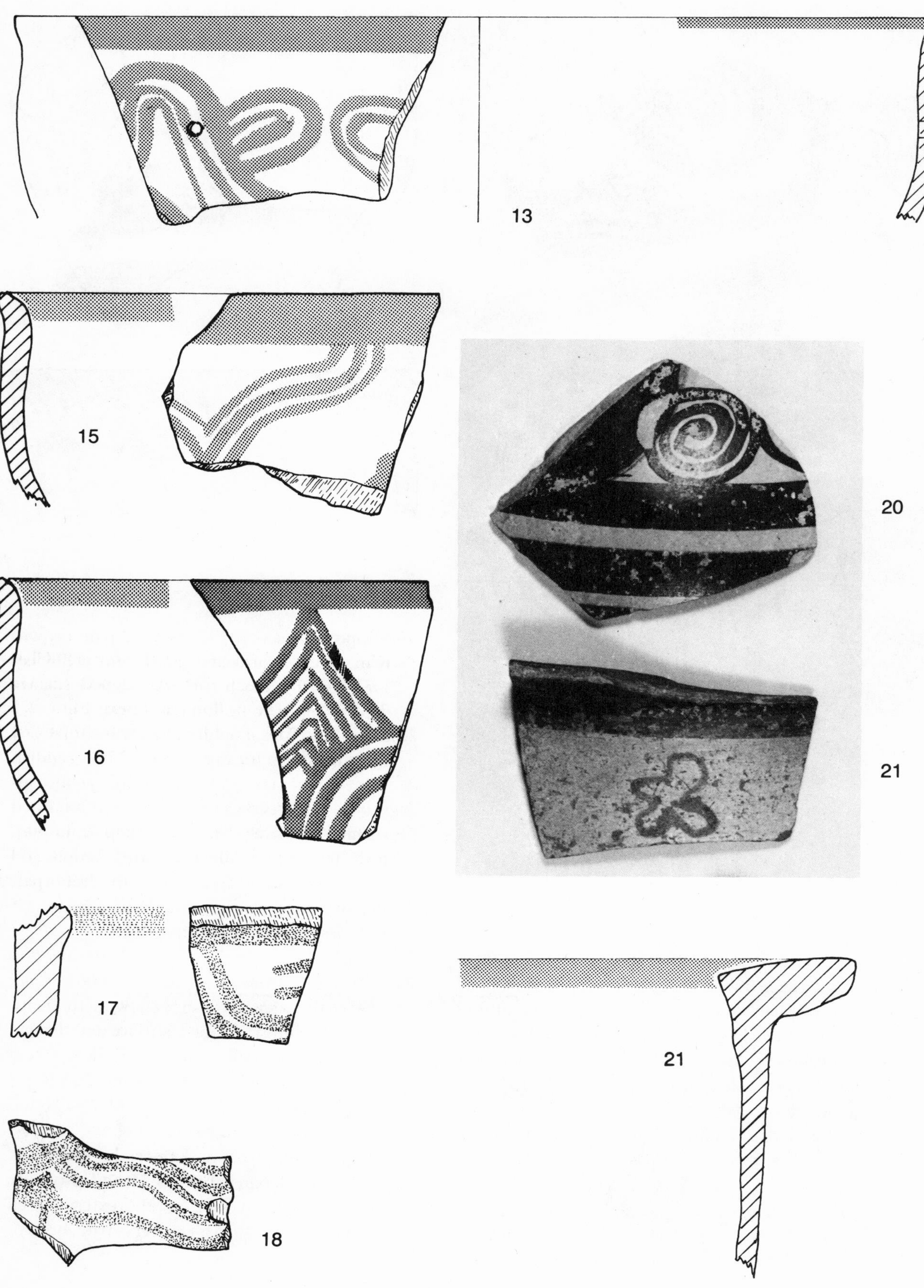

13
15
16
17
18
20
21
21

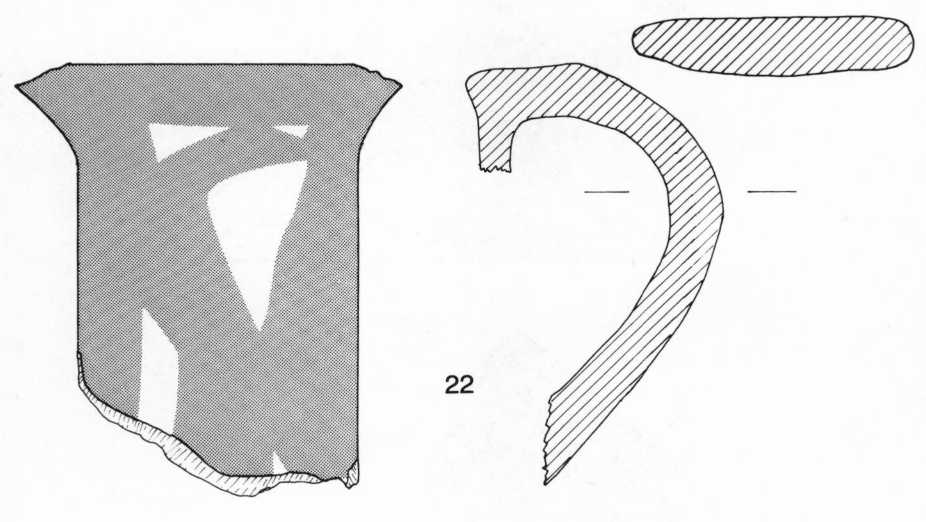

Slipped surface 10YR 8/4 very pale brown; matt paint black and 5YR 5/6 yellowish brown with a patch 10R 5/8 red. FM 22 (Argonaut) (?). FM 48 (Quirk). Local. Fig.

20 Sherd from the shoulder of a Piriform Jar (FS 35); l. 0.092. Clay 7.5YR 7/6 reddish yellow at center, 5YR 6/8 reddish yellow towards both surfaces; slipped and polished surface 10YR 8/3 to 8/4 very pale brown; lustrous paint 2.5YR 4/4 reddish brown and black. FM 46 (Running Spiral). Imported. Fig.

Trench II

In this trench were found short stretches of three walls, three fragments of painted plaster, a good deal of plain domestic pottery and a handful of painted sherds[3]. To the four Mycenean sherds published by Monaco there must be added three more sherds carrying the marking II in Roman numerals.

Both closed and open shapes are represented.

Closed Shapes

19 Two sherds from the shoulder of a Piriform Jar (?); l. 0.158; 0.167. Clay 5YR 6/6 to 6/8 reddish yellow with inclusions and mica.

Open Shapes

21 Rim sherd from a Krater; h. 0.063. Clay 5YR 6/6 to 6/8 reddish yellow with inclusions and mica; slipped surface on the exterior; slip partially vanished 7.5YR 8/4 to 7/4 pink, but see 22; matt paint 2.5YR 5/8 red. Filling quatrefoil motif FM 29 (Trefoil Rock-Work). Local. See 22. Fig.

22 Strap handle from a Krater; h. 0.089; w. 0.055. Similar in fabric to 21 and probably from the same vessel; on the exterior well preserved slip 10YR 8/3 very pale brown. Local. Fig.

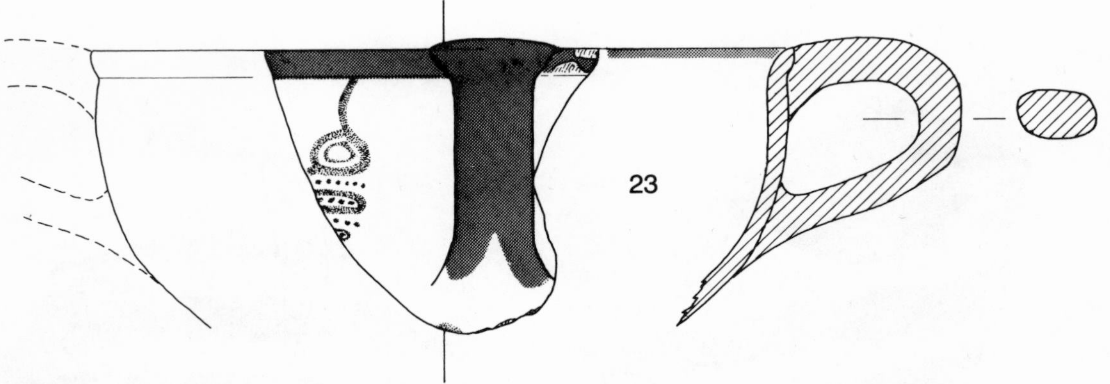

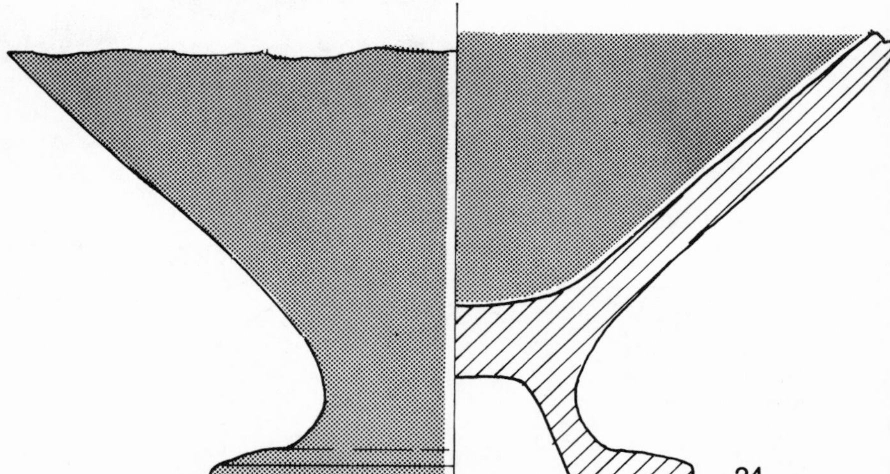

23 Body sherd from a Kylix (FS 257); h. 0.060. Clay 7.5YR 6/6 reddish yellow; slipped surface 10YR 7/4 very pale brown to 7/6 yellow; lustrous paint 5YR 5/6 yellowish red and 2.5YR 5/8 red. FM 23 (Whorl-Shell). Imported. Fig.

24 Stem from a Stemmed Bowl (FS 304); h. 0.062. Clay 5YR 6/6 reddish yellow; surface 10YR 8/3 very pale brown; lustrous paint 10R 3/4 dusky red to 3/6 dark red on the exterior, 3/6 to 4/8 red on the interior. Monochrome. Imported. Fig.

Trench V (House 3: Room A)[4]

The four Mycenean sherds from Trench V, not published by Monaco, have been identified through the marking V in Roman numerals. One closed and two open shapes are represented.

Closed shapes

25 Body sherd from a Piriform Jar (?); h. 0.108. Clay 2.5YR 6/6 to 6/8 light red with grits; slipped surface 10YR 8/3 to 8/4 very pale brown; lustrous paint 2.5YR 3/4 dark reddish brown to 3/6 dark red and black. FM 7 (Bird). Imported. See 26. Fig.

26 Base sherd from a Piriform Jar (?); h. 0.080. Similar in fabric to 25 and probably from the same vessel, paint 2.5YR 4/6 to 4/8 red. Imported. Fig.

Open Shapes

27 Rim sherd from a Krater; l. 0.077. Clay 7.5YR 7/6 reddish yellow; slipped and polished surface 10YR 8/3 to 8/4 very pale brown; lustrous paint black and 2.5YR 4/8 red. Imported. Fig.

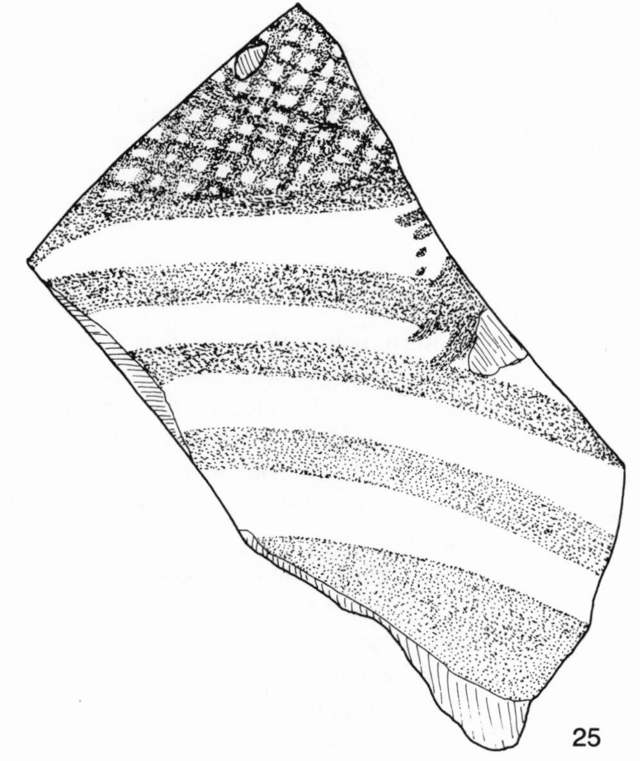

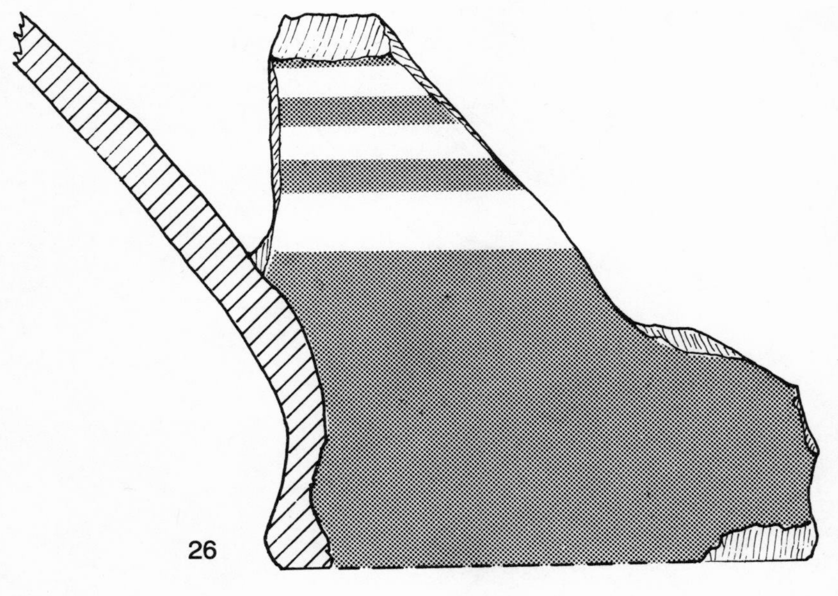

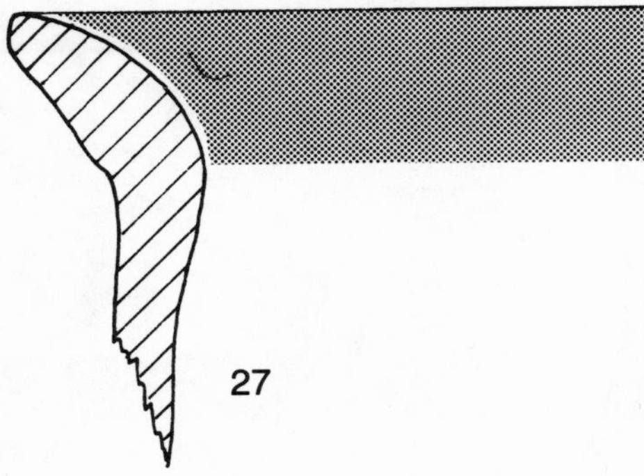

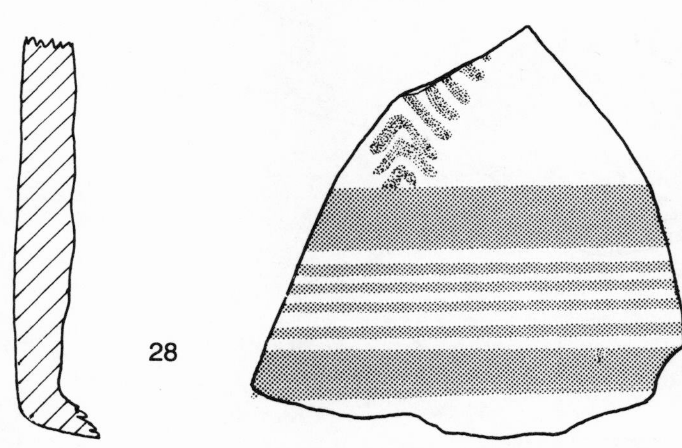

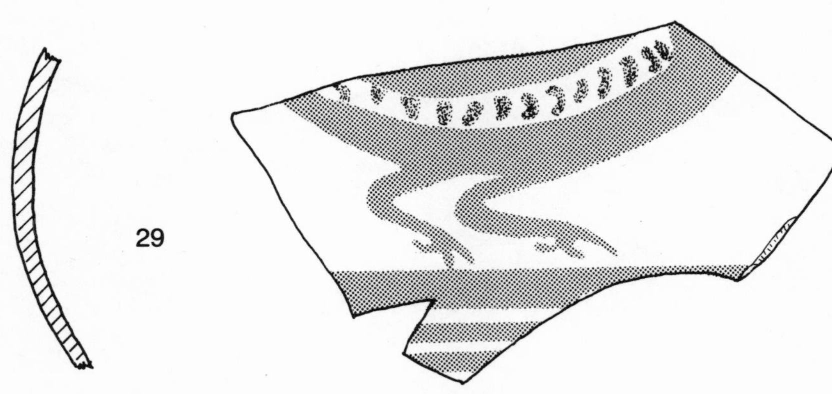

28 Sherd from the lower body of a Mug (FS 226); h. 0.055. Clay with a few mica 7.5YR 7/6 reddish yellow at center, 5YR 6/6 to 6/8 reddish yellow towards both surfaces; surface slipped on the exterior 5YR 8/4 pink; lustrous paint 2.5YR 5/8 red. FM 58 (Parallel Chevrons). Local (?). Fig.

Trench VI (House 1: Room 1 to 7)[5]

Eight of the eleven Mycenaean sherds from Trench VI belong to the same vessel (30); the two unpublished sherds 29, 32 have been attributed through markings. Both closed and open shapes are represented.

Closed Shapes

29 Sherd from the shoulder of a Piriform Jar (?) of medium size; h. 0.048. Clay 5YR 7/8 reddish yellow on the interior, 10YR 8/4 very pale brown on the exterior; lustrous paint black with shades ranging from 2.5YR 4/6, 4/8 red to 3/6 dusky red. Thin walled (th. 0.0025). FM 7 (Bird). Imported. Fig.

Open shapes

30 Eight sherds from a Krater (FS 6-7). Monaco, ClRh 10, 1941, fig. 11[6]. FM 57 (Diaper Net). Imported.

31 Body sherd from a Cup (FS 283 ?); h. 0.050. Clay 7.5YR 7/6 reddish yellow at center, 5YR 6/6 reddish yellow towards both surfaces; polished surface 7.5YR 8/6 to 7/6; lustrous paint 2.5YR 5/8 red. FM 64 (Foliate Band). Imported. Fig.

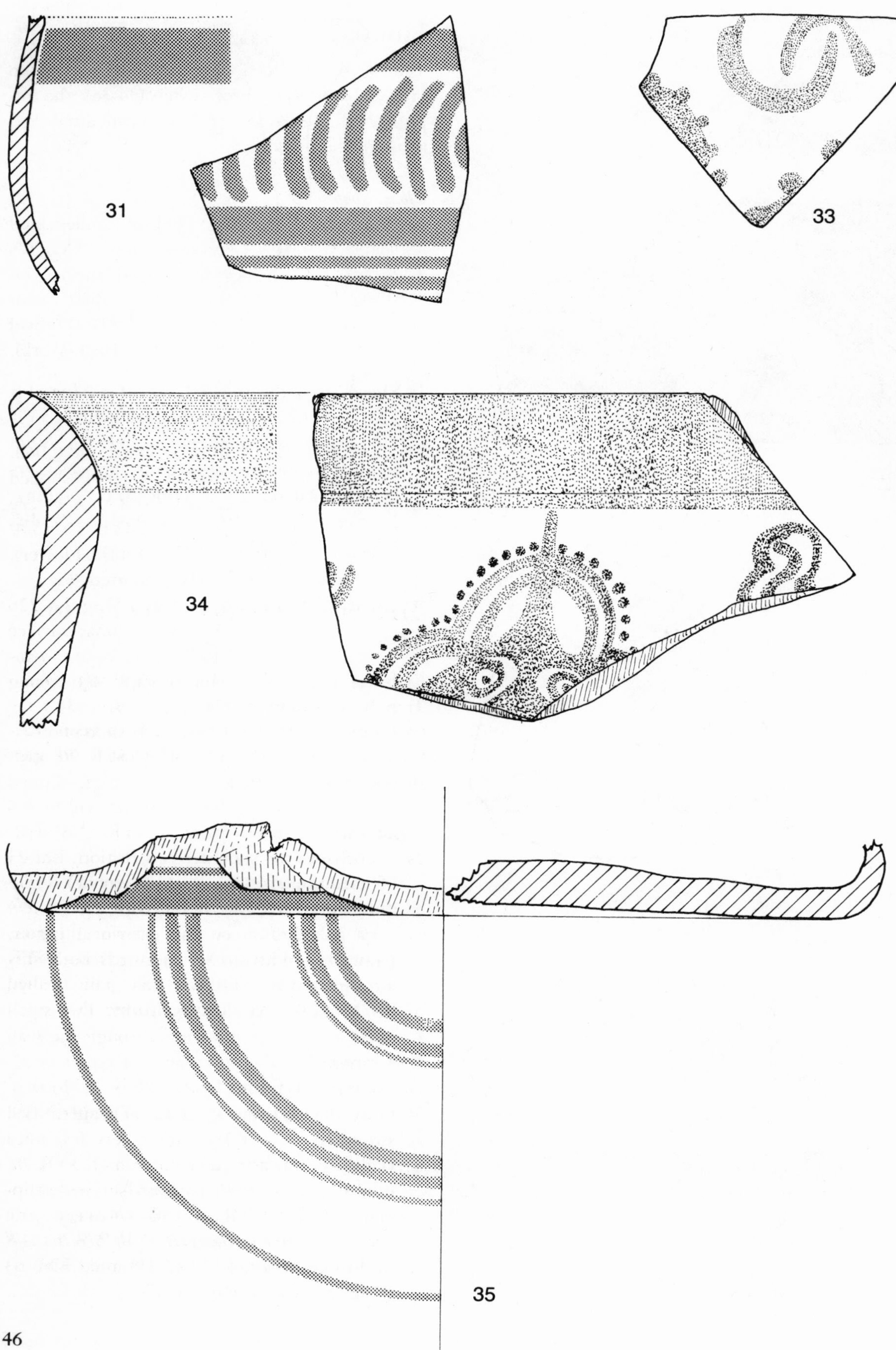

31
33
34
35

36

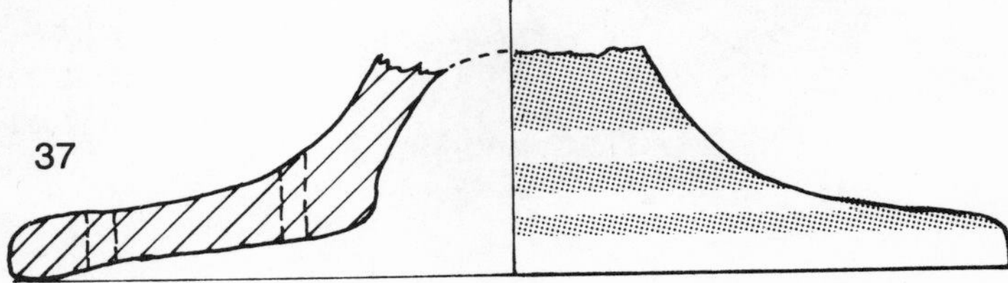

37

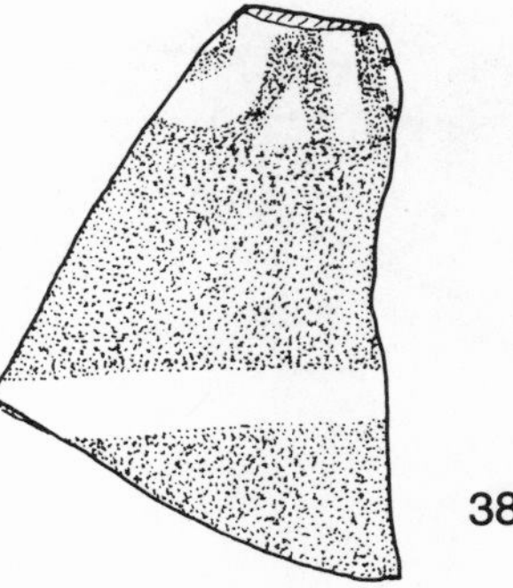

38

32 Sherd from the lower body and stem of a Kylix; h. 0.063. Clay 7.5YR 7/6 to 6/6 reddish yellow with a few mica. Slipped and polished surface 10YR 8/4 very pale brown; lustrous paint 2.5YR 4/8 red and black. Banded.

House 2

Ten of the thirteen Mycenaean sherds from House 2 belong to three vessels (34-36), the unpublished sherds 35, 38 have been attributed through the markings[7].

Closed Shapes

33 Body sherd from a vessel of unidentified shape; l. 0.053. Clay with mica 2.5YR 6/6 to 6/8 reddish yellow; slipped surface on the exterior 7.5YR 7/4 pink; matt paint 2.5YR 4/8 to 5/8 red. FM 18B (Hybrid Flower) (?). FM 29 (Trefoil Rock-Work). Local. Fig.

Open Shapes

34 Three rim sherds from a Krater, h. 0.060. Clay 7.5YR 7/6 reddish yellow; slipped and polished surface 10YR 8/3 to 8/4 very pale brown; lustrous paint 2.5YR 5/8 to 4/8 red and black. FM 18B (Hybrid Flower). FM 33 (Rock Pattern II). Imported. Fig.

35 Two sherds from the base of a Mug (FS 226 ?); d. 0.150. Clay 7.5YR 7/4 pink; surface 2.5Y 7/2 light grey to 7/4 pale yellow; vanished paint black and 7.5YR 4/4 strong brown. Imported. Fig.

36 Five sherds from the body and stem of a Kylix (FS 257); h. 0.115. Clay 5YR 7/8 reddish yellow with a very few mica; slipped surface 10YR 8/4 very pale brown to 8/6 yellow; lustrous paint 2.5YR 4/8 red. Whorl-shells in star-like composition. FM 23 (Whorl-Shell). FM 27 (Sea Anemone). Fig.

37 Sherd of Kylix foot. Clay with a very few mica 10YR 8/3 very pale brown at center, 5YR 6/8 reddish yellow towards both surfaces; surface 10YR 8/4 very pale brown; black and red semilustrous paint. Two small holes and traces of a third through the wall are probably due to an ancient repair or reuse. Local (?). Fig.

38 Body sherd from a vessel of unidentified shape; h. 0.037. Clay with a very few mica 10YR 7/6 reddish yellow at center, 5YR 7/6 reddish yellow towards both surfaces; slipped surface 10YR 8/3 to 8/4 very pale brown; lustrous paint 2.5YR 5/8 to 4/8 red. Floral motif. FM 18A (Voluted Flower) (?). Imported (?). Fig.

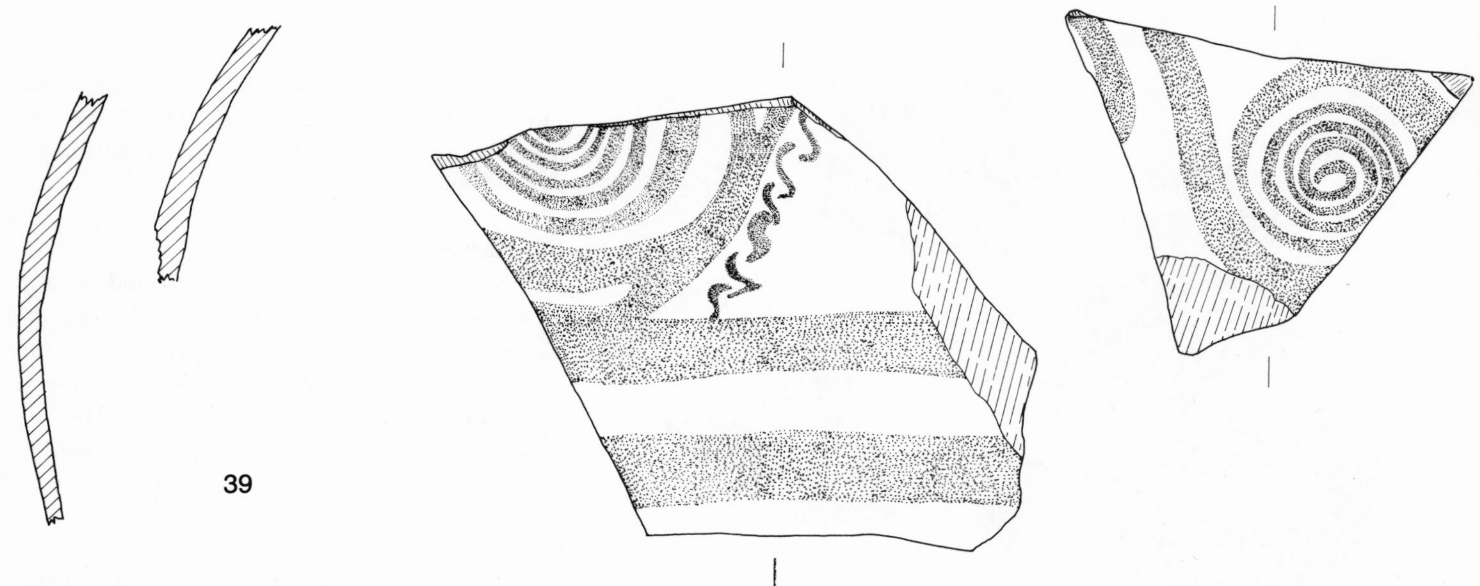

Unmarked Sherds

Closed Shapes

39 Two shoulder fragments from a big Piriform Jar (FS 34-35); l. 0.115; 0.083. Clay 5YR 7/6 to 6/6 reddish yellow with mica; surface 5YR 6/8 reddish yellow; matt paint 10YR 5/8 red. FM 22 (Argonaut). FM 48 (Quirk). Local. Fig.

40 Body sherd from a vessel of unidentified shape; l. 0.070. Clay 5YR 6/8 reddish yellow with a very few mica; polished surface 7.5YR 7/6 reddish yellow; lustrous paint 10R 5/8 to 4/8 red. FM 46 (Running Spiral) or FM 49 (Curved-Stemmed Spiral). FM 29 (Trefoil Rock-Work). Local (?). Fig.

Open Shapes

41 Body sherd from a Conical Rhyton (FS 199); h. 0.045. Clay with a few mica 2.5YR 6/6 light red at center, 7.5YR 7/6 reddish yellow towards both surfaces; slipped surface 10YR 8/4 very pale brown; matt paint black and 7.5YR 5/6 to 4/6 strong brown. FM 15 (Palm II). Local (?). Fig.

42 Body sherd from a Kylix (FS 257); h. 0.100. clay 7.5YR 7/6 reddish yellow at center, 5YR 7/8 reddish yellow towards both surfaces; surface 7.5YR 8/4 pink; lustrous paint 2.5YR 5/8 to 4/8 red. FM 18A (Voluted Flower). FM 62 (Tricurved Arch). Imported. Fig.

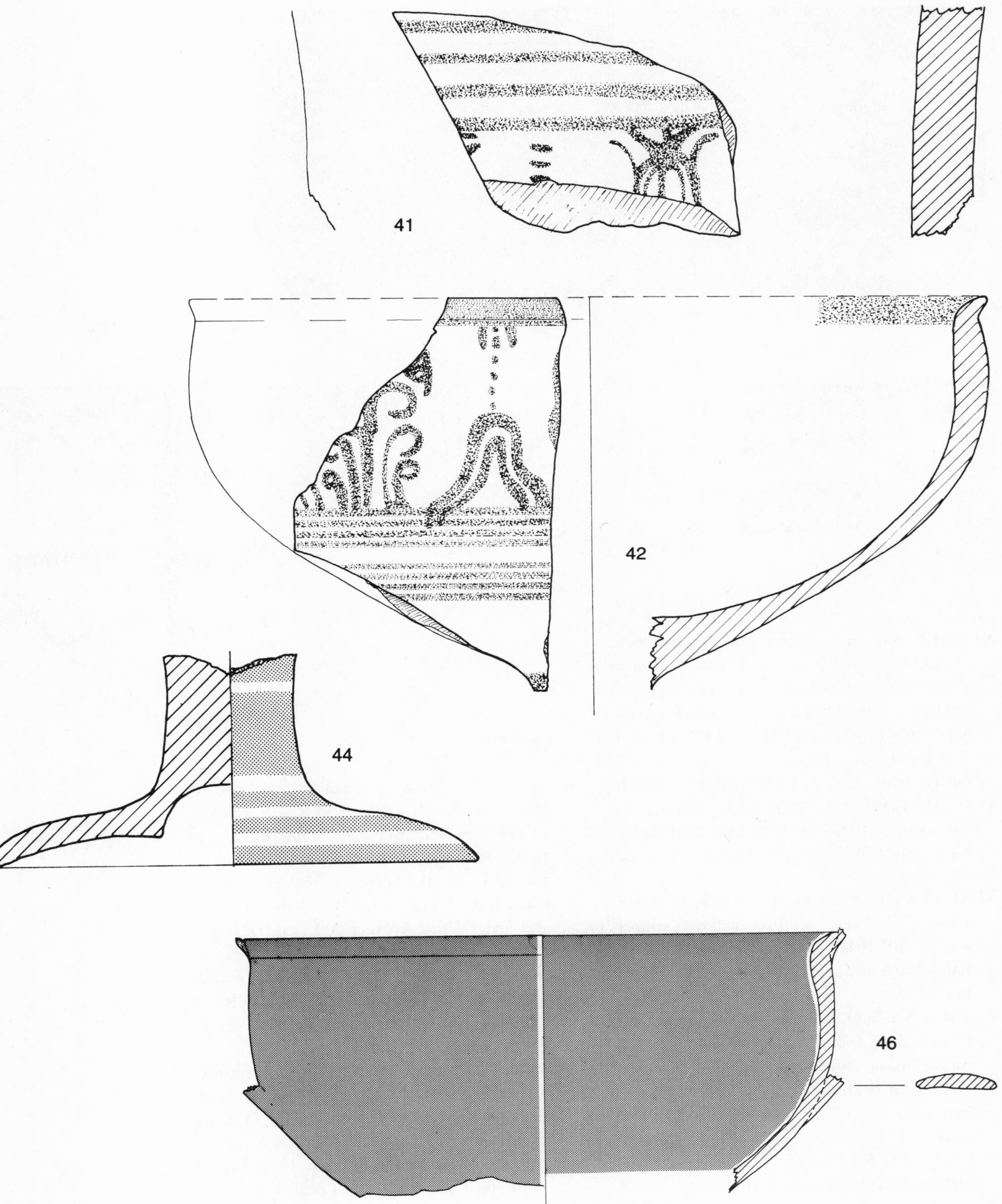
41
42
44
46

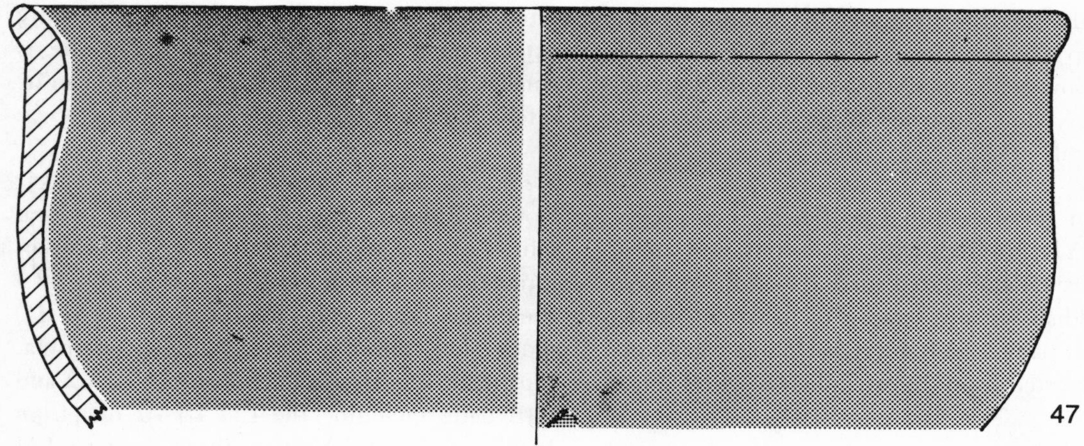

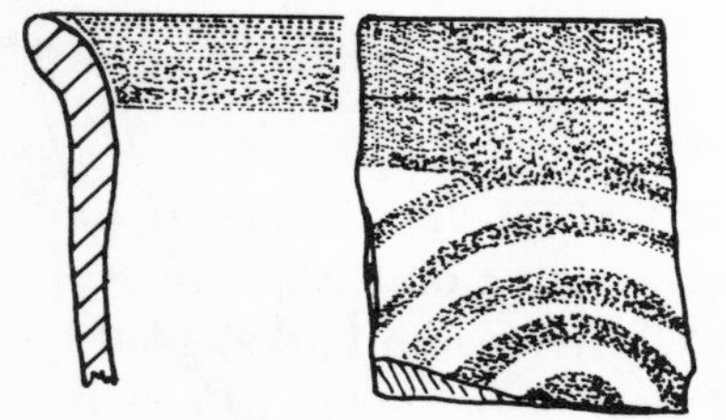

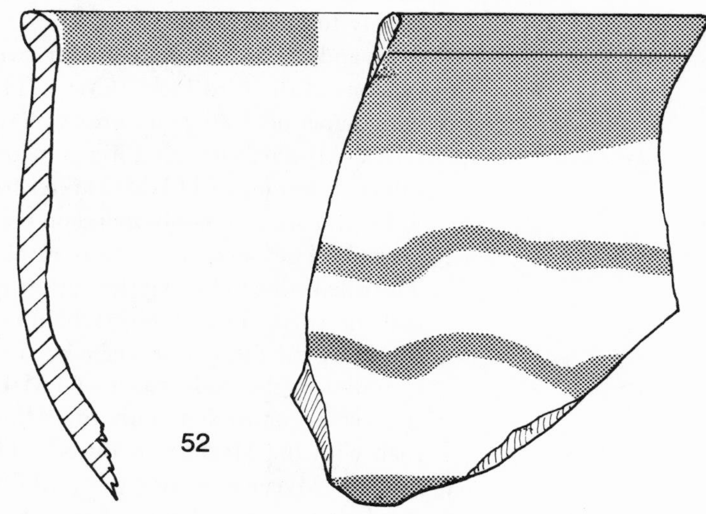

43 Sherd from the upper stem of a Kylix; h. 0.055. Clay 10YR 8/3 very pale brown at center, 5YR 7/6 reddish yellow towards both surfaces; slipped surface 10YR 8/4 very pale brown; lustrous paint 2.5YR 4/6 to 4/8 red and black. Imported.

44 Sherd from foot and stem of a Kylix; h. 0.045. Clay 5YR 7/6 reddish yellow; slipped surface 10YR 8/4 very pale brown; lustrous paint 10R 4/8 red. Domed foot. Imported. Fig.

45 Sherd from the stem of a Kylix; h. 0.058. Clay 7.5YR 7/6 reddish yellow; slipped surface 10YR 8/4 very pale brown; lustrous paint black and 5YR 4/6 yellowish red. Imported.

46 Kylix (FS 264), handles and stem missing; mouth d. 0.166. Similar in fabric to 24. Monochrome. Imported. Fig.

47 Rim sherd from a Kylix (FS 264) or from a Stemmed Bowl (FS 304); mouth d. 0.136. Clay 7.5YR 7/6 reddish yellow; lustrous paint 10R 4/8 red to 3/4 dusky red and black. Monochrome. Imported. Fig.

48 Body sherd from a vessel of unidentified shape; l. 0.052. Clay 7.5YR 7/6 reddish yellow with inclusions and a few mica; surface 7.5YR 7/6 reddish yellow to 7/4 pink, polished on the exterior; lustrous paint black and 2.5YR 5/6 red. Unidentified motif and FM 27 (Sea Anemone). Local (?). Fig.

49 Rim sherd from a vessel of unidentified shape; h. 0.029. Clay 5YR 6/6 reddish yellow with a few mica; surface 7.5YR 7/6 reddish yellow; lustrous paint 10R 4/6 to 5/8 red. Spiral (?). Local. Fig.

50 Body sherd from a vessel of unidentified shape; h. 0.043. Clay 5YR 6/8 reddish yellow with a few mica; surface 7.5YR 7/4 pink; lustrous paint 2.5YR 5/8 red on the exterior, black on the interior. Unidentified motif and FM 48 (Quirk). Local. Fig.

51 Body sherd with horizontal handle from a Cup (?); h. 0.055. Clay 5YR 7/6 reddish yellow with mica; surface 7.5YR 7/6 reddish yellow; lustrous paint 2.5YR 5/8 red. Local.

52 Rim sherd from a Cup (?); h. 0.067. Clay 2.5YR 5/6 red with inclusions and mica; polished and glazed surface 7.5YR 7/6 to 6/6 reddish yellow, traces of rotation inside; matt paint 2.5YR 5/8 red. Double wavy line. Imported from the Anatolian coast (?). Fig.

Closed Shapes
(19-20, 25-26, 29, 33, 39-40). The sherds are small and rather undiagnostic but should belong mainly to piriform jars.

25 and 29 are decorated with two different versions of the Bird motif (FM 7). The big Bird with diaper net filling on 25 fits well into the LH IIIA:2 Mycenaean series. Birds with the same filling appear on a LH IIIA:2 krater from Ialysos T 54[8] and are commonly found on kraters of this period[9]. The version on 29 is rather unusual. The filled zone following the outline of the body and the small filling blobs, which could be inspired by the filling transverse strokes commonly found in the body zones of LM IIIA Birds, suggest a connection with the Minoan rather than with the Mycenaean Birds[10]. The motif is rare on Mycenaean jars from LH IIIA:2 onwards; as far as I know, there are only three LH IIIB examples on jars of FS 36 from Cyprus[11].

The shoulder fragments 19, 39 are decorated with Argonauts (FM 22) similar to types 12, 13, which are found almost exclusively on piriform jars of FS 34-35. The slightly curved appendix shown on the right sherd of 19 is, however, somewhat puzzling; it looks like an appendix of the shell coil but, as far as I know, the appendix is found without exception on the left not on the right side of the shell coil. The vase is of local fabric and this could account for the unusual treatment of the motif. In Rhodes fifteen piriform jars are decorated with the Argonaut, none of them is later than LH IIIA:2[12].

20, an imported piece, comes very likely from the shoulder of a big jar of FS 35, as suggested by the fact that the decoration does not exceed the handle zone. The vase was very likely decorated with Running Spiral (FM 46); the only extant spiral, being placed beside the handle, is smaller than the main frieze. This sherd can be safely dated to LH IIIA:2.

Specialized Shapes
Conical Rhyton. Only 41, a small sherd of local fabric, may be assigned to this shape. The decoration consists of horizontal strokes and of a somewhat crude version of Palm II (FM 15) motif. This motif is not uncommon on rhyta. Furumark lists five examples of LH IIIA:2 and IIIB date, including the LH IIIA:2 one from Ialysos T 1[13]; in addition there are two LH IIIB:1 examples recently published by Mountjoy[14]. A LH IIIB dating of 41 cannot be excluded.

Open Shapes
Kraters (1-2, 21-22, 27, 30, 32). 1 is an outstanding piece decorated with a Bird which fits well into the LH IIIA:2 Mycenaean Bird series (FM 7:8). The motif seen in the upper part of the sherd should be a filling motif probably related to the "Bivalve Shell" (FM 25) rather than a wing. Although the piece looks Mycenean in style, its fabric is quite different from that of any other sherd in the deposit and recalls the fabric of a stirrup jar from Ialysos T 27, commonly regarded as a Minoan import[15]. The excellent rim sherd 34 is decorated with a Hybrid Flower (FM 18B) of type 33-34 well paralleled in LH IIIA:2 deposits at Mycenae[16]. There is no doubt that this is an import from the Argolid. Of the relatively well preserved Krater 30 only a few rim sherds survive. The Diaper Net (FM 57) decoration is rather unusual on this shape. The few examples so far known include two LH IIIA:1 Kraters from the Argolid[17] and a slightly later one from Iasos in Caria[18]. Nothing can be said of the decoration of 27, another fine imported piece. Three sherds may be assigned to local fabrics (2, 21-22). The first has a motif no longer identifiable. The rim sherd 21 and the strap handle 22 come from the same vessel. The only extant part of the decoration consists of a filling quatrefoil motif probably linked with the Trefoil Rock-Work pattern (FM 29).

Cups (4-5, 31, 51). No sherd may be safely assigned to any certain shape. 5 has a central motif flanked by Chevrons (FM 58); the central motif was probably the stem of some floral composition (FM 11:42 or FM 18A-B). On 4 there is a circumcurrent zone of alternating "U's" (FM 45) of type 4, which suggests a LH IIIA:2 dating. 31, an excellent imported piece, is decorated with a Foliate Band (FM 64) of type 19, commonly found in LH IIIA:2 deposits at Mycenae as well as on several LH IIIA:2 vessels from Rhodes[19].

Mugs (3, 28, 35). The ridged rim sherd 3 comes from a Mug of large size. Mugs with ridges at rim and waist are commonly found in LH IIIA:2 deposits at Mycenae[20] but continue in LH IIIB:1 as well[21].In Rhodes no less than five Mugs have ridges at rim and waist: three are LH IIIA:2[22], one from Pilona is LH IIIB[23], the last from Apollakia is dated by Furumark as late as LH IIIC but should be earlier[24]. The Quirk motif (FM 48) of type 5 is of no help for chronology. This is a rather uncommon motif on mugs but related linear designs such as U-Pattern, Wavy lines and N-Pattern occur on LH IIIA:2 as well as on LH IIIB Mugs[25]. 28 comes from the lower body of a Mug presumably decorated with circumcurrent Chevrons (FM 58) in two zones[26]. This motif appears on both LH IIIA:2 and IIIB:1 Mugs[27].Finally, the two joining base sherds 35 could belong to a Straight-sided Alabastron as well; the decoration consists of the usual groups of concentric circles commonly found on both shapes.

Kylikes (6-16, 23, 32, 36-37, 42-45). The patterned kylix is the most common shape.

(FM 18 Mycenaean Flower). Three sherds are decorated with floral motifs (6-7, 42). The remarkable imported piece 42, decorated with a central Voluted Flower (FM 18A) of type 15-16 flanked by isolated Tricurved Arches (FM 62), can be safely dated to LH IIIA:2. Although incompletely preserved, the Unvoluted Flowers (FM 18C) on 6-7 appear clearly related to the LH IIIA:2 series and compare well with examples of this period from the deposits at Mycenae and from tombs on Rhodes[28].

(FM 19 Mult.Stem). A hook-shaped version similar to types 49-50 appears on 8. It cannot be ascertained whether the motif was in a single row or alternating. Both versions are well represented on LH IIIA:2 pottery in Rhodes, especially on kylikes[29], and are commonly found in LH IIIA:2 deposits at Mycenae[30].

(FM 21 Cuttlefish). The two sherds 9-10 are difficult to date because kylikes with Cuttlefish decoration are common in Rhodes in the LH IIIA:2 as well as in the LH IIIB period[31]. 9 has added lines in white paint, a very common feature on cuttlefishes. In Rhodes dots and/or lines in white paint occur on ten cuttlefishes out of thirty attested before LH IIIC; seven of them are on LH IIIA:2 and B kylikes[32].

(FM 23 Whorl-Shell). This is the most common motif on kylikes (11-12, 23, 36). On 36, an unusually well preserved example of FS 257, the shells are arranged in a star-like composition of a type well paralleled in LH IIIA:2 deposits at Mycenae[33]. 23, decorated with rather undiagnostic vertical shells, should belong to FS 257. According to Hope Simpson and Lazenby, the rim sherd 11 with diagonal shells could be as late as LH IIIB:1, but the large band at lip and the elaborate design of the shells suggest a LH IIIA:2 dating[34].

(FM 24 Linked Whorl-Shell Pattern). Unusual versions of this motif appear on 13-14. On 13 the usual zig-zag design is replaced by Tricurved Arches; this version is unknown to Furumark and does not appear in the deposits at Mycenae. The very simple version on 14 could be as late as LH IIIB and recalls Minoan rather than Mycenaean variants. This is an altogether rare motif on Rhodes appearing on no more than five vessels[35].

(FM 62 Tricurved Arch) (15-16). 16 was very likely decorated with a disintegrated version of type 30, dated by Furumark to LH IIIB, but largely represented in LH IIIA:2 deposits at Mycenae[36]. Similar versions appear in Rhodes on two kylikes lacking a context[37] and on a LH IIIA:2 jug from Kameiros T 47[38]. On 15 there is a net pattern of a type attested in LH IIIA:2 as well as in LH IIIB; traces of a no longer identifiable filling motif are seen at the lower right edge of the sherd. On Rhodes Tricurved Arches in net pattern are a common motif on big jars, but are quite exceptional on kylikes[39].

Miscellaneous Open Shapes (17, 38, 48-50). Most of the sherds in this group are so undistinguished as to defy any close dating. The Tricurved Arch with filling Chevrons (FM 62) on 17 recalls net compositions of type 13. The Ladder motif flanked by a Curve-stemmed Spiral on 38 belongs to some floral composition rather than to a triglyph.

Monochrome Open Shapes (24, 46-47). In addition to the well preserved example 46, the monochrome Kylix FS 264 is represented by some unlisted rim sherds belonging to two or three more examples. This is a very common shape in LH IIIA tombs at Ialysos[40]. The short stem 24 has an high-domed foot and should belong to a Stemmed Bowl of FS 304 rather than to a Kylix. To the same shape should also belong the rim sherd 47 with short, rounded lip[41]. In the cemetery at Ialysos the shape was never popular; the monochrome version in particular is represented by no more than two examples[42]. Quite surprisingly four monochrome Stemmed Bowls come from the small, peripheral cemetery at Lelos[43]. All the sherds are painted in the black/red lustrous paint characteristic of the best LH IIIA fabrics.

Figurine
The fragmentary figurine 18 described by Monaco as "un idoletto fittile femminile" is, in fact, an animal figurine of Wavy Line Type 2. According to E. French, this type makes its appearance in LH IIIA:1 but becomes particularly popular from LH IIIA:2 to mid IIIB[44].

Non-Mycenaean Ware
The rim sherd 52, probably belonging to some large Bowl decorated with a double Wavy Line, is of particular interest. Its fabric looks completely different from both imported and locally produced Mycenaean wares. The clay is unusually rich in inclusions and mica; the surface is covered with a yellowish slip and has a glazed appearance; the paint is matt red. Sherds of similar or related shape, fabric and decoration appear on Kos and in the Vathy cave on Kalymnos and are quite common at Iasos[45]. This seems to be a characteristic fabric of the South-eastern Aegean area and its main production centre must be most probably located on the Anatolian coast.

Conclusions
In terms of chronology the evidence may be summarized as follows: most of the sherds are LH IIIA:2, a few could be as late as LH IIIB but none can be definitely attributed to this phase; characteristic features of LH IIIB such as deep bowls and panelled patterns are completely absent.

Evidence covering a wider time span has, however, to be expected from the new excavations. Last summer T. Marketou kindly showed me a good deal of the recently found sherds; most of them are LH IIIA:2, a few should be LH IIIB, and one could be as late as LH IIIC.

The few Mycenaean sherds published by Monaco were almost completely neglected by Furumark, who in fact assumed that the settlement was abandoned at some time during LM/LH IIIA:1[46].

Recently, the sherds from Trench I have been given more attention by scholars, especially by Hope Simpson and Lazenby, who, however, believe that from LH IIIA:2 onwards "the main Mycenaean centre in the Ialysos area was elsewhere, probably further inland and nearer to the Mycenaean cemeteries"[47].

What seems to me more impressive is that the sherds are scattered over so large an area as to rule out the possibility that they were removed by rain or running water from a more inland site. I think, indeed, that they should be regarded as *in situ* and testify the existence of a vanished Mycenaean settlement following Trianda IIB. The total absence of architectural remains attributable to the later settlement as well as the piecemeal character of the pottery can be reasonably explained, in my opinion, by the environmental conditions. Trianda is situated on a narrow alluvial plain edged on one side by a low, open sea-shore and on the other by the steep slopes of Prophitis Ilias and Philerimos. The plain is crossed by several short streams; three of them flow straight through the BA settlement area[48]. Under such conditions abundant rains may result in short-term but disastrous flooding of the coastal plain and in a severe erosion of the surface layers. In his 1925 study of the morphology of the island, the distinguished Italian geographer C. Migliorini observed that in the last centuries the hydrographic system underwent a radical change, resulting in augmented erosion against reduced deposition. According to Migliorini this is due to an increase in the flow of rivers following the extensive deforestation that took place in Rhodes in the preceding five or six centuries; more particularly he remarked that river-beds are more and more encroaching upon and eroding their alluvial plains[49]. At Trianda the more inland part of the settlement so far excavated, about one km from the coastal line, was buried under three m of alluvial deposit, while near the sea the walls of Trianda IIB are found one m under ground level. Furthermore it is interesting to remark that no traces of later occupation of any period are so far known from the BA settlement area.

Under such conditions it is quite difficult to ascertain whether the LH IIIA:2 sherds mark a continuity of occupation or a phase of reoccupation of the site. The archaeological evidence for the end of Trianda IIB is somewhat puzzling. According to Monaco, followed by Furumark[50], the inhabitants suddenly abandoned their houses leaving behind them the pottery and other objects, which were found still *in situ* on the floors. This is not an uncommon picture in the Aegean where other settlements were hastily abandoned by their inhabitants under the pressure of some natural catastrophe, but no traces of catastrophe of any kind have been noticed in Trianda IIB. On the other hand, the evidence from tombs speaks strongly in favour of a continuous use of the cemetery by the same people. Eleven of the 24 LH IIB-IIIA:1 tombs were in use in LHIIIA:2 as well; they constitute 45% of the LH IIB-IIIA:1 tombs (see Benzi, this volume). If the tombs re-used and largely cleared of their contents in LH IIIC are discounted, it appears that only three of the 16 LH IIB-IIIA:1 tombs excavated by the Italians were not used in the next phase[51].

In conclusion it seems to me that, at this stage of our knowledge, the settlement at Trianda is a more authoritative candidate to be connected with the cemeteries on Makra and Moschou Vounara than Mount Philerimos or a hypothetical more inland site or Moschou Vounara, where "a considerable amount of prehistoric coarse pottery... and some traces of rough walls" are reported by Hope Simpson and Lazenby[52].

It is not necessary to stress the provisional character of my conclusions. It is to be hoped that future excavations by the Rhodian archaeologists will solve the problem.

Mario Benzi
Dipartimento di Scienze Archeologiche
Sezione di Archeologia e Antichità Classiche
Via Galvani, 1
56100 Pisa
Italy

1. G. Monaco, ClRh 10, 1941, 49-53 and fig. 5:1-3 reports 80 conical cups, a high-spouted jug, a spouted jar, a jug, 7 flattened loom-weights and a lamp with vertical loop handle. On this deposit see J.L. Davis, AnatSt 32, 1982, 38; M. Benzi in Hägg – Marinatos 1984, 98, 100.
2. The identification of kylikes and cups proved particularly difficult. Since handles are missing, the identifications are founded on the decoration of the lower body where kylikes usually have a group of thin lines, while cups have a pattern of bands and lines. All the sherds not proved to be cups have been assigned to kylikes, but it is possible that some fragment identified as a kylix is in fact from a cup.
3. G. Monaco, ClRh 10, 1941, 53-56 and figs. 5:5-7, 9; 6; 14:3.
4. G. Monaco, ClRh 10, 1941, 57-60.
5. G. Monaco, ClRh 10, 1941, 60-64.
6. Only a few, small sherds are preserved.
7. For the published sherds see G. Monaco, ClRh 10, 1941, figs. 59:2-3; 87:3; 116:2.
8. A. Maiuri, ASAtene 6-7, 1923-24, 222, no. 6 not illustrated.
9. Prakt 1950, 220, fig. 23 from Mycenae; Slenczka 1974, pls. 23; 24:2a from Tiryns.
10. Furumark 1972, 195 ff., 250.
11. P. Åström, SCE IV. 1c, 1972, 385.
12. Mee 1982, 12-13.
13. Furumark 1972, 280, 282; A. Maiuri, ASAtene 6-7, 1923-24, fig. 5.
14. Mountjoy 1986, fig. 133:2,6.
15. A. Maiuri, ASAtene 6-7, 1923-24, pl. 3; Mee 1982, 14.
16. E. French, BSA 60, 1965, figs. 2:5, 8; 7:6; pls. 51b:2; 53c:1,3.
17. Mountjoy 1986, fig. 71:5 in panel; E. French, BSA 59, 1964, 253.
18. M. Benzi, "I Micenei a Iasos" in Studi su Iasos di Caria (Suppl. al Vol. 31-32 di BdA), Roma 1987, fig. 3:1.
19. Parallels restricted to open shapes include a shallow cup from Kattavia recently published in Lindos IV. 1, fig. 106, and two carinated conical cups from Ialysos, Mee 1982, pl. 18:5; Forsdyke 1925, fig. 199:840. Cfr. E. French, BSA 60, 1965, 173; Mountjoy 1986, fig. 109:6.
20. E. French, BSA 60, 1965, 176; Mountjoy 1986, 86.
21. E. French, BSA 61, 1966, 219; P. Mountjoy, BSA 71, 1976, 86; Mountjoy 1986, 112.
22. Mee 1982, pl. 18:1 from Ialysos T 19; G. Jacopi, ASAtene 13-14, 1930-31, fig. 96; CVA Danemark[2], pl. 48:11 from Kattavia.
23. G. Jacopi, ASAtene 13-14, 1930-31, fig. 89.
24. CVA Danemark[2], pl. 48:12.
25. Mountjoy 1986, 86, 112; the Quirk is listed by Mountjoy among LH IIIB:1 mug motifs but no example is illustrated; a vertical version of type 15 appears on a

LH IIIB:1 mug from the Prehistoric Cemetery deposit at Mycenae, E. French, BSA 61, 1966, fig. 2:27. In Rhodes a Quirk of type 5 is painted in white on the waist band of a LH IIIB or early IIIC mug from Pilona, G. Jacopi, ASAtene 13-14, 1930-31, fig. 90.

26. Cf. E. French, BSA 60, 1965, fig. 9:2 LH IIIA:2.
27. Mountjoy 1986, 86, 112.
28. E. French, BSA 60, 1965, fig. 2:6,11; pl. 53a:4; fig. 10:3, pl. 54d:2-4; M. Benzi, SMEA 23, 1982, pl. 3:a from Ialysos T 20; G. Jacopi, ClRh 6-7, 1932-33, fig. 153 from Kameiros T 46.
29. The variant in single row appears on kylikes from Ialysos T 19, A. Maiuri, ASAtene 6-7, 1923-24, fig. 53, and from Siana or Castellos, CVA Danemark[2], pl. 53:6,7; the alternating variant appears on a kylix from Apollakia, CVA Danemark[2], pl. 53:8.
30. E. French, BSA 60, 1965, 172, fig. 3:9-11 on kylikes, stemmed bowls and piriform jars; Mountjoy 1986, fig. 107:4.
31. Mee 1982, 25.
32. Forsdyke 1925, pl. 14:870 from Ialysos; CVA Danemark[2], pl. 51:1,2,4,6 from Rhodes, Vati and Apollakia; Lindos IV. 1, fig. 7 from Passia T 1.
33. A.J.B. Wace, Archaeologia 82, 1932, fig. 8:d; E. French, BSA 60, 1965, pl. 52d:4-5; Mountjoy 1986, fig. 107:7. See also Säflund 1965, figs. 19:2;24 from Berbati.
34. R. Hope Simpson – J.F. Lazenby, BSA 68, 1973, 135 footnote 42. Cfr. Mountjoy 1986, fig. 107:6.
35. Canonical Mycenaean versions appear on three kylikes and in the body zone of a LH IIIA:2 stirrup jar, Forsdyke 1925, pls. 14:894; 15:866 from Ialysos; CVA Danemark[2], pl. 53:5 from Siana or Castellos; Langlotz 1932, pl 2:39 from Rhodes. A Minoan version appears on a spouted bowl from Vati, CVA Danemark[2], pl. 56:11a-b.
36. E. French, BSA 60, 1965, 173, 182, figs. 8:4; 9:1; Mountjoy 1986, figs. 101:10,11;106:2;107:10.
37. One of u.p. in Rhodes Museum and CVA Danemark[2], pl. 53:4 from Vati.
38. G. Jacopi, ClRh 6-7, 1932-33, figs. 160-168. The chronology of this tomb is disputed, see Furumark 1941, 70 (LH IIIA:2/B); Mee 1982, 51 (LH IIIA:2 and B); M. Benzi, SMEA 23, 1982, 334 and footnote 34 (LH IIIA:2).
39. The only known example is on a kylix from Ialysos or Kameiros, Furtwängler – Loeschke 1886, pl. 11:70.
40. Mee 1982, 17-18. Monochrome kylikes are commonly found in LH IIIA:2 deposits at Mycenae, E. French, BSA 60, 1965, 177, fig. 4:8; see also Mountjoy 1986, 90.
41. Mountjoy 1986, 92.
42. Forsdyke 1925, pl. 10:862; A. Maiuri, ASAtene 6-7, 1923-24, 133, no. 20 from T 19, now missing.
43. A. Maiuri, ASAtene 6-7, 1923-24, fig. 153:3.
44. E. French, BSA 66, 1971, 152, 155, fig. 11.
45. M. Benzi, "I Micenei a Iasos" in Studi su Iasos di Caria (Suppl. al Vol. 31-32 di BdA), Roma 1987,31.
46. A. Furumark, OpArch 6, 1950, 166 footnote 8; 176 footnote 11; 180.
47. R. Hope Simpson – J.F. Lazenby, BSA 68, 1973, 135; Mee 1982,7.
48. G. Monaco, ClRh 10, 1941, fig. 1 and pl. 1.
49. C. Migliorini, L'Universo 6, 1925, 93-95.
50. G. Monaco, ClRh 10, 1941, 178; A. Furumark, OpArch 6, 1950, 180.
51. Makra V.: T 11, a badly damaged tomb without skeletal remains; T 37, containing about six burials. Moschou V.: T 74, a single burial tomb. On the re-use of earlier tombs in the Ialysos cemeteries, see W. Cavanagh – Ç. Mee, BSA 73, 1978, 36 ff; M. Benzi, SMEA 23, 1982, 323 ff.
52. R. Hope Simpson – J.F. Lazenby, BSA 68, 1973, 137.

The LH IIIB Period in the Dodecanese

Christopher Mee

LH IIIB has traditionally been regarded as a period of remarkable cultural and possibly even political uniformity, as the period par excellence of the Mycenaean koine, but I will argue that in the eastern Aegean at least there is evidence of instability.

The principal Mycenaean site on Rhodes is the chamber tomb cemetery at Ialysos. By LH IIIA2 there were no less than 59 tombs in use[1]. The quality of the grave offerings underlines the prosperity of the site at this time. Since LH IIIB is a much longer period[2], there should be an increase in the number of tombs, but in fact there were just 25 tombs in use[3]. The explanation could of course be a change of cemetery but the same phenomenon can be observed, if on a lesser scale, at Kalavarda and at Lelos: five tombs in use in LH IIIA2, only two tombs in LH IIIB[4].

It has been suggested that the LH IIIB tombs escape detection because much less pottery was included amongst the grave offerings[5] but this is not the case at Ialysos[6]. Another possibility is that the LH IIIB pottery style did not at first find favour on Rhodes because, as Furumark observed, "the IIIA2 tradition was firmly rooted"[7]. However, it would appear that a high proportion of the LH IIIB pottery from Ialysos was in fact imported[8] so conservative local potters cannot be held responsible for the discrepancy in the number of LH IIIA2 and LH IIIB tombs. I feel sure that the Mycenaean settlements in the north-west of Rhodes at least suffered a severe setback during the course of the LH IIIB period. The problem is that none of the settlements has been excavated, only their cemeteries.

There is in fact only one excavated Mycenaean settlement in the Dodecanese, the Seraglio on Kos. This is a complex site not least because Protogeometric and Geometric graves were cut into and consequently disturbed the LH III levels[9]. Moreover most of the original excavation records have been destroyed[10]. Nevertheless there is evidence of a destruction in LH IIIB. On a third city floor Morricone discovered a deposit of carbonised figs in a LH IIIB context[11] but the extent of this destruction level could not be ascertained, thus the settlement as a whole may not have been affected. In the associated chamber tomb cemetery at Eleona and Langada there is a slight increase in the number of tombs – 17 in LH IIIA2, 24 in LH IIIB[12] – but in the cemetery at Müsgebi, just north of Kos, the trend is quite the reverse – 24 tombs in use in LH IIIA2, only eight in LH IIIB[13]. At Miletus massive fortifications were constructed in LH IIIB after a fire had destroyed the settlement. It is suggested that this catastrophe was the result of "einen feindlichen Überfall"[14].

The concept of an LH IIIB koine is further undermined by the apparent reduction in the level of trade, at least in pottery which constitutes our primary source of evidence. In LH IIIA2 fine pottery had mainly been imported from the Argolid. Thus 13 of the 16 samples from Ialysos analysed by optical emission spectroscopy had an Argive clay composition[15]. In LH IIIB, and more especially in LH IIIB2, there is a change. As Lisa French has observed, there is an "absence of the standard types of LH IIIB2" in the Eastern Aegean[16]. The evidence has been fully marshalled by Sherratt[17] who points out that the features which define the LH IIIB2 pottery style in the Argolid – the deep band deep bowl, the rosette bowl and the heavy "filled style" decoration on bowls and kraters – do not penetrate the eastern Aegean, except for a single deep band deep bowl from Astypalaia[18]. In fact we would expect these LH IIIB2 innovations in the pottery from a settlement site rather than a cemetery, so it is their absence at the Seraglio and Miletus which is significant. Must we therefore assume that sites in the eastern Aegean lay deserted in LH IIIB2? Or is it the case that "shapes and decoration of early LH

IIIB origin continue as the main characteristics of a late LH IIIB pottery horizon"[19]? This is certainly a possibility and finds a precedent in the idiosyncratic use of certain LH IIIA2 shapes and motifs on LH IIIB1 pottery from Rhodes[20]. But if sites were still occupied there must have been a local IIIB pottery style, however derivative. I will admit that I could not isolate this[21] but in his study of the finds from the Passia graves Dietz has tentatively identified "the basis for a definition of late IIIB on Rhodes"[22]. This is firmly rooted in the local LH IIIB1 tradition. Analysis of LH IIIB pottery from Ialysos confirms the decline of the Argolid as the principal source of imported pottery. Of the 17 samples only 7 had Argive compositions, 41% whereas 81% of the LH IIIA2 samples were Argive imports[23].

The evidence which I have presented is suggestive rather than conclusive but gains credibility if considered in the context of the Aegean as a whole. In the Cyclades Barber notes "a marked decline, indeed cessation, of direct contact with and influence from the mainland centres of Mycenaean power" at this time[24]. At Phylakopi few LH IIIB2 imports can be identified and there is a consequent deterioration in the quality of the locally produced pottery[25]. This is also true of Ayia Irini[26] and suggests that trade between the mainland and the Cyclades may have been disrupted. It is surely no coincidence that the fortifications of Phylakopi were extended in LH IIIB1[27] and furthermore that a number of easily defensible sites were occupied[28]. Crete I will not discuss in detail but I would point out that Kanta records "a series of destructions and abandonments..... during LM IIIB"[29]. The sites affected include Ayia Pelagia, Chania, Gournia, Khondros Viannou, Knossos, Malia, Palaikastro and possibly Archanes.

I have concentrated on the Aegean but it is not out of the question that mainland Greece also suffered[30]. Traditionally, of course, disaster strikes late in LH IIIB but on a number of sites the destruction level cannot be precisely dated. This is true even of Pylos[31]. Was it because of events on the mainland that trade between the major Mycenaean centres and the Aegean collapsed in LH IIIB? Did the Aegean in fact escape unscathed? Obviously I do not think so and not simply because of the evidence of destruction and disruption which I have presented. Although my theme is LH IIIB we must briefly investigate the LH IIIC period.

At Ialysos there is a resurgence in the use of the chamber tomb cemetery[32]. Most of the pottery is in the Aegean koine style defined by Desborough[33] but was nevertheless locally produced[34] – exotic trinkets indicate that Eastern Mediterranean contacts had been resumed[35]. I believe that the explanation for this recovery must be sought in the high proportion of the LH IIIC chamber tombs which were reused[36] - the tombs had been constructed in LH IIIA or LH IIIB, abandoned and then reused in LH IIIC. The reuse of a chamber tomb is the act of displaced individuals and I have no doubt that these were "refugees" from the mainland[37]. They could settle at Ialysos because the site lay more or less deserted – only six of the LH IIIB chamber tombs were still in use in LH IIIC. The reuse of chamber tombs is also attested at Kalavarda, at Mandriko and on Kos at Eleona and Langada[38]. Again I would interpret this as evidence of an influx of mainland Mycenaean settlers who took advantage of an eastern Aegean which had never recovered from the disastrous events of LH IIIB.

Christopher Mee
School of Archaeological and Oriental Studies
The University of Liverpool
P.O. Box 147
Liverpool L69 3BX
England

1. Mee 1982, 11.
2. In the absolute chronology proposed by P. Warren – V. Hankey, BICS 21, 1974, 401. LH IIIA2 = 1385 or 1375/1370 – 1350/1340 or 1335/1325, LH IIIB = 1350/1340 or 1335/1325 – 1190.
3. Mee 1982, 22-23.
4. Mee 1982, 50-52 and 55-57.
5. E. French, BSA 64, 1969, 71.
6. There were on average 5.7 pots in each of the LH IIIA2 tombs and 4.4 pots in each of the LH IIIB tombs.
7. Furumark 1972, 541.
8. R. Jones – C. Mee, JFieldA 5, 1978, 469.

9. Cities III and IV in particular suffered "uno sconvolgimento degli strati" – L. Morricone, ASAtene 50-51, 1972-73, 388.
10. L. Morricone, ASAtene 50-51, 1972-73, 147-149.
11. L. Morricone, ASAtene 50-51, 1972-73, 227-229.
12. Mee 1982, 87-88.
13. C. Mee, AnatSt 28, 1978, 137-142.
14. W. Schiering, IstMitt 29, 1979, 87 – the catastrophe is dated circa 1300 but I would prefer a LH IIIB1 date for the fine krater from the destruction level, W. Schiering, IstMitt 28, 1979, 101 fig. 5.
15. R. Jones – C. Mee, JFieldA 5, 1978, 468.
16. E. French, in Proceedings of the X International Congress of Classical Archaeology. Ankara 1978, 167-168.
17. E.S. Sherratt, BSA 75, 1980, 192-193.
18. This deep bowl is from one of the Armenochori chamber tombs. E. Zervoudakis ADelt 26B, 1971, 550-551 – but has not yet been published.
19. E.S. Sherratt, BSA 75, 1980, 201.
20. Furumark 1972, 541.
21. Mee 1982, 88.
22. Lindos IV. 1, 113.
23. R. Jones – C. Mee, JFieldA 5, 1978, 469. – an additional 8 samples were identified as imports, from Attica, Boeotia and East Crete/Naxos. Subsequent multivariate analysis has confirmed that the samples were definitely not from the Argolid but comparison of their compositions and the controls for Thebes, Knossos, Palaikastro and Naxos proved inconclusive – R. Jones – C. Mee in Greek and Cypriot Pottery: A Review of Scientific Studies, Athens 1986, 501-508.
24. R.L.N. Barber, BSA 76, 1981, 11.
25. E.S. Sherratt, BSA 75, 1980, 191; P.-A. Mountjoy in MacGillivray – Barber (eds.) 1984, 225.
26. E.S. Sherratt, BSA 75, 1980, 191.
27. Renfrew (ed.) 1985, 81.
28. R.L.N. Barber, BSA 76, 1981, 11. cites Ayios Andreas on Siphnos, Koukounaries on Paros, Rizokastelia on Naxos, To Froudhi tou Kalamitsou on Siphnos and Akroterion Ourion on Tenos but the chronology of Koukounaries has since been revised – D. Schilardi in MacGillivray – Barber (eds.) 1984, 195. – a LH IIIC date being preferred for the initial settlement of the site.
29. Kanta 1980, 324.
30. E.S. Sherratt, BSA 75, 1980, 201-202.
31. E.S. Sherratt, BSA 75, 1980, 177.
32. Mee 1982, 27.
33. Desborough 1964, 227-228.
34. R. Jones – C. Mee, JFieldA 5, 1978, 469.
35. Mee 1982, 45-46.
36. The evidence for the reuse of chamber tombs at Ialysos is discussed in detail in W. Cavanagh – C. Mee, BSA 73, 1978, 36-38 and in Mee 1982, 28-29 and 89-90. It was suggested that at least sixteen of the 43 LH IIIC chamber tombs had been reused but this figure has been revised by M. Benzi, SMEA 23, 1982, 323-333 as a result of his meticulous study of the Ialysos cemetery. He has deleted two of the tombs from my list, NT4 and NT31, but has identified a further six instances of reuse: NT9, NT20, NT21, NT32A, NT71 and NT78. Thus the total stands at twenty. However it is not out of the question that a number of the other LH IIIC tombs were reused but had been thoroughly purified.
37. Mee 1982, 89-90.
38. W. Cavanagh – C. Mee, BSA 73, 1978, 39-40; M. Benzi, SMEA 23, 1982, 334-335.

Mycenaean Rhodes: A Summary

Mario Benzi

Evidence for the Mycenaean period in Rhodes is impressive but presents three serious drawbacks: lack of excavated settlement sites; extensive illicit excavations; summary accounts of the Italian excavations.

The large collection in the Rhodes Museum includes materials from ten cemeteries excavated by the Italian archaeologists (Ialysos, Tolo, Maritsa, Damatria, Zuccalades, Kameiros, Mandhriko, Lelos, Kariones and Pilona); a good deal of material from illicit excavations in the cemeteries at Phanes, Kameiros, Kritinia/Castellos, Siana, Kattavia, Lachania, Vati and Lardhos, formerly in the Biliotti, Karavella and Ghanotakis collections[1], and the substantial Akavi collection attributed by Morricone to the cemeteries of Vati: Apsaktiras and Anghio Vouno[2]. In addition there are several whole pots of unknown provenance and a good deal of sherd material probably from the dromoi and chambers of the Ialysos cemetery.

Only the cemetery of Ialysos has been relatively well recorded. In addition to the official reports four more sources are available: 1) the excavation note books, which provide sketch-plans of 42 tombs, from T 48 to T 89; 2) a catalogue of finds from T 1 to T 47; 3) the Italian inventory; 4) several photographs which proved useful for identifying unpublished or missing objects.

In southern Rhodes, except for some tomb groups from Kattavia and Passia recently published by Dietz[3] and the tomb investigated by the Italians at Pilona[4], evidence is critical depending almost exclusively on illicit excavations.

Materials from Rhodes are scattered in museums all over the world from Istanbul to Toronto, from Lund to Florence and Rome; outstanding collections are in the British Museum and in Copenhagen. The remarkable collection in Florence includes, alongside many purchased vases, the finds from Pace's excavations at Kouri and Asprovilo[5].

LH IIB-IIIA:1

The main historical problem of the LH IIB-IIIA:1 period is the arrival of the Mycenaeans in Rhodes. In his 1950 article, Furumark dated the first arrival of the Mycenaeans "at the end of Myc. IIB or at the very beginning of Myc. IIIA:1 period"; from the evidence of pottery in Trianda IIB, where fine Mycenaean pottery largely replaces the Minoan and plain domestic ware of Mainland type is found alongside the local Minoan, Furumark assumed that the two communities enjoyed friendly relations[6]. Sharing the same pottery types, however, does not necessarily imply that the two communities were on good terms. What seems more striking in Furumark's historical interpretation is that the Mycenaeans were allowed to settle in the pre-existing houses. This is such an astonishing example of friendly relations with foreign newcomers as to be strongly suggestive of an actual subjugation of the natives by the Mycenaeans.

At the same time the first chamber tombs of Mycenaean type appear on the two neighbouring hills of Makra and Moschou Vounara. Sixteen of the 79 datable tombs excavated by the Italians were in use in this period, to them must be added eight tombs excavated by Biliotti. They constitute 24% of the datable tombs.

In comparison with the list by C. Mee[7], I have included six more tombs and excluded one. The new additions are: T 11, T 21 on Makra V.; T 32A, T 35, T 45, T 78 on Moschou V. From the badly damaged T 11 comes a fragmentary alabastron of LH IIIA:1 type (fig. 1); according to the note book, T 45 contained two stirrup jars (now missing) and a small LH IIIA:1 jar (fig. 2); this is quite interesting because in the tomb were also found a leaf-shaped razor, a "cruciform" sword of type Di (fig. 4:2) and a spearhead of Höckmann's Group D[8]. I shall not deal with the four tombs re-used in LH IIIC (T 21. T 32A. T 35. T 78) which I have treated elsewhere[9].

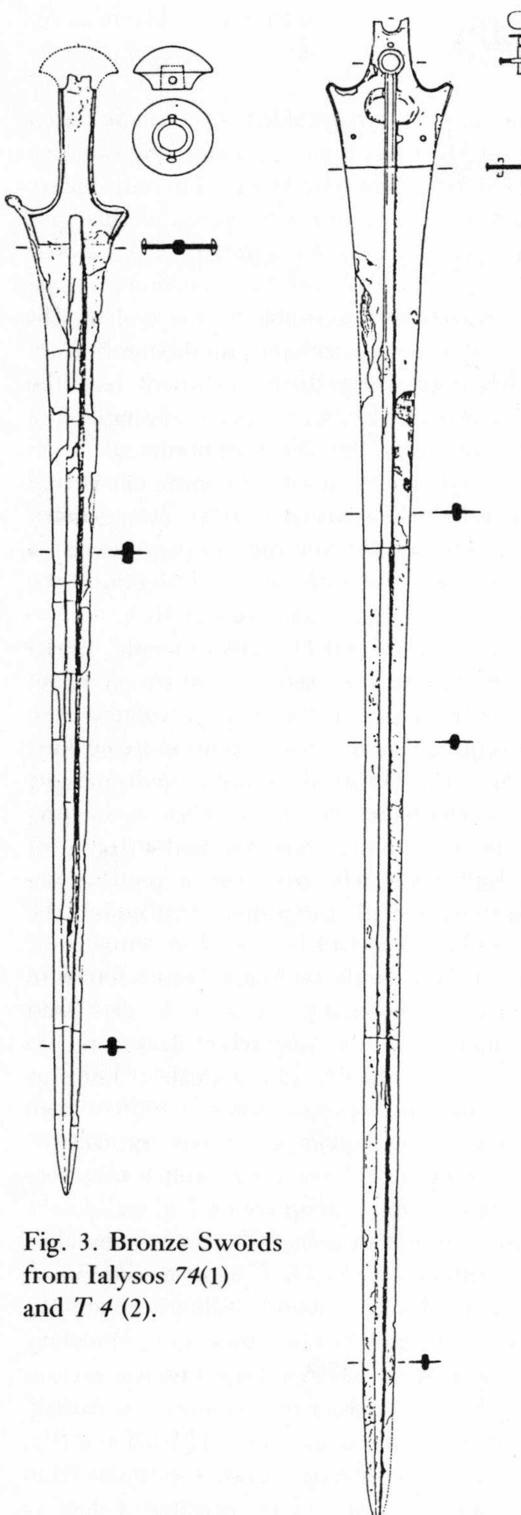

Fig. 3. Bronze Swords from Ialysos *74*(1) and *T 4* (2).

Fig. 1. Alabastron from Ialysos *T 11*.

Fig. 2. Jar from Ialysos *T 45*.

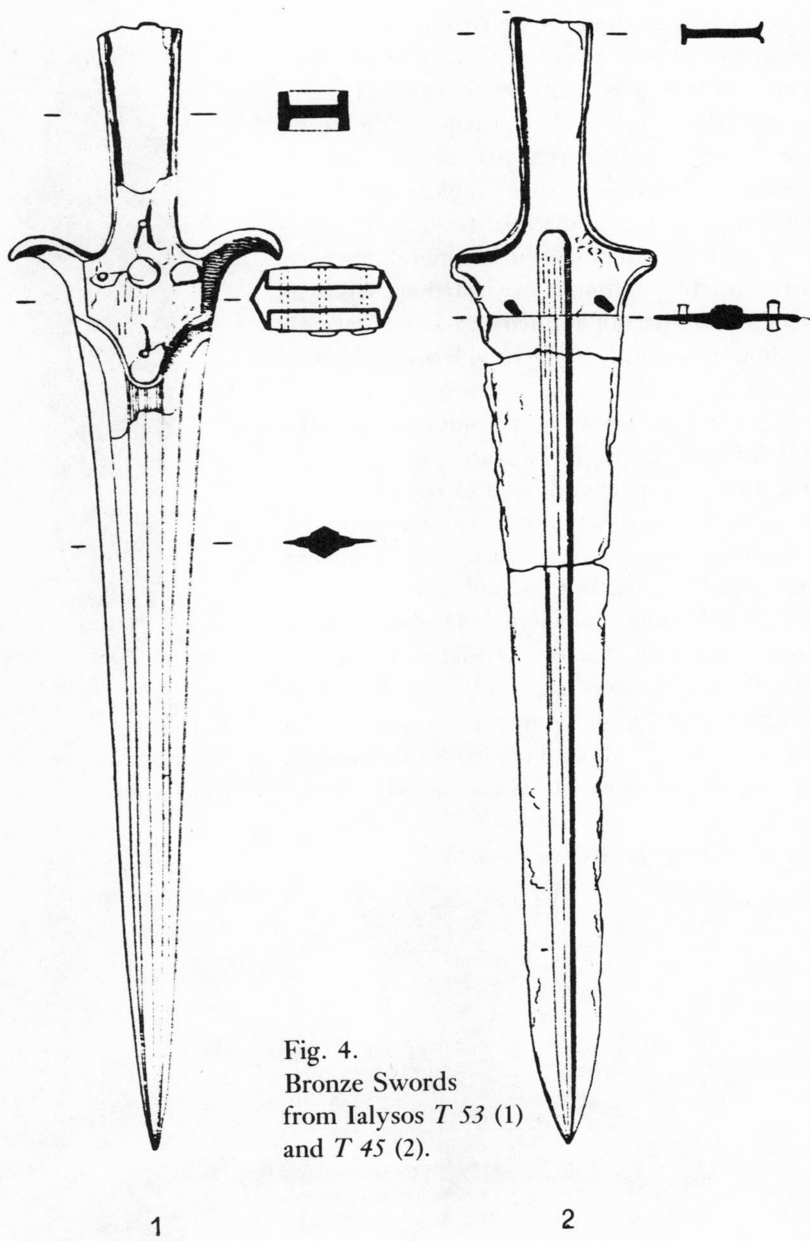

Fig. 4.
Bronze Swords
from Ialysos *T 53* (1)
and *T 45* (2).

A dating early in LH IIIA could also be suggested for T 65, T 76 and T 86 on Moschou V. In the single burial T 65, underlying a tomb reused in LH IIIC but containing a LH IIIA:2 piriform stirrup jar (T 15)[10], were found two bronze objects[11], an open-spring tweezer and a razor of the leaf-shaped type, which went out of use in the course of LH IIIA:2[12]. The two Cypriote tombs T 76 and T 86 on Moschou V., containing pottery contemporary with LH IIIA:1-2[13], should also belong to this early phase for connections between Rhodes and Cyprus are particularly well attested at the time of Trianda IIB[14].

The tomb I have excluded is the single burial T 18 on Makra V. Four vases and a figurine are assigned to this tomb by Maiuri, but only one jar is illustrated[15]. From the evidence of this vase Furumark included T 18 in his LH IIIA:1 closed find groups[16]; two of the remaining three vases, however, are datable to the end of LH IIIA:2 while a miniature jug and the figurine are LH IIIC. According to the note-book only the two LH IIIA:2 pots were actually found in the tomb. Some mixing must have occurred[17].

The important point in the argument is that weapons are not unusual in these early tombs. Ten of the 15 swords and daggers found in Rhodes come from LH IIIA:1-1/2 contexts or belong to types not later than LH IIIA.

From T 74, a LH IIIA:1 single burial "Warrior Tomb", comes a long sword intermediate between types Ci/Cii (fig. 3:1)[18]; in T 4, another "Warrior Tomb", were found two burials and a small group of bronzes, including a long sword of type Ci (fig. 3:2), a now missing "cruciform" sword of type Dii and a dagger of type Eii[19]. From the evidence of pottery, the earlier burial in the tomb must be dated to the very beginning of LH IIIA:2. The "cruciform" sword from T 45 (fig. 4:2) has been referred to previously. To a sword of type C or D should also belong a stone pommel with side-locking pin from T 31[20]; finally, a "pugnale", unfortunately lost, is reported from T 50[21]. From Biliotti's excavations come three "cruciform" swords of type Di and Dii[22] and a Cypriote rapier, dated by Catling to Late Cypriote I[23]. From outside Ialysos there are a Late Cypriote dagger from the LH IIIA:1 single burial tomb at Tolo (fig. 5)[24] and a sword of late B type from Kameiros in the British Museum[25]. Furthermore, spearheads were associated with swords in T 45, T 74[26] and other spearheads come from T 19 and T 62, both in use in LH IIIA: 1-2[27]. Three more spearheads of early type come from Biliotti's excavations. The first is one of the Cypriote type "with rat-tail and blade of four wing bayonet" dated by Catling to the Late Cypriote I period[28], the remaining two belong to Höckmann's group C and should not be later than LH IIIA[29].

The "militaris aura" surrounding the early tombs in the cemetery of Ialysos and the almost total disappearance of the Minoan culture on Rhodes after LM/LH IIIA:1 suggest that the first arrival of the Mycenaeans marks an actual and long-lasting conquest, probably due to a relatively small group of enterprising colonizers[30]. As pointed out by C. Mee, the pottery of this period is largely imported from the Argolid and should imply that the newcomers originated from the Peloponnese[31].

From other cemeteries in Rhodes there is little of this early phase (Table 1). On the north-west coast, in addition to the well known LH IIIA:1 tomb at Tolo[32], there are a LH IIB/IIIA:1 straight-sided alabastron from Kouri T 2 and a slightly later jar from Asprovilo T 6[33]. At Kameiros no pottery from regular excavations is earlier than LH IIIA:2, but the LH IIIA:1 jug published by Bossert[34] and the B type sword published by Sandars[35] point to an early occupation of the site. From Koskinou in north-east Rhodes comes a transitional LH IIIA: 1/2 jar[36].

In south Rhodes the evidence is scanty but casts some doubt on the largely accepted view that this part of the island was not settled by the Mycenaeans until LH IIIA:2. A surface sherd of possibly LH IIIA:1 date is reported from the settlement site at Ayios Minas near Kattavia[37]. In the Akavi collection, including pottery from the cemeteries of Vati:Apsaktiras and Anghio Vouno, there are three characteristic LH IIIA:1 jars[38]; from Lardhos comes a small jar decorated with early looking Stemmed Spirals[39].

LH IIIA:2

The LH IIIA:2 period marks the large-scale occupation of the island by the Mycenaeans. The number of inhabited sites rises suddenly to twenty-four against an estimated maximum of nine in the previous period (Table I). A substantial increase in the number of inhabited sites during LH IIIA:2 is by no means an exclusively Rhodian phenomenon but, as Rhodes, as far as we know, was so thinly settled in the previous period, it suggests the arrival of a second wave of Mycenaean settlers[40]. What is more impressive is that the settlement pattern as established in this period lasted almost unchanged until the early phase of LH IIIC inclusive. Furthermore, except for two or three sites that I will deal with later, LH IIIA:2 pottery is everywhere more abundant than that of any other period. The disappearance of Tolo and Asprovilo on the north-west coast may be fortuitous, because at Tolo evidence is restricted to a single burial tomb while a great deal of material from Asprovilo is no longer identifiable. Furthermore, Pace reports that the six tombs excavated at Asprovilo were a small part of a much larger cemetery extending between the modern villages of Villanova and Koupha[41].

Trianda (see Benzi, this volume), Damatria and Maritsa in the Ialysos area and Kariones near Lelos are new additions to the list of LH IIIA:2 sites and deserve some comment.

Inglieri[42] reports Mycenaean tombs at two sites near Damatria but the only extant vase is a LH IIIA:2 stirrup jar marked Damatria in the Rhodes Museum (fig. 6). At Maritsa some LH IIIA-B sherds have been collected by Hope Simpson and Lazenby near the remains of a chamber tomb on the hill named Kapsalovouno, supposedly the same site as a small Mycenaean

Fig. 5.
Cypriot Dagger from Tolo.

Fig. 6. Stirrup Jar from Damatria.

Fig. 7. Piriform Jar from Maritsa.

cemetery known to the Italian archaeologists as Coccala or Cocala[43]. In the Rhodes Museum there are three vases marked Maritsa: Coccala or Maritsa: a piriform jar (fig. 7), a quite exceptional tin-incrusted kylix (fig. 8) and a brazier[44].

A group of nine vases from Kariones was illustrated in 1933 by Jacopi and misleadingly labelled "the complete funerary equipment of a chamber tomb"[45]. Except for a LH IIIA:2 kylix, all vases are LH IIIB and the whole group was included by Furumark in his homogeneous LH IIIB find groups[46]. Five of the published pots carry markings consisting of number II in Roman numerals followed by an arabic number. From the evidence of similar markings on other vases in Rhodes Museum, it can be argued that two tombs, containing no less than 23 pots, were actually found at Kariones. Three of the 15 extant vases are LH IIIA:2, the published kylix, a big piriform jar (fig. 9) and a stirrup jar.

In 1937 a Mycenaean "tholos", no doubt a chamber tomb, containing two fine LH IIIA:2 vases, was discovered by a villager of Villanova at a place called Zuccalades. Hope Simpson and Lazenby were not able to locate this site[47]. According to Laurenzi, however, it was located near the crossing of the Peveragno road (Peveragno is the Italian name for Kalamona) with the coast road[48].

The increase in the number of tombs in the cemeteries on Makra and Moschou V. is impressive. Forty-one of the 79 datable Italian tombs were in use in this period: 33 on Makra V. and 8 on Moschou V.; with the addition of the 17 LH IIIA:2 tombs excavated by Biliotti on Moschou V. the total number rises to 58, which constitutes 52% of the datable tombs. Furthermore, 34 Italian tombs and 13 of Biliotti's tombs were built during LH IIIA:2; they constitute 43% of the datable tombs.

It is hardly necessary to stress that LH IIIA:2 marks a period of remarkable prosperity at Ialysos. Pottery is of consistently high quality and largely imported from the Argolid[49] while objects other than pottery are very common.

Fig. 8. Tin-incrusted Kylix from Maritsa.

Objects in gold including finger rings, rosettes and beads of various types have been found in eight tombs (T 1,T 4,T 28,T 31,T 43,T 46,T 56,T 60); objects in silver in three tombs (T 4, T 51,T 62); amber, notoriously a rare material in Rhodes, in three tombs (T 4,T 54,T 57). Bronze objects, including swords, spearheads, arrowheads, knives, razors and cleavers are reported from fourteen tombs (T 3,T 4,T 7,T 9,T 19,T 26,T 27,T 31,T 48,T 50,T 51,T 54,T 60,T 62 (?)); two bronze vessels, unfortunately missing, were found in T 56. Glass ornaments and beads of semiprecious stones appear in almost every tomb. Seals, on the contrary, are exceedingly rare; one only, unfortunately lost, is reported from T 50[50]. Outstanding groups of finds appear in no less than ten tombs (T 4,T 25,T 27,T 28,T 31,T 50,T 51,T 54,T 56,T 62), tombs with no small finds are five only (T 6,T 18,T 22,T 23,T 55). In addition there is the British Museum's remarkable collection from Biliotti's excavations.

Finds other than pottery from the peripheral sites are far less numerous. The list, including objects from LH IIIA:1 to IIIC inclusive, is as follows.

A few gold and silver objects have been found at Asprovilo[51], Vati:Apsaktiras and Passia[52]. Bronze objects are more common; they include the Cypriote dagger from Tolo (fig. 5) and the B type sword from Kameiros[53] mentioned previously, a razor or cleaver from Maritsa[54]; a cleaver and a tweezer from Kameiros[55]; the famous group of bronzes from Siana, now in Copenhagen[56]; two spearheads and a cleaver from Apollakia[57]; a knife from Lelos[58]; a knife and a fish-hook from Kattavia[59]; a sword of type Fii, a knife, an arrowhead and a finger ring from Passia[60]; four knives from Vati[61]; two "Trunnion Axes" from Lindos[62]; a spearhead and a knife from Pilona[63]; a cleaver from Archangelos[64].

Glass ornaments are reported from Asprovilo[65], Kameiros[66], Lelos[67], Kattavia[68], Vati:-Apsaktiras[69] and Passia[70]; beads in semiprecious stones from Kouri, Asprovilo[71] and Kattavia[72]. Finally, there are two seals from Kremasti, a suspicious provenance[73], and Lelos[74] and three scarabs from Kameiros[75] and Kattavia[76].

Although the list is far from impressive, objects other than pottery have come to light at almost every site where regular excavation has taken place. This suggests that the general level of prosperity was higher than we can now appreciate.

Fig. 9. Piriform Jar from Kariones.

LH IIIB

The main historical problem of the LH IIIB period on Rhodes is the unexpected and dramatic decrease in the number of tombs at Ialysos. Only 13 of the 79 datable Italian tombs are in use in LH IIIB against 41 in LHIIIA:2 and 39 in LH IIIC. Eight tombs are on Makra V. (T 5,T 10,T 24,T 30,T 49,T 53,T 59,T 60); five on Moschou V. (T 38,T 41,T 64,T 66,T 75); they constitute 16.5% of the datable Italian tombs. With the addition of the nine tombs excavated by Biliotti on Moschou V.[77], the total number of LH IIIB tombs rises to 22 and the percentage to 20%. The tombs built in this period are 13.

T 41 is a new addition to the number of datable tombs. This was a robbed pit tomb, containing two lost glass fragments, a small sherd from a cup or ladle and two almost complete vases, a kylix with Cuttlefish decoration and a stemmed bowl (fig. 10). The shape of the kylix and the small dimensions of the stemmed bowl suggest a dating at the very beginning of LH IIIB[78].

In the rest of the island the settlement pattern seems substantially unchanged (Table 1). A remarkable exception is the north-west coast, where LH IIIB is represented by no more than a few surface sherds from Maritsa[79]. The evidence for this area, however, has to be evaluated with caution, for most of the material from Kouri, Asprovilo, Maritsa and Damatria is no longer identifiable. Under such conditions Mee's suggestion that "Ialysos and possibly a number of other sites on the west-coast were destroyed during the course of LH IIIB" seems difficult to prove[80]. No less suspicious is the disappearance of sites such as Zuccalades and Mandhriko[81] on the west coast, and Kalovriou[82] and Asklipio[83] in the south, which are represented by a few pots or by a single tomb. On the other hand, no site can be safely regarded as a new foundation. Sites such as A. Isidoros[84] and Loryma[85], represented by single pots of doubtful provenance, should be discounted while the LH IIIB-C tomb at Pylona was part of a larger, plundered cemetery[86].

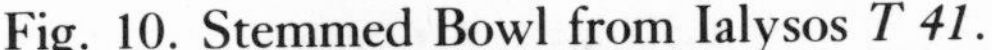

Fig. 10. Stemmed Bowl from Ialysos *T 41*.

A closer analysis of the evidence, however, shows that, in terms of quantity of pottery found, LH IIIB is at almost every site a far less productive period than LH IIIA:2.

In the area of Kameiros there should be LH IIIB pottery among the unpublished materials from Tzitzo and Kaminaki Lures[87], but only one tomb continued in use at Aniforo[88].

The two inland and neighbouring cemeteries at Lelos and Kariones show a striking contrast. At Lelos no more than eight LH IIIB vases of quite provincial character against 43 of LH IIIA:2 were found in three of the five tombs excavated by the Italians; at Kariones, on the contrary, LH IIIB pottery is comparatively more abundant and of far better quality, including a Zygouries kylix and a remarkable conical-piriform stirrup jar with decoration added in white paint, not unlike the famous examples from the Kadmeia[89].

In the south-western part of the island the contrast between LH IIIA:2 and LH IIIB is less marked but consistent with the general trend. From Kritinia/Castellos and/or Siana come four LH IIIB vases against 19 of LH IIIA:2[90]. In the remarkable cemetery at Apollakia LH IIIB pottery constitutes an altogether impressive 33.5% against 44% of LH IIIA:2[91]: At Kattavia there is no LH IIIB pottery among the extant burial material, but LH IIIB surface sherds have been collected at the settlement site of Ayios Minas[92].

In south-eastern Rhodes the balance is in favour of LH IIIB, especially in the Vati area. At Lachania there are six LH IIIB vases against two of LH IIIA:2. Of the 126 vases from Vati:-Apsaktiras now in Copenhagen 25% are datable to LH IIIA:2 and 46% are LH IIIB[93]; with the addition of the Akavi Collection the following, slightly less contrasting figures are obtained: LH IIIA:2 30%, LH IIIB 38%. Also at Passia the balance is largely in favour of LH IIIB[94].

The widespread decrease of LH IIIB pottery suggests that a large part of the island was involved in the same decline observed at Ialysos.

On the other hand, the increase of LH IIIB pottery in south-eastern Rhodes cannot compensate for the large depopulation of the main centre and of several minor sites.

Furumark suggested that the LH IIIA:2 pottery tradition lasted in Rhodes for a long time and gave rise to the so-called "Rhodo-Mycenaean Class", including vases LH IIIB in date but LH IIIA:2 in style. The existence of a class of local pottery cannot be denied; the question is to define its chronological range. Furumark himself pointed out that "much of this class comes from unknown contexts (mainly in southern Rhodes) and has to be dated by typological and stylistic criteria alone"[95]. Some local vases from LH IIIA:2 contexts, however, suggest that this class cannot be unquestionably regarded as later than LH IIIA:2. The vases in question are a krater[96], a piriform jar and a quite uncanonical jug (fig. 11)[97] from Ialysos T 4, T 6 and T 23; a straight-sided alabastron from Lelos T 7 (fig. 12), and a piriform jar from Mandhriko[98]. Several motifs commonly found on Rhodo-Mycenaean vases are paralleled on the most typical of the local shapes, the Basket Vase[99], which appears at Ialysos in LH IIIA:1-2 and seems to go out of use before the beginning of LH IIIC[100]. Moreover, much of the LH IIIB pottery from Ialysos as well as from the peripheral sites is up-to-date with the LH IIIB:1 developments in the Argolid; and analyses by Jones and Mee have shown that at Ialysos a high proportion of the LH IIIB vases was imported from the mainland[101]. A long-lasting LH IIIA:2 pottery tradition does not seem a convincing explanation for the decrease of LH IIIB tombs and vases.

In his 1982 study C. Mee has suggested that in Rhodes "The IIIB pottery style reflects the continuing influence of the Peloponnese....." but "stagnation set in because the influence of the Peloponnese diminished as the period progressed"[102]. As for Ialysos, I cannot see any trace of stagnation except for the absence of distinctive LH IIIB:2 features such as Rosette-and-Type B deep bowls. This is by no means a conclusive argument because attempts to extend the concept of LH IIIB:2 as defined in the Argolid to other areas and to grave groups has proved, with a few exceptions, highly problematic[103].

A different situation has been suggested in southern Rhodes, where a local late phase of LH

Fig. 11. Local Jug from Ialysos *T 23*.

Fig. 12. Local Straight-sided Alabastron from Lelos *T 7*.

IIIB has been tentatively defined by S. Dietz in Passia T4. Although Dietz's conclusions on the group as a whole may be correct, his assumption that stirrup jars of FS 182 with band-shaped Quirk (FM 48:12) must be regarded as a late IIIB product seems questionable. The motif is discussed at length by Dietz and a substantial list of parallels is provided in order to demonstrate that the pattern "occurs in the Argolid from the latest phase of LH IIIB:1 period"[104]. The pattern, however, does occur at Mycenae in the Prehistoric Cemetery deposit, commonly attributed to the very beginning of LH IIIB:1[105]. In Ialysos LH IIIB pottery maintains throughout such a distinctive metropolitan character as to rule out the possibility of defining a late IIIB phase in the same terms as those established by Dietz at Passia.

A general decline in the value of burial offerings in LH IIIA and especially in LH IIIB has been noted by many scholars, thus it could be suggested that some LH IIIB tombs in Rhodes were not provided with grave goods. A short review of the LH IIIB tombs on Makra and Moschou V., however, will demonstrate that austerity is not a satisfactory explanation.

In comparison with LH IIIA:2 the ratio of pottery per tomb is unchanged. Finds other than pottery are common; much are admittedly of poor value but some remarkable groups of bronze objects and jewellery come from three tombs on Makra Vounara. T 5 contained twelve glass rosettes, a gold necklace and some lost fragments of gold foil; the number of burials is unknown[106]. The two burials T 53 contained a sword of Sandars' type G (fig. 4:1), a two-handled bronze bowl and an unusually rich collection of small finds, all unfortunately lost but partially illustrated by Maiuri[107]. The Italian Inventory lists no less than one hundred beads in glass, rock crystal, amber and semiprecious stones; an unspecified number of small glass discs; two silver and one gold earring; a small piece of gold foil with Double Argonaut decoration and a lentoid seal with an ibex figure. T 59 contained a LH IIIA:2 and a LH IIIB burial. The original plan shows that the four bronzes found in the tomb were associated with the later burial. A "killed" knife was near the skull, another knife, a cleaver and a spearhead of the so-called "bayonet type" were at the feet[108]. The level of prosperity at Ialysos seems unchanged; depopulation was neither produced nor followed by an economic crisis.

LH IIIC

As can be expected, LH IIIC is the most problematic period in the history of Mycenaean Rhodes. At Ialysos, after the decline in LH IIIB, there is a sudden increase in the number of tombs. Thirty-nine of the 79 datable Italian tombs are in use in LH IIIC against 13 in LH IIIB; with the addition of Biliotti's tombs the total number rises to 47, which constitutes 43 % of the datable tombs.

Before attempting any explanation for the sudden recovery of Ialysos, a definition of the development of LH IIIC pottery in Rhodes is needed. Since Furumark's and Desborough's studies[109] our knowledge of LH IIIC pottery has much increased. The stratigraphic evidence now available from Tiryns, Mycenae, Lefkandi and other sites enables us to attempt a correlation between Rhodian and mainland IIIC pottery, in order to provide the Rhodian material with a sounder chronological framework[110]. Thus I have attempted to fit the Rhodian pottery into the four main LH IIIC phases as established in the Argolid: early, developed, advanced and late or final[111].

Several new features marking the early phase of LH IIIC in the Argolid appear in Rhodes.

From T 64 come a one-handled conical bowl of FS 242 with monochrome painted interior and large band at lip[112], and a semiglobular cup of FS 215, with a band at lip and linear decoration inside[113]. The carinated cup FS 240 is represented by a somewhat uncanonical example, missing the handle, from T 35[114]. The shallow angular bowl of FS 295 with banded decoration appears in a local variant painted with dots in place of lines. This shape is represented by five examples from T 21 and from T 40[115].

Deep bowls are comparatively rare in LH IIIC tombs at Ialysos: 17 come from six of the 39 tombs excavated by the Italians; four from Biliotti's excavations[116]. Rhodian IIIC deep bowls are rather conservative in decoration but some interesting novelties appear in early IIIC. From T 72 comes a "Rosette Bowl" with monochrome interior, which has very good parallels with early IIIC deep bowls from Tiryns[117]. Some patterned deep bowls have a medium band or a double banding at rim. These features appear in the Argolid in LH IIIB:2 and continue in early IIIC[118]. The Rhodian examples are difficult to date because with only one exception they lack context. The exception is the deep bowl from Passia T 4, which Dietz regards as "a representative of the late IIIB period in Rhodes"[119]. An early LH IIIC dating seems, however, preferable for three examples from Rhodes, in Florence. The new type of deep bowl having a monochrome interior and linear decoration on the exterior is represented by one example of FS 289 with vertical handles from T 21[120].

As can be expected, the high-stemmed kylix is a rare shape in Ialysos tombs. Four examples with monochrome interior and reserved handle zone come from T 32 and T 38[121].

The developed phase of LH IIIC is not particularly rich in novelties and is hardly detectable in Rhodes. However, two monochrome vases with reserved foot, a deep bowl and an amphoriskos from T 87, are characteristic of this phase[122].

The advanced phase of LH IIIC is characterized by a growing tendency to decoration in a dark ground scheme and to reserved decoration, especially on deep bowls[123]. Deep bowls of this type are completely absent in Rhodes, where the shape is usually decorated in a more traditional way. Reserved bands appear, however, on a stemmed bowl from T 32, on seven stirrup jars (from T 15, T 16, T 21, T 87), on a jug from T 17 with a remarkable decoration in a dark scheme, and on an unusual big jug of ovoid shape from T 20[124]. In addition there are two stirrup jars from Kameiros[125] and one from Phanes[126], which could be imported from the mainland. Reserved zones appear on eight amphoriskoi, which constitute no more than 6 % of the amphoriskoi from Ialysos. Outstanding examples come from T 32 and T 38[127].

Two neck-handled amphorae with scroll pattern, a combination very distinctive of the advanced to late phase of the period, come from T 17 and T 84[128]. A group of vases of closed shape with Wavy Line decoration is highly characteristic of the advanced to late phase of LH IIIC[129]. This group includes ten amphoriskoi (from T 20, T 21, T 42, T 70, T 87, T 88), a side-spouted jug with infusing spout from T 87[130], a feeding-bottle from T 72[131], a straight-sided alabastron with three legs from T 42[132] and a stirrup jar from T 16.

In conclusion there seems to be a continuous but thin thread between Rhodes and the Argolid throughout a large part of LH IIIC. Otherwise, the LH IIIC Rhodian pottery develops along different lines. The style is a rather open one and appears largely indebted to the traditional LH IIIB motifs. The influence of the Argive Close Style is negligible. Closeness in decoration is almost exclusively restricted to the "Octopus Style" stirrup jars, which are the hallmark of the IIIC period in Rhodes. The shape is represented by 35 examples coming from 14 tombs.

The LH IIIC development of the cemetery at Ialysos may be summarized as follows: 23 tombs are in use in the early phase of the period; 17 of them are in continuos use until the advanced phase; fourteen tombs (T 9, T 16, T 30, T 42, T 47, T 61, T 67, T 68, T 71, T 73, T 78, T 85, T 88, T 89)[132a]) belong exclusively to this phase; pottery datable to the advanced to late phase appears in eight tombs (T 13, T 17, T 20, T 21, T 40, T 42, T 84, T 87). Only seven of the 13 LH IIIB tombs are still in use in LH IIIC. Mee wonders whether these tombs were in continuous use[133]. As stated previously, I cannot see any break in LH IIIB at Ialysos but there is no doubt that the sudden increase in the number of tombs suggests some sort of break.

A point of interest arises from the re-use of earlier tombs. Twentytwo of the 39 LH IIIC Italian tombs were re-used: five on Makra V., where all LH IIIC tombs are in fact re-used, 17 on Moschou Vounara[134]. In 13 tombs the re-use took place in the early phase of LH IIIC; eight tombs (T 9, T 16, T 30, T 42, T 69(?), T 71, T 73, T 78) were re-used in the advanced phase of the period. The phenomenon is not restricted to Ialysos. At Kameiros three tombs were re-used in the advanced phase of the period[135], at Passia T 1 was re-used in the early phase[136]. C. Mee is probably right in suggesting that those reusing earlier tombs were newcomers. He also believes that they were from the Peloponnese and since the influence of the Argolid is apparent in the early as well as in the advanced phase of LH IIIC he assumes that this migration continued throughout the period[137]. This is a reasonable

Table I. Mycenaean Sites on Rhodes.

Site	Tomb Settl.	IIB-IIIA:1	IIIA:2	IIIB	IIIC
Trianda	S	x	x	?	?
Ialysos	T(134)	x	x	x	x*
Kouri	T(2)	x(1)	x(1)		
Asprovilo	T(6)	x(1)			
Zuccalades	T(1)		x(2)		
Damatria	T(2)		x(1)		
Maritsa	T(2)		x(2)	x(survey)	
Tolo	T(1)	x(2)			
Phanes	T(?)		x(3)	x(2)	x(1)*
Kameiros:					
Aniforo	T(5)		x(13+)	x(2)	x(11)*
Tzitzo	T(2)		x(4?)	x(2?)	x(2?)*
K. Lures	T(1?)		x(1)		
P. Lures	T(?)		x(1)	?	
Others	T(?)	x(1)	x(2)	x(2)	x(1)
Mandhriko	T(1)		x(1+1?)		
Kariones	T(2)		x(3+?)	x(8)	
Lelos	T (7+2)		x(43+/-)	x(8+?)	x(4)
Castellos	T(?)		x(1)	x(survey)	x(1?)
Cast/Siana	T(?)		x(15)	x(3)	x(1?)
Siana	T(?)		x(3)	x(1?)	x(1)
A. Isidoros	T ?			x(1)	
Chimaria	T				(survey)
Apollakia	T(12?)		x(44%)	x(33.5%)	x(11%)*
Kattavia	S(survey)	x	x	x	
	T(1+2)		x(19)		
	Others		x(2)		x(1?)
Lachania	T(?)		x(2)	x(6)	x(4)
Vati:					
Apsaktiras	S ?		x	x	x(*?)
	T(24?)				
Rhodes			x(6)	x(2)	x(1)
Copenhagen			x(25%)	x(46%)	x(15%)
Apsaktiras	T				
Anghio V.	T				
(Akavi Col.)		x(3%)	x(34%)	x(34%)	x(17%)
Kalovriou	T(?)		x(1)		
Passia	T(4)		x(5?)	x(12)	x(16)*
Asklepeio	T?		x(1)		
Lardhos	T(?)	x(1)	x(14)	x(6?)	x(10)
Pilona	T(1+?)			x(11)	x(6)*
Lindos	S		x	x	x
	Others		x(2)	x(1)	x(1)
Loryma	T ?			x(1)	
Archangelos	T(2)		x(8)	x(4?)	x(4)
Koskinou	T(?)	x(1?)	x(1)	x(3)	x(1)

Note on Table I. The sites are listed in roughly anti-clockwise order, from north-west through west and south-east to north-east. Sites where Mycenaean materials have been reported but are no longer in existence, have been disregarded.

Figures in brackets refer to the numbers of tombs and to numbers or percentages of vases. In the LH IIIC column the asterisk* refers to the presence of vases later than the early phase of the period.

explanation and might, to a certain extent, be the right one. Nevertheless, I wish to propose a different explanation, which seems to me more strongly supported by the evidence.

Except for Maritsa and Kariones, and discounting A. Isidoros and Loryma represented by single pots, the settlement pattern is unchanged (Table I). A closer analysis, however, points out two important facts.

The first is that LH IIIC pottery is almost everywhere less abundant than the LH IIIB material. At Apollakia, for instance, LH IIIC pottery constitutes only 11 % against 33% LH IIIB; at Vati: Apsaktiras 13 % against 38 %. At other sites the number of LH IIIC vases is almost negligible (Table I).

The second point is that at 10 or 11 of the 16 LH IIIC sites there is no pottery later than the early phase of the period. The only exceptions are Kameiros, Phanes, Apollakia, Passia, Pilona and possibly Vati[138].

In conclusion the evidence may be summarized in three main points:

1. In Ialysos a large increase in the number of tombs, both rebuilt or re-used, is seen in the early phase of LH IIIC.
2. At the same time the rest of the island appears largely depopulated and most of the sites are abandoned during the course of the early phase of LH IIIC.
3. Pottery influenced by the Mainland is largely submerged by pottery in the local traditional style and in the style of the "Aegean Koine".

It seems to me that the evidence suggests an internal migration from the peripheral areas to the main centre rather than an influx of settlers from the Mainland and/or from elsewhere in the Aegean.

Mario Benzi
Dipartimento di Scienze Archeologiche
Sezione di Archeologia e Antichità Classiche
Via Galvani, 1
56100 Pisa
Italy

1. A. Maiuri, ASAtene 6-7, 1923-24, 251-256.
2. L. Morricone, ASAtene 43-44, 1965-66, 305 footnote 4. Forthcoming publication in ASAtene by Mrs. L. Morricone.
3. Lindos IV. 1.
4. G. Jacopi, ASAtene 13-14, 1930-31, 336-343.
5. B. Pace, BdA 10, 1916, 87-94.
6. A. Furumark, OpArch 6, 1950, 181 followed by Mee 1982, 81.
7. Mee 1982, 8.
8. A. Maiuri, ASAtene 6-7, 1923-24, fig. 124. For the sword see N.K. Sandars, AJA 67, 1963, 124, 148; although attributed by O. Höckmann, JbZMainz 27, 1980, 25 C19 to his group C with socket longer than blade, the spearhead has in fact socket and blade of almost equal length and seems to fit better into Höckmann's Group D.
9. M. Benzi, SMEA 23, 1982.
10. M. Benzi, SMEA 23, 1982, 328, pl. 4:b.
11. G. Jacopi, ASAtene 13-14, 1930-31, 273, fig. 19.
12. N.K. Sandars, BSA 53-54, 1958-59, 235; Catling 1964, 230.
13. G. Jacopi, ASAtene 13-14, 1930-31, 304, 326-329; both tombs are discussed at length by Mee 1982, 22.
14. See G. Cadogan, Praktika tou protou Diethnous Kyprologhikou Synedriou, T. A', 1972, 5-13; Mee 1982, 22 and Åström (this volume).
15. A. Maiuri, ASAtene 6-7, 1923-24, 127-128, fig. 48; Mee 1982, pl. 3:3.
16. Furumark 1941, 53.
17. In fact I was able to attribute the two LH IIIC pieces to T 33, but I was unable to ascertain the provenance of the LH IIIA:1 jar.
18. G. Jacopi, ASAtene 13-14, 1930-31, 297-298, fig. 42. This sword has the tanged hilt and pronounced midrib characteristic of type Cii, see N.K. Sandars, AJA 67, 1963, 119, 121.
19. A. Maiuri, ASAtene 6-7, 1923-24, fig. 15; N.K. Sandars, AJA 67, 1963, 145, 149, 150.
20. A. Maiuri, ASAtene 6-7, 1923-24, 165, no. 28 not illustrated. The tomb is LH IIIA:1-2.
21. A. Maiuri, ASAtene 6-7, 1923-24, 211 and fig. 142: inv. number 4785. The tomb is LH IIIA:1-2.
22. Furtwängler – Loescke 1886, pl. D:11,13; N.K. Sandars, AJA 67, 1963, 148, 149, pl. 24:20.
23. Catling 1964, 112, fig. 12:12 rapier of "four-wing bayonet" type, with rat-tail tang.
24. Catling 1964, 125ff. type d, daggers with long-tongued butts.
25. N.K. Sandars, AJA 65, 1961, 28, pl. 19:6.
26. See supra notes 8, 18.
27. A. Maiuri, ASAtene 6-7, 1923-24, fig. 54; G. Jacopi, ASAtene 13-14, 1930-31, fig. 9.

28. Furtwängler – Loeschke 1886, pl. D:3; Catling 1964, 118; O. Höckmann, JbZMainz 27, 1980, 16.
29. Furtwängler – Loeschke 1886, pl. D:12,15; O. Höckmann, JbZMainz 27, 1980, 25.
30. Evidence for "Warrior Tombs" in the Aegean has been recently reconsidered by J. Driessen – C. Macdonald, BSA 79, 1984, 49-74.
31. Mee 1982, 82.
32. G. Jacopi, ClRh 6-7, 1931-32, 44 and fig. 46.
33. B. Pace, BdA 10, 1916, figs. 7, 8.
34. Bossert 1921, fig. 194.
35. See supra note 25.
36. S. Charitonidis, ADelt 18, 1963 A, 133, pl. 63a.
37. R. Hope Simpson – J.F. Lazenby, BSA 68, 1973, 148, pl. 39a:1.
38. Unpublished in Rhodes Museum. 1) FS 23, FM 9:16 (Lily); 2) FS 23, FM 70 (Scale Pattern); 3) FS 31, FM 70 (Scale Pattern). They compare well with LH IIIA:1 jars from the Atreus Bothros deposit at Mycenae, see E. French, BSA 59, 1964, 247, fig. 1:6, pl. 68a.
39. Unpublished in Rhodes Museum. FS 31, FM 49:10.
40. Mee 1982, 84.
41. B. Pace, BdA 10, 1916, 89.
42. Inglieri 1936, Foglio Nord, nos. 34, 36; R. Hope Simpson - J.F. Lazenby, BSA 68, 1973, 138.
43. R. Hope Simpson – J.F. Lazenby, BSA 68, 1973, 134-135.
44. L. Laurenzi, MemorieIst.FERT 2, 1937,51 reports three chamber tombs at Cocala but only two are described in the 1926 notebook. The second, excavated in 1926, was a very interesting tomb containing three burials lying on two levels, no less than thirteen vases and a bronze razor or cleaver. The notebook provides an unusually detailed plan of the tomb but no list of the finds, which are no longer identifiable.
45. ILN 20/5 1933, 714. For the location of the site, see R. Hope Simpson – J.F. Lazenby, BSA 68, 1973, 144.
46. A. Furumark 1941, 67, The FS 257 kylix is attributed by Furumark to his "Rhodo-Mycenaean Class" but the Chevron decoration has good LH IIIA:2 parallels, see Mountjoy 1986, fig. 106:1.
47. R. Hope Simpson – J.F. Lazenby, BSA 68, 1973, 138.
48. L. Laurenzi, MemorieIst.FERT 2, 1937, 49, pl. 40.
49. Mee 1982, 83.
50. A. Maiuri, ASAtene 6-7, 1923-24, 211.
51. B. Pace, BdA 10, 1916, 88 and fig. 5.
52. Lindos IV. 1, figs. 63; 26.
53. See supra note 25.
54. See supra note 44.
55. G. Porro, BdA 9, 1915, 300.
56. N.K. Sandars, AJA 67, 1963, 140 ff.
57. Lindos IV. 1, figs. 94-95.
58. A. Maiuri, ASAtene 6-7, 1923-24, 249, now missing, from T 5.
59. Lindos IV. 1, figs. 108-109.
60. Lindos IV. 1, figs. 25; 27-29.
61. Lindos IV. 1, fig. 62.
62. Lindos I, 67. nos 27, 27b, pl. 3:27.
63. G. Jacopi, ASAtene 13-14, 1930-31, fig. 84.
64. S. Charitonidis, ADelt 18, 1963A, fig. 4.
65. B. Pace, BdA 10, 1916, 88 and fig. 6.
66. Furtwängler – Loeschke 1886, pl. C:12.
67. A. Maiuri, ASAtene 6-7, 1923-24, 251, now missing, from T 6.
68. Lindos IV. 1, fig. 110.
69. Lindos IV. 1, figs. 63-64.
70. Lindos IV. 1, fig. 51.
71. B. Pace, BdA 10, 1916, 88 and fig. 6.
72. Lindos IV. 1, fig. 110.
73. I. Pini, CMS V:2, 1975, no. 659 said to be from Kremasti in the Italian Inventory.
74. A. Maiuri, ASAtene 6-7, 1923-24, 251, now missing, from T 6.
75. Mee 1982, 53; Furtwängler – Loeschke 1886, pl. E:42-43.
76. Lindos IV. 1, 86, fig. 110.
77. Mee 1982, 22-23.
78. Stemmed bowls with Wavy Line decoration have been found in LH IIIA:2 and B:1 deposits at Mycenae; several examples of small size are reported from the LH IIIB:1 Prehistoric Cemetery Central deposit, E. French, BSA 60, 1965, 177 and E. French, BSA 61, 1966, 222.
79. R. Hope Simpson – J.F. Lazenby, BSA 68, 1973, 139-140; see supra note 44.
80. Mee 1982, 88.
81. A. Maiuri, ASAtene 6-7, 1923-24, 252; Mee 1982,54; M. Benzi, SMEA 23, 1982, 335, pl. 7. The tomb contained a LH IIIA:2 jar FS 45 and a local piriform jar with Concentric Arcs; for the dating of the latter see supra p. 66.
82. According to Lindos IV. 1, 66, the well known kylix with Bird decoration CVA Danemark[2], pl. 54:8 comes from Kalovriou.
83. Mee 1982, 72.
84. Mee 1982, 60.
85. R. Hope Simpson – J.F. Lazenby, BSA 68, 1973, 151 footnote 149.
86. G. Jacopi, ASAtene 13-14, 1930-31, 335.
87. Mee 1982, 52, 53.
88. G. Jacopi, ClRh 6-7, 1932-33, 138, figs 169, 173 T 48, for the chronology of this tomb see M. Benzi, SMEA 23, 1982, 334.
89. See supra note 45; cfr. Symeonoglou 1973, figs. 127-171.
90. Mee 1982, 59, 60.
91. Mee 1982, 61 ff.
92. See supra note 37.
93. Mee 1982, 67 ff.
94. Lindos IV. 1, 96 ff.
95. Furumark 1972, 541 and footnote 1.
96. Mee 1982, pl. 17:1. For the chronology of this tomb, see M. Benzi, SMEA 23, 1982, 324.
97. The decoration consists of Hatched Triangles (FM 61A:6) on the shoulder and of two body zones filled with Zig-zag motifs.
98. The context included a LH IIIA:2 jar (see supra note 81), but association is not certain.
99. For lists of finds and motifs, see Mee 1982, 17, 24.
100. In Ialysos no Basket Vase has been found in IIIC contexts.
101. Mee 1982, 88.
102. Mee 1982, 88.
103. Cfr. E.S. Sherrat, BSA 75, 1980, 199 ff; Schachermeyr 1976, 266.
104. Lindos IV. 1, 102, 104, 114.
105. E. French, BSA 61, 1966, 229 lists fourteen examples from the body zone of stirrup jars.
106. A. Maiuri, ASAtene 6-7, 1923-24, 105-106.
107. A. Maiuri, ASAtene 6-7, 1923-1924, figs. 141, 142.
108. A. Maiuri, ASAtene 6-7, 1923-1924, fig. 147.
109. A. Furumark, OpArch 3, 1944, 194-265; Desborough 1964.

110. For discussion of the new evidence and full bibliography, see Lindos IV. 1, 111 ff; Mountjoy 1986, 134 ff. and Table II.
111. For a more detailed discussion of the problem, see M. Benzi "Rhodes in the LH IIIC Period", in Problems in Greek Prehistory. BSA Centenary Conference. Manchester, April 14-18, 1986 (forthcoming).
112. Mee 1982, pl. 39:1 the vase is wrongly attributed to T 4, see M. Benzi, SMEA 23, 1982, 324. Cfr. Chr. Podzuweit, AA 1978, 482; Chr. Podzuweit, AA 1979, 424 from early IIIC deposits at Tiryns; see also Mountjoy 1986, 172.
113. Mountjoy 1986, 146, fig. 183.
114. Mountjoy 1986, 147, fig. 185.
115. Mountjoy 1986, 153, fig. 197.
116. For a list, see Mee 1982, 43.
117. G. Jacopi, ASAtene 13-14, 1930-31, fig. 34. Cfr. Chr. Podzuweit, AA 1978, figs. 28:9;39.
118. For LH IIIB:2 see E. French, BSA 64, 1969, fig. 11:1,2 from Mycenae; Rutter 1980, 81-82; 129, fig. 39:1 from Korakou; for LH IIIC early, see Mountjoy 1986, 150, fig. 189.
119. Lindos IV. 1, 101.
120. Cfr. Mountjoy 1986, fig. 192.
121. A. Maiuri, ASAtene 6-7, 1923-24, figs. 102, 104, 113; Mee 1982, pl. 37:1-2. Cfr. Mountjoy 1986, 148, fig. 187.
122. G. Jacopi, ASAtene 13-14, 1930-31, fig. 79. Cfr. Chr. Podzuweit, AA 1983, 361.
123. Chr. Podzuweit, AA 1983, 368 ff.; Mountjoy 1986, 178, figs. 229,230.
124. A. Maiuri, ASAtene 6-7, 1923-24, fig. 56; Mee 1982, pl. 34:5.
125. G. Jacopi, ClRh 6-7, 1932-33, figs. 160, 167 from Aniforo T 47; Mee 1982, 52 from Tzitzo.
126. CVA Danemark[2], pl. 62:2.
127. Mee 1982, pl. 31:3,7.
128. Mee 1982, pl. 32:7; G. Jacopi, ASAtene 13-14, 1930-31, fig. 65. Cfr. Mountjoy 1986, 162, 185, fig. 239.
129. Chr. Podzuweit, AA 1983, 386 ff.; Mountjoy 1986, 181.
130. G. Jacopi, ASAtene 13-14, 1930-31, fig. 79.
131. G. Jacopi, ASAtene 13-14, 1930-31, fig. 34.
132. A. Maiuri, ASAtene 6-7, 1923-24, fig. 119.
132[a]. The number of tombs here attributed to LH IIIC advanced is remarkably higher than that I gave elsewhere (see supra footnote 111). This is due to two main reasons. The first is a more accurate definition of LH IIIC advanced; the second is that pottery in early IIIC style lasted throughout LH IIIC advanced. For instance in the single burial Tomb 61 only three vases out of seventeen are diagnostically LH IIIC advanced.
133. Mee 1982, 89.
134. See W. Cavanagh – C. Mee, BSA 73, 1978, 36 ss.; M. Benzi, SMEA 23, 1982, 323 ff., T 42 must be added to my previous ones.
135. See supra note 134.
136. Lindos IV. 1, 98.
137. Mee 1982, 89-90.
138. Some surface sherds from Apsaktiras are dated to the advanced phase of the period by S. Dietz in Lindos IV. 1, 106 and fig. 73:7-7a.

The Dodecanese and the Western Peloponnese in the Late Bronze Age: Some Thoughts on the Problem of their Relations

Thanasis J. Papadopoulos

In his great and well known work "The Last Mycenaeans and Their Sucessors" Desborough wrote: "As to contact (of the Dodecanese) with other areas, it is clear that there was communication over a very wide sphére, on the basis of the distribution of the Octopus Style stirrup jars, but that the South and West Peloponnese, and the islands adjoining it, seem to have been excluded from this sphere" (p. 157).

Indeed, up to the present time, no Octopus Style stirrup jar is known to me from the Western Peloponnese, but there are other elements which could probably be used as evidence for the links, which, I believe, existed between the two areas in the Late Bronze Age.

In outlining these links it is apparently essential to show what Western Peloponnesian elements occur in the Dodecanese as well as all the Dodecanesian ones that found their way to the Western Peloponnese. It is also necessary for a better understanding of the nature of these links that the similarities and common characteristics should, where possible, be presented. This is important since common elements usually indicate close and constant interconnections, while the exchange of goods surely reflects simple commercial links[1]. There is always the risk of being misled, as details concerning fabric and technique are in most cases unknown.

Nevertheless, I would suggest that:

A. Western Peloponnesian objects in the Dodecanese are rare and few, confined to some large two-handled storage jars of LH IIIC date from the cemeteries of Ialysos-Rhodes[2] and Eleona and Langadha-Kos[3], and possibly to three LH IIIC stirrup jars from Langadha-Kos[4] and Passia-Rhodes[5], which are very similar to LH IIIC-SM specimens from Achaea, Elis and Messenia[6], representing more clearly than anything else the local ceramic repertory. These may be considered as Western Peloponnesian imports or strongly influenced by West-Peloponnesian prototypes.

B. One might be a little safer in suggesting that at least five LH IIIA2-B large three-handled jars from Aigion, Kallithea, Olympia and Tragana, belonging to the type so frequently found in Rhodes (FS. 34-38)[7], are of Dodecanesian origin or influence. They are decorated either with evenly distributed plastic bosses set in rows, the space between them filled with painted flowers or with other motifs (tricurved and concentric arcs, argonauts), whose style corresponds exactly to the Rhodian conception and repertory of decoration.

For the jar from Aigion, I know that Dr Jones's analysis has shown that it was made locally, a view followed by Dr Mee in his "Rhodes in the Bronze Age", 1982, 12, 86. The result of this analysis did not surprise me, since the possibility cannot be excluded that the Aigion potters were commissioned to make vases, Achaean in technique but Rhodian in shape, purposely for trade with the island.

C. Turning now to the similarities and common elements, we find that though few, they are sufficient to show contacts between the West Peloponnese and the Dodecanese, rather than an independant and coincidental appearance and evolution.

For Achaea, I have already discussed them in my paper "Rhodiaka in Achaea"[8]. They are confined to some pots (two stirrup jars from Aigion with alternating upright and pendant semicircles in a subsidiary zone, a feature most prominent in Rhodes, five piriform stirrup jars (FS. 165-7), a shape quite common in Rhodes, four legged pyxides, one pilgrim flask, one based pyxis, one shallow spouted? cup with fish decoration, and one feeding bottle) which range in date from LH IIIA2 to LH IIIC, and find more or less good and close parallels in contemporary Dodecanesian pottery. The popularity of the amphoriskoi and less so of the composite vessels in both areas may constitute a link between them. Other common elements have been traced in some glass beads and plaques decorated with double rosettes, spirals and figure-of-eight shields, one fragmentary steatite pommel, one trunnion-axe and a spear butt-spike. Furthermore, the construction of Tomb 7 at Aigion shows close similarities with Tomb LXXV at Ialysos-Rhodes, and another probable common element between the two areas is the presence of stepped dromoi.

In the rest of the West Peloponnese (Elis, Messenia) similarities to and elements in common with those of the Dodecanese are less known, either because the excavated material has not been properly published[9] or because of inattention[10]. Thus, in Elis, some similarities may be seen in the occurrence of pottery shapes of LH IIIA2-C date from Olympia (a LH IIIB spouted cup)[11], Trypes (a LH IIIA2-B tripod brazier and a legged pyxis)[12], and Agrapidochori (a LH IIIC pyxis)[13], which are contemporary and can be compared with Dodecanesian specimens from Kameiros and Ialysos in Rhodes[14], and Langadha in Kos[15], respectively.

In Messenia some large three-handled jars (FS 35), amphoroid kraters (FS 9), tripod jars and "incense burners" (FS 315) from the Palace of Nestor[16] are more or less strongly reminiscent of LH IIIB-C Rhodian specimens[17]. So it is probable that they show the influence of these Rhodian vases, or that they are imports from the island.

Some negative evidence deserves cautious mention here: the impoverishment of the cemeteries[18] – gold and silver are extremely rare in both the Dodecanese and the West Peloponnese. This, if not a matter of chance, may indicate similar trends dictated by common burial habits, possibly deriving from existing links between the two areas.

The above observations in this brief survey perhaps justify the conclusion of:

1. Lord William Taylour, who first suggested[19] that relations existed between the Dodecanese and West Peloponnese in the Late Bronze Age, that along the western coast of the Peloponnese there were ports of call, visited by the Rhodians, on the route to Italy; and

2. my own view, based mainly on the Achaean evidence, which is roughly contemporary to that of Elis, Olympia and Messenia, that, (a), contrary to the opinions of Mrs Vermeule, Ålin and Desborough[20], Achaea and the rest of the West Peloponnese had long-lasting commercial and possibly cultural contacts with the Aegean, and especially with the Dodecanese, ranging in time from LH IIIA2 to and including the LH IIIC period; (b) apart from the trade route round the south-southwestern coast of the Peloponnese and the Ionian islands, as suggested by the evidence of Elis, Olympia and Messenia, the Dodecanesian seafarers and traders could follow a second, less expensive and dangerous, alternative trade route, which passed along the gulf of Corinth – with corresponding transport-stations in the Isthmus and Aigion – to reach their South Italian and Sicilian customers. The historical Greek routes to the West also passed either by the Isthmus of Corinth or the Southwestern Peloponnese and the Ionian islands, so there is no reason to suppose that the Dodecanesians travelled on a different course in the Late Bronze Age.

The lengthy distance between the Dodecanese and the West Peloponnese, and the negative results of the analysis of a few pottery samples cannot, in my opinion, be regarded as serious obstacles, since we know that the people of both areas travelled widely in the Mediterranaean and had relations over a wider sphere. Moreover the evidence of the analysis is only meagre and restricted to material from just two Achaean sites (Aigion, Aigeira) and one in Rhodes (Ialysos) and seems not to be definite and conclusive[21].

But even if we accept that the Peloponnese was the common source of both the Achaean and the Rhodian large three-handled jars (FS 34-38), which are the most characteristic shape in question, the possibility of an interconnection between these areas cannot be excluded.

Until more persuasive evidence is available to shed more light on the problem of these relations, I personally should prefer not to alter my previous view that the Dodecanese and the Western Peloponnese maintained contacts in the latter half of the Mycenaean period.

Thanasis J. Papadopoulos
69, Themistocleous Street
154 51 New Psychicon, Athens
Greece

1. Iakovidis 1970, B, 414.
2. Furtwängler – Loescke 1886, pl. IV:25XII.
3. L. Morricone, ASAtene 27-28, 1967, figs. 36:1330; 46:391 (Eleona T. 16,20); 73:30;143:84; 312:446 (Langada T. 5, 25, erratici).
4. L. Morricone, ASAtene 27-28, 1967, figs. 113, 115:60 (T. 18:shoulder-zone decorated with vertical wavy lines and all the rest of body with succesive bands).
5. Lindos IV. 1, 28, 97, fig. 11:1,7 (shoulder-zone decorated with joining semicircles (FM.43:33) in a "triangular patch").
6. See, e.g. Papadopoulos 1978-79, figs. 63-65, 74d-f, 104h; BCH 1956, 576, fig. 6; ADelt 17B, 1961-2, pl. 118b (Elis); Blegen 1966, fig. 373:1141, 818; Blegen et al. 1973, fig. 292:15 (Messenia-Palace of Nestor).
7. See Papadopoulos 1976, 18, pls. 48, 60; Papadopoulos 1978-79, fig. 123a; Taylour 1958, pl. 16:2-3; AEphem 1914, 110, fig. 18. Stubbings says (Levant, 14) that FS.34 and 35 piriform jars "have long been recognised as characteristic of Rhodes". Also, Taylour 1958, 128 "The large three-handled jar (FS.34-5) is found predominantly in Rhodes and is generally characteristic of that island".
8. OpAth 13: 15, 1980, 225 ff.
9. With the exception of some preliminary reports in ADelt, Prakt and BCH, the material from the excavations of Yialouris and Marinatos in Elis-Olympia and Pylos-Messenia still remains unpublished.
10. Blegen, e.g., makes no mention of parallels between the large three-handled jars from the Palace of Nestor and those from the Dodecanese.
11. Taylour 1958, 179.
12. ADelt 19B, 1964, pls. 184c, 186d.
13. AEphem, 1971, pl. 35a.
14. ClRh 6-7, 1932, 137, fig. 157; Mee 1982, pl. 14:5.
15. ASAtene 27-28, 1967, 184, fig. 194:149.
16. Blegen 1966, pls. 329 right, 377-378, 387, 395:457, 504, 580.
17. Cf. e.g. Mee 1982, pl. 4:1 and 6:1; Lindos IV. 1, fig. 36:4,1; BMA. 875.
18. Cf. Mee 1982, 87.
19. Taylour 1958, 179-180.
20. AJA 64, 1960, 21; Åلin 1962, 68; Desborough 1964, 6, 227.
21. See R. Jones's results and discussion of this analysis in OpAth 13: 15, 1980, 232-235.

Relations between Cyprus and the Dodecanese in the Bronze Age

Paul Åström

This paper discusses the evidence of contacts between Cyprus and Rhodes in the Early, Middle and Late Bronze Ages.

We begin with the Early Bronze Age, when four duck-vases were made in Cyprus in Red Polished III and Black Polished ware[1]. These were no doubt inspired by Early Cycladic prototypes, as pointed out by James R. Stewart, Søren Dietz and Robert Merrillees[2]. In Cyprus they occur in the third phase of the Early Cypriote Bronze Age at Lapithos and Ayia Paraskevi[3]. Søren Dietz has published two such vases from the Danish archaeological expedition to Rhodes. Another was found on Kalymnos[4]. The Cypriote duck vases show contact between the two areas. Perhaps Cypriote copper was exported at that time, although evidence of copper working is first surely attested in Cyprus at Ambelikou in Middle Cypriote I[5].

It may be mentioned that it was the Greek workmen at Phylakopi who called these vases *papies*, which was translated as "ducks". But Merrillees has pointed out that *papia* not only means "duck" but also "bed-bottle" or "chamber pot"[6]. He suggests that the workmen jokingly referred to these vases as bed-bottles rather than as ducks for, as Merrillees has observed, they have a striking similarity to hospital urinals "sharing the same enclosed body with side-spout set on the shoulder". The workmen at Eutresis called a similar vase somewhat anachronistically a "locomotive". We have no clue as to what they were used for in antiquity.

A White Painted jug of the Middle Cypriote Bronze Age in the Ashmolean Museum (Inv.no. 1927.655) was acquired as a gift from J.G. Milne and stated to be from Rhodes. It is a Cypriote vase dating from Middle Cypriote III. Such vases are also common at Ras Shamra. Dr. Robert Merrillees prefers to date the vase to Late Cypriote IA and does not like to dismiss the attribution to Rhodes out of hand[8]. The jug probably came to Rhodes in modern times, not in antiquity[8bis]. It may, however, be recalled that three Syrian vases of a similar shape and of the same date as the jug in the Ashmolean are preserved in the Thera Museum. These belonged to the Nomikos Collection and again we are not sure about their provenance[9]. We know that there were contacts between Crete, Cyprus and Syria in Middle Minoan times[10], and a Middle Cycladic sherd has also been found at Hala Sultan Tekke[11], so it is not impossible that the jug in the Ashmolean and the three jugs in the Thera Museum are ancient imports, but this cannot be proved.

We are on firm ground when we approach the Late Bronze Age. Contacts between Cyprus and Rhodes were established in Late Cypriote I, II and III.

In Late Cypriote I, covering the 16th and 15th centuries BC, two characteristic Cypriote fabrics – Base-ring I and White Slip I – and a Cypriote bronze rapier are attested in Rhodes.

A Base-ring I juglet was found at Ialysos in tomb LXXVI, a rectangular shaft grave containing the remains of a child[12]. This was the only object preserved in the tomb. Dr. Merrillees has suggested that Base-ring vases contained opium[13]. We know from Egyptian texts that one of the uses of opium was to calm crying children. It is tempting to suggest that this juglet - presumably containing opium – was placed in a tomb to relieve the pains of a child, who died prematurely from an illness of some kind.

Three White Slip I sherds decorated with framed lozenge decoration were found at Trianda associated with Late Minoan IB pottery[14]. Hector Catling collected a base of a White Slip I bowl from the Moschou Vounara cemetery at Trianda in 1953[15].

A rapier of four-wing type with rat-tail tang

from the old British excavations at Ialysos is a Cypriote import, according to Hector Catling[16], and contemporary with the Base-ring I and White Slip I vases. I cannot find any evidence of export from Rhodes to Cyprus in Late Cypriote I, unless the Late Minoan I vases in Cyprus came from Rhodes.

In Late Cypriote II, roughly the 14th and 13th centuries BC, White Slip II bowls were exported to Kos and Rhodes and two Base-ring II bull-vases were deposited in tombs at Ialysos. A glass jug is believed to be Cypriote or Syrian.

A Base-ring I juglet was found in a tomb, No. LXXXVI, at Ialysos, together with a Base-ring II bull-vase and a plain jug[17]. This chamber tomb dates from Late Cypriote II in Cypriote terms and the Base-ring I juglet may be regarded as a survival. The tomb is supposed to have contained the remains of a youth, presumably because of the small size of the chamber, 1 x 1.20 m. The bull-vase might have been a toy in this case. The plain vase seems to be a Mycenaean shape but the clay is described as rose-red and coarse (rosea grezza); one would expect the surface of a Mycenaean vase to be smooth. In fact Mee does not believe that the vase is Mycenaean, and I do not think it is Cypriote.

The other bull-vase was found in the rich Ialysos New Tomb XXXI, which contained Mycenaean IIIA1 to IIIA2 vases. The tomb contained at least three skeletons, but no plan was published[18].

A Base-ring II bull in Stuttgart and a Base-ring II jug in the Ashmolean Museum are alleged to be from Rhodes[19].

A sherd of a White Slip II bowl is on display in the Kos Museum[20].

I have so far omitted the Red Lustrous Wheel-made spindle bottles and lentoid flasks which have been found on Rhodes and Kos[21], partly because they occur both in Late Cypriote I and II, and partly because we do not yet know where they were made. They occur in Asia Minor, Crete, Cyprus, Syria, Palestine and Egypt, but analyses of the clay have not yet been published[22]. They may have come to the Dodecanese from Cyprus or via Cyprus.

D.B. Harden has suggested that a lip-spouted glass jug on base-disc, found during old British Museum excavations in a tomb at Ialysos, is Syrian or Cypriote[23]. Nolte includes it among her Egyptian types. As another specimen was found at Maroni in Cyprus, a Cypriote origin may be possible, but Egypt is not excluded as the place of origin. The date is mid- 14th to late 13th century BC.

Tanged mirrors found on Rhodes may have been Cypriote imports according to Catling[24]. They were found in Mycenaean IIIB-IIIC1 contexts.

Turning now to the Late Cypriote III period, *c.* 1190-1050 BC, we find again some evidence of contact.

The late Professor Arne Furumark found some vases in his excavations at Sinda which he believed to be imported from Rhodes. They date from the beginning of Sinda's second period, Late Cypriote IIIA1, *c.* 1190-1175 BC, after the first catastrophe befell the town. One is an amphoriskos and another a fine krater of the same fabric, both Mycenaean IIIC1a in Furumark's terminology[25].

A conical bowl with concave sides, of Mycenaean IIIC1b, FS 291, from Enkomi, has a parallel at Ialysos, from where it probably came, according to Dikaios, "although an importation from the mainland of Greece is not excluded"[26].

A "sub-elliptical barbless arrow-head with long narrow straight tang" of Near Eastern or Cypriote type was found in Rhodes, but not from a dateable context. In Cyprus the type occurs in Late Cypriote II and III. At Enkomi such arrowheads are not earlier than the beginning of the 12th century BC[27]. A tripod stone mortar of Cypriote manufacture was also found at Ialysos[28].

Furumark regarded two Mycenaean IIIC1c vases from Kourion Kaloriziki New Tomb 26 as "undoubtedly of Rhodian manufacture"[29]. Benson and others considered the amphoriskos to be a Cypriote product, but the classification of the three-handled jar seemed to him probable on the basis of the technique[30].

Other vases from Rhodes – for example a stirrup jar from Lindos, now in Copenhagen, and published by Søren Dietz[31] - have affinities with Cypriote Proto White Painted Ware which belongs to the latest phases of the Late Cypriote Bronze Age, c. 1150-1050 BC.

All this suggests contact between the two islands throughout the Bronze Age. Merrillees has suggested that "sea-borne trade in the Aegean was largely in the hands of independent entrepreneurs, who bought and sold goods and offered services wherever there was a profit to be made"[32]. Some of the vases mentioned here may have been acquired in this way.

Mee has even suggested that the tombs which contained Cypriote vases belonged to Cypriotes "possibly dependents of merchants who died suddenly and were buried at Ialysos"[33]. He pointed out that Rhodes was a convenient port en route between Greece and Cyprus, as it still is today.

Claude F.A. Schaeffer put forward the hypothesis of an invasion by Mycenaeans from Rhodes *c.* 1225-1200 BC. Gjerstad and Furumark believed that Rhodes was on the route of the migrants who colonized Cyprus. Benson argues on the basis of the consistent orientation of tombs, and of the occasional practice of cremation on Rhodes and at Kaloriziki in Cyprus, that the immigrants to Cyprus in LCIIIB came from or via Rhodes[34].

Whether or not Rhodians participated in a Mycenaean colonization of Cyprus is a difficult question. The objects from Rhodes of Late Cypriote III date which I have mentioned may have come by way of exchange but possibly with immigrants. There were two successive horizons of ash layers in Cyprus at the beginning and at the end of Late Cypriote IIIA1, *c.* 1190 and 1175 BC. A new element appears in Proto White Painted Ware about 1150 or so. This ware is so closely related to mainland and Rhodian equivalents that it suggests a large-scale immigration of Aegeans to Cyprus.

I believe that the Aegeans came in at least three waves in the wake of the two catastrophes and when the Proto White Painted Ware appeared. We can suspect that there were people from the Dodecanese among them.

Paul Åström
Klassiska Institutionen
Antikens Kultur och samhällsliv
Göteborgs Universitet
Västra Hamngatan 3
411 17 Göteborg
Sweden

1. J.R. Stewart, SCE IV:1A, 1962, 277, 278, 283, 312, type IIIBa, fig. XCVIII:6 and CLII:15; J.R.Stewart, SIMA 3 (forthcoming).
2. J.R. Stewart, loc.cit,; S. Dietz, Acta Arch 45, 1974, 133-143; R.S. Merrillees, in Acts of the International Archaeological Symposium "The Relations between Cyprus and Crete, ca. 2000-500 BC.", Nicosia 16th-22nd April 1978, Nicosia 1979, 8-55.
3. R.S. Merrillees, op.cit. (note 2), 14-15.
4. S. Dietz, Acta Arch 45, 1974, 133-143.
5. R.S. Merrillees, RDAC 1984, 6-11.
6. R.S. Merrillees, op.cit. (note 2), 9.
7. Åström 1957, 69 and 222.
8. Merrillees 1975, 5.
8 bis) According to Mrs Ann Brown there are five other vases which are said to have come from Rhodes besides 1927.655. These are a Base-ring I juglet, a Mycenaean IIIA2 pithoid jar, a White Painted III juglet with tubular spout, a Red Polished spouted bowl, MC, and a White Slip II jug. Nos (in order) 1927.656, 1927.657, 1927.658, 1927.659, 1927.660. The vases were acquired as a gift from J.G. Milne and on the base of 1927.658 was written Fairweather, Rhodes. On the catalogue card is the following remark: "1927.655-660 inclusive are said to be from Rhodes but 5 of the 6 are clearly Cypriote, it seems unlikely that a purchase of 6 vases from Rhodes would include 5 rare imports. It is probable enough that confusion arose between the two islands."
9. P. Åström, in Acta of the 1st International Scientific Congress on the Volcano of Thera held in Greece, 15th – 23rd September 1969, Athens 1971, 415-421.
10. Åström 1957, 257-260.
11. P. Åström, in The International Archaeological Colloquium "Cyprus between the Orient and the Occident", Nicosia 8-14th September 1985 (forthcoming).
12. G. Jacopi, ASAtene 13-14, 1930-31, 1933, 304, figs. 46 and 49; P. Åström, SCE IV:1D, 1972, 725; G. Cadogan, in Praktika tou protou diethnous Kyprologikou synedriou (Leukosia, 14-19 Apriliou 1969), A', Nicosia 1972, 6. Merrillees 1975, 6; Mee 1982, 22.
13. R.S. Merrillees, Antiquity 36, 1962, 287 ff.; Levant 11, 1979, 167-171.
14. ClRh 10, 1941, 58, 59, n.2, Fig. 8:1-2, Fig. 9:14, Fig. 41:12; Furumark in OpArch 6, 1950, 165f., 184; Cadogan, op.cit. (note 12), 6; Merrillees 1975, 6; Mee 1982, 6, 93, n. 39.
15. Catling 1964, 112, no. 5.
16. Catling 1964, 112, fig. 12:12; G. Cadogan, op.cit (note 12), 9.
17. ASAtene 13-14, 1930-31, 328f.; G. Cadogan, op.cit. (note 12), 6; Mee 1982, 22.
18. Gjerstad 1926, 326; Sjöquist 1940, 160, 162; G. Cadogan, op.cit. (note 12), 6; Mee 1982, 22 and 129.
19. SCE IV:1C, 149; IV:1D, 725, 854.
20. SCE IV:1D, 752.
21. SCE IV:1D, 741.
22. SCE IV:1D, 741-743; P. Åström, in MedelhavsMusB 5, 1969, 16-21.
23. Harden 1981, 34-35, No. 10.
24. Catling 1964, 227.
25. A. Furumark in OpAth 6, 1965, 114, pl. I, top.
26. Dikaios 1971, 267, fig. 74:2.

27. Catling 1964, 131.
28. H.-G. Buchholz, JdI 78, 1963, 1ff.; G. Cadogan op.cit. (note 12), 7.
29. A. Furumark, OpArch 3, 1944, 218, n. 4, 265.
30. Benson 1973, 25, no. 21.
31. Lindos IV. 1, 89 and 115.
32. Merrillees 1975, 8.
33. Mee 1982, 22.
34. Benson 1973, 23-25 (with references); Mee 1982, 92; Desborough 1964, 204-5. Cf. also F. Vandenabeele's paper in the Colloquium Thanatos, Liege 21st-23rd April, 1986.

Addenda: For a Cypriote bronze knife in a Mycenaean IIIA2 context from Tolo, see Mario Benzi's communication above. White Slip I and Base-ring I imports have also recently been found by Toula Marketou at Ialysos (supra p. 31). Benzi, McDonald and Mee have pointed out that sites in the southern part of Rhodes were abandoned early in Mycenaean IIIC. This may be connected with a population movement to the northern part of the island and, possibly, to Cyprus.

Chapter 2 . The Island of Rhodes

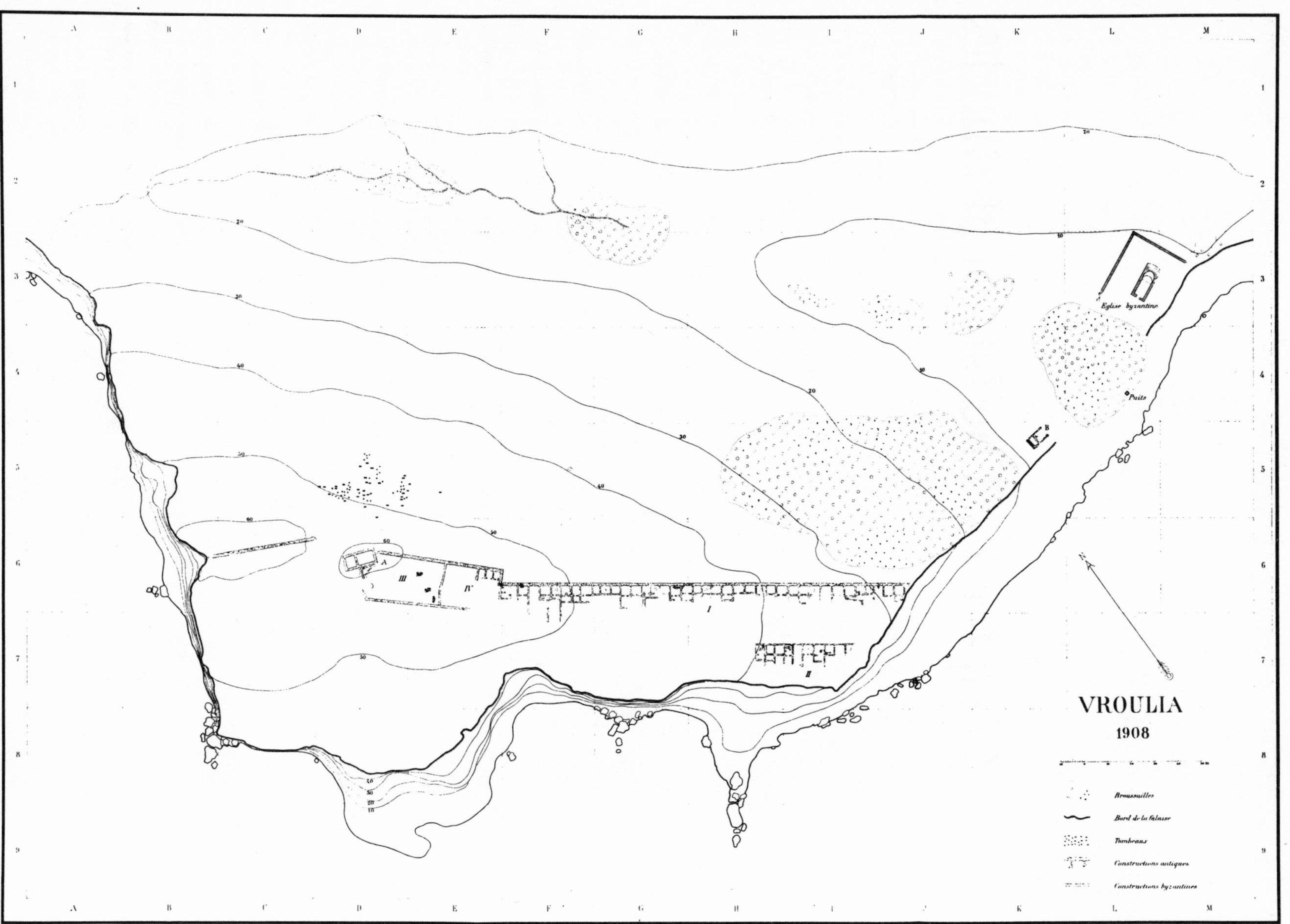

Fig. 1. Townplan of Vroulia, Rhodes. After Kinch 1914.

Vroulia: Town Plan and Gate

Torben Melander

In this preliminary paper it is my intention to reconsider some statements about the town of Vroulia on the very southern part of Rhodes.

In two seasons, 1907 and 1908, Vroulia was excavated by Karl Frederik Kinch, the permanent member of the Danish Rhodes Expedition 1902-09 and 1913-14[1].

The job of excavating was done in a rather hasty way one has to admit. More memorable is the ultra short time in which the results were published in what was to be the only comprehensive excavation report of a small town site in first millennium BC Greece for years to come[2]. In fact, only after the Second World War was something like this done with the British excavation in Emporio on the island of Chios[3], and the joint Turkish - British excavation in Old Smyrna or Bayrakli in Turkey[4], just to name a few outstanding cases. Maybe these newly excavated sites brought the old Danish excavation of Vroulia back in focus.

Anyhow, when Heinrich Drerup in 1969 wrote about the urban development in early Greece[5], Vroulia became the earliest town site of which enough was left to consider it a planned town. A type of town which for some time had been thought to originate in the Western Mediterranean during the 8th a 7th centuries colonization[6].

The foundation of Vroulia can be dated to around 700 BC by archaeological evidence[7]. Maybe Vroulia itself was a result of the above mentioned colonization movement. Perhaps Vroulia was a point of military interest as the last port of call on the territory of the city state or polis of Lindos before you left the Aegean for adventures father east[8].

This archaeological guesswork about the origins of Vroulia could very well turn out to be the historical reality of the site. It is not my intention here to follow this further. What I have in mind for the moment, is to consider one or two points of architectural interest.

My first topic is the plan of the town (fig. 1)[9]. – What we have left are two rows of houses, and of course the town wall. The western part of the town had never been built up, and I do not think it had ever been the intention to do so. It is a well known fact that in Greek town building in mountainous surroundings the amount of fortified area, more or less, were governed by the advantages in the terrain itself[10].

There have been speculations concerning the area empty of buildings inside the town gate. Already Kinch dared to explain the area in part as a sanctuary, in part as an *agora*[11]. All other parts of the town have fallen into the sea at some unknown time. But can you really deduce a whole town plan from two rows of houses? I am not sure. And I become really hesitant when I consider the way those two rows of houses came into being.

A brief glance at the map is enough to tell us how this happened. First of all the town wall was built. And as all well located Greek fortifications, the town wall was built with a view to the lines of the terrain. In the case of Vroulia the situation is extremely simple. You only have to follow the smoothly rising mountain ridge, which at some point breaks off from a southeast/northwest direction to a more east/west one. It is along the long eastern stretch of our wall that the two rows of houses had been laid out. And most important the lay-out was totally dictated by the wall.

But this is only what is to be expected from a Greek lay-out, as can easily be illustrated by a few well known sites, Olympia for example[12]. The lay-out of the sanctuary is totally governed by its site at the foot of Kronos, while the river Alphaios, in the distance, functioned as a reminder.

The Agora of Athens is another well known place[13]. Its triangular shape, at least for its first 150 years, was dictated by the two heights of Kolonos Agoraios in the west and the Areopagos

Fig. 2. Townplan of Karphi, Crete. After BSA 38, 1937-38.

in the south. To the east we have the Panathenaic Road. The road had since time immemorial for this part been running between the northern tip of Kolonos Agoraios and the eastern spur of Areopagos, before it continued further south[14].

My third example is the town of Thasos[15]. There too you will find the landscape outlines imposing enough to dictate the main lay-out of the town. A rather narrow piece of land is left between the foot of the hill and the seashore. The plan dictated by the landscape was to be the plan of the city of Thasos for all its history.

The confines of the individual houses in the rows in Vroulia are blurred by rebuilding over the years[16]. That means that it is impossible from both the town plan, as well as the excavator's report to say anything in general about the much discussed problem of the house lots in the colonized towns of the eighth and seventh century BC.

I will use this as maybe a weak excuse for a little discourse about another well known town plan, which is however much earlier: Eleventh century Karphi above the Lasithi Plain on Eastern Crete (fig. 2)[17]. What I have in mind is once more the architectural development.

When Heinrich Drerup in "Griechischer Baukunst" tried to explain the difference in the lay-out of the houses in the eastern and the western section of Karphi, he attempted an explanation from an ethnic point of view[18]. So Drerup thought of the western part of the settlement as built and lived in by the aboriginals, the so-called *Eteocretans*. They were thought to have built their houses in the agglutinative fashion[19], considered to be the Minoan way of building. The lay-out of the houses in the eastern part of the town following straight lines and with each section of the house clearly defined was considered Dorian. Of course there are other explanations. One of these comes easily to mind just by looking at the eastern row of houses in the western section. The lay-out of the rooms and the confines of each single room seem to represent an intermediate state between the two systems represented by the more western half and the eastern section.

What we see in Karphi is the most banal effect of urban dynamics, I think. The successive spreading from a center, in this case in the west, in one or more directions.

If this is the right explanation we are left with the problem of the wide empty area between the two parts of the town. The main function of the area was to lead the traffic from above down into the plain below. The first lay-out of Karphi (to the west) had not touched the road area. Later on when the eastern row was added the area almost touched, I guess. And so, when the inhabitants of Karphi had decided upon further town expansion they had to move to the other side of the cliff depression which from the beginning had been chosen as town site, with the road running through in the bottom of the depression.

Of course it is mere speculation to suggest that the area under consideration could have functions other than that of a road. – I think the area had additional space for some other social function. Some sort of an agora, for example. – I only have to remind you about the situation in Athens I mentioned above, when I tried to show that the roads were the very cause of the site itself; roads which had existed there as long as man had walked about in the area north of the Areopagos.

To what has already been said about the successive built up of an area, transfiguring the original more or less clearcut outline of its parts into a tight, almost amorphous mass of structure, I should add that this is nothing new. It seems to be just as old as city building in the Mediterranean.

We only have to look at the neolithic town of Çatal Hüyük near Konya, Southwestern Turkey. Here Ernst Heinrich and Ursula Seidl[20] demonstrated, some years ago, that what the excavator, James Mellart, believed to be a town at some time laid out after the principle of agglutinativity in fact can be shown to have originated in separate structures. These structures only gradually became more and more built into one big mass of houses, which in the end necessitated the inhabitants to enter their houses from the roof.

To return to Vroulia. Maybe something like the development at Karphi can be seen in its very beginning at Vroulia. From what is left, as already mentioned, it is extremely difficult to be sure where one house stops and where the neighbour takes over, perhaps because a determinable house plan never existed. Maybe the houses already had begun their frivolous "agglutination".

My second and minor topic is the town gate of Vroulia (figs. 3 and 4)[21].

In his publication of the town wall of Old Smyrna in the Annual of the British School of Archaeology at Athens, Mr. Nicholls has questioned the early dating of the town gate of Vroulia[22]. Mr. Nicholls may be right. For the moment, however, it is important that the question of age does not touch upon the more general archaic date of our gate, which after all still has to be placed it seems before the abandonment of the settlement in the first half of the sixth century BC. The ceramic date is MC[23]. (Of course the possibility exists that the construction of the gate is of a much later date, in connection with some use of the place as a refuge fortification).

It is of no less importance that the main entrance to the settlement – maybe the only one – always seems to have been on the same site. This we can deduce from the road coming up through the cemetery[24] just in front of what is now an opening in the wall – at least.

From the remains, then, we can believe in an early gate of the type following the so-called overlapping system, which is well known from other archaic fortifications[25].

Later on a new gate was constructed. This time with a bastion on the side towards the town. The gate house is placed in an obtuse angle with the eastern town wall. An overlapping western wall, continued from what exists, would together with the gate house make a gate of the funnel-shaped type. The effect of this is that an attacker is allowed to attack the gate itself with a great force. But when the gate is opened by the defenders the attackers are pressed back

Fig. 3. Towngate of Vroulia. Excavation photography.

and locked in, because of mere crowding. Caught in this way the attackers are easily slaughtered by the defenders. That is the theory.

Some years ago after new measurements had been made it was proven that this system had been used for the Dipylon gate in Athens[26]. As is well known, new phenomena attract great names. In this case the honour of introducing the use of the funnel-shaped gate into Greece was given to the *strategos* Themistocles.

Even if the gate at Vroulia should be shown one day to be of the type I have suggested in my paper, I am not postulating that Vroulia is the site where the funnel-shaped gate was introduced into Greece. But the existence at Vroulia of such a system is evidence, in my opinion, that something like this had existed in some of the major sites in Rhodes, or in some other part of Eastern Greece[27].

Torben Melander
Thorvaldsens Museum
Porthusgade 2
1213 Copenhagen K
Denmark

I am greatly indebted to Mrs Anne Sophie Urne who revised my English manuscript.

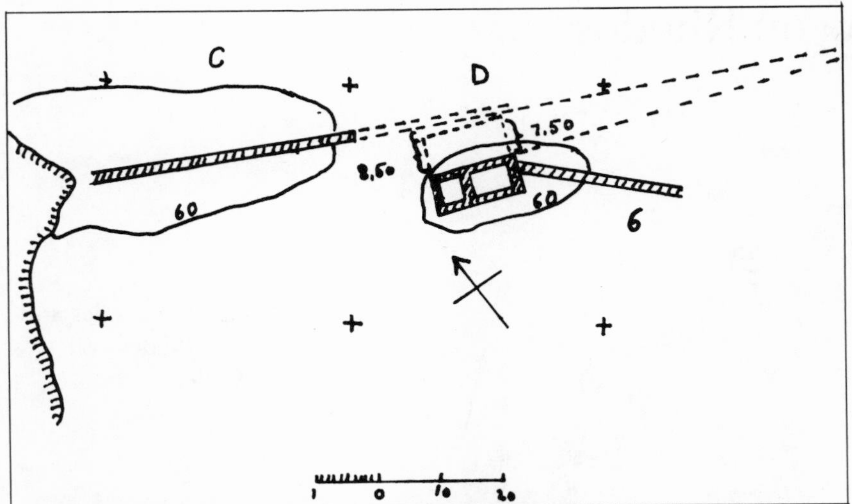

Fig. 4. Plan of towngate, Vroulia, Rhodes.

1. Lindos III, 13-28, with the earlier literature compiled p. 16, note 17. The history of the Danish Rhodes expedition has been surveyed most recently by S. Dietz in Dietz – Trolle 1974, 9-16.
2. Kinch 1914. For more recent treatment see Drerup 1969, H. Lauter, BJb 176, 1976, 455 (a review article).
3. Boardman 1967.
4. J.M.Cook and others, BSA 53-54, 1958-59, 1-81. For the dating of the city wall see now S.P.Morris, AJA 89, 1985, 177 (a review article).
5. Drerup 1969, 51-52.
6. Giuliano 1966, 38-40.
7. An early orientalizing skyphos, Kinch 1914, pl. 36, no. 39b ; Kardara 1963, 31.
8. For the city states of Rhodes in archaic time see H. von Gaertringen, RE, Suppl. 5, 1931, 731 ff.; Kirsten – Kraiker, 1967, 576, fig. 152. The polis of Lindos occupied all the southern half of the island of Rhodes, and thus was territorily the largest of the three Rhodian poleis. – For Lindian activity overseas see J.D.Bing, JNES 30, 1971, 99-109.
9. Plan of Vroulia after Kinch 1914.
10. Winter 1971, 102; 108-9. With a view to Vroulia this has also been put forward by E. Kirsten, AA 1964, 902 note 28.
11. Kinch 1914, 97-100 (the sanctuary) ; 108-9 (the agora).
12. A view of the Altis from the air is shown by Mallwitz 1972, 118-9; compare also Mallwitz 1972, 15, fig. 5, a model view with p. 78, fig. 70, the plan of the prehistoric Olympia.
13. Thompson – Wycherley 1972, pl. 4.
14. Travlos 1971, 422. For a possible 2. Mill. B.C. – more western placed – fore-runner of the Panathenaic Way, Hesperia 35, 1966, 45 (road material with MH pottery between the Middle Stoa and the South Stoa II). The Mycenean chamber tomb, Hesperia 35, 1966, 55-6, could indicate a removal of the road to the east between the road running in MH time and in the 1st Mill. B.C.
15. Daux 1968, 20-1, fig. 4.
16. Kinch 1914, 112-24 ; Drerup 1969, 98 ; A. Mallwitz, AA 1968, 610, note 51.
17. J.D.S.Pendlebury and others, BSA 38, 1937-38, 57 ff.; Drerup 1969, 39-41 ; A. Mallwitz, AA 1981, 610, 613; J.N.Coldstream; Rh. - Westfäl. Akad. d. Wissensch. 1984, 20.
18. Drerup 1969, 39-41.
19. E. Heinrich, AA 1958, 89 ff.
20. E. Heinrich – U. Seidl, AA 1969, 113-9.
21. Kinch 1914, 91-94.
22. R.V. Nicholls makes comments on the date of the gatehouse, BSA 53-54, 1958-9, 115, note 19.
23. For the date of the end of Vroulia see R.M.Cook, BSA 34, 1936, 88.
24. Kinch 1914, 34-6, fig. 14.
25. R.V. Nicholls. BSA 53-4, 1958-9. 116 and 117 ;Winter 1971, 208.
26. G. Gruben, AA 1964, 416-7.
27. I am most thankful to Dr. Hans Lauter who told me at the symposium that he had observed at the site some remains of the outer wall in front of the gate house. If the remains still exist it should be possible to trace and measure the gate itself.

Hippodamischer Stadtplan von Rhodos

Forschungsgeschichte

Grigoris Konstantinopoulos

Meinen jungen Kollegen und Mitarbeiter der Ephoreia von Dodekanes gewidmet.

Das Fehlen einer detallierten Beschreibung der Stadt Rhodos von Seiten eines antiken Periegeten macht sich besonders auf dem Gebiet der Stadtplanerischen Forschung bemerkbar. Dagegen haben sich einige wenige und zufällige antike Zeugnisse[1] erhalten, mit deren Hilfe bis in die 50er Jahre dieses Jahrhunderts versucht wurde, eine Vorstellung des antiken Stadtplans dieser bedeutenten Stadt zu gewinnen.

So gibt der Geograph Strabon[2] die genaue Lage der Stadt im östlichen Teil der Vorspringenden Landzunge an, spricht mit Bewunderung von ihrer Schönheit und unterstreicht dabei, dass es in der Antike keine bessere gab, die es mit ihr hätte aufnehmen können. Der Historiker Diodor charakterisiert ihre Lage anlässlich der Belagerung von 305 v.Chr. durch Demetrios Polyorketes[3] und der dritten Uberschwemmung 316 v.Chr. als theaterähnlich[4].

Ein späterer Rhetor, der bekannte Sophist Aelius Aristides, versuchte in einer öffentlichen Rede, die Rhodier zu bewegen, ihre beim Erdbeben 155 n.Chr. zerstörte Stadt wieder aufzubauen, und in dieser Rede sind uns wenige, aber nützliche Beschreibungen der Stadt erhalten: über das Gebiet der Akropolis, über die gerade angelegten Strassen, die die Stadt von einem bis zum anderen Ende durchlaufen, über die Geschlossenheit und Einheitlichkeit der Stadt, ihre Häfen, ihre hohen Mauern und ihre noch höheren Türme[5]. Schliesslich beziet sich Strabon auf die Überlieferung, dass Rhodos von dem selben Architekten erbaut sei, wie der Piräus, nämlich von Hippodamos[6].

Im 19. Jh., unter dem Eindruck der Städtebaulichen Entwicklung, in dem der orthogonale Plan dominierte, stellte man die sehr dürftigen Mitteilungen unserer Quellen über Hippodamos als Städtebauplaner in den Mittelpunkt der Betrachtungen[7] und im Zuge der allgemeinen Erforschung der Antike begannen sich die Wissenschaftler dafür zu interessieren. Als erster äusserte sich Hermann (1841) in einer Arbeit über Hippodamos auch kurz über Rhodos[8]. Systematisch stellte Erdmann (1883)[9] sämtliche antiken Quellen zusammen, dazu die wenigen Inschriften sowie die Beschreibungen von L. Ross[10], V. Guerin[11], dem Antiquar und Graveurs A. Berg[12], vor allem aber Newton[13]. Er hat auch die Karte[14] der englischen Marine übernommen, auf der Newton alle von ihm lokalisierten Altertümer verzeichnet hatte. Meines Erachtens hatte Erdmann auch persönlich Rhodos besucht und gab dann die erste, streng wissenschaftliche Beschreibung der antiken Stadt[15].

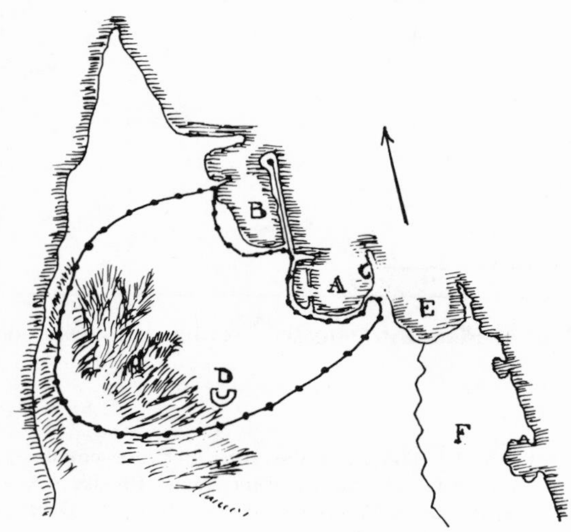

Fig. 1. Plan des antiken Rhodos von A. Berg.

Hinsichtlich ihrer Lage und Grösse stimmt er mit den Angaben von Berg[16] überein (Fig 1). Er nahm an, dass es "einen breiten Hauptweg längs der Hafenmauer... zum Dienste des Hafenverkers"[17] gegeben hätte und erschloss als erster, dass die mittelalterliche schnurgerade Ritterstrasse (Fig. 2) der nachfolger einer hippodamischen Strasse war. Die nach Westen verlaufende Achse der antiken Strasse meinte er ausserhalb der mittelalterlichen Mauern seitlich

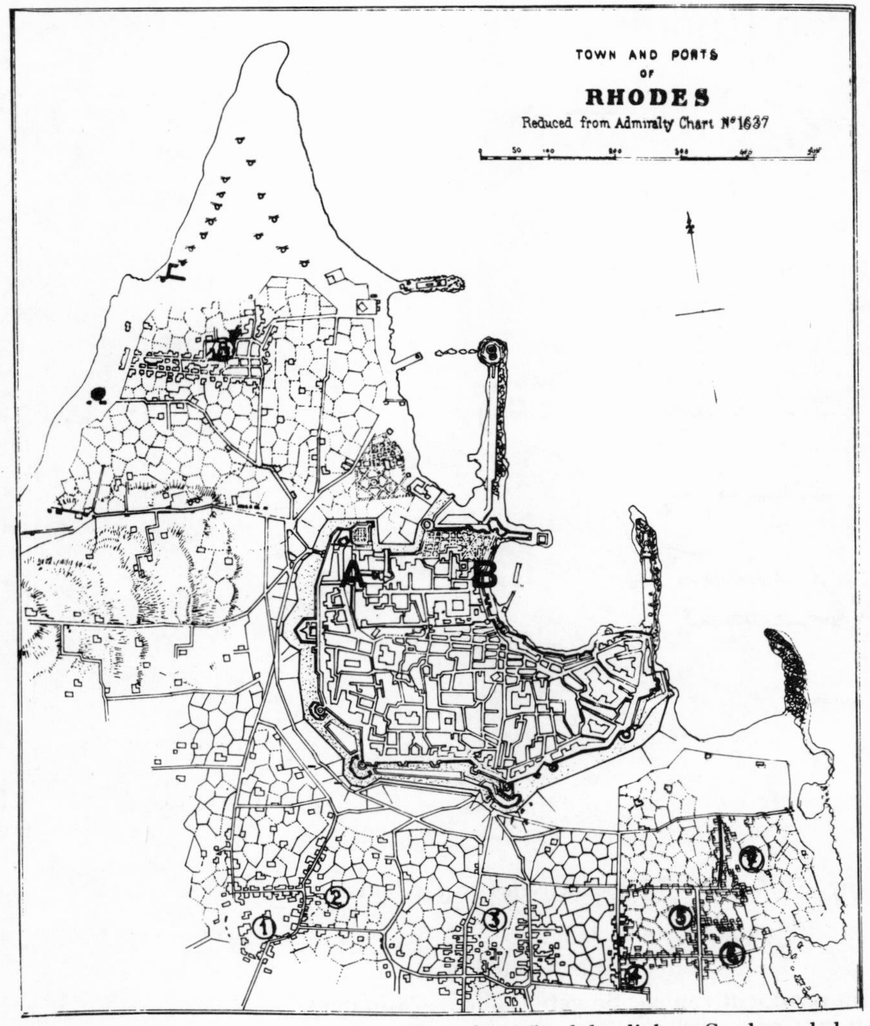

Fig. 2. Plan der mittelalterlichen Stadt und der Vororte von Rhodos mit den von C. T. Newton eingetragenen antiken Ruinen. A-B Ritterstrasse.

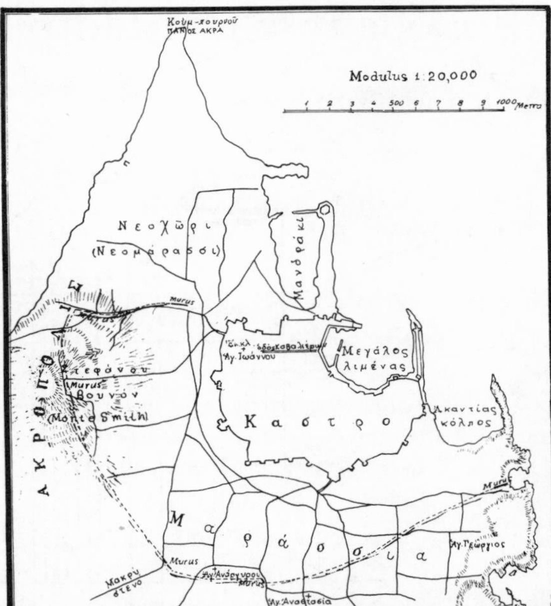

Fig. 3. Der von Fr. Hiller von Gaertringen festgestellte Mauerring.

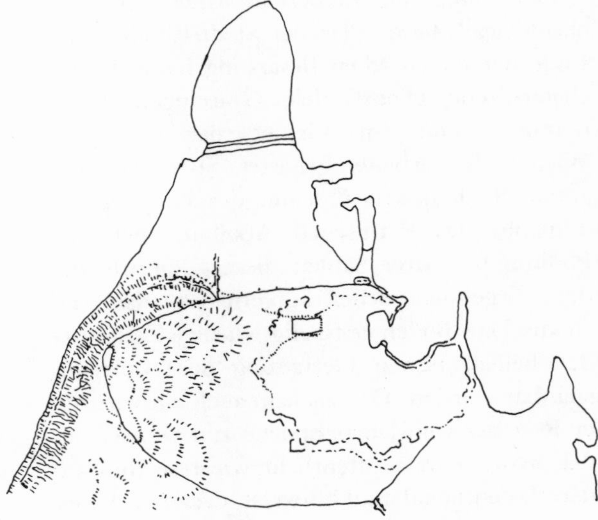
Fig. 4. Mauerring des antiken Rhodos von Schramm.

der erhaltenen Akropolis falsch in einem Feldweg[18] gefunden zu haben, den schon Newton auf seiner Karte verzeichnet und beschrieben hatte. Ausserdem erkannte er einen zweiten Feldweg, der auf der Karte erwähnt war[19] und nördlich von jenem parallel verläuft und eine antike Strasse überlagert. Er schrieb:"Wie wünschenwert wäre es, wenn durch Ausgrabungen und Aufnahmen eines Stadtterrainsplanes topographische Sicherheit geschaffen würde"[20], ausserdem betonte er die Notwendigkeit der genauen wissenschaftlichen Erforschung, "ob die Strassen nach Art der Theatertreppen auf die Agora hin konvergieren oder parallel gezogen waren"[21].

1895 fügte Hiller v. Gaertringen dem Corpus Inscriptionum von Rhodos[22] eine Planskizze bei (Fig. 3), auf der er den vermutlichen antiken Verlauf der Stadtmauer eingetragen hatte, deren überreste er selbst vor Ort aufgenommen hatte. Auf dieser Skizze war der Umfang der antiken Stadt deutlich grösser als der, den Berg eingezeichnet hatte. 1928 jedoch veröffentlichte Schramm anlässlich der Beschreibung der Belagerung durch Demetrios Poliorketes[23] einen Plan (Fig. 4) mit den Ausmassen der antiken Stadt, auf der er ihre Ausdehnung ohne bezug

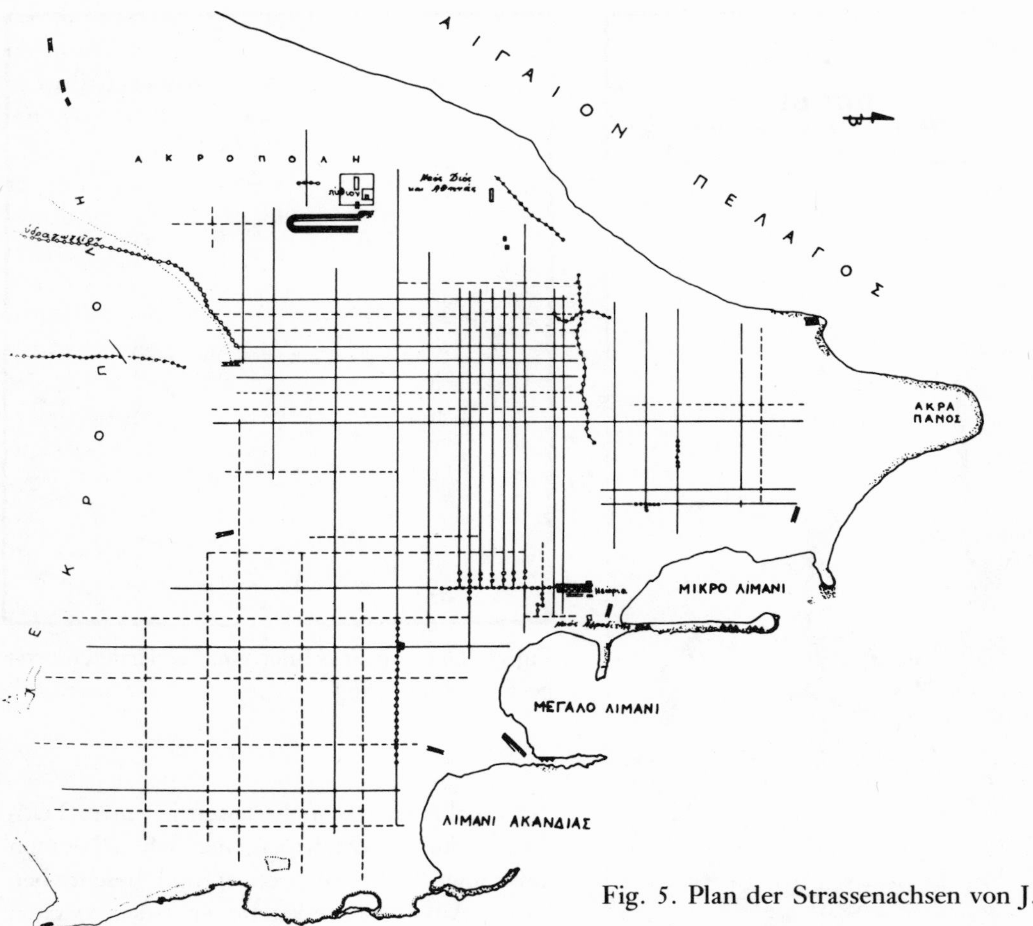

Fig. 5. Plan der Strassenachsen von J. Kontis.

auf die Skizzen von Hiller und Berg wieder eingrenzte[24].

Da kein neues literarischen oder epigraphischen Quellenmaterial hinzugekommen war, mussten sich alle Wissenschaftler, die sich mit Hippodamos oder antiker Stadtplannung beschäftigen, auf Annahmen oder Thesen beschränken, und zwar sowohl im Hinblick auf die amphitheatralische Lage der Stadt[25], als auch hinsichtlich der Frage, ob es überhaupt möglich war, dass Hippodamos im Jahre 408 v.Chr. noch gelebt hat, um Rhodos selbst gebaut haben zu können[26].

Obwohl die italienischen Archäologen von 1913 bis 1943 Ausgrabungen auf der ganzen Insel unternommen haben, wurde versäumt, systematisch einige der damals noch am Rande der modernen Stadt gelegene Gebiete zu ergraben, um den rhodischen Städtebau zu erforschen. Sie beschrängten sich auf Zufallsfunde, die bei öffentlichen und privaten Bauunternehmungen an das Licht kamen. So gab Maiuri 1928 in der Reihe Clara Rhodos[27] eine Zusammenfassung der Funde, die in der Stadt lokalisiert worden waren sowie eine Karte, auf der alle bis dahin gemachten Funde verzeichnet waren.

1936 unternahm Inglieri in seiner Carta Archeologica[28] diesen Plan der Stadt Rhodos. Am Ende der italienischen Besatzung hatte der archäologische Dienst viele Grabungen unternommen und im Gebiet der Akropolis Wiederaufbauarbeiten geleistet. So wurden das antike Stadion, das Odeion, der Umgang des Temenos des Pythischen Apollon sowie das Podium und drei Säulen dieses Tempels mit dem Ergebnis wieder aufgerichtet, dass auf rhodischem Boden erstmalig würdige Zeugnisse der hellenistischen Gestaltung der Akropolis sichtbar wurden. Damals kam auch ein wichtiger Rest der römischen Epoche zum Vorschein, der, obwohl unveröffentlicht wie fast alles andere[29], deutlich darauf hinweist, dass es sich hier um den vielleicht einzigen Eingriff der Römer in das ansonsten in jeder Hinsicht autarke Stadtgefüge handelt. Ich meine die Errichtung eines grossen Tetrapylons an hervorragender Stelle des kleinen Hafens und die Verlegung einer der zentralen gepflasterten Strassen, die mit Säulenhallen flankiert wurde und ihre nächste Parallelen in den grossen städtischen Zentren des Ostens oder vielleicht noch im benachbarten Kos findet[30].

Die Schwierigkeiten jener Kriegszeiten erlaubten den Forschern begreiflicherweise nicht, diese bedeutenden Grabungsergebnisse zu bearbeiten um für die rhodische Stadtplanung neue Erkenntnisse zu gewinnen. Daher wiederholt Dinsmoor noch 1950 die Ansicht von Hermann, dass Rhodos eine kreisrunde Anlage mit den Zentrum im Hafen war[31]. Die Geschicke der rhodischen Stadtplannung gelangten in die Hände des ersten griechischen Archäologen J. Kondis, der 1947 von dem letzten italienischen Kollegen, L. Morricone, Amt und Forschung übernahm. Da Kondis besondere Neigung zu Architektur, Städtebau und Raumplanung hatte, ordnete er das Grabungsmaterial und konnte so zur Klärung vieler Probleme in Städtebau und Strassenaufteilung von Rhodos beitragen: vor allem kontrollierte er zuerst mit dem Kompass die Ausrichtung von etwa 20 architektonischen Resten, die über verschiedene Punkte der Stadt verteilt waren und sicherte ihre Ost-West bzw. Nord-Süd Ausrichtung mit einer Abweichung von 3 Grad. Diese Feststellung widerlegte die Theorie, dass das alte Rhodos amphitheatralisch ausgerichtet war und so wurde nach 70 Jahren die Frage von Erdmann beantwortet, dass nämlich die von Ost nach West verlaufenden Strassen nicht am Hafen zusammentreffen, sondern parallel von Ost nach West laufen[32].

Ausserdem hat Kondis den Abstand zwischen den Mündungen von sieben Abwässerkanälen in den Zentralen Drainage der antiken Strasse gemessen, die von den Römern umgestaltet worden war. Dabei stellte er fest, dass diese Abstände fast gleichmässig waren und nur zwischen 31 und 32 Metern schwankten. Folglich entsprachen natürlich diese sieben Abwässerkanäle sieben jeweils darüberliegenden antiken Strassen. Als diese schrägen Abwässerkanäle im Strassenplan der neuen Stadt als Strassenachsen angelegt wurden, stellte man fest, dass zwei davon mit mittelalterlichen Strassen zusammenfielen und zwei weitere mit Strassen ausserhalb der Mauern[33].

Es folgten Vermessungen im neuen Stadtplan, aus denen deutlich wurde, dass mit grosser Wahrscheinlichkeit einige neue Strassen in gewisser Weise die Nachfolge der antiken Strassen angetreten hatten. Das Problem wäre nur durch neue Grabungen ganz gelöst worden, und man versteht, dass es in dieser Zeit sehr schwierig war, ausgedehnte Grabungen durchzuführen. Auf der anderen Seite hat sich die Antikenverwaltung damit begnügt, an solchen Plätzen Grabungen zu unternehmen, wo sich bei der Errichtung privater Häuser Antiken fanden. So kamen abermals antike Reste zum Vorschein, darunter auch Strassen, aus deren Untersuchung sich Hinweise auf ihren Strassenbelag, Abwässerkanäle, Fassaden oder Fundamente antiker Häuser, Teile von Wasserleitungen sowie auf Pflanzlöcher für Bäume ergaben[34].

All dies Material gab Kondis die Möglichkeit, eine Dissertation[35] zu veröffentlichen, in der sich eine Fülle von wichtigen Bemerkungen zu Stadtplannung von Rhodos finden. Vor allem aber erschien der erste Plan der antiken Strassenachsen (Fig. 5) von Rhodos. Da aber dieses Buch der nicht griechischsprachigen wissenschaftlichen Öffentlichkeit unzugänglich ist, hat er 1958 einen Artikel publiziert[36]. Damit wurde die Grundlage für die Beschäftigung mit Stadtplan von Rhodos gelegt[37].

Fast gleichzeitig mit Kondis ist der englische Archäologe J. Bradford ausgehend von Luftbildphotos zu ähnlichen Ergebnissen gelangt, die 1954 auf der International Classical Conference in Copenhagen vorgestellt wurden. Bradford hat auf den Luftbildaufnahmen von Rhodos sowohl in der bewohnten Stadt wie vor allem aber auch in den damals unbewohnten ländlichen Gebieten gerade Strassen festgestellt und in regelmässiger Anordnung Landgüter lokalisiert, deren Grenzen grösstenteils ebenfalls in geraden Linien verlaufen. Da Bradford sehr versiert im Lesen von Luftbildaufnahmen war, kam er zu dem Schluss, dass diese Grenzen auf die Existenz gerader antiker Strassen hinweisen mussten. Mit diesem Wissen zeichnete er die Karte der hippodamischen Strassen des antiken Rhodos (Fig. 6), die er zweimal veröffentlichte[38].

Ich muss an dieser Stelle daraufhinweisen, dass Bradford, bevor er seine Ergebnisse veröffentlichte, Rhodos besucht, wo er eng mit Kondis zusammengearbeitet hatte.

In den 60er Jahren – Kondis hatte schon Rhodos verlassen - erlebte Rhodos seine ersten Bauboom und ergab sich die Gelegenheit Grabungen in grossem Umfang in der ganzen Stadt durchzuführen, die die sorgfältige Erforschung jedes Grundstücks bis zum gewachsenen Boden beinhalteten. Danach begann auch die erste grosszügige finanzielle Unterstützung dieser Ausgrabungen durch das Ministerium. Die Ergebnisse waren ausgezeichnet: Wir stellten die Breiten vieler strassen fest, die an verschiedenen Stellen der Stadt ausgegraben wurden. Wir fanden neue Mauerabschnitte, Türme von enormen Ausmassen, das Vorwerk[39], neue Grabanlagen

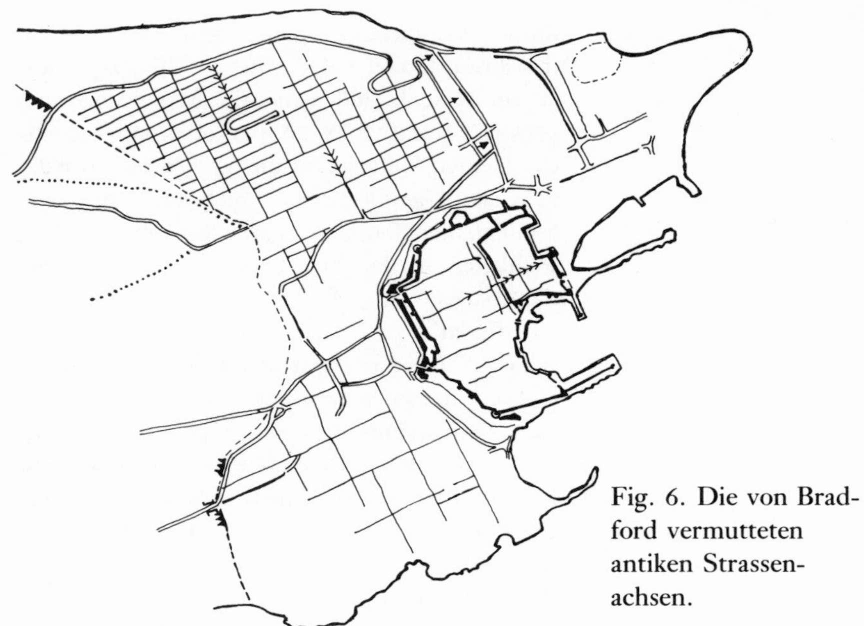

Fig. 6. Die von Bradford vermutteten antiken Strassenachsen.

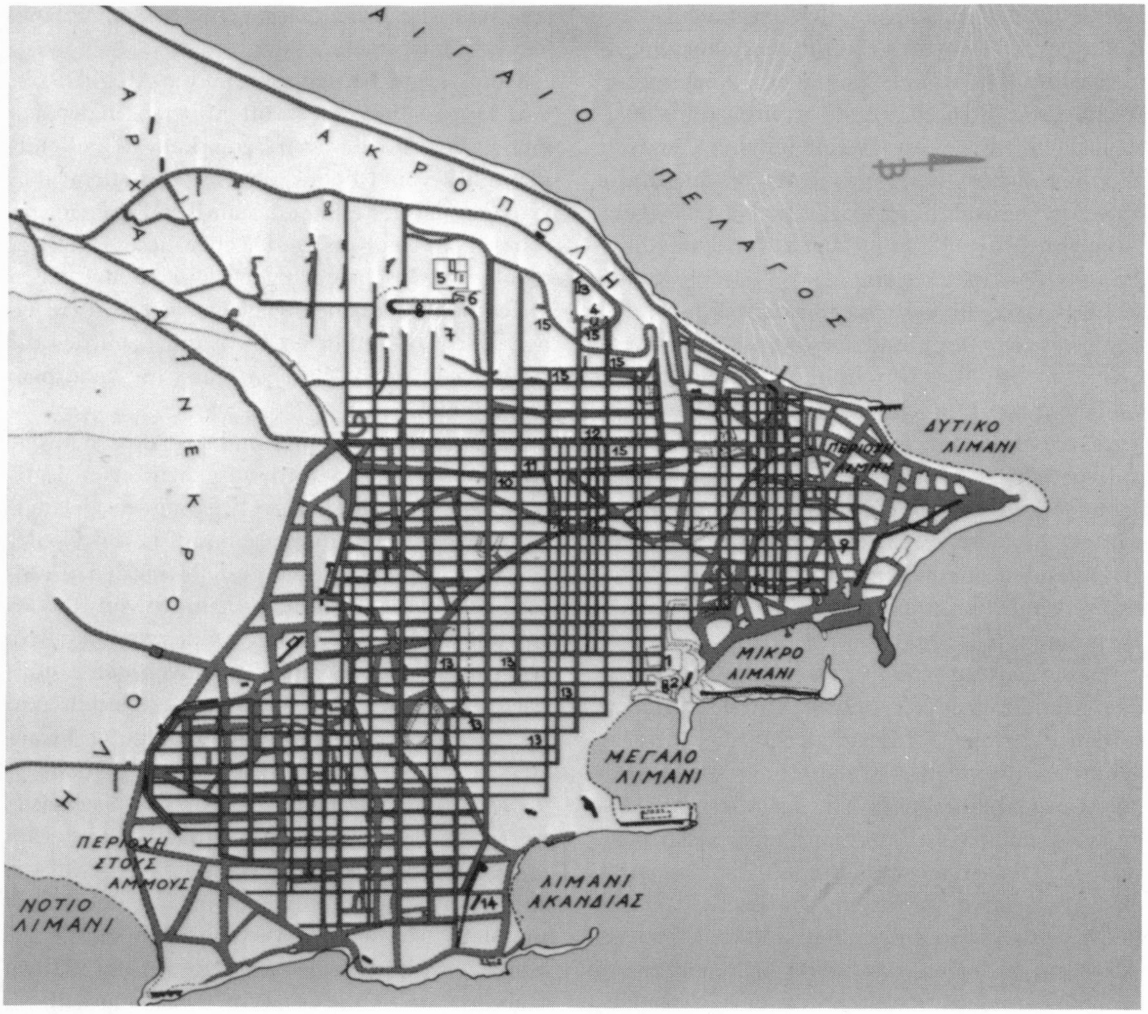

Fig. 7. Die antiken Strassen in Verhältnis zu den heutigen strassen der Stadt Rhodos.

und viele schwer zu deutende Funde[40]. Ich möchte betonen, dass viele dieser Ausgrabungen auch heute noch unter grossen Druck der Grundstückseigentümer durchgeführt werden müssen, die es eilig haben mit dem Bauen zu beginnen. Aus diesen Gründen war es uns nicht möglich, viele Areale erschöpfend zu erfassen. Trotzdem erstellten wir aber 1958 eine erste Zusammenfassung des Strassenplans von Kondis und veröffentlichten sie 1970[41] (Fig. 7).

In diesen Plan zeichneten wir alle bisher bekannten Strassen mit Länge und Breite ein, ebenso die Mauerabschnitte, die Türme und das Vorwerk und soviele Grabungsplätze wie möglich. Diesen Plan hätten wir nicht vervollständigen können ohne die grosszügige Hilfe unserer jüngst verstorbenen Freundin der Architektin Christa Grossnamm[42].

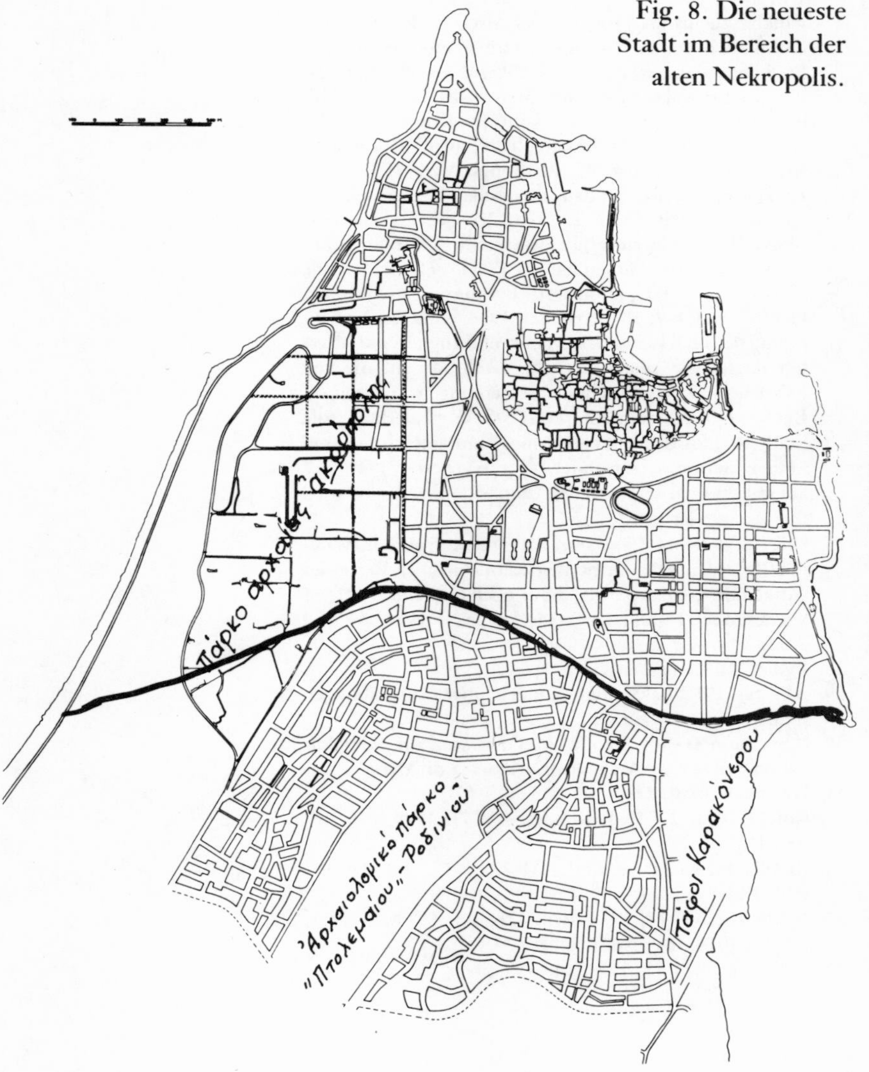

Fig. 8. Die neueste Stadt im Bereich der alten Nekropolis.

Als um 1970 der Bauboom im grossem Stil einsetzte, hatte sich die heutige Stadt bereits bis in das Gebiet der antiken Nekropole ausgedehnt (Fig. 8), so dass die genaue Untersuchung der Funde schwierig war, zumal es für dieses Gebiet keinen genauen Stadtplan gab[43]. Daher war es nötig, eine topographische Untersuchung durchzuführen, die die enorme Ausdehnung der Nekropole wiedergibt. In diesen Gebiet werden immer noch fast täglich einzelne Gräber aufgedeckt und erfasst, daneben aber auch Grabanlagen, die Strassen des antiken Friedhofs, Bezirke für den Totenkult und Grabheiligtümer. Was immer in Zukunft gefunden wird, nachdem in Übereinstimmung mit den geringen und fragmentarischen Quellen sich dort sowohl Erholungshaine[44] als auch Vorstädte[45] erfunden haben weiter in den Plänen eingetragen.

Ein vorläufiges Arbeitsergebnis haben wir für das Gebiet der antiken Akropolis, die von besonderem Interesse für das Leben in antiken Rhodos war und für ihre Gestaltung, die sie in hellenistischer, römischer und auch spätere Zeit erhielt[46]. Nach Quellenzeugnissen und den bis jetzt durchgeführten Ausgrabungen wissen wir, dass es hier grosse Heiligtümer, öffentliche Gebäude, Haine, Erholungsplätzte unterirdische Grotten[47] sowie grosse Statuengruppen[48] gegeben haben.

Die durch die Ausgrabungen gewonnenen Ergebnisse bestätigen die Quellen und bringen darüberhinaus neue, bisher unbekannte, ergänzende Angaben: z.B. die in der römischen Zeit dort errichteten grossen und prächtigen Stadtvillen[49].

Diese Arbeit ist natürlich von grossen Ausmass, aber die Begeisterung und der Eifer der jungen Archäologen, die in Rhodos arbeiten, lässt guten Erfolg erwarten.

Erlauben Sie mir, dass ich persönlich meine Hoffnung ausdrücke, dieses grosse Werk vollendet zu sehen.

Grigoris Konstantinopoulos
General Eforos I.R. der Altertümer
Serifou 3
Koliatsou
Athens 11254
Greece

1. J. Meursius hat in "Rhodus, Amstelodami 1675" alle griechischen und lateinischen Zeugnisse gesammelt. Das Buch erschien wieder unter dem Titel "Kreta-Cyprus-Rhodus" vielleicht in Florenz 1744?
2. (IΔ,652,5)
3. (XX,83,2)
4. (XIX,45,3)
5. XLIII. Rhodiacos 539-558. Für Datum des Erdbebens: Gelder 1900, 4, um 155 n. Chr.; L. Morricone, BdA 35, F IV, 1950, 56, um 142 n.Chr.; Papachatzis 1980, 374,3 um 153 n.Chr.
6. (IΔ,654,9)
7. I. Szidat, Bjb 18, 1980, 31.
8. C.F. Hermann, Disputatio de Hippodamo Milesio ad Aristotelis Politica, im Programm zum 20. August 1841, Marburg, 53. Durch den über Rhodos mit wenigen Worten eingefügten Text hat Hermann versucht nur zwei Punkte von der Rede des Aelios Aristeides hervorzuheben: a) Die Einheit der Stadtelementen von Rhodos, was gut zu dem klassischen, vielleicht auch dem ihm gleichzeitigen klassizistischen Geist passte. Darüber hat Kondis auch einige Ansichten in Kondis 1954, 4. und im Karousos 1973, 120 geschrieben. b) Die theaterförmige Gestalt der Stadt Rhodos, die Hermann mit der von Vitruv als "Theatri curvaturae similis" beschriebener Stadtform von Halikarnass verglichen hat. Das Vergleichen dieser beiden Städten hat der Forschung bis etwa 1950 Verwirrung gebracht, wie wir weiter sehen werden.
9. Das epigraphische Material ist auch bis heute noch spärlich und ohne besondere Bedeutung für die Stadtplanerische Forschung.
10. Ross 1840-52 und Ross 1861.
11. Guerin 1880.
12. Berg 1862, 67-68.
13. Newton 1865. Bemerkenswert ist die Beschreibung der Stadtanlage in S. 138: "The scenery round the town has a particular beauty. The land is formed in a succession of natural terraces down to the sea."
14. Die selbe Karte hat Biliotti 1881 publiziert. Ausserdem beschreibt er S. 22 und 23 einiges über die fünf Häfen der alten Stadt, was Kondis nicht bis zum seinem letzten Bericht (Karousos 1973, 119) beachtet hat. Inzwischen sind diese fünf Häfen bei den Ausgrabungen gefunden worden, und auf die Karte (Fig. 7) eingetragen.
15. M. Erdmann, Philologus 42, 1883, 193-227. Über Rhodos S. 219-227. 1900 hat Gelder 1900, 6-9 nach den Litterarischen Quellen, dem Text von Erdmann und anderen Gelehrten sehr interessante Beschreibung der Stadtform, Strassen, Häfen, Heiligtümer gemacht. Einiges davon stimmt noch heute.
16. Berg 1862, 22. Text S. 67.
17. M. Erdmann, Philologus 42, 1883, 224.
18. Newton 1865, 166; M. Erdmann, Philologus 42, 1883, 223. Es handelt sich um das westliche Ende der heutigen Odos Pindu, wo Kondis (Prakt 1951, 238) Ausgrabungen durchführte. Obwohl aber Kondis 1954, 13 richtig diese Strasse als rest einer parallelen und südlich von der Ritterstrasse liegenden feststellte, hat er die irrige Annahme von Erdmann nicht betont zurückzuwiesen. Über Kondis 1954, s. unten Anm. 32.
19. Newton 1865, 169; M. Erdmann, Philologus 42, 1883, 224.
20. M. Erdmann, Philologus 42, 1883, 224.
21. M. Erdmann, Philologus 42, 1883, 224.
22. I.G.XII,I.Hiller von Gaertringen hat später (RE Suppl. V (1931), 763-765, s.v. Rhodos) einiges über Stelle, Form, Strassen, Häfen und Akropolis geschrieben aber nichts über Mauerring. S.u. Anm. 26.
23. Kromayer – Weith 1928; S.J. Kondis, ADelt 18, 1963, 76-94.
24. Ich nehme an, dass Schramm nie auf Rhodos gewesen war.
25. Hier Anm. 8.
26. 1913 hat sich Fabricius, (RE I 8 2 (1913), 1732 s.v. Hippodamos) zum ersten Mal, nach Erdmann, mit dem Problem beschäftigt.
Lavedan 1924, 124, diskutiert nur, ob doch Hippodamos Gründer von Rhodos sein könnte; Gerkan 1924, 42; Cultrera 1924, 9, II besonders 13 und 20. "Il piano di Rodi, come poi quello di Alicarnasso, doveva necessariamente accostarsi allo schema semicircorlare con le vie piu o meno approssimativamente a reggiera, e non gia a quello ad angoli retti"; F. Tritsch, Klio 23 (N.F. IV), 1928 schreibt gar nichts über Rhodos und ganz wenig über hippodamisches System; Fabricius, RE III A2, 1929, p. 1992, 10 s.v. Städtebau (der Griechen) regelte zum ersten Mal nach 90 Jahren die von Hermann gemachte Verwirrung der Kreisförmigen Gestalt von Halikarnass und Rhodos, und formulierte Sp. 1993,60 seine Gedanken nach der Rede von Aristeides so:"Die ..... Stadt Rhodos dehnt sich hinter dem Haupthafen nach Westen sanft ansteigend aus, und die Strassen laufen keineswegs strählenförmig, sondern grösstenteils rechtwinklig zueinander von Norden nach Süden und von Osten nach Westen". – In unserem Symposion hat Dr. Poul Pedersen, gezeigt, dass Halikarnass auch Hippodamischer Stadtplannung war (unten 98-103) Obwohl Hiller von Gaertringen die von Maiuri publizierte Karte der alten Stadt Rhodos vor Augen hatte, alle Theorien und alle Texte kannte, hat sich RE Suppl. V, 1931, 764 s.v. Rhodos nicht ernst mit dem rhodischen Urbanismus beschäftigt S. hier Anm. 22. 1932 hat Al. Gabriel eine Skizze der Stadtmauer mit grösserem Stadtraum, fünf Häfen und eine Tür im Süden BCH 1932, 351, ohne Notizen im Text, publiziert; Erläuterungen darüber, Gelder 1900, 6-9, 387. Krischen 1938, ohne Berücksichtigung der inzwischen von Maiuri und Inglieri publizierten Karte, vor allem aber ohne Achtung auf die von Fabricius 1929 gemachten Bemerkungen, in seinem Buch "Die Griechische Polis" S.V. widerholt, die Stadt Rhodos durch Synoikismos "um einen grösserem Hafen herum.. gegründet sei; Wycherly 1949, 17 kommt zu dem schluss, "We cannot doubt that he used the rectangular plan".
27. ClRh 1, 1928, 44-45. Maiuri hatte schon früher in Maiuri 1918, 43 interessanten Bemerkungen über Reste der antiken Strassen gemacht, die er noch in Maiuri 1921, 35 wiederholte. Darauf hat auch Karousos 1949, 64 und 1973, 56 bezogen.
28. Inglieri 1936, 13-21.
29. Alle bis 1952 bekannten Notizen über Ausgrabungen und Wiederaufarbeiten, J. Kondis, Prakt 1952, 547-553.
30. Konstantinopoulos 1986, 244. Wir warten auf die Publikation der Scuola Archeologica Italiana di Atene.
31. Dinsmoor 1950, 214.
32. Kondis 1954, Taf II; J. Kondis, AM 73, 1958, 146-158, Taf. IV.
33. Kondis 1954, Taf. II und AM 73, 1958, Taf. IV P5, P12, P13.
34. J. Kondis, AM 73, 1958, Beil. 128, 2-3, 127 und 128,1.
35. Kondis 1954, hier Anm. 32.
36. J. Kondis, AM 73, 1958, 146-158.

37. Kirsten 1956, wusste noch nichts von der Forschung von Kondis; Castagnoli 1956 benutzt schon den Plan; S. weiter Martin 1956, 148; P.E. Wycherley, Historia 13, 1964, 135-139; J. Kondis, ADelt 18, 1963, Meletai s. 92; EAA 1963 s.v. Rodi, (Morricone); Kriesis 1965, 68,1; Giuliano 1966, 92-93; Schneider 1967, 387; Coppa 1968, 1093-1094; G. Konstantinopoulos, Archaeology 21, 1968, 116 mit Plan; Castagnoli 1971, 14-17; J. R. McCredy, in Studies Presented to George M.A. Hanfmann, 1971, 95-100; A.Burns, Historia 25, 1976, 414-428; J. Szidat, BjB 18, 1980, 31; Falciai 1982, 47-52; Greco – Torelli 1983, 283-285; Charl. Triebel-Schubert, Hephaistos, 5/6, 1983/84, 37-50. U. Muss, Politische Aspekte des hippodamischen Städtebaus, a.a.O.S. 50-59.

38. J. Bradford, AntJ 36, 1956, 57; Bradford 1957, 277-286. Meine Bemerkungen in AAA 3, 1970, 52-3.

39. Gr. Konstantinopoulos, AEphem 1967, 115-128.

40. Berichte der Ausgrabungen: ADelt 16, 1960, 237; ADelt 17, 1961-62, 301; ADelt 18, 1963, 322; ADelt 19, 1964, 462; ADelt 20, 1965, 577; ADelt 21, 1966, 436; ADelt 22, 1967, 541; ADelt 23, 1968, 432; ADelt 24, 1969, 451; ADelt 25, 1970, 500; Ergon 1960, 196; Ergon 1961, 216; Prakt 1960, 273; Prakt 1961, 215.

41. AAA 3, 1970, 52-55. Hier muss ich die von Kondis in Chr. Karousos 1973, 118 gemachte harte Kritik zu meinem Plan erwähnen. Denn Kondis konnte nicht von seinem theoretischen und abstrakten Achsenplan aus, wo er alle seinen Gedanken über hippodamisches System konzentriert hatte, meinen konkreten Plan akzeptieren. - 1979 habe ich unter anderen diesen Plan bei einem Referat im Louvre in Paris gezeigt, und 1983 in Neapel bei dem Kongress "Archeologia Urbana e centro antico di Napoli" vorgelegt. Dieses Referat wurde in Napoli in "Atti del Convegno 1983", 83-85 publiziert.

42. Bis jetzt weiss ich nur, dass die Dänischen Kollegen Dietz - Trolle 1974 die Karte benützt haben und Haugsted 1978 fast die selbe Karte publiziert hat. Sprachlich sind mir beide Bücher unzugänglich.

43. Fraser 1977, hat eine Skizze des Gebiets beigefügt.

44. H. Lauter, AntK 15, 1972, 49. Ab 4. In diesem Gebiet muss das von Etymol. Mag. Ἠλύσιον: Λέγεται δέ ἠλύσιον, καὶ ιερὸν πεδὶον περί Ρόδον, sein. Maiuri 1918, 43.

45. Hier müssen wir die προάστεια suchen: Appianus XII, IV, 24. Plutarch, Demetrios 22,2.

46. Für die neueren Forschungen, Gr. Konstantinopoulos, Prakt 1973, 127-136. Allgemeines über Akropolis, Konstantinopoulos 1986, 217.

47. Konstantinopoulos 1986, 124. Gr. Konstantinopoulos, Archaeology 21, 1968, 118 und Fig. 119.

48. Konstantinopoulos 1986, 112. Es handelt sich um das Original der Torro Farnese von Neapel, das meines Erachtens im Altertum irgendwo auf der Akropolis gestanden haben müsste.

49. Am Ostabhang des Akropolishügels haben wir bei den Ausgrabungen Ruinen von späthellenistischen, römischen und frühchristlichen Gebäuden gefunden.

Der Stadtplan von Rhodos

Wolfram Hoepfner

Ioannis Kondis und Gregoris Konstantinopoulos haben das grösste Verdienst daran, dass der antike Stadtplan von Rhodos in fast allen Einzelheiten wiedergewonnen werden kann[1]. Alle Archäologen des Antikendienstes, heute unter der Leitung von Ioannis Papachristodoulou, unter ihnen Melina Tsopotou-Filemonas, Thasia Dreliosi-Iraklidou, Maria Michalaki-Kollia, Vasso Patsiada, Angeliki Iannikouri-Pavlidi, Philippos Kostomitsopoulos, Toula Kostomitsopoulou-Marketou, Haris Kantzia und als Zeichner Sotiris Diakogeorgiou haben im Gebiet der alten Stadt mehr als 2000 Ausgrabungen durchgeführt, die in einem Plan im Massstab 1:5000 festgehalten sind. Melina Tsopotou-Filemonos hat auf Anregung von Konstantinopoulos eine Zusammenstellung aller archäologisch erschlossenen antiken Strassen begonnen. In 30-jähriger archäologischer Arbeit, die in dieser Systematik nicht ihresgleichen hat, konnten mehr als 70 Strassen nachgewiesen werden. Schwierig war diese Arbeit allein besonders deswegen, weil in erster Linie die Erfassung der klassischen Phase das Ziel war, diese aber durch Störungen und Überbauungen in römischer, byzantinischer oder mittelalterlicher Zeit gestört ist.

Der Stadtplan von Rhodos ist nach Auffassung von Konstantinopoulos schon 411 v.Chr. mit dem Beschluss zur Gründung der Stadt entstanden. Strabon (14,654) verbindet dieses Werk mit dem Erbauer des Piräus, fügt aber vorsichtig ein "wie es scheint" hinzu. Wenn auch aus chronologischen Gründen Hippodamos selbst für den Entwurf von Rhodos kaum in Frage kommt, so haben wir doch allen Grund, dieses Werk dem engsten Umkreis von Hippodamos, seinen Nachfolger oder seiner Schule zuzuschreiben. Soweit heute Vergleiche mit dem Piräus möglich sind, ergibt sich eine deutliche Übereinstimmung: Sie bezieht sich auf die alternierenden Strassenbreiten und auf die ungewöhnliche Kleinheit der Baublöcke oder Insulae.

Den bisherigen Unterlagen ist zu entnehmen, dass in Rhodos in Nord-Süd-Richtung die Strassen ganz besonders dicht aufeinander folgen (Fig. 1). Beträgt hier der Abstand 25 bis 26 m, so liegt er in Ost-West-Richtung mit ca. 48 m deutlich darüber. Das genaue Durchschnittsmass aller im Plan gemessenen Insulae liegt bei 25,50 m und 48,70 m. Wir dürfen also davon ausgehen, dass in Rhodos eine pythagoräische Stadtanlage mit einer proportionierten Einheitsinsula gegeben war, deren Seitenverhältnis 5:9 betrug. Ausgedrückt in ionischen Fuss von 29,4 cm, der Masseinheit, die dem städtebaulichen Entwurt zugrunde lag, beträgt die Breite 162 Fuss und die Tiefe 90 Fuss. Diese Insulae waren vermutlich im Normalfall in drei Parzellen aufgeteilt. Leider ist über die Häuser in der Frühphase der Stadt noch fast nichts bekannt.

Im Verhältnis zu anderen Poleis waren die Strassen in Rhodos unverhältnismässig breit. Gemessen wurden Werte zwischen 4,80 m und 20 m, Weitaus am häufigsten sind Strassenbreiten von 5,80 m und 6,30 m. Diese Wohnstrassen (die so breit sind wie die Hauptstrasse der Stadt Kassope) wurden in Ost-West-Richtung im Rhytmus 1:4 von einer doppelt so breiten Strasse unterbrochen. In Nord-Süd-Richtung ist jede neunte Strasse breiter, so dass sich Nachbarschaften oder Quartiere mit 4x9 = 36 Insulae oder etwa 1000 Häusern ergeben.

Drei besonders grosse Strassen führten auffallenderweise nicht durch das Zentrum der Stadt, sondern liegen in der Peripherie (Fig. 1). Die P 27 erschloss das Gebiet der Akropolis, die P 35 verband die beiden Häfen im Osten miteinander und die P 6 stellt eine Verbindung zwischen Westhafen und Kriegshafen dar. Diese Form von Dezentralisierung ermöglichte eine Umgehung des Zentrums und kann charakteristisch für Metropolen oder besonders grosse Städte gewesen sein. Rhodos hat jedenfalls von allen uns bekannten antiken Städten das dichteste Strassennetz überhaupt und eine auffällig grosse Strassenfläche im Vergleich mit den zu bebauenden Grundstücken. Das kann nur mit dem besonderen Charakter der Stadt als Handelsmetropole zusammenhängen. Hier kam es darauf an, ohne Umwege Waren von einer Ecke der Stadt in die andere zu schaffen.

Auch in ihren Inhalten muss sich eine Handelsstadt von den üblichen Bauern- und Bürgerstädten unterschieden haben. So dürfen wir vermuten, dass nicht der bäuerliche Haushalt mit Vorräten von landwirtschaftlichen Erzeugnissen vorherrschend war, sondern Häuser von Händlern, und vor allem mögen Warenhäuser und Warenlager das Bild der Stadt bestimmt haben. Bei Ausgrabungen im Norden von Rhodos unter der heutigen Touristenstadt sind vielfach Reste grosser Gebäude angetroffen worden. Ein Handelsmarkt, der in den kleineren Poleis oft neben der politischen Agora liegt, muss in Rhodos grosse Dimensionen gehabt haben, ja mag vielleicht sogar grösser als die politische Agora, das eigentliche Bürgerzentrum gewesen sein. Dem Gitternetz der Stadt entsprechend haben diese Platzanlagen rechteckige Form gehabt. Die berühmte "hippodamische Agora" im Piräus weist darauf hin, dass diesen Elementen beim Entwurf der Stadt grosse Aufmerksamkeit geschenkt wurde.

Bei der Einteilung der Stadt in regelmässige Quartiere ergeben sich Unregelmässigkeiten im Norden und Süden an den Stadträndern (Fig. 1) und eine deutliche Abweichung von der Regel stellt der grosse Strasse P 14 in der Stadtmitte dar, die eigentlich eine kleine Wohnstrasse sein müsste. Durch die beiden sehr breiten Strassen P 14 und P 15 wird in der Stadtmitte ein Geländestreifen von etwa 100 m Tiefe besonders hervorgehoben. Die Vermutung liegt nahe, dass dieser Geländestreifen für öffentliche Bauten reserviert war, dass sich hier die grossen Heiligtümer befanden und auch die Agora ihren Platz hatte. Es mag auch nicht zufällig gewesen sein, dass die Ritter bei der Anlage ihrer Stadt im 13.Jh.n.Chr. nicht den leicht zu verteidigenden Nordzipfel der Insel wählten, wo ihnen zwei Häfen zur Verfügung standen, sondern ein kreisförmiges Gelände um den grossen Hafen aussparten, in den das Gebiet eingezogen war, in dem wir die Agora der antiken Stadt vermuten. Diese lag auf einer ebenen Fläche und wurden von grossen antiken Strassen begrenzt, darunter von der P 15, auf der später die Ritter ihre Südmauer errichteten. Während in der klassischen Antike der Gedanke an monumentale Achsen und Strassenzüge fern lag, wurde in der römischen Kaiserzeit das Strassenbild in diesem Sinn verändert, indem die Strasse P 31 in eine monumentale Hallenstrasse umgebaut wurde, die ihren Anfang mit einem grossen Propylon am Hafen nahm, und in die Mitte der Agora einmündete.

In der Nähe der heutigen Pythagoras-Strasse hatte Kondis Teile einer grossen byzantinischen Mauer ausgegraben, in der Spolien eines bedeutenden klassischen dorischen Tempels verbaut sind. Diese zahlreichen Bauglieder stammen zweifellos nicht von der Akropolis, sondern von einem Gebäude, einem Tempel, der auf einem 20 m hohen Hügel dicht bei der Ausgrabung seinen Platz hatte. Dieses Heiligtum lag innerhalb des durch die P 14 und P 15 begrenzten Geländestreifens und ist dem Gebiet benachbart, das wir mit Vorsicht als Agora bezeichnen. Nach der Situation in anderen Städten kann es sich auch hier in Rhodos um den Haupttempel der Stadt, mithin um den Tempel des Helios, gehandelt haben.

Die topographischen Forschungen in Rhodos gehen weiter und die nächste Aufgabe wird es sein, mit gezielten Ausgrabungen weitere Aufschlüsse über die Struktur der antiken Stadt zu gewinnen.

Wolfram Hoepfner
Deutsches Archäologisches Institut
Podbielskiallee 69
Postfach 33 00 14
1000 Berlin 33

1. Vgl. auch Hoepfner – Schwandner 1986, 21 ff. das Kapitel über Rhodos, das zusammen mit G. Konstantinopoulos verfasst wurde.

Town-planning in Halicarnassus and Rhodes

Poul Pedersen

Only a few miles east of the Dodecanese islands is the coast of Caria. In the northern part of the area the Halicarnassus peninsula protrudes so far westwards that, from the island of Cos, one can actually distinguish the white houses of Halicarnassus on a clear day. It is no wonder that there were cultural interconnections between Halicarnassus and the cities of the Dodecanese, many of which had, furthermore, a Doric origin in common.

Nevertheless it has been the general opinion that, as far as town-planning is concerned, Halicarnassus differed very much from other contemporary cities in the area; for instance the city of Rhodes.

It is a generally accepted fact, based on literary evidence, that Mausolos – the Persian governor of Caria – made Halicarnassus his new capital and for that purpose carried out a synoikism of many of the smaller towns of the Halicarnassus peninsula to provide a large population for his new capital. As a part of this synoikism he completely refounded the town on a new and more monumental scale, suited for its future role as the capital of an important state.

This happened in the 370's or 360's B.C. – that is about the same time as the city of Cos was founded with an orthogonal plan, and about 30 or 40 years after the synoikism on Rhodes, when the city of Rhodes was given its famous Hippodamian plan.

For many years the lay-out of Halicarnassus, and town-planning in Hecatomnid Caria in general, has been assigned a very special and important role in the history of ancient Greek town-planning. It has been imagined that Halicarnassus had a very original non-Hippodamian plan.

For instance Simon Hornblower, in his new and very detailed study of "Mausolos", writes about Halicarnassus: "Certainly, there is nothing "Hippodamian" about it..."[1]. Hornblower does admit, though, that there are two features recalling the lay-out of Hippodamos' work on Rhodes. These are: "the stepped arrangement required by the theatri curvatura" – (both cities are described by ancient writers as theatre-like in their form) - and secondly "the integration of certain great monumental buildings into a plan embracing a large area of the city". In several other respects Hornblower finds the Halicarnassian synoikism comparable to that of Rhodes, and he suggests that Mausolos actually did copy aspects of the Rhodian synoikism[2]. But certainly not, he thinks, in the actual lay-out of the town.

This idea of a very special kind of planning in Hecatomnid Caria can probably be traced back to the important book of Roland Martin on "L'Urbanisme dans la Grèce Antique", and since its first edition in 1956 the theory has been repeated by many archaeologists, as, for instance, Ward-Perkins, Boëthius and Burkhardt Wesenberg[3].

In this book Roland Martin compares the plan of Rhodes with that of Halicarnassus and he concludes that the two cities represent two completely different trends in Greek town-planning. Rhodes represents the very strict Hippodamian system, which forces a regular orthogonal grid onto the site of a town, without regard to the natural configuration of the place. The most consistent, and Martin comes close to saying "worst" example of this type of plan is probably Priene, where the streets have become staircases[4].

Conversely Martin finds that Halicarnassus adapts itself, in a very sophisticated way, to the natural configuration of the site. The hills and slopes are used with great advantage for better presentation of monumental structures like the Mausoleum and the temples. Martin finds Halicarnassus and Carian planning in the late Classical period a very direct precursor of the

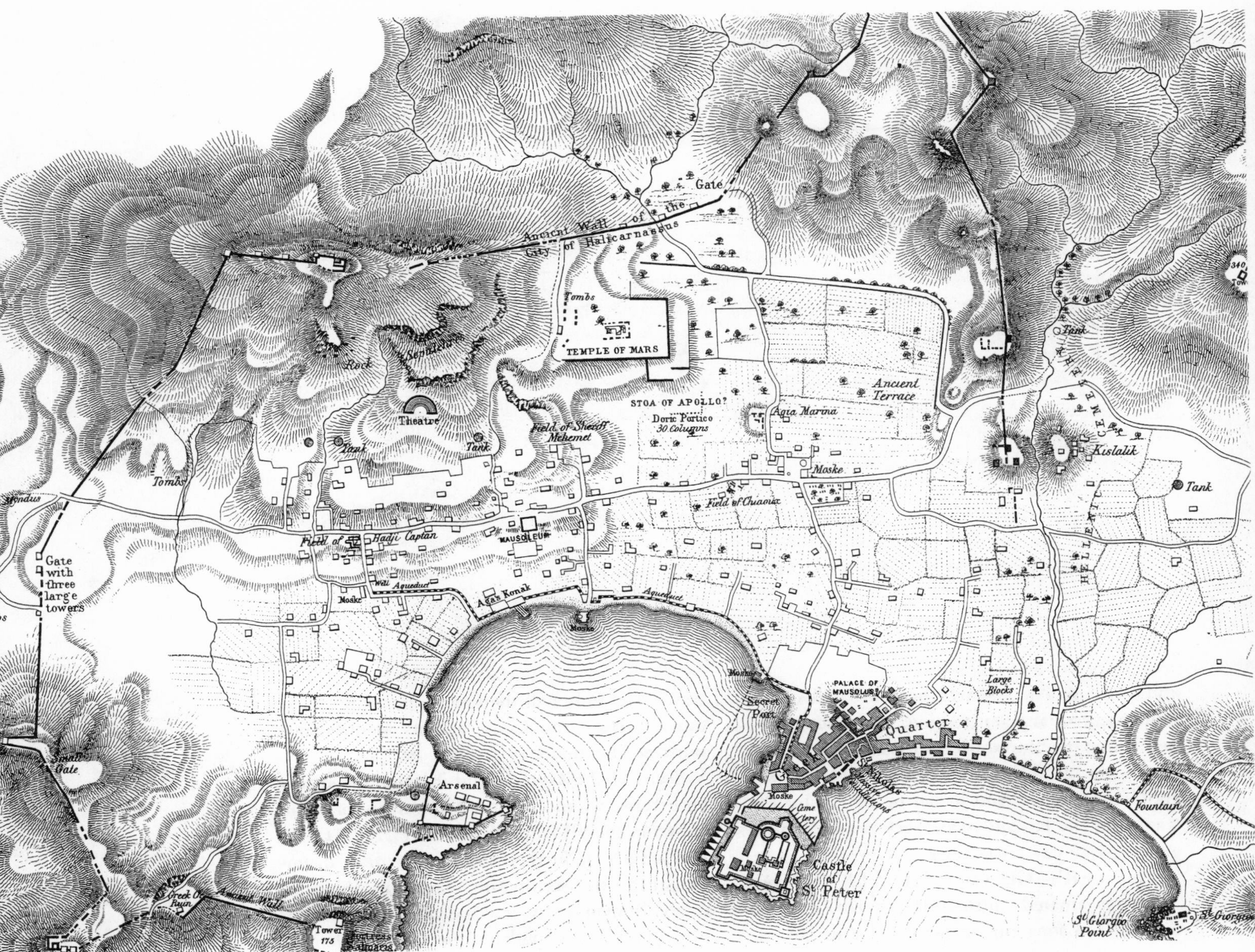

Fig. 1.

monumental urbanism of Hellenistic Pergamon. – Actually he does not explicitly say that the town-plan of Halicarnassus was *not* orthogonal, though this is the general idea that one gets.

Perhaps it would be wise to have a closer look at the actual remains found in Halicarnassus, as they have so far only played a minor role in the discussion.

Almost all of the ancient remains that I know of can be seen on Charles Newton's plan of Halicarnassus dating from the 1850's (fig. 1). These are: The MAUSOLEUM, the TERRACE OF MARS, the TERRACE OF HAGIA MARINA, the STOA OF THE THIRTY COLUMNS. The Sanctuary of Demeter and a Roman Villa are no longer visible. It must be admitted that these remains do not seem to be laid out according to an orthogonal plan, when one looks at Newton's plan. But let us take another look at the ruins:

Since the time of Newton knowledge concerning the MAUSOLEUM has greatly increased,

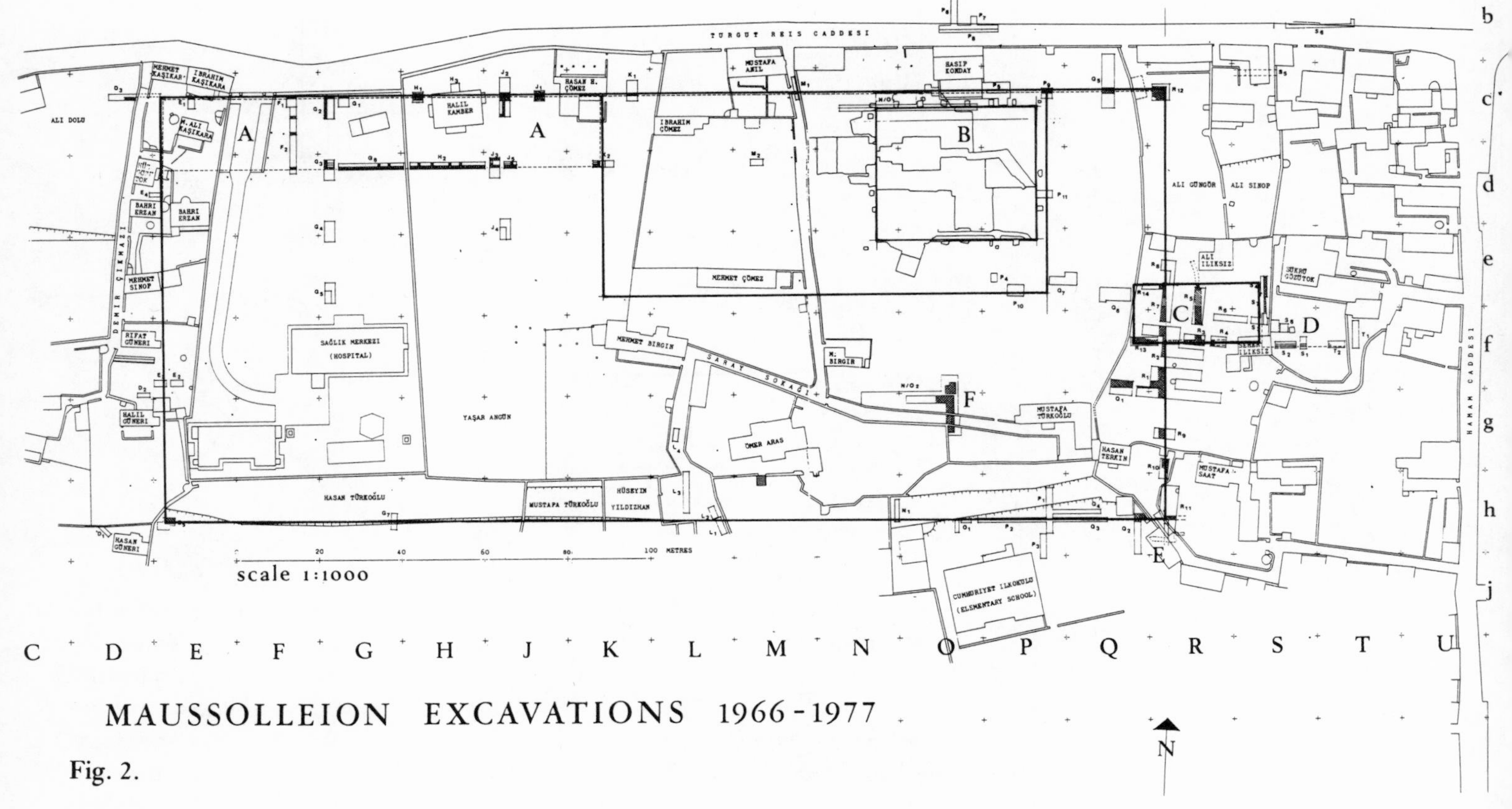

Fig. 2.

and we know now that it was situated on an immense, rectangular terrace, that must have dominated the central part of the city close to the Agora (fig. 2). The terrace is about 242 m long and 105 m wide. And it can be noted, by the way, that the lay-out is in every respect orthogonal.

The TERRACE OF THE TEMPLE OF MARS is situated a little further north. It is less than 100 m long but its width is also 105 m, exactly like the terrace of the Mausoleum, which is quite interesting. Of the temple itself only minor fragments can be seen lying around, but they would no doubt be worth studying.

The TERRACE AT TÜRKUYUSU or HAGIA MARINA, as this place was called by Newton, is much smaller. Many inscriptions on matters concerning a GYMNASION were found here by Newton, and by Bean and Cook[5]. It has therefore been supposed to be the site of the GYMNASION of Halicarnassus, but this has rightly been doubted by Delorme in his book on Greek Gymnasia, because he found the terrace too small[6]. To-day it can be seen from a recently exposed terrace wall that the terrace was in fact only half the size supposed by Newton and Bean and Cook, and its identification must be abandoned, I think.

Some of the Gymnasium inscriptions appear on certain column drums, presumably originating from the STOA OF THE THIRTY COLUMNS a little further west, where more drums are still to be seen in situ. Therefore this – no doubt Roman – stoa may be considered as part of a gymnasium, perhaps the early Hellenistic PHILIPPEION well known from inscriptions.

In the 18th and 19th centuries the state of preservation was far better, as can be seen on an engraving[7] and on a photo in the British Museum.

Apart from these few remains of larger structures and the recently excavated theatre, of course, I only know of a few very small remains of ancient walls in present-day Bodrum.

If all these remains are transferred to a map (fig. 3), the result is a picture very different from the map given by Newton. In particular it is evident that all remains are orientated in precisely the same direction. In this system NORTH is approximately 4 degrees west of the true north.

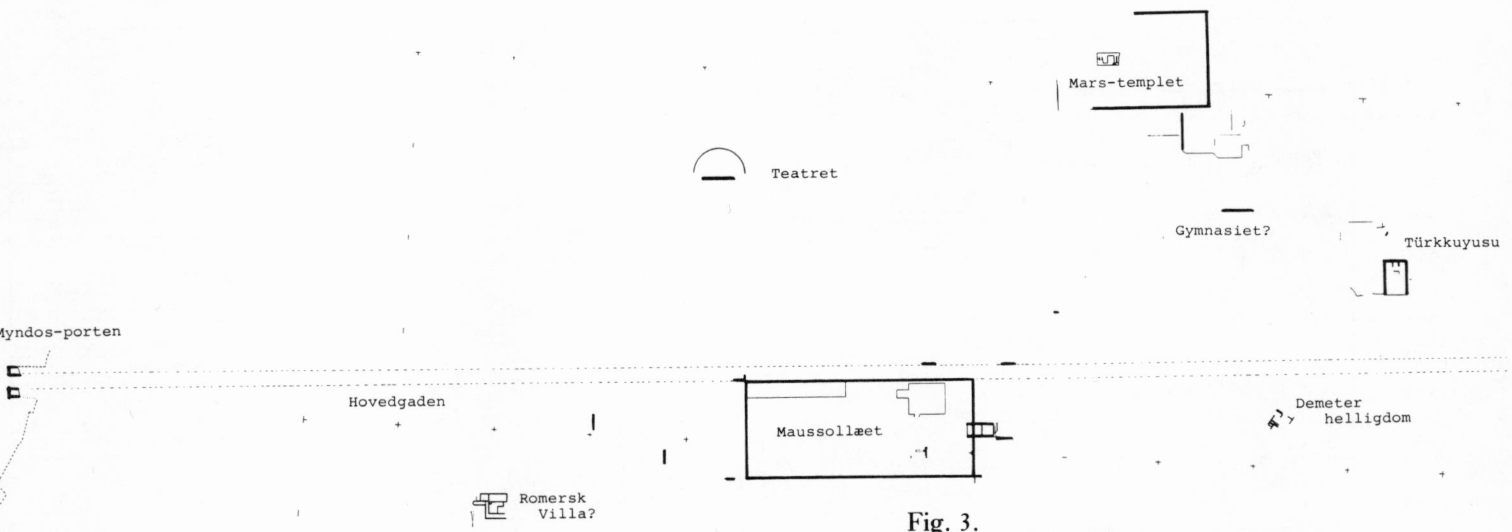

Fig. 3.

From this, I think, we can draw the important conclusion that the ancient town-plan of Halicarnassus was beyond doubt laid out on an orthogonal grid-system, and, as two great structures from the time of Mausolos are integrated in this system, the plan must date from the time of Mausolos.

The grid-system and town-plan of Rhodes, as reconstructed by Konstantinopoulos and Hoepfner, are well based on a knowledge of more than 50 streets, I think. For Halicarnassus there is very much less, but nevertheless I have made an experiment on determining the grid-system, in co-operation with Professor Bjarner Svejgaard from the Institute of Datalogy at the University of Aarhus (figs. 4-5). Professor Svejgaard has developed a special computer program for treating my measurements of distances between ancient remains at Bodrum. The results of this work showed a regularity that could hardly be mere coincidence, and it would agree well with a grid-system of units about 36,4 m in width and 54,6 m in length. The proportions of the grid-unit are therefore 2 to 3.

Interestingly the grid shows many cases of coincidence with modern streets. This I find

Fig. 4. Halikarnassos. Roads and lanes in the modern town.

Fig. 5. Halikarnassos. Hypothetical grid-system.

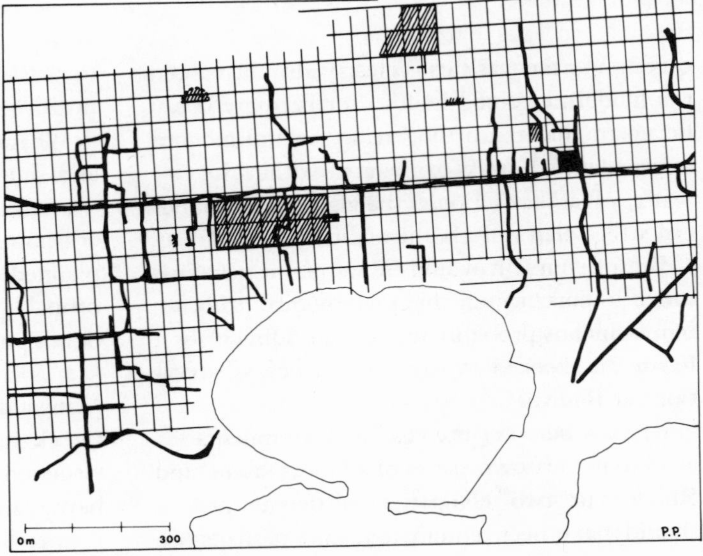

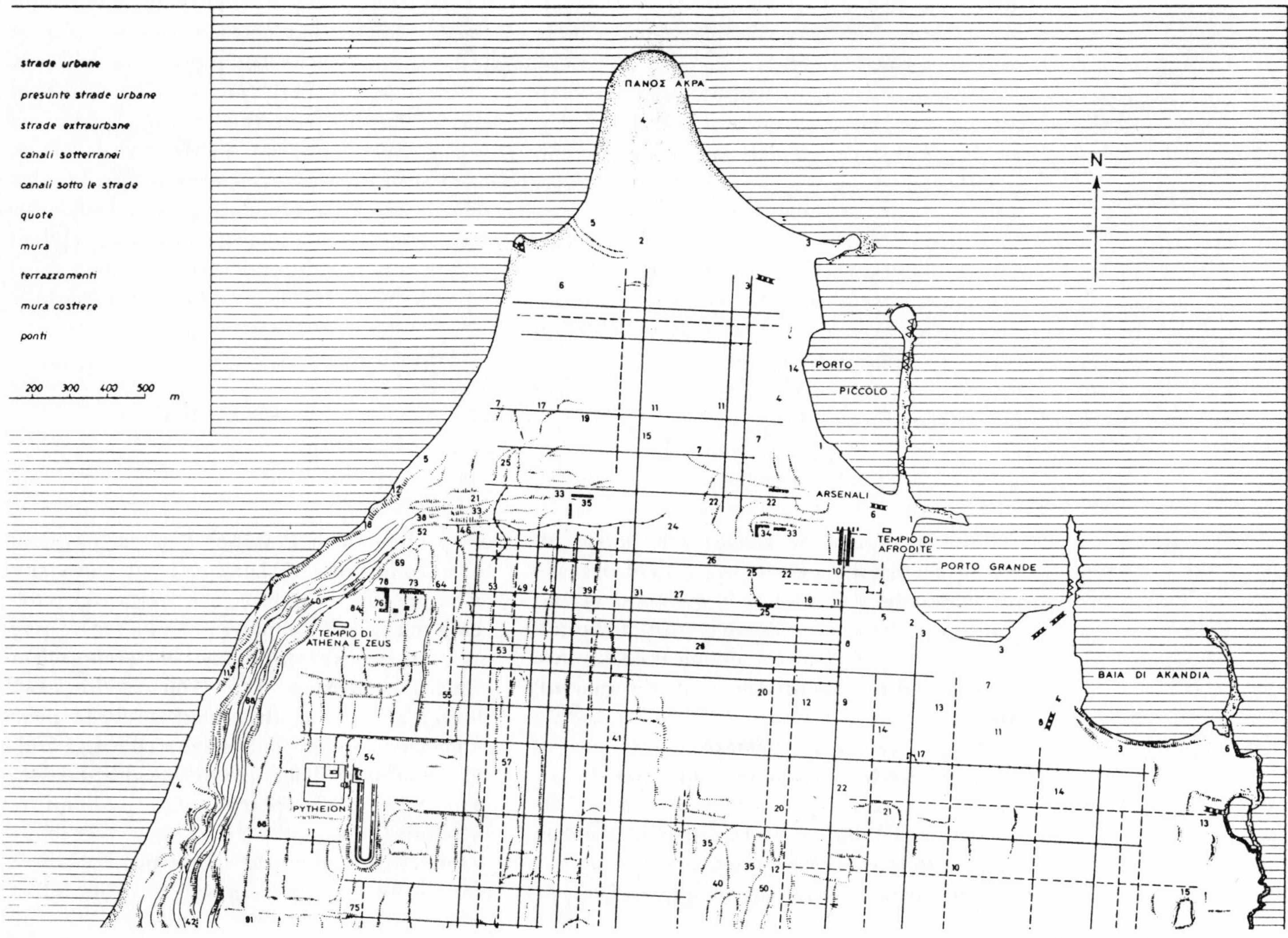

Fig. 6.

quite important, as this is clearly also the case in the modern city of Rhodes. Furthermore it can be noted that the orthogonality in the modern street-plan is limited to the area within the city walls, a fact that supports the view that the modern street-plan reflects the ancient.

But of course it would be wrong to place too much importance on this hypothetical grid-system, which is probably too regular. Obviously it has to be checked and refined by new observations at Bodrum.

By now some of the strongest arguments for assigning the town-plans of Halicarnassus and Rhodes to two completely different groups should have been eliminated, and perhaps we may look at the remaining evidence in a more positive way.

What city would be better suited than Rhodes as a source of inspiration for Mausolos when he was about to refound Halicarnassus on a modern, monumental scale (fig. 6)? Whether actually planned by Hippodamos or not, Rhodes was probably in many respects a culmination of the development in orthogonal planning that had taken place during the fifth century: and Mausolos, no doubt, wanted to keep up with Greek standards. By the 370's or 60's the construction of the city of Rhodes would surely have reached such a stage that its urbanistic qualities could easily be appreciated. On the other hand, the city of Cos, though closer at hand, would either have been still unfounded or in its very first stages.

As to the configuration of the two sites, both Rhodes and Halicarnassus are situated on a generally gentle slope, which becomes quite steep in some parts of the towns. The application of a Hippodamian orthogonal town-plan on such sites necessitates an extensive use of terracing, which is a characteristic feature in both places. Therefore it is probably not without significance that both towns are compared to a theatre in shape by ancient authors – though this is, of course, a rather vague term, used about other towns as well.

Turning to the detailed facts about the two cities we are really not in a position to make any comparisons. We know that the main street of Halicarnassus had the unusual width of 15 m and that one major street in Rhodes was about 16 m in width, but there are other parallels to this width, for instance in Alexandria and Peiraeus[8].

We think that the grid-unit in Halicarnassus had the same proportions, two to three, as in Rhodes, and almost the same dimensions: 34 to 50 m and 36 to 54 m, but these details are as yet very hypothetical as far as Halicarnassus is concerned.

Though we still know little about the town-plan of Halicarnassus, I think we can conclude that there is nothing in the actual remains of the city to prove that it differed from that of Rhodes. On the contrary, all evidence points towards a certain resemblance. In Halicarnassus the monumental terraces may have given the city an unusual character, but on the whole the plan of Halicarnassus has its logical place in the history of town-planning in this area in the late Classical period, together with Rhodes, Kos, Knidos and Priene. As terracing was a characteristic feature in most of these cities, it is quite possible that they inspired the town-planners of Hellenistic Pergamon, but in a general sort of way, and not in the way that Roland Martin had in mind when he wrote his book on Greek urbanism.

Poul Pedersen
Department of Classical Studies
Odense University
Campusvej 55
5230 Odense M
Denmark

This study of the plan of Halicarnassus is based on a survey carried out in 1978 by Susanne Høeg and myself. The survey was made possible by kind permission of the Department of Antiquities and Museums at Ankara. The Carlsberg and the Ny Carlsberg Foundations provided the necessary financial support.

In my communication "The Maussolleion-terrace at Halicarnassos and 4th cent. B.C. planning in south-western Asia Minor" given at the XII International Congress of Classical Archaeology, Athens 1983, some of the aspects discussed in this paper were also included.

1. Hornblower 1982, 300.
2. Hornblower 1982, 104.
3. Martin 1974, 147 f.; Ward-Perkins 1974, 19; Boëthius 1960, 40; B. Wesenberg, MarbWPr 1969, 1970, 37 f. and 40 f.
4. Martin 1974, 114.
5. Newton 1862, 319 ff. and pl. 48; G.E. Bean – J.M. Cook, BSA 50, 1955, 92 and 101.
6. J. Delorme, Gymnasium 1960, 126.
7. Choiseul-Gouffier 1882, pl. 99.
8. Gerkan 1924, 82.

La Stipe Votiva dell'Athenaion di Jalysos: Un Primo Bilancio

Marina Martelli

La Scuola Archeologica Italiana di Atene, grazie al nuovo impulso assunto con la dinamica direzione di Antonino Di Vita, intende saldare una serie di debiti scientifici contratti nei confronti dell'archeologia del Dodecanneso, portando a compimento quelle imprese che, precedenti il secondo conflitto mondiale, non hanno ancora trovato uno sbocco definitivo.

Fra queste si iscrive la pubblicazione integrale dei depositi votivi del santuario di Athena Ialysia, di cui mi è stato affidato il coordinamento: Eos Zervoudaki ha in corso di studio le terrecotte e i vasi plastici, l'egittologa statunitense Nancy Skon gli aegyptiaca; chi vi parla ha iniziato lo scorso anno, assieme a M.A. Rizzo, la schedatura e lo studio di tutto il materiale restante, numericamente ingente e ripartito in una vasta gamma di classi, dalla ceramica alle statuette in calcare, dai bronzi agli avori, dai sigilli in pietra dura ad una copiosissima serie di oggetti minori, dalle armi alle iscrizioni votive, etc.

Oltre 5.000 pezzi fanno parte di questa imponente stipe[1], che, per quantità e qualità, si preannuncia la più importante e ricca dell'isola, rispetto a quelle di Lindos e Kamiros, venendo al contempo ad occupare una posizione perspicua fra i complessi votivi del mondo greco.

Un primo problema da affrontare, sia pure in forma preliminare, riguarda l'ubicazione dei depositi, rinvenuti a più riprese in successive campagne di scavo condotte dal 1923 al 1926[2], campagne precedute da una ricognizione compiuta da Luigi Pernier nel febbraio 1913 e da saggi affettuati dalla Missione archeologica italiana a Rodi nell'anno stesso della sua istituzione, il 1914[3].

Dai giornali di scavo, assai sommarî e privi di adeguata documentazione grafica di supporto, risulta che l'area interessata dai rinvenimenti si trovava in una larga fascia situata a sud e a ovest del tempio ellenistico. Gli oggetti erano depositati, frammisti alla terra, in cavità naturali della roccia e i giacimenti più vicini alle fondazioni del tempio erano disturbati dai muri delle navate sinistra e centrale della prima basilica cristiana, oltre che da tombe di età bizantina e cavalleresca.

Nel 1923 vennero eseguiti saggi nel lato a sud del tempio, oltre la navata destra della basilica, mentre altri furono praticati in corrispondenza del lato occidentale dello stereobate, giungendo, al vergine, fino ad una profondità massima di m. 6,50. La situazione stratigrafica presentava strati di riempimento apparentemente intatti, che colmavano il fondo delle cavità rocciose, cui si sovrapponevano i detriti di lavorazione dei muri di fondazione dell'edificio templare. Negli strati intatti furono recuperati soprattutto materiali minuti, ora di difficile identificazione specifica, consistenti per lo più in fibule, spilloni e altri oggetti metallici, sigilli, scarabei, statuette e pendagli in faïence, vaghi di collana in pasta vitrea, ceramica di vario tipo.

Le esplorazioni del 1925 e del 1926, sempre stando ai giornali di scavo, non consentono di individuare con eguale certezza la situazione originaria dei giacimenti. Esse furono condotte più a valle del lato ovest del tempio, lungo il c.d. "muro arcaico", ancora visibile nelle fotografie dell'epoca: a quanto si può arguire, la concentrazione di oggetti di età orientalizzante e arcaica concerneva il settore meridionale, mentre quelli di età classica dovevano addensarsi nel settore settentrionale.

Alcune fotografie d'epoca riproducono il basamento del tempio, sgombrato dai muri della basilica che lo ricoprivano nella fronte sud, e il lato occidentale di esso prima e dopo i saggi condotti presso lo stereobate; una planimetria venne eseguita nel 1928 dall'arch. Fausto Franco.

Poichè il lavoro, almeno per quanto mi riguarda, è appena iniziato, in questa sede non posso

Fig. 1.

presentare che una campionatura dei materiali, per evidenziarne le principali categorie e per mettere in luce affinità e differenze rispetto alle altre stipi votive dell'isola.

La ceramica si dispone, nel suo nucleo più consistente, corrispondente alle fasi più antiche del deposito, fra la metà ca. dell'VIII e la fine del VI sec.a.C.

La più antica risale al geometrico rodio, in particolare al TG: accanto a forme comuni, quali lekythoi a corpo globulare di derivazione levantina, oinochoai (anche di piccole dimensioni), kotylai, altre ve ne sono assai più rare, come la mutila lekythos biansata 9748 (fig. 1), che, al pari di un puntuale omologo da una tomba camirese[4], coniuga i canonici partiti ornamentali ellenici del meandro tratteggiato, degli zig-zag, dei trattini sfalsati, etc., con la patente dipendenza morfologica da prototipi cipro-fenici in Black-on-Red, i quali del resto risultano importati a Jalysos, ad es. nella tomba 51[5].

Dei vari frammenti di kotylai, alcuni – come il 5233, a quattro metope, incluso il "Mäanderbaum", e il 5241, con meandro tratteggiato[6], di tipo ancora MG – sono specificamente attribuibili alla prima fase del Bird-kotyle Workshop[7], di cui vengono ad accreditare la supposta manifattura jalysia, mentre altri, pure riferibili al terzo quarto dell'VIII sec.a.C., non mancano di ampliare il repertorio di questa caratteristica classe di vasi potorî del Tardo Geometrico rodio, accostando agli ornati di rigore (losanghe a reticolato, sequenze di zig-zag, meandri a gancio, diaboloi alternati a trattini verticali, etc.) il capro o la schiera di uccelli dal corpo triangolare, in silhouette, dei nn. 5242 e 5244, questi ultimi replica di quelli di un esemplare dalla tomba, sempre jalysia, Marmaro 51[8].

D'altra parte, accanto a qualche importazione cipriota, come una lekythos Black-on-Red II (IV) con fascette orizzontali sul corpo (inv. 5188) ed una White Painted IV con cerchielli concentrici allineati verticalmente[9] (inv. 5187), cui fanno riscontro imitazioni dirette[10], un folto contingente è costituito dalle imitazioni locali di ceramica levantina e cipro-fenicia, che vengono ad incrementare le serie già individuate da Friis Johansen e Coldstream[11], contemplando una assortita gamma di flaconi per unguenti: si va infatti dall'aryballos e oinochoe conica con imboccatura androprosopa 6820 e 6821 – perfettamente allineati ad un gruppo locale, attestato in contesti tombali del terzo venticinquennio dell'VIII secolo, di ispirazione nord-siriana[12], per il quale significativi riscontri si colgono altresi' nella plastica rodia geometrica e la cui irradiazione investe anche la colonia di Gela[13] – alle brocchette con orlo a fungo esemplate sul Red Slip fenicio, come la 7176, che è replica di esemplari noti, dagli inizi ai decenni centrali del VII sec.a.C., in varie necropoli dell'isola e nel deposito di Lindos[14], e, ancora, ad una multiforme varietà di aryballoi a corpo globulare più o meno compresso o biconicheggiante, acromi ovvero con i filetti del "Kreis-und-Wellenband Stil" (come il 7155) oppure interamente verniciati in rosso o nero, del tipo che suole definirsi rodio-cretese e che, grazie anche alla documentazione riunita nella nostra stipe, andrà definitivamente assegnato a Rodi[15] (fig. 2).

Quanto poi a due aryballoi acromi di fine argilla color avorio, con collarino rilevato e minuscolo peduccio anulare (inv. 7153 e 7158: fig. 2, in basso a s.), di un tipo variamente designato come "orientale" o "levantino" o "nord-siriano"[16], la prevalente concentrazione a Rodi[17], rispetto a limitate attestazioni a Zinçirli e Pithecusa[18], sembra consigliarne, piuttosto che il riconoscimento di importazioni, l'immissione in una delle categorie di portaunguenti prodotte appunto nell'isola nella seconda metà dell'VIII sec.a.C. da quei metoikoi orientali, attivi

Fig. 2.

specificamente a Jalysos, che Coldstream ha validamente valorizzato.

Estremamente scarsa è la ceramica figurata orientalizzante rodia e, più in generale, greco-orientale, fra cui ricordo frammenti di una oinochoe in Wild Goat style (inv. 11325) con lepre in corsa, il cui corpo punteggiato, insieme ai riempitivi a crocetta e a uncino e al ductus della catena di fiori e boccioli di loto, rinvia alla serie che la Walter-Karydi ha assegnato alla "Ostdoris"[19].

Delle produzioni dei primi decenni del VI sec.a.C. meritano espressa menzione una lacunosa oinochoe a figure nere (inv. 11312), con fregi zoomorfi ravvivati da diffusi ritocchi in paonazzo, agevolmente inseribile nel chiota "Sphinx-and-Lion style"[20], del quale, con esemplari da Pitane[21], concorre ad ampliare il ventaglio morfologico, e vari frammenti di vasi di Vroulia, pertinenti non solo alle canoniche kylikes, ma anche a qualche forma chiusa, mentre per il terzo quarto del secolo vi è una situla frammentaria tipo Tell Defenneh, con guerriero, da riversare nel gruppo C di R.M. Cook[22].

Abbondante è invece la ceramica corinzia, consistente per lo più in aryballoi e alabastra dal PCM al CM, in stile lineare oppure con comasti, con parata di guerrieri, con volatili, con l'infrequente bucranio[23], o "quatrefoil" o a squame e baccellature, sovente graffite su fondo nero[24], etc., di contro a pochi frammenti di cratere e di anfora e ad un kothon decorato da motivi a sigma a quattro tratti intervallati da rosette ad anello, pressochè identico ad uno restituito da una tomba camirese[25].

La netta prevalenza di portaunguenti è altresi' evidenziata da taluni aryballoi laconici, compreso uno del raro tipo a tori[26], da un aryballos a bande "ionico"[27], da uno strigilato in bucchero "ionico"[28] e da svariati balsamari configurati a testa di guerriero, busto femminile, protome di toro o di leone, ariete, sirena, leone accovacciato, etc., di fabbricazione rodia.

Copiosa è pure la ceramica attica a figure nere e rosse, attualmente ancora in frammenti da ricomporre, uno dei più antichi documenti della quale è una lekane del Pittore KX (inv. 6747)[29], che fa da pendant a quella rinvenuta, sempre a Jalysos, in una tomba a cremazione[30].

Fra le sculture s'impone per consistenza e va-

Fig. 3.

Fig. 4.

rietà dei soggetti una novantina fra statuette e frammenti di statuette di tipo cipriota, in calcare tenero, importate dalla grande isola vicina o realizzate da artigiani itineranti[31] e anche qui, come a Lindos e Samos, affiancate da terrecotte cipriote[32]. Il lotto jalysio viene cosi' ad integrare il quadro di presenze già noto, al di fuori di Cipro, tanto a Rodi stessa (stipi di Lindos e Kamiros, nonchè qualche pezzo da Vroulia, Lardos e Kalathos), quanto a Samos, Chios, Delos, Knidos, Efeso, Smirne, Naukratis, in Siria, Fenicia, Palestina, e óra, a Policoro[33]; al pari di queste, si colloca fra l'ultimo quarto del VII e la prima metà del VI sec.a.C., secondo la cronologia rialzata, in base ai dati degli scavi di Samos[34], rispetto a quella fissata da Gjerstad per lo stile proto- e neo-cipriota[35].

Le nostre sculture dispiegano una tipologia assortita, largamente coincidente con gli ex voto lindii della stessa natura: oltre alle più comuni immagini di offerenti maschili (anche kriophoroi) e femminili – con capretti, uccelli (fig. 3b), fiori, conocchia, etc. – oppure di figure sedute, singole o in coppia, o di animali (leoni, sfingi alate, falchi, bovide), si hanno soggetti meno usuali, quali il suonatore di doppio flauto, il banchettante disteso con donna seduta frontalmente[36], un gruppo di donna e giovinetta (fig. 3a), la divinità criocefala assisa in trono[37] identificabile con il fenicio Ba'al Ḥammon.

La piccola plastica bronzea, dal canto suo, annovera alcune opere di eccezionale interesse, che riflettono esperienze diverse: se infatti un bronzetto maschile (inv. 8072) ed uno femminile (inv. 8064), con lunga veste scampanata, entrambi atteggiati nel tipico gesto cretese del saluto cultuale, con il braccio destro portato alla fronte, propongono una notissima formula iconografica minoica, altri, femminili, appalesano, negli occhi a incavo, nel naso e mento prominenti, nelle labbra spremute, nel risalto delle orecchie, nella stessa nudità, una forte impronta orientale, in specie nord-siriana, che si combina alle convenzioni proprie della plastica greca di età geometrica (fig. 4). Questi ultimi, mentre ribadiscono l'entità degli apporti levantini che pervadono la cultura figurativa rodia della seconda metà dell' VIII sec.a.C., ci consegnano l'efficace testimonianza di una produzione bronzistica locale, che non mi risulta finora individuata dalla letteratura specialistica, benchè non mancassero termini di riferimento nella stipe di Kamiros[38].

Caratteristiche consimili, sotto il profilo stilistico e tecnico, si colgono del resto in alcuni pendagli e in un pregevole gruppo di fibule, solo in parte pubblicate dalla Sapouna-Sakellarakis[39],

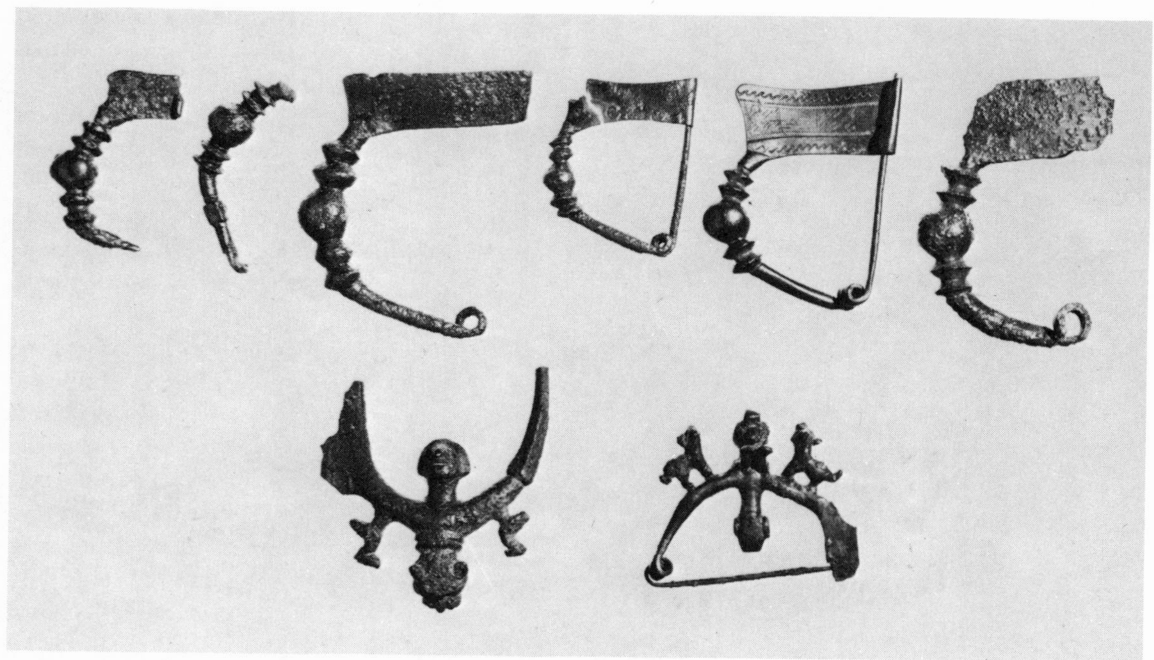

Fig. 5.

con arco ingrossato al quale sono saldate teste umane e/o protomi leonine, generalmente in contrapposizione, che la pressochè esclusiva concentrazione a Jalysos assicura ad un'unica officina dell'isola (fig. 5, in basso: inv. 8497 e 8501). Una ulteriore conferma in questo senso si ricava dalla concomitante occorrenza, in alcuni esemplari, di quegli stessi uccelletti plastici che, singoli o plurimi, connotano un altro gruppo di fibule (tipo VII b) di riconosciuta fabbricazione rodia[40] e che hanno i loro diretti corrispettivi dipinti sulla ceramica TG locale.

A proposito di fibule, la stipe del Monte Fileremo, con le sue duemila ca.[41], in bronzo ma anche in ferro, ne rinserra il più cospicuo dossier di tutto l'Egeo, superiore al pur nutrito contingente (ca. 1.600) del santuario lindio, e, in una area dorica quale questa, appare plausibile correlare tali accessori del costume, come d'altro canto alcune decine di spilloni, all'offerta rituale del peplo ad Athena o intenderli come simbolicamente sostitutivi di esso.

Dominano decisamente i tipi propri delle isole o di prevalente diffusione insulare, con staffa a piastrina alta e stretta e arco a sferette o elementi lenticolari giustapposti (fig. 5, in alto: inv. 11083-11088) o con una sola sfera al centro o rigonfio (tipi III, V, IV SS) e loro varianti (tipo VII), compresa quella con uno o più volatili dianzi ricordata (tipo VII b), ma, in misura più ridotta, vi sono anche diverse varietà di "Bogenfibeln" (tipo II), cosi' come tipi greco-continentali (VI, IX) e settentrionali (X), con qualche esemplare a occhiali o a quadruplice spirale o a disco e perfino uno con arco serpeggiante di foggia illirica[42] (tipo X B b). Ancora, fra le importazioni e le serie "esotiche" vanno menzionate fibule di tipo vicino-orientale e cipriota (XII B,C), con relative imitazioni di ambito egeo, nonchè fibule frigie e anatoliche (XII A), in articolata gamma di fogge, e loro imitazioni greco-orientali[43]. Nè mancano alcuni dei tipi detti "italici" (XI), di cui il più rappresentato è quello con staffa allungata e arco rivestito da elementi in osso e/o perline di pasta vitrea e dischetti bronzei[44] e fra i quali compaiono comunque esemplari sicuramente riconoscibili come realizzazioni greche, ad es. l'inv. 9082[45], caratterizzato come tale dalla anomalia dell'andamento serpeggiante nell'ardiglione, anzichè nell'arco, e da una particolare conformazione spiraliforme della molla, privi di riscontro in area tirrenica.

Infine, sempre in tema di fibule, vanno contemplate anche svariate "spectacle fibulae" in avorio o osso, con guilloches e cerchielli concentrici a incisione, i cui paralleli, distribuiti fra il tardo VIII e la metà ca. del VI sec.a.C., sono

Fig. 6.

Fig. 7.

facilmente reperibili nella stipe lindia e in molti altri santuari e siti della Grecia propria e coloniale, dell'Asia Minore, della Cilicia[46].

Fra gli oggetti di ornamento personale di pertinenza femminile deposti come offerte abbondano i pendenti di orecchini bronzei a spirale, nelle varietà diffuse nel TG e nel corso del VII sec.a.C. a Rodi, come in genere in ambito insulare e microasiatico, inclusa quella con estremità appiattite a dischetti[47].

Sempre in bronzo, vi sono poi parecchi pendagli, con puntuali confronti nelle stipi camirese e lindia, a doppia protome di capride[48] o a uccello[49] con base traforata, a sirena[50], a vasetto[51], a pesce[52], etc., mentre fra gli ex voto maschili si iscrivono sia armi difensive e offensive, quali elmi di tipo "ionico" – di cui restano le paragnatidi, congruenti con quelle di Lindos[53] -, frammenti di scudi in lamina con guilloches e decorazione figurata a sbalzo, foderi di spada, punte di freccia e di lancia (anche in ferro), ovvero loro riproduzioni miniaturistiche (bipenni, corazza, elmo di tipo cretese orientalizzante[54]), sia attrezzi per la pesca (ami[55]). Oltre a disparate categorie di instrumentum e vasellame frequenti nei santuari ellenici, quali pinzette[56], grattugie[57], phialai mesomphaliche – fra cui una (inv. 8601) fornita dell'iscrizione, in forma dorica, ἱαρά, tracciata all'altezza dell'orlo e capovolta rispetto al vaso[58] -, merita espressa segnalazione un arredo bronzeo ravvisabile come opera della metallurgia cretese del periodo tardogeometrico: si tratta infatti del frammento, decorato a giorno con figurine fuse di toro e cavallo saldate a verghette (inv. 8526: fig. 6), di uno di quei sostegni a quattro facce rinvenuti nell'Antro Ideo, in una tomba di Khaniale Tekke (Knossos), nel santuario di Hermes e Afrodite a Kato Syme Viannou, ma anche a Delfi[59], che, allo scorcio dell'VIII sec.a.C., rielaborano modelli orientali noti a Cipro, in area siro-palestinese e in Grecia nella tarda età del bronzo.

Senza soffermarmi sulle faïences di manifattura rodia e naukratita (vasetti configurati, pissidi, aryballoi, statuette e pendagli di varia forma, etc:), per le quali è al momento sufficiente il rinvio al lavoro della Webb[60], nè sugli alabastra appuntiti a invetriatura policroma di produzione rodia e/o nord-siriana[61], nè sui numerosissimi scarabei, scaraboidi e amuleti egizi ad egittizzanti, sottolineo invece lo speciale rilievo che assumono cinque elementi in faïence a nucleo bianco, lavorati su una sola faccia e quindi destinati in origine a decorare, a intarsio, un arredo o mobile ligneo (trono, forziere o simili) oppure una statua, nei quali N. Skon[62] ha individuato tre dei nomi reali, in caratteri geroglifici, di Necho II, che regnò in Egitto fra 610 e 596 a.C. (fig. 7).

Sembra trattarsi, in altri termini, piuttosto che di un prezioso oggetto importato per via commerciale, di un dono reale - esattamente databile, grazie alla titolatura del faraone, fra l'ultimo decennio del VII e il primo lustro del VI sec.a.C. - destinato al santuario di Athena da questo sovrano, del quale del resto Erodoto (II,159) espressamente ricorda l'invio come offerta all'Apollonion di Mileto della *esthés* indossata nella vittoriosa spedizione condotta in Siria nel 608 a.C. Nello specifico caso jalysio non è possibile conoscere le ragioni del dono votivo, ma si può congetturare un gesto di riconoscenza per un altro successo militare, conseguito forse anche con l'ausilio di mercenari greci, jalysii possibilmente inclusi, dal momento che lo stesso Erodoto informa (II,154) che già il padre, Psammetico I (664-610 a.C.), aveva ingaggiato fra le sue truppe pirati ionî e carî, che, *hoplisthéntas chalkô* (II,152), validamente contribuirono a sconfiggere i suoi nemici.

D'altra parte, la militanza di mercenari di Jalysos nell'esercito di Psammetico II (595-589 a.C.), figlio e successore di Necho II, è esplicitamente attestata dalle iscrizioni incise da due di essi, Telephos e Anaxanor, sulle gambe di due delle statue colossali di Ramesse II ad Abu Simbel, durante la campagna in Nubia del 591 a.C.[63], mentre ancora lo storico di Alicarnasso precisa (II, 163, 169) che Apries (589-570 a. C.), figlio e successore di Psammetico il Giovane, ebbe al soldo trentamila mercenari ionî e carî.

Si guadagnerebbe, insomma, la prima testimonianza archeologica diretta di uno di quei doni che, stando sempre ad Erodoto (II,180,182; III,47), non solo Necho II, ma, successivamente, un altro faraone della XXVI dinastia, Amasis (570-526 a.C.), fece a stati e santuari ellenici[64] (Lindos, Samos, Sparta, Delfi, Cirene).

Fra gli ex voto del Monte Phileremos sono inoltre comprese collane in pasta vitrea, delle quali restano decine di vaghi di forma e colore diversi: mi limito a ricordare, da un lato, quelli a tre protuberanze con "occhi" concentrici, ben documentati dal periodo geometrico all'arcaismo a Lindos, come in un più esteso ambito insulare e peninsulare greco[65], fino al santuario di Artemis Enodia in Tessaglia[66], ma anche a Cipro, Tarso e Zinçirli[67], e, dall'altro, un congruo numero di "Vogelperlen", la cui vastissima irradiazione nell'VIII sec.a.C. – dalla Siria alla Erigia, alla regione a sud-est del Lago di Urmia, da Cipro a Rodi (cui spetta la massima densità di presenze), a Perachora, all'Italia peninsulare (Lucania, Campania, Etruria villanoviana, onde vengono redistribuite nell'agro falisco, a Bologna e Este[68]) – utilmente riflette sul piano archeologico la mobilità di agenti levantini, in rapporto ai quali le evidenze restituite da Ischia e dall'Italia centrale possono a mio avviso meglio valutarsi proprio se correlate al complesso della documentazione di Rodi e alla compagine stanziata a Jalysos dalla metà ca. del IX sec.a.C.

Non va poi omesso un gruppo di sigilli-pendagli in steatite nera, grigio scuro, verde, screziata o in marmo bianco, di forma conica, parallelepipeda, tronco-piramidale, cilindroide, discoidale con presa, etc., provvisti di foro di sospensione e di intagli, non sempre accurati, con motivi geometrici e subgeometrici (zig-zag, chevrons, spirali, meandri, rettangoli multipli, croci, diagonali, puntini, globetti, cerchielli concentrici, stelle, rosette, etc.): al pari dei loro omologhi da Lindos e Kamiros classificati tipologicamente da Boardman[69], essi rientrano in una classe peculiarmente rodia di ispirazione orientale che, fra la fine dell'VIII e la prima metà del VII sec.a.C., si rifà in particolare alla sfragistica neo-hittita, assumendo la prevalente funzione amuletica rispetto a quella di sigillo.

In tema di sigilli, debbo segnalare una significativa novità, ossia l'occorrenza nella nostra stipe di oltre venti esemplari del "Lyre-Player Group", i quali incrementano quindi sensibilmente il corpus finora riunito[70], colmando una lacuna nella documentazione che, appunto per quanto concerne Jalysos, ho sempre giudicato inverosimile. Il tempo a disposizione non mi consente di presentarli partitamente, ma posso anticipare che si tratta di scaraboidi in serpentina rossa o verde e che il repertorio dei soggetti è alquanto ricco, offrendo sia tipi già noti e loro variazioni, anche infrequenti, sia tipi nuovi: trio di musicanti stanti, con liricine, suonatrice di

Fig. 8a+b.

Fig. 9.

tamburello e piccolo suonatore di doppio flauto[71] (inv. 7414), quest'ultimo sostituito in due esemplari rispettivamente da un alberello fogliforme[72] (inv. 7416) e da un ankh (inv. 7418: fig. 8a); liricine seduto, in atto di bere aspirando con un tubo da un recipiente posato su un tavolo a zampe incrociate[73] (inv. 7411: fig. 8b); liricine seduto e alberello[74] (inv. 7413); figura maschile fra due uccelli[75] (inv. 7409 e 7431) o sollevante per la bocca un grosso pesce[76] (inv. 7410); leone, fornito di "grembiule" e con una capra sul dorso, in lotta con un uomo, già atterrato[77] (inv. 7440), oppure gradiente, fra palmette, con un uccello sulla groppa[78] (inv. 7430); uccello e alberello[79] (inv. 7451); albero sacro di palma fiancheggiato da uccelli[80] (inv. 7417); simboli astrali (stella a dodici punte, disco alato schematico, punti) e due palmette (inv. 7424); motivi geometrici disposti su più registri[81] (inv. 7412 e 7453) o fitomorfi[82] (coppie di foglie e di palmette fra volute in diagonale; inv. 7420); e altri ancora. Speciale per la sua rarità è poi l'inv. 7421, un prisma a quattro facce che si affianca ai due soli finora conosciuti nella serie[83], da Carchemish e dalla Fenicia, con cui condivide alcuni dei soggetti: in A, fila di quattro uccelli sovrastati da disco solare alato[84]; in B, uccelli affrontati ai lati di una palma, fra doppio chevron, e disco solare alato in alto[85]; in C, capra con uccello sul dorso[86]; in D, cervo con uccello sul dorso[87].

In qualche caso inoltre sono conservati i castoni d'argento entro cui sono montati (il già citato 7417) o la verghetta che li attraversa longitudinalmente (il già cit. 7409), mentre l'inv. 8027, con tre uccelli sormontati da foglia a tratteggio[88], è pervenuto con l'intero pendaglio girevole in argento, di forma ellittica inflessa, munito di appiccagnolo a tubetto (fig. 9), che ha i suoi immediati corrispettivi a Pithecusa e in Etruria, oltre che naturalmente in area siro-fenicia[89].

Tale cospicua documentazione, che segna una decisiva impennata rispetto ai 18 esemplari sin qui noti da Rodi (15 a Lindos e 3 a Kamiros[90]), ampliando al contempo il repertorio tematico del Gruppo, non mi pare priva di conseguenze, soprattutto in rapporto alle evidenze occidentali e segnatamente di Pithecusa, che di questi sigilli-amuleti detiene il primato assoluto, con un centinaio di esempi in sepolture per lo più infantili del terzo e ultimo quarto dell'VIII sec.a.C.

Se infatti, da un lato, conviene ricordare l'ipotesi di una loro manifattura a Rodi ad opera di incisori orientali immigrati, emessa da un'eminente specialista di glittica quale Edith Porada[91], su cui ha poi prevalso quella nord-siriana o cilicia[92], dall'altro, e ancor più, è indilazionabile la correzione della pretesa, divenuta indiscutibile topos, di imputarne lo smistamento a Pithecusa e nell'Italia tirrenica agli Eubei. Una riconsiderazione dei vettori sgombra dal pregiudizio paneuboico e una più vigile attenzione agli indicatori di una frequentazione commerciale levantina s'impone invece valutando alcuni fatti obiettivi: rinvenimenti come quello di Francavilla Marittima, ove connessioni euboiche sono affatto fuori causa e ove, per converso, affluiscono importazioni orientali, in primis la coppa bronzea fenicia della tomba S[93]; l'elevata aliquota, nella Pithecusa della seconda metà dell' VIII secolo, di vasi TG di sicura fabbrica rodia, quali gli aryballoi con o senza "spaghetti" e le "bird-kotylai", e più in generale di oggetti che proprio nella grande isola dell'Egeo trovano diretto riscontro, quali gli aryballoi "levantini" dianzi discussi o gli scarabei e athyrmata vari egittizzanti in faïence, dei quali già von Bissing, Dunbabin e altri studiosi hanno localizzato una produzione a Rodi[94]; la stessa distribuzione del Gruppo del Suonatore di Lira tanto in Grecia, ove le presenze sono assai ridotte su suolo continentale e appena due in Eubea, di contro ad un'alta densità nelle isole (Delos, Paros, Chios, Samos, Rodi, Creta), quanto in Oriente, ove le percentuali maggiori spettano a Cipro, Tarso e Zinçirli, di contro ad un esemplare appena da Al Mina.

Non quindi agli Eubei dell'emporio alle foci dell'Oronte, ma piuttosto a Fenici o Aramei impegnati in attività mercantili afferenti anche ai porti di Rodi e collegati forse alla compagine orientale li' insediata ed attiva dal secolo precedente appare plausibile ricondurre almeno la diffusione dei sigilli in argomento.

Riferimenti obbligati all'ambiente siro-fenicio s'impongono, d'altro canto, per gli avori figurati, presenti nella stipe jalysia sia con importazioni[95] – come a Lindos, Samos, Creta (Antro Ideo), Thasos, etc. – sia con opere locali manifestamente dipendenti da modelli orientali.

Fra le prime si colloca un pannello quadrangolare lavorato a giorno, con triplice strombatura racchiudente una finestra con balaustra sorretta da colonnette e capitelli a foglie di palma (inv. 7955), attribuibile a scuola fenicia sia per lo stile sia per il soggetto, dato che la cornice aggettante rappresenta un partito tipico dell'architettura fenicia, allusivo ad un edificio templare, quale ricorre in stele e monumenti lapidei della Fenicia e di Cipro[96], e lo connette semanticamente, come versione abbreviata, priva della abituale ierodula affacciata, al noto tipo della "donna alla finestra", attestato a Nimrud (Palazzo di NO e Forte Salmanassar), Arslan Tash, Samaria, Khorsabad[97].

D'altra parte, prevalenti componenti di stile nord-siriano del IX-VIII secolo si colgono in una fine testa femminile a tutto tondo (inv. 7942), con lunga capigliatura cinta da corona, orecchini a tre pendenti e phylakterion (fig. 10), che trova validi referenti nelle testine e nelle statuette del gruppo Loftus dal Palazzo SE di Nimrud[98] ed è forse riconoscibile come divinità o come cortigiana sacra, in virtù del monile ricadente sulla fronte, simbolo di Ishtar[99], e degli orecchini, or-

Fig. 10.

Fig. 11.

Fig. 12a.

Fig. 12b.

namenti portati entrambi dalla divinità che campeggia sul famoso frontale equino eburneo dallo stesso palazzo assiro[100].

Dai medesimi prototipi levantini tradisce piena derivazione un nucleo, stilisticamente compatto, di figure femminili nude, stanti, singole o appaiate, con stephane, trecce ricadenti ai lati del volto, braccia allineate lungo i fianchi (fig. 11), che, accanto alle importazioni (includenti altre testine, statuette maschili, lastrine a rilievo e a incisione), utilmente evidenzia l'attività in loco nel VII sec.a.C. di intagliatori i quali combinano formule iconografiche e inflessioni prettamente nord-siriane con gli accenti formali un po' ingenui e rustici che avviano la piccola plastica del primo dedalico greco. Assegnabili alla stessa bottega da cui sono usciti esemplari rinvenuti dal Biliotti nel "pozzo" sull'acropoli di Kamiros, che forniscono i più calzanti confronti[101], esse rappresentano verosimilmente un'immagine divina e, nel caso di quelle affiancate, un duplice aspetto o natura, iconograficamente non differenziato, della dea, come a Creta, ove statuette e pinakes fittili con figure muliebri nude sia singole sia multiple compaiono nella stipe del santuario di Athena Poliouchos sull'acropoli di Gortina, e in altri luoghi di culto in Grecia e a Cipro, ove gruppi doppi o tripli ricorrono fra le offerte dedicate a varie divinità femminili[102].

Oltre a diverse altre categorie di oggetti in avorio o osso (pendagli, immanicature, stili, etc.) vanno infine ricordati frammenti di flauti, strumenti musicali che si trovano in molti siti e depositi votivi greci, da Lindos a Chios, all'Artemision di Efeso, a Sparta (Arthemis Orthia), Corinto, Egina, Atene, Brauron, etc., e grecocoloniali (Siracusa, Locri, Metauros)[103].

A conclusione della nostra rassegna, attenzione particolare va riservata alle iscrizioni votive, che ammontano a ca. 200 (compresi minuti frustuli), superando decisamente quindi quelle lindie, e che, registrando ripetutamente il nome di Athena, ci consegnano la sicura identificazione della divinità venerata nell'area sacra dell'acropoli di Jalysos.

Se si escludono un frammento di louterion marmoreo[104] (δεκ]άτας : ἀν [έθηκε], sull'orlo), un cippo in poros[105] e taluni oggetti bronzei, fra cui la phiale mesomphalos dianzi menzionata, si tratta di dediche vascolari, incise sul fondo esterno o sull'orlo di ceramiche prevalentemente attiche (kylikes, "stemless cups", skyphoi, qualche cratere, etc.) a figure nere o rosse o a vernice nera, scaglionate fra la seconda metà del VI e la metà ca. del IV sec.a.C., e, in misura assai minore, di vasi di altre fabbriche, rodia e grecoorientale, anche cronologicamente anteriori.

Il formulario è abbastanza fisso: le formule più semplici prevedono l'aggettivo *hiará*, riferito all'oggetto, oppure il nome di *Athanaia*, sempre nella forma dorica, in dativo, preceduto da quello del/la dedicante[106]; le più complesse comportano l'uso del termine "decima"[107] (*apò dekátas*, *dekátas*, *dekátan*, *dekáta*), frequentissimo e non di rado accompagnato dalla motivazione del "ricordo" (*mnamosynon*), o quello di "primizia", espresso però, in luogo della consueta *aparché*, come *ápargma*/*áparma*, che, rarissimo altrove[108], sembra connotarsi quale variante locale o regionale. Le norme paleografiche sono, nella stragrande maggioranza, quelle proprie dell'alfabeto rodio.

A titolo esemplificativo ho prescelto qualche testo:

a) 'Αθαναίας δεκάτας su kylix skyphoide attica a f. n. del Gruppo di Haimon (inv. 9874). 490-80 a.C. ca.;

b) τ'ἀθαναίαι Νόφυλος/δεκάτα sul collo di una kalpis attica a f. n. dello stesso Gruppo (inv. 9911);

c) Ξεναγόρας δεκάτας μναμόσυνον sotto il piede di una kylix attica (inv. 9901). V sec. a.C. (fig. 12a);

d) 'Αθαναίας ἄπαργμα Πείσιος ἀνέθεκε sotto il piede di un'altra kylix attica (inv. 9907). V sec. a.C. (fig. 12b);

e) Συβαρῖτις : 'Αθαν [αίαι] sull'orlo interno di un cratere attico a f. r. (inv. 9947), capovolto rispetto ad esso. Seconda metà del V sec.a.C.;

f) Βωλάκριτος : 'Αθαναίαι : ἄπαρμα sul fondo di uno skyphos attico a v. n. (inv. 9946). Fine V - inizi IV sec.a.C.;

g) ἱαρά

e

Θεομένης καὶ συνδαμιωργοὶ ἱαραὶ 'Αθάναι rispettivamente sull'orlo e sul fondo di uno skyphos attico a f. r. (inv.9871). Secondo quarto del IV sec.a.C. (fig. 13).

Fig. 13.

Fig. 14.

Si osserverà che quest'ultima è una dedica pubblica, effettuata dal presidente del collegio magistratuale e dai colleghi.

Dei molti altri documenti iscritti non si può passare sotto silenzio un frammento di vaso potorio (calice, piuttosto che kantharos o kyathos, data la posizione della solcatura impressa) in bucchero nero inconfondibilmente etrusco-meridionale, recante inciso un testo di cui restano due lettere, μα[109] (fig. 14).

Questa nuova attestazione, databile alla fine del VII – inizi del VI sec.a.C., è quanto mai preziosa in relazione al problema, sempre di attualità, della presenza di materiali etruschi in Grecia e della individuazione dei loro vettori[110]. L'iscrizione, benchè sinistrorsa, non è etrusca, ma certamente greca, connotata come tale dal *my* a quattro tratti, documentato a Rodi fin dalla seconda metà dell'VIII secolo, sulla kylix di Korakos[111], pure corredata di iscrizione retrograda. La rilevanza del pezzo risiede nel fatto che, dopo i due di Perachora[112], è questo il terzo vaso in bucchero etrusco iscritto rinvenuto in area ellenica e, analogamente a quelli, si configura come offerta compiuta in un santuario greco da un greco, nella sua lingua, che dunque, lungi dal suffragare il miraggio della presenza e dell'attività mercantile dei Tirreni nell'Egeo[113], viene invece a confermare come la circolazione di oggetti etruschi in Grecia sia l'effetto di un processo interno al commercio greco in Etruria[114].

Complementi di primario interesse alla prosopografia rodia vengono dall'onomastica restituita dalle iscrizioni votive, che costituiscono un precedente notevole quanto sconosciuto rispetto al corpus dei successivi titoli lapidari ellenistici, prospettando al contempo dati utili sull'estrazione sociale e il grado di litterazione dei devoti.

Dalla rapida presentazione sin qui condotta emerge chiaramente che la stipe dell'Athenaion di Jalysos, pur condividendo molteplici categorie di offerte con quelle di Lindos e Kamiros, è la più consistente e articolata dell'isola, e tale da suggerire, ancorchè in una fase di studio del tutto preliminare, qualche ipotesi di lavoro e valutazioni alternative in merito a talune classi di materiali e alle loro proiezioni, in specie occidentali. La documentazione non difetta certo, ma solo l'indagine più approfondita di essa consentirà di tracciare consuntivi meno provvisori.

Marina Martelli
Via Salaria 300/D
00199 Roma
Italy

Gratitudine vivissima tengo ad esprimere al Prof. A. Di Vita per avermi affidato questa ricerca, impegnativa quanto gratificante, e per la sollecita disponibilità con cui l'asseconda. Un sentito ringraziamento debbo inoltre al dr. Ioannis Papachristodoulou, Eforo del Dodecanneso, per le ampie agevolazioni concesse durante il lavoro nel Museo di Rodi; a E. Zervoudaki, membro della nostra équipe, per la cordiale collaborazione ed il valido aiuto nel reperimento del materiale, conservato nei magazzini del Museo stesso; ad Angeliki Jannikouri, epimelitis della Eforia, per la cortese assistenza.

Una prima missione per il riscontro autoptico e la catalogazione dei materiali ho effettuato a Rodi dal 9 al 26 settembre 1985, insieme alla dr. M. A. Rizzo.

Del compito di pubblicazione della stipe era stato in precedenza incaricato, dal 1953 fino al momento del suo decesso, il prof. G. Monaco.

1. Per cenni assai rapidi agli interventi di scavo e agli oggetti rinvenuti v. A. Maiuri, BdA, s. 2, a. 3, 1923, 237, figg. 7-8; A. Maiuri, BdA, s. 2, a. 4, 1924-25, 355, figg. 6-7; BCH 48, 1924, 513 s.; G. Jacopi, BdA, s. 2, a. 6, 1926-27, 331; H. Möbius - W. Wrede, AA 1927, c. 409; A. Maiuri, ClRh 1, 1928, 74-79, figg. 56-61; Jacopi 1932, 110-112; Inglieri 1936, 25, n. 12.
   Per alcuni oggetti – ceramiche, vasi in pietra, etc. – MM e della tarda età del bronzo dalla stipe o comunque dall'area del tempio di Athena v. M. Benzi, in Hägg – Marinatos (eds.) 1984, 93-104, con altra lett., e Mee 1982, 47; una placchetta eburnea di rivestimento micenea, con due leoni, retrospicienti, disposti in schema araldico ai lati di un altare sul quale appoggiano le zampe anteriori, è riprodotta da Barnett 1982, tav. 33 a, p. 37 (con generica indicazione di provenienza da Jalysos).
2. In merito va precisato che i giornali di scavo conservati si riferiscono agli anni 1923, 1925 e 1926; peraltro, in ClRh 1, 1928, 60, Maiuri elenca fra gli anni di scavo anche il 1924, ma il giornale relativo ad esso non è conservato o, almeno, non è al momento rintracciabile.
3. V. rispettivamente L. Pernier, BdA 8, 1914, 221-224 e A. Maiuri, ASAtene 2, 1916, 274, nonchè Maiuri 1921, 156.
4. ClRh 6-7, 1932-33, 35, n. 1, figg. 37-38. Limitatamente alla forma v. inoltre un ex. da Kamiros al British Museum, in Friis Johansen 1958, 89, nota 30, fig. 195. Sulle importazioni vascolari cipriote e cipro-fenicie a Rodi e Kos v. Coldstream 1968, 319 s., e J. N. Coldstream, BICS 16, 1969, 2 ss.; W. Culican, Levant 2, 1970, 33 s.; Coldstream 1977, 46, 68; L. Morricone, ASAtene 56 (n.s. 60), 1978, (1982), 405 ss.; J.N. Coldstream, RDAC 1984, 126.
5. ClRh 3, 1929, 87, n. 6, fig. 75, I da d. in alto. V. anche un ex. da Kos, t. 43 Serraglio, in L. Morricone, ASAtene 56 (n.s. 60), 1978, (1982), 231, n. 1, fig. 463.
6. Cfr. Coldstream 1968, 277, n. 1, tav. 61c, e soprattutto n. 2 (= I.A. Papapostolou, ADelt 23, 1968, tavv. 44b, 37a, I da d. in alto), entrambe da Jalysos, tt. 50 e 51; Walter 1968, 104, tav. 41, nn. 228, 232; C. Özgünel, in CGE, 22, tav. III, figg. 18, 20-21.
7. Coldstream 1968, 277-279, tav. 61 c-d, e Coldstream 1977, 247, fig. 78 b.
   Sulle "Mäander- e Vogelkotylai" v. inoltre Walter

1968, 40 s., 58, 104, nn. 228-232, 105-106, nn. 240-268, 118, nn. 467-475, tavv. 41-44, 84; ASAtene 47-48 (n. s. 31-32), 1969-70, (1972), fig. 59 a p. 508; IstMitt 23-24, 1973-74, 86 s., 96 s., tav. 23, 49-58; J.P. Thalmann, in E. Gjerstad et al. 1977, 67, n. 5, tav. I; C. Özgünel, in CGE, pp. 20-23, tav. III, figg. 8-25; Walter-Karydi et al. 1982, 10, nn. 2-4, tav. 1; A. Andreiomenou, ASAtene 59 (n.s. 43), 1981, (1983), 235 (due frammenti, con iscrizione, da Eretria); P. Pelagatti, ASAtene, 60 (n.s. 44), 1982, (1984), 139, figg. 12-14; G. Fiorentini – E. De Miro, ASAtene 61 (n.s. 45), 1983, (1984), 62, n. 1, 63 s., n. 2, 76, figg. 11b, 24 a-b; da Pithecusa, oltre alla celebre "coppa di Nestore" della t. 168, proviene un ex. in framm. dal quartiere suburbano di Mazzola: da ultima Dehl 1984, 244, c, con bibl. prec., cui adde G. Buchner, in La céramique grecque ou de tradition grecque au VIII*e* siècle en Italie centrale et méridionale (=Cahiers du Centre Jean Bérard 3) 1982, 107, e; Ridgway 1984, 112.

8. ClRh 8, 1936, 172, n. 1, fig. 161, fila superiore, III da s.; I.A.Papapostolou, ADelt 23, 1968, tav. 37 a, I da s. in alto.
9. Cenno in SCE, IV.2, 262.
10. Ad es., la brocchetta con sequenze di cerchielli multipli sulla spalla e sopra il fondo e fascette sul corpo riprodotta in ClRh 1, 1928, 76, fig. 58, fila inferiore, al centro, e in ADelt 23, 1968, tav. 41d.
11. Friis Johansen 1958, 148 ss.; Coldstream 1968, 275 s.; J.N.Coldstream , BICS 16, 1969; Coldstream 1977, 249, fig. 79; J.N.Coldstream, MB 8, 1982, 268 s.
12. Entrambi i nostri exx. sono riprodotti da I.A. Papapostolou, ADelt 23, 1968, 85 s., n. 3 a-b, tav. 40 c-d, mentre al solo 6821 ha accennato J.N. Coldstream, BICS 16, 1969, 3 e nota 30 a p. 7.
    Per quelli delle tombe jalysie 56 e 58 v. I.A. Papapostolou, ADelt 23, 1968, 85, tavv. 39 b-e, 40 a-b; Coldstream 1968, 276; J.N. Coldstream, BICS 16, 1969, 3, tav. II, a-e; Coldstream 1977, 249, fig. 79 e-f. Si tengano inoltre presenti un frammento di oinochoe dal "pozzo" di Kamiros e la sommità della presa del coperchio di una pisside stamnoide da Lindos, citati da I.A. Papapostolou, ADelt 23, 1968, 85, nn. 1-2, con bibl. prec. Il tipo dell'aryballos con volto umano all'altezza dell'imboccatura non è, d'altro canto, ignoto a Cipro: v. ad es. CVA Copenhagen[1] tav. 25,3.
13. Si veda un aryballos della stipe del Thesmophorion di Bitalemi, sul quale più di recente G. Fiorentini – E. De Miro, ASAtene 61, 1983, (1984), 79, fig. 40, con bibl. prec.
14. Friis Johansen 1958, 161 ss., con rifer.; I.A. Papapostolou, ADelt 23, 1968, 90 s., tav. 42 c, fila mediana, I da d., d, I da d. e I da s.; J.N. Coldstream, BICS 16, 1969, 2 s., 5, tavv. I f, III f, fila sup.; Coldstream 1977, 249, fig. 79 c; J.N. Coldstream, MB 8, 1982, tav. 27 a.
    Si consideri che un originale d'importazione è presente a Jalysos nella t. 132: J.N. Coldstream, BICS 16, 1969, 2, con bibl. prec., tav. I e.
15. Oltre al mio CVA Gela[2] commento a tav. 33, 1-4, con lett. e rifer. aggiuntivi, v. M. Martelli Cristofani, La ceramica greco-orientale in Etruria, in CGE, 151-153, con altri rifer., e M. Martelli Cristofani, in Atti del II Congresso Internazionale Etrusco (Firenze 1985), in corso di stampa; Coldstream 1977, 249, fig. 79d, e J.N. Coldstream, MB 8, 1982, 269, 369; F. G. Lo Porto, in Antichità cretesi. Studi in onore di Doro Levi (= CronAStorArt 13, 1974, [1978]), II, 176, figg. 1b, 2b; una carta di distribuzione ha elaborato B.B. Shefton, MB 8, 1982, 342, nota 1, Map A (fig. 1); D. Ridgway, in La céramique grecque ou de tradition grecque au VIII*e* siècle en Italie centrale et méridionale (=Cahiers du Centre Jean Bérard 3) 1982, 87, 98, A. 16. x, nonchè in Gli Eubei in Occidente. Atti del XVIII Convegno di Studi sulla Magna Grecia, Napoli 1979 (ma 1984), 75 e Ridgway 1984, 76, tav. 5, in basso al centro; degna di miglior causa l'ostinazione di G. Buchner, in La céramique grecque ou de tradition grecque au VIII*e* siècle en Italie centrale et méridionale (=Cahiers du Centre Jean Bérard 3) 1982, 107, d, a "non ritenere come sicuramente accertata la loro provenienza da Rodi", frutto di un'indomabile fede paneuboica che non si arrende all'evidenza; qualche ex. da Gela è stato ripubblicato da G. Fiorentini – E. De Miro, ASAtene 61, 1983, (1984), 79, figg. 38-39 e in Insediamenti coloniali greci in Sicilia nell'VIII e VII sec. a.C. (=Cronache di Archeologia 17, 1978), 1980, 95, tav. XII, 2, I da d.
16. J.N. Coldstream, BICS 16, 1969, 3, con accenno ai due exx. in argomento a p. 7, note 31, 35 (il n. inv. 7185 va rettificato in 7158); G. Buchner, MB 8, 1982, 280, II a, fig. 2 a-b; D. Ridgway, in Gli Eubei in Occidente. Atti del XVIII Convegno di Studi sulla Magna Grecia, Napoli 1979 (ma 1984), 77 s. = Ridgway 1984, 130, fig. 30; H.G. Niemeyer, JbZMusMainz 31, 1984, fig. 13.3 a p. 18.
17. Cfr. Lindos I, c. 300 s., nn. 1043-1046, tav. 48 ("3*e* type"); Friis Johansen 1958, 18, A 22-24, fig. 18, 25, B 9-10, figg. 44-45, 38, D 19, 161, 164 ("kugelige Aryballen, Form B"), in tre tombe tardo-geometriche; un ex. da Rodi è inoltre a Copenhagen, Nationalmuseet, H 201. Per una variante v. Kinch 1914, c. 62, n. 29, tav. 37 (t. 2).
18. V. rispettivam. Luschen – Andrae 1943, 153, tav. 27 b e G. Buchner, MB 8, 1982, l.c. a nota 16, nonchè G. Buchner-D. Ridgway, AnnAStorAnt 5, 1983, 5, n. 5, 7, 9, fig. 1, 3.
19. Cfr. Walter-Karydi 1973, ad es. tav. 135, nn. 1067, 1098, pp. 89 ss.
20. Cfr. Boardman 1967, 166, 168, fig. 115, tavv. 62-63; Boardman - Hayes 1973, 25 s., tav. 17, n. 2052; Walter-Karydi 1973, 68, tav. 97, nn. 703-706, 714, 717, 774; Alexandrescu 1978, 25 s., 43 s., nn. 67, 70-72, tav. 8, e P. Alexandrescu, in CGE, 56; C. Bayburtluoğlu, in CGE, 27, tav. V, figg. 2-4; P. Courbin, in CGE, 42, tav. XVIII, fig. 16; A.A. Lemos, in J. Boardman et al. (eds.) 1986, 244, 248, fig. 17.
21. Cfr. CGE, tav. V, fig. 2.
22. CVA British Museum[8] pp. 29 ss.: si noti che, dei 31 exx. elencati, 29 provengono da Tell Defenneh e gli altri due da tombe di Jalysos.
23. Fra uccelli e con girandola sul fondo (inv. 7117); è assegnabile al Lion Group di Payne: cfr. più di recente Stillwell - Benson 1984, 155, nn. 788-789, con rifer., tavv. 36, 105. Un alabastron con questo stesso motivo ricorre in una tomba camirese: ClRh 4, 1931, 363, n. 5 a, figg. 409, 411.
24. Questi ultimi sono piuttosto frequenti a Rodi e nella colonia di Gela: oltre a Lindos I, c. 319, nn. 1120-1122, tav. 50, v. il mio CVA Gela[1] tav. 12,2, con rifer.; A. Archontidou-Argiri, ASAtene 61 (n.s. 45), 1983, (1984), 19, fig. 2: due exx. da una tomba di Monolithos, indicati come imitazioni rodie. Sul tipo più di recente

Stillwell – Benson 1984, 75, n. 337, tav. 17.
25. Cfr. ClRh 4, 1931, 314, n. 7 a, fig. 347.
26. Cfr. CVA Gela[2] tav. 40, 2, con cfr., uno dei quali da Rodi; Chamay – Maier 1984, fig. a d. a p. 183.
27. Cfr. M. Martelli Cristofani, in CGE, 185 con nota 106, 188 s., con rifer.
28. Ma verosimilmente di fabbrica locale, stando ai molti esemplari da Vroulia (cfr. Kinch 1914, c. 152 s.), nonchè da Lindos (Lindos I, c. 278 s., n. 966) e Monolithos (A. Archontidou-Argiri, ASAtene 61 (n. s. 45) 1983, (1984), 27, fig. 13).
29. Beazley 1956, 24, n. 2.
30. ASAtene, 6-7, 1923-24, (1926), 296 ss., n. 27, figg. 191-192; Payne 1931, 197, n. 40; Beazley 1956, 24, n. 1, con altra bibl., e Beazley 1971, 14; Boardman 1974, 18, fig. 20; Burn-Glynn 1982, 3: Canciani 1984, 50, fig. 15 b.
31. Sulla plastica lapidea cipriota in generale, da ultime Lewe 1975 e L. Wriedt Sørensen, RDAC 1978, 111-121, con lett.
32. In corso di studio da parte di E. Zervoudaki. Qualcuna è riprodotta in ClRh 1, 1928, fig. 60 a p. 77 e menzionata in SCE IV.2, 330.
33. Lindos I, cc. 26, 401 ss.; SCE, IV.2, 318 ss.; Schmidt 1968, 54 ss., tavv. 95-120; Riis 1979, 15, fig. 24; per le presenze in centri costieri siro-fenici e palestinesi v. in ptc. A.M. Bisi, RStFen 10, 1982, 195, fig. 1. La prima attestazione in area greco-coloniale è adesso individuabile a Policoro, nel santuario di Demetra, e viene giustamente imputata a "bateau rhodiens sans doute" da C. Rolley, in Siris e l'influenza ionica in Occidente. Atti del XXI Convegno di Studi sulla Magna Grecia, Taranto 1981 (ma 1987), 176, tav. 34,1.
34. Schmidt 1968, 93 ss.
35. SCE IV.2, 207 ss.
36. Come a Lindos e a Samos: da ultimo v. Dentzer 1982, 155 ss., con bibl. prec.
37. Va rilevato che, al di fuori di Cipro, la diffusione di questo tipo di statuetta interessa esclusivamente Rodi, in particolare Lindos (cfr. Lindos I, cc. 400 s., 443, tav. 74, nn. 1793-1795 = Boardman 1980, fig. 181), il suo territorio (Lardos: cfr. Pryce 1928, 170, B 390, fig. 207, a destra) e, appunto, Jalysos.
Sull'iconografia di questo dio protettore delle greggi e l'eventuale sincretismo che essa presuppone con l'egizio 'Amun Reʿ v. più recentemente A.M. Bisi, in Barker et al. (eds.) 1985, 307 ss.
38. Cfr. ClRh 6-7, 1932-33, 345, n. 8, fig. 80.
39. Sapouna-Sakellarakis 1978, 100 ss., nn. 1448-1454 (indicate "o. Nr.", ma corrispondenti invece, nell'ordine, ai nn. inv. 8504, 8502, 8507, 8505, 8503, 8506, 8508), 1457-58, 1460, tavv. 40-42 (tipo VIII a,b). A queste occorre aggiungerne altre sei, inedite (inv. 8496-8501), due delle quali riprodotte qui a fig. 5, in basso. Si noti che le poche altre attestazioni riguardano Lindos, Kalymnos, Paros e Chios (Sapouna-Sakellarakis 1978, nn. 1455, 1456, 1461, 1462), mentre il n. 1459 è di prov. scon., ma acquistato a Smirne.
40. Sapouna-Sakellarakis 1978, 97-99, nn. 1349-1446, tavv. 38-40, nonchè Coldstream 1977, 250, fig. 80 a; Maass 1985, 102, 194, n. 69, con fig.
41. La tipologia cui si fa qui riferimento è quella della Sapouna-Sakellarakis, in quanto più di recente elaborata, anche se complessivamente risulta più tortuosa e meno funzionale di quella di Blinkenberg. Corre l'obbligo di avvertire che, nella sua monografia, la Sapouna-Sakellarakis ha riversato solo la metà ca. delle fibule della stipe jalysia.
42. Sapouna-Sakellarakis 1978, 115, n. 1555, tav. 47.
43. Oltre a Sapouna-Sakellarakis 1978, pp. 124, 125 s., 127, 129, nn. 1617, 1619-1622, 1632, 1633 A, 1676-1677, 1696, tavv. 50-54, v. Caner 1983, 78 e, per converso, 166.
44. Cos, ad es., gli exx., omessi dalla Sapouna-Sakellarakis 1978, inv. 10923 (erroneamente attribuito al suo 1633 A, che ha invece inv. 10929) e 10924.
45. Sapouna-Sakellarakis 1978, 118, n. 1583, tav. 49 (erroneamente indicata con l'inv. 9083)
46. Cfr. Lindos I, c. 90 s., n. 133, tav. 9; Blinkenberg 1926, 262 ss., 284 s. (gruppo XV); Dunbabin (ed.) 1962, 433 ss., A 124-194, tavv. 183-185, con aggiornamenti e aggiunte; Rubensohn 1962, 72, nn. 36-45, tavv. 11b-c, 13. 2-4; Boardman 1967, 211, nn. 231-239, tav. 86, con altri rifer.; Adriani (ed.) 1970, 89, 93, AO.1, tav. XXXIII, 4; Boardman – Hayes 1973, 80, 83, F 151-5, tav. 40; K. Kilian, HambBeitrA 3, 1973, 13 s., Karte 5; AttiMGrecia 15-17, 1974-76, (1977), 148 s., n. 17, tav. LXX,10 = AttiMGrecia, 24-25, 1983-84, 134, n. 20, fig. 46; Philipp 1981, 298, 303, n. 1099, tav. 21; Akurgal 1983, tav. 124 c, I da s., e tav. N, 2, I da s.
L'episodico attardamento oltre il VI sec. a.C. di fibule di questo tipo è documentato, fra l'altro, a Rodi, e precisamente a Kamiros, nella tomba XXVI di Makri Langoni (ClRh 4, 1931, 105, n. 8, fig. 89, fila centrale), il cui corredo include una pelike attica a f. r. del Pittore di Erittonio (Beazley 1963, 1218, n. 2).
47. Cfr. Lindos I, cc. 114 s., 119, n. 275, tav. 12; Kinch 1914, c. 101, tav. 19, 2; ClRh 6-7, 1932-33, 350, n. 50, fig. 82 (stipe di Kamiros); Boardman 1967, 221 s., nn. 352-360, fig. 144, tav. 91, con cfr.; Laffineur 1978, 189, C 5, nn. 49-50, 53, 57-62.
Per gli omologhi in metalli preziosi, di manifattura rodia, cfr. Laffineur 1978, 139 ss., 187, 189 (gruppo C 5), 231 ss., nn. 203-217, tavv. 23,4-6 – 25,6; Higgins 1980, 113 (var. 3), tav. 18 C.
48. Cfr. Walters 1899, 12 s., nn. 161-166; Lindos I, c. 103 s., nn. 223b-227, tav. 11; ClRh 6-7, 1932-33, 346, n. 14, fig. 80 (stipe di Kamiros).
49. Cfr. Lindos I, c. 104, nn. 228-230, tav. 11, con cfr.
50. Cfr. Walters 1899, 11, n. 145 (da Kamiros); Lindos I, c. 399, n. 1576, tav. 63.
51. Cfr. ClRh 6-7, 1932-33, 347, n. 25, fig. 81; v. anche Kilian-Dirlmeier 1979, 220.
52. Altri pendenti ittiomorfi della stipe sono in osso, come in quelle di Lindos (cfr. Lindos I, cc. 98, 101 s., nn. 210-214, tav. 10) e di Kamiros (ClRh 6-7, 1932-33, 342, n. 49, fig. 74).
53. Cfr. Lindos I, cc. 188 ss., nn. 571-577, tavv. 22-23, in ptc. il 571. – Sul tipo Kukahn 1936, 19 s., 43 ss.; CVA British Museum[8] 15 s., commento a tav. 3,3 (II D n); E. Kunze, Olympiabericht 7, 74 ss., figg. 37-38, con rifer.; Snodgrass 1964, 31 s.; Snodgrass 1967, 65 s.; Edrich 1969.
54. Armi miniaturistiche in funzione di ex voto, presenti anche a Lindos (Lindos I, c. 391 s., nn. 1562-66 b, tav. 63), sono frequenti a Creta. Per l'elmo, con la caratteristica alta cresta e privo di visiera, databile alla prima metà del VII sec.a.C., cfr. in particolare, oltre a Kukahn 1936, 15 s., BSA 40, 1939-40, (1943), 54, n. 31, tav. 28 (da Palaikastro), 57, nn. 17-22, tav. 31 (da Praisos), 79 s.; ASAtene 33-34 (n.s. 17-18), 1955-56, (1957), 260 ss., figg. 71-73 (stipe dell'acropoli di Gortina); Snodgrass 1964, 11 s., 16 ss., fig. 1 e (tipo B); Snodgrass 1967, 63; Hoffmann – Raubitscheck 1972, 1 s., con rifer. a nota 10, 22, tav. 41,4 (Gortina) e

5 s., H 5, tav. 13; A. M. Snodgrass, in Antichità cretesi (cit. a nota 15), 196, fig. 1 (Gortina).

55. Cfr. Buchholz et al. 1973, fig. 55, pp. 169 ss., con rifer. anche ad exx. in stipi votive (in ptc. p. 173 s. con nota 656); Chavane 1975, 109, n. 332, tav. 31.
Ami da pesca sono anche in contesti tombali arcaici di Jalysos e Kamiros: v. ad es. ClRh 8, 1936, 47 e 152, n. 1; ClRh 4, 1931, 74, n. 10, fig. 48.

56. Cfr. Lindos I, c. 148 s., nn. 416-7, tav. 15; Boardman 1967, 226,nn. 397-398, fig. 147, tav. 93.

57. Cfr. Lindos I, c. 215, n. 693, tav. 29; MonAnt 17, 1906, c. 81, n. 2, fig. 51 (Gela); Rubensohn 1962, 70 s., n. 32, tav. 12, 18, con rifer.; MuM, Sonderliste J, März 1968, 8, nn. 15-16, con rifer.; Kilian 1975, 215, tav. 94, n. 33 (santuario di Artemis Enodia a Pherai).
Esse sono state rinvenute anche in tombe camiresi (ClRh 4, 1931, 63 e 158, n. 7, fig. 156). Per la loro presenza in complessi tombali sicelioti, etruschi e italici v. M. Cristofani, MonPiot 63, 1980, 24 s., nota 48, con rifer.; Bailo Modesti 1980, 16 s., 162, n. 1, tav. 80; Bonghi Jovino 1982, 23, n. 5, 105, tavv. 7, fig. 4.9, 70.12, 42, nn. 22-23, tavv. 12, fig. 2.3, 88.5-6; Nieuw licht op een oude stad. Italianse en Nederlandse opgravingen in Satricum, Rome 1985, 117, n. 192, con fig.

58. Cfr. Lindos I, c. 223 s., nn. 749-752, tav. 31; Luschey 1939, 10 ss., 36 ss., fig. 6; SCE IV.2, 150, Bowl 4, fig. 28.7, 409, con rifer.; MuM, Sonderliste J, März 1968, 5, n. 4; Chavane 1982, 37, con altri rifer.
Per questo tipo di formula dedicatoria, in uso fra VI e V sec.a.C., v. M.L. Lazzarini, MemAccLincei, s. 8, vol. 19, 1976, 60, n.14, 127 s., 260-262.

59. Boardman 1961, 132-134, fig. 49 A; C. Rolley, RA 1975, 155 ss., figg. 1-4; Rolley 1977, 115 ss., figg. 37-58, tav. 9, 52-53; F. Canciani, in Acts of the International Archaeological Symposium "The Relations between Cyprus and Crete, ca. 2000-500 BC", Nicosia 1979, 270, tav. 48,1, con altra lett.; Boardman 1980, 37, fig. 10; Blome 1982, 25 ss., fig. 8, tav. 11; Rolley 1984, 67, figg. 46-47; H.W. Catling, RDAC 1984, 89 s., tav. XVII, 1-2; M.A. Rizzo, in Creta antica. Cento anni di archeologia italiana (1884-1984), Roma 1984, 55, fig. 10; Pilali-Papasteriou 1985, 78, fig. 41.

60. Webb 1978, passim; alcune sono riprodotte in ClRh 1, 1928, fig. 59 a p. 77.
Di fabbrica egizia è una "fiasca di Capodanno" (inv. 7082) in faïence verde, con figurazioni varie e iscrizioni geroglifiche, segnalata da von Bissing 1941, 5, nota 7, onde Hölbl 1979, I, 36, 38 e M. E. Aubet, CuadRom 14, 1980, 63, f.

61. Cfr. E.J. Peltenburg, Levant 1, 1969, 73 ss. (per gli exx. della stipe dell'Athenaion, ivi indicati semplicemente da Jalysos, in ptc. 90, nn. 13-15, 17, fig. 1 a); J.N. Coldstream, BICS 16, 1969, 5, tav. III c; Boardman 1980, 71, fig. 59, con aggiunte a p. 271, nota 142.

62. La quale ne ha dato notizia in una comunicazione sui "Votive Aigyptiaka from the Sanctuary of Athena at Ialysos on Rhodes", tenuta al 79° General Meeting of the Archaeological Institute of America (Atlanta, 28-30 dicembre 1977), come risulta dal programma stampato in AJA 82, 1978, 249; v. anche A. Di Vita, ASAtene 55 (n. s. 39), 1977, (1980), 349.
Uno dei cinque elementi è riprodotto in ClRh 1, 1928, fig. 59 a p. 77, in alto, al centro (sopra la collana).

63. Jeffery 1961, 348, 356, n. 4 a-b, tav. 67; Guarducci 1967, 329 s., n. 2; Meiggs – Lewis 1969, 12 s., n. 7 c,g; Jeffery 1976, 196, fig. 4, al centro; Boardman 1980, 115 ss., fig. 134.

64. Più di recente E.D. Francis – M. Vickers, AJA 88, 1984, 68 s.; E.D. Francis – M. Vickers, BICS 31, 1984, 119 ss.

65. Cfr. Lindos I, c. 93 s. (133 exx.), con cfr., tav. 10, 151, onde Fr. W. von Bissing, StEtr 16, 1942, 154 ss., tav. XIII, 40-41; Boardman 1961, 94, n. 416, fig. 39, tav. 31, 128, n. 553, fig. 47, tav. 48; Rubensohn 1962, 81, n. 69, tav. 10 h; Dunbabin (ed.) 1962, 518 s., F 29-31, tav. 194 (in pietra), con altri cfr.; Boardman 1967, 239, n. 552, fig. 161, tav. 95.
Di questo tipo è un ex. da Tarquinia, tomba 8 di Poggio Gallinaro, riconoscere come importazione: v. più di recente L'Etruria mineraria, Milano 1985, 76, n. 266, con fig.

66. Kilian 1975, 205, tav. 78, nn. 35-38.

67. SCE IV.2, 174, n. 2, fig. 38, n. 43 (Ayia Irini); von Luschen - Andrae 1943, 136, fig. 191; Goldman (ed.) 1963, 395, tav. 181, 8-9.

68. Più di recente Hölbl 1979, I, 264 s.; O.-H. Frey, in Este e la civiltà paleoveneta a cento anni dalle prime scoperte. Atti dell'XI Convegno di Studi Etruschi e Italici, Firenze 1980, 71, figg. 1.1 (t. 138 Casa di ricovero), 2 (carta di distribuzione); O.-H. Frey, in Kolloquium zur allgemeinen und vergleichenden Archäologie, Band 2, München 1982, 33, con note 53-54, fig. 8 (carta di distrib. aggiornata, ripresa poi da Niemeyer, JbZMusMainz 31, 1984, fig. 20 a p. 28), con rifer., cui vanno aggiunti almeno: ClRh 6-7, 1932-33, 60, n. 2, figg. 73-74 (t. 15 di Papatislures), 336, n. 10, fig. 70 (84 exx. della stipe di Kamiros); F.W. von Bissing, StEtr 12, 1938, 299 s., tavv. 59, nn. 61 A, C, 62 B; F. W. von Bissing, StEtr 16, 1942, 131 ss., fig. 4, tav. XIII, 42-43, con rifer.; Dohan 1942, 40, n. 53, tav. XX; StEtr 25, 1957, fig. 13 a p. 343 (collana di molti vaghi, di cui due ornitomorfi); gli exx. dalle tombe 93 Selciatello di Sopra di Tarquinia e 138 Casa di ricovero di Este, già noti a Frey, sono stati poi riediti, rispettivam., in Bonghi Jovino (ed.) 1986, 73, n. 106 (ove è ignorato Hencken 1968, 164, fig. 149 g) e in Chieco Bianchi – Calzavara Capuis 1985, 54, n. 9, tav. 8, mentre cinque da Capua, t. 248 Fornaci, sono stati pubblicati da Johannowsky 1983, 108, n. 13, tav. XIV,11 (capovolti). Inoltre le carte di distribuzione di Frey vanno integrate con Perachora, essendo infatti agevolmente riconoscibile come perla a uccello quella in Dunbabin (ed.) 1962, 519, G 7, tav. 194 (ivi non identificata).

69. Boardman 1963, 136 ss., fig. 14 (gruppo M); J. Boardman, JHS, 88, 1968, 7; Boardman 1970, 111, 113, fig. 160; Boardman - Vollenweider 1978, 1, 4 ss., nn. 11, 16-17, 21-23, fig. 1, tavv. III-V.

70. Fondamentali E. Porada, in The Aegean and Near East. Studies presented to Hetty Goldman on the Occasion of her Seventy-fifth Birthday, Locust Valley, NY, 1956, 185-211 e J. Boardman – G. Buchner, JdI 81, 1966, 1-62, con successive aggiunte di Boardman 1970, 110, fig. 158, 133, 399; Boardman 1975, 112, nn. 212-213; Popham et al. 1979-1980, 82, 86, n. 25, tav. 67 u; ARepLondon 1978-79, 1979, 9, fig. 7; J. Boardman, in Ladders to Heaven. Art Treasures from the Lands of the Bible. Toronto 1981, 166, nn. 137-138. – Sulla classe in generale o in riferim. ad exx. di Pithecusa e altri siti v. inoltre Wegner 1968, 13 s., 84, nn. 173-189, fig. 2 j; Snodgrass 1971, 346, fig. 109; Coldstream 1977, 229, fig. 75 f; A. Rathje, in Ridg-

way – Ridgway (eds.) 1979, 170 s., fig. X; Hölbl 1979, I, 222 s., II, 94 s., 126, 140, 194 s., 200, nn. 445, 525, 559, 852-855, 936, tav. 147, 2-9; Boardman 1980, 71, fig. 57; G. Buchner, MB 8, 279, I a, fig. 1; una carta di distribuzione di O.-H. Frey, in Kolloquium zur allgemeinen und vergleichenden Archäologie, Band 2, München 1982, fig. 3 a p. 26, onde Niemeyer, JbZMusMainz 31, 1984, fig. 21 a p. 28; Zazoff 1983, 59, 61 s., 64, fig. 24 i, tav. 11, 3,5-7; Ridgway 1984, 82, figg. 15, 34. Molto discusso l'ex., di grandi dimensioni, dalla t. 69 della necropoli di Macchiabate di Francavilla Marittima, a causa della iscrizione che lo correderebbe: fenicia e con il nome del proprietario, secondo P. Zancani Montuoro – M.G. Guzzo Amadasi, AttiMGrecia 15-17, 1974-76, (1977), 58-64, tavv. 22-23 e M.G. Guzzo Amadasi, VicOr 2, 1979, 3 ss., tav I b; aramaica e con la "firma" dell'incisore, a parere di G. Garbini, PP 33, 1978, 424-426; "imaginary", ad avviso di Boardman 1980, 277, nota 65.

71. Cfr. J. Boardman – G. Buchner, JdI 81, 1966, 33, 41, 49, nn. 103 (=Zazoff 1983, 61, nota 71, tav. 11,7), 161, figg. 36, 65.
72. Cfr. J. Boardman – G. Buchner, JdI 81, 1966, 49.
73. Il solo altro esemplare per ora noto con questa scena è edito da J. Boardman, in Ladders to Heaven. Art Treasures from the Lands of the Bible. Toronto 1981, 166, n. 137.
74. Variante di J. Boardman – G. Buchner, JdI 81, 1966, 34, 49, n. 118.
75. Cfr. ibidem, 28, 51, n. 53, ma con gli uccelli rivolti in senso opposto.
76. Cfr. ibidem, 25, 31, 36, 51, nn. 42, 92 (=Zazoff 1983, 61, nota 70, tav. 11,5), 135, fig. 30.
77. Variante, senza il falco, di J. Boardman – G. Buchner, JdI 81, 1966, 25, 53, n. 40 (=Hölbl 1979, II, 140, n. 559, tav. 147,9), figg. 30-31.
78. Cfr. J. Boardman – G. Buchner, JdI 81, 1966, 31, 39, 52, nn. 95, 140.
79. Cfr. ibidem, 28, 55, n. 57.
80. Cfr. ibidem, 16, 26, 28 s., 35, 55, nn. 27, 47, 55, 58, 63, 127, figg. 24-25, 37; Boardman 1975, 112, n. 212; Popham et al. 1979-1980, 1. c. a nota 70.
81. Cfr. J. Boardman – G. Buchner, JdI 81, 1966, 21, 39, 57, nn. 37, 139 B, 142, figg. 26, 51 b, 52.
82. Cfr. ibidem, 20, 29, 31, 33, 56, nn. 34-35 (=Hölbl 1979, II, p. 195, nn. 854-855, tav. 147, 2-3), 50, 87, 101, figg. 26, 28, 29, 41; Boardman 1975, 112, sub n. 212.
83. J. Boardman – G. Buchner, JdI 81, 1966, 33, n. 107, fig. 42 a-d, 39, n. 139, fig. 51 a-d, 42.
84. Cfr. ibidem, 25, 29, 33, 36,54, nn. 39 (registro inf.) (=Hölbl 1979, II, 200, n. 936, tav. 147,6), 68, 107 D, 136, figg. 30, 42 d.
85. Cfr. J. Boardman – G. Buchner, JdI 81, 1966, 40, 55, n. 155, fig. 61; v. inoltre rifer. supra, nota 80.
86. Cfr. ibidem, 13, 15, 33 s., 40 s., 54, nn. 18, 21, 109, 113, 149, 157, figg. 21-22, 36, 56, 63.
87. Cfr. ibidem, 15, 33, 40, 54, nn. 22, 106, 107 C, 150, figg. 21, 42 c, 57.
88. Cfr. ibidem, 16, 30, 36, nn. 24, 78, 129, figg. 21, 23; Boardman 1975, 112, n. 213.
89. Viene meno così l'esclusività sottolineata per Pithecusa da J. Boardman – G. Buchner, JdI 81, 1966, 42 s., con rifer. – Su questo tipo di pendagli v. più recentemente E. Lagarce, in Clerc et al. 1976, 168 ss., figg. 4-7D; Hölbl 1979, I, 147, 153 s,; Cristofani – Martelli (eds.) 1983, 37, 279, n. 94, con altri rifer.
90. J. Boardman – G. Buchner, JdI 81, 1966, 31, 33, nn. 88-105.
91. art.cit. (a nota 70), 192 ss.
92. J. Boardman – G. Buchner, JdI 91, 1966, 61 s.
93. Da ultimi Markoe 1985, 143 s., 161 s., Ca 1, con bibl. prec., fig. a p. 232; Niemeyer, JbZMusMainz 31, 1984, 14, 64, fig. 59.2, tav. 3.1.
94. Con diverso orientamento circa le maestranze immigrate, egiziane o fenicie, v. rispettamente von Bissing 1941, e Dunbabin 1957, 49; T.H.G. James, in Dunbabin (ed.) 1962, 462 s.; Markoe 1985, 94, 96, 124 s.
95. Per rapidi accenni v. R. D. Barnett, Iraq 2, 1935, 182, nota 1; E. Kunze, AM 60-61, 1935-36, 230; Freyer-Schauenburg 1966, 121; Marangou 1969, 287, nota 1177; Riis 1970, 170; Snodgrass 1971, 341; Barnett 1975, 51, 102, nota 10, 121, 128, 145, figg. 15, 55 (schizzi), e Barnett 1982, 47, 88 nota 45.
96. Barnett 1975, 129, 145, fig. 56; S.F. Bondì, in Atti del 1°. Convegno Italiano sul Vicino Oriente antico, Roma 1978, 147-155, tavv. VII-XII.
97. Barnett 1975, 145 ss., con rifer., 172 s., C 12 ss., tav. 4, e Barnett 1982, 48 ss., tav. 50 b; Phönizische Elfenbeine, Karlsruhe 1973, p. XXIII s., nn. 12- 15; I.J. Winter, Iraq 43, 1981, 116 ss., tav. 13 d,e; R. D. Barnett, ErIsr 18, 1985, 1, tav. I, 3.
98. Barnett 1975, 103 ss., 204 ss., S 172 ss., tavv. 70 ss.: stilisticamente la testina di Jalysos è prossima a 213, 215, S 294, S 308, fig. 85, tavv. 89, 91; per la bassa corona-polos cfr. in ptc. 104 s., 205 ss., 224, S 183, S 195, S 203-204, T 5, tavv. 70, 72, 73, 125. V. anche Barnett 1982, tavv. 43 d, 44 c.
99. Barnett 1975, 102 s., 128, 147 ss., figg. 57-58.
100. Barnett 1975, 101 ss., 202, S 146, tav. 63; ErIsr 18, 1985, tav. 1, 2.
101. Cfr. in particolare per la figura singola Hogarth 1908, 179, n. 5, tavv. XXX.16, XXXI.19 (che ha le stesse proporzioni), nonchè n. 8, tavv. XXX.9, XXXI.11; per quelle a coppia 179 s., n. 9, tavv. XXX.13, XXXI.16, oltre che archetipi di stile siriano, quali ad es. le "cariatidi" della coppa per unguenti eburnea Barnett 1975, 45, 226, U 10, tav. 125. – Ricordo inoltre che lo stesso tipo iconografico di estrazione orientale viene recepito in oreficerie etrusche orientalizzanti contemporanee a questi intagli: Cristofani – Martelli (eds.) 1983, 37, 284, n. 112.
Sugli avori camiresi in generale v. anche Poulsen 1912, 83 s., figg. 79-83; R.D. Barnett, JHS 68, 1948, 4 nota 26; Freyer-Schauenburg 1966, 124; Marangou 1969, 197, 204; Aubet 1971, 18.
102. V. in merito, con rifer., Demargne 1947, 299 ss.; D. Levi, ASAtene 33-34 (n. s. 17-18), 1955-56, (1957), 245 s.; S. Lagona, CronAStorArt 1, 1962, 28 ss.; Rizza – Santa Maria Scrinari 1968, 250 ss.; T. Hadzisteliou Price, JHS 41, 1971, 48 ss.; Blome 1982, 76 ss.
103. Cfr. Lindos I, cc. 153 ss., 750, nn. 448-454, 3239, fig. 17, tav. 16; Davidson 1952, 196 s., n. 1503, fig. 30, tav. 90, con rifer.; Dunbabin (ed.) 1962, 448 ss., A 394-432, fig. 29, tav. 190, con altri rifer.; J.G. Landels, BSA 58, 1963, 116-119, figg. 1-2, e J.G. Landels, Hesperia 33, 1964, 392 ss., fig. 1, tav. 70; Boardman 1967, 242, n. 598, fig. 164, tav. 97; A. Bélis, BCH 108, 1984, 111 ss.; A. Bélis, BCH Suppl. 9, 1984, 176 ss.; A. Bélis, RA 1986, 28 s., fig. 7; Lattanzi (ed.) 1987, 58; frammenti di flauti sono stati inoltre trovati sul relitto di nave naufragata nelle acque dell'isola del Giglio: v. M. Bound, in Il commercio etrusco arcaico. Atti dell'Incontro di Studio (=Quaderni del Centro di

Studio per l'archeologia etrusco-italica del Consiglio Nazionale delle Ricerche 9), Roma 1985, 67, fig. 4, nonchè ARepLondon 1985-86, 1986, 114, fig. 19. Sull'aulos in generale, oltre a Wegner 1968, 19 ss., v. ultimamente Paquette 1984, 23 ss. e la relativa recensione di A. Bélis, RA 1986, 171.

104. Mutilo e ricomposto da tre frammenti minori (inv. 9886), ha perfetti pendants negli esemplari, pure iscritti, Lindos II, cc. 201 ss., nn. 4 (=Jeffery 1961, 349, 356, n. 16; Dietz – Trolle 1974, 67, fig. 73; M.L. Lazzarini, MemAccLincei, s. 8, 19, 1976, 200, n. 161) -9, con rifer.

105. Con iscrizione bustrofedica, è stato pubblicato, con la sola indicazione di provenienza da Jalysos, da G. Pugliese Carratelli, ASAtene 33-34 (n. s. 17-18), 1955-56, (1957), 164, n. 13, fig. 13, cui adde fugaci cenni in BdA, s. 2, a. 4, 1924-25, 335 e in BCH 48, 1924, 514.

106. Per questi tipi di formula v. M.L. Lazzarini, MemAccLincei, s. 8, 19, 1976, 125 ss., 118.

107. Cfr. ibidem, 90 ss.; per *apò dekátas* cfr. in ptc. 92, 272, n. 684.

108. V. al riguardo L. Moretti, RivFil 111, 1983, 56, che cita un'attestazione a Istros (iscrizione in alfabeto ionico arcaico su un tegolone dall'area del tempio di Aphrodite) e due ad Atene.

109. I resti di due altre lettere che le affiancavano sono troppo esegui perchè se ne possa tentare un'integrazione fondata (incluso il pur allettante μ'ἀ[νέθηκε]). – Alla cortesia della prof. M. L. Lazzarini, che vivamente ringrazio, debbo utili consigli su questa e le altre iscrizioni.

110. Da ultimo Gras 1985, 651 ss., con lett. prec. e rassegna della documentazione archeologica, invero subordinata ad un'interpretazione a tesi tirrenocentrica in nessun modo condivisibile; in particolare, per altri buccheri etruschi a Rodi (Jalysos, Kamiros), 678, da integrare con Dunbabin (ed.) 1962, 386 nota 1, e Rasmussen 1979, 153 s., n. 31.

111. Jeffery 1961, 347, 356, n. 1, tav. 1; Guarducci 1967, 328 s., n. 1, fig. 163; Riis 1970, 174, fig. 64; Dietz – Trolle 1974, 47, fig. 38; M. L. Lazzarini, ArchCl 25-26, 1973-74, (1975), 346, n. 7, tav. 66, 1;0. Masson, ibidem, 428-431, tav. 81; Coldstream 1977, 299, fig. 95 b; Jeffery 1976, tav. 33.

112. Dunbabin (ed.) 1962, 385, nn. 4126 (Νέαϱ[χος ἀν]έθεκε, retrograda e in alfabeto corinzio) – 4126 bis ([---] εα [---]) = 396, nn. 43-44, tavv. 150, 160, 165; Rasmussen 1979, 152, Q; Gras 1985, 678, cui è sfuggito il secondo frammento iscritto.

113. Secondo l'aberrante tesi di Gras 1985.

114. Nella prospettiva indicata dalla scrivente, a proposito delle placchette eburnee tardo-arcaiche pertinenti a kibotia (uno dei quali restituito da una tomba jalysia), in Il commercio etrusco arcaico 1985, cit. (nota 103),237-238.

Lindian Sacrifice; An Evaluation of the Evidence Based on New Inscriptions*

Philippos Kostomitsopoulos

** I wish to dedicate this paper to the memory of the* ἄωρος και βιαιοθάνατος *Olaf Palme, who was buried on March 15, 1986, the day when the final draft was written.*

Two inscriptions, discovered recently at Lindos, may help us to understand better the Lindian religious life, particularly cult and ritual. The first inscription is part of a sacred law regulating sacrifice to Apollo; the second belongs to the "Boukopian group" of rock inscriptions.

Christian Blinkenberg devoted much attention to the first category. "Règlements de sacrifice rhodiens" was dedicated by him to M.P. Nilsson shortly before the outbreak of the Second World War in tribute to his pioneering work concerning Lindian epigraphical material. "Dragma Nilsson" appeared just in time to permit Mario Segre the writing of "Rituali rodii di sacrifici" (PPG, 1951, 139-53) before he was transported to a Nazi concentration camp, where he met his death. We owe very much to these studies.

Fig. 1.
New Lindian sacred law.

The newly discovered sacred law was found lying in the courtyard of a private house at Lindos, the former olive-oil press of the village, in March 1982. Mr. Ypsilantis, the owner, could not tell Toula Marketou and me how it came to be in his courtyard[1]. He thought the slab might have been brought to him by a villager some years ago, when he was repairing the building, in order to serve as a decoration. The inscribed surface was clearly readable.

It is a fragment of a stele of mottled-gray "Lartian" stone, broken on all sides except the left. (fig. 1). The fractures on the top and bottom seem to be old; small parts of the right side were freshly broken. Although nothing of the original surface is preserved at the right, it seems we miss only some mm on the top. The narrow left side is smooth, the back rough. The stele was probably built into the masonry of a wall or of an altar, maybe among other stelae at either side.

Preserved height: 0.20 m; preserved width: from 0.09 m (bottom) to 0.21 m (top). Thickness: 0.075 m[2]. Height of letters: 0.014 m; omicron: 0.010 m; space between lines: 0.010 m, the same as space at left.

Text	Transcription
ΑΠΟΛΛΩΝΙΕΝ‘	Ἀπόλλωνι ἐν
ΧΙΜΑΡΟΣΘΥΕΤ.	χίμαρος· θυέτ[ω
ΤΩΝΦΥΛΕΤΑ̣	τῶν φυλετᾶ[ν
ΟΓΕΡΑΙΤΑΤ̣	ὁ γεραίτατ[ος·
ΤΑΘΥΘΕΝΤ̣	τά θυθέντ[α αὐτεῖ
ΚΑΤΑΧΡΗ̣	καταχρῆ[σθαι.
vac	vac

Commentary

Rhodian inscriptions of this kind are usually short. The month and day of sacrifice and, probably, the name of the tribe would have appeared in the missing part.

1.1 There are traces of two more letters after the *nu*. The first is circular and smaller. It can be *omicron* or *theta*. The second looks like the lower left end of an *alpha* or another letter of similar shape. No more than three full letter spaces are missing, but there could be four letters, with an *iota* (like the one in the same line) squeezed in at the end.

A place-name in the dative, as well as the name of the place where the sacrifice was performed are equally possible[3]. What we expect naturally is an *epiklesis* of the god in this place, as is usual in Rhodian sacred laws[4]. *Enodiōi* or *Enolmiōi* are possible. The first would be wholly new for Apollo, the second is known only from Sophocles[5] but it is a better candidate because of its obvious connection with the cult of Apollo Pythios, prominent at Lindos[6]. I prefer to leave the space blank[7].

1.2 The name of the animal is in the nominative as always at Lindos, while at Camiros the accusative is the rule[8]. *Chimaros* is a he-goat older than *eriphos*[9] and, at least etymologically, "one winter old". *Eriphoi* fed on straw after harvest were called *diakalamásarkes* by the Rhodians according to Hesychius, who quoted a law, probably similar to the text under discussion. *Eriphoi diakalamásarkes* could not be sacrificed before late summer. Assuming the same precision of language in our text, we can venture to guess that the appropriate period for the sacrifice of a winter-old goat was early spring. The same animal was sacrificed to Apollo *Apotropaios* at Cyrene on two different occasions, once ordered to be of red colour[10] A choice *chimaros* sacrificed to Apollo at Sounion appears in the sacrificial calendar of Thorikos[11]. A *chimaros* excelling in beauty (*kallisteuon*) was offered to Dionysos Baccheus at Mykonos[12] A still unpublished inscription from Charaki near Lindos mentions the trieteric sacrifice of both a *chimaros* and a *tragos* to Dionysos[13].

1.3 The term *phylétas*, member of the tribe, appears for the first time on Lindian inscriptions. Tribes, even the mythical ones mentioned in the so-called Temple Chronicle, are known mostly in connection with contests. However at Kedreae (Rhodian Peraia) there is mention of *phyletai Dymanes*[14].

1.4 *Ho geraitatos* is the eldest member of the tribe, with a clear notion of dignity implicit in the word (Homeric connotations?).

1.5 The last word is restored after the identically formulated law of sacrifice to Athena *Apotropaia* at Lindos[15].

1.6 The use of *eta* instead of the diphthong appears also in the first part of the above-mentioned inscription, dated to the 4th cent. BC. This regulation is known also from Camiros, Cos and many other places[16].

Date: Letter forms and orthography suggest a date around the middle of the 3rd cent. BC.

The end of the first line is so dubious that it adds nothing positive to our knowledge about Lindian Apollo. Precious information is given, however, about sacrifice. What strikes one at first glance is the abnormality of sacrificial procedure. The sacrifice is carried out by the eldest member of the tribe, not by the priest, or *ierothytas*, as usual[17]. Why is a sacrifice in which a whole tribe is involved conducted in this peculiar way? Why are the state magistrates and cult officials not in charge?

In my opinion the sacrifice can take place only during the annual meeting of the tribe, at the moment when the tribesmen are proceeding to elect new officials. The eldest present undertakes a special sacrifice to Apollo, who will help, with his mantic power, to choose the best. A register of all *phyletai* has possibly just been completed, as was the case at the sanctuary of Apollo *Pythios* at Halasarna of Cos[18].

We now proceed to examine the new rock inscription of the "Boukopian" group. Blinkenberg published 40 inscriptions of this category in chronological order[19]. The new inscription is engraved on a vertical rock surface facing east, between No. 588 (1,30 m to the north) and No. 587 (4 m to the south) (fig. 2). They were numbered 39 and 40 by Kinch, the only two not included in Lieutenant Bagger's situation map. They face north, being on the eastern side of an outcrop of rock very close to the fortified hill, just west of the only path leading south, to the Spiliotissa caves. This rock is very schematically shown at sq. V-VI/17 of Rasmussen's 1905 general plan,

Fig. 2.
Eastern face of the rock with the 3 inscriptions.

20 m SE of the easternmost point of the medieval lower fortification[20].

We noticed the three inscriptions while working in this area in connection with the preparations for the restoration of the Acropolis. Another result of this work was the discovery of a wall, made with ample use of sherds, and probably medieval or Turkish[21].

The Ergias[22] inscription (No. 587) was depicted at 0,17 m above ground level in Fru Helwig Kinch's excellent drawing of May 1907[23]. The new inscription is 1,05 m above present-day ground level, which is now a little higher. In front of it is a small horizontal formation of the rock[24]. The Pythodoros inscription (No. 588) has a very narrow ledge at 1.30 m above ground level and it is carved 0.80 m above this. It is very exposed to northern winds and, consequently, badly damaged. This inscription, the first one of the group to be published, was discovered and copied by Symeon Georgiadis, a Lindian teacher at Massari, before 1886 and examined later by Hiller von Gaertringen, who also spotted the Ergias inscription (in 1892) and by Kinch[25].

Blinkenberg, who left Rhodes for good in the early years of the expedition (in 1905), probably did not know the exact location of the two inscriptions. He criticized[26] Georgiadis for describing the location as "in the castle", but Georgiadis was, at least partially, right[27]. Taking into account that the distance between No. 589 (inside the naiskos) and the rock face we are examining is about 200 m, the steepness of the ground where no direct path leads from one place to the other, and the difference in altitude (more than 35 m) we realize that our cluster of inscriptions lies in a different place. "Boukopion", Blinkenberg's proposal for the ancient toponym, cannot be accepted as valid for both areas[28].

The new inscription (fig. 3) has four lines, contrary to the neighbouring two-liners: Height of letters between 0,037 m (Π) and 0,050 m (Σ), space between lines 0,010-0,020 m[29]. The letters were first cut into the hard rock surface with a pointed tool, and the wide grooves must have been filled with colour if the inscription was meant to remain readable for any length of time.

Text	Transcription
ΠΡΟΧΑΡΑΙΟ	Πϱο(σ)χάϱαιο(ς)
ΠΡΑΤΑΡΧΟΥ	Πϱατάϱχου
ΘΥΣΙΑΟΥΒΟΚΟ	ϑυσία οὐ βοκο-
ΠΙΑ	πία.

Fig. 3.
New rock inscription of the Boukopian group.

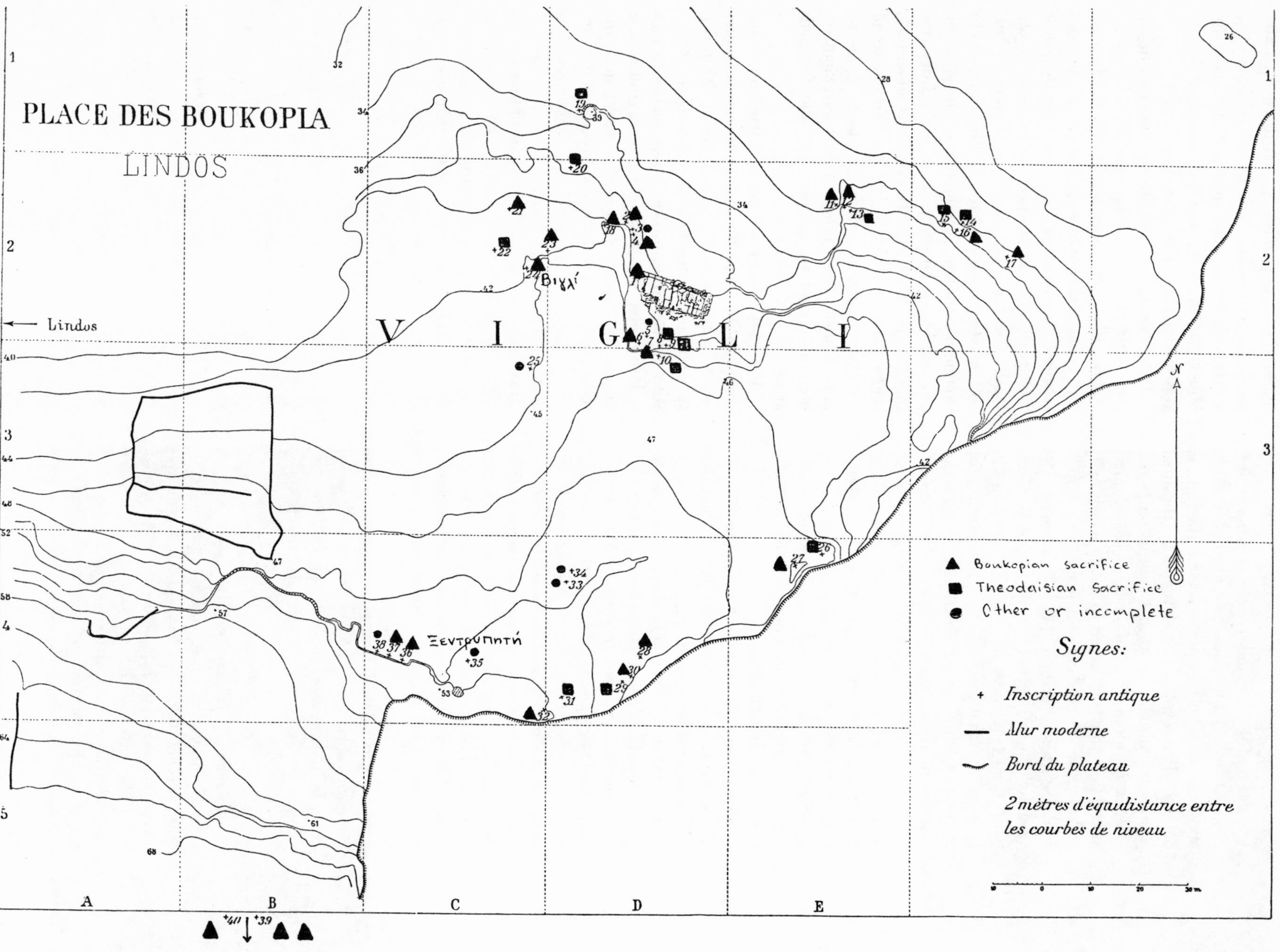
PLACE DES BOUKOPIA
LINDOS
Lindos
V I G L I
Boukopian sacrifice
Theodaisian Sacrifice
Other or incomplete
Signes:
Inscription antique
Mur moderne
Bord du plateau
2 mètres d'équidistance entre les courbes de niveau

Fig. 4

Commentary

1.1 The omission of *sigma* is unique in the group. No. 581 has double *sigma*, No. 612 has it added above *chi*. The surface of the rock at the right is convex. This explains, possibly, why the final *sigma* was omitted. *Proscharaios* appears on 28 out of 41 inscriptions, in 12 of them, including ours, as the first word separated from the word *thysia* by the name of the sacrificing person or group[30]. Hiller's interpretation of *proscharaios* as "freudig"[31] was rejected by Kinch and Blinkenberg, who explained the word as meaning "in front of the altar", with *eschara* substituting for the more common word *bōmós*. They proposed a derivation from pro+eschara, with krasis[32]. "Oe" is not, according to Schwyzer, contracted before two consonants; the composition could be possible only with hyphairesis[33]. If proscharaios qualifies the word thysia, as generally accepted, they should together form a sacrificial "terminus technicus". This problem will be further discussed below.

1.2 Genitives in *-ou* appear around the middle of the 4th cent. BC[34]. Pratarchos was the name of the natural father of Timogone in a Lindian inscription of 115 BC[35]. The name is new to the group, added to 26 fully preserved names, inter alia Hagesarchos (No. 607) and Timasarchos (No. 608). Some inscriptions mention other family members in a way that is interesting as evidence of the structure of the Lindian families[36].

1.3-4 The form *Boko-* is dated to the end of the 5th cent. BC[37]. *Ou* is put immediately before the word it negates. There is one parallel in the group, No. 612, although it was not recognised as such[38]. *Bokopaiá* is an adjective, as is *boukopia* in No. 612. *Theodaisia* is more common[39].

Date: The two published inscriptions on the same rock surface are dated to the end of the 5th cent. BC. *Boko-* belongs to this period but the genitive in *-ou* contradicts an early date. About 350 BC.

"*Proscharaios thysia*" as a sacrificial term creates serious difficulties. Literally it means – contrary to everything we know about sacrifices – that it should take place before the altar, not on it[40]. The ritual slaughter does indeed happen near the altar; parts of the victim always burn upon it. This burning is Greek *thysia* proper[41].

Blinkenberg's interpretation of the Boukopian inscriptions assumed the existence of a toponym, *Boukopion*, signifying the place where oxen were ritually killed for the sacrifice[42]. fig. 4 (map). The whole formula was not translated, but it was satisfactorily interpreted as:

"The carving up of the ox (for) the sacrifice of (NAME-S) in front of the altar".

Topographical objections apart, the new inscription in itself now produces a piece of unexpected information: beside the more common "Boukopian" sacrifice there existed also a "no Boukopian" type of sacrifice. We know now that *boukopia* refers strictly to the carving up of the sacrificial animal *after its ritual killing*, which is not expressed by this word. Having this in mind we are obliged to translate the texts differently:

"The sacrifice of (NAME-S) in front of the altar (has been accomplished by) 1) carving up 2) not carving up the ox" thus accepting *boukopia* as an integral part of the sacrificial formula.

The abnormality of sacrificial procedure becomes evident now. It is very difficult to understand how a sacrifice could be accomplished away from the altar, however near to it. Inevitably the victim could not be burned on the sacred fire. (We all agree, I hope, that *eschara* is impossible to conceive without fire; it is the altar of burnt offerings *par excellence*).

Lindian sacrificial procedure was famous for another reason in antiquity: during the sacrifice to Heracles the hero was constantly insulted by the participants[43]. This was known as "Lindian sacrifice". Killing the animal and carving up the meat in front of the altar without offering a part to the god would be regarded also, if it truly happened, as a serious insult. No literary sources mention such a procedure, with *aition* or not. The only excuse for such behaviour could be a sacred law forbidding any contact between the flesh of the sacrificial animal (either cut in pieces or the entire body) and the fire burning on the altar. Could Lindian law contain such a restriction? We have no Greek parallels for it.

What we have instead is information regarding the cult of Athena in Rhodes in general. According to Pindar[44], the sons of Helios, ordered by him to build Athena an altar that all may see (*bomon enargéa*) and to perform a sacred sacrifice (*semnán thysían*), forgot[45] to provide a means of making flame (*spérma flogos*) and they constructed a sanctuary for fireless sacrifices (*apyrois hierois*). This kind of sacrifice was really performed in Rhodes in historical times, as confirmed by various independent sources[46].

"*Apyra hierá*" could be offerings of fruit, grain and wine[47]. Blinkenberg, who attached great importance to Pindar's lines, believing they were relevant only to the acropolis of Lindos, supported this view[48]. He regarded Boukopion as the place of sanguinary Dorian sacrifices, while the top of the hill was restricted to the pre-Doric bloodless ritual of vegetable offerings identified with "*ápyra hierá*"[49]. Dyggve[50] and Konstantinopoulos[51] were in favour of animal sacrifices on the Acropolis, drawing attention to a stratum of charcoal and animal bones possibly connected with an altar[52].

If we accept as a working hypothesis that "*ápyra hierá*" means in Rhodian sacrificial usage simply that the slaughtered animal was not burned, we can regard the Boukopian formula as a possible confirmation of this rite. *Proscharaios thysia* in other words can be an expression equivalent to "*ápyra hierá*". Before we come to this point it is necessary to discuss whether Athena was the deity to whom a *proscharaios* sacrifice was offered.

The very early date of the naiskos was proven by excavation. Dyggve argued for the continnous use of this building and its close connection with the inscriptions around it[53]. Blinkenberg favoured Athena as the anonymous receiver of the cult in the naiskos[54]. This opinion seems valid to me, despite different views[55]. The fact that the sacrificial inscriptions are widely dispersed from the port area to the fortified sanctuary on the hill makes any other possibility unlikely. The vicinity of the naiskos area to the port lends support to this conclusion, indicating perhaps how the Danaids, who founded the sanctuary with the first aniconic statue of the goddess, sacrificed "on the coast, sailing by Lindos"[56].

Taking this into account we still have no other evidence that the sacrifice of the Boukopian inscriptions was anything but normal, except the possibility that *proscharaios* means the opposite of "burned sacrifice", which is the only way to explain this word in conformity with its accepted derivation.

As a matter of fact, I am not convinced that *proscharaios* really derives from *eschara*. Not only the difficulties of grammatical construction and inherent abnormalities of rite are against it: what troubles me more is the coexistence of two modal adjectives in a short text of this kind. The inscriptions were clearly commemorative in character, ordered by private persons, not by priests codifying rites.

I guess that *proscharaios* might be temporal instead of modal. It is perhaps a simple heading, meaning that the sacrifice takes place on a certain occasion. This could be the *Proschaireteria* or *Procharisteria*[57]: this day, according to the Suida, "at the end of winter, when the crops were beginning to grow, all the magistrates sacrificed to Athena and the sacrifice was called *procharisteria*. Lycurgus in his speech on the priestly office (speaks of) the most ancient sacrifice commemorating the return of the goddess and called *procharisteria* because the crops are beginning to grow"[58]. This feast is Athenian and it is connected with the agricultural character of the goddess. It is not attested at Lindos, but this happens with feasts of Athena in general, at Lindos and elsewhere. *Proscharaios* (and *procharaios* if the omission is not accidental) is indeed very far from the normal *proschaireterios*. Could it be a substandard dialectal form or an epigraphical contraction, as is the case with "*boukos*"[59] of some inscriptions? If this be so, we can say we know something more both about the cult of Athena and Lindian sacrifice.

Philippos Kostomitsopoulos
Ministry of Culture and Science
Archaeological Institute of the Dodecanese
Rhodes
Greece

1. Mr Ypsilantis is also the owner of a brick factory at Yennadi, south of Lindos, and he has a small collection of antiquities, mostly bought in Athens. He wanted no compensation for the stone given to Rhodes Museum, where it has the inventory No. E 2273.
2. A still unpublished intact inscription from Charaki near Lindos (inv. no. E 484) has the same thickness, a width of 0.217 m and a total height of 0.367 m with 0.14 m of empty space at the bottom.
3. Sanctuaries of Apollo at Kamyndos and Loryma are known from inscriptions. The place-names are in the accusative. The dative is used for sanctuaries of Asklepios in Kenchreai and Artemis in Kekoia (Lindos II, index).
4. Zeus Amalos, Poseidon Phytalmios, Apollo Pedageitnios appear on Rhodian sacred laws. Rare epithets of Apollo are known mainly from Camiros: Digenes, Epiknisios, Epimelidios, Petasitas, Pharmakios (Morelli 1959, 102-110).
5. Sophocles, the Fragments, vol. III, ed. A.C. Pearson, 1917, 145, fr. 1044. Cf. Burkert 1972, 140 n. 38 (*bolmos* and *enolmios*).
6. The priest of Apollo Pythios figures constantly from 293 BC on in the lists of *syniereis* second only to the priest of Athana (Morelli 1959, 108). Cf. M. Segre, PP 4, 1949, 72-82.
7. Prof. P.M. Fraser most kindly offered another possible end to the line – *enorchos*. The vertical stroke of a *rho* after *omicron* cannot be entirely excluded, although the stroke seems to me oblique.
8. M. Segre, PP 6, 1951, 149.
9. Ar. Byz. ap. Eust. 1625.33.
10. Sokolowski 1962, no. 115 A 1.7 (4th cent. BC); no. 116 A 1.1 (2nd cent. BC).
11. SEG XXVI, 1976-77, no. 136 1.20, dated 400-350 BC.
12. Sokolowski 1969, no. 96 1.27, about 200 BC.
13. Announced in ASAtene 33-34, 1955-56, 157 as "due leggi sacre" because the stele (see note 2 for dimensions) bears two texts.
14. Homeric tradition (Il. B 668) and Hellenistic usage (examples in BCH 99, 1975, 109) agree on the partition of the island between the three city states along tribal lines. A "phylá Argeia" (Lindos II, 199 1.6) homonymous to the Lindian *damos* creates some problems (ib. 1012-15). We also have evidence for a degradation of the term *phylá*, used in the partition of a *koinón* (IG XII 1, no. 127). On tribal cycles of the three (anonymous) Lindian tribes based on the triennial rule, P.M. Fraser in: Eranos 51, 1953, 23 ff. Improved text of the Kedreae Rhodian decree in Fraser-Bean 1954, 45 f. no. 42.
15. ASAtene 33-34, 1955-56, 169 f. with picture. Republished in Sokolowski 1962, no. 88.
16. Guarducci 1978, 43.
17. Blinkenberg commented on the number (Lindos II, no. 102 1.12) and the age (ib. no. 167,19) of Lindian *hierothytai*; M. Segre, PP 6, 1951, 153 observed their annual election to the office. Cf. D.R. Smith, ArchCl 41, 1972, 532-39.
18. Information as to the epithet kindly given by Mrs Charis Kantzia, who recently discovered an inscription mentioning it in the sanctuary of present-day Kardamaena.
19. Lindos II, nos 580-619.
20. Lindos III, 43.
21. The uncovered part measures 7.20 m in an E-W direction. This wall might originally have reached the easternmost bastion of the lower fortification.
22. Except the historian (Blinkenberg l.c.) the name appears also as a graffito on a 6th cent. BC burial pithos of the Camirean Makri Langoni cemetery (ClRh IV, 1933, 333, and Tituli Camirenses no. 175).
23. Lindos II, 909.
24. Similar to many described by Blinkenberg. It is 0.45 m high and almost square (0.70 X 0.90 m).
25. First published by Em. Loewy in: Archäologisch-Epigraphische Mitteilungen aus Oesterreich-Ungarn X, 1886, 220 no. 26 after the copy of Georgiadis.
26. Lindos II, 897.
27. Beside the existence of the above-mentioned wall (no. 21) which was mostly covered by recent débris but was probably still standing in Georgiadis' time, there is also literary evidence for the use of the word *kastro* in a wider sense (meaning the whole natural rocky stronghold) in the 10th cent. AD at Lindos (Anth. Pal. XV,11 description by Konstantinos the Lindian of the rock epigram near the road leading to the Acropolis, republished IG XII,1 no. 783).
28. Lindos II,897,907 et passim. Lindos III, 457 et passim. Hiller von Gaertringen, on the contrary, distinguished clearly between the two inscriptions "in arcis clivo orientali" and the twelve "in septentrionali arcis clivo supra portum magnum" in IG XII,1 p. 124.
29. Similar letter size in nos. 580, 585, 586, 588, 602.
30. This group of twelve inscriptions also includes nos. 581, 593, 596, 600, 607, 610, 611, 613, 614. Directly before the word *thysia*, *proscharaios* appears in nos 582, 584, 585, 592, 597, 601, 605. Directly after it, it appears in 612, after *thysia Boukopiou* in 608, in both cases before the name. Without the word *thysia* it appears in nos, 583, 590, 602, 604, 617. Two cases are indecisive because the inscriptions are not complete (586, 599). Seven inscriptions mention *boukopia* or *theodaisia* omitting *proscharaios* and sometimes also *thysia* (nos. 587, 588, 589, 591, 594, 603, 609).
31. In RE III 1 (1899) 1018 s.v. Βουκοπία Θευδαισια (Hiller v. Gaertringen)
32. Blinkenberg – Kinch 1903, 84; Lindos II, 908.
33. Schwyzer 1934, 398 and 402.
34. Lindos II, 909.
35. Lindos II, no. 252 1.146.
36. The name in the genitive is followed by anonymous sons (604, 614), grandsons (600, 608, 612), descendants (592) or brothers (613), who are probably minors. In these cases the person named is, I believe, present at the sacrifice. In other cases the person named is not present but his relatives are: sons (585, 593, 597, 601) or grandsons (582). The father of one of the anonymous grandsons in no. 582 was settled in Egypt. Some of the inscriptions of this category might belong to colonists returning temporarily. Cf. Lindos II, no. 44.
37. Lindos II, 909.
38. It was thought to be the beginning of the word *thysia*. This is totally excluded in our case, where the "mistaken" word is written just before OY on the same line.
39. It appears in nos. 582, 596, 597, 603, 605, 613.
40. Yavis 1949, 54-57 et passim. Blinkenberg in Lindos II, 908 draws a parallel with *probómios* quoting the Lex catharctica of Cyrene 1. 61, 67, 68 (Sokolowski 1962 no. 115 A) where this word has the meaning "placed on the altar beforehand as a preliminary sacrifice" Liddell-Scott, 9th ed. *Probómioi sfagai* in Eur. Ion 1.376 quoted also, refers to the slaughter of the sheep before the altar and preliminary to the sacrifice. It is interesting, however, that this sacrifice has no chance of success:

"Der Gipfel wäre es des Unverstands
Wenn wir durch Lämmerschlachten am Altar
durch Vogelflug die Götter zwingen, uns
Zu sagen, was ihr Wille uns verhüllt "
in the beautiful translation by Ernst Buschor (ed. Beck, 1963).

41. This is unanimously accepted by all scholars, based also on linguistic evidence. See recent discussions in Detienne – Vernant 1979 (with extensive bibliography by J. Svenbro) and Reverdin - Grange 1980. An important discussion of archaeological material may be found in Højlund 1981, esp. 83-87. Two relevant papers by J.-L. Durand and J. Svenbro are announced in Anthropozoologica 1985, 3, 22-23.
42. Lindos II, 897, 907.
43. Morelli 1959, 54-56.
44. Olympionikos 7, l. 40-50.
45. According to Bresson 1979, 48-50 the Heliads are immediately rewarded by Zeus because they brought themselves voluntarily into the pro-Promethean condition of mankind by "forgetting" to use fire during their sacrifice.
46. Philostratos, Eikones B.27.3 ; Diodoros V 56,5.
47. Eur. Fr. 912.4 : *thysian ápyron pankarpeias*.
48. Lindos I, 10.
49. Lindos II, 904-905.
50. Lindos III. 1, 179.
51. Konstantinopoulos 1972, 34-45.
52. Mr. Allan Bergfelt, student at Göteborgs Universitet, has recently (1986) made a new study of the subject: Athana Lindia - Kult med eller utan bränoffer?, which I had the pleasure to examine during the Symposium in Copenhagen.
53. Lindos III 2, 463.
54. Lindos II, 906.
55. To the list given by Blinkenberg in Lindos II, 904 n. 1 we may add: Hiller, GGA 204,5 1942, 164 (Dionysos); Eitrem, SOsl 23, 1944, 45 (Demeter); Pugliese-Carratelli, PP 1, 1946, 142 (Athena); Dyggve in Lindos III 2, 428 (anonymous); ib. 465 (more than one); Konstantinopoulos 1972, 43 is against Athena without offering a substitute.
56. Jacoby 1904, 17.
57. Deubner 1932, 17 n. 4 thought they are two different feasts because the writing differs. Nilsson ($GGrR^2$ I, 440 f.) believed they are identical because they both celebrate the Anodos of the goddess. I hold his opinion.
58. Suida 2928. The translation is Farnell's.
59. Blinkenberg suggested this possibility in Lindos II, no. 594. Cf. Nachmanson, Eranos 10, 1910, 101 ff.

Vorläufiger Bericht über die Terrakotten aus dem Demeter-Heiligtum der Stadt Rhodos

Eos Zervoudaki

Am nordöstlichen Stadtrand und etwa 50 m von der hellenistischen Stadtmauer entfernt wurde bei Rettungsgrabungen das Demeter-Heiligtum entdeckt[1]. Einen Tempel fand man nicht. Es wurden aber Reste von Rechteckbauten festgestellt. Von diesen sind drei nicht, wie für die Bauten der antiken Stadt die Regel, von Norden nach Süden orientiert. Ähnliche Bauten im unmittelbar nach Süden anschliessenden Grundstück[2] müssen mit diesem Heiligtum verbunden werden. Ein ausgedehntes, zum Demeter-Heiligtum gehörendes Areal ca. 100x100 m wird umschrieben durch: 1. Die kürzlich in einem nach Osten gelegenen Grundstück gefundenen über 200 Statuetten vom gleichen Typ wie jene im Heiligtum selbst, Lampen und Miniaturhydrien[3]. 2. Durch die über 100 Statuetten gleichen Typs, die zufällig nach einem Bombenabgriff des Zweiten Weltkriegs im Gelände des städtischen Gefängnisses gefunden wurden. Und 3. durch den freien Raum, den man durch früheren Grabungen im südwestlich anschliessenden Gelände bis zur antiken Strasse R 1a festgestellt hatte[4].

Die Ausgrabung im Heiligtum beschränkte sich auf zwei schmale, fortlaufende Schnitte von insgesamt 240 Quadratmetern Fläche, dort, wo die moderne Bautätigkeit nicht alle antiken Reste beseitigt hatte. Bereits in den obersten Schichten im Niveau der heutigen Strasse kamen zahlreiche, jedoch meist stark fragmentierte Statuetten zu Tage, hunderte von Miniaturhydrien, Olpen, Skyphoi und über dreitausend Lampen. Die Funde streuten über die gesamte Grabungsfläche und bis zum gewachsenen Boden. Funde gab es auch in den Gebäuden, in deren Aufschüttung Brandspuren und Tierknochen festgestellt wurden. Ich weise besonders darauf hin, dass in der Anlage III die Skeletten von drei Rindern begraben waren und dass die Anlage VIII aus einer Grube von 1,60x0,70 m besteht, die 1,12 – 1,65 m tief in den Felsen gegraben und mit Sandsteinplatten verkleidet ist; zugänglich war sie über drei Stufen.

Die Art der Votive – Hydrien, Lampen, Kernoi, Figuren mit Hydria, Schwein oder Korb, Kourotrophoi, Tänzerinnen, Koren usw. - zusammen mit dem Zeugnis der Weihinschrift auf dem Bronzeschöpfer aus der Anlage VIII lassen keinen Zweifel zu, dass es sich um ein Demeter-Heiligtum handelt[5]. Mit der Entdeckung dieses Heiligtums ist erstmals ein öffentlicher Demeter und Kore-Kult in Rhodos nachgewiesen. Bisher hatte man als Hinweis auf einen solchen Kult nur den Namen "Thesmophorios" für den ersten Monat des rhodischen Kalenders und den Verein der Thesmophoriasten neben einigen späteren Weihinschriften, die allerdings in Kamiros und Lindos gefunden sind[6].

Da die Keramik aus dem Heiligtum noch nicht bearbeitet ist, bleibt auch die Stratigraphie noch unklar. In groben Zügen lassen sich die zeitlichen Grenzen des Heiligtums festlegen mit einem Beginn spätestens im Anfang des 4. Jahrhunderts v.Chr. – das heisst die ersten Jahre nach der Stadtgründung – und Ende wahrscheinlich im frühen 2. Jh.v.Chr.

Während der langen und kontinuierlichen Benutzung des Heligtums scheinen ständig Tonfiguren geweiht worden zu sein, zumindest bis ins fortgeschrittene 3. Jh. Trotz der schlechten Erhaltung konnten etwa achthundert Figuren indentifiziert werden[7]. Diese Fundgruppe gewinnt damit besondere Bedeutung für Fragen nach der Entwicklung der rhodischen Koroplastik[8].

Wertvolle Informationen über die rhodische Koroplastik haben bisher die interessanten Fundgruppen aus den beiden Depots von Lindos geliefert[9]. Die Statuetten aus dem Grossen Depot zusammen mit den Funden aus Gräbern, vorallem der Nekropolen von Kamiros und Ialysos[10], gestatten es, ein recht klares Bild von der rhodischen Koroplastik des 6.-5. Jhs.v.Chr. zu entwerfen. Das kleine Depot mit 851 Statuetten umfasst das ganze 4. Jh.[11]. Die Übereinstimmung in Tonqualität, Farbgebung, technische Eigenheiten und die allmähliche innere Formentwicklung erlauben die Annahme, dass es sich überwiegend um Erzeugnisse nur einer und zwar wahrscheinlich lokalen Werkstatt handelt. Das Vorkommen nur weniger Typen von abweichendem Charakter bestätigt diese Annahme. Zugleich aber deutet sich an, dass die Typen aus dem Kleinen Depot nicht das ganze Spektrum der rhodischen Koroplastik repräsentieren. Das verdeutlichen auch weitere Funde aus anderen Grabungen in der Stadt Rhodos[12].

Ein beträchtlicher Teil der Figuren aus dem Demeter-Heiligtum sind Typen, die auch aus Lindos bekannt sind. Sie wurden nach den gleichen Archetypen hergestellet, aus gleichartigen oder ähnlichen Matrizen oder aus Matrizen mit kleinen Variationen. Einige dieser Typen gehören den gleichen Entwicklungsphasen an, wie jene von Lindos, aber viele von ihnen – und das ist besonders wichtig - entwickeln sich noch weiter als die von Lindos und bezeugen damit die Langlebigkeit von Kulttypen, die als Weihgeschenk in Heiligtümern bestimmt sind. Ebenso bedeutend ist der Anteil gleichzeitiger, aber für Lindos nicht nachgewiesener Typen. Sie geben eine Vorstellung von der Formenvielfalt, die kennzeichnend ist für die rhodische Koroplastik der spätklassischen und frühhellenistichen Zeit.

Die noch ausstehende Bearbeitung der Keramik aus dem Heiligtum und der Stratigraphie, zusammen mit der geringen Zahl an Statuetten aus Gräbern des 4. Jhs. erlauben es uns noch nicht, eine gesicherte chronologische Beurteilung der Verwendungsdauer einzelner Typen. Die Vielfalt und die Häufigkeit der Typen aus dem Heiligtum machen es jedoch deutlich, dass sich der typologische Wandel recht schnell vollzog.

Im allgemeinen sind die Figuren aus blassbraunem, weichen, feinen, nicht besonders stark gebranntem Ton hergestellt, der mit feinem Sand und wenig oder keine Mika gemagert sein kann. Unterschiede im Brand, in der Farbe (gelblicher Ton oder kräftigere Farbe bis orange) und in einigen Fällen in der Tondichte oder Tonhärte finden sich bei nicht lindischen (traditionellen) Typen und zwar vorallem des fortgeschrittenen 4. und des 3. Jhs.[13].

Gewöhnlich sind nur die Vorderseiten in Matrizen geformt. Die Rückseite wird mit einer flachen oder leicht gewölbten Platte verschlossen, meist ohne Brennloch. Die Verwendung von Matrizenserien des gleichen Typs is ein übliches Phänomen. Doppelte Matrizen für Vorder- und Rückseite lassen sich, wie zu erwarten, in späterer Zeit regelmässiger feststellen.

Die Basen sind gewöhnlich in einem Stück mit der Figur gearbeitet, nach vorne rechteckig und nach hinten gerundet, Höhe 1 cm. Bei eine Reihe traditioneller Typen des späten 4. und frühen 3. Jhs.v.Chr., die auch durch weitere gemeinsame Züge verbunden sind, so dass Herkunft aus der gleichen Werkstatt vermutet wird, ist die Basis zweimal gestuft und 2-3 cm hoch. Es gibt aber auch Figuren mit getrennt gefertigter Basis; es sind dann grosse Rechtecke mit profilierten Seiten oder Rundbasen u.ä.

Bemalung hat sich nur ganz selten erhalten. Sie unterscheidet sich nicht von jener der Statuetten aus Lindos[14].

Wie in anderen Demeter-Heiligtümern, z.B. in Kos, Priene, Pergamon, Troja, aber auch in Lindos[15], überwiegen weibliche Figuren. Männerstatuetten sind mit einem Anteil von 8 Prozent vertreten. Es gibt auch Tierfiguren, Ferkel, Tauben, ein Widder[16].

Bei den Frauenfiguren sind am häufigsten die Hydrophoren (etwa achtzig), es folgen die Tänzerinnen (sechunddreissig), deren Beziehung zu Demeter ja bekannt ist. Kourotrophoi, Kanephoren, Figuren mit Ferkel, Früchtekorb, Kranz, Protome, Phialenträgerinnen, Adorantinnen, verschiedene Typen von Himation- oder Peplosfiguren, freistehend oder angelehnt, Gliederpuppen, eine Menge Sitzende oder Thronende (an Zahl der Tänzerinnen gleich) bilden das weite Spektrum der Frauentypen. Viele von ihnen tragen eine Stephane und manche einen Polos. Es gibt einige Statuetten, die Statuentypen der Kore folgen. Es fehlt auch nicht eine thronende Kybele, sowie Frauen mit Tympanon. Daneben gibt es einige Typen der Aphrodite, Aphrodite mit Eros und Eroten, die übliche Weihungen in Heiligtümern von Demeter sind[17].

Die Männerfiguren sind begrenzt auf die ty-

Abb. 1:
Protome Nr. 648
(erh. H. 0,087 m)

pisierten Himationträger, bärtig oder unbärtig, mit oder ohne Polos, mit Phiale, Fackel o.ä., die sich auch in Lindos finden. Der hockende Knabe ist einmal und der reitende Heros in 2-3 Varianten belegt[18].

Schliesslich sind zu erwähnen die grosse Zahl und Vielfalt an Frauenprotomen in verschiedenen Grössen und Tonqualitäten. Nur ganz wenige Protomen sind ausreichend gut erhalten, meist haben wir nur kleine Fragmente.

Ich zeige hier eine Auswahl von wenigen Typen, um einerseits den Charakter der Votive deutlich zu machen, andererseits auch solche Typen vorzuführen, die in den Depots von Lindos nicht vertreten sind.

Ich beginne mit einigen Statuetten des 5. Jhs., die zu den ersten Weihungen im Heiligtum gehören müssen. Allerdings ist es im Augenblick noch nicht möglich, zu bestimmen, wie lange sie noch bis ins 4. Jh. fortleben. Jedenfalls beträgt ihr Anteil an den Votiven nicht mehr als vier Prozent.

Beispiele dafür gibt es mehrere bei den sitzenden Frauen. Einige davon sind weiterlebende ionische Typen archaischer Zeit[19], die im Grossen Depot von Lindos vorkommen, im Kleinen dagegen nicht mehr auftreten. Als Beispiele zeige ich die Polosträgerin (Nr. 229), die eine Granatapfel vor der Brust hält (vgl. Lindos 2165); von den Typen des fortgeschrittenen 5. Jhs. die Thronende mit den Klappern (Nr. 675) (vgl. Lindos 2245); Zu den frühen Votiven im Heiligtum gehört auch der nackte Knabe, der vor der Brust eine Frucht hält (Nr. 572). Dieser ostionischer Typ, der mit einer Entsprechung auch im Grossen Depot von Lindos belegt ist (Lindos 2380), dürfte dem frühen strengen Stil angehören und begegnet auch in Karien[20]. Ich erwähne noch den Jüngling mit Leier (Nr. 647), den es mit unterschiedlicher Frisur auch im Grossen Depot gibt (Lindos 2355). Eine weitere Gattung, die mit zahlreichen frühen Typen vertreten ist, sind die Protomen.

Unter den Protomen, bildet die Protome Nr. 648 eine Ausnahme (Abb.1). Mit dem hohen Polos, ursprünglich mit reichen Farben bemalt, und dem charakteristichen Schleier wird ein alter und weit verbreiteter Typ wiederholt, der zwar unterschiedlich benannt werden kann, im Fall dieses Heiligtums aber Demeter oder Kore darstellt, wie etwa in Selinunt Malophoros, im Nekyiomanteion von Ephyra und in Knidos Kore[21].

Zu den frühen Votiven im Heiligtum zählen auch Hydriaphoren, ein Motiv, das hier reichlich und in bedeutender Vielfalt belegt ist.

In Lindos begegnen Hydriaphoren im Kleinen Depot erstmals um 370 v.Chr. mit dem himationbekleideten Typ, bei dem das lange und gerade Himation vom Hals an den Körper und die Arme wie eine Kutte verhüllt (Lindos 3003 ff.)[22]. Im Demeter-Heiligtum setzen die Hydriaphoren viel früher ein. Die frühesten Beispiele tragen den charakteristischen ionischen Schrägmantel. Die erste Statuette (Nr. 28) ist massiv, aus dunkelbraunem, stark gemagertem Ton, der nicht rhodisch wirkt. Eine Figur gleichen Typs aus dem Depot vom Ialysos besteht aus dem typischen blassbraunen Ton rhodischer Statuetten und ist aus zwei Matrizen geformt. Der Typ der zweiten Hydriaphore (Nr. 230), zweimal im Demeter-Heiligtum belegt, tritt auch für einfache Schrägmantelträgerinnen vor (Abb.2).

Im beginnenden zweiten, oder noch am Ende des ersten Jahrhundertviertels, also um 380-370 v.Chr., setzt eine Serie neuer Typen ein, die bis zur Mitte des Jahrhunderts immer häufiger werden. In diese Zeit (380-370 v.Chr.) gehören zwei

Abb. 2: Hydriaphore Nr. 230 (erh. H. 0,12 m)

Abb. 3: Hydriaphore Nr. 118 (H. 0,165 m)

Kourotrophos-Typen, die jüngere Varianten eines lindischen Typs vom Beginn des Jahrhunderts sind (Lindos 2994)[23]. Die erste (Nr. 252), mit niedrigem, profiliertem Polos trägt ein Himation mit feinen, senkrechten Falten, das um die Hüfte befestigt ist, die Frau hält mit der Linken das auf ihre Schulter sitzende Kind; der rechte Arm ist unter der Brust abgewinkelt. Die Statuette, die mit ihrer quadratischen Basis in einem Stück gefertigt ist, zeigt den technischen Fehler rhodischer Terrakotten: Sie ist nach hinten verzogen, da die glatte Rückseite beim Brennen stärker schrumpfte. Bei der zweiten Variante (Nr. 610), bildet das Himation einen dreieckigen Überfall über dem Bauch und schräge Faltenbögen über dem Standbein. Der rechte Arm ist über den Leib gelegt. Diese Kourotrophos hat einen besonders grossen Kopf, ein Kennzeichen der Statuetten aus dem frühen 4. Jh.[24]. Die Art, wie diese Kourotrophoi das Kind tragen, und die charakteristische Haltung des rechten Arms, sind Besonderheiten des ionischen Kourotrophos-Typs[25]. Diese bleiben, wie wir noch sehen werden, auch bei viel späteren Beispielen erhalten.

In das Jahrzehnt 380-370 v.Chr. gehört auch die Frau mit Phiale (Nr. 594). Sie bedeutet eine neue Ausprägung des Motivs der Phialenträgerin aus dem Kleinen Depot von Lindos (Lindos 2910), aus dem vorangehenden Jahrzehnt. Dieser jüngere Typ trägt nicht mehr den Schrägmantel, sondern den Hüftmantel. Die Phiale ist für Männerfiguren sehr üblich, für Frauen dagegen ganz selten.

Mit den bekannten aus Lindos Typen des zweiten Viertels des Jahrhunderts wollen wir uns nicht aufhalten. Besonders hingewiesen sei aber auf den attischen Typus der Hydriaphore mit Peplos (Nr. 84). Wegen der tiefen Gürtung und der Gesichtsform muss sie ins zweite Viertel des 4. Jhs. datiert werden. Dieser attische Typ ist auf Rhodes auch durch jüngere Beispiele von Fundstellen im Stadtgebiet bekannt. Er begegnet sehr früh in Theangela und ist auf Knidos üblich[26]. In das Jahrzehnt vor der Jahrhundertmitte muss auch der neue Typ der Hydriaträgerin mit Schrägmantel (Nr. 118, Abb. 3) gehören. Der linke Arm ist vor dem Körper abgewinkelt. Dieser Typ lebt in gewandelter Ausprägung weiter in die zweite Hälfte des Jahrhunderts (Nr. 621, 696).

Die Tänzerin (Nr. 144) ist in den Depots von Lindos nicht vertreten. Mit erhobenem Kopf bewegt sich die Gestalt nach rechts. Das volle Gesicht ist uns schon von anderen rhodischen Statuetten bekannt. Hier ist der attische, z.B. durch die Tänzerin in Leiden vertretene Typ wiederholt, allerdings mit entgegengesetzter Bewegungsrichtung[27]. Es dürfte eine Schöpfung aus dem zweiten Viertel des Jahrhunderts sein, die auch aus Korinth bekannt ist[28]. Wir finden den Typ in der Troas, allerdings ganz ohne die Frische der rhodischen Statuette[29]. Die Tänzerin Lindos 2969 ist jünger, etwa Mitte des Jahrhunderts[30], ebenso die Manteltänzerin aus dem Demeter-Heiligtum (Nr. 370) des gleichen Typs. Es ist eine besonders grosse Figur (erhalten H. 14 cm), mit der viereckigen Basis in einem Stück gefertigt und mit rechteckiger Brennöffnung im glatt belassenen Rücken. Die Tonbeschaffenheit spricht nicht für auswärtige Herkunft. Die Qualität dieser Statuette, die sich von allen bisher gesehenen merklich unterscheidet, werden wir auch an anderen Figuren dieser Periode und späterer Zeit antreffen. Den gleichen Typ wiederholt eine Tänzerin im Louvre, die von S. Besques der kleinasiatischen Produktion der zweiten Jahrhunderthälfte zugewiesen wurde[31].

Um die Jahrhundertmitte und etwas später entsteht eine Reihe von weiblichen Figuren, die sich mit dem linken Ellbogen auf irgendetwas aufstützen. Die schöne Abgelehnte (Nr. 398,

Abb. 4: Angelehnte Figure Nr. 398 (erh. H. 0,132 m)

Abb. 5: Aphrodite mit Eros Nr. 182 (erh. H. 0,135 m)

Abb. 4) zählt zu den grossen Statuetten. Die Rückseite ist nicht in einer Matrize geformt und hat eine grosse, rechteckige Öffnung. Die Figur stützt sich auf einen Pfeiler mit Basis und Kapitell.

Die Gruppe Aphrodite mit Eros (Nr. 182, Abb. 5), gehört zu den schönsten Figuren aus dem Heiligtum; die erhaltene Höhe beträgt 13,5 cm. Sie ist aus zwei Matrizen hergestellt. Eine grosse, rechteckige Öffnung hinten sicherte für die Gruppe einen Brand ohne Verformung. Aphrodite stützt sich mit dem linken Ellbogen auf ein fein gearbeitetes ionisches Säulchen, auf dem Eros sitzt. Diese Gruppe ist nicht unbekannt. Sie wiederholt sich mit einer Statuette aus Myrina in Louvre, MYR 51[32]. Es bestehen einige Unterschiede in der Haltung des linken Arms, dem Pfeiler an Stelle der Säule und den Proportionen. S. Besques datiert sie in die zweite Hälfte des Jahrhunders. Ein älterer Typ, noch vor der Mitte des 4. Jhs., mit Unterschieden bei der Aphrodite und dem Pfeiler stammt aus der Kopais und befindet sich heute im British Museum[33]. Der rhodischen Statuette sehr ähnlich ist dagegen eine Figur aus Korinth, H. 20 cm, die Winter 1883 im Athener Kunsthandel sah[34]. Dass Werkstätten auf Rhodos korinthische Typen kopierten, ist nicht weiter überraschend. Auch die Manteltänzerin mit Tympanon schlagendem Eros aus dem Kleinen Depot von Lindos (Lindos 2985) ist die genaue Wiederholung einer korinthischen Gruppe im British Museum[35].

Ins dritte Viertel des Jahrhunderts muss ein neuer Typ der Ferkelträgerin datieren (Nr. 31), die mit der linken das Ferkel vor den Leib und in der Rechten eine grosse Fackel hält. Dieser Typ kommt in Lindos und Karien nicht vor, man kennt ihn aber aus Sizilien und aus dem Demeterheiligtum auf dem Akrokorinth, hier allerdings mit Umkehrung der Attribute[36].

Das Fragment einer Figur mit Himation (Nr. 211) gehört zu einer grossen Kore-Statuette (erh. H. 10,5), deren nach vorne gestreckte Arme eingestetzt waren. Die charakteristische Drapierung, die der Überfall des Himation unter der rechten Achsel durchführt, die rechte Brust frei lässt und die linke Schulter bedeckt, macht deutlich, dass diese Statuette den Typ der Urania im Vatikan kopiert[37]. In den angewinkelten Händen hielt sie wohl Fackeln. Dieser Typ kann nicht älter als Beginn des letzten Viertels des 4. Jhs. sein. Eine Reihe von Fragmenten zeigt, dass der Typ besonders beliebt war.

Die Mantelfigur (Nr. 565) gehört zu einem Typ, der auch aus dem Kleinen Depot von Lindos bekannt ist (Lindos 3069) und von anderen Fundstellen in Rhodos. Er ist in verschiedenen Grössen überliefert. Es handelt sich hier um die rhodische Umsetzung des tanagräischen Sophokles-Typ, wie das Işik ganz richtig gezeigt hat[38].

In der Mantelfigur (Nr. 569), aus zwei Matrizen, mit der schmalen rechteckigen Basis aus einem Stück gefertigt (H. 13 cm), erkennt man den Typ Lindos 3065-3068[39]. Hauptmerkmal ist der Fall des Himation von der rechten Schulter, das Anheben des Himation mit der rechten, verhüllten Hand und die auf die Hüfte aufgestützte Linke. Keine der Statuetten von Lindos kann jedoch mit der plastischen Ausformung und der Bewegung der Statuette aus dem Demeter-Heiligtum wetteifern. Hier haben wir die Übertragung eines Tanagra-Typs[40].

Eine Reihe von Fragmenten grosser Statuetten, die uns über das Ende des 4. bis ins 3. Jh. führen, sind Zeugen für eine weitere Übernahme und Aneignung von Tanagra-Typen.

Die Frauenfigur (Nr. 419), ist eine Variante der Kore in Florenz[41]. Sie muss ans Ende des 4. oder in den Beginn des 3. Jhs. datiert werden, ebenso wie die bekannte Kore-Statuette aus dem Heiligtum von Knidos im British Museum[42]. Weitere Fragmente zeigen dass der Typ ganz üblich war.

Neben diesen Figuren begegnen auch die alten, traditionellen Typen, jedoch in neuer Ausführung.

Die Hydriaphore (Nr. 295) vom Ende des Jahrhunderts[43], legt Zeugnis dafür ab, dass der Typ mit geschlossenem Mantel (Lindos 3003), der im Demeter-Heiligtum und in Lindos am häufigsten nachgewiesen ist, sich weiterentwikkelt. Mit anderen Funden aus der Stadt Rhodos können wir ihn bis ins 3. Jh. verfolgen.

Den Typ der Hydriaträgerinnen mit Schrägmantel aus der ersten Jahrzehnten des 3. Jhs. vertritt eine Reihe von Figuren, die alle aus der gleichen Werkstatt kommen dürfen. Auch die Fackelträgerinnen stammen aus der gleichen Werkstatt, von der wir gerade gesprochen haben. Dieses Motiv ist selten bei Frauenfiguren

Abb. 6: Polosfigur mit 'Liknon' und Ferkel Nr. Bo 30 (erh. H. 0,129 m)

Abb. 7: Himationträger Nr. Bo 35 (erh. H. 0,143 m)

aus dem Demeter-Heiligtum, die entsprechenden Männerfiguren dagegen kommen sehr häufig vor und sie müssen aus der gleichen Werkstatt kommen. – Aus der gleichen Periode stammt die Polosfigur mit Liknon in Schulterhöhe (Nr. Bo 30)(Abb. 6), der Sophokles-Typ (Nr. Bo 35)(Abb. 7), die Phialenträger (Nr. Bo 44, Bo 2)(Abb. 8).

Es ist von dem Gezeigten deutlich geworden, dass eine grosse Typenvielfalt erst im 2. Jahrhundertviertel und besonders um die Mitte des 4. Jhs. auftritt und sich ins 3. Jahrhundertviertel weiter fortsetzt, trotz manchen Einschränkungen, die kultische Gründe der Themenauswahl festlegten. Das Phänomen wird von einer bemerkenswerten Steigerung der Qualität begleitet. Neben der neuen Ausführung älterer treten neue Typen auf. Mehrere verraten ihre Verpflichtung den attischen und korinthischen Werkstätten. Der Einfluss der tanagräischen Terrakotten macht sich schon seit dem 3. Jahrhundertviertel bemerkbar. Auch werden statuarische Typen jetzt kopiert. Gleichzeitig werden die Tonstatuetten als Erzeugnisse verschiedener in der Stadt tätiger Werkstätten leicht erkennbar. Gegen das Ende des 4. und im 3. Jh. scheint die Vielfalt der traditionellen Kulttypen sich zu beschränken. Ihre Gleichförmigkeit zeigt, dass sie alle aus nur einer Werkstatt stammen, die anscheinend für den Bedarf des Heiligtums arbeitete. Jedoch fehlen die Statuetten, die nicht dem typisierten Kultrepertoire gehören, nicht. Sie zeugen mit ihrer Qualität und Form für die Existenz leistungsfähiger und schöpferischer Werkstätten in der Stadt. In der kurzen Zeit, die uns zur Verfügung stand, konnten wir nur einen kurzen Überblick anhand einer streng begrenzten Auswahl an Statuetten geben. So war es nicht möglich, die Menge an Informationen vorzuführen, die uns die Funde aus dem Heiligtum geben, Informationen, mit denen sich das Bild der rhodischen Koroplastik in spätklassi-

Abb. 8: Phialenträger Nr. Bo 2 (erh. H. 0,097 m)

scher und hellenistischer Zeit ausmahlen und ihr Charakter beschreiben lässt: Richtung und Intensität von Einflüssen während der einzelnen Phasen; der Grad der Assimilierung von jeweils neuen Elementen nach dem ersten Stadium des einfachen Kopierens; die Ausbildung und Fortentwicklung des eigentlich rhodischen Charakters inmitten der vielfältigen Beeinflussungen – man erkennt das nicht nur bei der konservativen Gattung von Kulttypen, sondern auch bei solchen, die nicht nur die Deckung des Kultbedarfs abzielten -; und schliesslich den Vorrang anderen Zentren gegenüber in der Aufnahme und Verbreitung von neuen Typen, sowie stilistische Einwirkungen auf die Regionen, die von Rhodos kulturell beeinflusst wurden.

Eos Zervoudaki
The National Museum
Tositsa 1
11256 Athens
Greece

Für die Übersetzung des Textes sei Frau Dr. Imma Kilian-Dirlmeier auch hier herzlich gedankt.

1. ADelt 28, 1973, B2, 622ff; ADelt 29, 1973-74, B2, 966ff.
2. ADelt 28, 1973, B2, 622ff "Grundstück Salachouri". Herr Dr. P. Pedersen machte mich aufmerksam auf entsprechend orientierte Bauten im Demeter-Heiligtum in Halikarnassos.
3. Die Ausgrabung des Grundstückes ist für 1986 geplant.
4. Prakt 1958, 236ff Plan 2; ADelt 28, 1973, B2, 624. Kontorini 1983, 44.
5. Für die anderen Kleinfunde s. ADelt 1.c. (Anm. 1). Für die Terrakotta-Typen in Demeter-Heiligtümern vgl. E. Töpperwein-Hoffmann, IstMitt 21, 1971, 131f mit Lit.; Thompson 1963, 9 f.; D. Thompson, Hesperia 23, 1954, 94 ff., 105; D. Levi, ASAtene 1967-68, 573ff; Raeder 1983, 26f; Metzger 1985, 23ff, 49ff.
6. D. Morelli, StClOr 8, 1959, 119ff.
7. Die Funde von 1985 werden nicht mitgerechnet.
8. Andere Aspekte der Bedeutung dieser Fundgruppe werden hier nicht berücksichtigt.
9. Lindos I, 459ff.
10. ClRh 3, 4, 6-7, 8; Higgins 1970, 43 ff.
11. Für die Datierung des Kleinen Depots s. Lindos I, 56; D. B. Thompson, Hesperia 21, 1952, 119 Anm, 13c; Higgins 1967, 61; Kleiner 1984, 93; Işik 1980, 22 mit Anm. 13, 144.
12. z.B. ADelt 23, 1968, B, Taf. 406c; ADelt 28, 1973, B, Taf. 581; ADelt 29, 1973-74, B, Taf. 720e, 734a-c; ADelt 22, 1967, B, Taf. 389d.
13. Für den rhodischen Ton bei Terrakotten s. Higgins 1967, 61; R.V. Nicholls, AJA 61, 1957, 304.
14. Bei den traditionellen Lindos-Typen gibt auf der weissen Grundierung, die meist nur die Vorderseite bedeckt, Rosa für das Inkarnat, für die Basis usw., Dunkelrot für die Haare, Schwarz zum Betonen von Augen und Augenbrauen usw., Hellrot, Blau, Gelb für Kleidung und Zierelemente. Rosa, Blau und Rot sind auf späteren Typen üblich.
15. Işik 1980, 179 glaubt, dass die Funde in Lindos einem, nur inschriftlich überlieferten Heiligtum der Damateres und Zeus Damatrios gehören. Dazu s. Morelli 1959, 121. – Für das Heiligtum in Kos s. R. Herzog, AA 1901, 134-136 und H. Kantzia in diesem Band. Für Priene und Troja s. hier Anm. 5. Für Pergamon s. Töpperwein 1976, 13ff.
16. Für die Bedeutung s. Raeder 1983, 26. Speziell für die Ferkel s. Sguaitamatti 1984, 52.
17. Thompson 1963, 9; E. Töpperwein, IstMitt 21, 1971, 131f.
18. Thompson 1963, 56, 59.
19. vgl. Higgins 1967, 62.
20. Işik 1980, 60 Taf. 7,5; Higgins 1970, Nr. 442.
21. Weill 1985, 193ff.
22. Zur Datierung Işik 1980, 118, Anm. 378. Die Hydrophoros Lindos 3011 ist eine jüngere Variation. Der Typ existiert auch im Demeter Heiligtum der Stadt Rhodos.
23. Işik 1980, 101 Anm. 319.
24. Vgl. Lindos 2988, 2953b, Lindos I, Taf. 139,137.
25. Işik 1980, 96.

26. Işik 1980, 87 f. Für Knidos s. Higgins 1967, Pl. 49D; Işik 1980, 23 Anm. 16.
27. Leyenaar-Plaisier 1979, Pl.5,27.
28. Hesperia 29, 1960, Pl.56,15.
29. Leyenaar-Plaisier 1979, Pl.23,132.
30. Işik 1980, 110.
31. Mollard-Besques 1971, 130 D 871, Pl. 160c.
32. Mollard-Besques 1963, Pl. 32d (H. 0,235 m), S.30, anders S. XII.
33. Higgins 1970, Nr. 887 (H. 0,195 m).
34. Winter 1883, Typen 2,94,2 (H. 0,205 m).
35. Lindos I, Taf. 138. Higgins 1970, Pl. 137, 970.
36. Sguaitamatti 1984, Pl. 41,145 und S. 57; Bell 1981, 33 ff.; Hesperia 34, 1965, Pl. 11a.
37. Neutsch 1952, Taf. 25,2.
38. Işik 1980, 144; vgl. hier Anm. 11.
39. Lindos I, 717 ff.
40. Vgl. eine jüngere Statuette aus Myrina in Wien, Winter 1883, Typen 2, 16,5 und eine italische Variation in Hannover, Liepmann 1975, 89 T 91.
41. Neutsch 1952, Taf. 27,1.
42. JHS 71, 1951, Pl. IXd; S. Mollard-Besques, RA 1981, 240 Fig. 22.
43. Vgl. Işik 1980, Taf 15, 104.

Adoption in Rhodian Society

E.E. Rice

Although a discussion of adoption perhaps falls more correctly under the aegis of social history than archaeology, my evidence for the subject is purely archaeological, being found in inscriptions on stone, and I therefore also face the problem of weaving the facts provided by archaeology into a sustained historical argument. These remarks are intended as a preliminary discussion of a complex topic which I plan to deal with more fully in a study of Rhodian society; consequently I can now only begin to consider various aspects of adoption as an institution in Rhodes, and I offer tentative hypotheses rather than conclusions. There are nearly 500 epigraphically-attested cases of adoption in the Rhodian state (by which I mean the island, its Peraea, and dependent islands), a very high number indeed. Adoption was of course practised elsewhere in the ancient world, and appears in inscriptions from various places, but most of our explanatory evidence about it comes from Athens (in legal speeches of the Attic orators), and from the law code from Gortyn in Crete (in which various provisions governing adoption are set out). Basically, adoption played a large role in civic and family law: a man with no natural heirs adopted a son who gave up rights of inheritance in his own family in order to become the heir of his adoptive father. At Athens, he was formally enrolled in his adoptive father's deme, and became for all intents and purposes a member of his adoptive family. In this way, an oikos and its property could be preserved intact if a couple produced no heirs. Given the unfortunate absence of Rhodian law codes or recorded legal speeches, we must rely on inference to understand how the system worked from the mere fact that it happened. This is by no means an easy task.

The surprising prevalence of adoption in Rhodes was remarked upon long ago by van Gelder[1], who suggested that its frequency meant that it had a particular function perhaps quite different from what we know at Athens and Gortyn. Indeed, the fact that at a certain period nearly one in three of the priests of Athana Lindia were adopted can hardly be explained merely on grounds of widespread infertility in the population as a whole! Blinkenberg[2], who made the important discovery of the triennial rule which governed the election of the priests of Athana Lindia (whereby priests of the same tribe succeeded each other in office in 3-yearly intervals), also observed that adoption could be used to circumvent this tribal cycle; for example, a priest of one tribe standing for election in a year which was restricted to a member of another tribe could be adopted by a man from a deme of the appropriate tribe, and so be eligible for the priesthood[3]. The fullest study of adoption at Rhodes was made by Gabriella Poma[4], and although her article contains many good points well made, I take issue with her over various arguments, and believe that the last word on the topic has yet to be said.

The first problem, and it is a major one, is chronological. Our earliest attested cases of adoption at Rhodes date from the middle of the third century BC. The earliest is a base from Kamiros (Segre-Pugliese Carratelli 1949-51, no. 20), dated by the damiourgos to c. 263 BC. In the inscriptions recording the names of successive eponymous magistrates, the first case appears under the year 240 BC in the list of the Kamiran damiourgoi (Segre-Pugliese Carratelli 1949-51, no. 3 sub ann.). At Lindos there is an adopted priest of Poseidon Hippios in the same year (Blinkenberg 1937, sub ann. 240 BC), and an adopted priest of Athana Lindia in 239 BC (Lindos II δ, 1 sub ann.). There is a variation in the style of titulature in these and other early cases, alternating between, for example, Ἁγησίας Τιμολέοντος καθ' ὑοθεσίαν δὲ Τιμαπόλιος, and Ἁγησίας Τιμολέοντος κατὰ γένεσιν, καθ' ὑοθεσίαν δὲ Τιμαπόλιος; this lack of a single standard formula seems to indicate that the use of the expressions is just beginning. Even though our earliest examples are restricted to public lists, which could be special cases, Poma[5] argues that had adoption existed earlier it would have been recorded in inscriptions of a private nature, such as tombstones and family dedications. I might note in this connection that very few inscribed documents of a public or private nature exist at all before the third century in Rhodes, and because of this we do not have any clear idea of what *was* inscribed then, but I agree that the early variation in terminology is significant. I think, however, that a truer explanation of it must be that adoption did exist before but was not recorded on stone before a certain date – for reasons we shall return to. The unfamiliarity of the new recording procedure in the middle of the third century accounts for the two parallel styles in use at this time.

The institution of adoption elsewhere in Greece arose in ancient times as a provision of family and testamentary law for the preservation of an oikos and its property; it is traced back to the time of Solon in Athens[6], and is attested in the earliest surviving inscriptions from Crete[7]. Given that the three old cities of Rhodes must have faced the same social problems of intestate succession and inheritance, it is reasonable to assume that adoption was used here too as a means of resolving the situation, especially in light of the fact that Rhodes had contact with Athens (where adoption was practised) both before and after the synoecism. The idea could even have been taken over from Athens, although to judge from the widespread practice of adoption in Greece, I do not think we need to hypothesize a direct borrowing. However, for all we know due to lack of evidence, the legal technicalities of the Rhodian system may have differed markedly from the Athenian, or any other, system.

I maintain that it is probably safe to see the origin of adoption in Rhodes over a century before we have epigraphical evidence for it. The strongest argument I can adduce is that the family need for a system such as adoption must have existed long before the middle of the third century in Rhodes, and since there is quite a family orientation in the later cases of Rhodian adoption, there is no reason to suppose that it did not arise naturally in the families of the classical or late classical period. It is worth emphasizing in this connection that nearly 100 adoptees appear to be adopted by close relatives, which happened also at Athens. It is certain that 8 men were adopted by their brothers, and 3 by their uncles. These are special cases because we happen to have chance information from other sources about the family in question, and they are a small minority of the total, but onomastic evidence is itself very telling and suggests a similar situation. In 27 cases a man is adopted by someone with the same name as himself, which I would say is almost certainly an indication of adoption by uncles; in 8 cases men are adopted by homonyms of their natural fathers, and I would suppose that these are additional examples of adoption by brothers. There are far more cases where I think it likely that a relative is involved because of more general onomastic links: in some 41 cases, parts of names are shared between adoptive sons and fathers, or between natural and adopted fathers. Another side of the question is female adoption, of which I am aware of 19 cases at Rhodes. Daughters were occasionally adopted and hence became epikleroi at Athens[8], but although it is impossible to know the circumstances of female adoption at Rhodes, it was surely wholly or largely a family concern, and was in no way relevant to eligibility for office which appears to be behind some cases of male adoption.

I am therefore satisfied that family circumstances were responsible for many cases of adoption at Rhodes in the hellenistic period, and I do not see why it should not have been so earlier. The real question we must address is why it only became desirable to record it from the middle of the third century BC. I shall return to this.

Poma believes that adoption only began at this late date in Rhodes, and tries to link it to the development of the deme system, probably a feature of the democratic Rhodian constitution. This argument has chronological and theoretical difficulties. The chronological question of course depends upon the date of the establishment of the Rhodian democracy. Although in the past the ghost of Alexander the Great has been seen to lurk behind this democratic constitution (because of his general support of democratic factions against the pro-Persian oligarchs in the Greek cities of the islands and Asia Minor which he "liberated" during his expedition), it has to my mind been convincingly argued that there is no evidence that Alexander was responsible for constitutional developments on Rhodes, however much we might perhaps like to see it from a romantic point of view[9]. Along these lines I believe that the most likely date for the introduction of the democracy and the deme system is the pro-Athenian revolution at Rhodes in the 390's, a few years after the synoecism. This revolution was inspired and executed by the Athenians, and we may note that in Athens, a demotic was the essential hallmark of a citizen, a practice not, in fact, common elsewhere. It could be argued that the Rhodian deme system looks Attic, and a likely time for it to have been introduced was at a period of palpable Athenian influence. I therefore cannot agree with the view that adoption arose as a result of the introduction of demes, and was linked to a consequent reform of the electoral system, argued to have happened in the middle of the third century at least at Kamiros[10]. The earliest known demotics in fact occur at Lindos in c. 325 BC, a list of subscribers to the restoration of the temple of Athana Lindia listed by demes (Lindos II 51; cf. a Lindian decree of about the same date which contains a list of names followed by demotics, SIG 340). This cannot be taken as proof that the demes did not exist before this date, but is a further unfortunate result of the lack of documentation in Rhodes generally in this period. Furthermore, demotics are not automatically recorded in all civic documents at Rhodes (as they are at Athens) – in fact, their appearance often seems arbitrary and inconsistent – so that their omission from any one document cannot be used to argue that the demes themselves did not exist at the date of the document in question.

The introduction of the deme system at whatever date does not in itself explain the corresponding rise of adoption. Poma would further attribute it to an aristocratic reaction against these new constitutional arrangements which replaced the earlier gentilicial organization of the population with new demes based on territorial divisions. I suppose that she envisages the citizens of the old cities adopting men of their own clan (irrespective of the new demes of either party) in order to consolidate their forces by keeping the old gentilicial groupings intact in the face of the new demes which could delimit their traditional power by dividing the clans for political purposes.

This will not, I think, quite do. The gentilicial structure of Rhodes before the synoecism is still only dimly understood, but certain divisions, perceived in names such as patrai, were probably gentilicial groups within the three original tribes of which we have reason to believe that the Dorian island of Rhodes was composed. Poma would champion the ktoinai, a division of the Rhodian population both before and after the synoecism, along with the tribes, as the residual body of aristocratic gentilicial feeling, but this is too simplistic a view. Although, as I have argued, the demes were a new civic administration established soon after the synoecism, presumably to give the old cities a sense of municipal autonomy, the tripartite tribal divisions somehow incorporated them (as is clear from the tribal cycle); their components were now the demes, but how the demes related to the surviving kinship groups is not understood. Nor is it possible to maintain that the surviving ktoinai were pitted against the artificial deme system by the old aristocratic families, because it seems that ktoinai were themselves territorial, not gentilicial, divisions[11]. There is, I think, no means of knowing if there was an aristocratic reaction to the establishment of the deme system, or, if so, how it manifested itself, but if the demes were established at the beginning of the fourth century, clearly a reaction of the type which Poma envisages could not be responsible for explaining our earliest epigraphical evidence for adoption some century and a half later. So we are no further along in explaining the sudden appearance of adoption at that date, nor its occasional relation to the manipulation of the tribal cycle in elections to office.

I would agree with Poma's basic view that adoption could have been a general measure intended to preserve the solidarity of the old families of the three old cities. But this poses a question rather than providing an answer. Preserve the solidarity against whom, and how? The need to preserve the solidarity of the citizen body can only have been in relation to the population of the new city Rhodos. (I use the convention of calling the island Rhodes and the city Rhodos.) Many resident foreigners availed themselves of the commercial advantages of the city (as indeed others had done at Athens in her heyday), with no access to citizen rights, and a process of naturalized citizenship is recorded in only very few cases: to some foreigners (of whom sculptors were one group), in circumstances which we cannot trace, the privilege of ἐπιδαμία (right of residence) was granted, and their children were entitled to use the civic title Ῥόδιος. (See, for example, Lindos II col. 54 no. 74, where the sequence of this change of status is clearly recorded.) It is not at all clear if these few known naturalized Ῥόδιοι (whose status is unambiguously stated in inscriptions) can be understood in the same terms as the large, wealthy mercantile class permanently resident in the city, descended from the original immigrants presumably called in to settle the site at the time of the synoecism, in addition, of course, to demesmen of the three old cities. Eligibility for some rights at Rhodos must have been an inducement for them to come, and their descendants could have retained those rights. We do not know if all members of this class had the right to use the civic title Ῥόδιος as the result of the privilege of ἐπιδαμία granted to older relations; if we can understand it to have been extended to this group as a whole, it is then clear that the title and the process of naturalization are recorded arbitrarily in only the tiniest number of cases (some 24 instances of ̓επιδαμία are known in comparison with the thousands of persons who are recorded in all types of Rhodian inscriptions with name and patronymic but without demotic, whose legal status therefore cannot always be ascertained)[12]. Whether or not we should see a technical difference in legal status between the naturalized foreigners and the original immigrants, the point at issue here is that these new inhabitants as a body were not demesmen of the three old cities. They were, it might be argued, a secondary class of Rhodian albeit with certain rights in the federal state. Although we cannot say what these rights may have comprised, nor indeed what political role, if any, the "Rhodioi" (by whom I mean all the permanent immigrants in the city) may have been able to play, they were certainly excluded from the inner circle of the federal state and from any public office which had to be filled by a demesman. To give only one example, the old cities took it in turn to provide a demesman to hold the priesthood of Halios, the eponymous magistracy of the state. However, even though the demesmen may have held the reins of power in the counsels of state by reason of their inherited status, as the commercial prosperity of Rhodes grew in the fourth century, so we might imagine that the urban-dwellers grew in number, and must have soon outnumbered full Rhodian citizens. The "aristocracy" of the state must therefore have been concerned with preserving the size of the families of the demesmen, perhaps taking the initiative by requiring that each adult male demesman had a sufficient number of heirs, natural or adopted, to meet its potential needs. Adoption by demesmen was therefore encouraged as a means of making up the requisite number of children. As such, it was a protective measure guarding against the extinction of inherited citizenship through the demes, which we might assume was a concern of considerable importance to the demesmen. The use of the institution was therefore extended beyond its normal function of keeping the inheritance of the oikos intact within the larger family circle.

If it had indeed been felt that the "Rhodioi" could potentially form a group powerful enough to engulf the demesmen, it is reasonable to suppose that this was not a problem until there was a substantial growth of the new city and its inhabitants, which would explain why adoption as a protective measure for inherited citizenship only became necessary by the mid-third century.

For the sake of argument, I wonder if there was a situation which at some time required the passage of a law to the effect that all married male demesmen should have (by nature or adoption) not less than X number of children. By this I do not suppose that young children were necessarily the adoptees, since cases of adult adoption are very common. In exchange for this there were no doubt some fiscal or similar mitigations to make the law less onerous to the adoptive father, on whom the burden would have fallen. Conversely, large families could have adopted out children in excess of the natural father's own quota. In view of patrimony and family holdings which were also involved, it was the list of the priests of Athana Lindia, men were adopted into a deme belonging to another tribe and so held office in a year in which they would not have been eligible under the tribe of their birth. Since demotics are not given in the priest list, this operation can be shown only in cases where the priest's natural and adoptive demes happen to be known from other evidence, such that their place within the tribal cycle in a given year can be ascertained. But these are the minority of all attested cases of adoption. As I have said, the use of the demotic was irregular at Rhodes, and the demotics of adopted men are given in only about 90 out of 500 cases, although it is clear that many more of these men *were* demesmen because they held offices in the old cities. Worse, there appears to have been no systematic method of recording the demotic when it does appear. (I cannot go into details here, but there are three different ways of recording the demotics of adopted men, and the distinction between two of them cannot be determined[14]). In other words, the different styles of terminology do not seem to have systematic meanings, and we therefore cannot base any firm conclusions on them. In only 18 cases is it made expressly clear by the terminology that the adoptee's deme was changed to that of his adoptive father (for example in the case Δαμαίνετος Σωκράτευς Ἄμιος καθ' ὑοθεσίαν δὲ Δαμοκράτευς Σιλύριος). These problems furnish ample proof of the profound state of our ignorance as to how this part of the system worked (although it might be argued that most cases of adoption within the family or clan would not involve a change of deme).

I suggest that the official encouragement of adoption as a measure to protect inherited citizenship through demes at the same time left the system open to abuse. Once adoption had an application wider than providing a legal heir for a childless man, and especially after the practice was encouraged, it could be exploited by those eager to hasten their careers by technically obeying but actually obviating the tribal cycle governing election to the most prestigious priesthood in Lindos. In a sense, then, the connection of adoption with the triennial rule perhaps emerged coincidentally. In these cases we might imagine that the impetus for adoption came from the prospective son, although he would be helpful obviously to the benefit of the adopting parties if the adoption could be kept within the family, and we have seen that it often was. Various collateral branches of families could be deliberately and artificially consolidated to ensure that there were always family members available for participation in public life in the cities and at Rhodos. It is indeed conceivable that in a few cases demesmen adopted "Rhodioi" if they had no available relatives, and that thereby "new" demesmen were enrolled[13]. In this way the population of the demesmen of the old cities could actually be increased through adoption, although, obviously, this practice, if taken to extremes, would have worked against the original purpose of protecting the integrity of the old families. I may also note that some 66 cases of adoption are attested from the dependent Rhodian islands and the Peraea, and suggest that if life was as hard in antiquity as it is in places there today, the resulting smaller families would have needed more frequent recourse to adoption to make up their quota of children. On the other hand, I suppose that the "Rhodioi" themselves, as well as demesmen, practised what we might consider the "normal" type of adoption when the childless among them needed to provide themselves with heirs, and that these cases number among the attested adoptions at Rhodes.

To ensure that these requirements were carried out by adult male demesmen with an insufficient number of natural offspring, the law may have demanded that adoptions be officially recorded; the practical outcome of the law would therefore be made public, and the law would be seen to be effective. A νόμος or ψήφισμα of the type I imagine must have been precipitated by an event which had demonstrated the insufficiency of the old citizen body, and a consequence of which was a review of the demographic condition of the city. Since our earliest records of adoption date to the middle of the third century, I suggest that this is the approximate date of the event, and of the law, the consequence of which was the registration of adoption on all public documents. But I shall have to leave speculation about the immediate cause to another occasion.

Let us briefly return to the relation of adoption to the tribal cycle. As I have said, it has been demonstrated that on occasion, at least in ing a man, albeit of the requisite tribe for electoral purposes, who needed to adopt in order to make up his quota of children. In these cases of adult adoption, the prospective adoptee might already have children of his own, with the result that the family of his birth would not be left without heirs.

Poma concludes with the suggestion that there could have been two concurrent types of adoption at Rhodes: the usual kind found in Athens which included a renunciation of rights in the family of birth, and a second merely formal kind which was intended to ease access to office and had no ties to patrimony or deme. I have indicated that adoption at Rhodes seems to have had more than one use, although it grew directly out of the adoption familiar for purposes of inheritance, but I find it difficult to imagine the practical application of a dual system in the real sense. For example, was it necessary to distinguish through terminology which type of adoption was entered into?

Some of the difficulty may be mitigated if we admit that there are perceptible peculiarities in the Rhodian system which are not paralleled by what we know of other systems. Given the wide variation in the appearance or omission of the demotic, and in the different ways in which it is recorded, it appears that there may have been at Rhodes no hard and fast rule about how adoption affected the deme to which one belonged (as there was in Athens). This suggestion may go some way in explaining the ambiguous placing of the demotic in cases of attested adoption as well as the fact that there was evidently a measure of choice regarding the demes of adopted men. For example, in the list of priests of Athana Lindia, priests sometimes stood in the deme of their birth according to the tribal cycle although it is known that they had been adopted into another deme and tribe[15]. A ceremony formally enrolling the adoptee into his adoptive father's deme obviously could only have taken place in cases where the deme *was* changed; in other adoptions presumably a religious or a family ceremony of some kind sufficed. That the system of adoption was peculiar in other ways at Rhodes is suggested by the observation that adoption seems only to have affected the person adopted in the cases where the deme is known to have changed. In most cases it appears that the children of adopted parents belong to the deme of their father's birth. For example, sons of priests of Athana Lindia are occasionally adopted out of their tribe for the purposes of election even though their fathers had already been adopted out previously. In a few cases there is a suggestion that children took their father's adoptive deme, but I suspect that this is an error of modern interpretation. Even if we admit a certain measure of laxity about the deme (since adoption was intended to preserve the old families in general, not the numbers of any one deme), there are hints of some distinction made between regular priests and adopted priests, possibly originating in opposition to those who abused the system of adoption solely to hasten their election. In Lindos II 419, a long decree of 22 AD which was trying to breathe life into the old cults, it is specified that adopted priests must by compulsion do everything that the other priests do or else be charged with impiety (lines 86-88)[16]. We have no means of knowing what may have been the former differences which are dispensed with in 22 AD, but they had evidently not been important enough to stop the abuse of adoption in those centuries when the institution was officially encouraged by the Rhodian state.

E.E. Rice
Wolfson College
Oxford, OX2 6UD
England

1. Gelder 1900, 284ff.
2. Lindos II, col. 95 ff.
3. See further P. M. Fraser, Eranos 51, 1953, 23ff.
4. Epigraphica 34, 1972, 169ff.
5. Epigraphica 34, 1972, 191.
6. Harrison 1968, 82ff.
7. Cf. Willetts 1967, 30-1, who shows that the institution had already been modified by the time the law code was drawn up in the middle of the fifth century.
8. Harrison 1968, 88.

9. See P. M. Fraser, PP 7, 1952, 192 ff.
10. G. Poma, Epigraphica 34, 1972, 203, points to the date of 279 BC which Pugliese Carratelli puts forward as the date of the substitution of demes for ktoinai in certain offices at Kamiros, StClOr 6, 1957, 69 ff., but he has not fully followed the consequences of the arguments of P.M. Fraser, PP 7, 1952, 192 ff.
11. Cf. G. Poma, Epigraphica 34, 1972, 191 ff., versus P. M. Fraser, PP 7, 1952, 205-6 ff.
12. See further the discussion in Fraser 1977, 47 ff. and note 246.
13. It is possible that this is reflected in one of the different ways in which adoption was recorded: Νικαγόρας Παμφιλίδα καθ' ὑοθεσίαν δὲ Νικαγόρα Λαδάρμιος could be interpreted to mean that the demotic accrued to the son only by virtue of his adoption. See further below on the ambiguity in terminology.
14. For example, what, if any, is the difference between Βασιλείδας Κλευμβρότου Βυβάσσιος καθ' ὑοθεσίαν δὲ Θευφάνευς, and 'Αγήσανδρος Πολυχάρμου καθ' ὑοθεσίαν δὲ 'Αγησάνδρου Καττάβιος?
15. Cf. P.M. Fraser, Eranos 51, 1953, 31-2.
16. This was pointed out by P.M. Fraser, Eranos 51, 1953, 35-6.

Richesse et pouvoir à Lindos à l'époque hellénistique[1]

Alain Bresson

Telle qu'on la voit apparaître dans les inscriptions à partir de 325 a.C. environ, la communauté de Lindos[2], au sein de l'Etat rhodien, comprenait d'une part des dèmes situés dans l'île de Rhodes (l'ancien territoire lindien d'avant le synoecisme) et d'autre part des dèmes situés à la fois dans l'île de Carpathos et dans la Pérée. L'opposition entre les deux composantes du territoire lindien, insulaire ou périphérique (Carpathos et la Pérée), n'était pas seulement géographique. A une date qui se situe autour de 325, les Lindiens de "vieille souche" avaient obtenu que les "nouveaux venus", habitants des dèmes lindiens de Carpathos ou de la Pérée, ne puissent avoir accès à la gestion et au service des cultes communautaires de Lindos[3]. L'exclusivisme lindien s'opposait en cela à ce qui apparaît être à travers nos sources l'attitude plus ouverte des Camiréens insulaires, puisque ces derniers admettaient à leurs côtés les habitants des dèmes péréens[4].

On sait aussi que l'effectif des dèmes de chacune des trois communautés rhodiennes (Lindos, Ialysos et Camiros) reste encore inconnu, en particulier (mais pas uniquement) du fait des obscurités qui demeurent autour des dèmes péréens. Pour ce qui est de la communauté lindienne, bon nombre de dèmes dont l'attribution à Lindos est certaine ne peuvent pas encore être localisés avec précision. Cette remarque vaut aussi pour le groupe des dèmes lindiens insulaires, dont on connaît pourtant à la fois l'effectif total et le nom de tous les dèmes qui le composent. Comme notre étude va avoir comme objet des données relatives à ces dèmes lindiens insulaires, nous commencerons par rappeler les principaux renseignements dont on dispose à leur sujet.

Le territoire lindien occupait environ 55 % des 1404 km² de l'île de Rhodes, soit grossièrement 775 km². Sur ces 775 km² se répartissaient douze dèmes (cf. fig. 1)[5]:

1. Lindopolitai: c'était naturellement le dème urbain de Lindos.
2. Nettidai: ce dème doit peut-être être localisé dans le secteur d'Apolakkia-Arnitha.
3. Brasioi: ce dème correspond peut-être à la règion Monolithos-Ayios Isidôros.
4. Pagioi: il est possible que les Pagioi aient occupé la région au sud d'Apollona.
5. Kamyndioi: les Kamyndioi occupaient peut-être la région de Vati.
6. Klasioi: il faut peut-être situer ce dème soit au nord de Lindos, dans la région Malona-Massari-Kalathos, soit au sud, dans le secteur Yennadi-Lachania (voir infra dème des Pedieis no. 12).
7. Ladarmioi: les Ladarmioi occupaient peut-être la région de Laerma.
8. Dryitai: les Dryitai sont peut-être à rechercher dans le secteur de Mesanagros.
9. Argeioi: ce dème se situait peut-être soit dans la région d'Asklipio, soit dans celle de Platania-Archipolis (cf. no. 10).
10. Boulidai: on peut faire pour les Boulidai la même remarque que pour le dème des Argeioi (no. 9): localisation soit dans la région d'Asklipio, soit dans celle de Platania-Archipolis.
11. Kattabioi: les Kattabioi occupaient le secteur du village actuel de Kattavia.
12. Pedieis: ce dème justifie des même remarques que le dème des Klasioi no. 6 (localisation dans le secteur Malona-Massari-Kalathos ou dans celui de Yennadi-Lachania).

Somme toute, pour ce qui est des localisations, le bilan est assez maigre puisque deux dèmes seule-

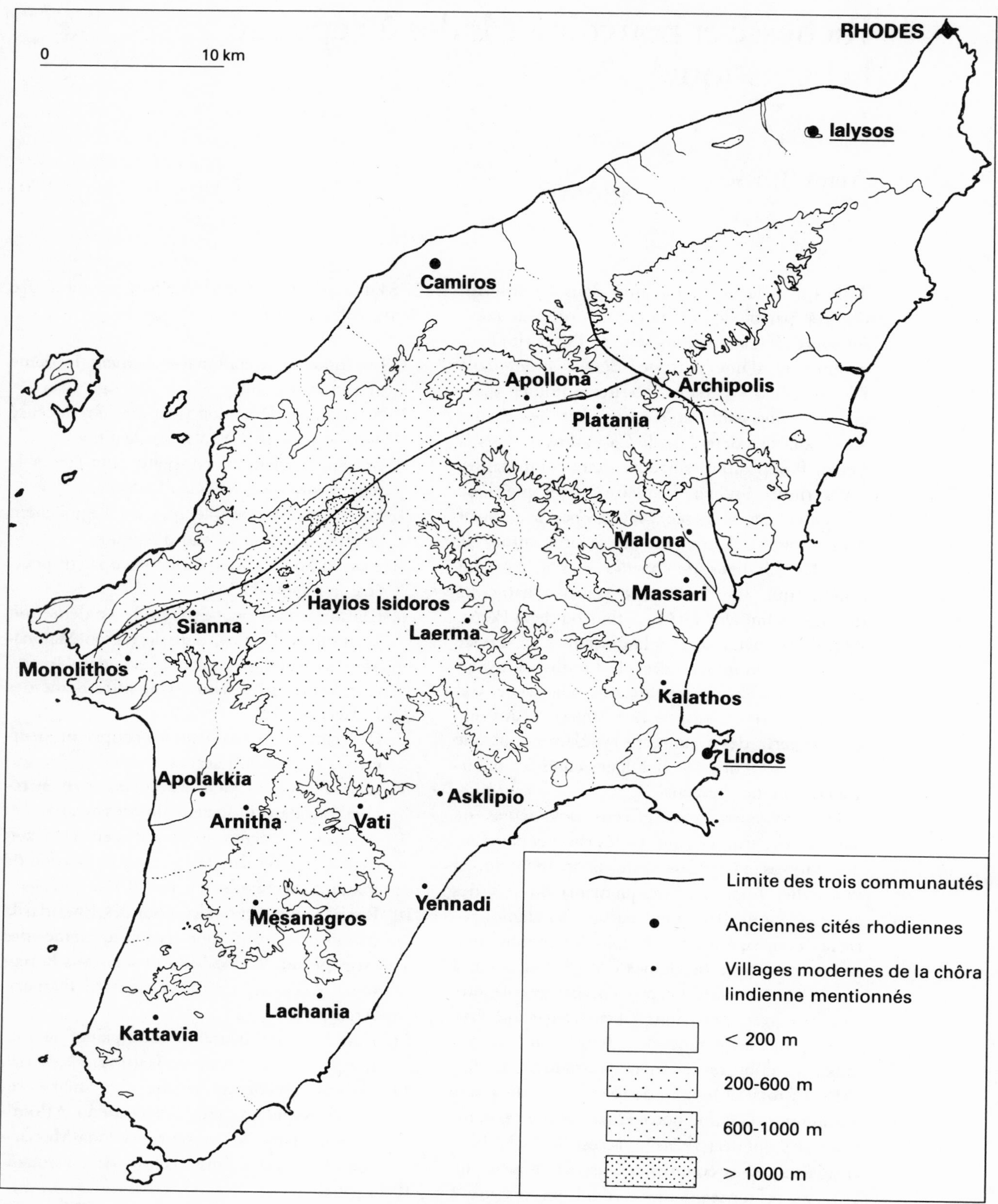

Figure 1: Lindos et la chôra lindienne

ment peuvent être situés avec certitude: celui des Lindopolitai et celui des Kattabioi[6].

Il nous paraît cependant que les données contenues dans deux groupes de deux inscriptions permettent d'éclairer sous un autre angle, économique et social et non pas strictement institutionnel, la vie des dèmes lindiens insulaires (le sens de cette restriction aux dèmes de l'île apparaîtra immédiatement).

Les deux premiers textes dont il s'agit sont deux inscriptions strictement contemporaines l'une de l'autre, qui datent toutes deux d'environ 325 a.C., *IG*, XII 1, 761 et *Lindos II*, 51 (les statistiques de base sont données dans le *Tableau no. 1*):

- *IG*, 761 est l'inscription à laquelle nous avons fait allusion précédemment[7]. Il s'agit d'un décret en l'honneur de trente citoyens de Lindos, appartenant tous à des dèmes de l'île, qui ont été responsables, manifestement devant le tribunal de l'Etat rhodien, de l'action judiciaire qui a permis aux Lindiens insulaires de continuer à se réserver l'exclusivité de leurs cultes. Leurs noms sont donnés dans le désordre, mais chaque personnage apparaît avec son démotique, ce qui permet des regroupements par dèmes.

- *Lindos II*, 51, est une liste de bienfaiteurs. Elle présente la liste de ceux qui ont accepté de verser une somme d'argent pour la parure et les coupes à boire du sanctuaire d'Athana. Cette liste est classée par dème, l'ordre de succession des dèmes ne paraissant pas avoir de signification particulière. Tous les donateurs sont des Lindiens insulaires, à l'exception d'un fort groupe de Physkioi (dème de la Pérée lindienne) et de trois Camiréens isolés. Malheureusement, cette liste est partiellement mutilée, et le nombre des donateurs de deux dèmes insulaires, ceux des Kattabioi et des Pedieis, ne peut être déterminé avec précision – du moins est-il quasiment certain que Kattabioi et Pedieis étaient effectivement représentés.

Or, si l'on opère un classement par dème des "avocats" des Lindiens insulaires de *IG*, 761, sur la base de la séquence des dèmes qui est celle de *Lindos II*, 51, et si l'on essaie de mettre en rapport les deux séries de chiffres, on aperçoit immédiatement, sur une simple représentation graphique par histogrammes comme celle de la figure no. 2, l'étroite corrélation qui existe entre elles. Mais on peut ne pas se satisfaire d'une impression subjective et souhaiter une confirmation mathématique de ce jugement. Un calcul simple montre alors qu'entre les effectifs des dix dèmes dont l'effectif d'"avocats" et de donateurs est connu avec certitude, on obtient en coefficient de corrélation r de 0.750. Comme on le sait, un taux de corrélation est dépourvu de signification intrinsèque. Ce taux doit évalué au moyen d'un test, le plus usuel étant le t de Student, qui évalue un taux de corrélation en fonction de l'effectif des individus (ou plus exactement du degré de liberté: si l'effectif est N, le degré de liberté est ici égal à $\nu = N - 2$). Pour rendre les choses plus concrètes, on peut dire que un taux de corrélation donné, même élevé, peut n'avoir aucune signification si le nombre d'individus est faible, il peut avoir une signification tout à fait positive si ce nombre est élevé. Le test t donne ici les résultats suivants:

$$r = 0.750 \qquad t\begin{cases}\alpha=0.01\\ \nu=8\end{cases} = 3.36$$

$$t = \frac{r}{1-r^2} \times (N-2) = 3.20$$

$$N = 10 \qquad t\begin{cases}\alpha=0.02\\ \nu=8\end{cases} = 2.90$$

La valeur de t étant comprise entre 2.90 et 3.36, le test montre que la corrélation entre les deux séries de chiffres est valable à 98%, ou en d'autres termes qu'il n'y a que deux chances sur cent pour que cette corrélation soit due au hasard, ce qui est largement satisfaisant.

Si, de manière hypothétique il est vrai[8], on attribuait à chacun des dèmes manquants dans *Lindos II*, 51, douze donateurs (il y a douze lignes effectivement manquantes, mais il ne s'agit que d'une fin de colonne), on aurait les résultats suivants:

$$r = 0.76 \qquad t = 3.69 \qquad t\begin{cases}\alpha=0.01\\ \nu=10\end{cases} = 3.17$$

On voit dès lors, avec un effectif de douze dèmes et une restitution hypothétique mais vraisemblable de douze individus par dème, que t étant supérieur à $t\ \alpha$ (pour $\alpha = 0.01$) le résultat est satisfaisant à 99%.

Tableau no. 1 (inscriptions d'environ 325 a.C.). Les effectifs du dème péréen des Physkioi dans *Lindos II*, 51, sont comptabilisés à part.

	IG, 761 "avocats"	*Lindos II*, 51 donateurs
Lindopolitai	8	65
Nettidai	3	15
Brasioi	2	8
Pagioi	0	10
Kamyndioi	1	17
Klasioi	7	26
Ladarmioi	3	4
Dryitai	0	17
Argeioi	2	18
Boulidai	2	16
Kattabioi	1	?
Pédieis	1	?
Physkioi		44

Tableau no. 2 (inscriptions d'époque hellénistique avancée). N.B. Les chiffres signalés entre parenthèses dans la première colonne renvoient à ceux de *Lindos II*, 346.

	Lindos II, 378 mastroi	*Lindos II*, 252 donateurs
Lindopolitai	4(7)	3
Nettidai	2(7)	4
Brasioi	5	4
Pagioi	1	2
Kamyndioi	5	4
Klasioi	6	7
Ladarmioi	6	7
Dryitai	3	1
Argeioi	9(8)	7
Boulidai	4	3
Kattabioi	4	2
Pédieis	2	3

La conclusion s'impose: il y avait à Lindos un lien étroit entre le poids politique et la richesse des membres des dèmes. Plus les membres d'un dème sont nombreux à apparaître dans une donation, plus on a de chance de voir des membres de ce dème jouer un rôle important dans la vie politique de la communauté. Si l'on admet que la richesse d'un dème était à la mesure du nombre des donateurs dans les souscriptions publiques, on doit également considérer que son influence politique était à la mesure de sa richesse.

Dans le détail, on peut encore faire une série d'autres remarques:

- Deux dèmes ont une position privilégiée, celui des Lindopolitai et celui des Klasioi. La place dominante des Lindopolitai, le dème urbain de Lindos, prouve sans aucun doute la richesse et la vitalité de la ville de Lindos en cette fin du 4ème siècle.

- Cinq autres sont en position moyenne, ceux des Nettidai, Brasioi, Ladarmioi, Argeioi et Boulidai.

- Les cinq dèmes restant, Kamyndioi, Kattabioi, Pedieis, Pagioi et Dryitai, et singulièrement les deux derniers nommés qui n'ont aucun représentant dans *IG*, 761, paraissent en position plus faible.

Deux autres inscriptions datant de la basse époque hellénistique, *Lindos II*, 252 et *Lindos II* 378, permettent de constater une corrélation semblable à celle qui a été relevée pour *IG*, 761, et *Lindos II*, 51 (les statistiques de base sont données dans le Tableau no. 2):

- *Lindos II*, 252 est une liste de donateurs qui ont versé une contribution pour la confection de couronnes d'or en l'honneur d'Athana Lindia, Zeus Polieus et Nika. Elle date de 115 a.C. Le texte fait apparaître les personnages sans ordre particulier mais avec l'indication de leur démotique. Il est donc aisé de les regrouper par dème. L'inscription n'est pas en très bon état et quelques noms ou démotiques sont perdus, mais en faible proportion. Nous ne prendrons en compte que les noms parfaitement assurés.

- *Lindos II*, 378 contient entre autres une liste de mastroi, magistrats que, de manière approximative, on peut plus ou moins assimiler à des bouleutes pour la vie interne de chacune des trois communautés rhodiennes. Cette liste est classée par dème. L'inscription est en bon état, mais elle date de 27 a.C. et elle est donc postérieure de 88 ans à l'inscription précédente.

Du fait de l'écart chronologique entre les deux textes, leur mise en rapport peut paraître périlleuse. D'emblée, cependant, une représentation graphique en histogrammes comme celle

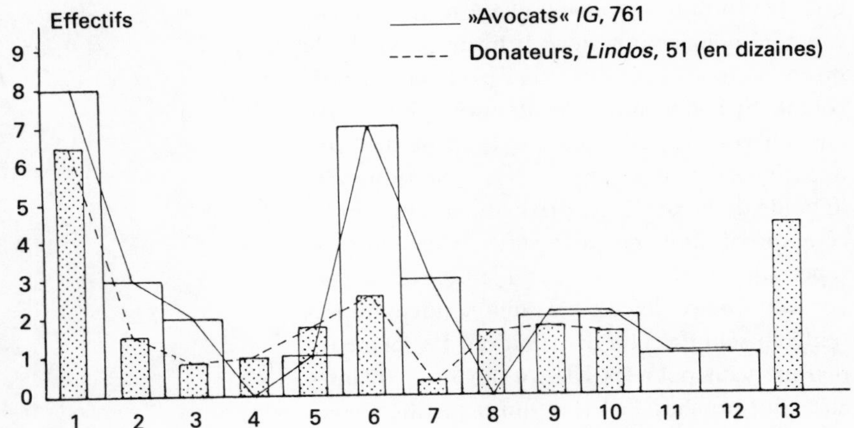

Figure 2: Représentation en histogrammes des données du tableau n° 1

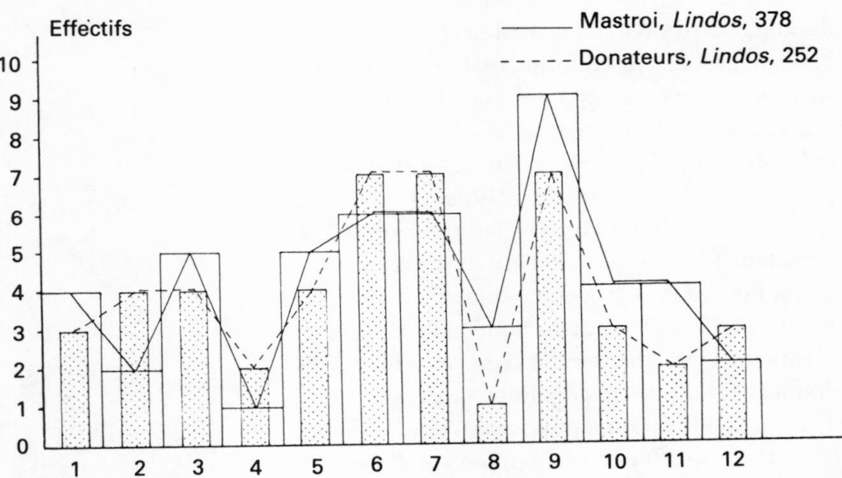

Figure 3: Représentation en histogrammes des données du tableau n° 2

Démes auxquels renvoient les numéraux des figures 2 et 3:

1 Lindopolitai
2 Nettidai
3 Brasioi
4 Pagioi
5 Kamyndioi
6 Klasioi
7 Ladarmioi
8 Dryitai
9 Argeioi
10 Boulidai
11 Kattabioi
12 Pédieis
13 Physkioi

de la figure no. 3 montre intuitivement l'étroite corrélation qui existe entre les effectifs classés par dème des mastroi de *Lindos II*, 252, et celui des donateurs de *Lindos II*, 378. Quant au calcul du coefficient de corrélation et à celui du t de Student, ils donnent les résultats suivants:

$$r = 0.754 \qquad t = 3.62 \qquad t\begin{cases}\alpha=0.01\\ \\ v=10\end{cases} = 3.17$$

Dans la mesure où t est supérieur à $t\alpha$ on obtient une nouvelle fois une corrélation très satisfaisante entre les deux séries d'individus statistiques puisqu'il n'y a guère qu'une chance sur cent pour qu'une telle corrélation soit due au hasard.

Il est vrai que dans une autre inscription, *Lindos II*, 346, datant de 43 a.C., qui donne une liste partielle des mastroi lindiens, on trouve pour trois dèmes des effectifs différents de ceux qui sont recensés dans *Lindos II*, 378: au reste, il n'est pas surprenant que d'une distribution à l'autre il y ait des variations d'effectif. Si, pour tenir compte de ces variations, on prend pour effectif des trois dèmes concernés, dans le calcul de la corrélation, la moyenne des chiffres de *Lindos II*, 346, et de *Lindos II*, 378, on obtient un taux de corrélation encore meilleur, avec des résultats suivants:

$$r = 0.783 \qquad t = 3.98$$

Il ne paraît donc pas niable qu'il y a effectivement une corrélation entre les effectifs par dème des magistrats qu'étaient les mastroi et ceux des donateurs dans une grande souscription publique. Une nouvelle fois, on est obligé de conclure que le nombre de mastroi qu'un dème parvenait à faire élire était fonction de la richesse et de l'influence de ses membres.

Pour ce qui est de la position des différents dèmes, on en voit émerger trois: ceux des Klasioi, Lardamioi et Argeioi. Deux dèmes occupent une position marginale, ceux des Pagioi et des Dryitai – comme dans les deux séries de la fin du 4ème siècle -, les sept dèmes restant étant dans une position moyenne.

La remarque que nous venons de faire sur la position marginale, dans les deux doubles séries statistiques, des deux dèmes des Pagioi et des Dryitai – outre qu'elle nous paraît pleinement justifier le bien fondé de notre démarche, puisque ce sont toujours les mêmes dèmes qui occupent la dernière place et qu'il serait bien étrange que cela soit dû au hasard – nous oblige à pousser plus loin notre analyse et à tenter de cerner la différence qui existe entre elles, ce qui revient à essayer de montrer l'évolution qui s'est produite entre la fin du 4ème siècle, date des deux premiers documents, et la fin du 2ème siècle et le 1er siècle, date des seconds.

Nous emploierons pour cela la méthode de l'analyse factorielle des correspondances[9]. Nous rappellerons brièvement en quoi consiste cette méthode. Elle est aussi fondée sur la notion de corrélation entre individus statistiques, à la fois "caractères" et "objets". Le but de la méthode est de produire une représentation plane de l'espace multidimensionnel dans lequel se trouvent projetés les individus statistiques. L'analyse de correspondance ne "transforme" en rien la réalité. Elle pernet seulement de visualiser les corrélations qu'on perçoit intuitivement en examinant un tableau de chiffres. Cette fois, chacune des quatre distributions est considérée comme un caractère prenant douze valeurs, et chaque dème comme un objet déterminé par quatre modalités. C'est un tableau à quatre colonnes et douze lignes (constitué en fait par la juxtaposition des deux tableaux no. 2 et 3) qui est traité par analyse de correspondance. Les résultats apparaissent sur la figure no. 4.

Nous rappellerons successivement deux des principes de base qui régissent l'interprétation d'un graphique d'analyse factorielle de correspondance, en appliquant ensuite ces principes au cas de notre diagramme et en essayant de tirer les conclusions historiques qui découlent de ces observations.

1) Le graphique retient les deux principaux axes d'inertie (représentés par l'axe horizontal et l'axe vertical) selon lesquels s'étire le nuage des points (objets ou caractères). L'axe horizontal (ou axe no. 1) représente la tendance dominante.

2) La proximité de deux points de catégorie différente (par exemple, dans le cas qui nous intéresse, la proximité d'un point représentant un dème avec un point représentant une distribution, A1, A2, etc) est l'indice d'une prédominance au sein de l'autre catégorie.

On remarque d'emblée que les deux séries de distributions A1 (*IG*, 761) et A2 (*Lindos II*, 51) d'une part, B1 (*Lindos II*, 252) et B2 (*Lindos II*, 378) d'autre part, ne voisinent pas l'une avec l'autre. La première série est, pour simplifier, en haut à gauche, la deuxième en bas à droite. *IG*, 761, et *Lindos II*, 51, sont plus éloignées l'une de l'autre que *Lindos II*, 252 et 378: c'est ce qu'on avait constaté précédemment en relevant une corrélation statistique meilleure entre les deux séries tardives qu'entre les deux séries de 325. Mais quoi qu'il en soit, c'est l'opposition entre les deux doubles séries qui avant tout mérite d'être relevée. Ainsi, la signification de l'axe no. 1 est claire: cet axe oppose d'une part les distributions A1 et A2 de la fin du 4ème siècle (à gauche), d'autre part les distributions B1 et B2 de la fin de l'époque hellénistique (à droite). Il est manifeste que l'évolution chronologique est un facteur essentiel pour comprendre la forme prise par le nuage des points-objets selon l'axe d'inertie horizontal. Si l'on examine les données plus en détail, on voit par exemple que le dème des Lindopolitai est tout proche de A2, c'est-à-dire que le poids de ce dème est prédominant au sein de cette distribution, ce qu'on vérifie aisément en se reportant au tableau no. 1 et à la figure no. 2 où l'on voit que ce dème est de loin le mieux représenté au sein de cette distribution. La même remarque vaut pour les Klasioi qui sont, quant à eux, plus proches de A1, ce qui se justifie pleinement si l'on se réfère aux données de base où l'on voit les Klasioi beaucoup mieux représentés dans A1 (*IG*, 761) que dans A2 (*Lindos II*, 51). Naturellement, les valeurs des dèmes des Lindopolitai et des Klasioi contribuent faiblement à l'inertie liée aux distributions B1 et B2. Des remarques inverses s'imposent pour les dèmes des Lardarmioi, Brasioi et Argeioi. Ce sont les dèmes qui sont prédominants dans les distributions B1 (*Lindos II*, 252) et B2 (*Lindos II*, 378), ce qu'une nouvelle fois on vérifie aisément en se reportant aux données de base du tableau no. 2 et à la figure no. 3. Si l'on examine maintenant le poids relatif des cinq dèmes que nous venons de mentionner successivement dans les tableaux de données et dans les histogrammes des figures no. 2 et no. 3, on voit que, pour ce qui est des dèmes cette fois, l'axe horizontal oppose les dèmes qui au fil du temps ont connu une *augmentation de leur richesse et de leur influence politique* à ceux qui, à l'inverse, ont connu une *dégradation*. A droite de l'axe vertical, Kattabioi et Kamyndioi (un peu), Argeioi, Brasioi et Ladarmioi (surtout) sont en meilleure position à la basse époque hellénistique qu'à la fin du 4ème siècle. En revanche, à gauche de l'axe vertical, Pagioi, Drytai et surtout Lindopolitai ont vu leur position relative en richesse et en influence politique se détériorer. Les dèmes situés en position moyenne, tout proches de l'axe vertical, n'ont pas vu leur position relative se modifier.

Quant au deuxième axe, sur lequel nous serons plus bref, manifestement il oppose entre elles les distributions, mais, de fait, pour ce qui est de l'interprétation, on doit retenir ici les oppositions deux à deux au sein du même groupe chronologique (opposition entre A1 et A2 d'une part, B1 et B2 d'autre part). B1 et B2 étant très

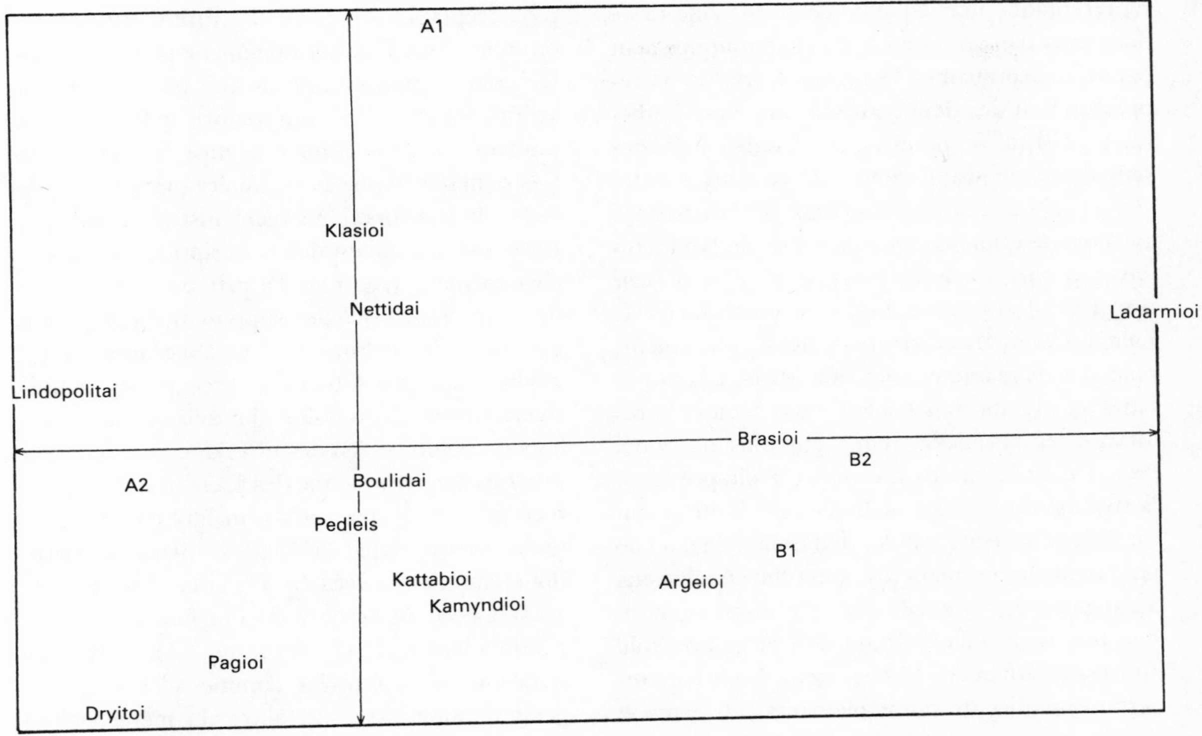

Figure 4: Analyse de correspondances N. B. A1 et A2 correspondent, respectivement aux deux distributions *IG*, 761, et *Lindos*, 51, B1 et B2 aux deux distributions *Lindos*, 378, et *Lindos*, 252.

fortement corrélés, ces deux séries sont très proches l'une de l'autre, comme nous l'avons relevé précédemment. En revanche, A1 et A2 sont moins homogènes l'une à l'autre. En fonction de ce qui a été dit plus haut sur le poids des Klasioi, proportionnellement "trop élevé" au sein de la distribution A1 (*IG*, 761), on peut largement comprendre la position excentrée de la distribution A1 et du même coup la distance qui sépare A1 et A2. Cependant, il n'est pas moins intéressant pour l'analyse historique de relever que Lindopolitai, Ladarmioi, Nettidai et Klasioi, qui sont au dessus de l'axe horizontal, ont proportionnellement nettement plus de représentants dans *IG*, 761, que le nombre de donateurs dans *Lindos II*, 51, ne pouvait le laisser présager. Pour ce qui est des Lindopolitai et surtout des Klasioi, qui sont les deux premiers dèmes pour le nombre de donateurs dans *Lindos II*, 51, il y a une nette "surreprésentation", comme si la fortune entraînait un poids politique plus que proportionnel. Cependant, si on admet cette interprétation, la surreprésentation des Ladarmioi dans *IG*, 761, par rapport à leur faible nombre de donateurs dans *Lindos II*, 51, peut paraître surprenante. Elle l'est sans doute moins si l'on constate que ce dème n'est certainement pas un dème marginal, puisqu'il est le deuxième en richesse et en influence politique à la basse époque. Il faut peut-être tenir compte de la part des variations dues au hasard pour expliquer le très faible nombre de donateurs Ladarmioi dans *Lindos II*, 51. En revanche, les dèmes qui sont dans tous les cas les plus faibles, à la fin du 4ème siècle comme à la fin de l'époque hellénistique, ceux des Dryitai et des Pagioi, n'ont aucun représentant dans *IG*, 761. On est bien tenté tout de même de conclure que la "fortune" entraîne une surreprésentation politique, la "pauvreté" une sous-représentation.

Dégager la signification historique globale des phénomènes que nous venons de dégager est moins simple qu'il n'y paraît. Nous tenterons néanmoins de tirer les quelques conclusions qui nous paraissent inévitables à la lumière des faits que nous venons de mettre en lumière.

1) Sur le plan institutionnel, tout d'abord, on peut légitimement se demander quelle signification accorder au fait qu'il y ait un lien entre le nombre des représentants officiels par dème, qu'il s'agisse des "avocats" de *IG*, 761, ou des mastroi de *Lindos II*, 378, et le nombre de donateurs dans des souscriptions publiques. A fortiori, l'évolution concomitante de l'effectif des

représentants de chaque dème et du nombre de donateurs dans des souscriptions publiques peut paraître surprenante. Dans son étude sur la représentation des dèmes au sein du conseil athénien, J. Trail[10] a montré que, depuis Clisthènes sans doute et jusqu'à une date se situant entre 200 et 193/192 a.C., il existait à Athènes un système de quotas fixes: le nombre de bouleutes envoyés chaque année par une dème à la *boulè* des Cinq-Cent était toujours absolument le même. Ces quotas correspondaient globalement, mais pas de manière stricte loin de là, à la population et à l'importance relative des dèmes. Après 193/192 en revanche, il n'y eut plus de quota fixe et c'est le hasard qui paraît avoir présidé à la fixation du nombre de bouleutes. Pour ce qui est de la représentation des dèmes lindiens, on ne peut malheureusement présenter des conclusions aussi précises, faute de pouvoir disposer, et il s'en faut de beaucoup, d'un dossier comparable au dossier athénien. Certes, nous possédons un certain nombre de renseignements sur le mode d'élection des mastroi au sein des trois communautés de Lindos, Camiros et Ialysos[11]. Mais en tout cas, à la lumière des deux inscriptions *Lindos II*, 252, et *Lindos II*, 378, il est tentant de conclure qu'à Lindos le nombre de mastroi était grosso modo proportionnel à l'importance d'un dème. Mais faut-il admettre que le nombre de mastroi de chaque dème était réexaminé périodiquement? Dans l'état actuel des sources, c'est un pas qu'il est impossible de franchir. On ne doit pas oublier que la liste *IG*, 761, n'est *pas* une liste de mastroi, qu'on ne sait même pas sur quelles bases étaient recrutés les mastroi à la fin du 4ème siècle. En revanche, il nous paraît clair que, fondamentalement, il existait un lien entre l'importance relative d'un dème et son poids dans le système politique.

2) Le nombre de donateurs d'un dème dans une souscription publique peut sembler être un critère aléatoire pour apprécier son importance. Ainsi, ne pourrait-on imaginer que, par exemple du fait de leur éloignement du centre politique de Lindos, les habitants d'un dème ou d'un groupe de dèmes, tels les Pagioi et les Dryitai, se soient désintéressés de ce genre de manifestations, tout de même qu'ils se seraient désintéressés de la vie de la communauté en fournissant peu de participants à la vie officielle de Lindos? Une telle affirmation ne nous paraîtrait pas acceptable. En effet, si à titre conservatoire on peut retenir ce raisonnement pour des souscriptions publiques, on ne voit pas comment il serait possible de comprendre que la communauté ait délibérément négligé des dèmes à la fois riches et importants numériquement dans le cadre de son fonctionnement institutionnel. Au reste, pour ce qui est des souscriptions publiques elles-mêmes, avec tout l'esprit de "montre" et de concurrence qu'elles supposent, on voit mal comment des habitants d'un dème auraient pu délibérément s'y soustraire. Pour rejeter définitivement cette hypothèse, ajoutons que les habitants du dème péréen des Physkioi, pourtant non intégrés dans le système des prêtrises lindiennes, n'en fournissent pas moins, malgré leur éloignement géographique de Lindos, quarante-quatre donateurs dans *Lindos II*, 51, et ce chiffre est le second pour le nombre de donateurs après les Lindopolitai (cf. Tableau no. 1). On voit pourquoi un argument comme "l'éloignement géographique" (ou tout autre du même genre) qui tendrait à justifier la faiblesse des effectifs de tel ou tel dème par des motifs purement circonstanciels n'est pas recevable. Il nous paraît certain que les chiffres de donateurs ainsi que ceux des "avocats" de *IG*, 761, et des mastroi de *Lindos II*, 378, nous renseignent effectivement sur l'effectif des membres d'un dème et, toutes choses égales, sur sa richesse relative.

3) Enfin, peut-on considérer que les évolutions que l'on constate dans l'importance relative des dèmes ont une signification, et si oui laquelle? Avant d'aller plus loin, il importe de remarquer que notre double série de documents ne nous permet en aucune façon de suivre une évolution, qui aurait pu éventuellement être très riche d'enseignement. Nous n'avons en quelque sorte qu'un point de départ et un point d'arrivée, sans étape intermédiaire. Ces réserves faites, sans reprendre en détail notre démonstration précédente, on peut dégager les conclusions suivantes:

- Argeioi, Brasioi et Ladarmioi ont vu leur position relative se renforcer.

- Kamyndioi, Kattabioi, Pedieis, Boulidai, Nettidai et Klasioi sont restés dans une position sensiblement identique - toujours très forte pour les Klasioi.

- En revanche, trois dèmes ont vu leur position se dégrader, mais leur situation présente des différences telles qu'elles ne sont pas directement comparables. Les Lindopolitai, qui étaient de loin le premier dème par ordre d'importance à la fin du 4ème siècle n'occupent plus à la fin de l'époque hellénistique qu'une position quelconque. La chute est nette et profonde. Pagioi et Dryitai, sont demeurés des dèmes marginaux, mais leur position relative s'est encore légèrement dégradée.

C'est ici que l'on regrette particulièrement que nos sources sur la localisation des dèmes lindiens soient si maigres. En effet, la pauvreté ou la richesse relative des dèmes pourrait éventuellement être mise en relation avec l'étendue et la richesse de leur terroir. Si les Pagioi occupent bien les régions intérieures du district situé au sud d'Apollona et les Dryitai la région de Mesanagros, elle aussi très accidentée, on pourrait mieux comprendre que ces dèmes ne jouent qu'un rôle marginal dans la vie lindienne. En revanche, le poids toujours remarquable des Klasioi conviendrait bien à une localisation dans une riche plaine côtière, au nord ou au sud de Lindos. Les incertitudes qui demeurent sur les localisations réelles rendent cependant toute conclusion précise par trop risquée. Ce n'est que pour les Lindopolitai, dont l'activité et la richesse étaient à coup sûr directement liées à l'activité portuaire et au commerce, que l'on peut avancer des conclusions plus nettes. Leur position dominante à la fin du 4ème siècle pourrait bien s'expliquer par une vitalité toujours maintenue de l'agglomération lindienne, moins d'un siècle après le synoecisme et alors que l'activité économique de Rhodes devait profiter à tous ses ports, y compris celui de Lindos. En revanche, à la basse époque hellénistique, alors que la vie économique rhodienne était durement affectée par les bouleversements successifs des courants d'échanges de la 2ème moitié du 2ème siècle et du 1er siècle avant notre ère, on peut comprendre aisément que le dème des Lindopolitai ait connu une dégradation de son poids relatif au sein de la communauté lindienne, y compris par une baisse de ses effectifs de population suite à l'installation définitive de membres de ce dème dans la ville de Rhodes ou par émigration à l'étranger.

Telles sont pour le moment les principales conclusions qui nous paraissent devoir être tirées de l'étude de la répartition par dèmes de la richesse et de l'influence politique au sein de la communauté lindienne à l'époque hellénisitique. D'autres investigations, et en particulier une investigation archéologique systématique de la chôra lindienne, permettront peut-être de préciser et de compléter ces analyses.

Alain Bresson
Institut d'Histoire
Université de Bordeaux III
Domaine Universitaire
33405 Talence Cedex
France

1. Nous remercions M. le Professeur Saingolet (Université de Bordeaux II) à qui nous devons ce que nous savons de statistique et d'analyse de données. Bien entendu, les positions défendues ici n'engagent que nous-même.
2. Nous employons le terme de "communauté" pour désigner les trois composantes tribales de l'Etat rhodien unifié postérieur au synoecisme de 408/407. Comme on le sait, ces trois "communautés" correspondaient aux trois anciennes cités d'Ialysos, Lindos et Camiros. Pour ce qui est des sources épigraphiques concernant Lindos, on trouve la plus grande partie d'entre elles dans le second volume des fouilles danoises de Lindos, magnifiquement publié par Chr. Blinkenberg dans Lindos II.
3. Cf. *IG*, XII 1, 761.
4. Cf. *Tituli Camirenses*, 110.
5. Pour les dèmes rhodiens, nous renvoyons à l'étude récente, riche et détaillée, de Papachristodoulou 1983, p. 64-80, et particulièrement p. 74-75, dont nous reprenons ici toutes les conclusions. On trouvera également dans ce travail toute la bibliographie antérieure que nous nous dispensons de donner ici. Nous remercions vivement M. l'Ephore Papachristodoulou de nous avoir fait parvenir un exemplaire de thèse avant la publication définitive.
6. Il convient cependant encore de rappeler (cf. P.M. Fraser, Eranos 51, 1953, 23-47) que, pour l'accès à la prêtrise suprême de Lindos, celle d'Athéna Lindia, il existait un "cycle triennal" de trois "tribus" regroupant les dèmes par groupes de quatre de la manière suivante: 1. Argeioi, Pagioi, Lindopolitai, Boulidai 2. Klasioi, Nettidai, Ladarmioi, Kamyndioi 3. Pedieis,

Brasioi, Kattabioi, Dryitai. Notre connaissance encore insuffisante de la localisation de ces dèmes ne nous permet cependant pas d'apprécier pleinement la signification de ces regroupements "tribaux".

7. Cf. supra, n. 3.
8. Sur l'analyse de correspondances, voir l'ouvrage de base de Benzécri et al. 1979.
9. A propos de l'absence des Kattabioi et Pedieis, Chr. Blinkenberg notait (Lindos II, 257, comm. ad. Lindos 51): "Manquent les Kattabioi et les Pedieis qui auront été nommés dans *b II*, 1-12 ou les parties manquantes de l'inscription". Notre proposition d'accorder douze dèmes à chacun des deux dèmes manquants comporte donc une bonne part d'arbitraire, mais on voit qu'elle a bien des chances de ne pas être très éloignée de la vérité.
10. Traill 1975, et en particulier les conclusions sur la représentation des dix tribus attiques originelles, p. 56-58. Les documents de base ont été publiés par Meritt – Traill 1974.
11. Nous ne pouvons aborder cette question dans les limites de cette étude.

Hellenistische Sepulkralarchitektur auf Rhodos

Mit einem Anhang: Rhodisch-koische Nikealtäre und die Bildhauerwerkstatt des Turmes der Winde zu Athen

Hans Lauter

Bis in spätklassische Zeit scheinen die Bewohner der Insel Rhodos eine eigentliche sepulkrale Architektur in Form grösserer Grabgebäude nicht gekannt zu haben[1]. Im Hellenismus hat sich dieses Bild gewandelt: Die bekannten Denkmäler rhodischer Grabbaukunst[2] – neue kommen regelmässig hinzu – besitzen für die allgemeine griechische Architekturgeschichte oft sogar eine Bedeutung, die weit über das lokale Interesse hinausgeht[3]. Gemeinsam ist diesen rhodischen Grabbauten jedoch hauptsächlich dies, dass sie untereinander kaum Gemeinsamkeiten typologischer Natur aufweisen. Dadurch unterscheidet sich Rhodos z.B. deutlich von dem verwandten Knidos – um nur eine Nachbarpolis zu nennen -mit seinen recht gleichförmigen Grabtemene[4], die wohl zumeist auch erst hellenistich sind. Selbst eine koloniale Stadt wie Alexandria zeigt trotz aller Varianten ein homogeneres Spektrum sepulkraler Grossarchitektur als Rhodos[5].

Es ist unter diesen Umständen klar, dass es nicht viel Sinn haben dürfte, innerhalb Rhodos' etwa entwicklungsgeschichtliche Massstäbe an die Grabbauten zu legen. Ihr Problem stellt sich m.E anders: Woher nehmen die Rhodier die Anregungen für ihre Realisationen, – wenn sie denn überhaupt etwas übernehmen; liegen neue Konzepte vor; was bedeutet die erwähnte Typenvielfalt für das Verständniss des hellenistischen Rhodos? Hierzu im Folgenden einige kurze Bemerkungen. Soweit möglich, seien die Grabbauten nach ihren Hauptgruppen zusammengefasst, ohne dass hiermit direkte Abhängigkeiten angedeutet werden sollen.

Tumulusgräber

Zwei grosse Tumulusgräber mit architektonisch gestaltetem Sockelgeschoss sind auf Rhodos erhalten, der Rundbau Hagios Milianos bei Lindos[6] und das sog. Ptolemaion von Rhodini[7]. Beide müssen dem Hellenismus angehören, ohne dass ihre Zeitstellung innerhalb dieser Epoche präzise zu bestimmen wäre[8].

Insbesondere der Rundbau repräsentiert einen Grabtypus, der während des ganzen Altertums in den verschiedensten Gebieten sei es sporadisch, sei es gehäufter auftritt[9]. Ein zeitlich und räumlich nicht allzu weit entferntes Beispiel wäre etwa der Tumulus von Belevi[10]. Jedenfalls handelt es sich bei dem Grabtyp von Hagios Milianos sozusagen um überall verfügbares "Gemeingut", das keine weiteren Schlüsse zulässt. Etwas anders verhält es sich mit dem sog. Ptolemaion: einesteils wegen seiner annährend quadratischen Grundform und der daraus resultierenden, vermutlich pyramidenförmigen Tumulusanschüttung, andernteils wegen der Verwendung der Blendsäulenordnung im Sockelgeschoss. Man ist versucht, hier an kleinasiatische Anregungen zu denken und wäre es noch mehr, wenn es Hinweise gäbe, dass der Tumulus wie auch immer als Stufenpyramide gestaltet war. Als Vergleich bietet sich das klassische Löwenmonument bei Knidos an[11] - wenn man einmal von der ganz unterschiedlichen Grösse und Proportionierung abzusehen geneigt ist. Pyramidale Elemente wies vielleicht schon das goldene Löwenvotiv des Kroisos in Delphi (Hdt. I 50) auf; später dürfte das Dach des Maussoleions eine Stufenpyramide gebildet haben. Interessant scheint vor allem auch der Hinweis auf das hellenistische Pyramidengrab des Diagoras bei Turgut, immerhin in der rhodischen Peraia[13]. Daraus die Vermutung abzuleiten, das sog. Ptolemaion gehörte einem aus Karien stammenden Rhodier, wäre aber wohl zu weitgehend. Was den Halbsäulenschmuck des Sockelgeschosses anbetrifft, so ist dies ein in der hellenistichen Koine wurzelndes Element, vertritt an diesem Grab also gewissermassen den allgemeinen Zeitgeschmack[14].

Felsfassadengräber
Unter den Felsfassadengräbern lassen sich die mit Halbsäulenscheinfassaden zu einer engeren Untergruppe zusammenfassen; zu ihnen zählt das grosse Familiengrab des Archokrates in Lindos[15], geschaffen um 200 v.Chr., das korinthische Grab in Rhodini[16] und in gewisser Weise die Hoffassade des Kammergrabs von Asgourou[17].

Ihre formal engsten Parallelen finden sich nun nicht in den räumlich benachbarten Gebieten Kleinasiens, die besonders reich an säulengeschmückten Felsfassadengräbern sind. Die lykisch-karischen Denkmäler[18] stellen in der Regel Tempelfassaden mit Giebeln vor. Die rhodischen Beispiele, – auf deren Unterschiede untereinander im Hinblick auf die Anordnung der Grablegen hier nicht eingegangen sei – lassen sich dagegen eher als Blendstoen beschreiben. Ein dem Wesen nach verwandter Fassadentypus wurde besonders in Kyrene überaus häufig benutzt[19]; selbst Einzelzüge wie die Existenz einer Attika am Archokrateion oder die Scheintüren des korinthischen Grabes von Rhodini finden dort Entsprechungen. Nun sind zwar intensive hellenistische Handelskontakte zwischen Rhodos und Kyrene bezeugt[20]; trotzdem zögere ich, direkte Anregungen zuzugeben. Das Motiv der fortlaufenden Halbsäulenordnung scheint zu allgemein "hellenistisch", als dass es nicht auch in Rhodos ad hoc für die Sepulkralarchitektur hätte "erfunden" werden können. Das zeigen auch strukturverwandte Grabfassaden in Illyrien[21] und jetzt sogar in der Peloponnes (Mamousia)[22]. Immerhin sind aufs Ganze der Antiken Welt gesehen derartige Felsfassaden auch wieder nicht so häufig, dass eine engere Beziehung zu Kyrene absolut auszuschliessen wäre. Die Frage sollte daher offen bleiben.

Nur mit einem Satz seien die Bogennischen über Grabloculi in Lindos[23] erwähnt, die sich aus entsprechenden Votiv- und Statuennischen im natürlichen Felsen ableiten, wie sie so häufig überall in der antiken Welt vorkommen; sie sind in Lindos freilich zu einer aussergewöhnlichen Monumentalität gesteigert.

Eingehendere Beachtung als ihr bisher zuteilgeworden verdient eine Felfassade in der Nekropole von Dokuz Sokak, deren augenfälligstes Merkzeichen ein Schildrelief ist[24]. Die Felsfassade war länger, als die mir bekanntgewordenen Veröffentlichungen zeigen, und besass architektonische Details, unter denen die beiden (Schein-)Türen, eine "Sitzbank" neben der einen Türe, ein erhaltener Eckpilaster sowie ein (nur ganz gering erhaltenes) Gesims, etwa in Höhe des Abschlusses des unteren "Geschosses", auffallen (Fig. 1, 2). Es leidet kaum einen Zweifel, dass mit diesen Angaben und durch die Unregelmässigkeiten des Ganzen hier eine ganz profane Hausfront nachgeahmt werden sollte. Ergänzt man sich die Fassade, fühlt man sich tatsächlich wie versetzt vor gewisse Häuser Pompejis aus seiner hellenistischen Phase. Diese Felsfasade von Dokuz Sokak ist damit m.W. ein Unikum in der gesamten hellenistischen Welt, insofern in keinem anderen Fall normale Wohnarchitektur in der Sepulkralarchitektur "abgebildet" worden sein dürfte (- so naheliegend ein solcher Gedanke auch manch einem erscheinen mag -). Wenn schon nicht anders, wird man dies Denkmal doch immer als Beispiel für die Versatilität im hellenistischen Rhodos gelten lassen müssen.

Felskammergräber
Es ist hier nur von solchen Kammergräbern die Rede, die architektonisch ausgestaltet sind, – etwa im Gegensatz zu dem schlichten Grabraum des Archokrateions in Lindos (s.o.). Von ihnen kenne ich zwei Beispiele: das Grab im Gehöft des R. Ratzikli zu Asgorou[25] und das nur flüchtig angezeigte, neue Rundgrab von A. Triada[26].

Bei ersterem scheint alexandrinischer Einfluss evident, handelt es sich doch um eine Kombination aus (unvollständigem?) Hof sowie Felssaal mit den eigentlichen Grablegen[27]. Entscheidend ist aber das segmentförmige Gewölbe des Felssaales, das endgültig auf Ägypten verweist[28]. In dem Grab von A. Triada ist es die Kreisform des überkuppelten Mittelteiles, die wiederum an Alexandria denken lässt, wo runde Kuppelgräber schon früh im Hellenismus Vorläufer haben[29] und wo in der grossen, spät- oder spätesthellenistischen Grabanlage von Abu Wardian[30] eine Saalarchitektur erhalten ist, die

Abb. 1.

in Wesen und Form dem rhodischen Grab am vergleichbarsten erscheint[31].

Verschiedene Hypogäen

Die Mehrzahl der rhodischen Grabbezirke, die oft viele Loculi vereinigen, lassen sich typologisch nicht weiter gliedern. Verschiedenste Plankombinationen treten auf; und wenn auch einzelne architektonische Elemente selten ganz fehlen, ist für die Hypogäen doch der insgesamt geringe künstlerisch-architektonische Anspruch kennzeichnend. Besonders gut erhaltene Beispiele bietet vor allem die Cova-Nekropole[32]; leider sind sie für eine tiefere wissenschaftliche Betrachtung zu schlecht publiziert, genauer: sie sind so gut wie unpubliziert. Nur so viel lässt sich vielleicht sagen: Die meisten architektonischen Elemente wie Gewölbe, Bögen etc. sind rein zweckhafter, unkünstlerischer Natur. Architektonische Kunstformen (Stufenanlagen, Sockel mit Gebälk o.ä.) bleiben im wahrsten Sinne des Wortes untergeordnet, indem sie nämlich Grabzeichen tragen sollten, insbesondere die endlosen Grabaltäre mit ihrem z.T. reicheren Reliefdekor. Die aesthetische Botschaft in den Hypogäen wird demnach von diesen im Sinn "plastischen", nicht eigentlich von baulichen Elementen getragen. – Es sei in die-

Abb. 2.

Abb. 3.

sem Zusammenhang gestattet, wieder einmal auf das grosse Hofgrab (?) in Karakonero mit seinem fast lebensgrossen, aus der Felswand gearbeiteten Relieffries dionysischen Inhalts hinzuweisen, das, an sich ein Unikum, das Überwiegen des plastischen Aspektes besonders anschaulich macht. Seine Publikation ist nach wie vor ein dringendes Desiderat[33].

Das bunte Bild der verschiedengestaltigen Hypogäen von Rhodos kann und soll hier nur als Folie für die viel weniger zahlreichen, eigentlichen Grabarchitekturen der Insel dienen. Als solche veranschaulicht es aber vielleicht noch einmal die Ausgangsthese dieser Betrachtungen über die Formen- und Typenvielfalt rhodischer hellenistischer Grabanlagen. Deren Problematik gilt es nun ins Auge zu fassen.

Zu Beginn der zusammenfassenden Uberlegungen zu den rhodischen Sepulkralbauten sei nochmals meiner Überzeugung Ausdruck verliehen, dass wir es mit Denkmälern aus einer relativ begrenzten Epoche von 100 bis 150 Jahren zu tun haben. Allein Hagios Milianos mag noch in die 1. Hälfte des 3. Jh.v.Chr. gehören, alles übrige wird im wesentlichen hochhellenistisch sein. Zweifellos entspricht das Aufkommen grosser Grabgebäude den speziellen Bedingungen der historischen Situation. Leitende oder auch nur einflussreiche Einzelne bzw. eher leitende Familien[34] wünschen nunmehr, ihre Rolle auch durch die sepulkrale Repräsentation in einer Weise zu dokumentieren, die hinter den Ausdrucksmöglichkeiten anderer führender Zentren nicht zurücksteht: Als Mitglied des aufgeblühten rhodischen Staatswesens, vielleicht sogar als Teilhaber der Macht, "ist man wer" und die vielfältigen internationalen Verflechtungen haben den reichen Rhodiern gewiss reichliche Möglichkeiten zum Vergleich und zur Anschauung geboten, wie sich andernorts die Oberschicht in Grabbauten selbst darstellt. – Grabgebäude sind nun einmal die aufwendigste Form sepukraler Selbstdarstellung. – Im Hinblick auf die älteren, eher bescheidenen Bestattungssitten der Rhodier dürfen die hellenistischen Sepulkralbauten dann wohl als abgeleiteter Brauch eingestuft werden, in dem auch ein gewisses Konkurrenzverhalten (gegenüber dem Ausland?) zu Buche schlägt. Die rhodische grosse Grabarchitektur ist nichts, das sich allein auf rhodischem Boden entwickelt hätte und aus bloss innerrhodischen Kausalitäten erklären liesse.

Es kommt dementsprechend auch zu keiner "gewachsenen" Typenbildung, sondern die einzelnen Monumente bleiben momentane Adaptionen nicht bodenständiger Vorbilder, – die es als solche ja auch gar nicht gab.

Einige Worte zu dem Problem der Vorbilder und der Adaptionen. Bei der Durchsicht der Grabbauten wurde es deutlich, dass präzise "Einflüsse" meist nur schwer zu definieren sind. Manches geht auf allgemein griechisches (Tumulustyp H. Milianos), anderes auf allgemein hellenistisches Repertoire zurück (Halbsäulenblendarchitektur), auf die künstlerische Koine der Epoche also. Lokal enger umschriebene Fremdanstösse könnten vielleicht im Pyramidengrab des sog. Ptolemaion erkannt werden (Südwestkleinasien); genügend gesichert erscheinen mir aber eigentlich nur die alexandrinischen Einflüsse auf die Felskammergräber von Asgourou und A. Triada. Und selbst in diesen Fällen handelt es sich nicht um "Kopien" fremder Vorbilder, sondern nur um excerptartige Übernahme einzelner, wiewohl oft wichtiger Elemente und Grundbestandteile, die dann einer Veränderungs- oder Vergesellschaftungsoperation unterworfen wurden[35]. Man griff demnach in Rhodos Anregungen auf, sei es aus dem allgemeinen Repertoire, sei es gelegentlich aus bestimmten Landschaften, imitierte aber die Vorbilder nicht, sondern adaptierte sie ad hoc. Für einen entwicklungsgeschichtlichen Prozess blieben die verschiedenen ad-hoc-Realisationen folgenlos, – ebenso wie übrigens auch die innovative Adaption des Hausfrontmotivs in Dokuz Sokak. Im Grunde stellen daher die Denkmäler rhodisch-hellenistischer Sepulkralarchitektur eine Anhäufung von isolierten, je für sich zu beurteilende Einzelschöpfungen dar; wenig verbindet sie miteinander; und dies Wenige ist nicht

Abb. 4.

Abb. 5.

"typisch rhodisch". Ein scheinbar negatives Ergebnis.

Auf der anderen Seite mag darin etwas zu Ausdruck kommen, das vielleicht in einem tieferen Verständnis für Rhodos charakteristisch ist. Die rhodische Sepulkralarchitektur zeigt also nicht ein enges, lokal oder provinziell geprägtes Gesicht wie oft andernorts, sondern ist offener, unbeschränkter, nicht "rhodisch", sondern eben "hellenistisch" in einem allgemeinen Sinn. Geht es zu weit, dies letztlich als eine kosmopolitische Tendenz zu werten? Es scheint mir in der Tat, als ob Rhodos auch auf anderen, wenn auch keineswegs auf allen Sektoren dem kosmopolitischen Ideal näher als sonst viele Städte, Mittelstaaten und Landschaften gekommen sei. Das kosmopolitische Ideal ist aber einer der vorgegebenen Fluchtpunkte hellenistischer Entwicklung überhaupt. Wie dem auch sei, die Betrachtung der grossen rhodischen Grabarchitektur führt notwendig auf das interessante Kapitel "Rhodos und die übrige griechische Welt", wobei in diesem Fall Rhodos rezeptiv, der nehmende Teil war, – aber doch so, dass sich hier sozusagen wie durch einen Brennspiegel wichtige Hauptströmungen in "autonomen" Bauschöpfungen bündelten.

Anhang:
Rhodisch-koische Nikealtäre und die Bildhauerwerkstatt des Turmes der Winde zu Athen.

Indem ich an den letzten Gedanken, – Beziehungen Rhodos' nach aussen – , anknüpfe, möchte ich noch eine kleine Beobachtung anschliessen, die zwar von meinem eigentlichen Thema der grossen Grabbauten wegführt, wenn sie sich anfänglich auch noch im Rahmen der Sepulkralkunst bewegt. Sie soll aber an einem kuriosen Fall aufzeigen, dass Rhodos durchaus gelegentlich auch gebender Teil war, dass von der Dodekannes aus Kunst sogar in die alte Hauptstadt griechischer Kunsttätigkeit, nach Athen, "exportiert" werden konnte.

Ausgangspunkt ist eine Reihe rhodischer Grabaltäre zylindrischer Form, die je vier schwebende Niken in recht hohem Relief aufweisen. Eine durchgehende Girlande verbindet die Niken; sie wird von ihnen zwischen (vorderer) rechter Schulter und rechtem Flügel hochgehoben, kommt hinter dem linken Flügel wieder zum Vorschein und hängt dann festonartig durch. Fraser hat die vier früher bekannten Stücke zusammengestellt[36] und noch eine weitere, in vielen Punkten freilich abweichende Ara angefügt[37]. Die Serie kann inzwischen um zwei Denkmäler vermehrt werden. E. Zervoudaki publizierte jüngst ein Stück aus Asgourou, das leider ohne Fundzusammenhang bei Bauarbeiten ans Tageslicht kam[38]. In den römischen Thermen von Kos befindet sich endlich noch ein gleichartiger, bisher m.W. unpublizierter Altar (Fig. 3-7)[39]. Die Unterschiede der beiden neuen Exemplare vor allem zu den bekannten Stücken aus der Cova-Nekropole und aus Kos in Istanbul sind sowohl faktisch wie gerade auch stilistisch so gering[40], dass sie allesamt als Wiederholungen angesprochen werden dürfen. Sie sind offentsichtlich innerhalb einer nur kurzen Zeitspanne von ein und derselben Werkstatt gearbeitet worden[41].

Diese auf der Dodekannes aktive Werkstatt[42] hat aber auch die Hochreliefs der Windgötter am Horologion des Andronikos zu Athen[43] gearbeitet. Diese Werke, die stilistisch einzuordnen bisher nicht gelungen ist, zeigen die frappantesten Übereinstimmungen mit den rhodisch-koischen Nikealtären: allgemein die Derbheit des plastischen Volumens und der Ausführung, näher die Art der Bewegung der Figuren, insbesondere der Zug, dass Beine und Unterkörper im Profil, die Brust aber frontal oder fast frontal gegeben wird. Im Einzelnen wiederholt sich etwa die gleichsam scherenförmig aufgefächerte Beinstellung, die "Schweben" oder "Fliegen" bezeichnet[44], usf. Am Schlagendsten beweist aber vielleicht ein Vergleich der Flügel der Windgötter[45] mit denen der koischen Niken (Fig. 6, 7), dass hier und dort dieselben Hände am Werke waren.

Es wird sich zeigen müssen, ob dadurch, dass

Abb. 6.

Abb. 7.

die athenischen Windgötter nunmehr aus ihrer Isolierung gelöst sind, Wege geebnet werden, um auch andere Fragen des noch immer problematischen Gebäudes, insbesondere die Frage seiner Datierung[46], mit grösserer Sicherheit beantworten zu können. Doch darum geht es uns an dieser Stelle nicht. Es kam hier nur darauf an, auf ein Beispiel des "Kulturaustausches" zwischen der Dodekannes und anderen hellenistischen Gebieten hinzuweisen, das die Betrachtungen zu der grossen Sepulkralarchitektur noch einmal von einer anderen Seite her beleuchten mag.

Hans Lauter
Archäologisches Seminar
Philipps-Universität Marburg
Biegenstrasse 11
3550 Marburg
West Germany

Vorliegender Beitrag wäre ohne wiederholtes Studium der Denkmäler vor Ort sogar in dieser knappen Form nie möglich gewesen. Ich danke daher auch an dieser Stelle dem vormaligen Ephoros, G. Konstantinopoulos, und dem jetzigen Ephoros, J. Papachristodoulou, für ihre stets herzliche Aufnahme und insbesondere für die Unterstützung, die sie meinen Anliegen ausnahmslos gewährten. Vor allem fühle ich mich jedoch I. Zervoudaki verpflichtet, die meine erste und gründlichste Lehrerin in rhodischer Topographie war und der ich überhaupt erst die Kenntnis so vieler Monumente und ihrer Probleme verdanke.

1. Das gilt gleichermassen für viele andere, aber keineswegs für alle griechischen Gebiete bzw. Randgebiete. Im näheren Umfeld von Rhodos, der dorischen Hexapolis, ist es freilich wohl nur das stets etwas aus dem Rahmen fallende Halikarnassos, das architektonisch gestaltete (autochthon kleinasiatisch beeinflusste?) Felsfassadengräber schon in der Archaik besass (oberhalb des späthellst. Theaters; mit äolischen Säulen?).
Für Rhodos-Stadt weist Fraser 1977, 7 auf die erstaunliche Tatsache hin, dass vor dem Hellenismus sogar Grabreliefs u.ä. spärlich vorkommen. Seine plausible Erklärung dieses Phänomens könnte auf Grabbauten schwerlich übertragen werden, zumal wenn man die ganze Insel in Betracht zieht.
2. Es ist hier zunächst nur von wirklichen "Bauwerken" (inklusive grossformatiger Blendarchitekturen wie Felsfassaden u.ä.) die Rede. Hellenistische Grabzeichen im engeren Sinne (Reliefs, Altäre etc.) sowie veritable Kleinarchitekturen (z.B. Ädikula: ClRh 1, 1928, 54, Abb. 37; Hesberg 1980, 46 Taf. 4.3. Vermutetes Säulendenkmal: H. Lauter, JdI 98, 1983, 294) bleiben im Wesentlichen ausser Betracht (hierzu Fraser 1977 passim; zur Interpretation eines aussergewöhnlichen Grabzeichens letzthin H. Lauter-Bufe, AM 98, 1983, 155-167). Zu einem Einzelproblem vgl. aber Anhang.
3. Auf das aesthetische Element "landschaftlich-romantischer" Züge und Wirkungen habe ich (AntK 15, 1972, 49ff.) hinzuweisen versucht. Die Erscheinung ist zwar nicht spezifisch rhodisch, aber dort doch besonders ausgeprägt. Dieses Problemfeld soll hier nicht weiter behandelt werden.
4. Breitgelagerte, in den Hang hinausterrassierte Bezirke (Grablegen in der Terrasse) mit mannshohen Umfassungsmauern, die zur talseitigen Front fehlen können; seitliche Türen; vor der Rückmauer Bank, die zur Aufstellung der Grabaren o.ä. diente. Genaue Untersuchungen fehlen m.W.
5. Vgl. hierzu Adriani 1966 passim.
6. Lindos III, 487; H. Lauter, AntK 15, 1972.
7. ClRh 2, 1928, 55 Abb. 38; Lindos III, 2 a.O. 514; H. Lauter, AntK 15, 1972, 55; Fraser 1977, Abb. 12, 13.
8. Der Mauerstil von H. Milianos schliesst vorhellenistiche Entstehung aus, wird aber auch in dieser Epoche nicht sehr spät sein, vgl. Lauter 1986, 275. Für das Ptolemaion geben etwa die glatten Säulenschäfte keinen irgendeiner Weise brauchbaren Fingerzeig.
9. Beispiele in Koenigs et al. 1980, passim, bes. 38 ff.
10. S. Kasper, AA 1975, 233ff.
11. F. Krischen, RM 59, 1944, 172 ff., Lawrence 1962, 197 Abb. 108.
12. Vgl. H. Büsing, JdI 97, 1982, 16.
13. Fraser – Bean 1954, 44 Nr. 41 Taf. 11.
14. Die Numidischen Tumuli des Medracen und des Tombeau de la Chrétienne kommen z.B. unabhängig, aber mit analogen Mitteln zu einem Bild, das dem Ptolemaion recht ähnlich ist (Horn – Rüger 1979, 132ff.).
15. Lindos III, 491 m.Lit.
16. ClRh 1, 1927, 53 Abb. 36; H. Lauter, AntK 15, 1972 Taf. 16.3.
17. H. Laüter-Bufe, RM 89, 1982, 45 Taf. 15.
18. Vgl. etwa Akurgal 1961, 128f., 161f.
19. Vgl. Stucchi 1975, passim; s.a. RM 89, 1982, 41ff.
20. SEG IX 2.
21. Illiria 1972, 179; P. Franke, AW, S.Nr. 1983, 35ff.
22. I. Dekoulakou bereitet die Publikation dieses wichtigen Denkmals vor.
23. H. Lauter, AntK 15, 1972, Taf. 15.3.
24. AAA 6, 1973, 116; Fraser 1977, Abb. 107 a,b.
25. H. Lauter-Bufe, RM 89, 1982, 155-167.
26. BCH 1982, 614.

27. Adriani 1966.
28. JdI 86, 1971, 171; Lauter 1986, 241, 251.
29. Adriani 1966, 123 Nr. 77, 78.
30. Adriani 1966, 162 Nr. 118; vgl. Lauter 1986, Abb. 73.
31. Der Kurosität halber sei darauf hingeweisen, dass Karyatiden wie im Grab von A. Triada jetzt auch in einem Grab in Sveschtari/Bulgarien bekannt wurden (Erwähnung R.A. Tomlinson, JHS 104, 1984, 254).
32. Z.B. ClRh 1, 1927, 51 Abb. 34 (über Loculi attika-artiger Sockel mit Triglyphon), 52 Abb. 35; Fraser 1977, Abb. 5,8.
33. Vgl. einstweilen Fraser 1977, 4 Abb. 9,10. Der Reiter sitzt nicht auf einem Pferd, wie Fraser meint, sondern zweiffellos auf einem Maultier. Damit ist, wie mir I. Zervoudaki vor Jahren nachwies, die Szene auf die Rückführung der Hephaistos zu deuten. Vgl. jetzt auch H. Mielsch, Gnomon 54, 1982, 574. Handelt es sich um das Temenos eines Dionysiasten-Koinons?
34. Die vielen hier anknüpfenden Fragen können zumeist nicht beantwortet werden: einheimische oder fremde Familie, Familie oder Koinon etc. Sicher ist nur das lindische Archokrateion (o.Anm. 15) als Grabanlage einer einheimischen Bürgerfamilie. Die meisten andern Bauten hatten mehr als eine Bestattung aufzuweisen; fraglich ist H. Milianos (o. Anm. 6).
35. Auf diese Operationen konnte hier im Einzelnen nicht eingegangen werden, da es nicht auf die spezifische, quasi persönliche Physiognomie eines jeden Denkmals ankam, die allerdings durch jene Operationen erst festgelegt wird.
36. Fraser 1977, 31 mit Anm., 164 Abb. 84f. Es handelt sich um die Stücke aus Kos in Istanbul, Mendel III Nr. 1150 (Neppi Modona, 1938, 161 Taf. 13a; Fraser 1977, Abb. 85 b,c.); aus der Cova-Nekropole (ClRh 5, 1931-32, 19, Nr. 6 Taf. 18ff.; Fraser 1977, Abb 84 c); von Plateia Symes (ClRh 5, 1931-32, 19 Taf. 22; Fraser 1977, Abb. 84 d); aus Trianda? (Fraser 1977 Abb. 85 a).
37. Fraser 1977, Abb. 84 a,b. Zu den Niken kommt zunächst eine fünfte Figur (auf einer Standplatte?) hinzu, nach den Abb. vielleicht der Geehrte. Die Ornamentik ist reicher als sonst. Bewegung und Stil der Niken weichen grundsätzlich von den übrigen Stücken ab.
38. ADelt 32, 1977 Chronika B2, 373 Taf. 224 d.
39. Die Attribute, die in Kos von den Niken in ihrer linken Hand gehalten werden, sind: 1. Palmzweig-Kranz – zweizipfelige Tänie, 2. grosser Kranz, 3. Palmzweig, 4. grosse eingerollte Tänie.
40. So ist anscheinend auf dem Altar aus Cova die Unterscheidung der Attribute nicht ganz so reinlich; eine Nike bewegt ausserdem ihren Kopf nach vorn zur rechten Schulter, während sonst durchweg der Kopf nach hinten gewandt ist. Das Istanbuler Stück, auf dem die Attribute anscheinend wie in Kos aufgeteilt sind, ist in seiner Arbeit wohl etwas weniger eckig, d.h. rundlicher und weicher als die drei anderen, – wenn hier nicht Verwitterung trügt. Das neue Stück von Asgorou scheint dagegen schwungvoller; die Köpfe der Niken sind nach vorne gewendet.
41. Die beiden (kleineren?) Altäre von der Plateia Symes und aus Trianda (o.Anm. 36) zeigen angearbeitetes, oberes Altarprofil, das bei den vier grossen Exemplaren gesondert gefertigt war. Nach den Abb. kann ich darüber hinaus weder faktische noch stilistische Unterschiede erkennen.
42. Ob die Bildhauer ursprünglich von hier stammten oder ob sie etwa aud dem rhodischen Einflussgebiet in Südwestkleinasien eingewandert waren, spielt keine entscheidende Rolle. Wichtig ist - besonders im Hinblick auf Athen – nur, dass sie nicht vom "ionischen" Kleinasien, nicht von den Kykladen und erst recht nicht aus dem "neu-attischen" Ambiente des Mutterlandes kommen.
43. Travlos 1971, 281; Freeden 1983.
44. Bes. der Lips: Freeden 1983 Taf. 32.2.
45. Freeden 1983, Taf. 39.
46. Die bisher übliche Datierung etwa in caesarische Zeit (etwas vorsichtiger Hesberg 1980, 53: 1. Hälfte bis Mitte des Jh.) ist letzthin bestritten worden, so durch Freeden a.O., passim (hierzu H. von Hesberg, Gnomon 57, 1985, 80ff.). Beachtenswert auch die Erwägungen von M. Verzar, DArch 9/10, 1976/77. 391 Anm. 41, über die varronische Überlieferung und Varro's frühen Aufenthalt in Athen. Verf. neigt ebenfalls einer Frühdatierung (nicht nach 100 v.Chr.) zu und wird dies in Kürze weiter zu begründen versuchen.

The Canon of Pliny for the Colossus of Rhodes and the Statue of Athena Parthenos

Thomas Thieme

Canon is a word with many meanings. From its Indo-European origin and the Babylonian qanu for cane (arundo donax) it was used for many purposes in antiquity as well as today[1]. In sculpture and architecture it became the rule for creating a work of art. For sculpture, the most famous example is Polycleitos' canon expressed in a statue where all the parts from the finger up to the whole were related in definite proportions.

I will here limit the expression to the total heights of representation of man and the total lengths of monuments and demonstrate the canonical qualities of the figures given by Pliny for the Colossus of Rhodes and the statue of Athena Parthenos.

After the siege of Rhodes in 305-304 BC under the command of Demetrios Poliorketes, a statue of Helios, the Colossus, was erected in Rhodes and this was to become one of the seven wonders of the world.

The sculptor was Chares of Lindos, a pupil of Lysippos, and the statue was cast in several stages, with an interior reinforced by stone blocks and a structure of iron.

Work on the statue started in 304 and it was completed after twelve years in 293. After 66 years it collapsed during the earthquake in 228.

The statue was broken at the knees, which were still standing until AD 653 when Muavija conquered Rhodes. In spite of the proverb minted at the collapse "one should not move a bad thing that is lying safely", he had the remains brought to the mainland where a Jew from Edessa bought the bronze as scrap. The Colossus finally disappears from history in a caravan of 900 loaded camels.

For the ancient writers the size and technique of the Colossus were more important than the exterior and the artistic values. Hence we know little more than that it was a statue of Helios. To us its appearance is based mainly on the Rhodian coins depicting the head of Helios and some amphora stamps showing a standing clothed statue. (fig. 1). This view is supported by the meaning of the word "colossus" at the time of its erection, when it was used for statues in an archaic fashion more or less shaped as a column or a pillar[2]. This interpretation of the word also gives sense to an 11th century miniature from Jerusalem where the statue is standing on a column[3].

Fig. 1. Rhodos, Tetradrachm 3rd Century B.C. (200-tallet f.Kr.) Kungliga Myntkabinettet Stockholm (SNG GVI A Nr 98).

The popular view of the Colossus straddling the entrance to the harbour is probably based on an incorrect reading of the dedication inscription.

The height of the Colossus is said to have been inscribed on its base. A problem is, however, that the height of 70 cubits/105 feet generally given is not consistent in the literary remains. The different figures are listed below. In the table 1 foot is equal to 16 fingers and 1 cubit equal 24 fingers, according to common Greek and Roman usage[4] (fig. 2).

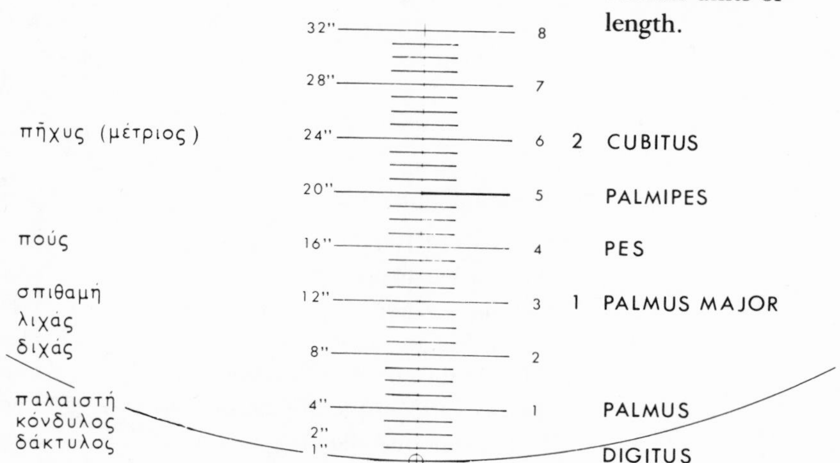

Fig. 2. Greek and Roman units of length.

Table 1

Overbeck No.	Source	Height in text	Cubits	Feet
1539	Plin. N.H. XXXIV.41.	70 cubits	70	105
1540	Strabo XIV. p. 652	11x10 cubits	110	165
	Eustath. ad Donys. Perieg. 504	70 cubits	70	105
	Anthologia Gr. I 75. 83	8x10 cubits	80	120
1541	Schol. Lucian. Icaromen 12	70 cubits	70	105
1542	Festus b. Paul. Diacon. p. 58	105 feet	70	105
1547	Philo Byzant. De sept mirac. mundi p. 14	70 cubits	70	105
1548	Hygin. Fab. 223.	90 feet	60	90
1549	Vibius Sequester in Append. Philon Byzant. ed Orelli p. 142.	105 feet	70	105
1551	Niceta in Append. Philon. Byzant. ed Orelli p. 144. According to Aristotle.	600 cubits	(60)	(90)
1552	Anonym. ibid. p. 145.	60 cubits	60	90
	According to Aristotle	19 cubits	19	27 1/2
1554	Constantin. Porphyr. De admin. imper. 21.	80 cubits	80	120

The different figures can be listed in the following way:

Table 2

Given heights for the Colossus of Rhodes			
2(3)	sources 90 feet	1	source 110 cubits
6	sources 105 feet	1	source 19 cubits
2	sources 120 feet		

The figure 105 feet is the most common and it was this number that first drew my attention to the problem when I met the figures 104/105 explicite and implicite in texts concerning heights of representations of man and lengths of monuments.

Pliny also gives a height for the Athena Parthenos statue by Phidias and states that it was 26 cubits[5]. The 26 cubits can be expressed as 26x24 daktyloi or 104x6 daktyloi. The figures 104/105 are further found in the following examples.

In South-Indian systems of proportion canons have been found with values of 120 and 104 angula (finger widths) for the height of man[6].

Cennino di Drea Cennini writes, about 1390, "E tutto l'uomo lungo otto visi e due delle tre misure" (The height of man is 8 2/3 face-lengths)[7]. With a face-length of 12 fingers, the height will be 8 2/3 x 12= 104 fingers.

For monuments Leo Ostienses (1046?-1115) gives 105 cubits for the Basilica of Montecassino and the same value is found in contemporary texts concerning the Great Mosque in Cordoba[8].

Finally there was a discussion in the years 1510-1580 in Bologna concerning the height of the facade of S. Petronio. The figures discussed were 100, 104 and 105 feet[9].

The examples mentioned are also listed in the table below.

Table 3

Statue/monument	Dimension	Number	Unit
Colossus of Rhodes	Height	105	feet
Athena Parthenos	Height	104	6 daktyloi
Cennini's canon	Height	104	fingers
South-Indian canon	Height	104	fingers
The Basilica of Montecassino	Length	105	cubits
The Great Mosque in Cordoba	Length	105	cubits
S. Petronio in Bologna	Height	104/105	feet

Numbers in ancient works of art can be considered as more or less speculative, or be given a more rational interpretation. In the following I will try to explain the practical, more earthbound functions of the numbers 104/105.

In Greek, Roman and later Byzantine metrology it is often said that the fathom is equal to the height of man. The standard division of the fathom is 4 cubits, 6 feet and 96 fingers. Beside the fathom of 96 fingers, fathoms of 108, 110, 111, 112 and 134 fingers are found in the metrological literature[10].

In Egypt figures in grid nets have the values 18 3/5, 19 and 22 1/2 squares in height[11].

In Roman times we have Vitruvius' value of 6 feet for the height of man and the statement of Diodorus of Sicily that the Egyptians made their statues 21 1/4 parts in height[12]. The numbers 104/105 are however not found as metrological fathom units.

One interpretation of the meaning of the numbers 104/105 is their use as approximations for $\sqrt{3}$ in connection with sides and heights in the equilateral triangle in the sexagesimal number system.

The number 105 first occurs as an $\sqrt{3}$ approximation in Babylonian Mathematics[13]. Later, Heron of Alexandria uses the same value beside 104[14].

In the sexagesimal system the expression is 1.45 and 1,44, which can be read as

$$\frac{60}{60} + \frac{45}{60} = \frac{105}{60} \text{ and } \frac{60}{60} + \frac{44}{60} = \frac{104}{60}$$

It can also be seen as the height of an equilateral triangle with the sides of 120 where the height is 60 x $\sqrt{3}$ = 103.92....with 104/105 as rational approximations. (fig. 3).

The examples demonstrated show that the knowledge of approximating the ratio between the height and side in the equilateral triangle was common during Antiquity and the Middle Ages.

In order to illustrate how these mathematical calculations can be used to establish a canon, I will give an interpretation of the so-called 2nd Egyptian Canon, or the Canon of the Egyptian Late Period from about 650 BC (fig. 4).

On wall paintings the underlying grid is preserved in several cases and the height of the figure is 22 1/2 squares. The navel is situated at a height of 13 squares. One square is supposed to be a hand of four fingers. The figure with net is now put into a vertical scale of 120 fingers, where one square corresponds to 4 fingers. The next step is to draw a circle with the center at the height of the navel touching the level of the feet similar to the description of Vitruvius' Circle Man in his chapter on temple planning. The following ratios can now be demonstrated. The diameter of the circle is 104 fingers and the height of the figure is 90 fingers. The height of

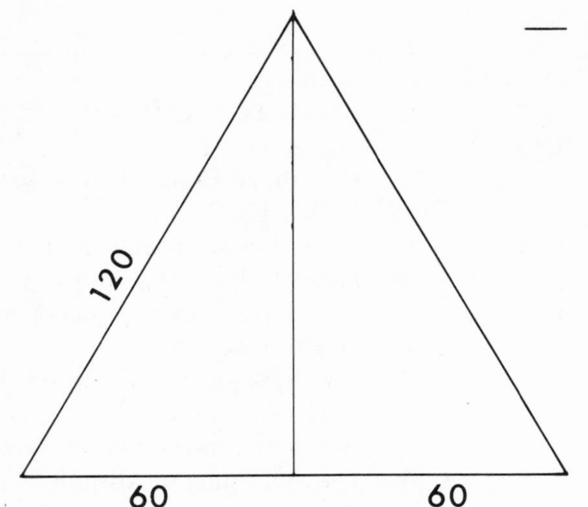

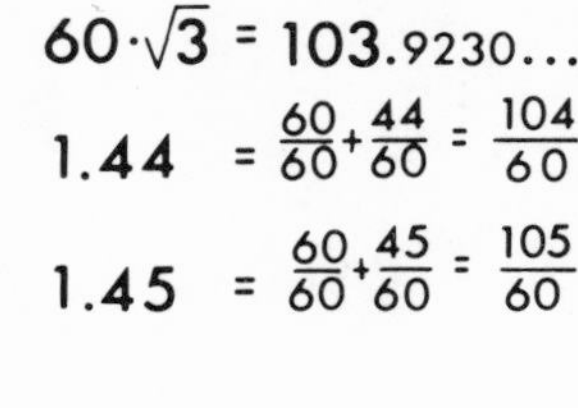

Fig. 3. Sides and height in the equilateral triangle with approximations in the sexagesimal system.

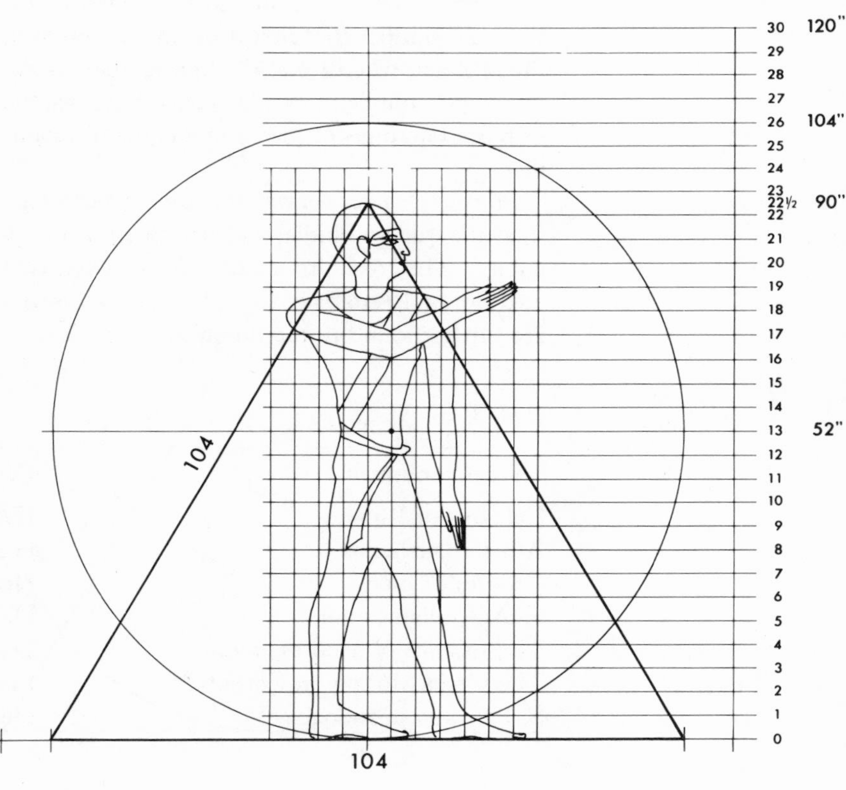

Fig. 4. The Canon of the Egyptian Late Period with superimposed circle and triangle showing rations between total and navel heights.

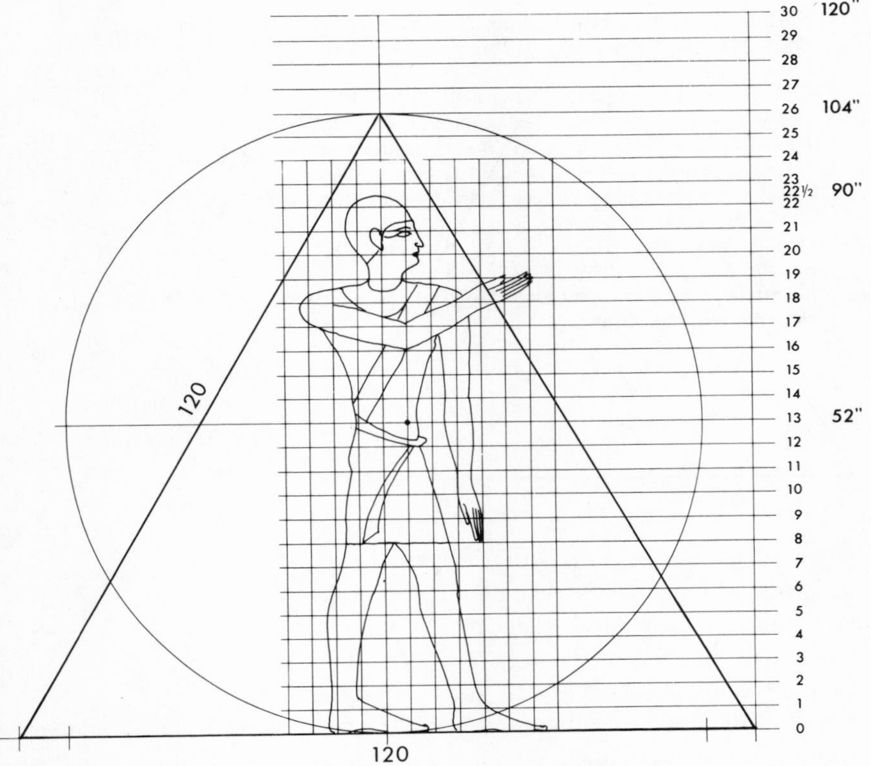

Fig. 5. The Canon of the Egyptian Late Period with superimposed circle and triangle (Circle diameter = triangle height).

an equilateral triangle with the side of 104 is $104/2 \times \sqrt{3} = 90.06\ldots$ The ratio between the total height 90 and the navel height 52 also seems to be a $\sqrt{3}$ approximation. Furthermore an equilateral triangle with the height of 104 will have the side of $104/\sqrt{3} \times 2 = 120.08\ldots$ (fig. 5).

In mathematical terms a geometrical series can now be demonstrated as

$$120 \times \left(\frac{\sqrt{3}}{2}\right)^{0},\ 120 \times \left(\frac{\sqrt{3}}{2}\right)^{1},\ 120 \times \left(\frac{\sqrt{3}}{2}\right)^{2} \text{ or } 120,\ 103.92\ldots,\ 90$$

$D \cdot \left(\frac{\sqrt{3}}{2}\right)^0$ 120

$D \cdot \left(\frac{\sqrt{3}}{2}\right)^1$ 103.9230

$D \cdot \left(\frac{\sqrt{3}}{2}\right)^2$ 90

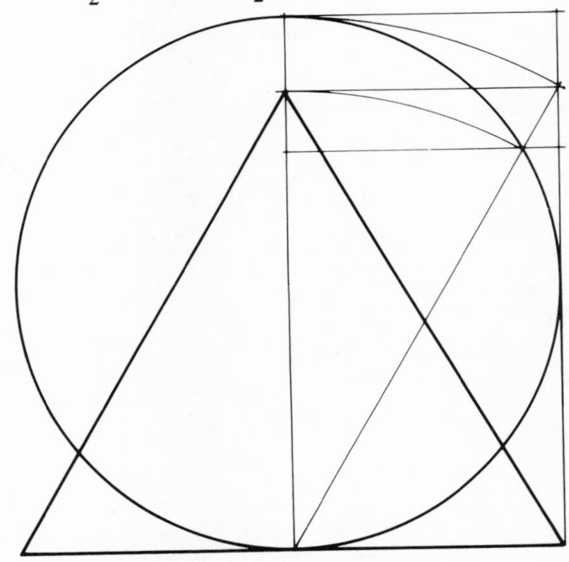

Fig. 6. Geometrical serie with the terms $\left(\frac{\sqrt{3}}{2}\right)^n$. D = 120.

With the approximated value of 105 for 60 x $\sqrt{3}$, we have here three of the heights given for the Colossus, and the values 120, 105 and 90 also indicate that such a method was current among the writers concerned with the Colossus[15].

The values 19 cubits and 110 cubits mentioned in the text also have canonical/metrological significance. 19 is the height of squares in the Canon of the Egyptian Middle Kingdom. The number 110 = 11 x 10 should be compared with a fathom of 11 x 12 fingers mentioned by Pediasimos[16].

What then was the real height of the Colossus? The different figures given indicate that the ancient writers estimated the monument by multiplying a canon with a suitable number of multiples. Furthermore in establishing the real height the given heights are not the only factors. Also the length of the foot/cubit unit used is uncertain. The value of the foot unit might have been between the Roman foot of 0.296 m and the Ptolemaic of 0.3552 m. The result of the investigation into the height of the Colossus is thus rather meagre for establishing an exact physical height.

What has been demonstrated above is more the tradition of organizing and systemizing the human body into metrological and mathematical terms and how this knowledge is used for representations of man.

In this tradition the Colossus of Rhodes is a central monument, both in time and no less in geography.

Thomas Thieme
Hedlundsgatan 12
413 21 Göteborg
Sweden

I wish to express my sincere thanks to Dr. Sven Tage Teodorsson for valuable help in reading the Greek and Roman texts, and to Dr. Eivind Lorenzen for many years discussion on modules and measurements of man.

The literary remains are collected in: Overbeck 1868, No. 1539-1554. See also M. P:n Nilsson, Historisk Tidsskrift 1910, 362-371; A. Gabriel, BCH 56, 1932, 331-359. With references to earlier literature.; H. Maryon, JHS 76, 1956, 68-86; D.E.L. Haynes, JHS 77, 311-312.; G. Kleiner in: Charites(1957) 101-104.; G. Roux, REA 62, 1960, 5-40.; P. Howell in: Athenaeum Pavia 46, 1968, 291-299; P. Moreno, ArchCl 25-26, 1973-74, 453-463; G. Hafner in: Tatort Antike (1979), 337-355; Ekschmitt 1984, 169-182.

1. Oppel 1937.
2. G. Roux, REA 62, 1960, 17-18.
3. Jerusalem, Greek Patriarchal Library, Codex Taphou 14, f. 312 v; dated in Galavaris 1969, 225-6.
4. Hultsch 1882.; Lorenzen 1966 and Lorenzen 1970.; Schilbach 1970.
5. Plin. N.H. XXXVI.18.
6. H. Ruelius, in Der "vermessene" Mensch. München 1973, 74-83.
7. Speich 1957, 130-31.
8. Chronikon Monasterii Casinensis, Chapter 26, Book III translated by Sciavo, in Atti del 2:o Convegno Nazionale di Storia dell'Arte, 1937, 162-4; Lehman-Brockhaus 1938, 476-80; Holt 1957, 8-17. See also T. Thieme, OpRom 11, 1976, 127-142.; F.H. Giménez, MM 1, 1960, 200.
9. Hecht 1979, 113-29.
10. Schilbach 1970, 22-28.
11. For the Egyptian canons see R. Lepsius in: Die Längenmasse der Alten, 1884, 99-104.; Lorenzen 1966 and Lorenzen 1970.; H.W. Müller in: Der "vermessene" Mensch (1973), 8-31.: Iversen 1975.
12. Diodorou Bibliotheke Historike, ed. L. Dindorf (1866), Bd. I, 141, Lib. I, Cap. XCVIII. See also Speich 1957, 3-5.
13. E.M. Bruins, Indaginationes Mathem 12, 1950, 370-1.; Bruins - Rutten 1961, TMS, Text 2, obverse, photo (pl. II) and hand copy (pl. 2).; E.M. Bruins, Còdex Constantinopolitanus Palatii Veteris, No. 1, Part 3 (1964), XI, pl. 2. Professor Jöran Friberg kindly drew my attention to the references above.
14. Heronis Alexandrini, Vol. IV, Ed. J.L. Heiberg (1912). See also Neugebauer 1969, 46-52.
15. Lorenzen's work is to a great extent based on a geometrical series with the terms

$$\frac{(\sqrt{5})}{2}^{n}$$

16. Schilbach 1970, 18.

The Anastylosis[1] of the Ancient Monuments on the Acropolis of Lindos

Past and present attempts

Vassos Papadimitriou

The excavations on the Acropolis, that revealed the ancient monuments, were carried out by Kinch and Blinkenberg during their first campaign, that is from April 1902 until the end of 1903. There were two principal aims. The first was to clear the area and reach the ancient remains as fast as possible, and the second was, in places where ancient remains were not found, to continue to dig as far as the virgin earth or the rock surface.

This procedure meant however, that the excavators were obliged to demolish buildings of later date, thus leaving no possibility of studying the evolution of the sanctuary during its history.

The only remains that survived demolition were the Byzantine church and the Commander's palace. Perhaps the fact that these buildings were some distance from the Hellenistic remains contributed to their survival.

The "clearing" and excavation began on the temple of Athena. Next was the wall that was visible in the centre of the site, Fig. 1. This was interpreted by Ross (1842) as a temple dedicated to Zeus Polieus, whereas Hiller (1892), as mentioned by Dyggve, considered it to be part of the ancient temple of Athena of the Geometric period.

Fig. 1. The stoa after the excavations (Photographic Archive of the Archaeological Service of the Dodecanese).

Kinch very soon realised that this wall was part of a stoa. Working towards the north-west and then the south-east, he gradually uncovered the whole stoa. He revealed seven column drums in situ, Fig.1, and a staircase of the Archaic era. Then he proceeded to reveal the area between the temple and the stoa. The remains brought to light here suggested the existence of the propylaia forming a unity together with a monumental staircase.

Because the parts of the monumental buildings that were revealed seemed to be in very bad condition, some pointing, small repairs and restoration were carried out.

Soon after 1912 the Italian archaeological service must have taken over responsibility for the site, but it seems that attention was focussed mainly on the towns of Rhodes and Kos, where large excavations were carried out at that time.

In the late thirties De-Vecchi, the Italian governor of the Dodecanese, ordered the restoration of the acropolis of Lindos. This was part of a larger scheme including other sites in Rhodes and other islands. The archaeologist Laurenzi and the "geometra" Paolini carried out the task.

The principles underlying the restoration were derived from the ideology then dominant in Italy. Since the twenties the Italian government had spent tremendous sums of money in the Dodecanese to build an exemplary new province, where the fascist ideal in architecture, town planning, organisation and life style would be applied and demonstrated.

The Classical and Roman world of antiquity would bring back glorious memories and support "national" pride. The revealing and restoration of ancient remains in an impressive manner seems to have been a general attitude at that time[2].

Restoration work started in 1938 and ended in 1940. The plans must have been changed during the work. The original drawings by Paolini (Fig. 2), show a different setting than that finally chosen (Fig. 3). It seems that Paolini was in favour of less impressive but more authentic intervention, closer to today's conception of restoration.

The ancient column drums and other architectural members were not replaced in their original position, and a large amount of new stone or reinforced concrete was used.

Laurenzi and Paolini used the archaeological and architectural results achieved by Kinch and Blinkenberg.

All joins were made using reinforced concrete. The new stone drums were pierced centrally by a square hole (18 x 18 cm), while the ancient ones were carved only near their upper and lower surfaces.

When the ancient and new column drums were joined in situ, the missing parts of the ancient drums were added either by means of mortar containing small stones, where required, or by larger right angle pieces.

The greatest problem facing the restored acropolis monuments today results from the way its members are connected. The oxidation of the steel of the reinforced concrete join produces expansion and cracking of the concrete and stone. Wind and earth tremors continue the destruction.

Apart from this "technical" problem, the carving (especially of the drums) that was used for this type of connection has destroyed the traces of the original dowels, which could have helped today for a better study of the monument and possibly for a more authentic positioning of the drums.

The use of reinforced concrete is related to the prestige that this "modern" building material had in the technical world at that time. Figure 4 shows the ruins in Berlin just after the end of the war. Here we can see an example of a similar technique of construction. The stone columns have a reinforced concrete core. It was believed more or less that reinforced concrete was the perfect and immortal building material, so it was the most appropriate for the construction of the monuments of the immortal "third Reich".

A similar technique of reassembling was practised during the same period in the acropolis of Rhodes, in Kamiros, and in the Asclepio of Cos. Moreover rather similar technique was used by

Fig. 2. Drawing of the restored Stoa (by Paolini).

Fig. 3. The restored monuments on the Acropolis of Lindos in early sixties.

Fig. 4. Ruins in Berlin just after the war.

Balanos for the construction of new drums during the great restoration carried out on the Parthenon.

Figure 5 shows the concrete core of a restored column on the acropolis of Lindos. The missing part of the drum is of the new sandstone, which has proved to have less resistance than the ancient.

Figure 6 shows the new conception for completing an architectural member by means of a Pantograph. A plaster-cast is made of the missing part and then, using a Pantograph (a device that transfers points), the points of the ruptured surface are transferred to the new piece of stone. Thus the new piece is an exact copy of the missing part and completes the member with a tolerance of approximately 2 mm. The new piece is placed in position using cement mortar as filling material, then sculpted externally to match exactly with the rest of the stone and, if necessary, secured with titanium reinforcements.

This new conception for the completions of architectural members expresses the new ideology that has been established since the Charter of Venice (1964). The restorers of the twenties and thirties were more concerned with the monument as a whole, and there was no sensitivity for the detail. Now concepts like reversibility, minimum intervention and authenticity apply even to each individual architectural member.

Today we accept that the Italian restoration in Lindos has an historical value. Unfortunately we cannot correct the majority of the previous errors. What we can do is to repeat the restoration using new technology when it does not contradict the principles of anastylosis today. So the use of titanium is considered instead of steel, the behaviour of stone with the binding materials is studied by means of ageing tests, and the best knowledge of the behaviour of the standing columns under earth tremors is acquired by using a seismic table.

Finally let it be said that there could be no progress in the ideas and methods related to restoration, if these attempts, which we tend to criticize, had not been made earlier.

Fig. 5. Restored column in Lindos today.

Fig. 6. Completion of architectural member today (Photograph by P. Psaltis).

Vassos Papadimitriou
Ioannou Theologou 63
Zografos
Athens 157 73
Greece

1. Article 15 of the international Charter of Venice describes the term anastylosis: "...all reconstruction work should however be ruled out a priori. Only anastylosis, that is to say, the reassembling of existing but dismembered parts can be permitted. The material used for integration should always be recognisable and its use should be the least that will ensure conservation of a monument and the reinstatement of its form."
2. It seems that intended exploitation of the island as tourist's resort may also have influenced the style and extent of the restorations.

Chapter 3 . The Island of Cos

1:4000
3
3
7
9
4
9
2
5
1
6
10
8
6

Recent Archaeological Finds from Kos

New Indications for the Site of Kos – Meropis

Charis Kantzia

In recent years there has been a great increase in building activity on Kos as a result of the rapidly growing influx of tourists. The Ephoria for Classical Antiquities in the Dodecanese is therefore controlling building operations,carrying out salvage excavations where construction is scheduled, in virtually all of the properties in the modern town of Kos and, as occasion requires, in the rest of the island. These excavations[1], continuing the large-scale German and Italian excavations have greatly increased our knowledge of virtually all eras, in particular the archaic period.

My main topic is Kos-Meropis, the settlement which was in the north-east tip of the island before the foundation of the new *polis* which, according to Diodoros (XV.76.2), was founded through metoecism in 366; most of the striking remains belong mainly to this *polis*. First, however, I would like to present a rapid review of the most significant finds in recent years.

Large sections of the Prehistoric settlement at Serraglio[2] have been investigated in quite a few properties; my colleague, Toula Marketou, is in charge of this work.

Six protogeometric and geometric graves were found in various spots above the Mycenaean settlement, one of which is an especially interesting early grave because it most probably is a cremation burial which, as is known, is lacking in the cemetery at Serraglio[3]. The burnt layer, measuring 2.20 by 1.35 m with a depth of 20 cm, contains carbonized matter, ash and pieces of burnt bones; two broken pots were found in this layer; one is a neck amphora, the other a round-bodied pyxis with Protogeometric patterns. A fragment of a bronze pin was also found.

Two other pyres also found in the graveyard cannot be graves; perhaps they have to do with funeral rites. An amphora and a lekythos were found broken at the edge of one of the pyres, which had no remains of bones whatsoever other than completely carbonized matter[4].

The absence of cremation burials up until now at the cemetery of Serraglio, where inhumation is the rule, has been interpreted in various ways. According to Morricone, who attributes the cemetery to the autochthonous inhabitants, the standard practice of inhumation, especially in contracted position, is accounted for as the continuation of the age-old custom of the natives of the island[5]. Desborough[6] and Snodgrass[7], on the other hand, link this phenomenon to the arrival of settlers from the Argolid where inhumation is the rule. According to the tradition these settlers arrived on the island at the beginning of the first millennium.

A late geometric grave of a little girl was particularly elaborate; it contained thirty-seven vases, most of which were outside and around the grave, an Egyptian faience amulet of Bes, six bronze pins, two pairs of earrings, one gold and one bronze, and beads of different kinds made of faience and glass paste[8].

The most interesting finds from this grave are two hollow terracotta fowl, obviously toys, of a type hitherto unknown in this cemetery, where a great many duck vases have been found, probably Cypro-Phoenician imports, as were the ring-necked black-on-red juglets from this cemetery[9].

A second also late geometric grave, unfortunately partly destroyed, had a remarkable wheel-made terracotta horse and a fragment of a hand-made terracotta figurine of a male, probably the horse's rider. The horse, a little smaller than the Centaur of Leukandi[10], from which it is descended, strongly resembles the wheelmade terracotta figurines of bovines found in quantities in the deposit at the temple of Apollo on Kalymnos[11]. The grave also contained a hand-

Fig. 1. Town of Kos.
1. Kalogerou property.
2. Sophou property.
3. The western mole.
4. Mouzakis property.
5. Stadium.
6. Western gymnasium.
7. Temple of Demeter.
8. Mylonas property.
9. Fortification wall of Kos-Meropis.
10. Investigated property.
• Investigated property.

made pot in which were burnt seeds, probably lentils.

The following investigations of the Hellenistic town were carried out: large sections of the fortifications[12] and the western mole[13] of the harbour (No. 3 in the plan of fig. 1) and many streets which provide new evidence for the city plan which seems to have features deriving from Hippodamos' grid plan[14] (see plan of fig. 1). In the western part of the town, however, there is a deviation from the north-south axis of the eastern section. Here the streets and the buildings are aligned northeast-southwest, perhaps dictated by the choice of the slope of the hill of Serraglio for the stadium site[15]. Two streets were found to meet at a pronounced acute angle east of the stadium on the Mouzakis property (No. 4 in the plan of fig. 1).

The divergence from the axis is especially noticeable in two large neighbouring buildings in the western district, the Stadium and the West Gymnasium (No. 6 in the plan) for which new evidence has come to light. Only the starting line (aphesis) and a few sections of the Stadium have been previously known[16]; now that the southwest end and three rows of stone benches have been found we know that the stadium (excavated by Eos Zervoudaki) was rectangular, not horseshoe-shaped[17]. The east stoa was all that was previously known of the western gymnasium; it had been identified as the covered running-track (Xestos dromos)[18]. After the northwest corner of the stoa had been uncovered[19], it turned out to be part of a large peristyle court measuring c. 200 m in length and c. 100 m in width.

Excavations carried out by Hersi Brouskari in two properties have uncovered wonderful mosaics of late antiquity showing that the city continued to be splendid and prosperous into early Christian times. One of the mosaics, more than 20 m long, has, within a circular frame, a female figure shown from the waist up, wearing a turreted crown and holding a Horn of Plenty; perhaps she is the personification of the city of Kos[20], corresponding to the representation of Constantinople on a mosaic found by Italian excavators[21].

At the modern village of Cardamena, on the ancient site of the deme of Halasarna, the famous temple of Apollo[22] has been discovered by chance and, unfortunately, partly destroyed. We now know Apollo's epithet from an inscription, referring to the festival celebrated there, the Pythaia; he was therefore worshipped as Apollo Pythaeus[23]. Amongst the finds are Attic sherds with graffiti giving the name of Apollo (fig. 2). The finds show that the temple flourished continuously from at least as early as the archaic period until Roman times. Beginning last year a team from the University of Athens has been conducting the excavations in this area.

The Settlement of Kos-Meropis

The most important result of recent excavations is, perhaps, the finding of a series of archaeological remains in and around the modern town; these finds date to the archaic and classical periods, which up until now have been obscure in the area of Kos, and they may be assigned to the settlement of Kos-Meropis[24].

The finds in question are: a large cemetery of the archaic and classical periods, new parts of the sanctuary of Demeter and sections of the walls with scattered remains of the settlement. Thucydides (VIII.41.2) reports a settlement by the name of Kos-Meropis in the course of an account of the last decade of the Peloponnesian War, when he describes the looting that went on there by the Spartan admiral Astyochos in 412 BC just after a terrible earthquake had laid it waste. "Descending at Kos-Meropis in his voyage, he sacked the city which was unwalled and in a state of ruin because of an earthquake which they had suffered (being the greatest in living

Fig. 2.

Fig. 3.

Fig. 4.

memory), the men having fled to the mountains, and cleared the country in forays, except for the free men". (Translated by Susan M. Sherwin-White, Ancient Cos, 1978, p. 36).

Diodoros (XIII.42) simply calls the place Meropis.

Merops is the eponymous founder of Kos and the early settlers of the island were called the Meropes who, as early as the fifth century BC onwards, were considered to be the original inhabitants.

The Mycenaean settlement at Serraglio has been identified as the Meropian settlement.

The geometric cemetery found above the Mycenaean habitation level comes to an end in the late 8th century BC and up until now there has been a big gap between the late 8th century and 366 BC, the year when the new city was founded. For the first two centuries of the gap there were no finds whatsoever; for the following period there were scattered finds as well as a series of archaeological data providing strong indications for a revival of the settlement in this area[25]. Although Bean and Cook[26] had correctly surmised that the settlement must be located at the site of the Hellenistic town, up until now Kos-Meropis had not been found.

This gap in the archaeological record has in the past given rise to a series of hypotheses[27]; it has been thought that the gap reflects a decline in Kos-Meropis after the 8th century BC and a corresponding development in the town of Astypalaia, located at the other end of the island[28]. Strabo (657) reports Astypalaia as the old capital of the island, the site where, according to Morricone, the Dorians settled[29].

The new archaeological evidence illuminates this obscure period and leads to the conclusion that the low hill of Serraglio never ceased to be inhabited.

The Cemetery (fig. 3)

The cemetery has been located in the area of Marmaroto, west of the modern town at a short distance outside the Hellenistic wall. From 1983 until today we have investigated two properties about a hundred metres apart, totalling 335 square metres[30]. Unfortunately the circumstances of the chance discovery meant that much of the cemetery was destroyed. Up until the present 300 graves of various types have been uncovered in stroses (fig. 4) dating from the 7th century BC to the 1st century AD. The cemetery is densely crowded and was in continuous use for at least five hundred years. The cemetery apparently began directly after the one at Serraglio came to an end, as shown by a scattering of sub-geometric sherds (fig. 5).

After the foundation of the new *polis* it continued to be used, but less frequently, until the second century BC. Two Roman graves of the first century AD are isolated burials but not unrelated to the Roman cemetery excavated a little to the south by my colleague Vasso Patsiada[31]. Uninterrupted use often resulted in complete or partial destruction of older graves and in reused sarcophagi, sometimes with extensions made of pots or slabs added on (fig. 6, 7). Most of the graves are archaic or classical. All types of burial are represented. In the 7th and 6th centuries BC adults received cremation burial of the same type as the geometric and archaic cremations of Rhodes[32]. The rectangular pits average 2.20 m in length, 1 m wide and 80 cm deep; at the four corners there are usually round pits in some of which offerings had been deposited (fig. 3).

During the same period children are buried in pots of various types and sizes according to their age, mainly in pithoi some of which have relief decoration, also in transport amphoras, chytras blackened by cooking during previous household use; and some of the funeral offerings bear traces of earlier use. Small cist graves with four orthostates are very common, like the geometric graves at Serraglio. From the end of the century and in the following centuries inhumation becomes the rule for adults who are buried either in built cist graves (one of which, interestingly enough, is narrower at one end, tapering like the Klazomenian sarcophagi) or in plain terracotta sarcophagi, many of the Klazomenian type, some with a hole in the lid obviously for sepulchral libations (fig. 5). The childrens' sarcophagi are either rectangular or tub-shaped. There is an interesting rectangular sarcophagus with three spouts and a row of holes in the upper section of the long side, originally used as a fountain basin or less likely as a bathtub[33](fig. 4).

Only one poros limestone sarcophagus was found; it has been looted and perhaps the fragments of Attic kraters found above came from it.

There are also simple pit graves, generally with no cover, sometimes covered with rooftiles enclosing a triangular area.

The general orientation is east-west. Usually a grave contains only one burial. The offerings are not especially rich; they are almost always placed inside the grave.

There are but few Attic vases, among them fragments of a kylix with the signature of Tleson, son of Nearchos: [Τλεσονhονεα] ϱχοεποεσεν[34]. Corinthian and orientalizing wares which are very significant for the study of

Fig. 5.

Fig. 6.

Fig. 7.

Fig. 8.

Fig. 9.

the East Greek workshops[35] occur more frequently; among them are many Ionic kylikes and kotylai from local workshops.

A pair of kylikes was typically placed at the shoulders or knees, a custom which was practised until a very late period also in other cemeteries on Kos[36]. Graves of small children usually contain two vases, one of which is always an oinochoe, the other being a drinking vessel, a feeder, mug or kylix. There were richer offerings only in a few cases (fig. 8, 9); in one cremation burial there was an offering of olives, the pits of which were found. There seem to have been plain unworked gravestones, one of which has been found in situ above a cremation burial. The outer enclosure wall has been located; there were also remains of smaller enclosures for groups of graves.

The Sanctuary of Demeter (no. 7 in the plan of fig. 1)

At the beginning of this century R. Herzog found west of the starting line of the stadium a small part of the sanctuary of Demeter, whose cult was widespread throughout the island[37]; he found a spring and many terracotta figurines, which he believed belonged to a small outdoor shrine, ranging from the end of the 6th to the 3rd century BC[38].

Excavations carried out in the same area in a series of properties[39] from 1980 onwards have uncovered parts of a large, very long narrow temple oriented east-west, the greater part of which is unfortunately hidden by adjoining buildings. The southeast corner of the stepped crepidoma has been found (fig. 10) as well as part of the cella and part of the southwest corner which enables us to calculate the dimensions: the length at 24 m and the width at 6 m, that is to say the proportion of width to length is one to four. The base of the cult statue was found at the

Fig. 10.

Fig. 11.

back of the cella at a distance of 17.50 m from the exterior wall and 6 m from the crosswall (fig. 11).

The base had three phases and so did the floor of the temple, the two oldest phases being pebbles set in lime cement. In the earliest phases the base was semicircular and was framed by two low walls; both base and walls were coated with stucco. In the two succeeding phases the base was rectangular. It is noteworthy that the phase two floor did not cover over the earliest base and that the old base remained visible at a lower level after the floor level had been raised several times, a sign of the sanctity of the old construction which, because of its form, may be associated with a circular pit or altar. A wall was found parallel with the temple, 3 m to the north, perhaps the foundation for a later colonnade. Part of the temenos wall was located 4 m farther north.

In its last phase the temple was made of a hard local travertine (amygdalopetra) and in the two preceding phases of a soft limestone, a material used since early (Mycenaean) times. The temple

Fig. 12.

Fig. 13.

rests on a Mycenaean structure but with about the same alignment; a Mycenaean terracotta figurine of the *psi* type was found in a burnt layer with animal bones, geometric bronze pins, beads, etc. The sanctuary whose earliest phase can be dated to the Mycenaean period, remained a cult centre until the Roman period, as shown by the stratigraphy and the dedications, mainly terracottas of the same type as those found by Herzog (fig. 12). Many conical cups, some with holes in the base, were found at a level lower than the Mycenaean wall; perhaps they may be associated with an earlier cult[40].

One of the most interesting finds is geison fragments from a terracotta model of a naiskos with dentils found in a late geometric stratum. Nothing of the superstructure of the temple architecture was found. The wing of an archaic marble sphinx was found near the base; it may, perhaps, come from an acroterion. A great many fragments of transport amphoras, found in a deposit at the southeast corner of the temple, must be associated with the Sacred Spring found by Herzog and with the purification rites mentioned in a sacred law of the early third century BC[41].

The Settlement

Morricone found a few sherds of the 7th and 6th centuries BC in his excavations at Serraglio[42]; these sherds were judged to be insufficient evidence for continued habitation at the site after the 8th century BC. During the recent excavations archaic and classical sherds were found in virtually all of the properties in this area; they resemble the pottery found in the cemetery.

A deposit full of archaic and classical pottery was found on the top of the hill on property owned by Mylonas; (no. 8 in the plan of fig. 1) the deposit was in a thick geometric layer 1 m deep and consisted mainly of fragments of relief pithoi, (fig. 13), one of which is identical with a fragment from the cemetery. This must belong to a sanctuary on the Acropolis, the existence of which Morricone had already discovered by chance[43].

The same property produced clues as to the site of the geometric settlement. The deep protogeometric and geometric layer, containing a great number of high quality sherds, some from large vases, should not be related to the cemetery. By observing the disposition of the graves around the hill, Morricone was able to figure out that the settlement was located in the centre of the hill, where however, he had no opportunities of excavating, with the graves placed around the circumference of the settlement[44]. It seems that Morricone's conjecture is confirmed by the thick geometric layer on the Mylonas property; this layer also contained some slight remains of walls. But a child's grave was found on the same property, on the floor of the deposits which had disturbed it. A second children's burial in a chytra containing two skeletons of very young children was found a little below the top of the hill on property owned by Thalassinou. Both of these graves are in the heart of the area thought to be the site of the settlement and may be accounted for by the custom of burying children *intra muros*.

The archaelogical evidence, which still requires much thinking out, reveals that habitation on the hill of Serraglio, beginning long before the Mycenaean period, continued uninterrupted until our own time.

In the geometric period the dwellings seem to be limited to the middle of the hill with the cemeteries ranged around the circumference. In the following period the habitation site was still the same but the cemeteries were moved 1 km farther west, where they remained even after the foundation of the new *polis*.

The foundations of a very strong wall have been found running north to south along the west side of Serraglio hill[45] (no. 9 in the plan of fig. 1). This wall may surely be identified as the fortification wall of Kos-Meropis which, according to Thucydides (VIII.108.2) was fortified by Alcibiades in 411/410 BC to serve as a base for the Athenians against Rhodes. The wall has a thickness of more than 1.40 m and the section found has a length of around 60 m; it is built of large, rectangular poros limestone blocks laid down in a Mycenaean layer around 2 m deep (fig. 14).

The identification is based on the following evidence: the sturdy construction, the great depth of the foundation and the fact that the wall was dismantled in the early Hellenistic period, as we see from the filling of the foundation trench. The dimensions and material of the blocks used to construct the Hellenistic drain just to the east show that they must have been taken from the wall. It is clear that the wall was taken down to provide building material needed for construction in the new *polis*, once it had ceased to function as a fortification.

Charis Kantzia
Curator of Antiquities
Museum of Cos
Greece

Fig. 14.

I should like to thank warmly Dr. J. Binder, member of the American School of Classical Studies, who kindly translated the text into English.

1. Bibliography up to 1957 in Susini 1957, 47 ff; Sherwin-White 1978, 23-28.
2. L. Morricone, ASAtene 50/51, 1975, 139ff.
3. The pyre was found on the Kalogerou property, Hephaistou street, excavated 1984, no. 1 in the plan of fig. 1.
4. This grave was found on the Sophou property excavated 1980; to be published in ADelt 1980, Chronika; no. 2 in the plan of fig. 1.
5. L. Morricone, BdA 35, F. IV, 1950, 322-323; idem, ASAtene 56, 1982, 47, 49.
6. Desborough 1952, 224.
7. Snodgrass 1971, 163, 330.
8. Excavated on Sophou property; this grave and other excavations from the same year were briefly mentioned by N.A. Winter, AJA 86, 1982, 555 pl. 71, fig. 23.
9. N. Coldstream, MB 8, 1982, 264, 268.
10. For the development of wheel-made animal figures from the Late Bronze Age onwards see V.R. Desborough, R.V. Nicholls, M. Popham, BSA 65, 1970, 26f; Mortzos 1985, 88-90; for representations of horses – and – rider in the Mycenaean period see H.W. Catling, RDAC 1974, 108-109 with bibliography.

11. Stored in the Kalymnos Museum, not published.
12. See AAA 13, 1980, 102-104 for a short report on the south city walls.
13. Excavated on the properties belonging to Adamantidis and Patatoukos, Kountouriotou coastal district; to be published in ADelt 1980, 1982, Chronika; for the western mole, see L. Morricone, BdA 35, 1950, 219; E. Zervondaki, ADelt 26, 1971, Chronika 542-3.
14. L. Morricone, BdA 35 F. IV, 1950, 70-71; Susini 1957, 11-19.
15. L. Morricone, BdA 35 F. IV, 1950, 222.
16. R. Herzog, AA, 1901, 134, fig. 2; L. Morricone, BdA 1950, 222-224.
17. E. Zervoudaki, ADelt 27, 1972, Chronika 680.
18. L. Morricone, BdA 35 F IV, 1950, 224-227; E. Zervoudaki, ADelt 26, 1971, Chronika 543, plan 5.
19. Excavated on Kamaterou property, M. Alexandrou street; about 100 m of the stylobates of the western stoa was found in several properties along the western side of M. Alexandrou street (Bakaloglou, Papakonstantinou, Sevastopoulou properties), see ADelt 1978, 1979, 1983, Chronika, to be published.
20. This suggestion was made by Elias Kollias, Ephor of the Byzantine Antiquities of the Dodecanese.
21. L. Laurenzi, BdA 30, 1936-37, 141.
22. R. Herzog, AA 1903, 4; idem SBBerlin 1901, 470-494. Herzog did not find the temple itself but only architectural pieces and inscriptions reused in the early Christian Basilica of Aghia Theotes. It is therefore incorrect to believe that the temple of Apollo has been located at the church of Ag. Theotes.
23. It has been suggested that he was Apollo Dalios because the festival falls in the month of Dalios; see Sherwin-White 1978, 300.
24. For the bibliography see Sherwin-White 1978, 47-48 notes 95, 96.
25. Sherwin-White 1978, 52-54, where all the archeological data are reported.
26. G.E. Bean – J.M. Cook, BSA 52, 1957, 121.
27. Sherwin-White 1978, 45, 49; L. Morricone, ASAtene 1982, 50.
28. D. Mackenzie, BSA 4, 1897-8, 95ff; G.E. Bean – J.M. Cook, BSA 52, 1957, 121-123.
29. L. Morricone, ASAtene 56, 1982, 50.
30. The Koutouzi and Kalergi – Mamouzelou properties.
31. In the property belonging to the ERGOBETON company.
32. Friis Johansen 1958, 9-11 with bibliography.
33. For the symbolic use of the bathtubs as sarcophagi see Andronikos 1968, 39; Ginouvès 1962, 32-35, 244.
34. J.D. Beazley, JHS 52, 1932, 176, 195-196.
35. See E. Walter-Karydi, in Milet 1899-1980, Kolloquium ed. W. Müller-Wiener, Tübingen 1986, 76, who locates the centre of the East-Dorian ware on Cos and Kalymnos.
36. E. Zervoudaki, ADelt 27, 1972, Chronika, 684.
37. Sherwin-White 1978, 305-312; R. Kabus-Preisshofen, AntPl 15, 1975, 31-64.
38. R. Herzog, AA 1901, 134. For the votive offerings see Diehl 1964, 191; Mendel 1979, 128-133 no 1635-1706. pl. III 8-16; other terracotta figurines from this site are in Tübingen and have been treated in an unpublished MA dissertation by Regine Kleinknecht, Archäologisches Institut.
39. Excavated on the Hatzistergou, Tsoulfa, Demopoulou properties, Veriopoulou street.
40. For the conical cups connected with the cult (Kultnäpfchen) from the area of the altar of the Samian Heraion see H. Walter, AM 72, 1957, 36 pl 49,1.
41. Herzog 1928, No. 8.
42. L. Morricone, ASAtene 56, 1982, 50; some of these sherds are published by Walter 1968, No. 496-499 pl. 89 and Walter-Karydi 1973, 1 No. 1049-1052, 1065, 1110, pl. 136-137.
43. L. Morricone, BdA 35 F IV, 1950, 316.
44. L. Morricone, ASAtene 56, 1982, 45.
45. Excavated on Sophou and Mouzaki properties, P. Tsaldari street; for the excavation on Sophou property see ADelt 1980, Chronika (to be published), where this wall had been interpreted as connected with the stadium, situated below.

Fig. 1. Amazon fragment of the Mausoleum frieze (Kos, Kastro).

Fig. 2. The slab 1022 in the British Museum and the adjoining fragment from Kos (photomontage).

The Kos Fragment and the Genoese Slab from the Mausoleum

Nicholas Chr. Stampolides

The join between the fragment from Kos (fig. 1) and slab no. 1022 in the British Museum, leaving aside possible objections[1], can be considered in itself fortunate (see fig. 2); nevertheless it raises certain questions about the fate of the component parts of the Mausoleum after the monument's collapse. Although tracing the history of an ancient monument subsequent to its destruction frequently presents a difficult task for research[2], we shall here attempt as precise a reconstruction as possible. For slab 1022 in particular a number of facts are known which make a fairly detailed reconstruction of its history to some extent possible[3].

At the end of 1865 the Marquis Serra sold the slab to the British Museum as a result of the efforts of the British Consul in Genoa, Montague Brown. The Marquis had only been in possession of it for eight years, after inheriting it from the Marquis G.C. Di Negro – a cousin on his mother Laura's side – who died in 1857. It seems, however, that the ancient relief did not belong to Di Negro, even though its display over a number of years in the Villetta Di Negro had made it known to a series of savants, archaeologists, historians and art critics from 1832 onwards[4]. Di Negro, according to two letters he addressed to S. Betti[5], acquired the Mausoleum frieze slab from his cousin, Vincenzo Spinola, the son of his mother's sister, Benedetta Serra, who had in his turn legally inherited it from his grandfather, of the same name. The latter was a distinguished collector of antiquities, who died around 1750, and whose collection in the Palazzo in the Via Canneto il Lungo originally included the slab.

From this date – that is, from about the second quarter of the 18th century onwards, the history of the slab is conjectural, but there are enough indications to enable us to form some idea of who brought it to Genoa.

As Bettini[6] notes, "Nessuna notizia certa ci è giunta riguardo alla data e alle modalità del suo arrivo a Genova". Nevertheless, Di Negro writes in one of his letters "Si crede que uno di lui (ancestor of the Spinola family) antenato l'abbia portato della Grecia", a fact that led the Genoese historian, D. Bertolotti[7], to put forward the suggestion that the slab had probably been brought to Genoa by Pietro Spinola, who captured Andros and Naxos in 1432. This view received further support from Berri in 1950[8]. On the other hand, E. A. Brawn[9], who published the slab, maintained at some length that one of the Spinolas might have brought it to Genoa from Antioch at the time of the Crusades. In Newton's more carefully expressed view[10], which was later followed by Smith[11], the slab must have been brought to Genoa at the end of the 15th or beginning of the 16th century by some Knight of St. John. This last theory seems the most probable in view of the fact that "tra l'altro si conoscono anche i nomi di due Cavalieri di S. Giovanni, Battista e Bartolomeo Spinola, che parteciparono nell 1522 alla difessa di Rodi ed avrebbero quindi potuto far parte precedentemente della guarnigione del Castello di Bodrum"[12].

Brawn's supposition seems on logical grounds to be out of the question[13], while the weakness in Bertolotti's theory derives more from the distance separating Naxos from Halicarnassus than to the reasoning behind it because, in regard to the actual pillaging of the slab and its possession by the Spinola family, he takes the same line as the, to my mind, more correct view of Newton, Smith and Bettini. Their theory, moreover, seems to be supported not only by the subsequent history of slab 1022 and its possession until the middle of the 19th century by members and descendants of the Spinola family[14], but also from the following facts:

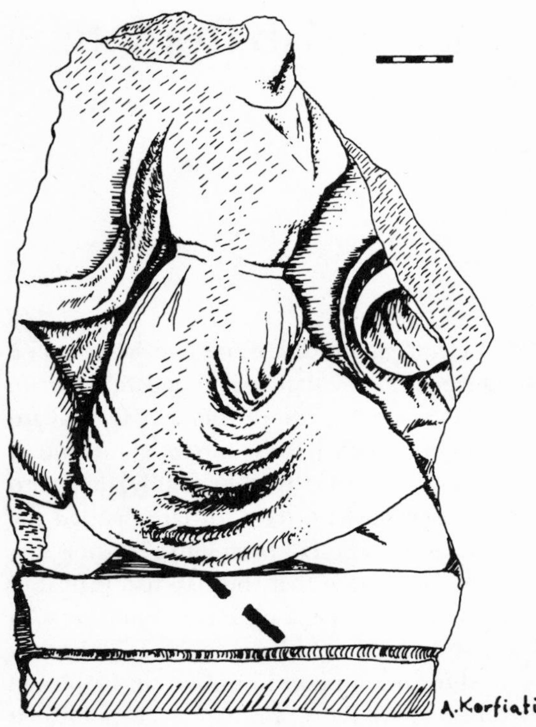

Fig. 3. Amazonomachia fragment of the Mausoleum frieze (archaeological Museum of Rhodos).

The two pieces of slab 1023 that travelled to old Albion on being purchased by the British Museum in 1876 are well known, as already noted elsewhere[15]. These fragments, "that have suffered considerably from fire", undoubtedly belong to the frieze of the Mausoleum[16] even though they were found "in the courtyard of a Turkish house in Rhodes... (which) was certainly one of the old houses of the Knights of St. John, and it is therefore presumed that... (they) had been conveyed from Bodrum to Rhodes while the Knights still held the Castle of St. Peter"[17]. Furthermore, these two pieces are not the only ones that come from Rhodes. In the island's archaeological museum is displayed yet another fragment which appears to have once been an integral part of a frieze slab with an Amazonomachy from the Mausoleum (fig. 3)[18]. The fragment has a rather eroded surface and measures 0.475 m high, 0.36 m long and about 0.17 m thick. The stone, a grey-blue veined marble, has a composition similar to that of the plaques at Halicarnassos and Kos. It preserves its concavo-convex cymatium and taenia and a large part of the scene: in the centre, a headless, kneeling Amazon turned to the right and wearing a small chiton and a himation; on the left, part of the leg[19] of another figure; and, on the right, the edge of a garment and traces of a probable third figure can be distinguished. This fragment, we now realise, became known after its discovery in one of the Rhodes Museum storerooms after the Second World War. It probably arrived there during the time of the Italian occupation of the Dodecanese, although it certainly does not appear to have been known at the end of the last century – otherwise it, too, would have ended up in the British Museum like the previous ones. It therefore seems most likely that before the Knights of St. John departed from Rhodes and the surrounding region at the end of 1522 and the beginning of 1523[20], some parts of the sculptured decoration of the Mausoleum – and perhaps not only these – had already travelled far from Halicarnassos. When and for what reason were pieces of the Mausoleum carried so far from the place where the monument was set up?

The best evidence available to answer this question is provided by re-examination of the history of the Mausoleum[21] in connection with the construction of the Castle of St. Peter. The Mausoleum apparently survived in good condition during the 12th century[22]. It is not certain whether it was destroyed in the earthquake of 1222[23], or whether it was still surviving at the end of the 13th century[24]. What does appear certain, however, is that it was in ruins by the 15th century[25]. According to Newton[26], material from the Mausoleum was already being pillaged when the construction of the Castle first began[27]. No sections, however, of the monument's sculptured decoration, at least, appear to have been incorporated into the earlier parts of the castle[28]. This means that in the castle's first phase of construction the builders used the nearest available material from the ancient harbour, buildings and city wall[29]. Only later, when the ancient material in the neighbourhood of the fortress had been exhausted, would some incidental robbery of material from the Mausoleum have occurred[30], while systematic dismantling of the monument would not appear to have taken place until the great additions and repairs were made to the castle in the last two decades of the 15th and the

Fig. 4. Walls and gates of St. Peter's castle (Halicarnassus) decorated with reliefs from the Mausoleum frieze (cf. Mayer's Views of the Ottoman Empire).

Fig. 5. The castle of St. Peter, the thicker lines show the newer parts and annexes of the construction.

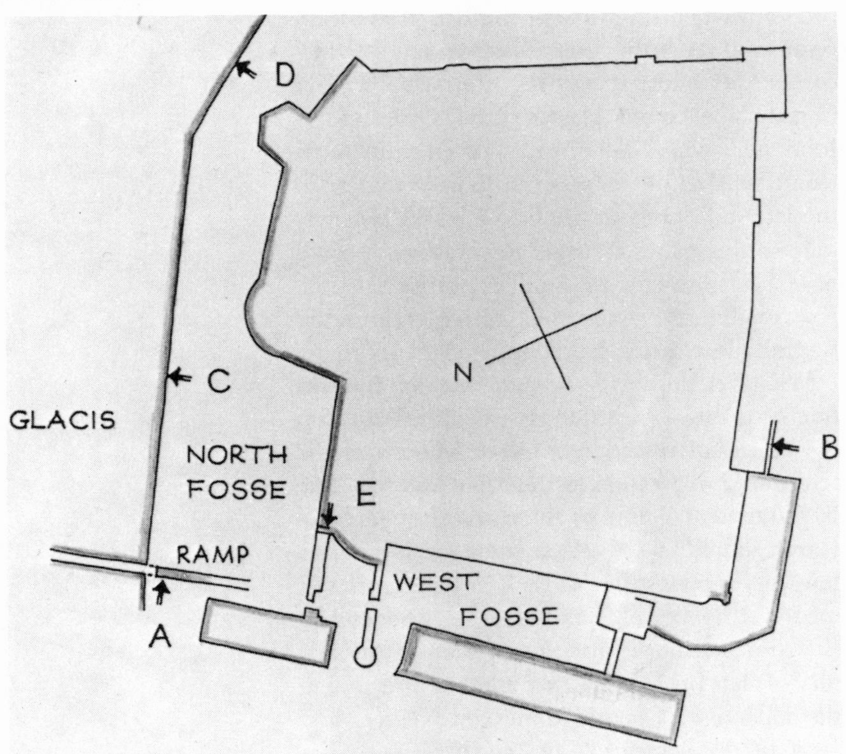

beginning of the 16th century[31]. That, at least, is what is indicated by the evidence of the frieze slabs built into the structure and the lions from the Mausoleum[32], which, together with the Knights' escutcheons, adorned the walls and gates of the Castle of St. Peter[33] – as we know from the accounts of travellers in the preceding centuries[34] and from the sketches of others during the 18th and 19th centuries[35] (see fig. 4). Even more convincing are the relatively recent extractions of sections of the frieze and sculptured decoration of the Mausoleum from the unquestionably newer parts and annexes to the castle (see also fig. 5)[36]. It is therefore in the period between 1472 and 1522[37] that sections of the sculptured decoration of the Mausoleum were removed, however this was done, and taken away from Halicarnassos. This removal may be explained by the fact that "the Knights had taste enough to save (the slabs).. according to a fashion very prevalent in Italy in the 15th c."[38].

The reason for the growth of this fashion,

mainly manifested in the Knight's castles in SW Asia Minor and the Islands, where the architect-builders were Italian[39], must be sought in the ideas of the Renaissance. These were already prevalent at the end of the 15th and beginning of the 16th century, and met with a definite response from the educated Knights, as we know from contemporary historians[40]. Furthermore, frequent communication with Renaissance centres such as Rome and Venice, is attested by a series of business dealings between the Knights and the Pope and the Venetian merchants[41]. Moreover connections with the Genoese[42], and particular the bankers, and the frequent appearance of the Genoese fleet[43] in the area, are facts that must be accorded due weight. Finally, we also know that in the early years of the 16th century, collectors of antiquities arrived from Italy[44], among them the well-known Sabba di Castiglione[45].

Slab 1022 found its eventual destination in some Genoese palazzo, but how is the existence of the Kos fragment in the piles of stones from the medieval castle on that island to be explained? Should we perhaps suppose that the fortunes of the Genoese slab and the Kos fragment diverged after a certain point in time? An affirmative answer to this question would seem to appear from the following observations: slab 1022 from Genoa, the piece from the Rhodes Museum and the fragments 1023, 1.2 in the British Museum preserve only one half of their original thickness, which is not the case with the slabs at Halicarnassus, the Kos fragment and slabs in London from Newton's excavations. This seems to be a definitive feature that perhaps distinguishes those sections of the Mausoleum's sculptured decoration that were transported over great distances, for ornamental purposes during the Renaissance: they had to be loaded onto the galleys of the period and any unnecessary bulk of weight would have prevented the transport of other necessary cargo. If in fact some Knight of St. John, whether or not of the Spinola family, or some merchant and collector of antiquities had marked slab 1022 for transport to Rhodes or Genoa, considering it suited to contemporary taste, he does not appear to have bothered about the other slab, either because he could not transport it too[46], or, more probably, because the two slabs did not happen to be together at the time for him to mark them both. The theory that both slabs were first transported in their original thickness as far as Kos, and that one of them was left on the island possibly because it broke during the cutting away of half of its bulk, while not entirely impossible, does not appear very likely. This reduction would have had to be carried out, one way or another, at Halicarnassus before the ship transporting them set sail. It would therefore seem that the two neighbouring slabs suffered different fates after the destruction of the monument to which they had belonged. Whether the Kos fragment (or the slab of which it was a part) originally lay with the pieces transported to the harbour for the building of the Castle of St. Peter and, in the end, was not used, or whether at some point it was carried away from there as ship's ballast and unloaded at the first port of call after Halicarnassus, it is difficult to say, because the Kos fragment does not appear to have suffered the same damage as other stones sometimes employed for this purpose[47].

The above observations, however, and the objections on grounds of reason to the theories mentioned above, add weight to the probability that the fragment was transported as either building or decorative material by the Knights of St. John when the walls of the Kos castle were reinforced and the great bastion on the SW corner was built. It was the time when F. Del Caretto was Grand Master of the Order of St. John and when, as already noted[48], material from the Mausoleum was transported for use in the later additions to the Castle of St. Peter. It follows that material from the Mausoleum could have been brought for similar purposes to the Kos castle[49], which would better explain the finding place of the fragment[50].

Whatever the correct answer may be, the Kos fragment throws a little, but hopeful, light[51] on the efforts of research to locate sections of the sculptured decoration of the Mausoleum[52]. The Kos fragment points to the direction which research should take, because some, even if only a few, pieces may still exist built into the castles or medieval houses of Halicarnassus, Rhodes and Kos. Furthermore, the investigation of the history of slab 1022 leads in yet another direction to the Palazzi of Genoa, Rome and Venice, and even to the cemeteries of North Italian cities where, according to evidence, ancient reliefs were employed to adorn more recent funeral monuments[53]. Perhaps, however, most important of all is that the Kos fragment can still look across to the place from which it came.

Nicholas Chr. Stampolides
Department of History and Archaeology
University of Crete
741 00 Rethymno, Crete
Greece

1. If in fact any such exist, they are due to the problems created by more recent operations carried out on the surface of the front and right sides of slab No 1022. For the join between the fragment and the slab, see my contribution to Αμητός, Τιμητικός τόμος για τον Καθηγητή Μ. Ανδρόνικο, 1986, 813-829, pl. 166-172.
2. Cf. for example studies by L. Beschi, ASAtene 31/32, 1969/70, 417-433 and ASAtene 34/35, 1972/73, 479-502.
3. Very useful from this point of view is the article by A. Bettini, Xenia 1, 1981, 71-77.
4. See A. Bettini, Xenia 1, 1981, 72.
5. They are now in the National Library of Rome (A. Bettini, Xenia 1, 1981, 71 fn. 3 and 4).
6. Xenia 1, 1981, 71.
7. Viaggio nella Liguria Marittima II, 1834, 244ff.
8. Bolletino Linguistico 11.3, 1950, 71-77.
9. AdI 21, 1849, 74f, and 22, 1850, 285f.
10. Newton 1862, 234.
11. Smith 1900, 112-113.
12. A. Bettini, Xenia 1, 1981, 73.
13. See above p. 186 for the history of the monument and its probable destruction in the 13th century.
14. For the family's history, see also Deza 1644. Hereby I want to express my thanks to Pr. Chr. Maltezou for being so kind to discuss with me problems of medieval history concerning this article.
15. See N.Chr. Stampolides in Αμητός, Τιμητικός τόμος για τον Καθηγητή Μ. Ανδρόνικο, 1986, 820 n. 17.
16. The stone they are made from is the same as that of the frieze slabs with the Amazonomachy; their dimensions match and so do the details of technique and style.
17. Smith 1900, 112-113.
18. B. Ashmole and D. Strong expressed interest in this fragment, according to K. Jeppesen and D. Strong, Discoveries, 200- 201. Gr. Konstantinopoulos, 1986, 104 No. 97 insists that the piece does not belong to the Mausolean Amazonomachia-frieze.
19. The left one, if the figure is frontal, the right one, if shown from the rear.
20. See Kingsley 1978, 50-53; Alpözen , 78.
21. Unfortunately, up till the time that this article was released for publication, the end of March 1986, the book by Luttrell 1985, which Professor E. Zachariadou from Canada kindly drew my attention to, had not reached any libraries or archaeological institutes in Athens. I have thus been obliged to go ahead with the facts that I have been able to assemble myself, and I hope that there are no important differences concerning the history of the monument. The announcement of A. Luttrell's book appeared in Jeppesen 1981, 1.
22. See Ευστάθιος Θεσσαλ. (12th. c. AD), Σχόλ. στήν Ιλιάδ. I298, 256: καί ὁ μέν τοῦ Μαυσώλου μάλα πολλός τάφος ἄκρως περιείργασται, καί θαῦμα ἦν καί ε'στιν. And cf. Newton, 1862, 72f. RE 24, 1963, 374.s.v.Pytheos (Riemann).
23. See Waywell 1978, 15.
24. See Treu 1960, 163 col. 43-44, 176 col. 143-146, 234 and esp. 265-266. A considerably later destruction seems to be implied by evidence – from a certain Greek Demetrios (Chalkokondyles?) - available to C. Caesariano, professor of architecture in Milan at the beginning of the 16th century. Cf. Jeppesen 1958, 11 and fn. 39.
25. Most probably from the erosion it would have suffered over the centuries, or from one or more earthquakes, in spite of the fact that the Halicarnassians were proud in antiquity of the fact that their region did not suffer from Enceladus (cf. Tacitus, Annales IV, 55. Jeppesen 1958, 60 fn. 73).
26. Newton 1862, 74-75.
27. The commencement of the work should be placed somewhere between 1402 (date of the capture of Smyrna by the Tatars; cf. Luttrell 1978 I, 308. XXIII, 48f) and 1409 (when, we learn from the archives of the Knights, "....procuratores ad recipiendas elemosinas ad fortificationem Castelli S. Petri, tunc temporis constructi contra Turcas", in Delaville Le Roulx 1883, chap. 251; and "Fontenay H. de ....châtelain des Rhodes et capitaine du château S. Pierre (1409-1420) in J. Delaville Le Roulx, Mélanges sur l'ordre de S. Jean de Jér. 1910, XVII, 10). The date given by de Buodelmondi 1824, 104, of around 1400, does not seem to be correct. For a date before 1408, cf. also Luttrell 1978, I, 310, and Zachariadou 1983, 87 fn. 381.
28. G. Karo, AA 34, 1919, 61f.
29. A similar practice was followed in the building of the Kos castle, Stampolidis 1987, 161-162. Cf. also the dismantled sections east of the wall of the ancient city of Halicarnassus, near the castle (K. Jeppesen, Ist Mitt 27/28, 1977/78, 171, 193.).
30. See G. Karo, AA 34, 1919, 64.
31. Although the visit of the Venetian captain C. Cepio in 1472 does not appear to refer to Halicarnassus (cf. RE 24, 1963, 379.s.v. Pytheos (Riemann). For the opposite view see Guichard 1581, III, 5. 378f; Newton 1862, 74-75; and Classical Museum V, 182-183), this date in the decade 1470-80 will be kept here as the terminus post quem for the works of repairing and enlarging the Castle of St. Peter; see G. Karo, AA 34, 1919, 61f., and especially 70f; RE 24, 1963, 376f.s.v. Pytheos (Riemann); and finally Jeppesen 1981, 23; "but it was certain that it was demolished after 1494, by the Knights....", and Alpözen 86.
32. At least those marble sculptures and other parts that escaped the kiln into which such material was thrown in order to make lime (cf. the document of 1502 where mention is made of a "forno della calcina" that was to be used for the building necessities of the Castle of St. Peter; G. Karo, AA 34, 1919, 74 fn. 3). That a considerable number of sculptures and reliefs had the misfortune to end up in a kiln seems clear also from slab 1008+1010 in the British Museum, which was cut in two for easier

transport to the lime kiln, but which escaped the disaster in the end (for the joining of the two parts of the slab, see B. Ashmole, JHS 89, 1919, 22-23, pl. 1. For the destination of sculptures in the kiln see also B.F. Cook, BSA 71, 1976, 51). A similar practice occurred with the sculptures of the Pergamum altar; H. Winnefeld, AvP III, 2, 1910, 2.

33. See Newton 1862, II 649. A. Maiuri, ASAtene 4/5, 1921/1922, 318-319 fig. 31; G. Karo, AA 34, 1919, 71 fig. 2,0 and Alpözen, 26.
34. Thévenot 1664/5, 211, 215.
35. Dalton 1749. Sketches published in Views in Greece and Egypt (1751-1781).L. Mayer in: Antiquities of Ionia II (1797) expanded, fig. 2; Mayer 1803, pl. 18 (see our fig. 4); Devereux 1847, pl. 16.
36. See above 186.
37. This date, which is given by Guichard 1581, fn 91, for the narrative of the Knight of St John de la Tourette, who supervised the transport of material from the Mausoleum to the Castle of St Peter, must be erroneous, as G. Karo, AA 34, 1919, 75, has already shown and as Jeppesen 1958, 12-13, admits. We keep it, however, as the last possible chronological limit for the removal of material from Halicarnassus while the Knights of St. John were still dominant. Of course, pillaging and removal of material could also have occurred after the capture of Halicarnassus by the Turks (cf. the use of marble from ancient Knidos in Alexandria to build the palace of Mechmet-Ali of Egypt in 1841-43; Benndorf-Niemann 1884, 13 n. 5), but it would not have been employed for ornamental purposes as in the Renaissance. The Knights, furthermore, seem to have exhausted the material from the Mausoleum in completing the castle, as indeed was shown by the excavations of Newton, Billioti and Jeppesen. As far as the first date (1472) is concerned, the significant fact has to be noted here that refugees were removed from the Petronion area on 52 galleys, on which a great amount of property could have been transported from the region (cf. Zachariadou 1985, XVII, 193).
38. See Newton 1862, 79.
39. See G. Karo, AA 34, 1919, 70 fn. 3.
40. Thus, for example, Fontanus 1527, I par. BII also mentions Fabrizio del Carretto (Carectanus) as "doctus literas latinas". The importance in this case lies in the fact that Carretto was the Grand Master of the Knights of St. John on Rhodes from 1513-1521, the period when, as has been said, parts of the Mausoleum were being used for repairs and additions to the Castle of St. Peter. A removal of the sculptures from the Mausoleum to Rhodes and the areas under their jurisdiction therefore seems very probable in general.
41. See also Delaville Le Roulx 1883, chaps. XXIV-XXXV.
42. See Delaville Le Roulx 1883, chap. XX, p. 40 and 44-45; chap. XX VII no. 2 etc, Also Zachariadou 1983, 10-12, 48 and 52. For Genoa, her interests in the East during the Middle Ages and her relations with Venice etc., see also Delaville Le Roulx 1885 and comments on him by C. Desmioni in the Archivo Storica Italiano (1887). Foglieta 1585. Giustiniani 1855. Canale 1858-1864. Heyd 1879, and Heyd 1885.
43. See Delaville Le Roulx 1885, 407, 418, 470, 473 e.a. especially for the Carretto and Grimaldi families and their relations and ranks in the Genoese fleet. Also Bosio 1697, XLII, mentions that F. del Carretto, before becoming Grand Master, was an admiral in the Genoese navy at the end of the 15th and beginning of the 16th century. One can thus see the connection in the carrying away of slab 1022 at the end of the 15th or beginning of the 16th century to Genoa by some Knight or collector of antiquities in a Genoese galley.
44. It would be interesting to know whether their arrival was connected with some important event, such as, for example, their being informed about the finding of valuable objects in the burial chamber of the Mausoleum, in which case the date of the event described by de la Tourette would certainly come down to the first decade of the 16th century.
45. See also RE 24, 1963, 378 s.v. Pytheos (Riemann). Riemann - Hasluck, BSA 18, 1911-12, 214 also think it possible that slab 1022 was removed at that time. Nor must we forget that the first owner of slab 1022 known from evidence, Vincenzo Spinola (died 1750), was an eminent collector of antiquities in Genoa. It is useful from this standpoint to consult Meisner – Röhrricht 1837.
46. For reasons of expense or because it was not found in good condition, as at least slab 1022 was.
47. For "pierres errantes" see the works of L. Robert concerning the subject published mostly in REG and Bull. Epigr. (e.g. REG 1929, 23 ff., REG 1932, 199 ff., REA 62 (1960) 276 ff. and lately D. Knoepfler, BCH 108 (1984) 230 fn. 5 etc.)
48. See notes 40 and 43.
49. See accordingly the remarks by Newton, Classical Museum V, 185-186 and note, although he was referring to an earlier period. Further, similar transportations of building material, and indeed to near-lying places, are recorded by Byzantine writers (cf. Doukas) independently of the correctness or not of the occurrences or, finally, of the impossibility of confirming them.
50. See above note 1.
51. Contrary to B.F. Cook's pessimistic words in BSA 71, 1976, 50 and 54.
52. For distribution of free-standing sculpture material from the Mausoleum on the island of Kos, see also Waywell 1978.
53. See A. Bettini, Xenia 1, 1981, 75 fn. 49.

Honorary Statues on Kos (320 BC – AD 15/20)

Kerstin Höghammer

This study aims to examine the function, on Kos, of statues as marks of honour during the Hellenistic period and the period transitional to the Roman Empire (i.e. c. 30 BC to AD 15/20). The inscriptions on the statue bases are the foundation of this work.

I will begin with a few cautionary remarks. My source material is not very large and derived only from published material. I don't know how many unpublished inscriptions there are. Also, my work is still in progress and I may later find reason to revise some of my opinions.

THE INSCRIPTIONS

To date I have collected sixty-four inscriptions, some fragmentary, which, with a reasonable degree of certainty can be accepted as belonging to statue bases (see List of inscriptions). Thirty-eight, the greater part, are honorary in character and nineteen are dedicatory. Five are both honorary and dedicatory, and two are of uncertain character.

As can be seen from fig. 1, Table 1 there is a converse line of development for the two kinds of inscription. The great majority of the dedicatory ones falls within period 1, 320-200 BC, whereas a majority of the honorary inscriptions falls within period 4, 30 BC to AD 15/20. As quite a large number of inscriptions of all types have been found to date from c. 300 - 150 BC and 50 BC – AD 15/20 this development does not seem to be entirely fortuitous.

PROVENIENCE

Thirty-two of the inscriptions were found in the town of Kos. Twenty come from the Asklepieion and twelve from other parts of the island. Five of the latter are from Halasarna, three from Chiparissi, two from Hippia, and one each from Isthmos and the modern village of Mesaria, 6 km west of Kos town.

The majority of the inscriptions from the town of Kos was found built into the walls of different buildings and other structures, notably the fortress (nine items), and so, unfortunately, their original provenience is unknown.

As to the Asklepieion, no inscriptions are known to have been found on the uppermost of the three terraces.

Fifteen honorary inscriptions were found in the Asklepieion. This is a surprising number when compared with the four dedicatory inscriptions. The dedications may have been located on terraces I and II where the altar and temples were situated. There they would presumably have been the first to fall prey to Medieval stone robbers, as the upper terraces are less likely to have been filled in and covered with earth after the complete collapse of the sanctuary following the severe earthquake of AD 554.

IMPLICATIONS CONCERNING THE ECONOMIC STATUS OF WOMEN

Before coming to my main topic, I would like to point out that the number of statues representing men does not exceed that of women to the extent that might be expected: twenty-four as compared to fifteen. For statues put up by the damos in the Augustan era, the difference is indeed very small: twelve represented men and ten women. However, because of the small number of inscriptions involved a few more on either side might radically alter any conclusions drawn. Nevertheless I still think it likely that the relatively large number of women is significant. We know from other sources[2] that women in the Hellenistic age had more personal control over their own economic resources than they had, for instance, in classical Athens. This should be the fact reflected in the large number of honorary inscriptions to women on Kos and other places set up during the 1st century BC and the beginning of the 1st century AD. That a social and political amelioration of women's situation went

Figure 1 Kos Island

Table 1. *Type of inscription*

	Period 1 320-200	Period 2 200-100	Period 3 100-30	Period 4 30BC-AD20	uncert. date.	Total
Dedicatory	9	3	1	1	5	19
Honorary	4	5	7	19	3	38
Dedicatory and Honorary				5		5
Uncertain	1				1	
Total	14	8	8	25	9	62

Table 2. *Provenience*

	Period 1 320-200	Period 2 200-100	Period 3 100-30	Period 4 30BC-AD20	uncert. date.	Total
Kos Town	3	5	5	13	6	32
Asklepieion	6	3	4	7		20
The rest of the island	5			4	3	12
						64

Table 3. *Statues put up by the Damos to*

	Period 1 320-200	Period 2 200-100	Period 3 100-30	Period 4 30BC-AD20	uncert. date.	Total
Men		1	3	8	1	13
Women			1	7		8
The people of Myndos		1				1
Unknown				1	1	2
						24

Table 4. *Statues representing*

	Period 1 320-200	Period 2 200-100	Period 3 100-30	Period 4 30BC-AD20	uncert. date.	Total
Men	2	3	5	12	2	24
Women	2	1	2	10		15
Men & Women	1					1
Children	3					3
Unknown					1	1
						44

Table 5. *Nationality of the persons honoured by the damos.*

	Period 1 320-200	Period 2 200-100	Period 3 100-30	Period 4 30BC-AD20	uncert. date.	Total
Kos			1	5	1	7
Knidos			2			2
Myndos		1				1
Rome		1	2	7		10
Uncertain				2	2	4
						24

Figure 2. Kos Town

Table 1. *Type of Inscription*

	Period 1 320-200	Period 2 200-100	Period 3 100-30	Period 4 30BC-AD20	Uncert. date	Total
Dedicatory		3	1	1	3	8
Honorary	3	2	3	9	2	19
Dedicatory and Honorary				4		4
Uncertain					1	1
Total	3	5	4	13	6	32

Table 2. *Provenience*

	Period 1 320-200	Period 2 200-100	Period 3 100-30	Period 4 30BC-AD20	Uncert. date	Total
In the fortress	1			6	2	9
Near the theatre	1	2		2	1	6
Kumburnu				1	1	2
Other	1	3	4	5	2	15
						32

Table 3. *Statues put up by the damos to*

	Period 1 320-200	Period 2 200-100	Period 3 100-30	Period 4 30BC-AD20	Uncert. date	Total
Men				2	1	3
Women				2		2
Unknown				1		1
Total						6

Table 4. *Nationality of the persons honoured by the damos*

	Period 1 320-200	Period 2 200-100	Period 3 100-30	Period 4 30BC-AD20	Uncert. date	Total
Kos				2	1	3
Knidos			1			1
Rome				1		1
Uncertain					1	1
						6

hand in hand with an economic improvement for them is, I think, true, but the evidence for this remains to be collected and analysed.

TITULI HONORAII

There are thirty-eight honorary inscriptions, twenty-four of which were set up by the damos. Of the remaining fourteen, six were put up by private individuals, three by nonofficial bodies and five by donors unknown to us.

Dating of the damos inscriptions

Period 1 (320-200 BC)

No damos inscriptions from this period have been published. (There are two set up by private individuals and two by unknown donors.)

Period 2 (200-100 BC)

Of a total of five honorary statues, two were set up by the damos: one to honour the people of Myndos (the reason for this honour is not stated) and one to Titus Quinctius Flamininus (here the reason is obvious as the Koans fought on the same side as the Romans against Philip V).

Period 3 (100-30 BC).

Four of the seven honorary inscriptions from period 3 were set up by the damos. Two of them

Figure 3. The Asklepieion

Table 1. *Type of inscription*

	Period 1 320-200	Period 2 200-100	Period 3 100-30	Period 4 30BC-AD20	Uncert. date	Total
Dedicatory	4					4
Honorary	1	3	4	7		15
Unknown	1					1
Total	6	3	4	7		20

Table 2. *Provenience*

Terrace II	1					1
Terrace III			4	6		10
Unknown	5	3	1			9
						20

Table 3. *Statues put up by the damos to*

Men		1	3	5		9
Women			1	2		3
The people of Myndos		1				1
Total		2	4	7		13

Table 4. *Nationality of the persons honoured by the damos*

Kos			1	3		4
Knidos			1			1
Myndos		1				1
Rome		1	2	2		5
Uncertain				2		2
						13

date from the period 50 to 30 BC, one to Gaius Julius Theopompos from Knidos, a friend of Caesar, and the other to Junia, wife of Publius Servilius Isauricos, pro-consul in Asia 46-44 BC.

Period 4 (30 BC – AD 15/20)

Of the three honorary inscriptions not from Kos town and the Asklepieion, one is from Isthmos and two from Halasarna. The Isthmos inscription is in honour of Julia, daughter of Augustus, as is one from Halasarna too. The other from Halasarna depicts Augustus as Apollo Soter.

R. Herzog mentions another inscription from Halasarna[3], apparently unpublished. If we include it here, then four inscriptions date from period 4.

Between 30 BC and AD 15/20 the damos erected sixteen statues: seven in the Asklepieion, five in Kos town, three in Halasarna, and one in Isthmos. Three honoured victors in *enkomioi*, eulogies in honour of the Roman emperor. Four were in honour of Koan citizens, four honoured members of the Imperial family, two Romans of pro-consular status, one an imperial freedman, and two were in honour of persons of unknown status. As can be seen the overwhelming majority of honorary statues voted by the damos is late. Sixteen of a total number of twenty-four, i.e.

about 65%, date to period 4. There are no damos inscriptions from period 1. Two from period 2 and four from period 3. Of these last four, two are from c. 50 BC to 30 BC. A third (Pa 2) is also rather late, i.e. the second half of the first century BC, period 3 or 4. This means that about 65% of the damos inscriptions date from c. 30 BC to AD 15/20 and another 12% (three inscriptions) from after 50 BC.

REASONS FOR THE ERECTION OF HONORARY STATUES BY THE DAMOS.

Excluding the victors in *enkomioi*, the reason given for distinction is, in eight cases, the *areta* of the honoured person and, in most of these cases, *areta* together with *eunoia*, i.e. good deeds and favour towards the damos. In two cases Augustus is described as *soter*, saviour, and in four cases we do not know the reason for the honour, either because it is not stated, or because of the fragmentary state of the inscription.

Economy of Kos

We know that society on Kos was affluent during most of the Hellenistic period. This can be seen from the extensive building programs both in the Asklepieion and in the town of Kos during the 3rd and 2nd centuries BC.

The wine trade prospered and the harbour dues must have provided the state with ready cash. In times of particular need the state was strong enough to demand and receive extra donations from rich citizens, as shown by the wartime subscription lists of c. 200 BC.

From the latter part of the 2nd and the first part of the 1st century BC., there is less material, but nothing indicates decreasing affluence. Kos was *not* hard hit by the Mithridatic wars in the 80s and when the victorious Romans arrived, they had no particular reason to punish the Koans. The *Romaioi* had been protected in the asylum of the Asklepieion when Mithridates put in to the island; the Koans appear to have purchased their peace and the Romans' security with the treasure left on Kos for safe-keeping by the Egyptian queen Cleopatra III in 102 BC. The heir to the Egyptian throne, the son of Ptolemy IX, Alexander I, had been entrusted to the Koans by the same queen; he too was surrendered to Mithridates.

During the civil war following Caesar's death, the Koans were however hit harder, since this time they supported the losing side. Octavian/Augustus forced them to pay tribute and the sum of 100 talents is mentioned in this connection. A series of earthquakes during the last quarter of the 1st century BC made the situation even more difficult[4].

Statues as reward and payment

Under such difficult circumstances the state was obliged to rely to a greater degree on voluntary economic help from private individuals. The state was no longer in a position to demand contributions from wealthy citizens, especially not from the *Romaioi*. Some inducement was necessary to get the rich to help the community. What more appropriate than a statue of the donor, forever commemorating his or her honour and or virtue?

The same trend has been noted in Athens, although there it occurs much earlier, during the course of the 4th century BC[5].

It is my opinion, therefore, that the large number of honorary statues put up by the damos in the period from 50 BC to AD 15/20 is a sign of the weakened state of the Koan community, i.e. the Koan damos, and that honorary statues of the kind discussed filled the function of reward and payment expected and received for gifts given.

Kerstin Höghammer
Institut för Antikens kultur och samhällsliv
Gustavianum
S-752 20 Uppsala
Sweden

1. See R. Herzog, AA 1903, 194, col. 2.
2. Schaps 1979, 96.
3. R. Herzog, HZ 125, 1922, 217 note 2.
4. See Sherwin White 1978, esp. chapter 6.
5. Stewart 1979, 123-124.

List of inscriptions

(arranged according to provenience, type and date)

Period 1 320-200
Period 2 200-100
Period 3 100-30
Period 4 30 BC – AD 15/20

Kos town (32 inscriptions)

	Honorary	Dedicatory	Honorary & Dedicatory	Uncertain
Per 1	Paton – Hicks 1891, nos. 221, 227 Herzog 1942, 19 Stampolides 1982, 299			
Per 2	Paton – Hicks 1891, nos. 73, 133.	Paton – Hicks 1891, nos. 54, 56.		
Per 3	Paton – Hicks 1891, 117, 134, 206. Degrassi 1941, 203.		Paton – Hicks 1891, no. 58.	
Per 4	Paton – Hicks 1891, nos. 75, 81-83, 115, 116. Maiuri 1925, no. 466. Herzog 1899, no. 35.	Paton – Hicks 1891, no. 55. Maiuri 1925, no. 447. Levi della Vida 1938, 140 f.	Paton – Hicks, 1891, nos. 124, 125, 127.	
Uncertain date	Paton – Hicks 1891, no. 126. Maiuri, 1925, no. 457.	Paton – Hicks 1891, no. 60, 61.		Maiuri 1925, nos. 451, 474, 475.

The Asklepieion (20 inscriptions)

	Honorary	Dedicatory	Honorary & Dedicatory	Uncertain
Per 1	Patriarca 1932, no. 22.	Herzog 1930, 207-209, 3 inscript. Schazmann 1932, 22 f.		

Per 2	Patriarca 1932, nos. 24, 25. Paton – Hicks 1891, no. 128.			Paton – Hicks 1891, no. 137
Per 3	Patriarca 1932, nos. 1, 2, 13, 28.			
Per 4	Patriarca 1932, nos. 3, 4, 5, 7, 8, 9, 10.			
Uncertain date				

Kos island except for Kos town and the Asklepieion (12 inscriptions)

	Honorary	Dedicatory	Honorary & Dedicatory	Uncertain
Per 1		Kabus-Preisshofen 1975, 39, 50, 57. Laurenzi 1938, 24-26. Konstantinopoulos 1970, 250 f.		
Per 4	Herzog 1899, no. 223. Herzog 1922, 217, no. 1. Paton – Hicks 1891, no. 373 (= Herzog 1899, 139, no. 373) Pugliese Caratelli 1969, 129, no. 4.		Herzog 1901, 494, no. 7.	
Uncertain date		Hauvette-Besnault-Dubois 1881, 198, nos. 1, 4.		

Abbreviations

Degrassi 1941 Degrassi, A., ClRh 10, 1941, 201-213.

Hauvette-Besnault – Dubois 1881 – Hauvette-Besnault, A. – Dubois, M., BCH 5, 1881, 201-240.

Herzog 1901 Herzog, R., SBBerlin 21, 1901, I, 170-194.

Herzog 1922 Herzog, R., HZ 125, 1922, 189-247.

Herzog 1942 Herzog, R., RivFil 70, 1942, 1-20.

Kabus-Preisshofen 1975 Kabus-Preisshofen, R. AntPl 15, 1975, 31-64.

Konstantinopoulos 1970 Konstantinopoulos, G., AAA 3, 1970, 249-251.

Laurenzi 1938 Laurenzi, L., ClRh 9, 1938, 24.

Levi della Vida 1938 Levi della Vida, G., ClRh 9, 1938, 139-148.

Patriarca 1932 Patriarca, G., BMusImp 3, 3-34 apud Bull-Com 60, 1932.

Pugliese Carratelli 1969 Pugliese Carratelli, G., PP 24, 1969, 129.

Segre – Pugliese Carratelli 1949-51.

Segre, M. – Pugliese Carratelli, G., ASAtene 27-29 (n.s. 11-13), 1949-51, 141-318.

Stampolides 1982 Stampolides, N., AAA 15, 1982, 297-310.

Chapter 4 . The Dodecanese

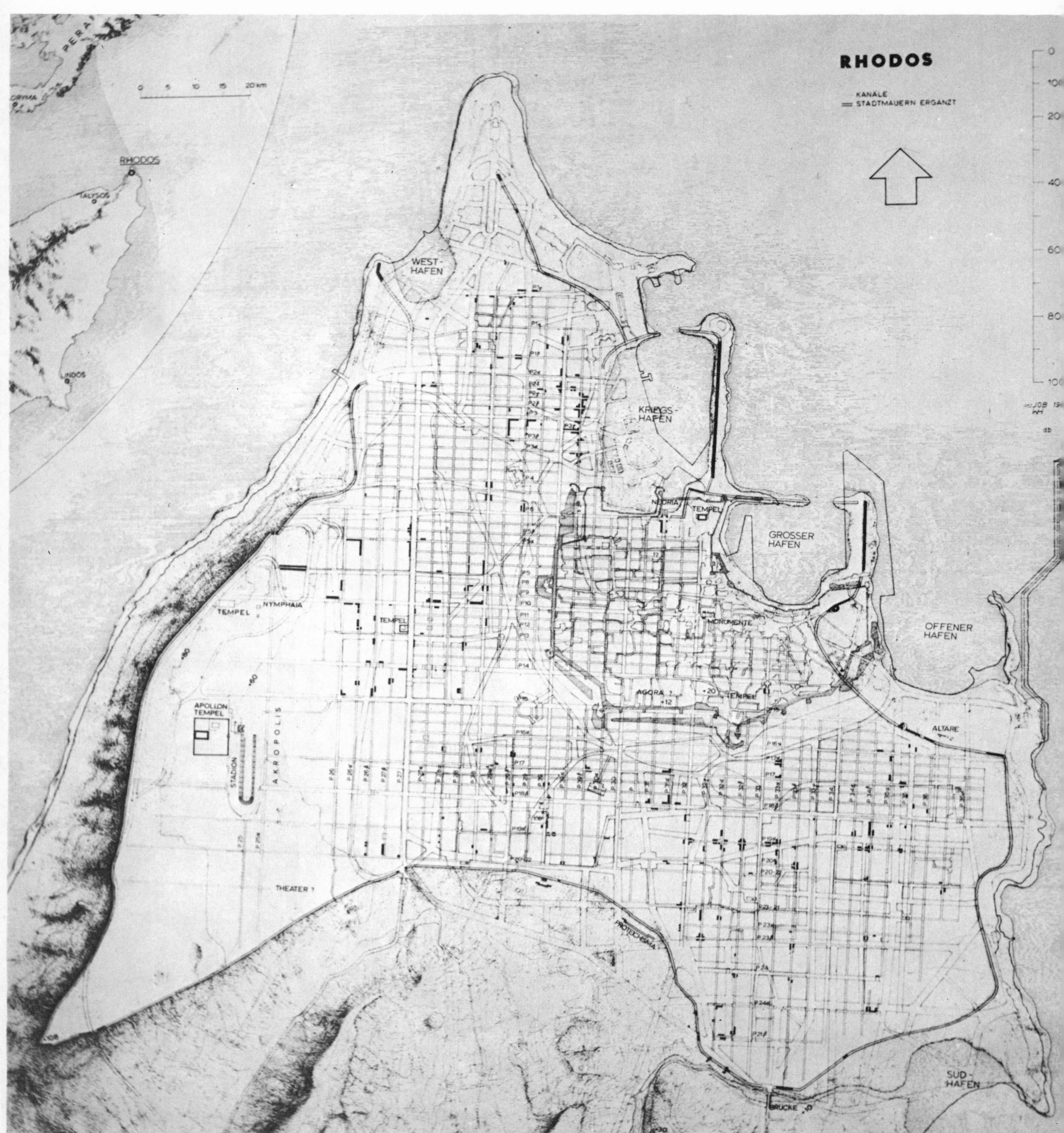

Plan of the ancient city of Rhodes

Recent Investigations and Activities carried out by the Archaeological Service of the Dodecanese*

Ioannis Papachristodoulou

This communication aims to give a brief survey of the activities of the Archaeological Service of the Dodecanese during the last twelve years. The presentation will necessarily be very condensed. As our investigations are constantly in progress, and since systematic study of the finds from the various sectors by a number of excavators is not yet complete, it is not a question of presenting final results but only of preliminary, partial findings. This paper deals only with antiquity and thus disregards the important work carried out by the Service relating to the excavations and monuments of early Christian and Byzantine times, and the era of the Knights of St. John.

The work carried on by the Service in recent years continues along lines laid down by our predecessors, especially by I. Kontis, the founder of the Dodecanese Department of the Greek Archaeological Service[1]. As always the main target of our investigations is the ancient city of Rhodes, the capital of the unified Rhodian State after the synoicism of 411-408 BC (p.200). It should be borne in mind that such investigations are almost always salvage operations. Excavations are put in hand before construction starts on private property or when public buildings are erected, and in connexion with various technical projects, such as harbour installations and trenches dug by the electricity, water and telephone companies, etc. These salvage operations, nevertheless, often lead to more extensive systematic excavation campaigns; furthermore, every single find, even the smallest and seemingly insignificant, acquires scientific value when incorporated in the framework of the long-range goals set by the Service: investigation of the city street network, water supply and drainage systems, locating civic buildings and sanctuaries, ancient harbour installations, the line of the city walls, houses, industrial districts and cemeteries.

Thanks to investigations carried out over decades, our knowledge of the ancient city of Rhodes has considerably increased and there is now a rich collection of archaeological material which has already been profitably studied by a number of scholars. In recent years the systematic study of this material has accelerated so that we may hope for a very substantial scholarly harvest in the next few years. The main features of the developments within the last eight years are as follows: 1. In the city of Rhodes priority was given to exploring cemeteries as a result of the steady expansion of the modern town in the direction of the ancient necropoleis. 2. Exploration of the Minoan settlement of Ialysos (Trianda) was resumed. 3. Extensive investigations of the ancient city of Kos where numerous excavations were carried out. 4. Inauguration of systematic research on the prehistoric period in the Dodecanese with excavations mainly in caves.

The preceding speakers have already delivered communications on the last three topics, as also on the city street plan of ancient Rhodes, so I shall not touch on these subjects. Work accomplished in locating and investigating public buildings and sanctuaries may be summarized as follows, beginning from the north: scientific research on the remains of the ancient sanctuary of Demeter has been completed. The sanctuary, located west-north-west of the National Theatre, just inside the line of the ancient city wall has already been the subject of a communication. To the south-west, near the church of the Presentation of the Virgin (Eisodia), in the Neochori quarter, another important sanctuary has been located by combining information from earlier finds with new finds such as a series of statue bases – one of which, still in situ, carried the

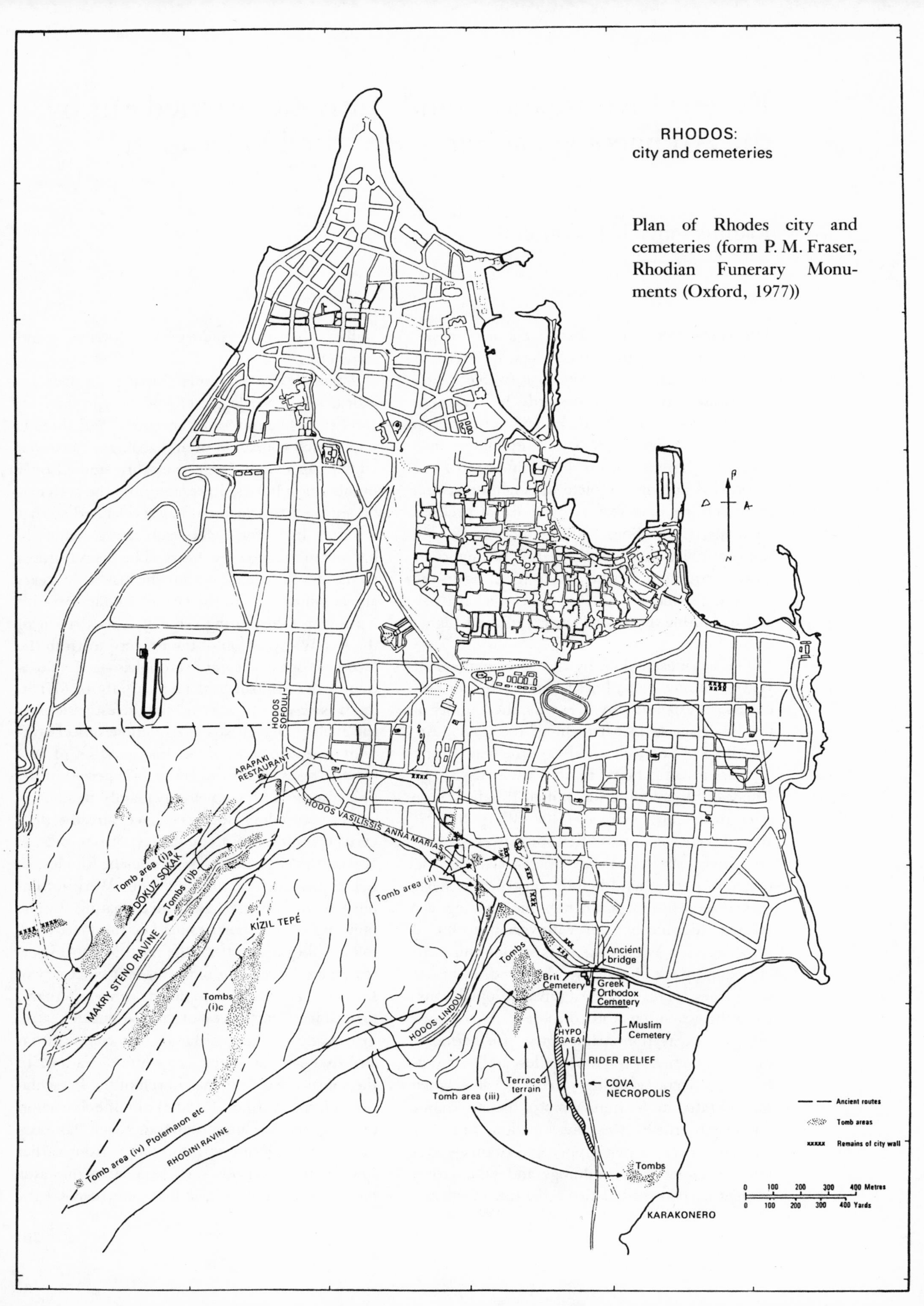

Plan of Rhodes city and cemeteries (form P. M. Fraser, Rhodian Funerary Monuments (Oxford, 1977))

signature of the sculptor Phyles from Halicarnassus – tiny clay lamps, and an inscription giving a catalogue of names, probably of priests[2]. In the Acropolis area (Monte Smith) the chance find of an inscription, now being studied, again brings the Library of the Gymnasium into the limelight; inscriptions found earlier mention this library[3]. Another inscription, found in the excavation of a lot near Diagoridon Street (Ancient Street P 15), may be derived from the famous Ptolemaion, which perhaps should be sought for in this area. Farther east, also near Diagoridon Street, new finds of dedicatory bases belong to another sanctuary, the location of which was already known.

Remains of a bronzecasting workshop for overlifesize bronze statues, the well known Rhodian colossi, have been found and preserved in the basement of a building owned by Nassos Mylonas[4]. At the intersection of present-day Them. Sophouli and Cheimarras Streets (Ancient streets P 27 and P 13) work was completed in the area of an ancient sanctuary where votive bases were found mentioning the god Helios (῞Αλιος)[5]. In the area of the medieval town, exploration of sections of monumental buildings continues on Platonos Street near the mosque of Ibrahim Pasha, at the eastern extension of an earlier excavation[6]; one of these buildings, rectangular in plan, does not conform to the grid of the city street network. It should be noted that the ancient Agora and the Deigma are probably to be found in this general area. A large building was located in the south central section of the ancient city, near the New Stadium, west of Haghias Anastasias Street, which runs approximately on the line of ancient street P 32; to judge from epigraphic data this building is probably a Gymnasium. Farther east, one of the most important ancient houses in Rhodes has been excavated, that with two large mosaic floors, one showing a centaur, the other Bellerophon and the Chimaira[7]. Another inscription found in the central Venetokleon street east of the new stadium and west of Canada Street, indicates that the sanctuary of Isis, known from literary sources[8], must have been somewhere here. The find-spot is neither very near nor very far from the north-eastern line of the city wall. Regarding harbour installations, new excavations and finds in the vicinity of the Catholic Church Santa Maria may be linked to the north-west harbour, today filled in[9]. In the same area, a little farther south, a large building was found; it has interior supports and was probably a kind of arsenal (fig. 1). In the area of the southern harbour, in the district now called Zephyros, a large wall was discovered in the area of the Central Vegetable Market; it is probably part of a jetty.

Fig. 1. Part of an arsenal(?) seen from the north.

During recent years many sections of the city wall have come to light, significantly adding to our previous knowledge about the fortifications of Rhodes. We report the most remarkable finds, beginning at the north and proceeding eastwards: a stretch of the ancient city wall about 40 m long was explored in two adjoining properties west of the previously excavated section preserved north of the National Theatre, very near the sanctuary of Demeter[10]. A section of the circular ancient street P 40 was discovered on the south-eastern side of the town at Australias Street; this ancient street circles the ancient town just inside the line of the city wall[11].

In the post war period a considerable stretch of the Hellenistic wall was uncovered at its southern part, near the intersection of Anna Maria Street and Gregory the Fifth (Grigoriou Pemptou) Street, north-west of the point where a section of the wall already found during the Italian period is still visible in a fenced area. More recent excavations have uncovered the continuation of the wall to the south, and also the proteichisma, the outer line of defense parallel to the wall. Another short stretch of the wall and proteichisma was uncovered farther north at the square Epta Chourmadies[12]. But the largest and most impressive section of the city wall and proteichisma were uncovered a little farther northwest, in the block of buildings bounded by Megalou Konstantinou, Garibaldi and Stephanou Kazoulli Streets. The wall and proteichisma are preserved to a length of 160-180 m with plus or minus 20 m between them (figs. 2-3). The wall is of solid masonry 3.50 m wide, with the typical buttresses on the inner face of the wall[13]; the superstructure of the proteichisma is preserved with remains of stairs, postern gates and drainage channels. A thick layer of murex shells, previously noted at other points in the area, covered the wall and the proteichisma in early Roman times when the fortifications seem to have fallen into disuse. What appears to be a purple dye factory was investigated in 1979 just outside the proteichisma. After the investigation is complete, the Service plans to preserve this extremely important section of the ancient fortifications and to organize it as an archaeological site. Lastly, another important stretch of the fortifications was uncovered in both earlier and more recent excavations to the northwest, across from the old Venetokleion Highschool for boys; a monumental tower and sections of the wall, the proteichisma and the circular street P 40 were revealed here[14].

Fig. 2. Wall and proteichisma seen from northwest (M. Konstantinou Street).

Fig. 3. Wall seen from southwest (M. Konstantinou Street).

As noted above, much richly rewarding archaeological work has recently been accomplished in the area of the cemeteries, the general lay-out and distribution of which was previously known (p.202). Beginning at the west we report rectangular rock-cut tombs of the fourth century BC just south of the wall. This district is known for its early graves, which date to the first period of the city. Another district yielding many finds during recent years is the ravine Makry Steno, today called Tzenio, extension of Sophouli Street, or recently Michail Petridi Street, and the Dokuz Sokak District, nearer to the wall. During recent years the town has expanded particularly into the Kizil Tepé district, today called Haghia Triada and Analipsi, providing an opportunity for intensive investigation of the crowded cemeteries in this district; numerous excavations brought to light many tomb complexes and hundreds of graves. At the start of the road leading to Haghia Triada (recently named Tsaldari Street), just south of the fenced-in archaeological area known as the "tombs of Ai Yanni", a rectangular structure was investigated, measuring about 30 by 11 m; inside were rectangular raised platforms built of stone and coated with stucco; two inscribed sepulchral altars were found in situ near the southwest corner (fig. 4). The site, the shape and the

Fig. 4. Sepulchral structure seen from the east.

Fig. 5. Inscription painted on a potsherd.

Fig. 6. Kerameas – Tsikkis sepulchral monument (detail).

contents of this late Hellenistic structure show that it must have been a gathering-place for the performance of sepulchral rites. To the north, a deep filling of black earth was partly explored; it contained much evidence of burning, disintegrated skeleton remains, skulls and various ancient artefacts including an interesting series of inscriptions painted on potsherds (fig. 5). In a series of adjoining lots west of the structure a crowded group of about three hundred rectangular tombs was investigated. Most of them were pit-graves of the 4th century BC and the Hellenistic Period. In the north-east section of this cemetery was a rectangular area measuring about three by one metres, containing a layer of bones above which were three layers of skulls in eight rows[15].

Amongst the finds from the Haghia Triada district is a remarkable Hellenistic sepulchral monument found on property owned by Kerameas and Tsikkis, on the east slope of Kizil Tepé. It consists mainly of a square chamber, sides measuring 4.62 m, carved out of the living rock, a type of sandstone, with the entrance at the east. Along three of the walls are rock-cut couches (klinai) provided with cushions and footstools and adorned with relief friezes (fig. 6). The domed ceiling was coated with sky-blue stucco and supported by four youthful female figures. The statues are of the same material as the building and were also coated with stucco.

Fig. 7. Vases from the necropoleis.

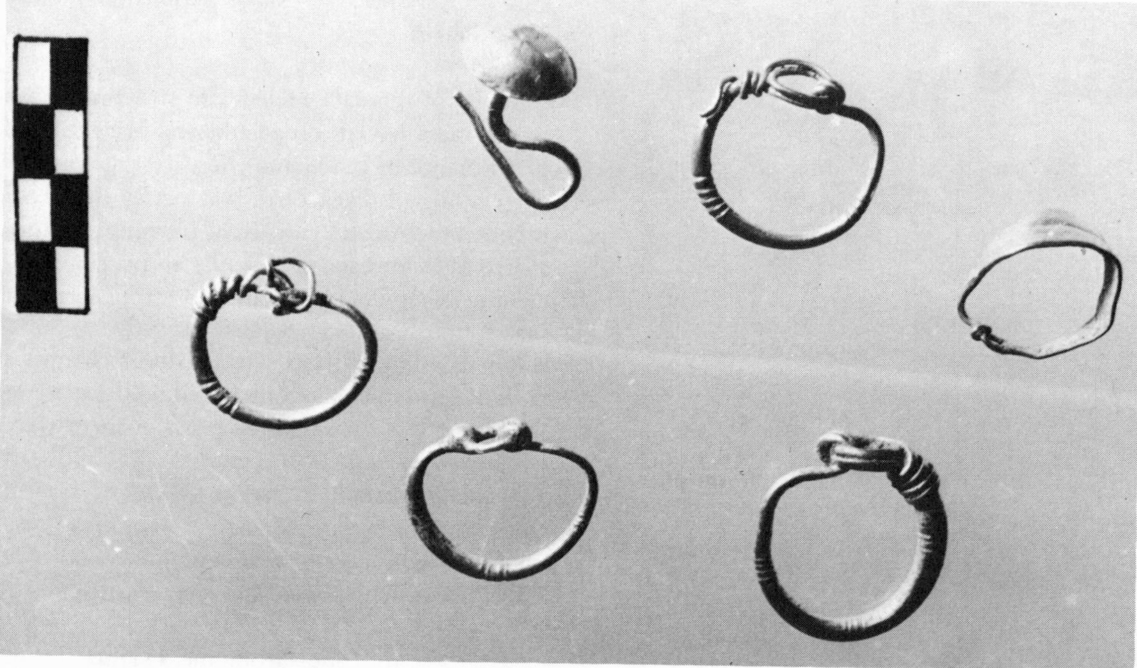

Fig. 8. Jewelry from the necropoleis.

The monument was enclosed in a peribolos and had a badly destroyed monumental façade on the east. Amidst the great number of graves and tomb complexes, the Kerameas Monument and a few others demonstrate the high level attained by Rhodian cemeteries.

The area around the Lindou Street was previously known to have particularly important grave assemblages and monuments. East of Lindou St., on the extension of Anna Maria Street, part of an imposing grave monument, 31.50 m long, was investigated and preserved below a modern apartment building; a series of vaulted tombs open onto the inner, west side[16]. West of Lindou Street, on Anna Maria Street, another interesting sepulchral ensemble has recently been explored; it has rock-cut graves, funeral tables and remains of klinai. Farther south, excavation of another important grave monument started at the corner of Lindou and Anastasiadi Streets. It consists of a chamber with klinai, in front of which was a monumental façade with

Doric columns. An especially noteworthy inscription found in this excavation mentions the word: *temenos*.

Other interesting tombs were found on the same property, some of them going back to the fourth century BC, and also well-preserved sepulchral structures above ground. Quite a number of tombs have recently been excavated near the Korakonero necropolis along the Rhodes-Kallithea road, in the vicinity of the Phaneromeni Church. Graves were also found and investigated opposite Rodini and the so-called Ptolemaion, east of the Rhodes-Lindos road.

The suburb of Asgourou, a few kilometres south of the town on the Rhodes-Lindos road, has long been known for notable finds of tombs. In 1976-77 four subterranean rock-cut tomb complexes of the third to first centuries BC were located and excavated near the seven-kilometre mark beside an ancient road, probably the Rhodes-Lindos road. Among the finds special mention may be made of a gold wreath with myrtle leaves and little round berries of glass paste. The wreath comes from a grave dated to the first half of the third century BC[17].

It is interesting to observe that the graves of the 4th century BC, that is those belonging to the early period of the city, are found not only close to the city wall, as one would expect, but also at considerable distances from the ancient city.

Excavation of the cemeteries yielded a quantity of movable finds: pottery, sculpture, inscriptions, coins, glass, gold ornaments and small objects (figs. 7-8), the systematic study of which will illuminate various aspects of the history and development of the cemeteries, of the history and the institutions of the city, and of the artistic life and development, and will also provide new information about relations with other centres far and near. In general it constitutes an important chapter in the study of Hellenistic history and art. Besides the documentation of each excavation by means of photography, plans and drawings, a detailed general topographical plan of the cemeteries of Rhodes is being drawn up; by means of this plan the quantities of finds will be uniformly recorded.

We conclude our review with a brief look at the activities of the Service in the countryside of

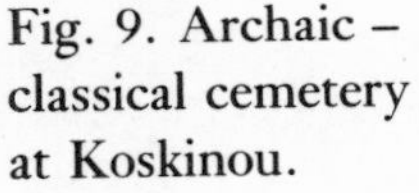
Fig. 9. Archaic – classical cemetery at Koskinou.

Fig. 10. Líndos, lower town. Part of a wall.

Rhodes and on other islands of the Dodecanese. In the village of Koskinou, where in the past Hellenistic and Roman graves and also Mycenaean remains[18] have been found, a cemetery of the archaic and classical periods has recently been investigated; it resembles cemeteries of the historic period at Ialysos (fig. 9). At Ialysos, already famous for its recent finds of the Minoan-Mycenaean period, activity was renewed in the area of the town cemeteries of historic times, amidst the small country towns of Trianda and Kremasti where, in the area of the Drakidis property[19], also remains of an early Christian basilica have recently been excavated. In Lindos, where intensive efforts are now being made to preserve the Italian restoration of the Acropolis monuments, remains of the lower town were investigated during recent years. The main find is a section of a wall dating to the late archaic – early classical period, the first example of a fortification in the lower town (fig. 10). A small cemetery ranging from the geometric to the Roman period was located and investigated in south-east Rhodes, at the village of Vati, in the "Kaourokampos" area. Main finds were two graves of the early 8th century BC with rich goods typical of the geometric graveyards of the island[20].

Turning now to *Karpathos*, we report a grave with rich finds of the Late Minoan III A1-III B period located between the villages of Menetés and Arkasa (ancient Arkaseia)[21].

On *Telos* Minoan finds were discovered near Megalo Chorio, the ancient capital of the island[22]. On the island of *Leros* a prehistoric settlement was discovered and partly explored at Partheni, where there was a sanctuary of Parthenos and an early Christian basilica has been found[23]. On *Nisyros* graves of the sixth and fourth centuries BC and of the Hellenistic period were found in connection with the construction of an Athletic Centre in the district of Ai Yanni, where excavations were previously carried out in 1932[24]. The finds include cremation burials of the archaic period, classical pithoi and sarcophagi and Hellenistic cist graves. The recent archaeological activity on the island of *Astypalaea* is presented elsewhere, so my report finishes at this point[25].

Ioannis Papachristodoulou
Ephor of Antiquities
Archaeological Service
Rhodes 85100
Greece

*I am indebted to Mrs. Judith Binder for her kind and valuable help in the English translation of the text.

1. For the activities of the Service in the post-war period see mainly Ergon, Praktika, Deltion and I. Kontis, AM 73, 1958, 146 ff.
2. See ADelt 32, 1977, Chronika 346.
3. Maiuri 1925, no. 4 and 11; RivFil 63, 1935, 214 ff.; RivFil 64, 1936,40.
4. ADelt 30, 1975, 363.
5. Prakt 1975 A', 238 ff.
6. ADelt 25, 1970, Chronika 507 ff.; ADelt 32, 1977, 356.
7. ADelt 32, 1977, 360 ff.; Ergon 1976, 166 ff.; Prakt 1976 B', 334 ff.
8. See Morelli 1959, 58, 155 and 174, sv. ''Ισις and Σάραπις.
9. ADelt 30, 1975, 366; ADelt 33, 1978, 397-8.
10. ADelt 20, 1965, 594-5; ADelt 31, 1976, 386; ADelt 32, 1977, 346; see also ADelt 33, 1978, 396.
11. ADelt 29, 1973-4, 974; ADelt 32, 1977, 346.
12. ADelt 30, 1975, 366; ADelt 31, 386; ADelt 32, 1977, 344 ff.
13. ADelt 28, 1973, 610 ff.; ADelt 29, 1973-74, 959; ADelt 32, 1977, 344; ADelt 33, 1978, 397.
14. ADelt 28, 1973, 608 ff.; ADelt 29, 1973-74, 959, 968-970.
15. ADelt 30, 1975, 361 ff.; ADelt 32, 1978, 367 ff.
16. ADelt 30, 1975, 369.
17. ADelt 32, 1977, 373 ff.
18. ADelt 18, 1963, Meletai 133-4; cfr. BSA 68, 1973, 155.
19. For the Italian excavations see ASAtene 3, 1916-20, 252 ff.; ASAtene 6-7, 1923-24, 257 ff.; ClRh 3, 1929, 7 ff.; ClRh 8, 1936, 64 ff.
20. See preliminary reports in AAA 8, 1975, 223 ff.; ASAtene 61, 1983, 9 ff.
21. ADelt 33, 1978, Meletai 249 ff.; Melas 1985, 39 ff.
22. AAA 13, 1980, 68 ff.
23. BSA 52, 1957, 134; Benson 1963, 18-19.
24. ClRh 6-7, 1932-33, 469 ff.
25. I wish to thank all the archaeologists of the Ephoreia for Prehistoric and Classical Antiquities of the Dodecanese for their collaboration in the preparation of this communication.

Telian and Other Names

P. M. Fraser

I am very glad to have this opportunity to tell you about an aspect of Dodecanesian onomastics that I have abstracted from the material assembled for the *Lexicon of Greek Personal Names*, edited by myself and E. Matthews assisted by many collaborators, the first volume of which, containing the personal names from the islands of the Aegean and Cyrenaica, will appear, I hope, within the next nine months.* It contains some 70000 separate entries, comprising about 13500 different names, almost half of them from the Dodecanese, notably about 15000 Rhodians. Although there is not a great deal of epigraphical material from the smaller islands of the Dodecanese such as Nisyros, Telos and Chalke, it is nevertheless sufficient to reveal some significant features of the history of these small communities, both in themselves and in relation to their great neighbour, Rhodes.

In general the onomastic pattern of these islands is of a local Dorian nomenclature, differing, as we shall see, in some respects from island to island, with a substratum of common Dorian and pan-Hellenic names. This pattern continues long after the incorporation of the islands into the Rhodian state before and during the Hellenistic age. Then the same names appear borne by Rhodian citizens, and proclaim their Telian or Nisyrian, or whatever it may be, origin. In the examples that follow I shall focus particularly on Telos, the island that, apart from the offshore islands, lies closest to Rhodes, but I shall use the onomastic evidence from some of the other islands, in particular, of course, Rhodes, for purposes of comparison. The same exercise could very easily be carried out for Nisyros, Karpathos and other islands. We have to bear in mind that Telos was incorporated in the Rhodian state as a deme of Kamiros some time about 200 B.C.; an independant community hitherto, it had at a much earlier stage been a subject-member of the Athenian Empire.

Of course, as might be expected, Telos, the total onomastikon of which comprises some 330 different names spread among about 400 persons, contains a good number of ordinary Dorian names such as we find in abundance in the South Dorian region, and from which therefore no particular historical conclusions can be drawn. Let us look, however, at another group of names which are also regular Dorian formations, but, so far as we can tell, exclusively, or almost exclusively, local Telian names. I chose first of all two names with the first element, Ἀριστ-, one of the most productive of all adjectival roots, and then half a dozen or so less familiar ones.

First, Ἀριστανδρίδας. This occurs eight times on Telos, on Rhodes at the most twice and elsewhere in the Dodecanese not at all. Next, Ἀριστόδοκος, seven times on Telos, once on Rhodes, and not elsewhere in the Dodecanese. Next, two names in Ἑρμ – the theophoric Hermes-names, one with the same second element as the Arist-name, Ἑρμανδρίδας, and Ἑρμόδοκος; of these the former occurs nine times on Telos but only four times on Rhodes, and not elsewhere, while Ἑρμόδοκος occurs eleven times on Telos and thrice on Rhodes. Next, an odd pair, Εὐανδρίδας – the same patronymic termination again – six times on Telos, five times on Rhodes (four at Lindos), and not recorded elsewhere; and Νικᾶναξ – an isolated instance of that large group of names compounded with -άναξ – four times on Telos, once at Lindos, never elsewhere in the Dodecanese.

These figures constitute both a lesson and a warning. The lesson is that localisation of certain Dorian names, normal in form but rare in themselves, is clearly attested within the individual small islands of the Dodecanese, and at the same time when we see, for example, people named Εὐανδρίδας or Ἑρμανδρίδας attested as Rhodians we may suspect that they are either themselves Telians or descended from Telians. The warning is, correspondingly, that by reason of the social and political complexity of the Rhodian state we must always analyse Rhodian names "in depth", beyond their general Rhodian context, and try to find a more precise location for them, in a way that is not possible if we are dealing with a single homogenous state – for instance, Cyrene. The same procedure can also be followed for Athens or, for example, Eretria in Euboea, the deme system of which is fairly fully known. This localisation is further emphasised by the pattern in Telos and elsewhere of names deriving from κλειτός, "famous", "glorious". At Rhodes (as elsewhere) we find a large series of such names, among others Κλειτανδρίδας – note, once more, the patronymic termination -, once at Lindos, Κλειτάνωρ, three times at Rhodes, Κλείταρχος, Κλειτόμαχος. At Telos of these names we find only one Κλειτόμαχος, but we find instead four names of which none occurs at Rhodes, namely the masculines Κλειταίνετος and Κλειτογένης (also found on Nisyros), and the feminines Κλειταγήτα and Κλειτάνασσα. These examples all belong to the Hellenistic period, and mostly to the time when Telos was simply a deme of Kamiros. The Telians, then, preserved their own onomastic features within the Rhodian state. A subtle distinction between the nomenclature of Telos and that of Nisyros is revealed by the pattern of two masculine names in Καλλιστ-, Καλλισταίνετος and Καλλιστόδικος. The former occurs six times on Nisyros, never on Telos while Καλλιστόδικος occurs five times on Telos, never on Nisyros (though, unexpectedly, it does occur twice, of a father and son, at Methymna on Lesbos). These statistics may to some extent be due to chance, as statistics often are, but I hardly think they can be wholly misleading. The phenomenon seems to be simple and unmistakable; it is that of a strictly insular, localised society that remained remarkably conservative, as far as name-giving was concerned, and unaffected by the influence of its populous neighbour, Rhodes, of which it formed an integrated part, and of the rest of the Dodecanese.

It is important to stress that the singularity of the names I have singled out consists only in the *combination* of the two elements in any single name, not in the elements themselves. For example, names in ---δοκος, of which we have looked at two instances, 'Αριστόδοκος and 'Ερμόδοκος, are not uncommon: the name Ξενόδοκος occurs eight times in the Aegean, and there are other examples. Names in ---αίνετος, of which we have noted Καλλισταίνετος as Nisyrian, are numerous: Πολυαίνετος and Πανταίνετος are frequent from an early date at Thasos, 'Ἀρισταίνετος is essentially Rhodian, and Δημαίνετος and Δαμαίνετος are both widely spread. It is thus even more striking that Telos should have produced the particular variants indicated. One may ask if we cannot draw the net a little tighter still, and establish that these rare variants are confined to a specific family, as in England, for example, some rare first names, mostly of mediaeval French origin, are confined to a single family.

The whole matter is well illustrated by an inscription from Telos, with which I must close this brief analysis. *IG*,xii[3], 40 is inscribed on a marble base of the second century BC, which supported a statue set up by a certain Χαρσίφιλος, the son of 'Αλεξίμαχος, commemorating his wife Νικάνασσα (I have already mentioned that Νικᾶναξ occurs only on Telos, save for one example at Lindos, as far as the Dodecanese is concerned; here we have the feminine form Νικάνασσα), the daughter of 'Ερμόδοκος, a name we have also already encountered. The seven children of this fecund pair join in the dedication (see the stemma at the end of the article). They are 'Αλεξίμαχος, named after his paternal grandfather, 'Ερμόδοκος, named after his maternal grandfather, and the rest named presumably after other relatives, 'Αριστόφιλος, Χαρσίφιλος, Κυδαίνων, (otherwise known only from one instance at Rhodes), Κλείτων and lastly Κλειτάνασσα. Two particular points are to be noted here. First, let us look at 'Αριστόφιλος a little more closely. Of course, a very obvious non-dialectal pan-Greek name. I agree, but let us look at it in depth. In the Aegean there are 36 examples of the name, and of these 36, 16 occur on Rhodes and 12 on Telos. The Rhodian-Telian bias is very clear. Secondly, as an example of the exclusiveness of names, we may note that the name Χαρσίφιλος, borne here by a father and son, is attested apart from this pair only once in all the Aegean islands – at Paros in the third century A.D., an Αὐρ. Χαρσίφιλος: was he of Telian ancestry? In any case, probably a family name, but who can say how it originated ? The simple name Χάρσιος occurs once at Methymna, but the root is not Greek, so far as I know. Thirdly, the daughter, Κλειτάνασσα, "The Glorious Queen", has been named after her mother, Νικάνασσα, in a slightly different way, the mother being "The Victorious Queen". They are descended from some noble ancestor of the time when Kings (we may fancy) ruled on rocky Telos, half a millenium or more perhaps before the rise of the new Rhodian Republic. This noble family, its traditions surviving during the period of Rhodian domination, sharply reflects a social tradition preserved in its names from a distant past. We should not forget this aristocratic element in Rhodian society, more clearly identifiable in its old cities, its demes and its islands, than in the more mixed population of the great city founded by Dorieus of Ialysos.

P. M. Fraser
All Souls College
Oxford, OX1 4AL
England

* Since this volume has now appeared, (A Lexicon of Greek Personal Names, by P. M. Fraser and E. Matthews, vol. I, Oxford 1987), and all instances of the name discussed are included in it, I need not do more than refer the reader to it for the evidence.

IG xii (3) 40, Family tree:

Ἀλεξίμαχος Ἑρμόδοκος

Χαρσίφιλος ~ Νικάνασσα

Ἀλεξίμαχος Ἑρμόδοκος Ἀριστόφιλος Χαρσίφιλος Κλειτάνασσα Κλείτων Κυδαίνων

The Greek Imperial Coinage from Cos and Rhodes

Anne Kromann

Whereas nine of the Dodecanese islands had a coinage of their own in archaic and classical times, only three of them were still striking coins under the Roman empire, and the so-called Greek imperial bronze coins are confined to Astypalaea, Cos and Rhodes[1].

The coinage of Astypalaea was rather short-lived, coming to an end after Tiberius, but Rhodes and Cos continued minting until the second and the third century respectively.

The silver coinage of Cos begins in the seventh century and continues until the middle of the first century BC. From the fourth to the second century Herakles is the most common motif (fig. 1). The crab on the reverse is often seen together with Herakles' club, and some scholars see a connection between the crab and the cult of Herakles[2], but as the crab is earlier than the hero as coin motif, it seems more reasonable to regard it as a symbol of the island. It may later have been absorbed into the local Herakles cult.

Fig. 1.

The transition from a bimetallic coinage of silver and bronze to a plain bronze coinage is marked by the tyrant Nikias, who was installed by Antony about 40 BC[3]. He struck rather large bronze coins of about 20 grammes weight with the healing god Asclepios and an eponyme magistrate's name on the reverse. On the obverse was Nikias himself, a youngish man wearing the diadem of the Hellenistic kings (fig. 2).

Fig. 2.

The size of the coins seems to make up for the abandonment of the silver, but after the death of Nikias the large bronze coins disappear. No coin from the early imperial period weighed more than 10 grammes, and most of them weighed far less. But there is a general renovation of the types. Herakles is a well known motif, but here (fig. 3) we meet him bare-headed and with a club on the shoulder. There are two different reverses, one of which represents the famous Coan physician Hippokrates (fig. 3). The other, showing two doves drinking from a basin, bears a great resemblance to a mosaic in Pergamon, and A. Blanchet[4] has suggested that the artist was Coan (fig. 4).

Fig. 3. Fig. 4.

Fig. 5. Fig. 6.

The veiled woman's head (fig. 5) is readopted from the silver coins of the 4th century, where she is alternately identified with Demeter and Artemisia, wife of Mausolos[5]. Here she is given the name of Boule – or Boula to remain in the Doric tounge - the Coan Council. The embodi-

Fig. 7.

Fig. 8.

Fig. 9.

Fig. 10.

Fig. 11.

ment of the council is no uncommon motif on the coins of the Greek city states in imperial times. The reverse of the Boule coin reveals Herakles seated with a child on his knee. The child is tentatively called Telephos by Head[6], but a more probable identification is Thessalos[7], the son of Herakles and the Coan princess Chalkiope. On the leg of Herakles is the Coan crab.

If we turn to the coins with emperors' heads, the reverse motifs are mostly confined to the heads of Herakles or Asclepios and only once in a while do we meet some other god (fig. 6). Later on the gods are shown in full figure (fig. 7-10) and it is easy to imagine that some of them represent statues.

Throughout the 1st century the imperial bronze coins were rather small, but from the time of Hadrian the weights started to increase and under the Antonines we again find large pieces of bronze weighing about 20 grammes (fig. 8). In the 3rd century the weights decreased slightly and after Philip I the Coan bronze coinage seems to have come to an end.

Rhodes

The best known Rhodian coins are without doubt the tetradrachms with the facing Helios and the rose, which with minor variations of types were struck from the 5th to the 2nd century BC, whereafter the issue of tetradrachms ceased owing to economic decline. Drachms and hemidrachms were still minted, but some time in the middle of the first century the silver coinage was totally abandoned and replaced by bronze[8]. The bronze coins were very large, 20-25 grammes, and struck with the same types as the silver coins they succeeded; that is: facing Helios on the obverse and a rose within an oak wreath on the reverse. And it is highly probable that they were meant to have the same value as the silver drachms (fig. 11-12).

Fig. 12.

The use of silver might have ceased because of Cajus Cassius' capture and plundering of Rhodes during the civil war in 43 BC. The first bronze drachms were followed by other heavy issues with a – sometimes radiate – head of Dionysos on the obverse (fig. 13, scheme I,1), while the reverse showed various representations of an alighting Nike – probably inspired by the Rhodian masterpiece Nike of Samothrace. There is no doubt that the issues date from early imperial time, and it must be possible to elucidate their internal chronology by a comparison of dies. A third heavy bronze series weighing slightly less than the other two (fig. 14, scheme I,2) shows Helios in profile on the obverse and has two

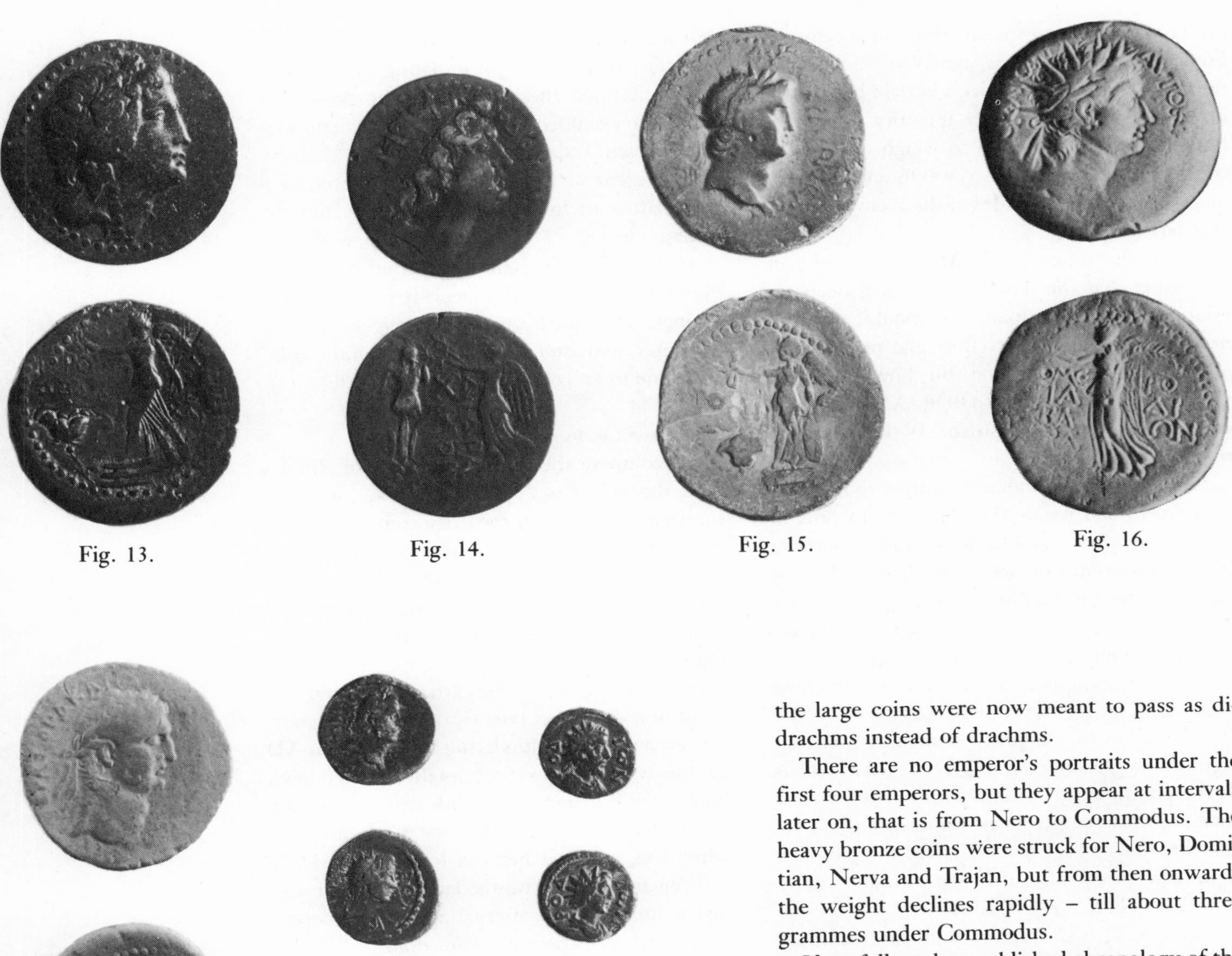

Fig. 13. Fig. 14. Fig. 15. Fig. 16.

Fig. 17. Fig. 18. Fig. 19.

reverses: either a standing Nemesis (scheme I,3) or a Nike crowning a trophy (scheme I,2). There are no magistrate names: the reverse inscription is ΡΟΔΙΩΝ ΔΙΔΡΑΧΜΟΝ and the Nike-trophy issues have on the obverse ΥΡΕR ΤΩΝ SEBASTΩΝ, that is: "On behalf of the Augusti" (fig. 14).

Marks of value are not common on Greek coins, but they do occur now and then on the Greek imperials especially in Asia Minor and the nearby islands[9]. The legend on the Rhodian bronze coins can only be a sign of reduction; the large coins were now meant to pass as didrachms instead of drachms.

There are no emperor's portraits under the first four emperors, but they appear at intervals later on, that is from Nero to Commodus. The heavy bronze coins were struck for Nero, Domitian, Nerva and Trajan, but from then onwards the weight declines rapidly – till about three grammes under Commodus.

If we follow the established chronology of the coins (scheme I) it appears that the legend DIDRAXMON is abandoned on the coins of Nero and Domitian only to reoccur under Nerva (fig. 17) and Trajan. What can be the reason for this?

In his publication of two Domitian coins[10] the Belgian scholar Marc Bar draws attention to the fact that Domitian's Rhodian bronzes (fig. 16) are slightly heavier than both the Helios didrachms and the Nero coins, and suggests that as Domitian raised the weight of the coins in Rome, he may well have done so too in Rhodes. According to M. Bar the absence of DIDRAXMON on Domitian's coins signifies that they were again worth one drachm. However in the first place we have not many examples of Roman emperors interfering with the weights of the local Greek bronze coins[11]. In the second place it is difficult to draw conclusions from the weights of bronze coins struck "al marco" - that is the mintmasters had to produce a certain number of bronze coins from a certain quantity of bronze, but they were not bound to weigh each single coin. Thus it is necessary to weigh several specimens to get a qualified idea of the average weight of a series.

If, on the other hand, M. Bar is right in supposing that the drachm value had been re-established by Domitian, we should expect a new coin legend to that effect and not just the abolishment of the old one. But how, then, can we explain the absence of DIDRAXMON on the coins of Nero and Domitian? Without further research we cannot do so.

Nevertheless it is indeed tempting to make an experiment and redate the Helios didrachms to the period after the Domitian coins. Nothing seems to prevent the Nero coins from following directly after the Dionysos/Nike issues. In fact they have a reverse type in common: Nike on prow alighting towards a rose (figs. 13, 15) which does not appear on the Helios didrachms (fig. 14). The legend: ΥΠΕΡ ΤΩΝ ΣΕΒΑΣΤΩΝ "On behalf of the Augusti" is unclear. It cannot signify a single emperor, as ΤΩΝ ΣΕΒΑΣΤΩΝ is in the plural, and it is highly improbable that it means: "those emperors in Rome (we don't remember their exact names)". But the Rhodian Domitian coins mention not only ΔΟΜΕΤΙΑΝΟΣ ΑΥΤΟΚΡΑΤΟΡ but also ΔΟΜΕΤΙΑ ΣΕΒΑΣΤΑ, the wife of Domitian. Actually Domitia is the only empress whose name appears on Rhodian coins. In spite of Plutarch's allusion to a conflict with the Rhodians, Domitian's relationship with the island seems not to have been too bad, and both he and Domitia were given statues with flattering inscriptions[12].

If ΤΩΝ ΣΕΒΑΣΤΩΝ refers to Domitian and his wife – and in fact the Helios on the didrachms bears some likeness to the emperor - the didrachm coinage must have started in the reign of Domitian. And a bronze hoard, probably from Rhodes, seems to confirm our theory[13]. The composition is as follows: c. 4 facing Helios didrachms, c. 240 Dionysos/Nike coins, c. 21 Nero/Nike coins, perhaps – but not certainly – one or two Nerva coins, but no Helios didrachms at all. Thus we have reason to believe that the Helios didrachms were later than Nero, and perhaps we are right in dating them to Domitian, but on the other hand the possibility cannot be excluded that they are later than Nerva and even Trajan.

At present we can find no special reason for a coin reduction in the late 1st century but the general decline of the coinage may well have started then. In the following period it becomes even more pronounced, especially under the Antonines, when the heaviest coin weighed about 5 grammes, and after Commodus, when the coinage came to an complete end (figs. 19-20).

Rhodes and Cos in imperial times

If we compare the imperial bronzes of Rhodes with those of Cos, we come across some dissimilarities in so far as the Coan coins in contrast to the Rhodian ones grow immensely in size in the period between Nero and the Antonines. And whereas the Rhodian coinage ceases after Commodus, Coan coins were struck as late as Philip I (244-49).

In the Hellenistic times Rhodes was far the wealthiest and most famous of the two islands, and even after the plundering by Cassius in AD 43 the economy was not totally undermined. Under the Roman empire both islands lost their freedom and became tributary to Rome, but while Cos regained her freedom about AD 70 and remained free until the late empire, Rhodes had an unstable fate, alternating between dependency and short periods of freedom.

During the economic upswing of Asia Minor in the second century AD Rhodes and Cos declined in importance, as Ephesos, Smyrna and other large coastal cities took the lead in commerce and effectuated all trade between Asia Minor and the Mediterranean world. But in spite of the competition Cos was still able to find a market for her domestic products, above all the Coan silk, and prospered though on a lesser scale than previously[14]. Rhodes, however, with her brilliant position between East and West was first of all a commercial community and owed her wealth to an extensive transit trade more than to her own products – which she nonetheless took the opportunity of exporting to her customers in conjunction with the foreign goods[15]. But as the transit trade was taken over by the coastal cities of Asia Minor, Rhodes found it difficult to sell her own products. It is probably the economic decline of the island in imperial times that we find reflected in the languishing coinage.

Anne Kromann
The Royal Collection of Coins and Medals
The National Museum
Frederiksholms Kanal 12
1220 Copenhagen K
Denmark

Scheme I.
Rhodes: The alleged chronological order of the heavy bronze coins.

Date	Obv.	Rev.	Weights
1) 1st cent. AD	Dionysos. Magist. name.	Nike alight. ʽΡοδιων	21-34 g
2) 1st cent. AD	Helios Ροδιοι ὑπερ των σεβατων	Nike, trophy Διδραχμον	17-20 g
3) 1st cent. AD	Helios –	Nemesis (?) Ροδιων διδραχμον	17-22 g
4) Nero (54-68)	Portrait Καισαρ Αυτοκρατωρ Νερω	Nike alight. Ποδιων	23-26 g
5) Domitian (81-96)	Portrait Καισαρ Αυτοκρατωρ Δομετιανος	Nike alight. Δομετια σεβαστα Ροδιων	23-26 g
6) Nerva (96-98)	Portrait Αυτοκρατωρ καισαρ σεβαστος Νερυας	Helios, Tyche Ροδιων διδραχμον	17-23 g
7) Trajan (98-117)	Portrait Αυτοκρατορα καισαρα Νερουαν Τραιαν	Dionysos Ροδιων διδραχμον	17-18 g

The weights are approximate and after no. 3 taken from very few specimens.

1. Head 1887, 544.
2. Head 1897, XC.
3. Cf. Strabo, Chrest. 14,658.
4. A. Blanchet, RevNum 1907, LXXXIII ff.
5. Cf. J. Zahle, Numismatisk Rapport 1985, 76.
6. Head 1911, 634.
7. Homer, Il. 2,677 ff.
8. On the coin history of Rhodes, cf. Head 1897, CIII-CXVIII.
9. Cf. T. Jones, Proceedings of the American Philosophical Society 107 no. 4, 1964.
10. M. Bar, Cercle d'etudes numismatiques, 15, 3, 1978, 41-48.
11. Even if the right of coinage was acquired by imperial permission – cf. Howgego 1985, 88 f. – there is no reason to believe that the emperor controlled the local bronze weights.
12. Cf. Gelder 1900, 175 note 5.
13. Mr. Richard Ashton, who is publishing the hoard, has kindly informed me of some details (in a letter of 31/3 – 1986) as the list in Coin Hoards, vol. II, 1976 no. 136 is incorrect.
14. Sherwin White 1978, 52, 52.
15. Cf. M. Rostovtzeff in CAH VIII, 1930, 628 f.

Fig. 1.

Fig. 3.

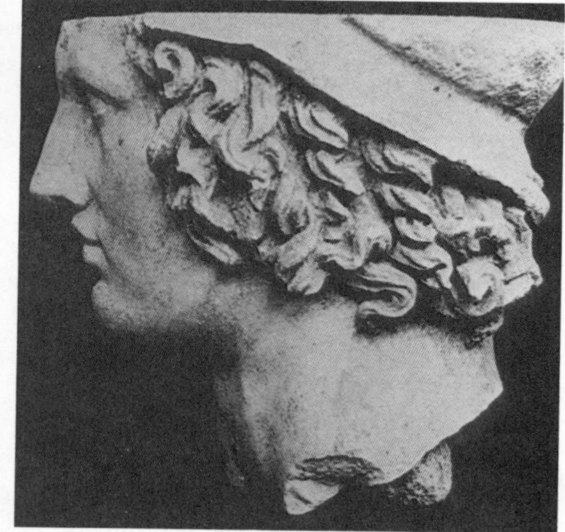

Fig. 2.

Fig. 4a.

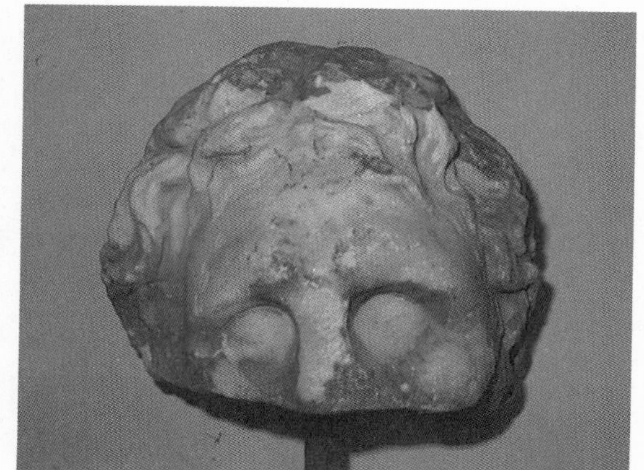

Portraits of Alexander the Great in the Dodecanese:

Some Questions – Some Answers?

Anne Marie Nielsen

Speaking quite frankly, I feel as if I am stirring up a hornets' nest when I venture to comment on the iconography of Alexander the Great. But two portraits from Cos do, however, illustrate some of the problems concerned in a very vivid manner. Accordingly, I have added a few words to my original title: Some questions – some answers?

One portrait poses questions of style and dating; the other gives a lesson in the academic exercise of identifying sculpture famed in literature.

There is a third portrait of Alexander the Great from Cos[1], but it is of the common mass-produced variety found all over the ancient world.

Although Alexander never set foot on Rhodes it is remarkable that, to the best of my knowledge, no portrait has been found in that island. I am, of course, aware of the Helios controversy, but I do not intend to consider it in this connection, because I doubt that it is possible to reach any conclusion.

This lack of a portrait is the more noteworthy, since Alexander was honoured as a god in Rhodes in the "Alexandreia" at least from the 3rd century BC, and from the 2nd century BC also in connection with the Dionysia.

The well known helmeted Alexander from Cos should arouse new interest after the remarkable finds from Vergina[2](figs. 1-2). Hitherto, there has been no agreement as to whether this portrait really represents Alexander at all, divine or not, or Ares as Alexander, or Alexander as Ares, or just Ares as Ares[3] – take your choice! This could be debated ad nauseam because, to my mind, we cannot expect to discover what Alexander really looked like; we shall always see him – at least in his later portraits -the way he wanted us to. He created his own image, he was the inventor of the political portrait!

When we try to identify portraits of Alexander I think it is necessary to follow the German school of Kleiner and especially of von Graeve[4], i.e. we should try to establish a set of formal criteria – the exterior form revealing the mean-

Fig. 4b.

Fig. 4c.

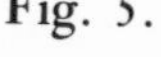

Fig. 5.

Fig. 6.

Fig. 7.

Fig. 8.

ing. These criteria could be the representation of the hair, the turn of the neck, the position of the lips, etc. Incidentally, this is probably the way Alexander himself "built" his own portrait. He visualized his own personality, and in this case reality, art and style are inseparable. Without these distinct criteria any heroic representation of a beardless young man may qualify as Alexander, which indeed has often been the case in the past.

The discovery of an Alexander portrait in ivory at Vergina, however, has confirmed, at least to my mind, the identification of the Cos portrait as an Alexander[5](fig. 3). The similarities are striking. We see the same facial contour, his upturned glance, the turn of the head, the muscular neck – all well known characteristics of Alexander. The Vergina profile shows an aquiline nose never seen in any other portrait. The anastolé, the cowlick, is of course missing in both cases, but later we shall have the opportunity of discussing this feature in more detail.

The new Vergina Alexander, however, adds a new intricate problem to the manifold problems of the Alexander iconography. The style of the portrait with its pathetic rather baroque character we normally date at least a hundred years later – it is almost Pergamene! – the period when the Cos head was probably created. Therefore it is rather disturbing that this Vergina Alexander, idealized and marked by the formulas of the Hellenistic ruler portrait, could have been created in the 4th century BC, whether in the thirties or after 320 BC[6].

The most interesting of the Alexander heads in the Dodecanese is, alas, the most fragmentary[7]. Only the top of the skull, the fillet, the front hair, the brows, eyes and upper part of the nose are preserved of this impressive head (figs. 4a-c).

The fragment is 20 cm high, thus the head was larger than life, and made of local marble. Around the hair is a fillet. The curly hair is parted in front, a little to the right. The brows are very prominent making the eyes deep-set in the shadows below. The eyes are very close set. The nose was broad. The rendering of the eyebrows makes you suspect a bronze original. The

Fig. 9.

Fig. 10.

Fig. 11.

provenance - the Muslim quarter of the city of Cos – tells us nothing, but the style is early Hellenistic.

I agree with Laurenzi, who published the head, in identifying it with Alexander the Great[8].

In our search for parallels we end up in Alexandria, where this special variety of Alexander is found in abundance.

Before going any further may I remind you of the two different anastolés of Alexander. We have the genuine cowlick well known for centuries from the Alexander Azara to the Tarsus Alexander[9]; and we have the more subdued parting of his "leonine" hair. The latter is not very common outside Egypt, but an example is the Alexander statuette from Priene[10]. In Egypt, and especially in Alexandria, there are examples galore: the well known portrait in the British Museum (fig. 5), the Sieglin head (fig. 6), the Guimet head, a limestone head, a small head of clay (fig. 7), a large granite head (fig. 8), the Alexander Bastis, the Copenhagen Glyptotek head no. 441 (figs. 9-10) – all from Alexandria proper – a head in the British Museum reflecting the same original (figs. 11-12), a small head in

Fig. 12.

Fig. 13.

Fig. 14.

Fig. 15.

Fig. 16.

Fig. 18.

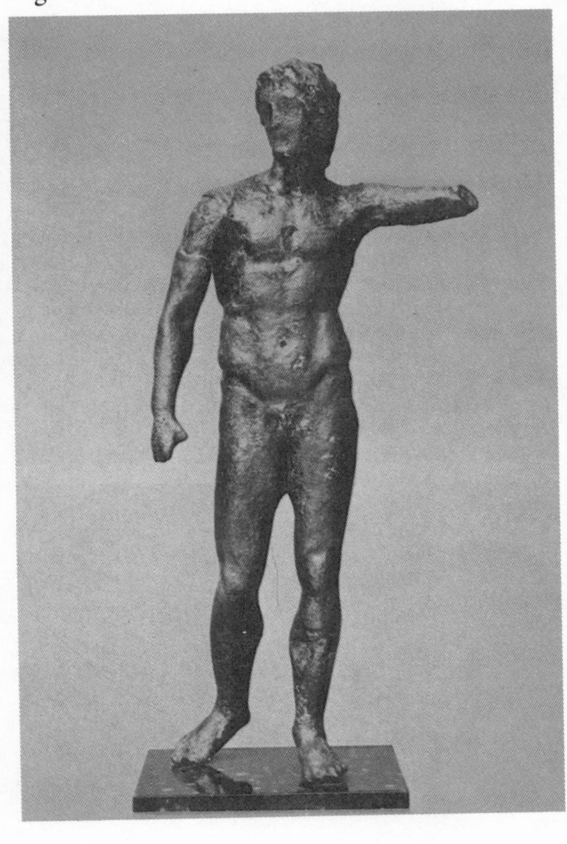

Cairo (fig. 13), and finally a colossal head from Ashmunim[11].

Apart from the hair, a common feature is the turning of the head towards the spectator's right, the slightly open mouth, and the prominent frontal bone. In all cases Alexander is looking slightly upwards.

Thus, I think there can be no doubt that we are faced with a portrait of Alexander the Great in the style, later on characteristic of the city of Alexandria, this the most famous of Alexander's foundations.

That the island of Cos should be under the influence of Alexandria is no wonder – the wine trade between Cos and that city was very intense, and a lot of Coans lived in Alexandria[12]. The only connection between Alexander himself and the island of Cos is the fact that Alexander's personal doctor was a Coan.

Who then is the master of this Coan fragment? Here I must slightly disagree with Laurenzi, as I am convinced that it must be Lysippos himself or someone very close to him[13]. One look at the corresponding parts of Agias, the Apoxyomenos or the Ny Carlsberg Glyptotek athlete is very convincing (figs. 14-16).

We do not know for sure of any connection between Lysippos and Alexandria, but several Alexander scholars, for example Bieber and Kleiner[14], have suggested that Lysippos made a

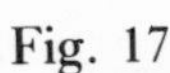

Fig. 17.

young Alexander with the Lance for the newly founded city in the years around 330 BC, whereas the famous Alexander with the Lance was created in Babylon by Lysippos just before Alexander's death.

The statue might be reflected in the small figure seen behind two young men in a tondo mummy portrait from Antinopolis in the Cairo Museum[15] (fig. 17), while the Fouquet statuette, found in Egypt, may be a reversed version[16]. The head is reflected in all the heads from Egypt just cited.

To conclude I venture the suggestion that the Cos fragment may be a copy of a statue of Alexander with the Lance made by Lysippos for Alexandria around 330 BC. In Egypt, where Alexander was honoured as a god, many versions have occurred – of this particular statue as well as others – in all sizes for public and private use. Someone from Cos may have returned to his native island with the wish and means to produce a statue of Alexander the Great locally, either for his own house or for some public use, sacred or temporal. The statue should reflect the greatest cosmopolitan center of the Hellenistic age – Alexandria.

Anne Marie Nielsen
Kaplevej 62
2830 Virum
Denmark

1. ASAtene 33-34, 1957, 79, no. 12.
2. M. Bieber, JdI 40, 1925, 167 ff.
3. K. Kraft, JfHG 15, 1965, 7 ff. with additional literature. Kraft maintains that the Corinthian helmet precludes the identification as Alexander. Dr. N. Stampolidis, University of Crete, very kindly supplied me with information on a helmeted Alexander-Ares on a painted Macedonian tomb in Toumba Bella, still unpublished.
4. AM 89, 1974, 231 ff. V. von Graeve attributes the group to Leochares. Below I shall try to demonstrate why I disagree on this particular point.
5. The Search for Alexander 1980, no. 171.
6. For this controversy, cf. AJA 86, 1982, 437 ff. with references.
7. ClRh 9, 1938, 13 ff. I find Holden's attribution of the head to Scopas unfounded, cf. Mills Holden 1984.
8. ClRh 9, 1938, 13 ff.
9. Bieber 1964, figs. 13-17 and 92-93.
10. Bieber 1964, figs. 47-49.
11. Guimet head: Bieber 1964, fig. 11; limestone head, AM 89, 1974, Taf. 90:4; Bastis 1982-83, no. S 65; Ashmunim, AM 89, 1974, Taf. 90:1-2. The so-called Inopus (Bieber 1964, fig. 86) that may be an Alexander, has this particular hair. The statue is an Alexandrian dedication to Delos.
12. Fraser 1972, passim.
13. ClRh 9, 1938. Laurenzi decides it is one of Lysippos' pupils.
14. Bieber 1964, 35. G. Kleiner, in Studies in Classical Art and Archaeology. A Tribute to P.H. von Blankenhagen, 129-138.
15. This suggestion appears in The Search for Alexander, 120, no. 41. For another interpretation, cf. Parlasca 1966, no. 7.
16. Bieber 1964, fig. 18.

Céramique incisée de tradition géometrique trouvée dans l'île d'Astypalée*

Maria Michalaki-Kollia

La céramique qui va nous occuper provient de l'île d'Astypalée[1] (fig. 1) – située dans la partie Ouest du Dodécanèse – et a été trouvée dans la région de Chôra, capitale de l'île. Ce site, qui se trouve à l'extrémité Est d'un haut promontoire dominant les golfes de Skala et de Livadia, occupe l'emplacement de l'ancienne capitale[2]. Sur l'acropole antique subsiste aujourd'hui le château médiéval de Quirini[3]. Si nous possédons, sur la ville classique, beaucoup d'informations historiques, fournies par les inscriptions et les auteurs anciens[4], ainsi que par les vestiges remployés dans les constructions modernes, nous ne disposions, en revanche, jusqu'à une date très récente, d'aucun document archéologique dont le contexte exact nous soit connu[5]. Les chercheurs anglais Dawkins et Wace, traitant de la région de Chôra, ont décrit les différents vestiges (mur polygonal dans le Castro, dédicace à Apollon, fragments de sculptures) et rapporté un témoignage oral selon lequel de nombreuses terres cuites avaient été trouvées près de l'église des Saints-Anargyres (fig. 1, no. 1), à l'extérieur de la ville, à l'Ouest du Castro[6]. Hope Simpson et Lazenby y ont ajouté un catalogue des tessons ramassés à l'intérieur et en contrebas du Castro, matériel dont la datation s'échelonne entre le Géométrique Récent et l'époque hellénistique, ce qui suggère une occupation ininterrompue du secteur pendant toute cette période[7]. Il faut encore ajouter à cela l'ensemble de vases et de figurines du IVe-IIIe siècle av. J.-C. trouvés par hasard, en 1971, lors de la construction d'une maison, sur le flanc de la colline de Katsalos et provenant apparemment de tombes[8]. C'est cette dernière découverte qui a suggéré à E. Zervoudaki que la nécropole devait être recherchée à cet endroit[9]. Or c'est justement là, à quelques mètres des trouvailles précédentes, qu'ont été découverts, en octobre 1981, les vases incisés que nous présentons dans les pages qui suivent. Le lieu-dit Katsalos se trouve à droite de la route qui mène à Livadia, non loin des dernières maisons de Chôra (fig. 1. no. 2). La découverte fortuite de quelques tessons (Fig. 2) sur le flanc du talus[10], a entraîné une fouille limitée. Celle-ci a permis de recueillir, mêlés à de la terre noire et à des fragments d'ossement brûlés, plusieurs vases brisés, dont trois phiales disposées l'une dans l'autre (Fig. 3). Après l'enlèvement d'une mince couche de terre brûlée qui se trouvait au-dessous, est apparue une fosse creusée dans le rocher[11], qui semble bien être une tombe à crémation[12].

Ainsi l'hypothèse selon laquelle la nécropole de l'ancienne ville d'Astypalée devait être cherchée sur cette colline[13] est maintenant confirmée par cette première trouvaille archéologique, mais aussi par une seconde exploration, menée pendant l'été 1985[14]. Comme l'habitat, la nécropole fut donc en usage de façon continue depuis le Géométrique Récent jusqu'à l'époque hellénistique[15].

Le matériel[16].

Il s'agit de six petits vases incisés, tous plus ou moins fragmentaires, et de deux petites oenochoés sans décor, également incomplètes.

Des six vases incisés cinq sont des petites phiales. Trois d'entre elles, de profil très ouvert, sont décorées sur la face interne; les deux autres, qui sont à peine plus profondes, sont pourvues d'un omphalos et décorées sur la face externe. Le sixième vase n'est que partiellement conservé.

Les trois petites phiales à décoration intérieure (catalogue, no. 1, 2, 3) (Fig. 4 a, b, c et Fig. 5-7), quoique de dimensions légèrement différentes, sont pratiquement identiques par la forme et le décor: une svastika[17] hachurée, inscrite dans un cercle, occupe le centre du médaillon; autour du cercle deux motifs, reproduits trois fois, alternent pour former comme six rayons: le premier

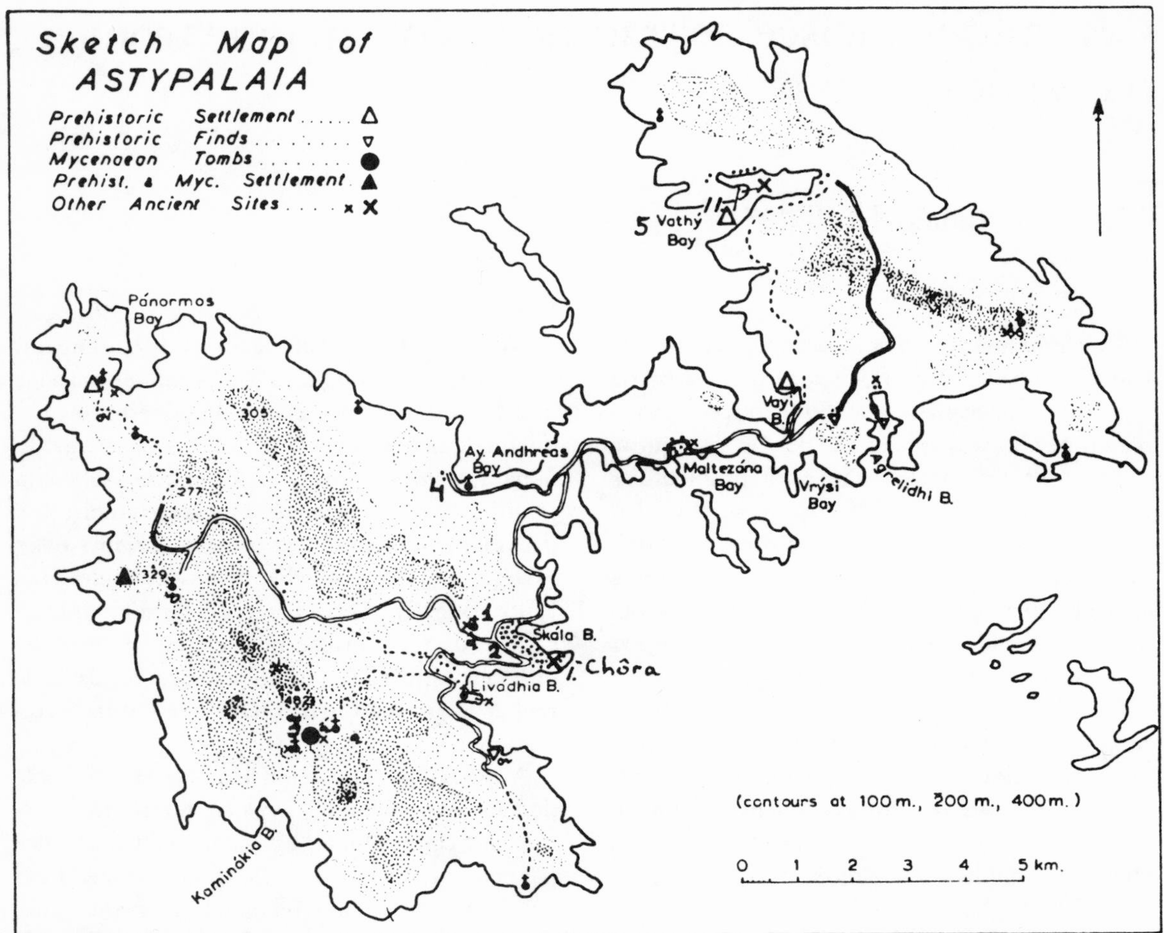

Fig. 1. Carte d'Astypalée. (D'apres R. Hope Simpson et J. F. Lazenby, BSA 68, 1973, p. 160).

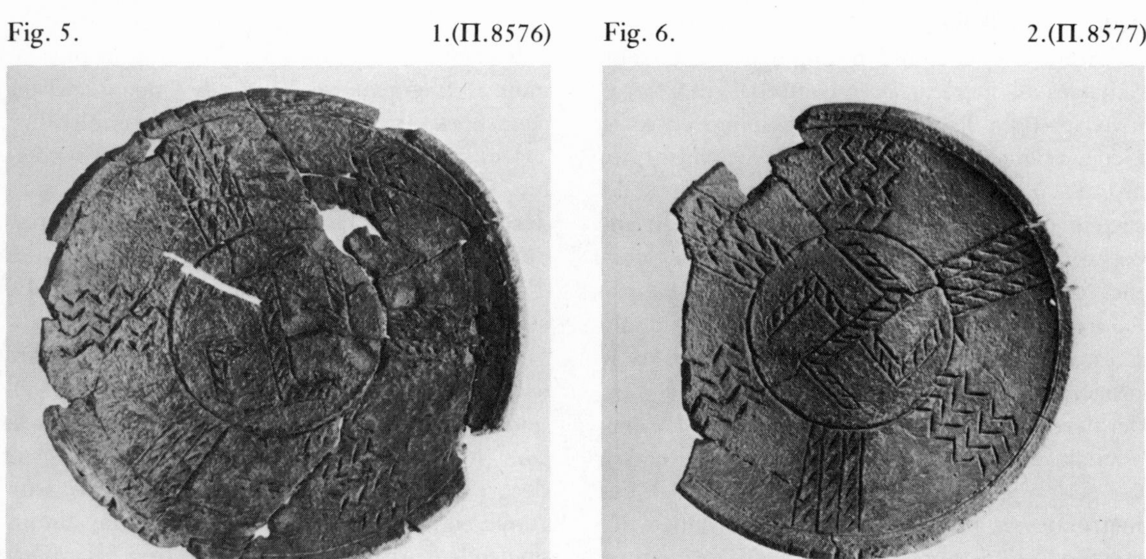

Fig. 5. 1.(Π.8576)

Fig. 6. 2.(Π.8577)

Fig. 2.

Fig. 3.

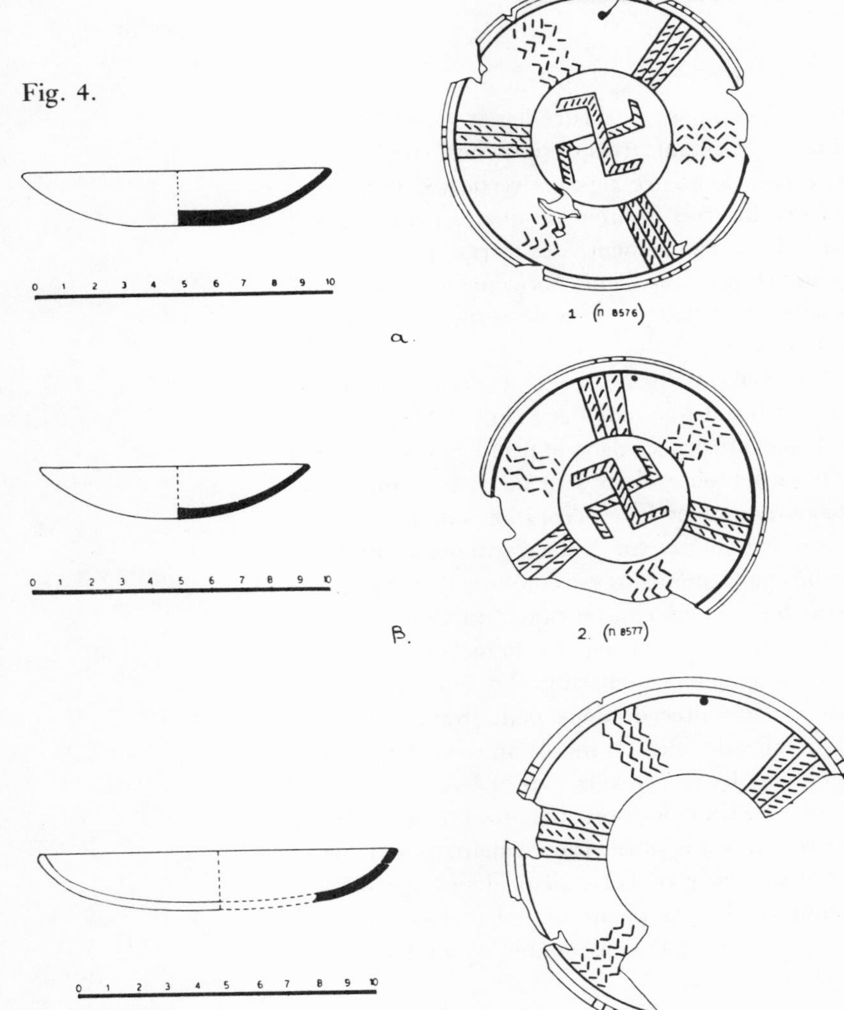

Fig. 4.

Fig. 7. 3.(Π.8578)

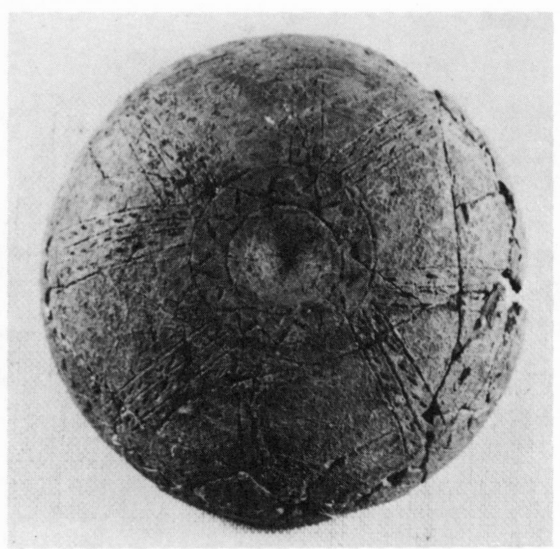

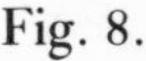
Fig. 8.
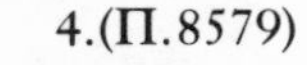
4.(Π.8579)

Fig. 9. 4.(Π.8579)

Fig. 10. 5.(Π.8580)

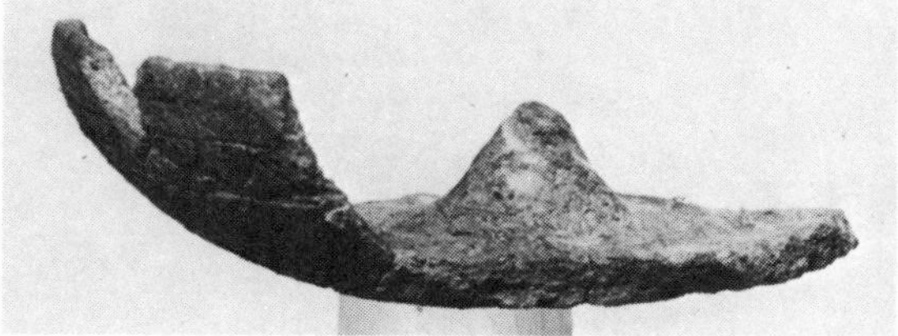

Fig. 11. 5.(Π.8580)

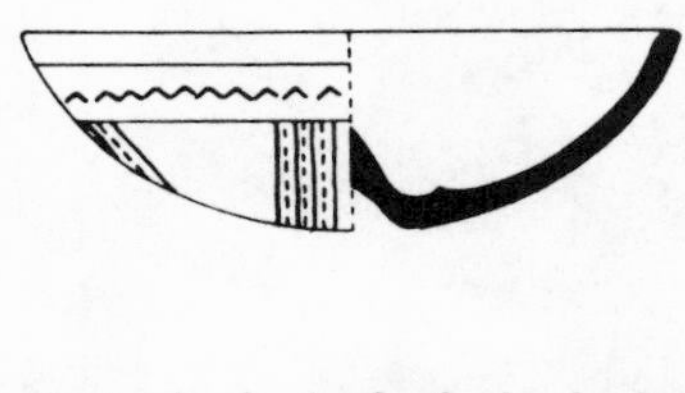

Fig. 12.

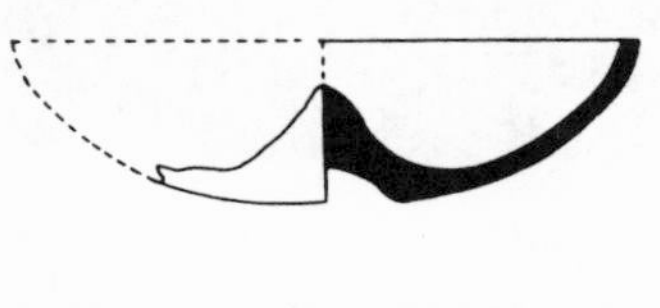

4. (Π 8579)

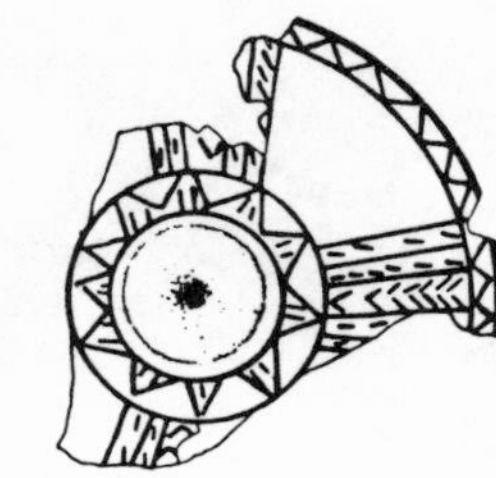

5. (Π 8580)

motif se compose de quatre lignes verticales parallèles dessinant trois "triglyphes" hachurés, le second de quatre zig-zags verticaux; la lèvre, décorée de trois groupes de quatre petits traits dans le prolongement des "triglyphes", est soulignée par une ligne horizontale. Ces trois phiales possèdent un trou de suspension[18] près de la lèvre.

Les deux petites phiales à décoration extérieure (catalogue, no. 4 et 5)(Fig. 8-12) présentent des différences dans le profil et les dimensions, mais toutes deux sont pourvues d'un omphalos pointu et leur décoration ont plusieurs points communs: sur la face externe la cavité formée par l'omphalos est entourée d'un zig-zag entre deux cercles concentriques qui dessine une sorte d'étoile (à 11 ou 13 branches); sur la phiale fragmentaire chacune des branches d'étoile est hachurée de deux petits traits, ce qui donne plus de relief au motif; un second zig-zag entre deux lignes cercle la lèvre. La vasque porte un motif en métopes rayonnantes qui se répète quatre fois: sur la phiale fragmentaire (no. 5) une bande de chevrons entre deux doubles bandes hachurées; sur la phiale complète (no. 4) un triangle bordé par une double – ou triple – bande hachurée.

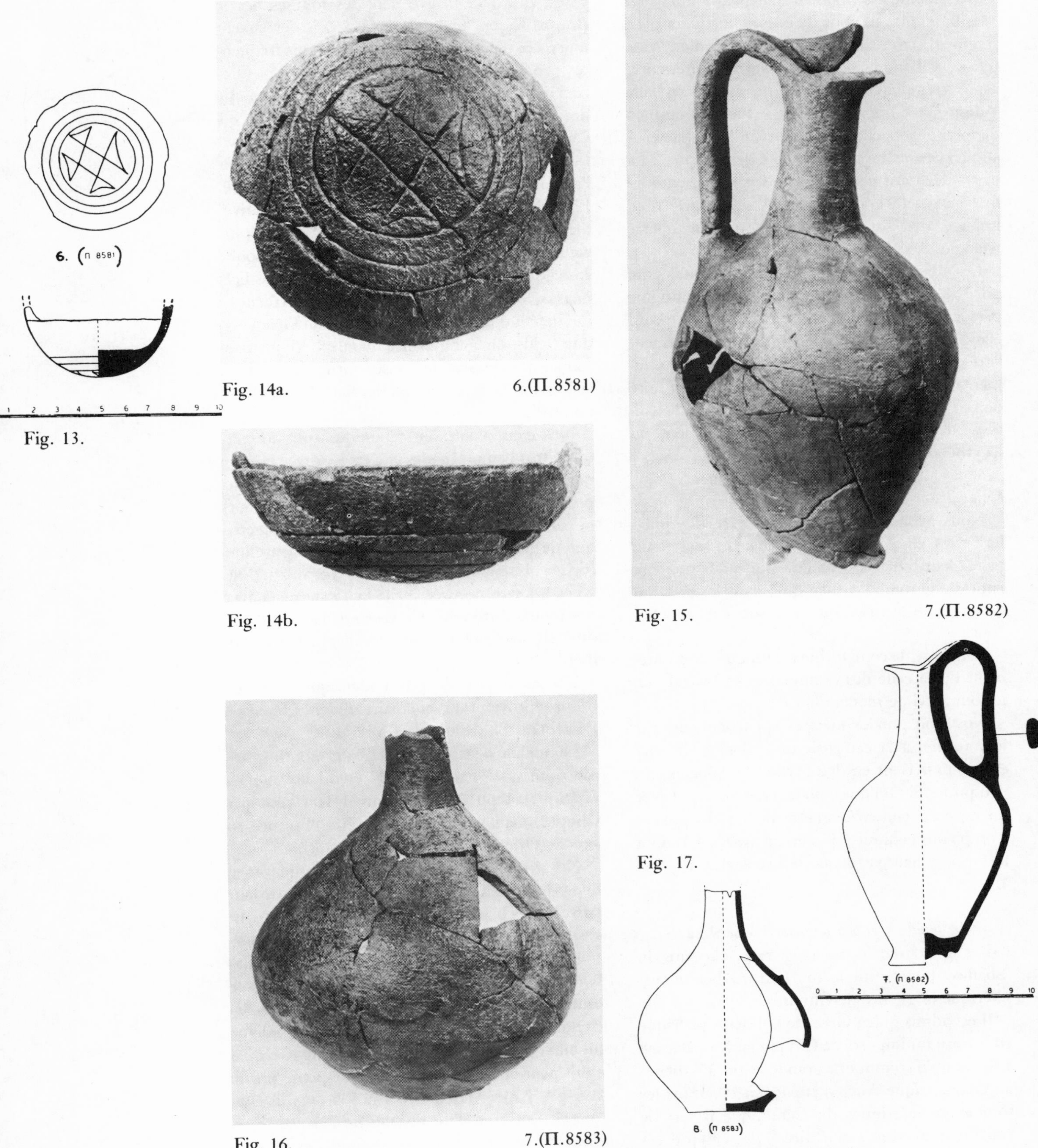

Fig. 13.

Fig. 14a. 6.(Π.8581)

Fig. 14b.

Fig. 15. 7.(Π.8582)

Fig. 16. 7.(Π.8583)

Fig. 17.

Du sixième vase incisé (catalogue, no. 6). (Fig. 13a, b, et 14a, b) nous ne possédons qu'un petit fragment circulaire. Il doit s'agir d'un vase fermé, si l'on en juge par sa surface intérieure, assez irrégulière: peut-être une sorte d'aryballe – dont notre fragment serait le fond[19] – ou bien de petite oenochoé globulaire ou de flacon – auquel cas on aurait ici un côté de la panse[20]. Le motif décoratif central de ce fragment, entouré de trois cercles concentriques[21], se compose d'un losange des sommets duquel partent quatre triangles isocèles à base concave.

Les deux petits vases sans décor (catalogue, no. 7, 8), qui complètent la trouvaille sont d'une part une oenochoé (Fig. 15 et 17,a) de profil élancé, à embouchure trilobée et anse légèrement surélevée, d'autre part un petit vase fermé fragmentaire (Fig. 16 et 17,b). Ce dernier peut faire penser à un aryballe globulaire, mais, vu l'étroitesse de son col, c'est plus probablement un lécythe aryballisque.

Les phiales

Nous avons désigné du nom grec de "phiales"[22] les cinq petits vases ouverts, soulignant par là leur fonction rituelle - puisqu'ils proviennent d'une tombe -, bien que, dans les publications, cette forme soit très souvent appellée "bol".

L'histoire de cette forme céramique est étroitement liée à celle des exemplaires en bronze qui lui ont servi de modèle[23].

Nos cinq phiales incisées appartiennent, par leur forme, à la catégorie des "shallow bowls" et se subdivisent en deux types: A) phiales très peu profondes ou quasi plates (vases 1, 2, 3) avec un rapport hauteur/diamètre de 1/5; B) phiales à omphalos conique à l'intérieur (vases 4,5) dont le rapport hauteur/diamètre est égal à 1/3,5 et 1/4.

A. – *Les phiales très peu profondes (Vases 1, 2, 3).*

Il s'agit d'une forme assez rare, variante du "shallow bowl", lui même issu du bol hémisphérique originaire de Chypre.

Il est admis qu'en Grèce le bol hémisphérique en bronze fut importé de Chypre au Xe siècle av. J.-C. et qu'il connut une grande vogue à Athènes au Géométrique Ancien et Moyen I[24]. Dans les tombes géométriques du Céramique il sert de couvercle aux vases cinéraires[25]. A Chypre ces vases, que l'on trouve dans les tombes dès le Bronze Récent (± 1500 av. J.-C.)[26], deviennent une pièce du mobilier funéraire des plus fréquentes pendant toute l'époque géométrique[27]. Elles coexistent dès lors avec des vases en céramique de même forme[28], l'existence probable, à Chypre, dès le Bronze Récent III, de manufactures de bols en bronze[29] pouvant expliquer l'apparition précoce d'imitations en céramique. En Grèce les exemplaires en céramique, relativement rares au Protogéométrique[30], sont plus courants au Géométrique Récent et à l'époque archaïque. Parmi les plus anciens citons les bols incisés du Céramique[31] et de l'Agora d'Athènes[32] qui datent du Protogéométrique et du Géométrique[33]. Ils ont une panse hémisphérique profonde, une décoration incisée sur la face externe et leur fond est tantôt bombé, tantôt plat, tantôt pointu[34].

Nos trois phiales en céramique sont au contraire très peu profondes et c'est leur face interne qui porte un décor incisé[35]. Le parallèle le plus proche se trouve dans le Dodécanèse. Il est fourni par un vase trouvé dans une tombe géométrique de Ialysos à Rhodes[36], phiale en céramique incisée présentant le même profil très aplati, (Fig. 18 et 19) mais décorée sur la face externe et avec des motifs différents. Ce vase est daté du début du VIIe siècle av. J.-C. et considéré comme rhodien[37].

Un autre vase de profil identique, mais en bronze, provient du sanctuaire d'Héra Liménia à Pérachora. Sa datation est incertaine[38].

Le modèle de ce type très peu profond, (comme celui du "shallow bowl" et du bol hémisphérique) a pu être transmis à la Grèce par Chypre, mais son origine doit être cherchée au Proche-Orient ou en Égypte.

Nos trois petites phiales en céramique – en dépit de légères différences dans la forme de leur base[39] – peuvent être rapprochées d'un petit vase chypriote en bronze de profil et de proportions à peu près semblables, vase trouvé à Idalion, dans le sanctuaire d'Athéna sur l'acropole Ouest et daté par le contexte du Chypro-Archaïque I[40] (Fig. 20, no. 1). Matthäus souligne lui aussi la rareté de cette forme et suggère qu'il s'agit peut-être de l'imitation d'une petite phiale votive[41]. La très faible convexité des parois évoquerait la forme d'un plateau de balance, récipient de petite taille, peu profond, en bronze,

Fig. 18.

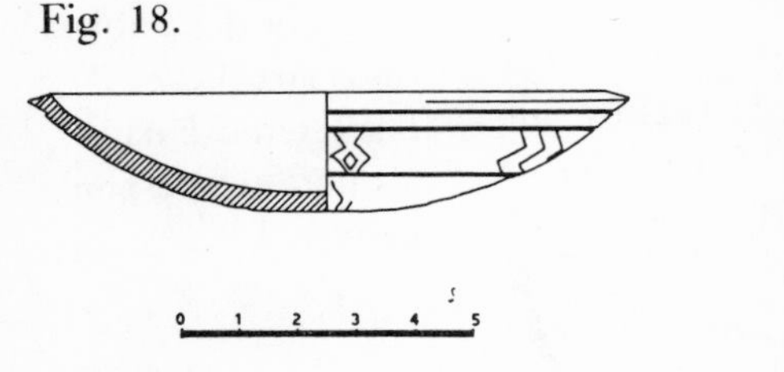

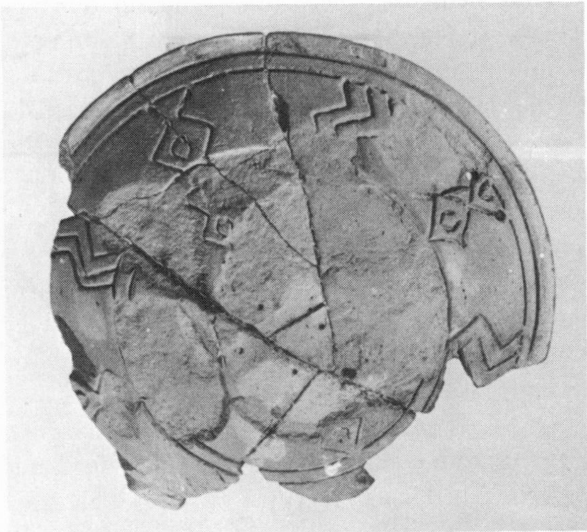

Fig. 19.

percé de quatre trous, que l'on trouve, à la même époque et plus tard, dans de nombreuses tombes de Chypre[42]. Il est donc possible que ce type de phiale, qui est exceptionnel à l'époque géométrico-archaïque, soit apparu de façon tout aussi épisodique aux époques antérieures. De fait, pour le Bronze Récent, on n'a jusqu'à présent trouvé que deux petits vases en bronze de ce type, tous deux à Chypre, l'un dans une tombe de Kourion (Épiskopi), l'autre dans une tombe d'Enkomi. Catling, qui les désigne sous le nom de "small saucer"[43], pense qu'ils sont de fabrication locale et souligne l'absence de parallèles, à cette époque, en Égée et au Proche-Orient.

Il est cependant intéressant de noter, pour l'histoire de cette forme, qu'au Proche-Orient on trouve un petit vase en bronze de ce type dès le Bronze Récent II, dans une tombe de Meggido[44], et, au même endroit, un autre exemplaire, encore plus petit, que son contexte permet de dater du Bronze Ancien IV[45]. Ce dernier ayant été trouvé, avec d'autres bols, près d'un autel, sa fonction cultuelle remonterait donc à cette époque[46]. Signalons aussi qu'en Égypte des vases de ce type (très peu profonds avec un trou ou de profil hémisphérique), sont connus dès le troisième millénaire[47]. Et Howes Smith, dans son étude récente, attribue au bol peu profond (type IA), qui apparaît à Chypre avec la plus grande fréquence aux VIIIe-VIIe siècles av. J.-C., une origine égyptienne[48]. C'est sous ce type (fig. 20, no. 2). – dans sa variante la moins profonde – que peuvent se ranger nos trois premières phiales en céramique incisées.

B. – Les phiales à omphalos (vases 4, 5).

Les deux phiales à omphalos d'Astypalée peuvent elles aussi, d'aprés leur profil, être classées dans le type IA de Howes Smith, bien que, dans l'étude de ce dernier, les vases de cette classe soient répertoriés sous le type IE parce qu'ils sont généralement un peu plus profonds[49] (fig. 20, no. 3).

Il n'y a depuis longtemps plus personne pour défendre la théorie de Luschey selon laquelle la phiale à omphalos conique - précurseur de l'omphalos arrondi – fit son apparition en Grèce vers 700 av. J.-C.[50], date qui reposait sur les deux petites phiales à omphalos en céramique du trésor de Tirynthe[51] (fig. 20, no. 4). Cette datation a dû en effet être remontée de deux siècles environ (vers 900 av. J.-C.) à la suite de plusieurs découvertes: a) une phiale en bronze de Corinthe, datée de 750 av. J.-C.[52] (fig. 20, no. 5); b) une phiale en bronze d'Athènes assignée au Protogéométrique[53] (fig. 20, no. 6). La phiale en bronze du même type découverte plus tard à Drépano, en Achaïe, doit, elle aussi, dater du début de la période[54].

Nous avons vu plus haut que le type du "shallow bowl" ou du bol hémisphérique plus profond provenait de Chypre et que son origine était peut-être à chercher en Syro-Palestine ou en Égypte. L'omphalos conique, qui apparaît sur les phiales les plus anciennes, semble bien, pour sa part, être originaire du Proche-Orient et plus particulièrement de la Syrie septentrionale[55]. De fait, dans cette région, il se rencontre sur des vases de formes diverses[56], et surtout c'est là que se trouvent la plupart des exemples, dont le plus ancien date du XVIIe-XVIe siècle av. J.-C. et le plus récent du XIIe[57] (un exemple fig. 20, no. 7).

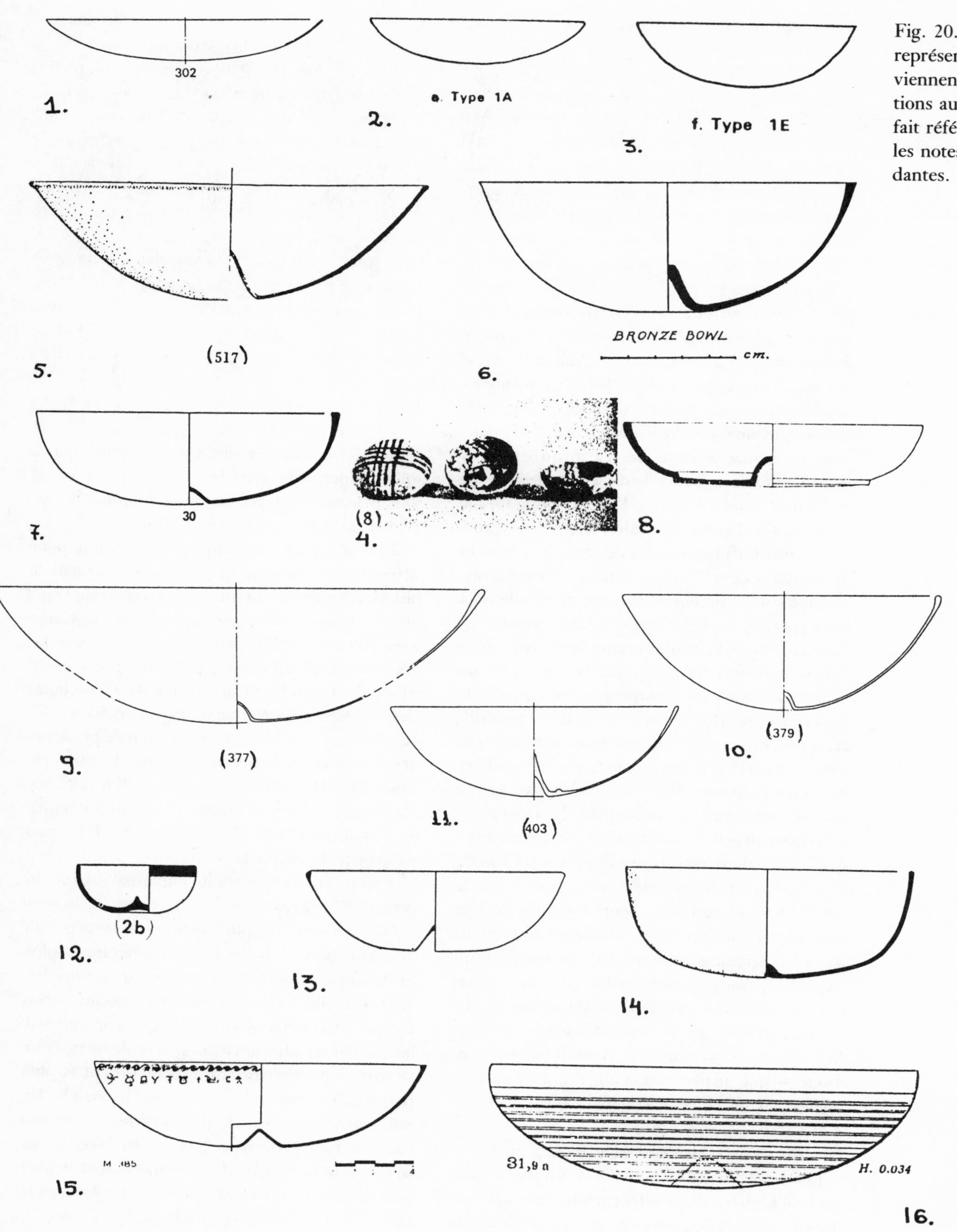

Fig. 20. Les figures représentées ici proviennent des publications auxquelles il fait référence dans les notes correspondantes.

En Égypte, au contraire, c'est l'omphalos arrondi qui est le plus fréquent[58].

A Chypre l'omphalos conique apparaît pour la première fois sur un vase des environs de 1250 av. J.-C. trouvé à Kition[59] (fig. 20, no. 8), vase qui n'appartient pas au type chypriote habituel IA – IE de Howes Smith et que son fond plat désigne peut-être comme une pièce importée[60]. Les exemples locaux de bols peu profonds ou hémisphériques à omphalos conique sont plus tardifs. Les plus anciens sont en bronze (du Chypro-Géométrique III à l'époque archaïque[61] (fig. 20, no. 9, 10, 11), et c'est seulement au Chypro-Archaïque I qu'apparaissent les imitations en céramique[62] (fig. 20, no. 12). Au Proche-Orient, au contraire, où les phiales à omphalos en céramique de profil hémisphérique existent dès le Bronze Récent[63], il semble que ce type soit plus ancien[64].

En Grèce il est intéressant de noter que, dès avant l'époque géométrique, on trouve quelques exemples de vases à omphalos, en Crète et à Mycènes. Mais il s'agit toujours de bols hémisphériques à une anse et omphalos arrondi[65], qui n'ont, du point de vue de la forme aucun rapport avec les vases qui nous occupent ici. Or, le type du "bol" hémisphérique à omphalos conique, il faut le signaler, apparaît en Grèce plus tôt qu'à Chypre, comme en témoignent les deux phiales protogéométriques en bronze, d'Athènes[66] et de Phères[67], et surtout les deux exemplaires en céramique de Cos[68] (fig. 21 a, b), qui ont été trouvés dans une tombe protogéométrique et portent, comme les phiales 3 et 4 d'Astypalée, un décor incisé à l'extérieur. Cela suggère que l'omphalos est venu directement d'Orient à l'époque protogéométrique, sans passer par Chypre, où il est plus tardif[69]. Ainsi les deux exemplaires de Cos, si leur datation est exacte, seraient les premiers vases en céramique de ce type trouvés en Grèce. Mentionnons encore un fragment de bol à décor incisé, du Céramique, pourvu, à l'intérieur, d'une sorte d'omphalos et daté du Géométrique Moyen I[70]. Un autre vase en bronze de Gordion[71] (fig. 20, no. 13), daté du milieu ou de la fin du VIIIe siècle av. J.-C., ressemble, par son profil et son omphalos conique, aux vases 3 et 4 d'Astypalée comme à la plupart des exemplaires grecs et chypriotes précédemment cités. La phiale à omphalos de Lefkandi[72] (fig. 20 no. 14) en revanche, présente un profil et un omphalos tout à fait différents, qui renvoient à une autre sphère d'influences.

Il semble que la phiale en bronze à omphalos conique du musée de la Canée, qui a été récemment publiée[73] (fig. 20 no. 15) – pour autant que ce vase, vendu à un collectionneur privé par des trafiquants d'antiquités, soit authentique – puisse être considérée comme le plus ancien des vases de ce type dans le domaine grec au sens large[74].

D'après Luschey[75] l'omphalos conique, apparu le premier, fut vite remplacé par l'omphalos arrondi, le premier ne se trouvant plus, à partir de la fin du VIIe siècle av. J.-C., qu'à Rhodes et parfois en Italie[76]. De fait des vases à omphalos conique d'époque archaïque ont été trouvés à Rhodes (un exemplaire en bronze à Camiros[77], un en céramique à Vroulia[78] (fig. 20, no. 16), mais aussi à Géla[79], qui se trouve dans la sphère d'influence de Rhodes.

Ainsi les deux phiales en céramique à omphalos conique et décoration incisée d'Astypalée, en liaison avec les deux exemplaires archaïques de Rhodes et les deux échantillons protogéométriques de Cos[80] – qui proviennent tous de tombes nous amènent à penser que ce type de vase était probablement traditionnel dans les îles de l'Est égéen et qu'il y reflète peut-être une influence orientale précoce. Cette suggestion est renforcée par la présence, à Samos[81] et à Lesbos (Antissa)[82], de vases similaires à omphalos conique: il est clair que nous avons affaire à un faisceau d'influences venues d'Orient[83].

La décoration

D'une manière générale, le décor incisé des vases d'Astypalée ne ressemble pas du tout, dans son esprit, à celui des vases protogéométriques du Céramique (tombe 48)[84] ou de l'Agora d'Athènes[85], différence qui existait déjà au niveau des formes. Il présente en revanche des points communs avec les fragments de bols géométriques de ces deux sites[86]. Ainsi, par exemple, le motif anguleux (motif no. 4) du vase no. 4 d'Astypalée (fig. 22) - motif dont la pointe est tournée vers le centre – rapelle de près celui du fragment de bol no. 55 de l'Agora[87] (fig. 23) ou du fragment K 8 du Céramique[88] (fig. 24) qui ont été datés tous deux du Géométrique Moyen I[89].

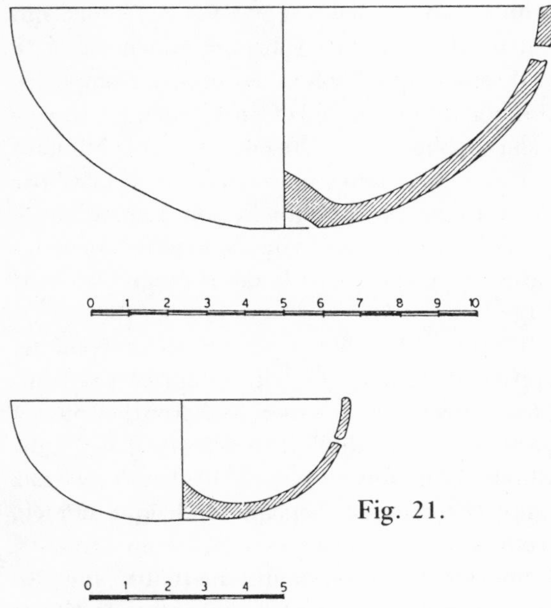

Fig. 21.

On observe également une ressemblance entre le motif qui orne la vasque de la phiale à omphalos n°. 5 d'Astypalée (Fig. 22,3) et celui qui décore la zone située sous la lèvre du fragment K 7 du Céramique[90] (fig. 24). Mais le décor de notre fragment est plus proche encore, par son esprit et par la disposition des motifs de celui du bol fragmentaire de l'Agora d'Athènes no. 54[91] (fig. 23): même bande horizontale avec zig-zag sous la lèvre, même alternance de motifs rayonnants sur la vasque. Le vase d'Athènes présente cependant deux motifs supplémentaires, qui n'existent pas sur le nôtre: une bande hachurée soulignant la bande avec zig-zag sous la lèvre, des cercles concentriques entre les motifs rayonnants de la vasque[92].

Il est clair que la décoration des vases d'Astypalée est plus simple que celle des vases géométriques d'Athènes, qui est elle même plus simple que celle des vases protogéométriques. Les quelques ressemblances qui ont été relevées peuvent difficilement, à notre avis, être interprêtées en termes d'influence ou de parenté. Nous ne doutons pas, en revanche, qu'elles puissent être liées à la fonction de ces vases dans les rituels funéraires[93].

Les deux phiales incisées de Cos[94], qui sont datées - comme on l'a dit – du Protogéométrique, n'ont rien de commun avec la décoration "sophistiquée" des bols d'Athènes qui leurs sont contemporains. Celles de Cos portent un décor assez simple (une grande croix hachurée en quadrillage sur l'une des phiales, sur l'autre une alternance de bandeaux rayonnants, remplis de chevrons ou de losanges), mais ici l'esprit décoratif et la disposition des motifs sont tout autre de ce qu'on observe sur les vases que nous étudions[95].

La décoration des vases d'Astypalée s'insère, beaucoup plus facilement que leurs profils, dans des limites chronologiques plus restreintes. La plupart des motifs, pris isolément sont attestés dès le début du Géométrique (surtout dans les séries peintes). Cependant la façon dont ils sont ici composés – inscrits dans un cercle (fig. 22, motifs no. 7, 8), sur une bande circulaire (motifs no. 5, 5a, 6), ou disposés en panneaux rayonnant (motifs no. 1, 2, 3, 4) – trahit d'emblée un stade esthétique plus avancé, proche du style du Géométrique Récent et plus particulièrement de celui de Rhodes. Ainsi, par exemple, le motif no. 3 (bande de chevrons entre deux "triglyhes"), qui fait sa première apparition au Géométrique Moyen I en Attique et à Corinthe[96], devient très courant, au Géométrique Récent, en Attique, à Argos, et à Rhodes[97]. De même le motif no. 1 (zig-zag vertical), caractéristique du Géométrique Récent et du Subgéométrique de Béotie[98], se

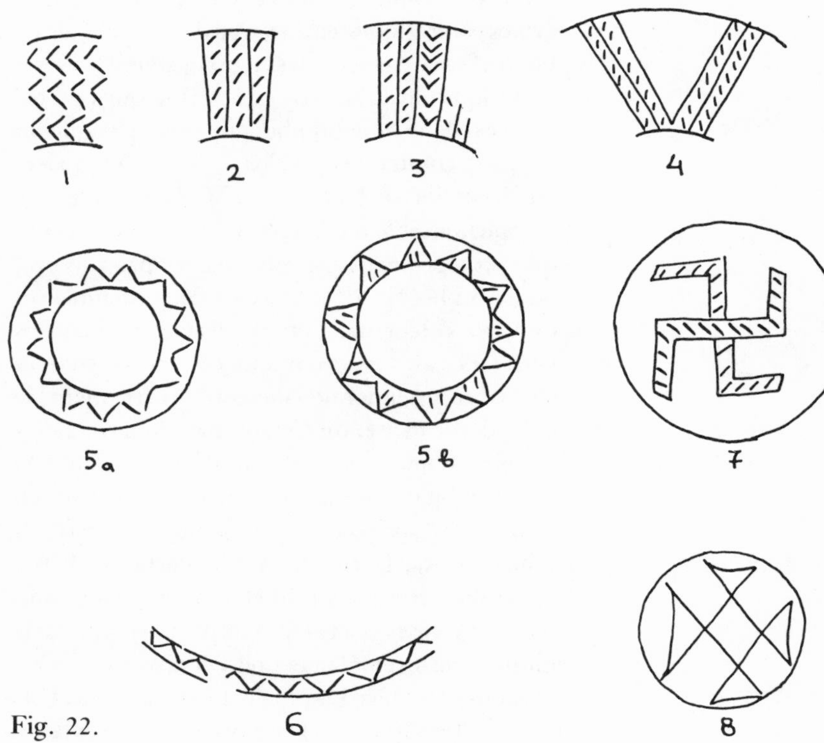

Fig. 22.

Fig. 23.

rencontre très fréquemment, à Rhodes, à la même époque sous forme de ligne ondulée[99] ou de ligne brisée angulaire[100], motif qui se rencontre aussi sur des petits vases incisés de fabrication locale[101]. Le motif du zig-zag vertical encadré de deux ou trois bandes lisses (motifs no. 1 et 2), qui est très commun au Géométrique Récent (à Argos[102], en Béotie[103], à Chios[104] et ailleurs), a dû inspirer la décoration des trois petites phiales d'Astypalée no. 1, 2, 3, où il est cependant dissocié et intégré dans une composition originale. Rappelons que ces trois vases d'Astypalée sont, jusqu'à présent, les seuls – parmi les exemples connus de céramique incisée – qui soient décorés à l'intérieur[105].

La petite phiale de Ialysos[106] (fig. 18-19), qui est decorée à l'extérieur, porte elle aussi des groupes de zig-zags verticaux, mais ils alternent avec des losanges. Ce vase paraît à la fois plus récent que les exemplaires d'Athènes et de Cos que nous venons de citer et plus ancien que ceux d'Astypalée qui nous occupent.

Le motif no. 5a, b, (fig. 22) qui cerne l'omphalos des vases 4 et 5, se rencontre fréquemment, dès le Protogéométrique, autour de médaillons, que ce soit sur des vases en céramique, des bijoux ou d'autres objets. Bien qu'un peu différent, il rappelle le motif en étoile ornant la base d'un pinax du Géométrique Récent trouvé dans une tombe de Ialysos[107], qui contenait encore un autre vase incisé. On ne peut totalement exclure que ce motif ait une connotation symbolique, comme c'est souvent le cas pour ceux qui décorent les vases funéraires[108].

Il en va peut-être de même de la svastika[109] qui, à notre connaissance, du moins, ne se présente jamais ailleurs, comme ici, inscrite dans un cercle, que ce soit en céramique peinte ou incisée[110].

Faite d'une double ligne incisée et inscrite dans un carré formant une métope, elle orne le col de deux petites amphores trouvées dans une tombe d'Anavyssos[111]. Celles-ci étaient associées à d'autres vases incisés, non tournés, vraisem-

Fig. 24.

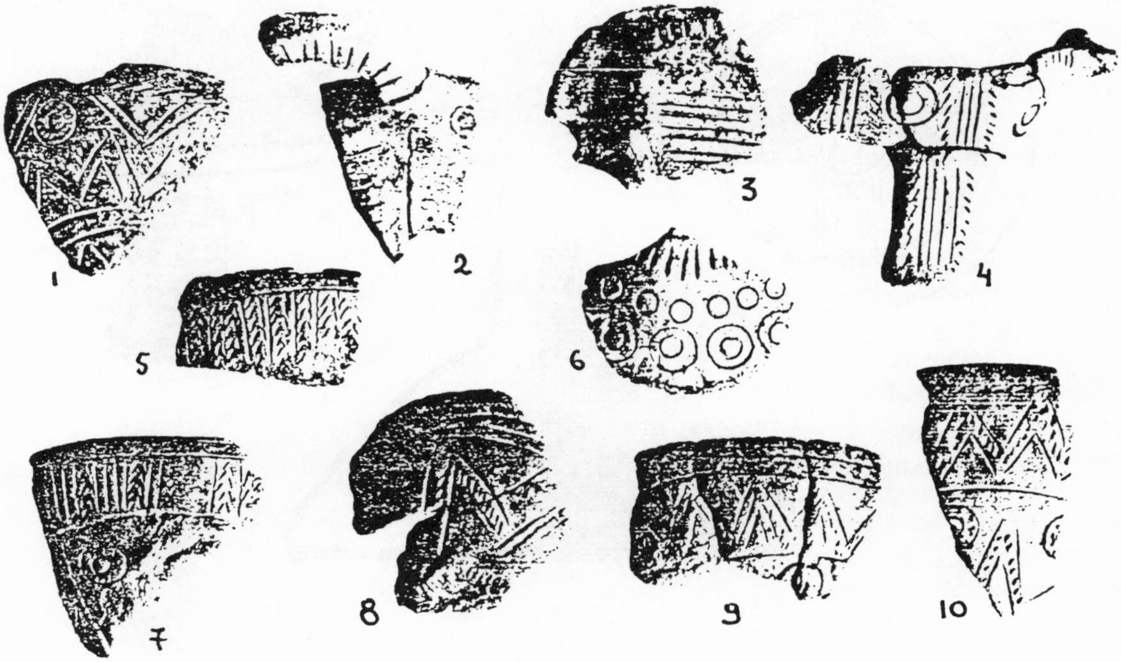

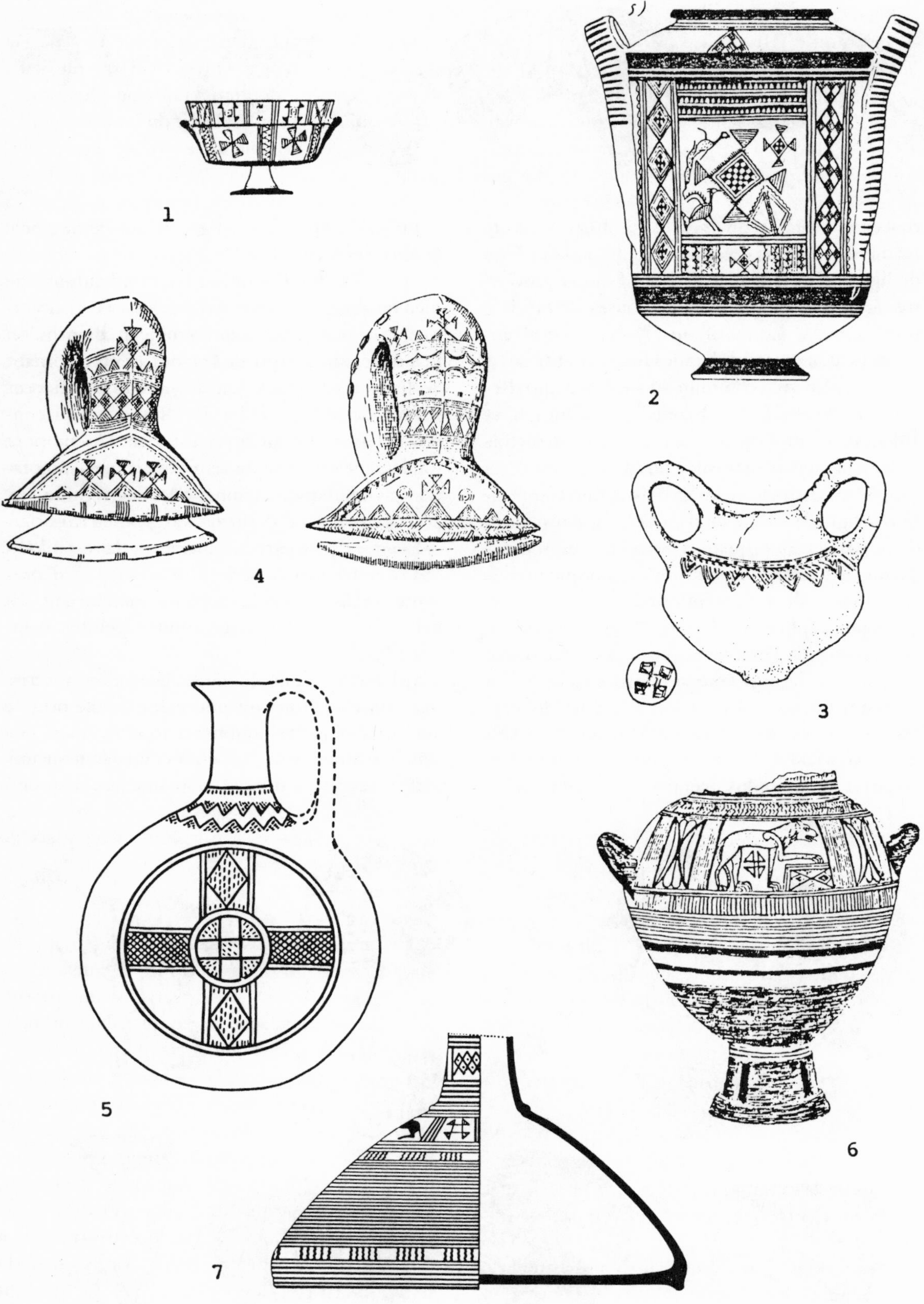

Fig. 25. Les figures représentées ici proviennent des publications auxquelles il fait référence dans le notes correspondantes.

blablement produits par un atelier local et datés de la fin du VIIIe siècle av. J.-C.[112].

Hachurée, comme ici, elle se trouve déjà sur un vase peint du Géométrique Ancien I d'Athènes[113]. Là elle devient, au troisième quart du VIIIe siècle av. J.-C., l'un des motifs le plus souvent reproduit, en métopes, sur les parois des pyxides peintes[114]. A Argos, où la variante avec branches à gauche est la plus commune, c'est un motif décoratif assez fréquent de la céramique du Géométrique Récent[115]. Il est bien connu que, sur la céramique de Naucratis et de Rhodes, il est également fondamental[116].

Mais le motif le plus intéressant des vases d'Astypalée est celui qui apparaît sur le fragment du vase fermé no. 6 (fig. 22, motif no. 8). Sous la forme qu'il revêt ici – c'est à dire linéaire, inscrit dans un cercle, et avec la base des quatre triangles concave – il est sans parallèle exact. Toutefois, si on l'analyse, il rappelle le motif bien connu des deux paires de lignes parallèles se coupant à angle droit ou obliquement et qui, selon le traitement décoratif des quatre triangles ainsi formés (remplissage à la peinture, hachures ou autre), donne plusieurs variantes, inscrites dans un cercle ou dans un carré.

Dès le Protogéométrique, ce motif apparaît sur un vase de Marmariani en Thesssalie, hachuré, inscrit dans le tondo d'une coupe peinte[117], mais aussi à Cnossos[118] et à Fortetsa[119]. A Chypre il se rencontre dès le Chypro-Géométrique I, linéaire, non inscrit, répété trois fois sur une amphore cylindrique en White Painted I[120], (fig. 25, n° 2) ainsi qu'au Chypro-Géométrique I et II, inscrit dans le médaillon d'un grand nombre de pinakes provenant de tombes[121]. Dans une autre variante linéaire, il se trouve également ici-même, à une date ultérieure, sur un vase du Chypro-Géométrique III[122] (fig. 25, n° 1).

Ce motif quelque peu énigmatique, qui apparaît sur les vases primitifs de Macédoine et de Thessalie[123], se rencontre également dans les Balkans, dès le début de l'âge du fer, non seulement sur la céramique[125] (fig. 25, no. 3), mais aussi sur des casques métalliques[125], (fig. 25, no. 4).

Anne Roes, qui a étudié le symbolisme et la provenance des motifs de l'art Géométrique, rattache cet ornement en forme de croix de Malte à une tradition proto-élamite[126].

A Rhodes on le trouve, peint sur le médaillon d'un flacon de type chypriote trouvé à Massari et daté du Géométrique Moyen[127] et sur plusieurs autres exemples, contemporains ou plus tardifs provenant de Camiros, de Lindos et d'Exochi[128].

A Cos cet ornement se trouve également, peint[129] ou incisé[130] (fig. 25, no. 5) sur des vases du type de flacon. C'est pourquoi nous avons proposé d'attribuer à ce type de vase le fragment d'Astypalée qui porte ce décor[131].

A Chios (Emporio), ce motif est également très fréquent au Géométrique Récent. Il décore généralement, dans une métope située près des anses, la zone de la panse des cratères ou des oenochoés. Le plus souvent ses branches sont asymétriques[132].

Mais les parallèles les plus proches du motif *tel qu'il se présente sur notre fragment* sont fournis d'une part par une amphore de Théra[133] (fig. 25, n° 6) assignée à l'époque géométrico-orientalisante, du style dit «linéaire insulaire»[134], daté du premier quart du VII. s. av. J.-C., d'autre part par une oenochoé à panse conique (fig. 25, no. 7), trouvée dans les fouilles d'Aétos à Itaque[135] et que son profil[135a] invite à placer au cours de la première moitié du même siècle, enfin par deux fragments de vases du même site, datés de l'époque subgéométrique[136].

C'est le même motif vraissemblablement qui, schématisé, aboutira à l'époque archaïque, à l'ornement de remplissage reproduit inlassablement sur les vases de Fikellura et les plats de Nissyros et de Rhodes[137].

Conclusion

La céramique incisée se rencontre à toutes les époques, dans presque toutes les régions, et cela dès l'époque préhistorique, car c'est une technique souvent plus facile à pratiquer dans un petit atelier local que celle de la céramique peinte[138].

La céramique incisée d'Astypalée, malgré certaines ressemblances avec celle d'Attique, de Cos et de Rhodes, possède, semble-t-il, un caractère bien particulier qui pourrait être interpreté comme le signe d'une production locale. Cette impression tendrait à se confirmer grâce à l'existence d'un autre vase incisé, découvert aussi à Astypalée dans une tombe de Vathy, dans la partie Nord de l'île[139] (fig. 1, no. 5). Il s'agit d'une petite pyxide à couvercle décorée de cercles concentriques; son profil concave, qui évoque celui des vases corinthiens, invite à la dater, au plus tôt vers le milieu du VIIe siècle av. J.-C.[140].

C'est, en première approximation, la datation qu'il convient d'assigner aux vases de Chôra. La panse peu profonde des trois petites phiales, qui rappelle celle des petits bols chypriotes en bronze, géométrico-archaïques, déposés par paire dans les tombes, les deux phiales à omphalos conique dont le type, apparu à Cos dès le Protogéométrique, n'est vraiment courant à Rhodes, à Samos et à Lesbos qu'au VIIe-VIe siècle av. J.-C., les motifs décoratifs, qui appartiennent au répertoire du Géométrique Récent/Subgéométrique et dont l'un a même des chances de descendre plus bas, – tous ces éléments nous amènent à dater les vases incisés d'Astypalée du premier quart jusque vers le milieu du VII siècle. De cette époque, à peu près, ou peut-être d'un peu plus tard, peuvent être datés aussi les deux petits vases sans décor, l'oenochoé no. 7 de profil élancé et le lécythe aryballisque no. 8[141].

Le fait qu'à Rhodes le Géométrique Récent s'arrête en 680[142] n'empêche pas que cette tradition décorative demeure vivante jusqu'au milieu ou, même jusqu'à la fin du siècle[143].

Ainsi pour les vases d'Astypalée, si la petite pyxide de Vathy, qui présent un profil plus récent est issue du même atelier que les exemplaires de Chôra, cela confirmerait une datation assez basse pour cet atelier, qui pourrait même déscendre jusqu'à la fin du siècle.

Les ressemblances observées, dans la forme des vases comme dans leur décor, avec d'autres régions – d'Ithaque à Chypre, en passant par Chios, Théra et la Crète – témoignent de contacts commerciaux et artistiques étroits. Elles confirment à noveau des relations avec l'Orient[144] et posent encore une fois le problème de l'origine de l'art géométrique que nous avons rencontré ici avec l'apparition du motif no. 8 dans l'art de la région des Balkans[145].

La petite île d'Astypalée qui, à l'époque classique comme plus tard à l'époque médiévale, contrôlait un carrefour de voies maritimes[146], etait peut-être déjà, à cette époque, un relais important[147].

Des conclusions intéressantes sur les coutumes funéraires peuvent être également tirées des rapprochements évoqués. Ainsi, par exemple, se trouve désormais attestée, à Astypalée la pratique - illustrée jusqu'à présent au Céramique et à l'Agora d'Athènes, à Cos, à Rhodes et aileurs – qui consiste à déposer des petits vases incisés dans les tombes à crémation. La trouvaille d'Astypalée ne permet pas de vérifier si, comme on le prétend[148], ces vases accompagnaient les sépultures enfantines ou féminines. Mais la disposition des vases, emboîtés l'un dans l'autre, qui est celle que l'on trouve ici, semble être une pratique funéraire assez courante à l'époque géométrique, en Grèce[149] mais aussi à Chypre[150] où elle pourrait bien avoir une origine ancienne[151].

La trouvaille d'Astypalée montre enfin que, l'habitude de placer des petits vases incisés dans les tombes a survécu, dans cette île, bien après le Géométrique Moyen I. L'hypothèse de Smithson, selon laquelle les bols incisés furent alors remplacés, dans le mobilier funéraire, par les "red cross-bowls"[152], reposait sans doute, sur le fait qu'on n'avait jusqu'alors trouvé aucun exemplaire incisé dans des tombes postérieures. Il est intéressant de noter qu'à Rhodes, à l'époque où, dans certaines tombes de Ialysos, sont déposées des phiales incisées, dans d'autres tombes nous trouvons la forme évoluée des "red-cross bowls" qui maintenant sont faits au tour[153].

Catalogue

1. (π 8576) Petite phiale très peu profonde.

H. 1,8 cm. Diam. lèvre 10,5 cm. Diam. fond 3/3,2 cm.

Argile grise à coeur plus clair, sous-cuite mais brûlée. Vase tourné, surface d'aspect irrégulier. Recollé à partir de 35 petits fragments, profil complet.

Vasque très ouverte à parois convexes et fond aplati. Lèvre coupée obliquement vers l'extérieur. Un trou de suspension sous la lèvre. Décoration incisée sur la face intérieure: un médaillon central avec svastika vers la gauche, à partir duquel rayonnent trois groupes de quatre zig-zags alternant avec trois "triglyphes" hachurés.

2. (π 8577) Petite phiale très peu profonde.

H. 1,8/2 cm. Diam. lèvre 9,4 cm.

Argile gris-brun, brun-jaune par endroit. Vase tourné, surface lissée. Recollé à partir de six fragments, profil complet. Semblable au précédent mais avec fond arrondi. Trou de suspension près de la lèvre. Décor incisé sur la face intérieure identique au précédent.

3. (π 8578) Petite phiale fragmentaire identique aux deux précédentes.

H. conservée 1,5 cm. Diam. lèvre 12,4 cm.

Argile grise. Traces de couverte noire à l'intérieur. Recollé, profil incomplet (manquent le fond et une partie de la vasque). Trou de suspension sous la lèvre. Face intérieure incisée: trois "triglyphes" hachurés alternant avec trois groupes de quatre zig-zags.

4. (π 8579) Petite phiale à omphalos peu profonde.

H. 3 cm. Diam. lèvre 10,1 cm. Diam. cavité omphalos 1,4 cm. H. omphalos 1 cm.

Argile gris foncé. Traces de tour à l'intérieur. Recollé à partir de plusieurs petits fragments, profil complet.

Vasque ouverte à parois convexes. Omphalos conique avec dépression concave à l'extérieur. Décoration incisée sur la face extérieure: bande avec zig-zag formant un motif en étoile à 13 branches autour de l'omphalos. Quatre triangles pointe en bas, en disposition rayonnante, sur la vasque; les côtés de trois d'entre eux sont bordés d'une double bande hachurée, ceux du quatrième d'une triple bande hachurée. Une bande ornée d'un zig-zag cercle la lèvre, répondant à celle qui entoure l'omphalos.

5. (π 8580) Petite phiale à omphalos fragmentaire.

H. 2,5 cm. Diam. lèvre ± 9,6 cm. Diam. cavité omphalos 2 cm. H. omphalos 1,2 cm.

Argile brunâtre. Surface gris foncé avec traces de couverte noire sur la face externe. Sont conservés le fond (avec l'omphalos) et une partie de la panse. Cinq fragments recollés, profil complet.

Vasque à parois convexes de même profil que la précédente. Omphalos conique avec dépression concave à l'extérieur. Décor incisé sur la face extérieure: étoile à onze branches – chacune hachurée de deux petits traits – autour de l'omphalos; quatre métopes rayonnantes sur la vasque (une bande verticale de chevrons bordée de part et d'autre d'une double bande hachurée obliquement); une bande avec zig-zag au-dessous de la lèvre.

6. (π 8581) Fragment de petit vase fermé à panse convexe.

H. conservée 2,5 cm. Diam. conservé 6,4 cm.

Argile brun foncé. Surface flammée (brun à gris-noir) par l'incinération. Face intérieure irrégulière avec traces de tournage. Face extérieure décorée d'un motif incisé: à l'intérieur de trois cercles concentriques, une sorte de croix de Malte dont le centre est constitué par un losange et les branches par quatre triangles isocèles à base incurvée partant des quatres sommets du losange.

7. (π 8582) Petite oenochoé à bec trilobé.

H. 14,5 cm. Diam. max. 7,3 cm. Diam. base 3,3 cm. Diam. min. col. 2,2 cm.

Argile brun clair. Surface flammée (gris/brun-jaune clair) par l'incinération. Vase presque complet (manquent une partie de la lèvre, de la base et de la panse), recollé à partir de nombreux petits fragments.

Base annulaire conique avec fond renflé, panse ovoïde, col haut et étroit à embouchure trilobée, anse en ruban légèrement surélevée de la lèvre à l'épaule. Sans décor.

8. (π 8583) Petit vase fermé à col (lécythe aryballisque?).

H. conservée 10 cm. Diam. max. 8,5 cm. Diam. base 3,6 cm. Diam. col. 1,9 cm.

Argile gris-brun, surface de même couleur. Fragmentaire (manquent l'embouchure, une partie du col et un côté de la panse), recollé.

Base plate légèrement concave, panse piriforme presque biconique, col étroit. Trace d'attache d'anse verticale sur l'épaule. Sans décor.

Maria Michalaki-Kollia
Ministry of Culture and Science
Archaeological Institute of the Dodecanese
Rhodes
Greece

* Je remercie Nota Kourou, Angéliki Lebessi et Eos Zervoudaki pour leur aide et leurs intéressantes observations. Ce texte pourtant, n'aurait jamais pu aboutir sans la contribution essentielle et amicale de Odile Didelot, de Martin Kreeb et surtout de Gilles Touchais. J'exprime à tous trois ma plus sincère gratitude.

1. Pour Astypalée voir: E. Oberhummer, RE II 2, 1896, 1873-5 avec bibliographie; R.M. Dawkins – A.J.B. Wace, BSA 12, 1905-6, 151 avec bibliographie; R. Hope Simpson – J.F. Lazenby, BSA 68, 1973, 157, avec bibliographie; E. Zervoudaki, ADelt 26, 1971, Chron. B'2, 549, avec bibliographie; E. Zervoudaki, ADelt 27, 1972, Chron. B'2, 676-7; Chr. Doumas, ADelt 20, 1975, Chron. B'2, 372; art. "Astypalaia (Chora)" dans The Princeton Encyclopedia of Classical Sites, 1976, 105-6, avec bibliographie (G. Korres).
2. R.M. Dawkins – A.J.B. Wace, BSA 12, 1905-6, 152; R. Hope Simpson – J.F. Lazenby, BSA 68, 1973, 159; The Princeton Encyclopedia of Classical Sites, 1976, 105.
3. G. Gerola, ASAtene 2, 1916, 71-73, fig. 60-61.
4. Les sources écrites nous apprennent que l'île a d'abord été habitée par les Cariens, puis conquise par Minos (Ovid. Met. VII 461-2); qu'à l'époque historique elle fut colonisée par les Mégariens et par les Doriens d'Argos; qu'à l'époque Classique elle joua un rôle important dans le bassin égéen et qu'elle possédait un Prytanée, une Agora, un Théâtre ainsi que des Sanctuaires d'Athéna et d'Asklépios, d'Apollon et d'Artémis. Pour d'autres informations historiques et pour les références concernant les inscriptions, voir les articles déja cités dans RE, BSA 1973 et The Princeton Encyclopedia of Classical Sites.
5. Des fouilles ont été menées en deux endroits seulement de l'île: a) à Arménochori (fig. 1, no. 3), à l'intérieur des terres, où l'on a trouvé deux tombes mycéniennes richement dotées; b) à Synkairo (fig. 1, no. 4), sur la côte N.O. de l'Isthme, où l'on a mis au jour deux autres tombes mycéniennes.
6. R.M. Dawkins – A.J.B. Wace, BSA 12, 1905-06, 154.
7. R. Hope Simpson – J.F. Lazenby, BSA 68, 1973, 159, 160 et 169 pour les tessons.
8. E. Zervoudaki, ADelt 27, 1972, Chron. B'2, 676 et suiv. pl. 631, 632.
9. E. Zervoudaki, ADelt. 27, 1972, Chron. B'2, 677.
10. A 1.20 m. au-dessus du niveau de la route. D'après les informations du gardien des antiquités N. Manolakis, qui a attiré mon attention sur cet endroit, toute cette zone a été perturbée il y a quelques années, lors de l'élargissement de la route et les tessons sont apparus à la surface sous l'effet du ruissellement.
11. 0.90 m. de long, sur 0.30 m. de large et à peu près 0.30 m. de profondeur au centre.
12. Il semble que l'une au moins des tombes classiques, qui se trouvaient à proximité, était aussi une tombe à crémation. Voir E. Zervoudaki, ADelt 27, 1972, Chron. B'2, 676.
13. Voir plus haut et note 9.
14. C'est, une fois de plus, lors du percement d'une voie privée sur la colline qu'ont été découvertes et détruites deux nouvelles tombes à crémation taillées dans le rocher, non loin de la tombe fouillée en 1981. On a également mis au jour la partie inférieure d'une tombe, rectangulaire, dont la couche d'incinération contenait des vases peints du Géométrique Récent.
15. Voir plus haut et note 7.
16. Les restaurateurs Antonis Gatsaras et Manolis Vassilaras ont mené à bien le travail délicat du recollage des vases. Cathérina Kokonou a exécuté les dessins (profils et décor). Je les remercie tous trois chaleureusement.
17. Ou "sauvastika" appellée ainsi lorsque les branches sont tournées vers la gauche, variante qui est d'ailleurs plus fréquente. Voir Courbin 1966, 380; voir aussi Schliemann 1880, 345 et suiv., où est établie la distinction entre les deux variantes et où sont indiquées l'origine et l'étymologie de ces mots.
18. Les vases de cette forme, en céramique ou en bronze, sont généralement percés d'un ou deux trous de suspension. Cf. J. Bouzek, SborPraha 1, 1974, 11, note 34 et 44-45 note 125.
19. Le fragment évoque les aryballes corinthiens avec motif floral sur le fond. Voir aussi le petit flacon dans Brock 1957, 96, no. 1051, pl. 71: "Fabrique des aryballes gréco-chypriotes", daté de l'époque orientalisante.
20. A rapprocher des vases chypriotes: Deshayes 1963, pl. 56,9 (daté du Chypro-Géométrique III), p. 117 (daté du Chypro-Géométrique II). Voir aussi L. Morricone, ASAtene 56, 1978, 265, fig. 551, 552 et p. 377, fig. 823.
21. Précisons que la cassure coïncide avec un quatrième cercle incisé qui entourait la panse du vase. C'est pourquoi elle est rectiligne.
22. Pour le terme de "phiale", voir la signification chez Homère déjà, qui d'après Liddell – Scott, serait un "flat bowl or saucer for drinking or pouring libations". Voir aussi la monographie de Luschey 1939, intéressante mais dépassée en ce qui concerne certaines chronologies; Sparkes – Talcott 1970, 105 avec bibliographie; la bibliographie plus récente donnée par M. Tiverios, dans: Sindos, Catalogue de l'exposition, 1985, 167 (en grec).
23. La plupart du temps nous renverrons à des prototypes en bronze, car ils sont plus nombreux que les exemplaires en céramique et ils ont été plus étudiés. Nous nous référerons aux études de Catling 1964, Gershuny 1985, P.H.G. Howes Smith, IrAnt 21, 1986, 1-88 et Matthäus 1985.
24. Coldstream 1977, 32, fig. 4a. Voir aussi Kübler 1943, pl. 38, et Kübler 1954, pl. 163.
25. Coldstream 1977, 58-59, où il est mentionné comme couvercle d'amphores cinéraires pour hommes.
26. Catling 1964, 147-148, provenant d'Enkomi, de Kouklia et de Kition; reférences aux notes 2-8.
27. Catling 1964, 148, provenant d'Amathonte, de Polis, de Lapithos et de Kastros, voir notes 9-12. Cf. E. Gjerstad, SCE IV 2, 1948, 151, fig. 28, types de bols 1a, 2a.
28. SCE II 1, 1935, pl. XI 1, de la tombe 7 d'Amathonte; pl. XXIII 1, de la tombe 15 d'Amathonte.
29. Catling 1964, 148 et note 8.
30. Frödin – Persson 1938, 427, fig. 275, non tourné; autre exemple p. 430, fig. 282. Voir aussi J. Bouzek, OpAth 9, 1969, 53, fig. 7 B 1; Kübler 1943, 23 no. 1092, à propos duquel Blegen (dans Hesperia 21, 1952, 287) pense qu'il est fait sur le prototype du bol en bronze M 1 dans Kübler 1943, pl. 38.
31. Kübler 1943, pl. 29 et 30.
32. H.A. Thompson, Hesperia 21, 1952, 108 pl. 27 c; D. Burr, Hesperia 2, 1933, 564-6, fig. 24-25. Voir aussi E. Lord Smithson, Hesperia 37, 1968, 108, pl. 30, nos. 54-5.
33. E. Lord Smithson, Hesperia 30, 1961, 171; J. Bouzek, SborPraha 1, 1974, 1 et suiv. C'est l'article le plus complet sur la céramique incisée trouvée jusqu'alors, avec toute la bibliographie antérieure.
34. Kübler 1943, pl. 29 et 30. Pour des ressemblances avec la céramique d'autres régions voir E. Lord Smithson,

Hesperia 30, 1961, 171 note 19 et J. Bouzek, SborPraha 1, 1974, 1 n. 4 et p. 2.

35. Il existe un très petit vase appelé "saucer" (D. 52 cm) avec un décor estampé à l'intérieur: une croix composée de petits cercles. Il provient du dépôt près du Sanctuaire d'Héra Liménia à Pérachora. Voir Dunbabin (ed.) 1962, 299, no. 3006, pl. 127.
36. G. Jacopi, ClRh 3, 1929, 102, no. 21, fig. 93.
37. J. Papapostoulou, ADelt 23, 1968, Mel. A', 92, pl. 43c., où il est considéré comme un exemplaire de céramique bucchero.
38. Payne et al. 1940, 159, pl. 62,3. Il est mentionné comme couvercle de pyxide (D. 16 cm); il a été trouvé dans le dépôt d'Héra Liménia, dans un contexte du 8e-5e s. av. J.-C. Voir aussi P.H.G. Howes Smith, IrAnt 21, 1986, 18, note 70.
39. Sur deux phiales le fond est conservé: la base de l'une est arrondie, celle de l'autre est un peu aplatie.
40. Matthäus 1985, 105, no. 302, pl. 17 (H. 17 cm., D. 12 cm.). Daté du Chypro-Archaïque I, ± 725-625 av. J.-C.
41. Matthäus 1985, 106.
42. Matthäus 1985, 287, variante B, pl. 86, no. 633-642. Ils on été trouvés par paire dans des tombes à Idalion, à Salamis, ainsi que trois paires trouvées dans une tombe de la région de Kapsalos de Limassol. Cf. note 149.
43. Catling 1964, 148, fig. 17, no. 7: celui de Kourion H. 24 cm., D. 13 cm., celui d'Enkomi D. 75 cm., trouvé dans un contexte du Chypriote-Récent III.
44. Gershuny 1985, 14 no. 105, pl. 9 (H. 22 cm., D. 99 cm.), et p. 39.
45. Gershuny 1985, 14, no. 104, pl. 9, et p. 39.
46. Gershuny 1985, 39, 56.
47. Radwan 1983, pl. 1, no. 1, 2, 3, 16A, 16B; voir aussi pl. 47, 48.
48. P.H.G. Howes Smith, IrAnt 21, 1986, 6, 17, 18. Cf. tableau des formes, 19, fig. 1.
49. P.H.G. Howes Smith, IrAnt 21, 1986, tableau des formes, p. 33, fig. 2f; type IE: p. 37-38, à propos de l'omphalos.
50. Luschey 1939, 35.
51. Luschey 1939, fig. 8.
52. Davidson 1952, 68-70, fig. 1, 517.
53. C. Blegen, Hesperia 21, 1952, 287-288, fig. 4, pl. 77b. Jusqu'alors on ne connaissait que deux autres exemples du même type, mais mal datés: la phiale de Delphes, Demangel 1926, 46, pl. 56, et la phiale de Pérachora, Payne et al. 1940, pl. 55,1. Voir les anciennes théories concernant les phiales à omphalos conique, selon l'ordre de parution: Luschey 1939, 35-38; E. Hall Dohan, Compte-rendu de l'étude de Luschey, AJA 45, 1941, 125-127; Dunbabin in Payne et al. 1940, 148-156; Davidson 1952, 68-70; C. Blegen, Hesperia 21, 1952, 287-8.
54. Ph. Petsas, ADelt 26, 1971, Chron. B'1, 186, pl. 166c.
55. P.H.G. Howes Smith, IrAnt 21, 1986, 80-81.
56. Gershuny 1985, 4-5, pl. 3, nos. 29-36; pl. 9, no. 108.
57. Gershuny 1985, pl. 3, no. 34-5.
58. Radwan 1983, pl. 49-50, nos. 262-268; pl. 54, nos. 304-306; pl. 60-61, nos. 333-4, 336.
59. Karageorghis 1974, pl. 165, 20.
60. Gershuny 1985, 5.
61. Matthäus 1985, 137-139: no. 377, pl. 28, de la tombe 7 d'Amathonte, daté du Chypro-Géométrique III au Chypro-Archaïque I, (ici fig. 20, no. 9); no. 378 de Kouklia; no. 379, pl. 28, de la tombe 403 de Kastros à Lapithos, daté du Chypro-Géométrique III, (ici fig. 20, no. 10). Il existe aussi un "bol" plus profond, à omphalos conique, daté du Chypro-Géométrique III, cf. Matthäus 1985, 147, no. 403, pl. 30, (ici fig. 20, no. 11).
62. SCE II, 1935, 26 no. 37, pl. VIII 1, de la tombe 5 d'Amathonte; profil du même vase SCE IV 2, 1948, fig. 28, 3, type 2b, qui, d'après le tableau des formes de P.H.G. Howes Smith, IrAnt 21, 1986, 33, il pourrait être classé au type "Palestinien" 1D.
63. Tufnell 1958, pl. 72, 625.
64. Amiran 1970, 42, ph. 22. Il s'agit de petites phiales en céramique, à omphalos conique, datées du début de l'âge du Bronze. Nous mentionnons ces exemples seulement pour l'histoire de la forme de ce vase, sans prétendre à des influences dès cette époque. (Voir aussi P.H.G. Howes Smith, IrAnt 21, 1986, 80 et note 213). Il faut seulement émettre l'hypothèse – si en effet ces exemples céramiques se datent si haut – que ces formes céramiques pourraient avoir été à l'origine des prototypes de bols en bronze de cette même forme, contrairement à ce qu'on croit communément. C'est un problème qui serait à étudier.
65. Matthäus 1980, 227-235, nos. 349, 351 et 350, provenant de tombes: les deux premiers de Phaires en Achaïe, le troisième de Mycènes, cf. pl. 41 et 42.
66. Cf. note 53.
67. Cf. note 54.
68. L. Morricone, ASAtene 56, 1978, 87, fig. 82 et 83; 88 fig. 84 et 85, provenant de la tombe 10 à Serrallia. Cf. Desborough 1972, 175-6.
69. Cf. plus haut et note 61.
70. Kübler 1943, pl. 30c, no. 8; cf. Bouzek, SborPraha 1, 1974, 24, pl. VII 8.
71. Young 1981, 206, fig. 124, pl. 90E.
72. Popham et al. 1979-1980, 185-186, pl. 186, no. 31, 20 et pl. 243, e.
73. M. Tsipopoulou, dans: Actes du 5e Congrès des Études Crétoises, 1981, (1986), 373 et suiv., pl. PZ' et PIΓ', 1; cf. M. Tsipopoulou – L. Godart – J.-P. Olivier, SMEA 23, 1982, 61 et suiv.
74. Par sa forme, il entre dans la catégorie I c – II de P.H.G. Howes Smith, IrAnt 21, 1986, 33, de type "palestinien". Il peut être comparé à des phiales provenant du Proche-Orient qui présentent un profil et un omphalos conique semblables (cf. Gershuny 1985, pl. 3, no. 30). (ici fig. 20, no. 7).
75. Luschey 1939, 35.
76. P.H.G. Howes Smith, IrAnt 21, 1986, 80-81, avec un esprit différent.
77. G. Jacopi, ClRh 6-7, 1932-33, 104, fig. 116. Provenant de la tombe 30 à Kechraki, il a été trouvé avec des vases du type Fikellura. Daté du dernier quart du 7e s. av. J.-C. (H. 45 cm., D. 14 cm.).
78. Kinch 1914, 86, no. 9, provenant de la tombe 31 (H. 34 cm., D. 11,9 cm). Selon Dunbabin (Dunbabin (ed.) 1962, 80, note 4), ce vase est corinthien et doit dater, d'après le contexte, de la seconde moitié du 7e s.
79. D'après la référence de Kinch, p. 86: "Coupe à libation assez semblable, à Géla, tombe 49", avec indication bibliographique.
80. Voir note 68 (ici fig. 21 a, b).
81. H. Walter,.AM 72, 1957, 35 et suiv., pl. 71, nos. 1 et 2, datés du 7e et du 6e s. av J.-C.
82. W. Lamb, BSA 32, 1931-32, 41 et suiv.: a) 52-54, pl. 21, no. 6, daté fin de l'époque géométrique / début de l'époque archaïque. b) 63, pl. 21, no. 11, trouvé dans un contexte Protocorinthien, associé à des "bucchero cups".

83. Cette forme en bronze, on la trouve aussi en Asie Mineure: mis à part l'exemple de Gordion, déjà cité, et un autre de forme plus profonde (cf. Matthäus 1985, pl. 131,1), ils existent encore deux petites phiales très plates avec un petit omphalos conique qui se trouvent toutes deux au Musée de Philadelphie (cf. Matthäus 1985, 147, note 5).
84. Kübler 1943, pl 29 et 30 a, b. J. Bouzek, SborPraha 1, 1974, 11-14 et 18-20.
85. H.A. Thompson, Hesperia 21, 1952, pl. 27c.
86. Kübler 1943, pl. 30c (Nous énumérons les tessons représentés ici de 1 à 10, de haut en bas et de gauche à droite). E. Lord Smithson, Hesperia 37, 1968, pl. 30, 54 et 55, à propos des exemples de l'Agora.
87. Voir note précédente.
88. Voir note 86.
89. E. Lord Smithson, Hesperia 37, 1968, 104; J. Bouzek, SborPraha 1, 1974, 20-25.
90. Voir note 86.
91. Voir note 86.
92. Ces derniers existent aussi sur le fragment no. 55 de l'Agora et manquent également sur la phiale no. 4 d'Astypalée.
93. On sait depuis longtemps que les petits vases incisés (à l'époque préhistorique et Protogéométrique souvent non tournés mais modelés à la main), étaient généralement placés dans les tombes à crémations et que certaines formes de vases (p. ex. phiales, aryballes sans décor ni vernis etc.) étaient consacrées à des rites funéraires précis en rapport avec le sexe, l'âge, etc. Sur ce sujet, il y a une vaste bibliographie dont voici quelques références: A. Skias, AEphem 1898, 99-101; E. Lord Smithson, Hesperia 30, 1961, 170-171 et note 17 et 19; E. Lord Smithson, Hesperia 37, 1968, 42, 46 et 48; J.F. Daniel, AJA 41, 1937, 74-5.
94. Voir note 68.
95. A propos des bols incisés attiques on a fait références à des théories qui y voient des influences venues du Nord (cf. J. Bouzek, SborPraha 1, 1974, 1 note 4, et p. 48). Pour les bols de Cos, par contre, il semble qu'il y a plutôt une influence venue d'Orient. Nous avons déjà mentionné la relation de l'omphalos conique avec la Syrie du Nord. En ce qui concerne la décoration, il pourrait y avoir une influence de la Phénicie (cf. Coldstream 1977, 68) ou plus généralement de l'Orient et de Chypre.
96. En Attique, sur toute la surface du corps d'un petit vase peint (Coldstream 1977, 62, fig. 17, F); ainsi que sur les fragments des bols incisés K5 et K7 du Céramique (Kübler 1943, pl. 30c) (ici fig. 24). A Corinthe, motif très fréquent (Coldstream 1977, 84 et fig. 26, h.).
97. D'Attique (Coldstream 1968, pl. 10, j; 12, e; 15, b); d'Argos avec des chevrons ouverts vers le haut (Coldstream 1968, pl. 28, d; 30, c), ou bien vers le bas (Coldstream 1968, pl. 31, d); de Rhodes, de la tombe 2 de Kechraki, ClRh 4, 1931, 342 et fig. 380); sur le grand cratère du British Museum, Friis Johansen 1958, 103, fig. 203, ou Walter 1968, pl. 51; très courant sur les anses (Friis Johansen 1958, 52, fig. 109) et sur deux oinochoés (Friis Johansen 1958, 63, fig. 129; 65, fig. 132).
98. Coldstream 1977, 201-202.
99. J. Papapostolou, ADelt 23, 1968, Mel.A´, pl. 41b etc; ils appartiennent à une catégorie spéciale de vases de la phase subgéométrique du style Rhodien (J. Papapostolou, ADelt 23, 1968, 86).
100. ClRh 4, 1931, 274, fig. 301.
101. Il s'agit surtout de petits aryballes: cf. ClRh 3, 1929, 46, fig. 32, de Ialysos; 89, fig. 79, de Ialysos également; aussi le petit aryballe no. 10885 qui se trouve dans les réserves du Musée de Rhodes.
102. Coldstream 1968, pl. 27a; 30c.
103. Coldstream 1968, pl. 45a-b; Coldstream 1977, fig. 65a, c et e.
104. Boardman 1967, pl. 22 nos. 39, 41, 42; pl. 23 no. 47.
105. La petite phiale de Pérachora, citée note 35, porte une décoration estampée. Avec décor peint, il existe une série de petites phiales, non tournées, décorées de deux séries de quatre lignes en forme de croix: Voir Waldstein 1905, 96, fig. 32a (où il est appelé mycénien); Frickenhaus 1912, 99, fig. 31; Ch. Dugas, BCH 45, 1921, 420, fig. 61, no. 241; Luschey 1939, fig. 8 (ici fig. 20, 4); cf. Bouzek, SborPraha 1, 1974, 45 note 126, 46 note 134. Selon Smithson, ces petits vases ont remplacé, après le Géométrique Moyen I, les bols incisés faits à la main (Hesperia 37, 1968, 103).
106. Voir note 36 et 37.
107. ClRh 3, 1929, 89 fig. 79, 90 fig. 80, provenant d'une tombe à crémation de Ialysos.
108. Cf. E. Lord Smithson, Hesperia 30, 1961, 171 note 19; J. Bouzek, SborPraha 1, 1974, 10 et note 33.
109. Cf. note 17. Voir aussi Courbin 1966, 149 pour des notes stylistiques; 476 pour le symbolisme. Pour d'autres théories, cf. Walters 1905, 214.
110. Sur les fibules, on la voit souvent dans un cercle: p.ex. Ch. Dugas, BCH 45, 1921, 384, fig. 45. En ce qui concerne les exemplaires à décor peint, M. Courbin (avec qui l'ai eu la chance de discuter, quand ce travail prenait fin), m'a montré un exemple de petite svastika linéaire, encerclée représentée sur le corps d'un petit oiseau qui se trouve sur un fragment de vase provenant de l'Héraion (voir Courbin 1966, pl. 147, no. 6). Mais il s'agit ici d'une svastika utilisée comme motif secondaire et non pas comme élément essentiel du décor.
111. P. Kastriotis – A. Philadelpheus, Prakt 1911, 124, nos. 26 et 28 (p. 126).
112. Young 1939, 199 note 1. D'après l'information qu'a bien voulu me donner l'épimélète Olga Kakavogianni, d'une tombe de Markopoulo, en Attique, provient un petit vase-biberon qui est décoré d'une svastika incisée et qui est probablement sorti du même atelier que les vases incisés d'Anavyssos. (Rapport de fouille à paraître dans les Chroniques de l'ADelt 1983.)
113. Coldstream 1968, pl. 1, k.
114. Coldstream 1977, 115, fig. 34. nos. d,e,f. Bohen 1979, 151-2 et note 18, pl. 17, 20, 22-29, 32.
115. Courbin 1966, 380-1.
116. Walters 1905, 214.
117. W.A. Heurtley – T.C. Skeat, BSA 31, 1930-31, pl. 8, no. 127; cf. le tableau des motifs, p. 45.
118. J.N. Coldstream – P. Callaghan – J.H. Musgrave, BSA 71, 1981, 147, nos. 4, 5, 30; pl. 19, 31; datés du Géométrique Moyen et du Géométrique Récent.
119. Brock 1957, voir l'"analysis of patterns" gao et gar qui se rapprochent le plus de notre motif et qui sont datés du Protogéométrique B et du Géométrique Récent.
120. SCE IV 2, 1948, fig. III, 2a (à comparer avec les motifs autour du médaillon du plat no. 26 de la tombe 19 d'Amathonte, SCE II 1, 1935, pl. 25,1).
121. SCE IV 2, fig. XII 3; SCE II 1, pl. 9, plat de la tombe 7 d'Amathonte; cf. SCE I, pl. 46, de la tombe 408 de Lapithos; Karageorghis 1974, pl. 98, nos. 22, 24 et 17-19. (Le motif se trouve sur la base des plats que se soit dans un cercle ou dans un carré).

122. SCE IV, fig. XVIII, 8.
123. W.A. Heurtley, BSA 28, 1926-27, 176, fig. 24.
124. Jevtic 1983, pl. V 8, XXIII 6, XXIX 4, XXXVII 8, ce dernier porte le motif sur la base du vase. (ici fig. 25, no. 3).
125. Garasanin 1954, pl. LXI 1 et 3-8. (ici fig. 25, no. 4 a, b).
126. Roes 1933, 37 fig. 29.
127. CVA Danemark[I] 6, pl. 65,7 (cf. Friis Johansen 1958, 129, fig. 211). Pour ce type de vases voir J. Papapostolou, ADelt 23, 1968, Mel. A´, 81.
128. Avec toutes ses variantes, que se soit en deux lignes parallèles se recoupant dans un cercle, ou dans un carré, cf. ClRh 6-7, 1933, 352, fig. 100: sur deux fragments provenant du bothros de l'Acropole de Kamiros. ClRh 4, 1931, 344, fig. 380: sur une oinochoé de la tombe 2 de Kechraki. Lindos I, nos. 81, 952; 868, 894, 941 et 1859. Friis Johansen 1958, 27, fig. 39; 32, fig. 48, 107, fig. 206. Cf. Kinch 1914, 173, fig. 56.
129. L. Morricone, ASAtene 56, 1978, 377, fig. 823.
130. L. Morricone, ASAtene 56, 1978, 265, fig. 551-2.
131. Comparer aussi à une oenochoé globulaire, non tournée, provenant de Chypre: SCE II 2, pl. CLXIV, 3. Cependant il y a un problème: le fragment du vase 6 qui est convexe et sur lequel se trouve le motif en question, est assez épais vers le centre. De ce fait, peut-il vraiment appartenir à une panse? Ou bien faut-il revenir à l'idée que c'est un aryballe du type corinthien piriforme, ou d'un type chypriote comme par ex. le vase dans SCE IV, fig. III, 16.
132. Boardman 1967, 104, fig. 61 D (cf. p. 106 et 107). Cet ornement appelé "diamond" est plus courant à la période I et II, c.à.d. 690-660 (voir introduction, p. 101). Cf. pl. 19, nos. 6 et 15; pl. 21, nos. 34-37; pl. 25, nos 71a,c; pl. 49, no. 551.
133. Hiller von Gaertringen 1903, fig. 209 et 409 (cf. EAA II, 1959, 588, fig. 802).
134. A. Lebessi, ADelt 22, 1967, Mel. A´, 112 et suiv. N. Zaphiropoulos, ASAtene 61, 1983, 153 et suiv.
135. S. Benton, BSA 48, 1953, 336, fig. 30, no. 1018 (texte 322-323).
135a) Pour l'oenochoé conique voir: CVA Gela[I], 3, pl. 1. Coldstream 1968, 97. Dunbabin (ed.) 1962, 35.
136. M. Robertson, BSA 43, 1948, pl. 34, no. 491a; pl. 35, no. 520 (où le motif en question – 491a – est caracterisé "unusual").
137. ClRh 4, 1931, fig. 391; 371, fig. 417. ClRh 6-7, 1933, 480-481; 489, fig. 16; 509, fig. 36.
138. Pour la céramique incisée, l'article de Bouzek dans SborPraha, 1, 1974, reste le travail le plus complet où se trouvent réunis tous les exemples connus jusqu'alors. Dans notre étude nous nous sommes occupés seulement de documents comparables à notre matériel et non pas des autres types de céramique incisée - par ex. poupées, pyxides, boules, poids, pesons – placés couramment dans les tombes à crémation. Nous ne nous sommes pas non plus occupé de la technique de l'incision du décor car cela nous aurait entraîné trop loin. Ce pourrait être l'objet d'une autre recherche sur l'ensemble de la céramique incisée du Dodécanèse, en effectuant en plus des analyses d'argile.
139. E. Zervoudaki, ADelt 26, 1971, Chron. B´2, 552, pl. 560, d.
140. Le type de pyxide à parois concaves apparait pour la première fois à l'époque protocorinthienne.
141. Des vases analogues sont également traditionnels dans les tombes à crémation (cf. N. Skias, AEphem 1898, 28-122, fig. 21, 23, 25, 26; Weinberg 1943, pl. 2, nos. 16-18). Leur origine est vraisemblablement argienne ou corinthienne (Coldstream 1977, 78). On a aussi dit (E. Lord Smithson, Hesperia 30, 1961, 171 et E. Lord Smithson, Hesperia 37, 1968, 103 note 67) que ces vases, après le Géométrique Moyen II, ont remplacés dans les tombes d'Athènes les pyxides incisées. Pourtant, sur d'autres sites, de petits vases à verser peints, coexistent déjà dès l'époque Protogéométrique (par ex. tombe 10 à Cos, cf. ASAtene 56, 1978, 90) avec des bols incisés, parce que comme les phiales, ce sont des vases indispensables pour les libations au cours des cérémonies funéraires.
142. Coldstream 1977, 249.
143. L'esprit géométrique est présent non seulement sur les vases du type "bird bowl", pendant toute la phase Subgéométrique (Coldstream 1977, 247), ou sur un type de vases décorés de cercles concentriques et de lignes ondulées (J. Papapostolou, ADelt 23, 1968, 87 et note 50), mais il est aussi sensible sur les plus anciens exemples de vases archaïques Rhodiens (ClRh 4, 1931, 57, fig. 28).
144. Coldstream 1977, 249.
145. Il est intéressant de noter l'apparition du motif no. 8 en Italie aussi (cf. Mayer 1914, pl. 18, no. 11; 21, no. 4a; 23, nos. 8 a et 14) qui y arrive peut-être par la voie des Balkans.
146. R. Hope Simpson – J.F. Lazenby, BSA 68, 1973, 157. Cf. G. Susini, ASAtene 41-2, 1963-64, 228, fig. 28, la carte des voies maritimes.
147. Même la petite île de Syrna (cf. A. della Seta, BdA 4, 1924-25, 87-8) à quelques milles de distance au Sud d'Astypalée, perdue dans la mer et aujourd'hui désertée, porte les ruines d'une tour ou d'un phare (phrykroria) d'époque classique, et elle est jonchée de fragments d'obsidienne.
148. E. Lord Smithson, Hesperia 30, 1961, 171, et E. Lord Smithson, Hesperia 37, 1968, 103 note 66. J. Bouzek, Sbor Praha, 1, 1974, 48.
149. Pour l'un des exemples cf. D. Evangélidis, AEphem 1912, 127. Nous avons déjà dit que ces vases étaient disposés par paire dans les tombes; cf. Bouzek, art. cit., 48, voir aussi note 42. Cf. pour l'époque classique, G. Richter, AJA 54, 1950, 357 et note 3.
150. SCE II p. 41, de la tombe 7 d'Amathonte, où le bol en bronze no. 242 était dans le bol en céramique no. 213. Cf. Matthäus 1985, 287 où sont mentionnées une paire de Idalion (633-634), une paire de Salamine (641-642) et trois paires de Limassol (635-640). Cf. Catling 1964, 148, note 8.
151. Radwan 1983, pl. 23, nos. 124 D et 125 A-B.
152. E. Lord Smithson, Hesperia 37, 1968, 103, note 67.
153. ClRh 3, 1929, 49, fig. 39 et ClRh 6-7, 1932-33, 200, fig. 240.

1313a

1313a

Notes on the Rhodian Vases found on the Island of Lemnos[1]

Aglaia Archontidou

The plates numbered 1313a[2] and 1313b[3] in the museum on the North Aegean island of Lemnos were found in 1929 in a deposit in the Tyrenean sanctuary of the Great Goddess at Hephaistia, together with Corinthian, Chian, Attic and local pottery[4].

The plates belong to well known Rhodian types of footless ware with wide ring base and flat horizontal lip[5]. The type of decoration on plate number 1313a – a meander pattern on the lip and a garland of lotus flowers and buds inside arranged around a central star-shaped emblem – is already known from plates found at Vroulia in Rhodes, as well as on plate lids and crater rims from Naucratis[6].

The type of lotus flower depicted on the Hephaistia plate number 1313a has its prototype in the Vrouli and Fikellura[7] style, in which ornament appears compact and the decorative scheme better organized. On later ware, the flower loses its shape and appears broken up; its heart assumes the common rhomboid shape, which either breaks up into three parts or is completed by a palmette[8]. The flowers on the Lemnos plate combine the "classical" form of flower with the unenclosed palmette, also a motif associated with Rhodian pottery.

This type of floral ornament is found on an earlier oinochoe[9] and on the lip of a "dinos" from Vrouli[10], as well as on plates from Naucratis[11]. On the Leningrad oinochoe[12], the lotus flower with palmette, in place of the heart, constitutes the main decoration on the vase's shoulder, in conjunction with a motif of "broken meanders".

A checkerboard pattern is also a common decorative device on Rhodian wares, examples of which are found on a "dinos" base, crater base, oinochoae from Vrouli[13], pottery fragments from Miletus[14], from Cyrene[15] and frequently on local Corinthian[16] pottery.

Both the type and the arrangement of decorative designs, such as the meander, the checkerboard pattern, the garland of lotus flowers and buds surrounding a central star-shaped emblem, are common on other Rhodian pottery such as the Vrouli plate[17]. A checkerboard pattern combined on the same vessel with the lotus flower and palmette is encountered on other Rhodian wares, just to mention here the skyphoi found in Cyrene[18].

The type of decoration and arrangement of motifs on plate number 1313b is also found on the Vrouli[19] wares, such as on the lekanis with a centrally placed star. The star's rays have assumed the form of drops, which both Kardara and Kinch identify as lotus buds[20]. This appears to be true also of the rays depicted on the Hephaistia plate.

A lekanis from grave 5 in Vrouli has a more complex design as the rays, in the form of lotus buds, issuing from the center, are denser and more numerous.

On the lekanis from grave 9 at Vrouli the star's rays have a more elongated form and cover the entire surface of the vessel, spreading from the centre towards the circumference.

While the star-shaped emblem of the previous lekanis seems to toss ifself towards the edges, the star's rays on plate number A710 in the British Museum – also in the form of lotus buds[23] - appear as those on the Lemnos plate number 1313b, where larger rays alternate with smaller ones and are enclosed by two bands. The so-called horror vacui is not so obvious in the British Museum plate where there is a sprinkling of filling ornament. This is entirely absent in our Lemnos plate.

Kinch indicates that star rays of this kind are not commonly found on Rhodian vessels[24]; however, we encounter a number of them, for example, around the bases of the Boston

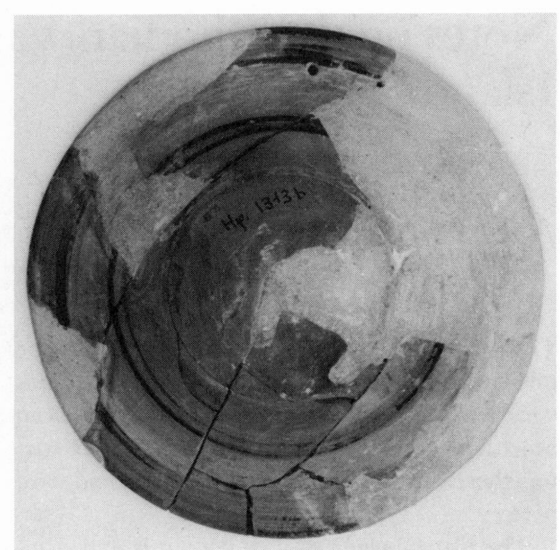

1313b

oinochoe[25] and on the oinochoe of grave 18 from Vrouli, replacing the lotus chains or types depicted on vases of earlier date.

The type of meander on the Lemnos plate is identical to that depicted on the London oinochoe, no. 65-5-8-925 in the Blacas[26] collection, which, according to Kardara, should be classified with the groups of pottery decorated in "shadow and outline" technique (ca. 610-600 BC). The same type of meander is seen on plate rims from Naucratis, which Price identifies as Rhodian[27].

The checkerboard pattern on the Lemnos plate with added white slip is also found on a plate from Naucratis; this type of decoration is commonly associated with Rhodian aryballoi of the "Early Corinthian" type dated ca. 600 BC[28].

A lotus flower combined with an unenclosed palmette (in place of its heart) of the same type as that on the Lemnos plate, is also found on a vessel rim from grave no. 6 at Vrouli. Kinch considers it contemporary to the "dinos" of the "chapel area" at Vrouli and classifies it with the Camiran pottery of the so-called third period, that is, ca. 650-550 BC[29].

It is of interest that on the "dinos" from the "chapel area" is depicted a chain of lotus flowers, the hearts of which form a rhombus broken into three parts[30]. Kardara notes that this motif – of the so-called School of the Parisian dinos – imitates decoration associated with Vroulian pottery. On the evidence of the destruction level of Smyrna, the vessel is dated by Cook ca. 610-600 BC[31].

The type of lotus flower with wide open petals which separate immediately above the stem and the heart-shaped bud with the characteristic central line closely recalls the Louvre oinochoe, dated by Kinch to ca. 600 BC[32]. The broad meander of the "broken meander" is a motif well known in Rhodian vase painting of the 6th century BC[33]. The lotus buds, having assumed the form of a star in the Vrouli example, show rays racing in opposite directions. Kinch classes this piece with polychrome pottery, and Kardara with the group of vessels of mixed technique dating from the end of the 7th century BC. She also places the Louvre oinochoe in this group.

I think that the Lemnos plate is later in date than these specimens, on the grounds that the type of lotus bud is closer to that of the plate from grave 9 at Vroulia. On the other hand, the arrangement of the ornaments, heavy, concentric circles with blank spaces in between, around the centrally placed star, recalls the plate from Vrouli, which has incised rather than heavy painted circles.

Chronologically, I consider the plate in the British Museum from the site of Kalavarda in

Rhodes to be earlier. Kinch classes this specimen with the so-called Camiran ware. Vessels decorated with star-emblem and lotus buds in the position of rays are distinguished by Kardara as ware executed in the "drawing in outline and incision technique". Plate no. 1313a is later in date than the Louvre and Vrouli oinochoe, but slightly earlier than the Leningrad oinochoe. The two Rhodian plates from Lemnos are contemporary and should be dated ca. 600 or 590 BC.

The sanctuary of the Great Goddess at Hephaistia on the island of Lemnos flourished between the middle of the 8th until the end of the 6th century BC, when it was devastated by fire attributed to the invasion of the Persian Satrap of Asia Minor, or the colonisation of Miltiades on Lemnos and the expulsion of the local population to the Chalcidike[33].

The sanctuary's deposit has been dated by Di Vita to between the second half of the 7th century to the end of the 6th century BC. This is of great importance for the history of the sanctuary. The imported pottery is dated to ca 600 to 590 BC.

The fact that only a few Rhodian vessels have, to date, been found on Lemnos, and that these came exclusively from the deposit of the Tyrenean sanctuary at Hephaistia – along with other imported wares – implies that such vessels were probably precious and were purchased strictly for votive purposes.

The scarcity of Rhodian ware on Lemnos, on Lesbos, where a few sherds were found in the ancient city of Antissa, and on Chios, where only a few sherds were found at Emporio, is rather firm evidence of trade rélations and the sea-routes between Rhodes and the North-Eastern Aegean at the end of the 7th and the beginning of the 6th century BC.

Aglaia Archontidou-Argyri
Curator of Antiquities
Mytilene Museum
Eftalioti 1
81100 Mytilene
Greece

1. I would like to thank Dr. Antonino Di Vita and Dr. Luigi Besci for allowing me to study and present here the Rhodian vases from Lemnos.
2. No 1313a Rhodian plate, restored. Flat base with band-shaped ring. Horizontal, flat lip. Clay: brown-reddish without mica. Slip: creamy white. Decoration in dark brown to black glaze. Outside: concentric, heavy circles. Inside: star-shaped emblem surrounded by checkerboard pattern, garland of lotus flowers and buds. Flattened lip: "broken meander" pattern and, on the edge of the lip, hatched lines.
   Dimensions: Height 0.052. Diameter 0.285. Diameter of base 0.097.
3. No 1313b Rhodian plate, restored. Flat base. Horizontal, flat lip. Two suspension holes. Clay: brown-reddish without mica. Decoration: dark brown. Outside: Fine concentric circles. Inside: central star-shaped emblem with rays in the form of lotus buds. Wide brown bands, blank between. On the rim, serpentine lines.
   Dimensions: Height 0.023. Diameter o.155. Diameter of base 0.06.
4. A. della Seta, AEphem 1937, 629-654; A. di Vita, ASAtene 55, 1977, 344-348.
5. Kinch 1914, 212-218, F 105, 106.
6. Kinch 1914, 218, pl. 5,6,8,9; E. Price, JHS 44, 1924, 196, 198, pl. VII, 14, pl. VII, 6; Fairbanks 1928, pl. XXXV, 324.7, 324.1, 323.5.
7. Kinch 1914, pl. 5, 8 and fig. 85 and pl. 12; Kardara 1963, 253.
8. Kinch 1914, pl. 6, 8.
9. Kinch 1914, pl. 24,5, fig. 104.
10. Kinch 1914, pl. 24.6a; Kardara 1963, eik. 253-254.
11. E. Price, JHS 44, 1924, 196, fig. 28.
12. Kardara 1963, sel. 238, eik. 197.
13. Kinch 1914, fig. 73, fig. 108.
14. Kardara 1963, eik. 54', 53a, 175.
15. Fairbanks 1928, pl. XXXIII, 315, 316 and pp. 105, 106.
16. Kinch 1914, pl. 44, 43; Arkontidou, ASAtene 45.
17. Kinch 1914, fig. 134.
18. Fairbanks 1928, pl XXXIII no 313.
19. Kinch 1914, pl. 10.
20. Kinch 1914, pl 11,5a.
21. Kinch 1914, pl. 9.
22. Kinch 1914, 250,5, fig. 129.
23. Kinch 1914.
24. Fairbanks 1928, 235, pl. XXXV.
25. Kardara 1963, sel. 27, eik. 178 and sel. 299'183.
26. E. Price, JHS 44, 1924, pl. VII, 2, 6, p. 198; Fairbanks 1928, pl. XXXIII, 313.
27. Kinch 1914, pl. 24, 6, pp. 132, 194; Arkontidou, ASAtene 45, J.M. Cook, BSA 53-54, 1958-59, 25-27.
28. Kinch 1914, pl. 13 226, 195 fig. 76c.
29. Kinch 1914, fig. 115, 108, 227.
30. Kardara 1963, sel. 24.
31. Kinch 1914, pl. 17, 193.
32. Kinch 1914, fig. 24, 193-194.
33. Her. 5,26ss; Her. 6, 136, 140; Thucc. IV, 109; A. di Vita, ASAtene 55, 1977, 345.

Land and Underwater Excavations in the Bodrum Area

Oguz Alpözen

Bodrum is in the southwest corner of Anatolia, across from the island of Kos, a distance of 9 miles by sea. Founded on the ruins of ancient Halicarnassos, Bodrum's most important structure is the 15th century castle. Built by the Knights of St. John, this is the best preserved castle in the Aegean at the present time. When the Knights built the castle they named it after St. Peter. The name of Halicarnassos was forgotten during the Middle ages and the city around the castle was called "Petronium". This word became Bodrum in Turkish. The Bodrum Museum of Underwater Archaeology is located in the castle. (Alpözen, 1983). The towers and outbuildings of the castle are used as museum exhibition halls, depots, workshops and laboratories. The gardens and terraces are used for open air exhibitions. The Museum of Underwater Archaeology is responsible for an area about the size of the ancient province of Caria encompassing all of the area of the present province of Mugla, excepting Fethiye.

Turkish and foreign teams excavate on land and underwater with the permission of the General Directorate of Antiquity and Museums. The ancient theatre in Bodrum is being excavated under the scientific consultancy of the Museum's retired Professor Umit Sedaroglu[1]. This theatre is one of the oldest in Anatolia. In August and September 1985 one of the places most visited in Bodrum was the Mausoleum. Excavated by Kristian Jeppesen, Professor at Aarhus University in Denmark, (Jeppesen, 1981) the Mausoleum, one of the seven wonders of the ancient world, now has it's own small museum exhibiting some of the friezes. In October 1985 Jeppesen was still working on some of the marble pieces[2].

Sixty km from Bodrum, on the Milas-Mugla road, is an important ancient city of the Hellenistic period, Stratonikeia. This site, presently known as Eskihisar, has been under excavation since 1977 under the direction of Professor Yusuf Boysal. The city, which existed during Hellenistic, Roman and Byzantine times also has some houses from the Ottoman period. Because this city, which was very important in ancient times, is situated on the site of rich coal reserves and a power plant has been established near it, excavations have to be completed very quickly. The Western Aegean Lignite Corporation wishes to remove coal from this area and our Museum, under the orders of the General Directorate of Antiquity and Museums, wishes to save the city. An interesting war may break out between the Museum and the coal company, between archaeology and energy. Under an agreement made with the coal company regarding the city's necropolis, a rapid excavation was made to save the graves, and nearly 100 were excavated. The graves which date from the 8th century BC through Byzantine times, have yielded gold, elephant tusks and various objects[3].

Although there is a coal source 3.5 m beneath the ancient Stratonikeia its border is 30 m away from the city wall, and so the city has been preserved for the world of archaeology. In reply to a request from the General Directorate of Antiquity and Museums and our Museum, the General Directorate of State Highways changed the route of the road which passed near the city. A city wall, dated to the 3rd century BC, was found when the road was constructed. It has been assumed that this place could be the upper Gymnasium mentioned in the ancient sources. Professor Boysal will continue in 1986, his studies of the upper Gymnasium and of the temple discovered in the 1985 excavation[4].

Labranda is another ancient site with which our museum is concerned. This is a mountain village, 13 km from the old capital city of Mylasa, which is also the site of a sacred temple city of the Hekatomid period. During that period some sacred buildings were set up by Mausolos and Idrieus. The city has been excavated by a Swedish team. Measurements, pictures and drawings of four buildings, dated to the Hekatomid period, were made by Professor Pontus Hellström and his team in 1985. One building is a Dorian style of construction built by Idrieus; it is not known for what purpose it was used. A study of marble blocks from the structure that became a Roman bath during the Roman period has been completed[5].

Nowadays Labranda is one of the most magnificent and well-cared for cities of the area.

One of the ancient Karian coastal cities near Bodrum is Iassos. The excavation has been carried out by Professor Celia Laviosa and her Italian team since 1979. In 1985 Professor Fede Berti excavated the agora and periphery and reached the Mycenaean level[6]. We hope that more attention will be given to the restoration studies made by the team.

Another coastal city important in the Classical period is Knidos. The excavation, which had been conducted by the American Professor Iris Love[7], was brought to an end by the General Directorate of Antiquities and Museums because no proper scientific approach and method were used on the site.

Our Museum deals both with underwater and land excavation. Near Adana, at Karatas, local fishermen located a lifesized statue of a Roman Senator, dated 2nd century AD, which was then excavated by our underwater archaeological team[8].

One duty of our staff is to instruct local sponge divers what to look for when they perform their dives. Visits are made to their villages and instruction given through slides and video shows. Sponge divers make two or three daily dives from May to October. Most of the information about ancient shipwrecks has been provided by sponge divers. In October 1982 the sponge diver Mehmet Cakir came to our museum and reported that he had seen "metal biscuits with ears" around 50m deep near Ulu Burun. Shortly after our Museum Directorate, under my direction, drove to Kas with Mehmet Cakir. The Turkish archaeologist Feyyaz Subay joined this survey on behalf of the Institute of Nautical Archaeology. The wreck was found after a second dive on the 23rd of October and a copper ingot, typical of the Late Bronze Age, was raised from it. Mehmet Cakir was rewarded by our Museum and the INA. The copper ingot

The Bodrum Museum of Underwater Archaeology is housed in this medieval castle.

An archaeologist working on ancient shipwreck.

A general view of the ancient city of Labranda.

conforms to the second type of Buchholz. The shipwreck provisionally dated by us to the 15th century, was later dated to the 14th century BC by Professor G.F. Bass. In 1983 Cemal Pulak was given permission to survey the Kas area on behalf of the INA and subsequently made a ten day inspection of the site. The wreck lay on an east-west axis at a depth of 44 to 51 m, on a steep and rocky bottom. Some one hundred copper ingots lay scattered over an area measuring 10 by 8 m. In 1984 excavation of the Kas-Ulu Burun wreck was commenced by the INA with Professor George F. Bass as consultant at the beginning of July and continued to the end of August. It is assumed that the study will continue for 3 years. During the last 25 years the INA has discovered many wrecks around the Aegean and Mediterranean coasts using scientific methods. Bodrum Museum of Underwater Archaeology was established when the artifacts of the Cape Gelidonya shipwreck, dated to the 12th century BC, were taken to Bodrum castle[9]. The underwater archaeologists of Bodrum Museum are also working on the Kas wreck. The Virazon, belonging to an American team, was moored semi-permanently above the wreck and most of the staff camped on the shore nearby. The ship was 50 m from the shore. There were two daily dives to the wreck and in a short time many artifacts were raised. Three types of copper ingots were mainly found: ox-hide, bun and pillow-shaped ingots in addition to tin ingots of ox-hide type. At the lower end of the site was a slightly tapered stone-weight anchor with a hole at its narrower end. This is the first of its type to be found with a shipwreck. Under one of the stone anchors fragments of keel and planking belonging to the Bronze Age shipwreck were found. The planking and keel are made of fir wood. Planking is joined together with mortise and tenon joints. Some Syro-Palestinian amphoras known as the Canaanite type were raised from the wreck. A study was made of their contents. One of the amphoras was filled with beads. Some beads appear to be of glass and others of amber. Another amphora contained, among other things, orpiment or yellow arsenic, a common pigment. One pithos contained 18 pieces of pottery consisting of 5 milk-bowls, 3 base-ring II bowls, 3 white-shaved juglets, 3 buchero jugs and 4 Canaanite lamps. Other interesting artifacts are elephant and hippopotamus ivory. Two lentoid seals, originally Mycenaean were also found. The most important artifact is a kylix found next to a gold chalice. Stone weights, in the form of frogs, bronze weights, stone trays, gold and silver ornaments, glass ingots, bronze instruments and weapons show how wealthy was this merchant ship of the Late Bronze Age. Professor George F. Bass dated this wreck to the beginning of the 14th Century BC. It seems likely that her final voyage took place during the reign of Amenophis III, or during the early years of the reign of Amenophis IV, or ca. 1375 BC. It is understood that she started her voyage from the Syro-Palestinian shore past Cyprus. Perhaps it was her intention to reach the Mycenaean shore. This merchant ship contained raw materials that were bought in the east, but it is thought that, on the way to Rhodes, close to Kas, she sank. From the artifacts recovered from this wreck much is being learned about the trading relationship between the Mycenaean area, Anatolia, Syria and Egypt[10]. These artifacts will be on display in the Bodrum Museum of Underwater Archaeology in a few years time.

Oguz Alpözen
Bodrum Museum of Underwater Archaeology
Bodrum
Turkey

1. Reports of this excavation are yet to be published.
2. Other publications about the Mausoleum include: – Newton 1862, Newton 1865, Højlund 1981, Luttrell 1985.
3. Yusuf Boysal, in *Kazı Sonuçları Toplantısı*. Vol's III – VII (1979-1984) T. C. Kültür veTurizm Bakalığı. (Annual Excavations Reports. Turkish Culture and Tourism Ministry.)
4. Yusuf Boysal, in *Kazı Sonuçları Toplantısı*. Vol. VIII. 1985.
5. Pontus Hellström, in *Arastırma Sonuçları Toplantısı*. Vol. IV. 1985. (Annual Survey Reports.) T. C. Kultur ve Turizm Bak, also other reports include: P. Hellström. Labraunda II:1, Pottery of Classical and Later Date Terracotta Lamps and Glass. Lund 1964. *Skrifter Utgivna Av Svenska Institutet Athen*, 4"V II:1. A. Westholm. Labraunda I:2. The Architecture of the Hieron. *Skr. Ut. Sv. Inst. Athen*. Lund 1963. A. W. Persson: Swedish Excavations at Labraunda. *Bulletin de la Société Royale des Lettres de Lund*. 1948-1949, III. Lund 1949.
6. Celia Laviosa, *K.S.T.* Vol. VII, Fede Berti *K.S.T.* Vol. VIII.
7. See Iris Cornelia Love: A Preliminary Report of the Excavations at Knidos, 1970. AJA *76*.
8. Unpublished. The statue is now displayed in the Adana Museum.
9. George F. Bass. Cape Gelidonya: A Bronze Age Shipwreck. *Transactions. American Philosophical Society.* Dec. 1967.
10. The first report of the Ulu Burun shipwreck has now been published in *National Geographic 172* (6) Dec. 1987, by George F. Bass of the Institute of Nautical Archaeology.

Bibliography

Besides abbreviations suggested in Archäologische Bibliographie 1986, X-XXXIX and in Archäologischer Anzeiger 1985, 757 ff. the following are used here:

CGE Les Céramiques de la Grèce de l'Est et leur diffusion en Occident. Paris – Naples 1978.

Lindos I Blinkenberg, Chr., Lindos, Fouilles de l'Acropole 1902-1914, Les petits objects. Berlin 1931.

Lindos II Blinkenberg, Chr., Lindos, Fouilles de l'Acropole 1902-1914 II, Inscriptions. Publiées en grande partie d'après les copies de K.F. Kinch. Berlin 1941.

Lindos III Dyggve, E., Lindos, Fouilles de l'Acropole 1902-1914 et 1952 III. Le sanctuaire d'Athana Lindia et l'architecture lindienne. Berlin 1960.

Lindos IV. 1 Dietz, S., Lindos IV. 1. Excavations and Surveys in Southern Rhodes: The Mycenaean Period. Odense 1984.

Adriani, A. 1966
Repertorio d'Arte dell'Egitto Greco-Romano. Ser. C, Vol. I. Palermo.

Adriani, A. (ed.) 1970
Himera, I. Campagne di scavo 1963-1965. Roma.

Akurgal, E. 1961
Die Kunst Anatoliens von Homer bis Alexander. Berlin.

Akurgal, E. 1983
Alt-Smyrna, I. Wohnschichten und Athenatempel. Ankara.

Alexandrescu, P. 1978
Histria IV, La céramique d'époque archaïque et classique (VIIe-VIe s.). Bucureşti.

Alpözen, O.
Bodrum.

Amiran, R. 1970
Ancient Pottery of the Holy Land from its beginnings in the Neolithic to the end of the Iron age. New Brunswick, N.J.

Andronikos, M. 1968
Totenkult. (ArchHom III, W). Göttingen.

Angel, L. 1959
Early Helladic Skulls from Aghios Kosmas, (Appendix), in G. Mylonas, Aghios Kosmas, an Early Helladic Settlement and Cemetery.

Angel, L. 1971
The People of Lerna. Princeton N.J.

Atkinson, T.D. et al. 1904
Excavations at Phylakopi in Melos. Society for the Promotion of Hellenic Studies, Suppl. Pap. 4. London.

Aubet, M.E. 1971
Los marfiles orientalizantes de Praeneste. Barcelona.

Bailo Modesti, G. 1980
Cairano nell'età arcaica. L'abitato e la necropoli. Napoli.

Barber, R.L.N. (ed) 1984
The Prehistoric Cyclades. Contributions to a workshop on Cycladic Chronology. Edinburgh.

Barker, G. et al. (eds.) 1985
Cyrenaica in Antiquity. Oxford.

Barnett, R.D. 1975
A Catalogue of the Nimrud Ivories with other examples of Ancient Near Eastern Ivories in the British Museum (2nd ed.). London.

Barnett, R.D. 1982
Ancient Ivories in the Middle East. Jerusalem.

Bastis, A. 1982-1983
The Search of Alexander. Suppl. to the catalogue. The Metropolitan Museum of Art. 1983

Beazley, J.D. 1956
Attic black-figure vase-painters. Oxford.

Beazley, J.D. 1963
Attic red-figure vase-painters (2nd ed.). Oxford.

Beazley, J.D. 1971
Paralipomena. Additions to "Attic black-figure vase-painters" and to "Attic red-figure vase-painters". Oxford.

Bell, M. 1981
The terracottas. Morgantina Studies Vol. 1. Princeton.

Benndorf, O. – Niemann, G. 1884
Reisen im Südwestlichen Unterasien I, Reisen in Lykien und Karien. Wien.

Benson, J. 1963
Ancient Leros. Durham.

Benson, J.L. 1973
The Necropolis of Kaloriziki. (SIMA 36). Göteborg.

Benzécri, J.-P. et al. 1979
L'analyse des données I-II (3rd ed). Paris.

Berg, A. 1862
Die Insel Rhodus. Braunschweig.

Bieber, M. 1964
Alexander the Great in Greek and Roman Art. Chicago.

Biliotti, E. 1881
L'Ile de Rhodes. Rhodos.

Bissing, Fr.W. von 1941
Zeit und Herkunft der in Cerveteri gefundenen Gefässe aus ägyptischer Fayence und glasiertem Ton. SB München, II. 7.

Blegen, C.W. 1966
The Palace of Nestor at Pylos in Western Messenia, Vol. I. Princeton.

Blegen, C.W. et al. 1973
The Palace of Nestor at Pylos in Western Messenia, Vol. III. Princeton.

Blinkenberg, Chr. 1926
Fibules grecques et orientales. (Lindiaka 5). Det Kgl. danske Videnskabernes Selskab. Historisk-filologiske Meddelelser 13, 1. København.

Blinkenberg, Chr. 1937
Les Prêtres de Poseidon Hippios. Étude sur une Inscription lindienne. (Lindiaka 6). Det Kgl. danske Videnskabernes Selskab. Archaeologisk-Kunsthistoriske Meddelelser 11, 2. København.

Blinkenberg, Chr. – Kinch, K.F. 1903
Exploration archeologique de Rhodes I. Det kgl. Danske Videnskabernes Selskabs Forhandlinger. København.

Blome, P. 1982
Die figürliche Bildwelt Kretas in der geometrischen und früharchaischen Periode. Mainz.

Boardman, J. 1961
The Cretan Collection in Oxford. The Dictaean Cave and Iron Age Crete. Oxford.

Boardman, J. 1963
Island Gems. A Study of Greek Seals in the Geometric and Early Archaic Periods. London.

Boardman, J. 1967
Excavations in Chios 1952-1955, Greek Emporio. BSA Suppl. 6. Oxford.

Boardman, J. 1970
Greek Gems and Finger Rings. Early Bronze Age to Late Classical. London.

Boardman, J. 1974
Athenian black figure vases. A handbook. London.

Boardman, J. 1975
Intaglios and Rings. Greek, Etruscan and Eastern from a private Collection. London.

Boardman, J. 1980
The Greeks Overseas. Their early Colonies and Trade. (3rd ed.). London.

Boardman, J. – Hayes, J. 1973
Excavations at Tocra 1963-1965. The archaic Deposits II and later Deposits. (BSA Suppl. 10). Oxford.

Boardman, J. – Vollenweider, M.L. 1978
Ashmolean Museum, Oxford. Catalogue of the engraved Gems and Finger Rings, I. Greek and Etruscan. Oxford.

Boardman, J. et al. (eds.) 1986
Chios. A Conference at the Homereion in Chios 1984. Oxford.

Bohen, B.E. 1979.
Attic Geometric Pyxis

Bonghi Jovino, M. 1982
La necropoli preromana di Vico Equense. Cava dei Tirreni.

Bonghi Jovino, M. (ed.) 1986
Gli Etruschi di Tarquinia. Modena.

Bosio, J. 1697
Gli Statuti della Sacra Religione di S. Giovanni Gierosolimitano.

Bossert, H. 1921
Alt Kreta. Kunst und Kunstgewerbe im ägäischen Kulturkreise. Berlin.

Buondelmondi, Chr. de 1824
Liber Insularum Archipelagi.

Boyd Hawes, H. 1908
Gournia, Vasiliki and other prehistoric sites on the Isthmus of Hierapetra, Crete. Philadelphia.

Boëthius, A. 1960
The Golden House of Nero. Ann Arbor.

Bradford, J. 1957
Ancient Landscapes. Studies in Field Archaeology. London.

Bresson, A. 1979
Mythe et contradiction: Analyse de la VIIIe Olympique de Pindare.Paris.

Brock, J.K. 1957
Fortetsa. An Account of the excavation of early greek tombs near Knossos. (BSA Suppl. 2). Cambridge.

Brothwell, D. 1981
Digging Up Bones. (BM-NH-OVP).

Bruins, E.M. – Rutten, L.M. 1961
Textes mathématiques de Suse. Paris.

Buchholz, H.-G. et al. 1973
Jagd und Fischfang (ArchHom II, J). Göttingen.

Burkert, W. 1972
Homo necans. Interpretation altgriechischer Opferriten und Mythen. Berlin - NY.

Burn, L. – Glynn, R. 1982
Beazley Addenda: Additional references to ABV, ARV2 & Paralipomena. Oxford.

Canale, M.G. 1858-1864
Nuova istoria della republica di Genova I-IV. Firenze.

Canciani, F. 1984
Bildkunst II. (ArchHom N, 2). Göttingen.

Caner, E. 1983
Fibeln in Anatolien I. (PBF XIV, 8). München.

Castagnoli, F. 1956
Ippodamo di Mileto e l'Urbanistica a Pianto Orthogonale. Roma.

Castagnoli, F. 1971
Orthogonal Town Planning in Antiquity. London.

Catling, H.W. 1964
Cypriot Bronzework in the Mycenean World. Oxford.

Chamay, J. – Maier, J.-L. 1984
Céramiques corinthiennes. Collection du docteur Jean Lauffenburger. Genève.

Chavane, M.-J. 1975
Les petits objets. Salamine de Chypre VI. Paris.

Chavane, M.-J. 1982
Vases de bronze du Musée de Chypre (IXe-IVe s. av.J.-C.). Lyon.

Chieco Bianchi, A.M. – Calzavara Capuis, L. 1985
Este I. (MonAnt. S. Monografica II). Roma.

Choiseul-Gouffier, M.G.F.A. 1882
Voyage pittoresque dans l'Empire Ottoman en Grèce, dans la Troade.. (2nd ed.)

Clerc, G. et al. 1976
Fouilles de Kition II, Objects égyptiens et égyptisants: Scarabes, amulettes et figurines en pâte de verre et en faïence, vase plastique en faïence: Sites I et II, 1959-1975. Nicosia.

Coldstream, J.N. 1968
Greek Geometric Pottery. A Survey of ten local Styles and their Chronology. London.

Coldstream, J.N. 1977
Geometric Greece. London.

Coldstream, N. – Huxley, G.L. (eds.) 1972
Kythera: Excavations and Studies. London.

Coppa, M. 1968
Storia dell'Urbanistica.

Courbin, P. 1966
La céramique géométrique de l'Argolide. Paris.

Cristofani, M. - Martelli, M. (eds.) 1983
L'oro degli Etruschi. Novara.

Cultrera, G. 1924
Architettura Ippodamea. Roma.

Cummer, W. – Schofield, E. 1984
Keos III. Ayia Irini: House A. Mainz am Rhein.

Daux, G. 1968
Guide de Thasos. Paris.

Davidson, G.R. 1952
The Minor Objects. (Corinth XII). Princeton.

Dehl, C. 1984
Die korinthische Keramik des 8. und frühen 7. Jhs. v.Chr. in Italien. Berlin.
Delaville Le Roulx, J. 1883
Les Archives, la Bibliotheque et le Trésor de l'Ordre de St. Jean de Jérusalem á Malte.
Delaville Le Roulx, J. 1885
La France en Orient au XVI siècle. Expéditions du Maréchal Boucicaut.
Delorme, J. 1961
Les Palestres. (Exploration Archeologique de Délos XXV). Paris.
Demangel, R. 1926
Le Sanctuaire d'Athéna Pronaia. (Fouilles de Delphes II 3). Paris.
Demargne, P. 1947
La Crète dédalique. Études sur les origines d'une renaissance. Paris.
Dentzer, J.-M. 1982
Le motif du banquet couché dans le Proche-Orient et le monde grec du VIIe au IVe siècle avant J.-C. Roma.
Desborough, V.R.d'A. 1952
Proto-Geometric Pottery. Oxford.
Desborough, V.R.d'A. 1964
The Last Mycenaeans and their Successors. An Archaeological Survey c. 1200-c. 1000 BC. Oxford.
Desborough, V.R.d'A. 1972
The Greek Dark Ages. London.
Deshayes, J. 1963
La Nécropole de Ktima. Paris.
Detienne, M. – Vernant, J.-P. (eds.) 1979
La cuisine du sacrifice en pays grec. Paris.
Deubner, L. 1932
Attische Feste. Berlin.
Devereux, W.M. 1847
Views on the Stories of the Mediterranean.
Deza, M. 1644
I storia della famiglia Spinola descritta dalla sua origine fine al secolo XVI.
Diehl, E. 1964
Die Hydria. Formgeschichte und Verwendung im Kult des Altertums. Mainz.
Dietz, S. – Trolle, S. 1974
Arkæologens Rhodos. København.
Dikaios, P. 1971
Enkomi. Mainz.
Dinsmoor, W.B. 1950
The Architecture of Ancient Greece. (3rd ed.). London.
Dohan, E. Hall 1942
Italic Tomb-Groups in the University Museum. Philadelphia.
Δουβίτσας, Γ. – Λαγουβάρδος, Π. 1984
Οδοντική Χειρουργική 1.
Doumas, Chr. 1983
Thera: Pompeii of the Ancient Aegean. London.
Doumas, Chr. (ed.) 1978-1980
Thera and the Aegean World I-II. London.
Drerup, H. 1969
Griechische Baukunst in geometrischer Zeit. (ArchHom II, O). Göttingen.
Duday, H. 1970
La Pathologie Dentaire de Hommes de Kitsos, (Appendix).
Dunbabin, T.J. 1957
The Greeks and their Eastern neighbours: Studies in the relations between Greece and the countries of the Near East in the eighth and seventh centuries B.C. London.
Dunbabin, T.J. (ed.) 1962
Perachora II. The Sanctuaries of Hera Akraia and Limenia. Oxford.
Edrich, K.H. 1969
Der ionische Helm. Diss. Göttingen.
Effenterre, H. van 1980
Le Palais de Mallia et la Cité Minoenne. (Incunabula Graeca 96). Paris.
Ekschmitt, W. 1984
Die Sieben Weltwunder. Ihre Erbauung, Zerstörung und Wiederentdeckung. Mainz am Rhein.
Elvy, N. 1980
Human Teeth from Kition. Opuscula Atheniensia XIII:13. Stockholm.
Evans, A. 1921-1935
The Palace of Minos I-IV. London.
Fabricius, E. 1929
Die griechische Polis.
Fairbanks, A. 1928
Catalogue of Greek and Etruscan Vases I. Museum of Fine Arts. Boston.
Falciai, P.B. 1982
Ippodamo di Mileto, Architetto e Philosofo.
Fischer, P. 1980
Eine Untersuchung der Kieferfragmente und Zahne aus Zwei Graben von Trypes der Dromolaxia, Zypern. Stockholm.
Foglieta, O. U. 1585
Historia Genuensium Libri 12.
Fontanus 1527
De Bello Rhodio.
Forsdyke, E.J. 1925
Catalogue of the Greek and Etruscan Vases in the British Museum I, 1: Prehistoric Aegean Pottery. London.
Fraser, P.M. 1972
Ptolemaic Alexandria. Oxford.
Fraser, P.M. 1977
Rhodian Funerary Monuments. Oxford.
Fraser, P.M. – Bean, G.E. 1954
The Rhodian Peraia and Islands. London.
Fraser, P.M. – Matthews E. 1987
A Lexicon of Greek Personal Names, vol. I, Oxford.
Freeden, J. van 1983
ΟΙΚΙΑ ΚΥΡΡΕΣΤΟΥ. Studien zum sogenannten Turm der Winde. Rom.
Freyer-Schauenburg, B. 1966
Elfenbeine aus dem samischen Heraion: Figürliches, Gefässe und Siegel. Hamburg.
Frickenhaus, A. 1912
Tiryns I, Die Hera von Tiryns. Athens.
Friis Johansen, K. 1958
Exochi. Ein frührhodisches Gräberfeld. København. Acta Arch. 28, 1957, 1-192.
Frödin, O. – Persson, A.W. 1938
Asine. Results of the Swedish excavations 1922-1930. Stockholm.
Furtwängler, A. – Loeschke, G. 1886
Mykenische Vasen. Vorhellenische Thongefässe aus dem Gebiet des Mittelmeeres. Berlin.
Furumark, A. 1941
A. The Mycenaean Pottery. Analysis and Classification. Stockholm.
Furumark, A. 1941
B. The Chronology of Mycenaean Pottery. Stockholm.
Furumark, A. 1972
The Mycenaean Pottery. Analysis and Classification. (Reprint.). Stockholm.

Galavaris, G. 1969
The Illustrations of the Liturgical Homilies of Gregory Nazianzenus. Princeton.
Garašanin, D. 1954
Katalog der vorgeschichtlichen Metalle.
Gejvall, N. ?
The Human Remains in Dendra Greece.
Gelder, H. van 1900
Geschichte der Alten Rhodier. Den Haag.
Gerkan, A. von 1924
Griechische Städteanlagen. Berlin - Leipzig.
Gershuny, L. 1985
Bronze Vessels from Israel and Jordan. (PBF II 6-7). München.
Gesell, G.C. 1972
The archaeological evidence for the Minoan House cult and its survival in Iron Age Crete. (Ph.D.) Michigan.
Gesell, G.C. 1985
Town, Palace and House Cult in Minoan Crete. (SIMA LXVII). Göteborg.
Ginouvès, R. 1962
Balaneutikè. Recherches sur le bain dans l'antiquité grecque. Paris.
Giuliano, A. 1966
Urbanistica delle Città Greche.
Giustiniani, A. 1855
Annali della Republica di Genova.
Gjerstad, E. 1926
Studies on Prehistoric Cyprus. Uppsala.
Gjerstad, E. et al. 1977
Greek Geometric and Archaic Pottery found in Cyprus. Stockholm.
Goldman, H. (ed.) 1963
Excavations at Gözlü Kule, Tarsus. 3. The Iron Age. Princeton.
Graham, J.W. 1972
The Palaces of Crete. Princeton.
Gras, M. 1985
Trafics tyrrhéniens archaïques. Paris.
Greco, E. – Torelli, M. 1983
Storia dell'Urbanistica. Bari.
Guarducci, M. 1967
Epigrafia Greca I. Roma.
Guarducci, M. 1978
Epigrafia Greca IV. Roma.
Guichard, C. 1581
Funérailles et diverses manières d'ensevelir des Romains, Grecs etc. III.
Guérin, V. 1880
Ile de Rhodes. (2nd ed.). Paris.
Harden, D.B. 1981
Catalogue of Greek and Roman Glass in the British Museum I. London.
Harrison, A.R.W. 1968
The Law of Athens: The Family and Property. Oxford.
Haugsted, I. 1978
Hippodamos fra Milet: Antikke græske byplaner fra det 5. årh. f.Kr. København.
Head, B.V. 1887
Historia Nummorum. A manual of Greek numismatics. (1st ed.). Oxford.
Head, B.V. 1897
Catalogue of the Greek Coins of Caria and the Islands in the British Museum. London.
Head,B.V. 1911
Historia Nummorum. (2nd ed.). Oxford.
Hecht, K. 1979
Mass und Zahl in der gotischen Baukunst. Hildesheim - NY.
Hencken, H. 1968
Tarquinia Villanovans and Early Etruscans, Cambridge (Mass.).
Herzog, R. 1899
Koische Forschungen und Funde. Leipzig.
Herzog, R. 1928
Heilige Gesetze von Kos. Berl.Abh. No. 8. Berlin.
Herzog, R. 1930
Epigramm der Kinderstatue eines Lysippos in Kos, in Schumacher Festschrift. Mainz.
Hesberg, H. von 1980
Konsolengeisa der Hellenismus und der frühen Kaiserzeit. (RM Ergh 24). Berlin.
Heyd, W. 1879
Geschichte des Levanthandels im Mittelalter I-II.
Heyd, W. 1885
Histoire du Commerce du Levant au Moyen-Age I-II. Leipzig.
Higgins, R.A. 1967
Greek Terracottas. London.
Higgins, R.A. 1970
Catalogue of the Terracottas in the Department of Greek and Roman Antiquities in the British Museum, Vol. I. London.
Higgins, R.A. 1980
Greek and Roman Jewellery (2nd ed.). Berkeley – Los Angeles.
Hiller von Gaertringen, Fr. 1895
Inscriptiones Graecae Insularum Rhodi, Chalkes, Carpathi cum Saro, Casi. Fasc. I. Berlin.
Hiller von Gaertringen, Fr. 1903
Thera. Untersuchungen, Vermessungen und Ausgrabungen in den Jahren 1895-1902. II. Theraeische Gräber. Berlin.
Hoepfner, W. – Schwandner, L. 1986
Haus und Stadt im Klassischen Griechenland (Wohnen in der klassischen Polis I). München.
Hoffmann, H. – Raubitscheck, A.E. 1972
Early Cretan armourers. Mainz am Rhein.
Hogarth, D.G. 1908
Excavations at Ephesus. The Archaic Artemisia. London.
Holt, E.G. 1957
A documentary history of art. Vol. 1-2. NY.
Hood, S. 1981
Prehistoric Emporio and Ayio Gala I. (BSA Suppl. 15). London.
Horn, H.G. – Rüger, C.B. 1979
Die Numider. Köln - Bonn.
Hornblower, S. 1982
Mausolus. Oxford.
Hourmouziades, G. 1968
Eisagogi stis ideologies tis ellinikis proistorias. Polites.
Howgego, C.J. 1985
Greek Imperial Countermarks. London.
Hultsch, F. 1882
Griechische und römische Metrologie. Berlin.
Humphreys, S.C. – King, H. (eds.) 1981
Mortality and Immortality.
Hägg, R. – Marinatos, N. (eds) 1984
The Minoan Thalassocracy: Myth and Reality. (Skrifter utgivna av Svenska Institutet. Athen, 4, 32). Stockholm.
Hölbl, G. 1979
Beziehungen der ägyptischen Kultur zu Altitalien, I-II. Leiden.

Højlund, Fl. 1981
The Maussoleion at Halikarnassos, vol. 1. The Deposit of Sacrificed Animals at the Entrance to the Tomb Chamber. Copenhagen.

Iakovidis, S.E. 1972
Peratí, to nekrotapheíon. Athens.

Inglieri, R.U. 1936
Carta Archeologica dell'Isola di Rodi. Firenze.

Işik, F. 1980
Die Koroplastik von Theangela in Karien und ihre Beziehungen zu Ostionien zwischen 560 und 270 v.Chr. (Ist Mitt Beiheft 21).

Iversen, E. 1975
Canon and Proportion in Egyptian Art. Warminster.

Jacoby, F. 1904
Das Marmor Parium. Berlin.

Jacopi, G. 1932
Lo Spedale dei Cavalieri e il Museo Archeologico di Rodi. Roma.

Jeffery, L.H. 1961
The local Scripts of Archaic Greece. Oxford.

Jeffery, L.H. 1976
Archaic Greece: the City-States c. 700-500 B.C. London.

Jeppesen, K. 1958
Paradeigmata: Three mid-fourth century main works of Hellenic architecture. Aarhus.

Jeppesen, K. 1981
The Maussoleion at Halikarnassos 1. København.

Jevtic, M. 1983
The Early Iron Age Pottery at the Central Balkan Region. Beograd.

Johannowski, W. 1983
Materiali di età arcaica dalla Campania. Napoli

Kanta, A. 1980
The Late Minoan III Period in Crete: A survey of sites, pottery and their distributions. (SIMA 58). Göteborg.

Karageorghis, V. 1974
Excavations at Kition, I: The Tombs. Nicosia.

Kardara, Ch. 1963
Rhodiaki Angeiographia. Athens.

Karousos, Chr. 1949
Rhodos.

Karousos, Chr. 1973
Rhodos (2nd ed).

Kilian, K. 1975
Fibeln in Thessalien von der mykenischen bis zur archaischen Zeit (PBF XIV, 2). München.

Kilian-Dirlmeier, I. 1979
Anhänger in Griechenland von der mykenischen bis zur spätgeometrischen Zeit. (PBF XI, 2). München.

Kinch, K.F. 1914
Fouilles de Vroulia (Rhodes). Berlin.

Kingsley, R. G. 1978[2]
The Order of St. John of Jerusalem.

Kirsten, E. 1956
Die Griechische Polis als Historisch-Geographisches Problem des Mittelmeerraumes. Bonn.

Kirsten, E. – Kraiker, W. 1967
Griechenlandkunde: Ein Führer zu klassischen Stätten. (5th ed.). Heidelberg.

Kleiner, G. 1984
Tanagrafiguren. Untersuchungen zur hellenistischer Kunst und Geschichte. (2nd ed.). Berlin.

Koenigs, W. et al. 1980
Rundbauten in Kerameikos. (Kerameikos XII). Berlin.

Kondis, J. 1954
Symboli eis tin meletin tis rymotomias tis Rhodou. Rhodos.

Konstantinopoulos, G. 1972
Ho rodiakos kosmos I, Lindos. Bibliotheke Archaeol. Hetaireias no. 74, Athenai.

Konstantinopoulos, G. 1986
Archaia Rhodos.

Kontorini, V. 1983
Inscriptions inédites relatives à l'histoire et aux cultes de Rhodes au IIe et au Ier s. av.J.-C.: Rhodiaka 1. Louvain.

Kriesis, A. 1965
Greek Town Building. Athens.

Κριχος, A. 1935.
Η Εξέλιξις της Τερηδόνας των Οδόντων εν Ελλάδι απο των Αρχαιοτάτων Χρόνων Μέχρι των Καθ' ημάς Χρόνων. Πρακτικά Ελληνικής Ανθρωπολογικής Εταιρειας.

Krischen, F. 1938
Die Landmauer von Konstantinopel. Berlin.

Kromayer, J. – Weith, G. 1928
Heerwesen und Kriegsführung der Griechen und Römer.

Krzyszkowska, O. – Nixon, L. (eds.) 1983
Minoan Society. Proceedings of the Cambridge Colloquium 1981. Bristol.

Kukahn, E. 1936
Der griechische Helm. Marburg - Lahn.

Kübler, K. 1943
Neufunde aus der Nekropole des 11. und 10. Jahrhunderts. (Kerameikos IV). Berlin.

Kübler, K. 1954
Die Nekropole des 10. bis 8. Jahrhunderts. (Kerameikos V, 1). Berlin.

Laffineur, R. 1978
L'orfèvrerie rhodienne orientalisante. Paris.

Langlotz, E. 1932
Griechische Vasen in Würzburg. München.

Lattanzi, E. (ed.) 1987
Il Museo Nazionale di Reggio Calabria. Roma – Reggio Calabria.

Lauter, H. 1986
Architektur des Hellenismus. Darmstadt.

Lavedan, P. 1926
Histoire de l'Urbanisme. I. Antiquité - Moyen Age. Paris.

Lawrence, A.W. 1962
Greek Architecture. 2nd ed. Hammondsworth.

Lehman-Brockhaus, O. 1938
Schriftquellen zur Kunstgeschichte der 11. und 12. Jahrhunderts für Deutschland, Lothringen und Italien. Berlin.

Levi, D. 1976
Festós e la Civiltà Minoica I. Roma. (Incunabula Graeca, 60).

Lewe, B. 1975
Studien zur archaischen kyprischen Plastik. Diss. Frankfurt.

Leyenar-Plaisier, P. 1979
Les terres cuites grecques et romaines. Catalogue de la Collection du Musée National des Antiquités à Leiden.

Liepmann, U. 1975
Griechische Terrakotten, Bronzen, Skulpturen. Bildkataloge des Kestner-Museums XII. Hannover.

Lloyd, S. – Mellaart, J. 1962
Beycesultan I. The chalcolithic and early bronze age levels. London.

Lorentzen, E. 1966
Technological studies in ancient metrology. København.

Lorentzen, E. 1970
"along the line where columns are set", Technological studies in ancient metrology, book 11. København.

Lound, D. 1983
Lemba Lakkous: Report on the Human Dentitions.

Luschen, V.F. von – Andrae, W. 1943
Die Kleinfunde von Sendschirli, Ausgrabungen in Sendschirli V. Berlin.
Luschey, H. 1939
Die Phiale. Berlin.
Luttrell, A. 1978
The Hospitallers in Cyprus, Rhodes, Greece and the West 1291-1440. London.
Luttrell, A. 1985
The Later History of the Mausoleion and its Utilization in the Hospitaller Castle at Bodrum. (Jutland Archaeological Society Publications XV, 2). Aarhus.
MacGillivray, J.A. – Barber, R.L.N. 1984
The Prehistoric Cyclades. Contribution to a workshop on Cycladic Chronology. Edinburgh.
Maiuri, A. 1918
Rodi, Guida dei Monumenti.
Maiuri, A. 1921
Rodi, Guida. Roma-Milano-Firenze-Napoli.
Maiuri, A. 1925
Nuova Silloge Epigrafica di Rodi e Cos. Firenze.
Mallwitz, A. 1972
Olympia und seine Bauten. Darmstadt.
Marangou, E.-L.I. 1969
Lakonische Elfenbein- und Beinschnitzereien. Tübingen.
Marinatos, S. 1968
Excavations at Thera I. Athens.
Marinatos, S. 1969
Excavations at Thera II. Athens.
Marinatos, S. 1970
Excavations at Thera III. Athens.
Marinatos, S. 1971
Excavations at Thera IV. Athens.
Marinatos, S. 1972
Excavations at Thera V. Athens.
Marinatos, S. 1974
Excavations at Thera VI. Athens.
Marinatos, S. 1976
Excavations at Thera VII. Athens.
Markoe, G. 1985
Phoenician bronze and silver bowls from Cyprus and the Mediterranean. Berkeley-Los Angeles-London.
Martin, R. 1956
L'Urbanisme dans la Grèce Antique.
Martin, R. 1974
L'Urbanisme dans la Grèce Antique. (2nd ed.).
Maass, M. 1985
Badisches Landesmuseum, Wege zur Klassik. Karlsruhe.
Matthäus, H. 1980
Die Bronzegefässe der kretisch-mykenischen Kultur. (PBF II, 1). München.
Matthäus, H. 1985
Metallgefässe und Gefässuntersätze der Bronzezeit, der geometrischen und archaischen Periode auf Cypern. (PBF II, 8). München.
Mayer, L. 1803
Views in the Ottoman Empire.
Mayer, M. 1914
Apulien vor und während der Hellenisierung. Berlin.
Mee, C. 1982
Rhodes in the Bronze Age. Warminster.
Meiggs, R. – Lewis, D. 1969
A Selection of Greek historical inscriptions to the end of the fifth century B.C. Oxford.
Meisner, H. – Röhuricht, R.V. 1837
Mémoires de la Societé des Antiquaires de l'Ouest I-IV.
Melas, E.M. 1985
The Islands of Karpathos, Saros and Kasos in the Neolithic and Bronze Age. (SIMA 68). Göteborg.
Mellaart, J. 1970
Excavations at Hacilar. Edinburgh.
Mendel, G. 1912-1914
Catalogue des figurines Grecques de terre cuite des Musée Imperiaux Ottomans. T. I-III. Constantinopel.
Meritt, B.D. – Traill, J.S. 1974
Inscriptions. The Athenian Counsellors. The Athenian Agora 15. Princeton.
Merrillees, R.S. 1975
Trade and Transcendence in the Bronze Age Levant. (SIMA 49). Göteborg.
Metzger, I. 1985
Das Thesmophorion von Eretria. Eretria VII. Bern.
Mills Holden, B. 1984
The Metopes of the Temple of Athena at Ilion.
Mollard-Besques, S. 1963
Catalogue raisonné des figurines et reliefs en terre-cuite grecs, étrusques et romains du Musée National du Louvre. 2. Myrina. Musée du Louvre et Collections des Universités de France. Paris.
Mollard-Besques, S. 1971-1972
Catalogue raisonné des figurines et reliefs en terre-cuite grecs, étrusques et romains du Musée National du Louvre. 3. Époques hellénistique et romaine, Grèce et Asie Mineure (Vol. 1-3). Paris.
Morelli, D. 1959
I culti in Rodi, Studi classici e orientali vol. VIII. Università di Pisa.
Mortzos, Ch. 1985
To Elleniko iero A ston Kastello Apodexis 1. Athens.
Mountjoy, P.-A. 1986
Mycenaean Decorated Pottery: A Guide to Identification. (SIMA 73). Göteborg.
Neppi Modona A. 1938
Isola di Cos nell'antichità classica.
Neugebauer, O. 1969
The Exact Sciences in Antiquity. (2nd ed). NY.
Neutsch, B. 1952
Studien zur vortanagräisch-attischen Koroplastik. (JdI Ergh. 17). Berlin.
Newton, C.T. 1862
A History of the Discoveries at Halikarnassos, Cnidus and Branchidae.
Newton, C.T. 1865
Travels and Discoveries in the Levant I. London.
Niemeyer, W.D. 1984
Die Palaststilkeramik von Knossos. Archäologische Forschungen, 13. Berlin.
Nilsson, M.P. 1950
The Minoan – Mycenaean Religion and its survival in Greek Religion. Lund.
Oppel, H. 1937
Kanon. Zur Bedeutungsgeschichte des Wortes und seinen lateinischen Entsprechungen. Leipzig.
Overbeck, J. 1868
Die antiken Schriftquellen zur Geschichte der bildenden Künste bei den Griechen. Leipzig.
Papachatzis, N. 1980
Pausanias, Achaïká - Arkadiká. Athens.
Papachristodoulou, I.Ch. 1983
Symboli stin Archeologiki Erevna ton Dimon tis archaias Rodiakis Politias. I Ialysia. (Ph.D). Ioanina.
Papadopoulos, Th.J. 1976
Excavations at Aigion. (SIMA 36). Göteborg.

Papadopoulos, Th.J. 1978-1979
Mycenaean Achaea. (SIMA 55). Göteborg.
Paquette, D. 1984
L'instrument de musique dans la céramique de la Grèce antique. Études d'organologie. Paris.
Parlasca, K. 1966
Mumienporträts und verwandte Denkmäler. Wiesbaden.
Paton, W.R. – Hicks, E.L. 1891
The Inscriptions of Cos. Oxford.
Payne, H. 1931
Necrocorinthia. A study of Corinthian Art in the Archaic Period. Oxford.
Payne, H. et al. 1940
Perachora I. Architecture – Bronzes – Terracottas. Oxford.
Philipp, H. 1981
Bronzeschmuck aus Olympia. (Olympische Forschungen 13). Berlin.
Pilali-Papasteriou, A. 1985
Die bronzenen Tierfiguren aus Kreta. (PBF I, 3). München.
Platon, N. 1971
Zakros, the discovery of a lost palace of Ancient Crete. NY.
Podzuweit, C. 1979
Trojanische Gefässformen der Frühbronzezeit in Anatolien, der Ägäis und angrenzenden Gebieten. Heidelberger Akademie der Wissenschaften Monographien 1. Mainz.
Popham, M.R. et al. 1979-1980
Lefkandi I, The Iron Age. (BSA Suppl. 11).
Poulsen, Fr. 1912
Der Orient und die frühgriechische Kunst. Leipzig – Berlin.
Preziosi, D. 1983
Minoan Architectural Design. Formation and Signification. Berlin.
Pryce, F.N. 1928
Catalogue of Sculpture in the Department of Greek and Roman Antiquities of the British Museum. Vol. 1, Part 1. Prehellenic and Early Greek. London.
Radwan, A. 1983
Die Kupfer- und Bronzegefässe Ägyptens. (PBF II, 2). München.
Raeder, J. 1983
Priene. Funde aus einer griechischen Stadt. Bilderhefte der Staatlichen Museen Preussischer Kulturbesitz. Berlin.
Ramage, E.S. (ed.) 1978
Atlantis. Fact or Fiction? Bloomington.
Rasmussen, T.B. 1979
Bucchero Pottery from Southern Etruria. Cambridge.
Renfrew, C. (ed) 1985
The Archaeology of Cult: The Sanctuary at Phylakopi. (BSA Suppl. 18). London.
Reverdin, O. – Grange, B. 1980
Le sacrifice dans l'antiquité. (Entretiens XXVII. Fondation Hardt.). Genève.
Ridgway, D. 1984
L'alba della Magna Grecia. Milano.
Ridgway, D. – Ridgway, F. (eds.) 1979
Italy before the Romans. The Iron Age, Orientalizing and Etruscan Periods. London-New York-San Fransisco.
Riis, P.J. 1970
Sukas I: The North-East sanctuary and the first settling of Greeks in Syria and Palestine. Copenhagen.
Riis, P.J. 1979
Sukas VI: The Graeco-Phoenician Cemetery and Sanctuary at the Southern Harbour. Copenhagen.
Rizza, G. – Santa Maria Scrinari, V. 1968
Il santuario sull'Acropoli di Gortina. Roma.
Roes, A. 1933
Greek Geometric Art, its Symbolism and Origin.
Rolley, C. 1977
Les trépieds à cuve clouée. (Fouilles de Delphes V, 3). Paris.
Rolley, C. 1984
Die griechischen Bronzen. München - Freiburg.
Ross, L 1861
Archäologische Aufsätze II. Leipzig.
Ross, L. 1840-1852
Reisen auf den griechischen Inseln des Ägäischen Meeres. I-IV. Stuttgart - Tübingen.
Rubensohn, O. 1962
Das Delion von Paros. Wiesbaden.
Rutter, J. 1980
The Late Helladic IIIB and IIIC Periods at Korakou and Gonía in the Corinthia. Ann Arbor.
Sampson, A. 1983
Topographical survey of prehistoric sites in the Dodecanese, in D.R. Keller and D.W. Rupp, Archaeological survey in the Mediterranean area, BAR 155. Oxford.
Sampson, A. 1986
I neolithiki periodos sta Dodecanisa.
Sapouna-Sakellarakis, E. 1978
Die Fibeln der griechischen Inseln. (PBF XIV). München.
Schachermeyr, F. 1976
Die mykenische Zeit und die Gesittung von Thera (Die Ägäische Frühzeit II). Wien.
Schaps, D.M. 1979
Economic rights of women in Ancient Greece. Edinburgh.
Schazmann, P. 1932
Asklepieion. Baubeschreibung und Baugeschichte. Berlin.
Schilbach, E. 1970
Byzantische Metrologie. München.
Schliemann, H. 1880
Ilios: The city and country of the Trojans. London.
Schmidt, G. 1968
Kyprische Bildwerke aus dem Heraion von Samos. (Samos VII). Bonn.
Schneider, C. 1967
Kulturgeschichte des Hellenismus I-II. München.
Schwyzer, E. 1934
Griechische Grammatik. (Handbuch d. Altertumswissenschaft II 1,1) München.
Sguaitamatti, M. 1984
L'offrante de porcelet dans la coroplathie géléenne. Étude typologique. Mainz am Rhein.
Sherwin White, S. 1978
Ancient Cos: A historical study from the Dorian settlement to the Imperial Period. (Hypomnemata 51). Göttingen.
Shulte-Campbell, C.
The Human Skeletal Remains from Palaepaphos-Skales (Appendix XII).
Shulte-Campbell, C. 1979
The Jaws and Teeth of a Bronze Age Skeleton from Hala Sultan Tekke, Cyprus.
Sjöquist, E. 1940
Problems of the Late Cypriote Bronze Age. Stockholm.
Slenczka, E. 1974
Tiryns VII. Forschungen und Berichte. Mainz am Rhein.
Smith, A.M. 1900
Catalogue of Sculpture in the Department of Greek and Roman Antiquities of the British Museum II. London.

Snodgrass, A.M. 1964
Early Greek Armour and Weapons from the end of the Bronze Age to 600 B.C. Edinburgh.

Snodgrass, A.M. 1967
Arms and armour of the Greeks. London.

Snodgrass, A.M. 1971
The Dark Age of Greece. Edinburgh.

Sokolowski, Fr. 1962
Lois sacrées des cités grecques (Supplément). Travaux et mémoires des anciens membres étrangers de l'Ecole Française d'Athènes Fasc. XI. Paris.

Sokolowski, Fr. 1969
Lois sacrées des cités grecques. Travaux et mémoires des anciens membres étrangers de l'Ecole Française d'Athenes Fasc. XVIII. Paris.

Sparkes, B. – Talcott, L. 1970
Black and Plain Pottery of the 6th, 5th and 4th centuries B.C. (The Athenian Agora 12). Princeton.

Speich, N. 1957
Die Proportionslehre des menschlichen Körper. Andelfingen Z. H.

Stampolidis, N. Chr. 1987
Ο βωμός του Διονύσου στην Κώ. Συμβολή στη μελέτη της ελλενιστικής πλαστικής και αρχιτεκτονικής. Αθήνα.

Stewart, A. 1979
Attica. Studies of Athenian Sculpture in the Hellenistic Age. London.

Stillwell, A.N. – Benson, J.L. 1984
The Potter's Quarter. The Pottery. (Corinth XV, 3). Princeton.

Stucchi, S. 1975
Architettura cirenaica. Roma.

Susini, G. 1957
Nuove scoperte sulla storia di Coo. Bologna.

Symeonoglou, S. 1973
Kadmeia I. Mycenaean Finds from Thebes, Greece. (SIMA 35). Göteborg.

Säflund, G. 1965
Excavations at Berbati 1936-1937. Stockholm.

Ταραμίδης, Γ. 1983
Τα Δόντια των Κυπρίων της Νεολιθικής Εποχης. Οδοντοστοματολογική Πρόοδος.

Taylor, Lord W. 1958
Mycenaean Pottery in Italy and Adjacent Areas. Cambridge.

Theocharis, D.R. (ed.) 1973
Neolithic Greece. Athens.

Thompson, D. Burr 1963
The Terracotta Figurines of the Hellenistic Period. Troy Supplementary Monograph 3. Princeton.

Thompson, H.A. – Wycherley, R.E. 1972
The Agora of Athens. The Athenian Agora 14. Princeton.

Thévenot, J. de 1664-1665
Relations d'un voyage fait au Levant. Rouen.

Traill, J.S. 1975
The Political Organization of Attica. (Hesperia Suppl. 14). Princeton.

Travlos, J. 1971
Bildlexikon zur Topographie des Antiken Athen. Tübingen.

Treu, M. 1960
Maximi Monachi Planudis Epistulae.

Tufnell, O. 1958
Lachisch IV. The Bronze Age.

Töpperwein, E. 1976
Terrakotten von Pergamon. (PF 3). Berlin.

Verlinden, C. 1984
Les statuettes anthropomorphes crétoises en bronze et en plomb du IIIe millénaire au VIIe siècle av. J.-C. Louvain-La-Neuve.

Waldstein, Ch. 1902-1905
The Argive Heraium I-II. Boston - NY.

Walter, H. 1968
Frühe samische Gefässe. (Samos V). Bonn.

Walter-Karydi, E. 1973
Samische Gefässe des 6. Jahrh. v. Chr. (Samos VI, 1). Bonn.

Walter-Karydi, E. et al. 1982
Ostgriechische Keramik. (Alt-Ägina, II. 1). Mainz.

Walters, H.B. 1899
Catalogue of the Bronzes, Greek, Roman, and Etruscan in the Department of Greek and Roman Antiquities, British Museum. London.

Walters, H.B. 1905
History of Ancient Pottery. Vol. 1-2. London.

Ward-Perkins, J.B. 1974
Cities of ancient Greece and Italy. NY.

Waywell, G.B. 1978
The Free-standing Sculpture of the Mausoleum at Halikarnassus. A Catalogue. London.

Webb, V. 1978
Archaic Greek Faience: miniature scent bottles and related objects from East Greece, 650-500 B.C. Warminster.

Wegner, M. 1968
Musik und Tanz. (ArchHom 3 U). Göttingen.

Weill, N. 1985
La plastique archaique de Thasos. Figurines et statues de terre cuite d'Artemision I. Le haut archaisme. Paris.

Weinberg, S.S. 1943
The Geometric and Orientalizing Pottery. (Corinth VIII, 1).

Willetts, R.F. 1967
The Law Code of Gortyn. Berlin.

Winter, F. 1883
Die Typen der figürlichen Terrakotten. Berlin.

Winther, F.E. 1971
Greek Fortifications. London.

Wycherley, P.E. 1949
How the Greeks built cities. (1st ed.). London.

Yavis, C.G. 1949
Greek Altars. Origins and Typology. St. Louis.

Young, R. 1939
Late Geometric Graves and a Seventh Century Well in the Agora. (Hesperia Suppl. 2). Princeton.

Young, R.S. 1981
Three Great Tumuli. The Gordion Excavations Final Reports I.

Zachariadou, E. 1983
Trade and Crusade.

Zachariadou, E. 1985
Romania and the Turks c. 1300-c. 1500.

Ζαφειράτος, Κ. 1982
Θέματα Εργαστηριακών Ασκήσεων φυσικής Ανθρωπολογίας. Πανεπιστήμιο Αθήνας.

Zazoff, P. 1983
Die antiken Gemmen. (HdA). München.

Zois, A.A. 1973
Kriti. I epochi tou lithou. Athens.

Ålin, P. 1962
Das Ende der mykenischen Fundstätten auf dem griechischen Festland. (SIMA 1). Göteborg.

Åström, P. 1957
The Middle Cypriote Bronze Age. Lund.